Eighth
Edition

BUSINESS FORECASTING

John E. Hanke
Eastern Washington University, Emeritus

Dean W. Wichern
Texas A&M University

PEARSON

Prentice
Hall

UPPER SADDLE RIVER, NEW JERSEY 07458

Library of Congress Cataloging-in-Publication Data

Hanke, John E.
  Business forecasting / John E. Hanke, Dean W. Wichern—8th ed.
    p. cm.
  Includes bibliographical references and index.
  ISBN 0-13-141290-6
   1. Business forecasting. I. Wichern, Dean W. II. Title.

  HD30.27.H37   2005
  658.4'0355—dc22   2003058109

Executive Editor: Tom Tucker
Editor-in-Chief: P.J. Boardman
Editorial Assistant: Dawn Stapleton
Senior Media Project Manager: Nancy Welcher
Executive Marketing Manager: Debbie Clare
Marketing Assistant: Amanda Fisher
Managing Editor (Production): John Roberts
Production Editor: Kelly Warsak
Production Assistant: Joe DeProspero
Manufacturing Buyer: Michelle Klein
Cover Design: Bruce Kenselaar
Cover Illustration: Getty Images
Composition: Laserwords Private Ltd, India
Full-Service Project Management: Tempe Goodhue/nSight, Inc.
Printer/Binder: Hamilton Printing Company
Cover Printer: Phoenix Color Corp.

Credits and acknowledgments borrowed from other sources and reproduced, with permission, in this textbook appear on appropriate page within text.

Microsoft® and Windows® are registered trademarks of the Microsoft Corporation in the U.S.A. and other countries. Screen shots and icons reprinted with permission from the Microsoft Corporation. This book is not sponsored or endorsed by or affiliated with the Microsoft Corporation.

10 9 8 7 6 5 4 3 2
ISBN 0-13-141290-6

Dedicated to
the memory of Harry
(who really didn't want to read it);

Geri
(who doesn't need to);

Donna and Dorothy
(who probably won't);

Katrina, Michael, and Andrew
(who might);

Kevin
(who says he did);

and all of our students
(who better).

Contents

CHAPTER 3   Exploring Data Patterns and Choosing a Forecasting Technique   57

Preface

The goal of the eighth edition of *Business Forecasting* remains the same as that of the previous editions: to present the basic statistical techniques that are useful for preparing individual business forecasts and long-range plans. The book is written in a simple, straightforward style and makes extensive use of practical business examples. Fifty-three cases appear at the end of chapters to provide the student with the necessary link between theoretical concepts and their real-world applications. The emphasis is on the application of techniques by management for decision making. Students are assumed to have taken an introductory course in statistics and to be comfortable with using the computer to access software packages such as word processors and spreadsheets.

ORGANIZATION

All chapters have been revised to enhance the clarity of the writing and to increase teaching and learning effectiveness. The content is organized into six sections.

The first section (Chapters 1 and 2) presents background material. The nature of forecasting and a quick review of basic statistical concepts set the stage for the coverage of techniques that begins in the second section.

The second section (Chapter 3) emphasizes the exploration of data patterns and the choosing of a forecasting technique. The third section (Chapters 4 and 5) covers averaging, smoothing techniques, and an introduction to time series decomposition in terms of underlying components. The fourth section (Chapters 6 and 7) emphasizes causal forecasting techniques, such as correlation, regression, and multiple regression analysis.

The fifth section (Chapters 8 and 9) looks at techniques used to forecast time series data. The book concludes with a final section (Chapters 10 and 11) on judgmental forecasting and forecast adjustments, along with a discussion of managing and monitoring the forecasting process.

CHANGES IN THE EIGHTH EDITION

The eighth edition has been completely rewritten. Although the "flavor" of earlier editions has been retained, added emphasis has been placed on the most recent theoretical developments and empirical findings. Outdated material has been eliminated and the book has been completely reorganized with the addition of new problems, examples, data sets, and cases.

The following features are either new or improved in this edition:

- Seven new cases have been added.
- An example of how to use Minitab (Version 14) in a forecasting situation is demonstrated at the end of most chapters.

- A student solutions manual consisting of answers to odd-numbered problems in the chapters is included on the CD.
- An updated instructor's manual is available from Prentice Hall, Upper Saddle River, NJ 07458.
- An example of how to use Excel 2000 to solve a forecasting problem is demonstrated at the end of most chapters.
- Examples using Crystal Ball's CB Predictor (an Excel add-in) are included in Chapter 4, "Moving Averages and Smoothing Methods," and Chapter 9, "The Box-Jenkins (ARIMA) Methodology."
- Data sets for Minitab, Excel, or other programs are available on the CD included with this book. These data sets are also available on the Internet.
- The student version of CB Predictor is included on the CD.
- Several new problems have been added to this edition.
- Data sets have been updated.
- Material on growth curves has been moved from Chapter 10 to Chapter 6.
- An expanded discussion of the Delphi method is included in Chapter 10.

THE ROLE OF THE COMPUTER

In the first seven editions, the computer was recognized as a powerful tool in forecasting. The computer is even more important now, and managers take advantage of the ease and availability of the sophisticated forecasting afforded by desktop, laptop, and notebook computers and networking capabilities.

The authors have spent several sleepless nights deciding what to do about the computer. A nationwide research study of all AACSB member institutions conducted by the authors to determine what faculty do about using computers to teach forecasting showed (1) that most forecasting faculty (94.2%) attempt to provide students with hands-on experience in using the computer, and (2) that several statistical packages and specific personal computer forecasting packages were mentioned in the survey. The packages mentioned most frequently were Minitab, SAS, Eviews, and spreadsheets.

The authors have tried several different approaches to help faculty and students use the computer for forecasting. This edition features the following:

1. Minitab instructions are presented at the end of most chapters.
2. Excel instructions are present at the end of most chapters.
3. CB Predictor instructions are presented at the end of Chapters 4 and 9.
4. Three data collections are available on the CD included with this book and on the Internet (Minitab, Excel, other programs). Each collection contains data from the text examples and problems. To access the data sets on the Internet, go to the Prentice Hall Web site at *www.prenhall.com/hanke*.
5. Example of different computer outputs are placed throughout the text.

ACKNOWLEDGMENTS

The authors are indebted to the many instructors around the world who have used the first seven editions and have provided invaluable suggestions for improving the book. Special thanks go to Professor Frank Forest, Marquette University; Professor William Darrow, Townsend State University; Susan Winters, Northwestern State University; Professor Shik Chun Young, Eastern Washington University; Mark Craze, Judy Johnson, Steve Brandon, and Dorothy Mercer for providing cases; and Jennifer Dahl for constructing the index.

Portions of this text, particularly several data sets, are adapted from those that appeared in the second edition of *Understanding Business Statistics* by Hanke and Reitsch (1999), published by Richard D. Irwin, whom we here credit for this reuse.

We also thank reviewers John Liechty, University of Michigan; John Tamura, University of Washington; and Ted Taukahara, St. Mary's University for their very constructive comments in the revision of the book. Other reviewers deserving of our thanks are Perry Sadorski, York University; Shady Kholdy, California State Polytechnic University–Pomona; Michael Niemira, New York University; Fred Zufryden, University of Southern California; and Haizheg Li, Georgia Institute of Technology. If we were talented enough to accomplish everything our reviewers suggested, the book would be improved 100 percent.

Finally, we thank our computers and wonder how we ever wrote a textbook without one. We, not the computers, are responsible for any errors.

1

INTRODUCTION TO FORECASTING

This book is concerned with methods used to predict the uncertain nature of business trends in an effort to help managers make better decisions and plans. Such efforts often involve the study of historical data and the manipulation of these data to search for patterns that can be effectively extrapolated to produce forecasts.

In this text, we regularly remind readers that sound judgment must be used along with numerical results if good forecasting is to result. The example in this chapter and the cases at the end of this and the remaining text chapters emphasize this point. There are discussions of this matter in this chapter and in the concluding chapter.

THE HISTORY OF FORECASTING

Many of the forecasting techniques used today and discussed in this book were developed in the nineteenth century; regression analysis procedures are an example. By contrast, some of the topics in this book were developed and have received attention more recently. The decomposition, smoothing, and Box-Jenkins procedures fall into this category.

With the development of more sophisticated forecasting techniques, along with the advent of computers—especially the proliferation of the personal computer (PC) and associated software—forecasting has received more and more attention. Every manager now has the ability to utilize very sophisticated data analysis techniques for forecasting purposes, and an understanding of these techniques is essential. For this same reason, consumers of forecasts (managers) must be alert to the improper use of forecasting techniques because inaccurate forecasts can lead to poor decisions.

New techniques for forecasting continue to be developed as management concern with the forecasting process continues to grow. A particular focus of this attention is on the errors that are an inherent part of any forecasting procedure. Predictions of outcomes are rarely precise; the forecaster can only endeavor to make the inevitable errors as small as possible.

THE NEED FOR FORECASTING

In view of the inherent inaccuracies in the process, why is forecasting necessary? The answer is that all organizations operate in an atmosphere of uncertainty but decisions must be made today that affect the future of the organization. Educated guesses about the future are more valuable to organization managers than uneducated guesses. This book discusses various ways of making forecasts that rely on logical methods of manipulating the data that have been generated by historical events.

This is not to say that intuitive forecasting is bad. On the contrary, the "gut" feelings of persons who manage organizations often provide the only forecasts available. This text discusses forecasting techniques that can be used to supplement the common sense and management ability of decision makers; judgmental elements in the forecasting process are discussed in Chapter 10. It is our view that decision makers are better off understanding both quantitative and qualitative forecasting techniques and using them wisely than they are if forced to plan for the future without the benefit of valuable supplemental information.

The role of judgmental forecasting has changed in recent years. Before the advent of modern forecasting techniques and the power of the computer, the manager's judgment was the only forecasting tool available. However, according to Makridakis (1986), forecasts generated using only judgment are not as accurate as those involving the judicious application of quantitative techniques:

> Humans possess unique knowledge and inside information not available to quantitative methods. Surprisingly, however, empirical studies and laboratory experiments have shown that their forecasts are not more accurate than those of quantitative methods. Humans tend to be optimistic and underestimate future uncertainty. In addition, the cost of forecasting with judgmental methods is often considerably higher than when quantitative methods are used.[1]

It is our belief that the most effective forecaster is able to formulate a skillful mix of quantitative forecasting techniques and good judgment and to avoid the extremes of total reliance on either. At the one extreme we find the executive who, through ignorance and fear of quantitative techniques and computers, relies solely on intuition and feel. At the other extreme is the forecaster skilled in the latest sophisticated data manipulation techniques but unable or unwilling to relate the forecasting process to the needs of the organization and its decision makers. We view the quantitative forecasting techniques discussed in most of this book to be only the starting point in the effective forecasting of outcomes important to the organization: Analysis, judgment, common sense, and business experience must all be brought to bear on the process through which these important techniques generate their results.

Because the world in which organizations operate has always been changing, forecasts have always been necessary. However, recent years have brought about increased reliance on methods that involve sophisticated data manipulation techniques. New technology and new disciplines have sprung up overnight; government activity at all levels has intensified; competition in many areas has become more keen; international trade has stepped up in almost all industries; social help and service agencies have been created and have grown; and the Internet has become an important source of data and decision-making information. These factors have combined to create an organizational climate that is more complex, fast-paced, and competitive than ever before. Organizations that cannot react quickly to changing conditions and cannot foresee the future with any degree of accuracy are doomed to extinction.

Computers, along with the quantitative techniques they make possible, have become more than a convenience for modern organizations; they have become essential. The complexities just discussed generate tremendous amounts of data and an overwhelming need to extract useful information. The modern tools of forecasting, along with the capabilities of the computer, have become indispensable for organizations operating in the modern world.

---

[1] Makridakis (1986), p. 17.

Who needs forecasts? Almost every organization, large and small, private and public, uses forecasting either explicitly or implicitly, because almost every organization must plan to meet the conditions of the future for which it has imperfect knowledge. In addition, the need for forecasts cuts across all functional lines as well as all types of organizations. Forecasts are needed in finance, marketing, personnel, and production areas, in government and profit-seeking organizations, in small social clubs, and in national political parties. Consider the following questions that suggest the need for some forecasting procedures:

- If we increase our advertising budget by 10%, how will sales be affected?
- What revenue might the state government expect over the next 2-year period?
- How many units might we sell in an effort to recover our fixed investment in production equipment?
- What factors can we identify that will help explain the variability in monthly unit sales?
- What is a year-by-year prediction for the total loan balance of our bank over the next 10 years?
- Will there be a recession? If so, when will it begin, how severe will it be, and when will it end?

A passage from Bernstein (1996) effectively summarizes the role of forecasting in organizations.

> You do not plan to ship goods across the ocean, or to assemble merchandise for sale, or to borrow money without first trying to determine what the future may hold in store. Ensuring that the materials you order are delivered on time, seeing to it that the items you plan to sell are produced on schedule, and getting your sales facilities in place all must be planned before that moment when the customers show up and lay their money on the counter. The successful business executive is a forecaster first; purchasing, producing, marketing, pricing, and organizing all follow.[2]

TYPES OF FORECASTS

When managers are faced with the need to make decisions in an atmosphere of uncertainty, what types of forecasts are available to them? Forecasting procedures might first be classified as for the long term or the short term. Long-term forecasts are necessary to set the general course of an organization for the long run; thus they become the particular focus of top management. Short-term forecasts are used to design immediate strategies and are used by middle management and first-line management to meet the needs of the immediate future.

Forecasts might also be classified in terms of their position on a micro–macro continuum, that is, on the extent to which they involve small details versus large summary values. For example, a plant manager might be interested in forecasting the number of workers needed for the next several months (a micro forecast), whereas the federal government is forecasting the total number of people employed in the entire country (a macro forecast). Again, different levels of management in an organization tend to focus on different levels of the micro–macro continuum. Top management would be interested in forecasting the sales of the entire company, for example, whereas individual salespersons would be much more interested in forecasting their own sales volumes.

---

[2] Bernstein (1996), pp. 21–22.

Forecasting procedures can also be classified according to whether they are more quantitative or qualitative. At one extreme, a purely qualitative technique requires no overt manipulation of data. Only the "judgment" of the forecaster is used. Even here, of course, the forecaster's "judgment" is actually a result of the mental manipulation of past historical data. At the other extreme, purely quantitative techniques need no input of judgment; they are mechanical procedures that produce quantitative results. Some quantitative procedures require a much more sophisticated manipulation of data than do others, of course. This book emphasizes the quantitative forecasting techniques because a broader understanding of these very useful procedures is needed in the effective management of modern organizations. However, we emphasize again that judgment and common sense must be used along with mechanical and data-manipulative procedures. Only in this way can intelligent forecasting take place.

MACROECONOMIC FORECASTING CONSIDERATIONS

We usually think of forecasting in terms of predicting important variables for an individual company or perhaps for one component of a company. Monthly company sales, unit sales for one of a company's stores, and absent hours per employee per month in a factory are examples.

By contrast, there is growing interest in forecasting important variables for the entire economy of a country or for the global economy. Much work has been done in evaluating methods for doing this kind of overall economic forecasting, called *macroeconomic forecasting*. Examples of interest to the government of the United States are unemployment rate, gross domestic product, and the prime interest rate. Economic policy is based, in part, on projections of important economic indicators such as these. For this reason, there is great interest in improving forecasting methods that focus on overall measures of a country's economic performance.

One of the chief difficulties in developing accurate forecasts of overall economic activity is an unexpected and significant shift in a key economic factor. Large changes in oil prices, inflation surges, and broad policy changes by a country's government are examples of shifts in a key factor that can affect the global economy.

The possibility of such significant shifts in the economic scene has raised a key question in macroeconomic forecasting: Should the forecasts generated by the forecasting model be modified using the forecaster's judgment? Current work on forecasting methodology often involves this question.

Much work, both theoretical and practical, continues on the subject of macroeconomic forecasting. Considering the importance of accurate economic forecasting to economic policy formulation in this country and others, continuing attention to this kind of forecasting can be expected in the future. A good introductory reference for macroeconomic forecasting is Pindyck and Rubinfeld (1998).

CHOOSING A FORECASTING METHOD

The preceding discussion suggests several factors to be considered in choosing a forecasting method. The level of detail must be considered. Are forecasts of specific details needed (a micro forecast)? Or is the future status of some overall or summary factor needed (a macro forecast)? Is the forecast needed for some point in the near future (a short-term forecast) or for a point in the intermediate or distant future (a long-term forecast)? And to what extent are qualitative (judgment) and quantitative (data-manipulative) methods appropriate?

The overriding consideration in choosing a forecasting method is that the results must facilitate the decision-making process of the organization's managers. Rarely does one method work for all cases. Different products (for example, new versus established), goals (such as simple prediction versus the need to control an important business driver of future values), and constraints (such as cost, required expertise, immediacy) must be considered when selecting a forecasting method. With the availability of current forecasting software, it is best to think of forecasting methods as generic tools that can be applied simultaneously. Several methods can be tried in a given situation. The methodology producing the most accurate forecasts in one case may not be the best methodology in another situation. However, the method(s) chosen should produce a forecast that is accurate, timely, and understood by management so that the forecast can help produce better decisions.

Choosing a forecasting technique is discussed in Chapter 3 and summarized in Table 3-6. The forecasting methodologies considered in this book are summarized in Table 11-1 (Chapter 11). These tables, along with additional discussion available in Chase (1997), can help the forecaster select an initial set of forecasting procedures to be considered.

FORECASTING STEPS

All formal forecasting procedures involve extending the experiences of the past into the future. Thus they involve the assumption that the conditions that generated past data are indistinguishable from the conditions of the future except for those variables explicitly recognized by the forecasting model.

A human resource department is hiring employees, in part, on the basis of a company entrance examination score because, in the past, examination score seemed to be an important predictor of job performance rating. To the extent that this relation continues to hold, forecasts of future job performance—hence hiring decisions—can be improved by using examination scores. If, for some reason, the association between examination score and job performance changes, then forecasting job performance ratings from examination scores using the historical model will yield inaccurate forecasts and potentially poor hiring decisions. This is what makes forecasting difficult. The future is not always like the past. To the extent it is, quantitative forecasting methods work well. To the extent it isn't, inaccurate forecasts can result. However, it is generally better to have some reasonably constructed forecast than no forecast.

The recognition that forecasting techniques operate on the data generated by historical events leads to the identification of the following five steps in the forecasting process:

1. Problem formulation and data collection
2. Data manipulation and cleaning
3. Model building and evaluation
4. Model implementation (the actual forecast)
5. Forecast evaluation

Step 1, problem formulation and data collection, are treated as a single step because they are intimately related. The problem determines the appropriate data. If a quantitative forecasting methodology is being considered, the relevant data must be available and correct. Often accessing and assembling appropriate data is a challenging and time-consuming task. If appropriate data are not available, the problem may have to be redefined or a nonquantitative forecasting methodology employed. Collection and quality control problems frequently arise whenever it becomes necessary to obtain pertinent data for a business forecasting effort.

Step 2, data manipulation and cleaning, is often necessary. It is possible to have too much data as well as too little in the forecasting process. Some data may not be relevant to the problem. Some data may have missing values that must be estimated. Some data may have to be re-expressed in units other than the original units. Some data may have to be preprocessed (for example, accumulated from several sources and summed). Other data may be appropriate but only in certain historical periods (for example, in forecasting the sales of small cars one may wish to use only car sales data after the oil embargo of the 1970s rather than data over the past 50 years). Ordinarily, some effort is required to get data into a form that is required for using certain forecasting procedures.

Step 3, model building and evaluation, involves fitting the collected data into a forecasting model that is appropriate in terms of minimizing forecasting error. The simpler the model, the better it is in terms of gaining acceptance of the forecasting process by managers who must make the firm's decisions. Often a balance must be struck between a sophisticated forecasting approach that offers slightly more accuracy and a simple approach that is easily understood and gains the support of—and is actively used by—the company's decision makers. Obviously, judgment is involved in this selection process. Because this book discusses numerous forecasting models and their applicability, it is our hope that the reader's ability to exercise good judgment in the choice and use of appropriate forecasting models will increase after studying this material.

Step 4, model implementation, consists of the actual model forecasts that are generated once the appropriate data have been collected and possibly reduced and an appropriate forecasting model has been chosen. Forecasting for recent periods in which the actual historical values are known is often used to check the accuracy of the process. The forecasting errors are then observed and summarized in some way and is included in Step 5.

Step 5, forecast evaluation, involves comparing forecast values with actual historical values. In this process, a few of the most recent data values are often held back from the data set being analyzed. After the forecasting model is completed, forecasts are made for these periods and compared with the known historical values. Some forecasting procedures sum the absolute values of the errors and may report this sum, or divide it by the number of forecast attempts to produce the average forecast error. Other procedures produce the sum of squared errors, which is then compared with similar figures from alternative forecasting methods. Some procedures also track and report the magnitude of the error terms over the forecasting period. Examination of error patterns often leads the analyst to a modification of the forecasting procedure. Specific methods of measuring forecasting errors are discussed near the end of Chapter 3.

MANAGING THE FORECASTING PROCESS

The discussion in this chapter serves to underline our belief that management ability and common sense must be involved in the forecasting process. The forecaster should be thought of as an advisor to the manager rather than as the monitor of an automatic decision-making device. Unfortunately, the latter is sometimes the case in practice, especially given the aura of the computer. Again, quantitative techniques in the forecasting process must be seen as what they really are, namely, tools to be used by the manager in arriving at better decisions. According to Makridakis (1986):

> The usefulness and utility of forecasting can be improved if management adopts a more realistic attitude. Forecasting should not be viewed as a substitute for prophecy but rather as the best way of identifying and extrapolating established patterns or relationships in order to forecast. If such an attitude is accepted, forecasting errors must be considered inevitable and the circumstances that cause them investigated.[3]

Given that, several key questions should always be raised if management of the forecasting process is to be properly conducted.

- Why is a forecast needed?
- Who will use the forecast, and what are their specific requirements?
- What level of detail or aggregation is required, and what is the proper time horizon?
- What data are available, and will the data be sufficient to generate the needed forecast?
- What will the forecast cost?
- How accurate can we expect the forecast to be?
- Will the forecast be made in time to help the decision-making process?
- Does the forecaster clearly understand how the forecast will be used in the organization?
- Is a feedback process available to evaluate the forecast after it is made and to adjust the forecasting process accordingly?

COMPUTER FORECASTING PACKAGES

The development that has had the greatest impact on forecasting in the past several years is that of computer software packages specifically designed to deal directly with various forecasting methods. Two types of computer packages are of interest to forecasters: (1) statistical packages that include regression analysis, time series analysis, and other techniques used frequently by forecasters, and (2) forecasting packages that are specifically designed for forecasting applications.

Examples of stand-alone software packages with forecasting tools include Minitab, SAS, EViews, and SPSS. In addition, there are now many add-ins or supplemental programs that provide forecasting tools in a spreadsheet environment. For example, the Analysis ToolPak add-in for Microsoft Excel provides some regression analysis and smoothing capabilities. More comprehensive add-ins such as Crystal Ball (CB) Predictor and Forecast X provide an (almost) full range of forecasting capability.

Managers with PCs on their desks and knowledge of forecasting techniques are no longer dependent on staff for their forecasts and can take advantage of the ease and availability of sophisticated forecasting methods. Forecasting software is consistently updated with enhanced ease of use. It is now fashionable, particularly in a spreadsheet setting, to have "automatic" forecasting available. That is, the software selects the best model or procedure for forecasting and immediately generates forecasts. We caution, however, that this functionality comes at a price. Automatic procedures produce numbers but rarely provide the forecaster with real insight into the nature and quality of the forecasts. We believe that the generation of meaningful forecasts requires

---

[3] Makridakis (1986), p. 33.

human intervention, a give and take between problem knowledge and forecasting procedures (software).

Many of the techniques in this book will be illustrated with Minitab 14 and Excel 2000 with the CB Predictor add-in. You will find descriptions and screens for these programs throughout the text. On occasion, we will display selected output from EViews.[4] Other forecasting packages will have the same basic functionality, although the input and output windows will be somewhat different. The programs we use in this book were chosen primarily for their ease of use and widespread availability.

A recent summary of forecasting software is contained in the survey of statistical analysis software found in the INFORMS publication *ORMS Today*, Vol. 30, No. 1, February 2003.

ONLINE INFORMATION

Information of interest to forecasters is available on the World Wide Web. Perhaps the best way to learn about what's available in cyberspace is to spend some time searching for whatever interests you using a browser such as Netscape or Microsoft's Internet Explorer.

Any list of Web sites for forecasters is likely to be outdated by the time this edition appears; however, there are two Web sites that are likely to remain available for some time. B&E DataLinks, available at *www.econ-datalinks.org/*, is a Web site maintained by the Business and Economic Section of the American Statistical Association. This Web site contains extensive links to economic and financial data sources of interest to forecasters. The second site, Resources for Economists, sponsored by the American Economic Association at *rfe.wustl.edu/EconFAQ.html*, contains an extensive set of links to data sources, journals, professional organizations, and so forth.

FORECASTING EXAMPLE

Discussions in this chapter emphasize that forecasting requires a great deal of judgment along with a mathematical manipulation of collected data. The following example shows the kind of thinking that often precedes a forecasting effort in a real firm. Notice that the data values that will produce useful forecasts, even if they exist, are not apparent at the beginning of the process and may not have been identified. In other words, the initial efforts may turn out to be useless to management. The computer results of the forecasting effort using the identified variables are not shown here as they involve topics that are described throughout this text. However, look for the techniques described in later chapters to be applied to these data. Example 1.1 will be resolved in Chapter 11. For the moment, we hope that this example illustrates the scope of the forecasting effort that real managers face.

Example 1.1

Alomega Food Stores is a retail food provider with 27 stores in a midwestern state. The company engages in various kinds of advertising and, until recently, has never studied the effect its advertising dollars have on sales, although some data had been collected and stored for 3 years.

The executives at Alomega decided to begin tracking their advertising efforts along with the sales volumes for each month. Their hope was that after several months the collected

---

[4] EViews, a popular forecasting software package, is available from Quantitative Micro Systems LLC, Irvine, CA.

data could be examined to possibly reveal relationships that would help in determining future advertising expenditures.

The accounting department began extending its historical records by recording the sales volume for each month along with the advertising dollars for both newspaper ads and TV spots. They also recorded both sales and advertising values that had been lagged one and two months. This was done because some people on the executive committee thought that sales might depend on advertising expenditures in previous months rather than in the month the ads appeared.

It was also believed that sales experienced a seasonal effect. For this reason a dummy or categorical variable was used to indicate each month. Management also wondered about any trend in sales volume.

Finally, it was believed that Alomega's advertising dollars might have an effect on its major competitors' advertising budgets the following month. For each following month it was decided that competitors' advertising could be classified as a little (1), a moderate amount (2), or a great amount (3).

After a few months of data collection and analysis of past records, the accounting department completed a data array for 48 months using the following variables:

- Sales dollars
- Newspaper advertising dollars
- TV advertising dollars
- Month code where January = 1, February = 2, through December = 12
- A series of 11 dummy variables to indicate month
- Newspaper advertising lagged one month
- Newspaper advertising lagged two months
- TV advertising lagged one month
- TV advertising lagged two months
- Month number from 1 to 48
- Code 1, 2, or 3 to indicate competitors' advertising efforts the following month

Alomega management, especially Julie Ruth, the company president, now wants to learn anything it can from the data it has collected. In addition to learning about the effects of advertising on sales volumes and competitors' advertising, Julie wonders about any trend and seasonal effects on sales. However, the company's production manager, Jackson Tilson, does not share her enthusiasm. At the end of the forecasting planning meeting, he makes the following statement: "I've been trying to keep my mouth shut during this meeting, but this is really too much. I think we're wasting a lot of people's time with all this data collection and fooling around with computers. All you have to do is talk with our people on the floor and with the grocery store managers to understand what's going on. I've seen this happen around here before, and here we go again. Some of you people need to turn off your computers, get out of your fancy offices, and talk with a few real people."

Summary

The purpose of a forecast is to reduce the range of uncertainty within which management judgments must be made. This purpose suggests two primary rules to which the forecasting process must adhere:

1. The forecast must be technically correct and produce forecasts accurate enough to meet the firm's needs.
2. The forecasting procedure and its results must be effectively presented to management so that the forecasts are used in the decision-making process to the firm's advantage; results must also be justified on a cost-benefit basis.

Forecasters often pay particular attention to the first rule and expend less effort on the second. Yet if well-prepared and cost-effective forecasts are to benefit the firm, those who have the decision-making authority must use them. This raises the question of what might be called the "politics" of forecasting. Substantial and sometimes major expenditures and resource allocations within the firm often rest on management's view of the course of future events. Because the movement of resources and power within an organization is often based on the perceived direction of the future (forecasts), it is not surprising to find a certain amount of political intrigue surrounding the forecasting process. The need to be able to effectively sell forecasts to management is at least as important as the development of the forecasts.

The remainder of this book discusses various forecasting models and procedures. First we review basic statistical concepts and provide an introduction to correlation and regression analysis. Then one chapter is devoted to methods of collecting data and exploring data sets for underlying patterns. Many specific forecasting methods are detailed in the chapters that follow, and the final two text chapters are devoted to aspects of judgmental forecasting and management of the forecasting process.

CASES

CASE 1-1   MR. TUX

John Mosby owns several Mr. Tux rental stores, most of them in the Spokane, Washington area.[5] His Spokane store also makes tuxedo shirts, which he distributes to rental shops across the country. Because rental activity varies from season to season due to proms, reunions, and other activities, John knows that his business is seasonal. He would like to measure this seasonal effect, both to assist him in managing his business and to use in loan repayment negotiations with his banker.

Of even greater interest to John is finding a way of forecasting his monthly sales. His business continues to grow, which, in turn, requires more capital

and long-term debt. He has sources for both types of growth financing, but investors and bankers are interested in a concrete way of forecasting future sales. Although they trust John, his word that the future of his business "looks great" leaves them uneasy.

As a first step in building a forecasting model, John directs one of his employees, McKennah Lane, to collect monthly sales data for the past several years. In the chapters that follow, various techniques are used to forecast these sales data for Mr. Tux. In Chapter 11 these efforts are summarized, and John Mosby attempts to choose the forecasting technique that will best meet his needs. ■

CASE 1-2   CONSUMER CREDIT
COUNSELING

Consumer Credit Counseling (CCC), a private, nonprofit corporation, was founded in 1982.[6] The purpose of CCC was to provide assistance to consumers in planning and following budgets, to assist consumers in making arrangements with creditors to repay delinquent obligations, and to provide money management education.

Private financial counseling was provided at no cost to families and individuals who were experiencing financial difficulties or who wanted to improve their money management skills. Money management educational programs were provided for schools, community groups, and businesses. A debt management program was offered as an alternative to

---

[5] We are indebted to John Mosby, the owner of Mr. Tux rental stores, for his help in preparing this case.

[6] We are indebted to Marv Harnishfeger, executive director of Consumer Credit Counseling of Spokane, and Dorothy Mercer, president of the board of directors, for their help in preparing the case. Dorothy is a former M.B.A. student of JH who has consistently kept him in touch with the use of quantitative methods in the real world of business.

bankruptcy. Through this program, CCC negotiated with creditors on behalf of the client for special payment arrangements. The client made a lump-sum payment to CCC that was then disbursed to creditors.

CCC had a blend of paid and volunteer staff; in fact, volunteers outnumbered paid staff three to one. Seven paid staff provided the management, clerical, and about half of the counseling needs for CCC. Twenty-one volunteer counselors fulfilled the other half of the counseling needs of the service. CCC depended primarily on corporate funding to support operations and services. The Fair Share Funding Program allowed creditors who received payments from client debt management programs to donate back to the service a portion of the funds returned to them through these programs.

A major portion of corporate support came from a local utility that provided funding to support a full-time counselor position as well as office space for counseling at all offices.

In addition, client fees were a source of funding. Clients who participated in debt management paid a monthly fee of $15 to help cover the administrative cost of this program. (Fees were reduced or waived for clients who were unable to afford them.)

This background will be used in the chapters that follow as CCC faces difficult problems related to forecasting important variables. ∎

Minitab Applications

Minitab is a sophisticated statistical program that improves with each release. Described here is Release 14.

Figure 1-1 shows you four important aspects of Minitab. The menu bar is where you choose commands. For instance, click on Stat and a pull-down menu appears that contains all of the statistical techniques available. The toolbar displays buttons for commonly used functions. Note that these buttons change depending on which Minitab window is open. There are two separate windows on the Minitab screen: the data window where you enter, edit, and view the column data for each worksheet, and the session window that displays text output such as tables of statistics.

In the following chapters specific instructions will be given to enable you to enter data onto the Minitab spreadsheet and to activate forecasting procedures to produce needed forecasts.

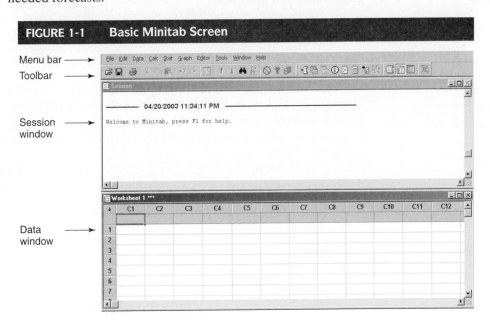

FIGURE 1-1   Basic Minitab Screen

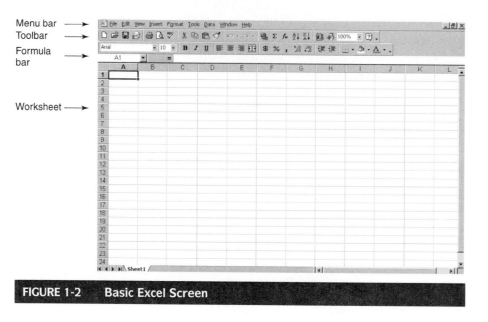

Menu bar →
Toolbar →
Formula bar →

Worksheet →

FIGURE 1-2   Basic Excel Screen

Excel Applications

Excel is a popular spreadsheet program that is frequently used for forecasting. Figure 1-2 shows the opening screen of Version 2000. Data are entered in the rows and columns of the spreadsheet (note that row 1, column A has been highlighted in Figure 1-2), and then commands are issued to perform various operations on the entered data.

For example, annual salaries for a number of employees could be entered into column 1, and the average of these values calculated by Excel. As another example, employee ages could be placed in column 2 and the relationship between age and salary examined. The chapters that follow will show you how to use Excel to solve these and other forecasting problems.

There are several statistical functions available on Excel that may not be on the drop-down menus on your screen. To activate these functions, click on the following:

```
Tools>Add-Ins
```

The Add-Ins dialog box appears. Select Analysis ToolPak and click OK. The functions available under ToolPak will be called on in later chapters.

It is strongly recommended that an Excel add-in be used to help with the multitude of statistical computations required by the forecasting techniques discussed in this textbook.

We recommend the Excel add-in Crystal Ball (CB) Predictor to expand the forecasting capabilities of Excel. We will illustrate the use of CB Predictor in Chapters 4 and 9.

References

Bernstein, P. L. *Against the Gods: The Remarkable Story of Risk.* New York: John Wiley & Sons, 1996.

Carlberg, C. "Use Excel's Forecasting to Get Terrific Projections." *Denver Business Journal* 47 (18) (1996): 2B.

Chase Jr., C. W. "Selecting the Appropriate Forecasting Method." *Journal of Business Forecasting* (Fall 1997): 2.

Diebold, F. X. *Elements of Forecasting*, Third Edition. Cincinnati, Ohio: South-Western, 2004.

Georgoff, D. M., and R. G. Mardick. "Manager's Guide to Forecasting." *Harvard Business Review* 1 (1986): 110–120.

Hogarth, R. M., and S. Makridakis. "Forecasting and Planning: An Evaluation." *Management Science* 27 (2) (1981): 115–138.

Makridakis, S. "The Art and Science of Forecasting." *International Journal of Forecasting* 2 (1986): 15–39.

Newbold, P., and T. Bos. *Introductory Business and Economic Forecasting*, Second Edition. Cincinnati, Ohio: South-Western, 1994.

Ord, K., and S. Lowe. "Automatic Forecasting." *American Statistician*, 50 (1996): 88–94.

Perry, S. "Applied Business Forecasting." *Management Accounting* 72 (3) (1994): 40.

Pindyck, R. S., and D. L. Rubinfeld. *Econometric Models and Economic Forecasts*, Fourth Edition. New York: McGraw-Hill, 1998.

Wright, G., and P. Ayton, eds. *Judgemental Forecasting*. New York: John Wiley & Sons, 1987.

CHAPTER 2

A REVIEW OF BASIC STATISTICAL CONCEPTS

Most forecasting techniques are based on fundamental statistical concepts that are the subject of business statistics textbooks and introductory statistics courses. This chapter reviews some of the basic concepts that will serve as a foundation for much of the material in the remainder of the text.

Most statistical procedures make inferences about the items of interest, called the *population*, after selecting and measuring a subgroup of these items, called the *sample*. Careful selection of a representative sample and the use of a sufficiently large sample size are important components of a statistical inference process that has an acceptably low degree of risk.

In forecasting we usually work with historical data in an attempt to predict, or forecast, the uncertain future. For this reason we will concentrate on examining sample data, manipulating these data in some way, and using the results to make forecasts.

DESCRIBING DATA WITH NUMERICAL SUMMARIES

The purpose of descriptive statistical procedures is to briefly describe a large collection of measurements with a few key summary values. The most common summary is obtained by averaging the values. In statistics the process of averaging is usually accomplished by computing the *mean*, which involves adding all values and dividing by the number of values.

The sample mean (X-bar) is computed using Equation 2.1.

$$\bar{X} = \frac{\Sigma X}{n} \tag{2.1}$$

where

$\bar{X}$ = sample mean

ΣX = sum of all the values of the sample

n = sample size

To simplify the computations in this text, some shorthand notation is used. In the simplified notation for summing all X values (see Equation 2.1), the summations are understood to extend from 1 to n. A more formal notation system for this procedure is

$$\sum_{i=1}^{n} X_i$$

15

where the subscript i varies from its initial value of 1 to n in increments of 1. Since almost all sums run from 1 to n, the starting and ending (n) indices will be suppressed, and the simpler notation will be used except where the more complete notation is needed for clarity.

In addition to measuring the central tendency of a group of values by computing the mean, the extent to which the values are dispersed around the mean is oftentimes of interest. The *standard deviation* can be thought of as a unit of measurement for measuring distance from the mean. Equation 2.2 is the formula for the standard deviation:

$$S = \sqrt{\frac{\Sigma(X - \bar{X})^2}{n - 1}} = \sqrt{\frac{\Sigma X^2 - \frac{(\Sigma X)^2}{n}}{n - 1}} \tag{2.2}$$

where the numerator represents the sum of squared differences between the measured values and their mean.

Many statistical procedures make use of the sample *variance*. The variance of a collection of measurements is the standard deviation squared. Thus the sample variance (S^2) is computed as

$$S^2 = \frac{\Sigma(X - \bar{X})^2}{n - 1} = \frac{\Sigma X^2 - \frac{(\Sigma X)^2}{n}}{n - 1} \tag{2.3}$$

Example 2.1
Consider the following collection of people's ages:

$$23, 38, 42, 25, 60, 55, 50, 42, 32, 35$$

For this sample, $n = 10$ and

$$\sum_{i=1}^{n} X_i = X_1 + X_2 + \cdots + X_{10} = 23 + 38 + \cdots + 35 = 402$$

$$\bar{X} = \frac{\Sigma X}{n} = \frac{402}{10} = 40.2$$

$$S^2 = \frac{\Sigma(X - \bar{X})^2}{n - 1} = \frac{(23 - 40.2)^2 + \cdots + (35 - 40.2)^2}{10 - 1} = \frac{1339.6}{9} = 148.84$$

$$S = \sqrt{S^2} = \sqrt{148.84} = 12.2$$

The computations are shown in Table 2-1. The sample mean is 40.2 years, the sample variance is 148.84, and the sample standard deviation is 12.2 years.

The term *degrees of freedom* is used to indicate the number of data items that are free of each other in the sense that they cannot be calculated from each other and can therefore carry unique pieces of information. For example, suppose the following three statements are made:

> *I am thinking of the number 5. I am thinking of the number 7. The sum of the two numbers I am thinking of is 12.*

At first glance three pieces of information are presented. However, if any two of these statements are known, the other one can be determined. It could be said that there are

TABLE 2-1	Calculation of S^2 ($\bar{X} = 40.2$)	
X	$X - \bar{X}$	$(X - \bar{X})^2$
23	−17.2	295.84
38	−2.2	4.84
42	1.8	3.24
25	−15.2	231.04
60	19.8	392.04
55	14.8	219.04
50	9.8	96.04
42	1.8	3.24
32	−8.2	67.24
35	−5.2	27.04

$$\Sigma(X - \bar{X})^2 = 1,339.60$$

$$S^2 = \frac{1,339.60}{10 - 1} = 148.84$$

only two unique pieces of information in the three statements or, to use the statistical term, there are only two degrees of freedom because only two of the values are free to vary; the third is not.

> *Degrees of freedom* refers to the number of data items that are independent of one another and that carry unique pieces of information.

In the example presented in Table 2-1, the ages of 10 people constitute a sample with 10 degrees of freedom. Anyone's age could have been included in the sample and, therefore, each of the ages is free to vary. When the mean is calculated, all 10 ages are used to account for a total mean age equal to 40.2 years.

The computation of the sample standard deviation differs. When the sample standard deviation is calculated, an estimate of the population mean is used (the sample mean $\bar{X}$). By using the sample mean as an estimate of the population mean in the computation, a standard deviation that is smaller than the population standard deviation will usually be obtained. However, this problem can be corrected by dividing the value $\Sigma(X - \bar{X})^2$ by the appropriate degrees of freedom. Once the sample mean is computed, only nine of the deviations $X - \bar{X}$ are required, in this example, to calculate the sample standard deviation. Given nine of the deviations, the last deviation is fixed since $\Sigma(X - \bar{X})$ must equal zero. Consequently, we say that the sample standard deviation (or sample variance) has nine degrees of freedom. In general, whenever a sample statistic is used as an estimate of a population parameter in a computation, one degree of freedom is lost.

Summary statistics can be defined for populations. To distinguish population statistics from sample statistics, we use a different notation. Table 2-2 shows the symbols used for both population and sample statistics.

The mean and standard deviation are the most common ways of describing sample data in a brief and meaningful way. However, other descriptive summary measures are sometimes used as well. The *median* is sometimes used to indicate a central value in a data collection. The median is that value such that half the values in the collection are greater than it and half are less.

TABLE 2-2	Notation for Population and Sample Statistics	
Statistic	*Population Symbol*	*Sample Symbol*
Mean	μ	$\bar{X}$
Variance	σ^2	s^2
Standard deviation	σ	S

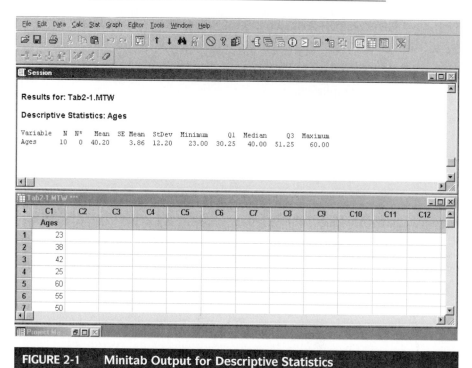

FIGURE 2-1   Minitab Output for Descriptive Statistics

Sometimes the *range* of the data is presented as a rough measure of dispersion. The range simply indicates the difference between the minimum and maximum values. The range of ages in Table 2-1, for example, was 37 ($60 - 23$).

The *quartiles* divide the data collection into four equal parts, after the numerical values have been arrayed from smallest to largest. The median divides the array into two equal parts, and is sometimes called the *second quartile* and denoted by Q_2. The *first quartile* (Q_1) divides the lower half into two equal parts and the *third quartile* (Q_3) divides the upper half into two equal parts. The collection of ages in Table 2-1, for example, has a first quartile of $Q_1 = 30.25$, a median (or second quartile) of $Q_2 = 40$, and a third quartile of $Q_3 = 51.25$.

Finally, the *interquartile range* provides an indication of the variability of a data set. It is simply the difference between the third quartile and the first quartile, ($Q_3 - Q_1$), or the range for the middle 50% of the data values. For the age data the interquartile range is 21 ($51.25 - 30.25$).

Minitab and Excel can be used to compute most of the descriptive statistics presented so far. Figure 2-1 shows the Minitab output for the age data presented in Table 2-1. The instructions for computing descriptive statistics using Minitab and Excel are presented in the Minitab and Excel applications sections at the end of this chapter.

DISPLAYS OF NUMERICAL INFORMATION

In forecasting we are concerned with two types of data: *cross-sectional* data in which all observations are from the same time frame, and *time series* data that consist of a sequence of observations over time. Table 2-3 shows an example of cross-sectional data: the net income as a percentage of equity for a sample of 209 companies from the Fortune 500 survey. Other examples are corporation executives' yearly incomes and selling prices for homes in a particular city. Some examples of time series data are the number of visitors at the Coulee Dam Visitor Center per month, monthly sales for the Sears Corporation, daily IBM stock price, and annual U.S. wheat production.

One of the most important things to do when first exploring a variable is to visualize the data through charts and graphs. Basic features of the data including unusual observations and unique patterns are most easily seen visually. At times, graphs even suggest possible explanations for some of the variation in the data.

A *dot plot* is one of the simplest ways to visualize data graphically. In Figure 2-2 a horizontal axis displays the range of values for net income as a percentage of equity from Table 2-3. Each observation is represented by a dot placed above the axis. Dot plots show the details of the data and also allow a forecaster to compare two or more sets of data.

A *box plot*, also called a box-and-whisker plot, is useful for displaying the distributional characteristics of data. Figure 2-3 shows a box plot for the net income as a percentage of equity data. A line is drawn across the box at the median. This line divides the data into two equal sections. The lower edge of the box is the first quartile (Q_1) and the upper edge is the third quartile (Q_3). Additional limits using the interquartile range, ($Q_3 - Q_1$), can be constructed. The lower limit is located at $Q_1 - 1.5(Q_3 - Q_1)$ and the upper limit at $Q_3 + 1.5(Q_3 - Q_1)$. *Outliers* are points outside of the lower and upper limits and are plotted with asterisks. In Figure 2-3 the first quartile is 8, the

TABLE 2-3	Net Income as a Percentage of Equity for a Sample of 209 Companies from the Fortune 500 Survey								
17	23	22	18	8	7	12	2	49	14
14	36	16	7	3	8	10	11	20	17
15	25	18	12	20	7	5	11	0	22
14	10	14	19	8	12	13	21	3	22
11	18	2	18	14	11	36	16	7	14
12	14	10	8	20	13	8	23	6	21
9	23	7	14	25	12	12	8	11	5
18	13	14	9	16	2	19	21	18	9
14	2	20	17	11	16	13	12	22	16
7	6	14	10	1	21	35	20	18	28
17	15	9	12	5	10	14	1	17	14
14	14	6	22	16	13	14	8	12	6
15	10	22	19	16	4	20	18	2	3
20	7	15	39	4	3	10	7	15	16
12	13	12	11	18	10	13	7	13	12
14	8	11	17	11	22	16	11	12	11
9	11	13	0	12	3	9	9	13	27
1	16	18	12	11	0	10	9	12	22
18	44	4	3	17	12	8	16	7	16
27	11	19	12	22	3	14	14	7	8
11	1	3	17	8	7	5	19	22	

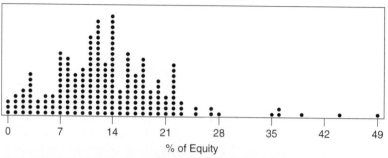

Dotplot of % of Equity

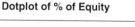

FIGURE 2-2   Dot Plot for Net Income as a Percentage of Equity

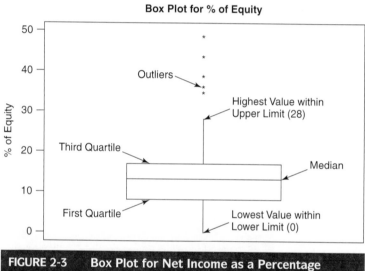

Box Plot for % of Equity

FIGURE 2-3   Box Plot for Net Income as a Percentage of Equity

median is 13, the third quartile is 17, and the interquartile range is 9 ($17 - 8$). The lower limit is -5.5 ($8 - 1.5 \times 9$) and the upper limit is 30.5 ($17 + 1.5 \times 9$). Note that the lowest value within the lowest limit, -5.5, is 0 and the highest value within the highest limit, 30.5, is 28. Six values (35, 36, 36, 39, 44, and 49) exceed the upper limit of 30.5 and are outliers.

The *histogram* condenses the data by grouping similar values into classes. A histogram can be constructed by placing the variable of interest on the horizontal axis and the frequency, relative frequency, or percent frequency on the vertical axis. By looking at a histogram such as Figure 2-4, you can tell the proportion of the total area above an interval of the horizontal axis. A total of 61 out of the 209 companies, or 29.2%, had net income as a percentage of equity in the interval between 7.5% and 12.5%. Consequently, the third rectangle in Figure 2-4 contains .292 of the total area represented by the shaded vertical bars.

Although histograms provide good visual descriptions of data sets, especially very large data sets, they do not let us identify individual observations. In contrast, in a dot plot each of the original values is visible.

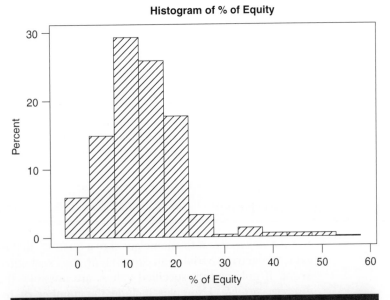

FIGURE 2-4   Histogram for Net Income as a Percentage of Equity

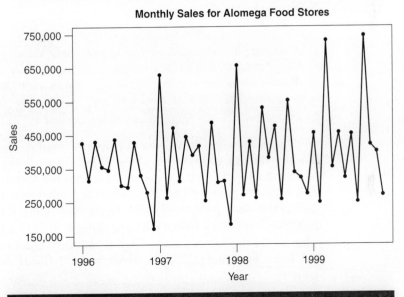

FIGURE 2-5   Monthly Sales for the Alomega Food Stores of Example 1.1

Scatter diagrams are used to visualize the relationship between two variables. They will be discussed later in the chapter in the correlation analysis section.

For chronological data, the most frequently used graphical form is a *time series plot* in which the data are plotted over time. Figure 2-5 shows a time series plot of monthly sales for the Alomega Food Stores discussed in Example 1.1. A time series plot reveals the variability of the data and the time at which peaks and valleys occur.

It also shows the relative size of the peaks and valleys compared with the rest of the series.

One important step in selecting an appropriate forecasting technique is to identify the data patterns that exist within a time series. Once the data patterns have been identified, the forecasting methods most appropriate to those patterns can be used. Four types of time series data patterns can be identified: horizontal, trend, cyclical, and seasonal. Each type will be discussed in depth in Chapter 3.

A tool that is often used to help identify time series data patterns is the correlogram, or autocorrelation function. It is a graphical tool for displaying the correlations between various time lags of a time series. Correlograms will also be discussed in Chapter 3.

PROBABILITY DISTRIBUTIONS

A *random variable* is the name given to a quantity that is capable of taking on different values from trial to trial in an experiment, the exact outcome being a chance or random event. If only certain specified values are possible, the random variable is called a *discrete variable*. Examples include the number of rooms in a house, the number of people arriving at a supermarket checkout stand in an hour, and the number of defective units in a batch of electronic parts. If any value of the random variable is possible within some range, it is called a *continuous variable*. Examples of this type of variable are the weights of people, the length of a manufactured part, and the time between car arrivals at a tollbooth.

A *discrete random variable* can assume only values from a predetermined set. These outcomes are often represented numerically by integers. A *continuous random variable* can assume any value within a specified range. These outcomes are represented numerically by an interval of values.

The *probability distribution* of a discrete random variable lists all possible values that the variable can take on, along with the probability of each. The *expected value* of a random variable is the mean value that the variable assumes over many trials. The expected value, $E(X)$, for a discrete probability distribution can be found by multiplying each possible X value by its probability $P(X)$ and then summing these products. Equation 2.4 shows this calculation:

$$E(X) = \Sigma[X \times P(X)] \tag{2.4}$$

The *expected value* of a random variable is the mean value of the variable over many trials or observations.

Example 2.2
The number of no-sales days for a salesperson during a month is described by the probability distribution shown in Table 2-4. These values are based on the salesperson's past experience and will be used to forecast future sales activity. The X column lists all values (no-sales days) that are possible, whereas the $P(X)$ column lists the corresponding probabilities. Note that, since all possible values of X are listed, the probabilities sum to 1.00, or 100%. This is true for all probability distributions, disregarding rounding errors.

TABLE 2-4	Discrete Probability Distribution
X	P(X)
1	.10
2	.20
3	.25
4	.15
5	.30

For the probability distribution given in Table 2-4, the expected value is

$$E(X) = 1(.1) + 2(.2) + 3(.25) + 4(.15) + 5(.30) = 3.35$$

Thus if this salesperson were observed for a very large number of months and the number of no-sales days were recorded, the mean would be 3.35 if future activity is correctly predicted by the historical data on which the probability distribution is based.

Notice that the mean falls near the middle of the X values. It is pulled toward the upper end of the probability distribution because of the relatively large probability associated with $X = 5$.

For a continuous distribution the probability of obtaining a specific value approaches zero. For instance, the probability of anyone weighing 150 pounds may be considered zero since this would mean that this weight is exactly 150.0000—no matter how accurate a scale is used. In the continuous distribution case, probabilities are assigned to intervals, or ranges of values. The probability that a person's weight falls in the interval 145 to 155 pounds might be computed, for example.

Some theoretical distributions occur over and over again in practical statistical applications, and for this reason it is important to examine their properties. One of these is the *binomial distribution*, often used to represent a discrete random variable. The requirements for a binomial experiment are:

1. There are n identical trials, each of which results in one of two possible outcomes, say, success and failure.
2. The probability of success for each outcome remains fixed from trial to trial.
3. The trials are independent.

The interest is in finding the probability of X successful occurrences in the n trials, where a successful occurrence is arbitrarily defined to be one of the two possible outcomes. The various values of X, along with their probabilities, form the binomial distribution. These probabilities can be found from the following binomial formula:

$$P(X) = \binom{n}{X} p^X (1-p)^{n-X} \qquad \text{for } X = 0, 1, \ldots, n \qquad \textbf{(2.5)}$$

where

$\binom{n}{X}$ = the number of combinations of n things taken X at a time

p = the probability of success on each trial

X = the particular number of successes of interest

n = the number of trials

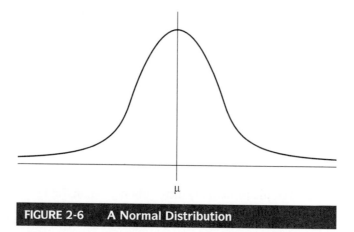

μ

FIGURE 2-6   A Normal Distribution

The *binomial distribution* is a discrete probability distribution describing the likelihood of X successes in n trials of a binomial experiment.

An easier way to find binomial probabilities than using Equation 2.5 is to refer to a binomial distribution table such as the one found in Appendix C, Table C-1. Blocks that represent n group the probabilities. Each block has a column headed by p and a row indicated by X.[1]

Example 2.3
Suppose eight items are randomly drawn from a production line that is known to produce defective parts 5% of the time. What is the probability of getting exactly zero defectives? The answer, from the binomial table in Appendix C-1, is .6634. (Here $n = 8$, $p = .05$, and $X = 0$.)

An important continuous distribution of interest to us, because many useful populations of numbers can be approximated by it, is the *normal distribution*. Knowledge of the mean and the standard deviation is necessary to identify a specific normal distribution. A normal curve is symmetrical and bell-shaped as shown in Figure 2-6. This distribution represents many real-life variables that are measured on a continuous scale.

Probabilities of values drawn from a normal distribution falling into various intervals are found by first converting all intervals to units of standard deviation called *Z-scores*.[2] The Z-score of any X value is the number of standard deviations from the central value of the curve (μ) to that value. Thus the formula is

$$Z = \frac{X - \mu}{\sigma}$$ **(2.6)**

where

> X = the value of interest
>
> μ = the mean
>
> σ = the standard deviation

---

[1] Excel and Minitab will also calculate binomial probabilities.

[2] It can be shown that if the random variable X has a normal distribution with mean μ and standard deviation σ, then the random variable $Z = (X - \mu)/\sigma$ has a normal distribution with mean 0 and standard deviation 1. This particular normal distribution is called the *standard normal distribution*.

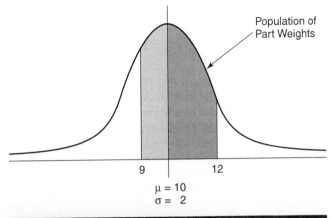

FIGURE 2-7   **Normal Curve Areas for Example 2.4**

After the Z-score has been computed, the normal curve table can be consulted to find the area under the curve between the center of the original curve (μ) and the value of interest X.[3]

The *normal distribution* has a bell shape and is completely determined by its mean and standard deviation.

Example 2.4
The weights of a population of parts made by a certain machine are normally distributed with mean 10 pounds and standard deviation 2 pounds. What is the probability that a part drawn at random from the machine weighs between 9 and 12 pounds? The normal curve with the appropriate area shaded is shown in Figure 2-7.

Since normal curve tables are often designed to give areas from the center of the curve to some point, two separate areas must be found: one on each side of the mean. These areas are then added together. This process will produce the probability of a value falling in this interval. The two Z-scores are

$$Z_1 = \frac{X_1 - \mu}{\sigma} = \frac{9 - 10}{2} = -.50$$

$$Z_2 = \frac{X_2 - \mu}{\sigma} = \frac{12 - 10}{2} = 1.00$$

Consequently, the area under the normal curve between 9 and 12 in Figure 2-7 is the same as the area under the normal curve of Z (see Footnote 2) between $-.5$ and 1. For the normal table in this book, the negative sign on the first Z-score is disregarded since the area under the normal curve for Z between $-.5$ and 0 is the same as the area between 0 and .5. These two Z-scores are referred to the normal curve table in Appendix C, Table C-2, to yield the two areas, which are then added together:

$$Z_1 = -.50 \rightarrow .1915$$
$$Z_2 = 1.00 \rightarrow \underline{.3413}$$
$$.5328$$

It is concluded that there is about a 53% chance that a part randomly drawn from this population of parts will weigh between 9 and 12 pounds.

[3] Normal probabilities can be computed using Excel or Minitab.

SAMPLING DISTRIBUTIONS

In most statistical applications a random sample is taken from the population under investigation, a statistic is computed from the sample data, and conclusions are drawn about the population on the basis of this sample. A *sampling distribution* is the distribution of all possible values of the sample statistic that can be obtained from the population for a given sample size. For instance, a random sample of 100 persons might be taken from a population and weighed and then their mean weight computed. This sample mean ($\bar{X}$) can be thought of as having been drawn from the distribution of all possible sample means of sample size 100 that could be taken from the population. More generally, each sample statistic that can be computed from sample data can be considered as having been drawn from a sampling distribution.

> A *sampling distribution* is the array of all possible values of a sample statistic that can be drawn from a population for a given sample size.

The *central limit theorem* states that as the sample size becomes larger, the sampling distribution of sample means tends toward the normal distribution, and that the mean of this normal distribution is μ, the population mean, and the standard deviation is $\sigma/\sqrt{n}$, the population standard deviation divided by the square root of the sample size. This quantity $\sigma/\sqrt{n}$ is known as the *standard error* of the sample mean. Thus the sampling distribution of the sample mean will tend toward normality regardless of the shape of the population distribution from which the samples were drawn. Figure 2-8 demonstrates how such a sampling distribution might appear.

The central limit theorem is of particular importance in statistics since it allows the analyst to compute the probability of various sample results through knowledge of normal curve probabilities.

Example 2.5

What is the probability that the mean of a random sample of 100 weights drawn from a population will be within 2 pounds of the true population mean weight if the standard deviation of the population is estimated to be 15 pounds? Figure 2-9 illustrates the appropriate sampling distribution.

The standard error is $\sigma/\sqrt{n} = 15/\sqrt{100} = 1.5$, yielding a Z-score of $Z = (\bar{X} - \mu)/(\sigma/\sqrt{n}) = 2/1.5 = 1.33$ and an area from the normal curve table of .4082. Doubling this area to account for both sides of the mean results in a total area of .8164. Chances are about 82% that the sample mean will be within 2 pounds of the true mean, given the sample size

FIGURE 2-8   Sampling Distribution of $\bar{X}$

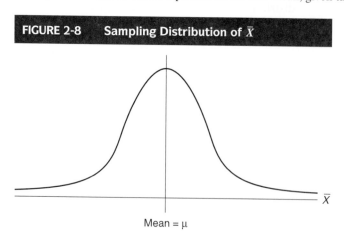

Mean = μ

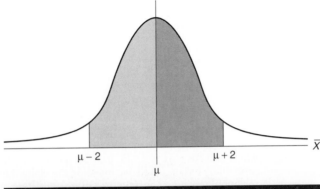

FIGURE 2-9   Sampling Distribution Areas for Example 2.5

of 100 and the estimated variability of the population, $\sigma = 15$. As will be seen, this ability to calculate probabilities of sample results will enable an analyst to make inferences about the population from the sample, with direct applicability to forecasting.

For small sample sizes, the sample means may not be normally distributed. However, if the population from which the sample is selected is essentially normal, and the population standard deviation is estimated by the sample standard deviation S, the sampling distribution of the ratio

$$t = \frac{\bar{X} - \mu}{S/\sqrt{n}} \tag{2.7}$$

is known. It is called *Student's t distribution* (or simply the t distribution) with $n - 1$ degrees of freedom (abbreviated df). The t distribution is centered at 0 and has a bell shape but with fatter tails than a normal distribution. However, as the number of degrees of freedom (equivalently, the sample size n) increases, the t distribution looks more and more like a normal distribution with a mean of 0 and a standard deviation of 1.

Appendix C, Table C-3 shows values taken from the t distribution. Note that only one value need be specified before referring to the table, namely, the degrees of freedom. Once the degrees of freedom value is known, the t values that exclude desired percentages of the area under the curve can be found. For example, if the t distribution of interest has 12 degrees of freedom, then a t value of 2.179 on each side of 0 will include 95% of the area under the curve and exclude 5% of it, that is, 2.5% in each tail.

Example 2.6
A manager of a credit card company claims the mean time to resolve disputed claims is 30 days. To test this claim, data were collected on a sample of 15 disputed claims. The 15 claims had a mean time to resolve of 35.9 days and a standard deviation of 10.2 days.

If the data are regarded as a random sample from a normal population, do they cast suspicion on the manager's claim?

If the manager's claim is correct, the population mean is $\mu = 30$ and the random variable

$$t = \frac{\bar{X} - \mu}{S/\sqrt{n}}$$

has Student's t distribution with $n - 1 = 15 - 1 = 14$ degrees of freedom. The manager's claim would be suspect if the value of this variable is too large or too small because this occurs when the value of $\bar{X}$ is far from μ. Consulting Table C-3 for 14 degrees of freedom, we see that $t_{.025} = 2.145$. Before the sample is obtained, the probability that t will exceed 2.145 is .025. Similarly, the probability is .025 that t will be less than -2.145. Adding these two equal probabilities, the probability is $.025 + .025 = .05$ that t will be larger than 2.145 or smaller than -2.145. Now we are ready to determine whether the value of $\bar{X}$, 35.9, is far from μ, 30. The observed value of t is

$$t = \frac{35.9 - 30}{10.2/\sqrt{15}} = 2.240$$

which exceeds $t_{.025} = 2.145$. Rather than accept the explanation that an event with a small probability has occurred, we question the claim that the mean is 30 days. A larger value for the hypothesized mean would be more consistent with the data.

INFERENCE FROM A SAMPLE

Estimation

There are two major reasons for examining sample evidence when it is not feasible, or even possible, to measure the entire population of interest. The first of these is called *estimation*, where the sample results are used to estimate unknown population characteristics. Although estimation is the common statistical term for this task, it could as well be called forecasting in many business situations because the data consist of collected historical observations, and the value for which the estimate, or forecast, is desired lies in the unknown future. The second major purpose of examining sample evidence will be discussed in the next section.

A *point estimate* of a population parameter (a forecast) is a single value calculated from the sample data that estimates the unknown population value. A point estimate is a "best guess" of a population parameter computed from the sample. Often the best guess of a population parameter is provided by the corresponding sample quantity. For example, the best guess of the value of the population mean is given by the value of the sample mean. Table 2-2 contained three population parameters and the sample statistics that provide point estimates of them.

An *interval estimate* is an interval within which the population parameter of interest is likely to lie. It is found by constructing an interval around the point estimate of the form

Point estimate $\pm$ Multiple $\times$ (Estimated standard deviation of point estimate)   **(2.8)**

where the "multiple" is often a normal distribution percentage point or a t distribution percentage point.

Ideally, we would like to obtain a sample and then determine an interval that would, for instance, definitely contain the population mean μ. However, because of sample-to-sample variability, this goal is unattainable. Instead we specify a high probability, say .95 or .99, that a proposed interval will cover the true value of the population parameter of interest. Because this probability pertains to the interval before the sample is observed, it is called the *level of confidence*. An interval obtained by a procedure satisfying the probability requirement is called a *confidence interval*. The quantity to the right of the $\pm$ sign in Equation 2.8 is sometimes called the *error allowance*, and its size will depend directly on the level of confidence (through the multiple) and the information in the sample (through the estimated standard deviation of point estimate).

A *point estimate* is a single-valued estimate of a population parameter.
An *interval estimate* is an interval within which the population parameter is likely to lie.

Example 2.7

A random sample of 500 shoppers is selected from Northgate Shopping Center to determine the average distance they traveled to the mall. An analysis of the sample results reveals: $\bar{X} = 23.5$ miles, $S = 10.4$ miles.

The point estimate for the unknown population mean distance for all shoppers at the mall is 23.5 miles, the sample mean. The interval estimate for μ using a 95% confidence level, and using Equation 2.9 below, is

$$\bar{X} \pm Z\frac{S}{\sqrt{n}} \tag{2.9}$$

or

$$23.5 \pm 1.96\frac{10.4}{\sqrt{500}}$$

$$23.5 \pm 1.96(.465)$$

$$23.5 \pm .91 \rightarrow (22.6, 24.4)$$

Notice that the multiple in Equation 2.8, in this case, is the upper .025 (2.5%) point of a standard normal distribution (see Footnote 2), and $S/\sqrt{n} = 10.4/\sqrt{500}$ is the estimated standard deviation of $\bar{X}$ for a sample of size $n = 500$.

It can be stated, with 95% confidence, that the mean number of miles traveled to the shopping mall by the population of shoppers is somewhere between 22.6 miles and 24.4 miles. The 95% confidence refers to the fact that if, say, 100 samples of size 500 were selected, sample means and standard deviations computed, and interval estimates constructed, 95 out of 100 of the intervals would, in fact, contain the actual population mean. Consequently, it is highly likely that the particular interval constructed above contains the population mean miles traveled to the mall.

HYPOTHESIS TESTING

In many statistical situations, including forecasting, the interest is in testing some claim about the population rather than estimating or forecasting one of its parameters. This procedure is called *hypothesis testing* and is the second major purpose of examining sample evidence. Hypothesis testing involves the following steps:

Step 1. Formulate the hypothesis being tested (called the null hypothesis, symbol H_0) and state the alternative hypothesis (the one concluded if H_0 is rejected, symbol H_1).

Step 2. Collect a random sample of items from the population, measure them, and compute the appropriate sample test statistic.

Step 3. Assume the null hypothesis is true and determine the sampling distribution of the test statistic.

Step 4. Compute the probability that a value of the sample statistic at least as large as the one observed could have been drawn from this sampling distribution.

Step 5. If this probability is high, do not reject the null hypothesis; if this probability is low, the null hypothesis is discredited and can be rejected with a small chance of error.

When these steps are followed, two types of error can occur, as shown in Table 2-5. It is hoped that the correct decision concerning the null hypothesis will be reached after

TABLE 2-5   Results of a Hypothesis Test

		Action	
		Do Not Reject H_0	Reject H_0
State of Nature	H_0 *True*	Correct decision	Type I error: probability α
	H_0 *False*	Type II error: probability β	Correct decision

examining sample evidence, but there is always a possibility of rejecting a true H_0 and failing to reject a false H_0. The probabilities of these events are known as alpha (α) and beta (β), respectively. Alpha is also known as the *significance level* of the test.

Example 2.8

A job-shop foreman suspects that the mean weight of parts produced by a certain machine has decreased. It is desired to test the hypothesis that the mean weight of parts produced by the machine is still 50 pounds, the mean weight of the parts in past years. A random sample of 100 parts is taken. It is assumed that the standard deviation of part weights is 5 pounds regardless of the mean weight because this value has remained constant in past studies of parts. We will use the sample mean as our test statistic and take as the null hypothesis the status quo; that is, the mean part weight μ is 50 pounds. Consequently, if the null hypothesis H_0 is true, the central limit theorem says the sampling distribution of $\bar{X}$ is, in this case, normal with mean $\mu = 50$ and standard deviation $\sigma/\sqrt{n} = 5/\sqrt{100} = .5$. A value of the sample mean, $\bar{X}$, close to or larger than 50 is support for H_0, and a value of $\bar{X}$ far below 50 is evidence against H_0, because such an event is unlikely if H_0 is true. A sensible decision rule, then, is one that rejects H_0 for a value of $\bar{X}$ far below 50. However, with this rule it is possible we could make a Type I error, that is, reject a true H_0. We can control the chance of rejecting a true H_0 by selecting alpha, the significance level. Suppose we make alpha small, say .05 (5%). Then we will reject H_0 if the observed value of our test statistic $\bar{X}$ falls beyond the lower .05 (5%) point of its sampling distribution under H_0. The test is demonstrated in Figure 2-10.

FIGURE 2-10   Hypothesis Test for Example 2.8

$H_0: \mu = 50$ pounds (the null hypothesis)
$H_1: \mu < 50$ pounds (the alternative hypothesis)

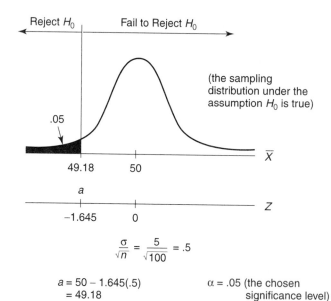

$$\frac{\sigma}{\sqrt{n}} = \frac{5}{\sqrt{100}} = .5$$

$a = 50 - 1.645(.5)$
$\quad = 49.18$

$\alpha = .05$ (the chosen significance level)

The decision rule for this test is:

If $\bar{X} < 49.18$, reject the null hypothesis H_0: $\mu = 50$

If the sample mean turns out to be 49.6 pounds, we could not reject H_0 at the 5% level. On the other hand, if the sample mean weight turned out to be 48.6 pounds, we would reject H_0. Note that for $\bar{X} = 48.6$, the probability of getting a value this extreme (far below 50) if H_0 is true is $P(\bar{X} < 48.6) = P(Z < \frac{48.6 - 50}{.5}) = P(Z < -2.8) = P(Z > 2.8) = (.5000 - .4974) = .0026$, an unlikely event indeed.

In hypothesis testing, there is always some ambiguity associated with selecting the null and alternative hypotheses. In general, the null hypothesis is the status quo or "no change" hypothesis. The alternative hypothesis is the research or change hypothesis. To discover if what we have done has made a difference or has resulted in a change from the status quo or current procedures, we formulate the difference or change as the alternative hypothesis. The goal is to see if we can reject the null hypothesis, with a small chance of a Type I error, in favor of the alternative.

p-Value

In Example 2.8, we calculated the probability of getting a value of the sample mean as extreme as $\bar{X} = 48.6$ if the null hypothesis H_0: $\mu = 50$ is true. The probability turned out to be .0026. This probability is called the *prob-value*, or *p-value*, of the test. Rather than select a significance level, it is now common practice to compute and report the *p*-value for the test; in fact, statistical software packages routinely report *p*-values associated with test statistics. *p*-values and their use in hypothesis testing are discussed in Steps 4 and 5 of our hypothesis testing steps at the beginning of this section. A small *p*-value suggests a strong rejection of the null hypothesis. The *p*-value can be regarded as evidence for (large *p*-value) or against (small *p*-value) the null hypothesis. Typical cutoff points for small *p*-values are .05 or .01.

In Example 2.8, if a two-tailed test had been performed, H_0: $\mu = 50$ versus H_1: $\mu \neq 50$, and $\bar{X} = 48.6$, the *p*-value is $P(\bar{X} < 48.6 \text{ or } \bar{X} > 51.4) = 2P(Z > \frac{51.4 - 50}{.5})$, or twice the area under the standard normal curve to the right of $Z = 2.8$. In this example, the *p*-value would equal $2(.0026) = .0052$.

> The *p-value*, or *significance probability*, is the probability of getting at least as extreme a sample result as the one actually observed if H_0 is true.

Example 2.9

Suppose it is desired to test the hypothesis that the mean score of students on a national examination is 500 against the alternative hypothesis that it is less than 500. A random sample of 15 students is taken from the population and produces a sample mean score of $\bar{X} = 475$. The standard deviation of the population is estimated by the sample standard deviation, $S = 35$. Assume the population of test scores is normally distributed.

We want to know if mean test scores are less than their historical value of 500. We will make a decision on the basis of the sample evidence and, in particular, on the value of the sample mean. The competing hypotheses are

$$H_0: \mu = 500$$
$$H_1: \mu < 500$$

If H_0 is true, we would expect to see a value of the sample average close to or larger than 500. If H_0 is false (H_1 is true), we would expect to see a value of the sample average quite a bit less than 500. Because the sample size is small, the population is normal, and the population standard deviation is estimated by the sample standard deviation, an appropriate

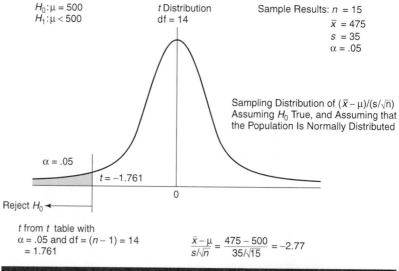

$H_0: \mu = 500$
$H_1: \mu < 500$

t Distribution
df = 14

Sample Results: $n = 15$
$\bar{x} = 475$
$s = 35$
$\alpha = .05$

Sampling Distribution of $(\bar{x} - \mu)/(s/\sqrt{n})$
Assuming H_0 True, and Assuming that
the Population Is Normally Distributed

$\alpha = .05$

$t = -1.761$

0

Reject H_0

t from *t* table with
$\alpha = .05$ and df $= (n - 1) = 14$
$= 1.761$

$\dfrac{\bar{x} - \mu}{s/\sqrt{n}} = \dfrac{475 - 500}{35/\sqrt{15}} = -2.77$

FIGURE 2-11   Hypothesis Test for Example 2.9

test statistic is the *t* statistic given in Equation 2.7 with $n - 1 = 15 - 1 = 14$ df. A large negative value of the *t* statistic is evidence against H_0 (the sample average is much less than the hypothesized population average of 500). First, let us construct the test for a significance level of $\alpha = .05$. The test (decision rule) is shown in Figure 2-11.

Because

decision rule: if observed $t < -1.76$, reject H_0: $\mu = 500$

and the observed *t* statistic is

$$t = \frac{\bar{X} - \mu}{S/\sqrt{n}} = \frac{475 - 500}{35/\sqrt{15}} = -2.77$$

we would reject the null hypothesis and conclude that the mean test score of students on the national exam is less than 500. Alternatively, the *p*-value in this case is *p*-value $= P(t < -2.77)$. Using Table C-3 with 14 df and the symmetry of the *t* distribution, this probability is between .010 and .005. Our observed test statistic is very unlikely if H_0 is true. The *p*-value tells us we should reject the null hypothesis.

CORRELATION ANALYSIS

In building statistical models for forecasting, it is often useful to examine the relationship between two variables. Two techniques, correlation and regression analysis, are reviewed here. In addition, special cases of correlation and regression are also considered in later chapters. This emphasis on correlation and regression is justified in view of the widespread use of these techniques in all sorts of forecasting applications.

Scatter Diagrams

A study of the relationship between variables begins with the simplest case, that of the relationship existing between two variables. Suppose two measurements have been taken on each of several objects. An analyst wishes to determine whether one of these measurable variables, called Y, tends to increase or decrease as the other variable, called X, changes. For instance, suppose both age and income have been measured for several individuals, as shown in Table 2-6. What can be said about the relationship between X and Y?

From Table 2-6 it appears that Y and X have a definite relationship. As X increases, Y increases. From this sample of five persons, it appears as if the older a person becomes, the more money that person makes. Of course, it is dangerous to reach conclusions on the basis of a small sample size, a subject to be pursued later. Yet given these observations, a definite relationship appears to exist between Y and X.

These five data points can be plotted on a two-dimensional scale, with values of X along the horizontal axis and values of Y along the vertical axis. Such a plot is called a *scatter diagram* and appears in Figure 2-12.

A *scatter diagram* is a plot of X–Y data points on a two-dimensional graph.

The scatter diagram helps to illustrate what intuition suggested when the raw data were first observed, namely, the appearance of a linear relationship between Y and X. This relationship is called a *positive* relationship because as X increases, so does Y.

In other situations involving two variables, different scatter diagram patterns might emerge. Consider the plots in Figure 2-13.

Diagram (a) of Figure 2-13 suggests what is called a *perfect, positive, linear relationship*. As X increases, Y increases also, and in a perfectly predictable way. That is,

TABLE 2-6	Income and Age Measurements	
Person	*Y, Income ($1,000s)*	*X, Age (years)*
1	27.8	22
2	28.5	23
3	30.0	26
4	35.0	27
5	36.4	35

FIGURE 2-12 **Scatter Diagram for Age and Income**

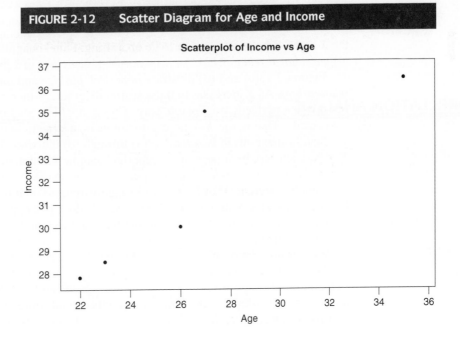

Scatterplot of Income vs Age

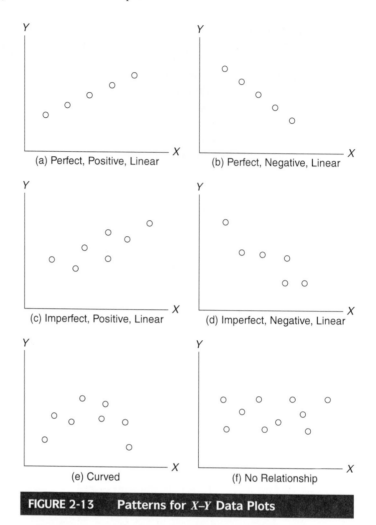

FIGURE 2-13   Patterns for *X–Y* Data Plots

the *X* and *Y* data points appear to lie on a straight line. Diagram (b) suggests a *perfect, negative, linear relationship*. As *X* increases, *Y* decreases in a predictable way.

Figures 2-13(c) and (d) illustrate *imperfect, positive* and *imperfect, negative, linear relationships*. As *X* increases in these scatter diagrams, *Y* increases (c) or decreases (d) but not in a perfectly predictable way. Thus *Y* might be slightly higher or lower than "expected." That is, the *X–Y* points do not lie on a straight line.

Scatter diagrams in Figures 2-13(a) through (d) illustrate *linear relationships*. The *X–Y* relationship, be it perfect or imperfect, can be summarized by a straight line. In comparison, a *curved relationship* appears in diagram (e).

Finally, diagram (f) of Figure 2-13 suggests that no relationship of any kind exists between variables *X* and *Y*. As *X* increases, *Y* does not appear to either increase or decrease in any predictable way. On the basis of the sample evidence that appears in diagram (f), it might be concluded that, in the world containing all the *X–Y* data points, there exists no relationship, linear or otherwise, between variables *X* and *Y*.

Now consider the two scatter diagrams in Figure 2-14. Both scatter diagrams suggest imperfect, positive, linear relationships between *Y* and *X*. Figure 2-14(a) shows a strong relationship because the data points are all quite close to the straight line that passes through them. In Figure 2-14(b) the data points are farther away from the

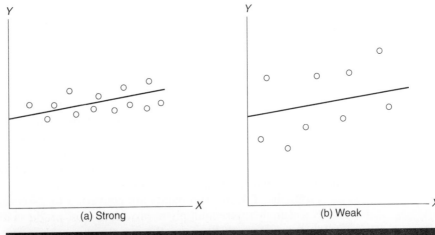

FIGURE 2-14   Strong and Weak Linear Association for *X–Y* Data Plots

straight line that passes through them, suggesting a weaker linear relationship. Later in this chapter we will demonstrate how to measure the strength of the relationship that exists between two variables.

As the two scatter diagrams in Figure 2-14 suggest, it is frequently desirable to summarize the relationship between two variables by fitting a straight line through the data points. You will soon learn how this is done, but at the moment it can be said that a straight line can be fitted to the points in a scatter diagram so that a "good" fit results. A question of interest for forecasting is: How rapidly does this straight line rise or fall?

Answering this question requires the calculation of the slope of the line. The slope of any straight line is defined as the change in *Y* associated with a one-unit increase in *X*.

To summarize, when investigating a relationship between two variables one must first know whether the relationship is linear (a straight line) or nonlinear. If it is linear, one needs to know whether the relationship is positive or negative and how sharply the line that fits the data points rises or falls. Finally, the strength of the relationship is needed, that is, how close the data points are to the line that best fits them.

CORRELATION COEFFICIENT

The strength of the linear relationship that exists between the two variables is measured by the *correlation* that exists between them. The *coefficient of correlation* measures strength as follows. Two variables with a perfect negative relationship have a correlation coefficient equal to −1. At the other extreme, two variables with a perfect positive relationship have a correlation coefficient equal to +1. Thus, the correlation coefficient varies between −1 and +1 inclusive, depending on the amount of association between the two variables being measured.

> The *correlation coefficient* measures the extent to which two variables are linearly related to each other.

Scatter diagram (a) of Figure 2-13 illustrates a situation that would produce a correlation coefficient of +1. Scatter diagram (b) has a correlation coefficient of −1.

Diagrams (e) and (f) demonstrate two variables that are not linearly related. The correlation coefficients for these relationships are equal to 0; that is, no linear relationship is present.

Forecasters are concerned with both population and sampled data. In the *population* containing all of the *X–Y* data points of interest, there is a correlation coefficient whose symbol is ρ, the Greek letter rho. If a random sample of these *X–Y* data points is drawn, the correlation coefficient for these sample data is denoted by *r*.

Frequently, *X* and *Y* are measured in different units, such as pounds and dollars, sales units and sales dollars, or unemployment rate and GNP dollars. In spite of these differing units of measure for *X* and *Y*, it is still important to measure the extent to which *X* and *Y* are related. This measurement is done by first converting variables *X* and *Y* to standardized units, or *Z*-scores.

After the *X–Y* measurements are converted to *Z*-scores, the *Z*-scores for each *X–Y* measurement are multiplied, providing cross products for each case. These cross products are of interest because the mean of these values is the correlation coefficient. The calculation of the correlation coefficient as (essentially) the mean cross product of *Z*-scores will produce the correct value, but in most cases the correlation coefficient is computed directly from the *X–Y* values. Equation 2.10 shows how to compute the sample correlation coefficient *r* from the *Z*-scores and from the *X–Y* measurements. Here $Z_X = (X - \bar{X})/S_X$ and $Z_Y = (Y - \bar{Y})/S_Y$.

$$
r = \frac{1}{n-1}\Sigma Z_X Z_Y = \frac{\Sigma(X - \bar{X})(Y - \bar{Y})}{\sqrt{\Sigma(X - \bar{X})^2}\sqrt{\Sigma(Y - \bar{Y})^2}}
$$

$$
= \frac{n\Sigma XY - (\Sigma X)(\Sigma Y)}{\sqrt{n\Sigma X^2 - (\Sigma X)^2}\sqrt{n\Sigma Y^2 - (\Sigma Y)^2}} \tag{2.10}
$$

A table such as Table 2-7 facilitates the calculation of *r*.

Example 2.10

If the relationship between age and income is being studied (see Table 2-6), it might be of interest to know the value of *r* for these data. The required computations appear in Table 2-7. The totals from Table 2-7 are substituted into Equation 2.10, providing:

$$
r = \frac{n\Sigma XY - (\Sigma X)(\Sigma Y)}{\sqrt{n\Sigma X^2 - (\Sigma X)^2}\sqrt{n\Sigma Y^2 - (\Sigma Y)^2}}
$$

$$
= \frac{5(4,266.1) - (133)(157.7)}{\sqrt{5(3,643) - (133)^2}\sqrt{5(5,035.05) - (157.7)^2}}
$$

$$
= \frac{21,330.5 - 20,974.1}{\sqrt{(18,215 - 17,689)}\sqrt{(25,175.25 - 24,869.29)}} = \frac{356.4}{401.17} = .89
$$

It can be seen that the sample correlation coefficient confirms what was observed in Figure 2-12. The value for *r* is positive, suggesting a positive linear relationship between age and income. Also, on a scale of 0 to 1, the value of *r* is fairly high (.89). This result suggests a strong linear relationship rather than a weak one. The remaining question is whether the combination of sample size and correlation coefficient is strong enough to make meaningful statements about the population from which the data values were drawn.

Two important points in the discussion of correlation should now be made. First, it must always be kept in mind that *correlation,* not *causation,* is being measured. It may

TABLE 2-7		Computations for the Correlation of Age and Income in Example 2.10			
Person	*Y*	*X*	Y^2	X^2	*XY*
1	27.8	22	772.84	484	611.6
2	28.5	23	812.25	529	655.5
3	30.0	26	900.00	676	780.0
4	35.0	27	1,225.00	729	945.0
5	36.4	35	1,324.96	1,225	1,274.0
Totals	157.7	133	5,035.05	3,643	4,266.1

be perfectly valid to say that two variables are related on the basis of a high correlation coefficient. It may or may not be valid to say that one variable is causing the movement of the other; that is a question for the analyst's judgment. For instance, it may be true that the sales volume of a country store in a sparsely populated area is highly correlated with the average stock market price in New York City. It might be concluded after examining a large sample of these two variables that such a high correlation exists. It is probably not true that one of these variables is causing the movement of the other. In fact, the movements of both these variables are probably caused by a third factor, the general state of the economy. Politicians, advertisers, and others frequently make the error of assuming causation on the basis of correlation.

Second, note that the correlation coefficient is measuring a *linear* relationship between two variables. In the case in which the correlation coefficient is low, it can be concluded that the two variables are not closely related in a linear way. It may be that they are closely related in a nonlinear, or curved, fashion. Thus a low correlation coefficient does not mean that the two variables are not related, only that a linear or straight-line relationship does not appear to exist.

FITTING A STRAIGHT LINE

As mentioned earlier, it is often of interest to fit a straight line through a collection of *X–Y* data points in such a way that a "good fit" results. As will be shown in later chapters, such a good-fitting line can be used to forecast unknown values of *Y*, the variable of interest.

In practice, a well-defined mathematical procedure is used to calculate both the *Y*-intercept and the slope of the best-fitting straight line. The most common approach to determining such a best-fitting line is called the *method of least squares*. In this procedure, a line is formulated that minimizes the sum of the squared distances between the data points and the line, as measured in the vertical (*Y*) direction.

The method of least squares chooses the values for slope and *Y*-intercept to minimize the sum of squared errors (distances), *SSE*, between the *Y* values and the line:

$$SSE = \Sigma(Y - \hat{Y})^2 = \Sigma(Y - b_0 - b_1 X)^2 \qquad \textbf{(2.11)}$$

where $\hat{Y} = b_0 + b_1 X$ is the estimated *Y* value on the fitted line.

Using calculus (see Appendix A), specific algebraic expressions can be derived for the least squares values. In particular,

$$b_1 = \frac{\Sigma(X - \bar{X})(Y - \bar{Y})}{\Sigma(X - \bar{X})^2} = \frac{n\Sigma XY - \Sigma X \Sigma Y}{n\Sigma X^2 - (\Sigma X)^2} \qquad (2.12)$$

$$b_0 = \bar{Y} - b_1\bar{X} = \frac{\Sigma Y}{n} - \frac{b_1\Sigma X}{n} \qquad (2.13)$$

where

b_1 = slope of line

b_0 = Y-intercept

The *method of least squares* is used to calculate the equation of a straight line that minimizes the sum of squared distances between the X–Y data points and the line, as measured in the vertical (Y) direction.

Example 2.11

Example 2.10 suggested a strong positive linear relationship between age and income. Substituting the totals from Table 2-7 into Equations 2.12 and 2.13, the equation of a straight line that best fits the points is computed:

$$b_1 = \frac{n\Sigma XY - \Sigma X \Sigma Y}{n\Sigma X^2 - (\Sigma X)^2} = \frac{5(4,266.1) - (133)(157.7)}{5(3,643) - (133)^2} = \frac{356.4}{526} = .678$$

$$b_0 = \frac{\Sigma Y}{n} - \frac{b_1\Sigma X}{n} = \frac{157.7}{5} - \frac{(.678)(133)}{5} = 31.540 - 18.035 = 13.505$$

The line that best fits the data, $\hat{Y} = 13.505 + .678X$, is shown in Figure 2-15.

FIGURE 2-15   Fitted Straight Line for Example 2.11

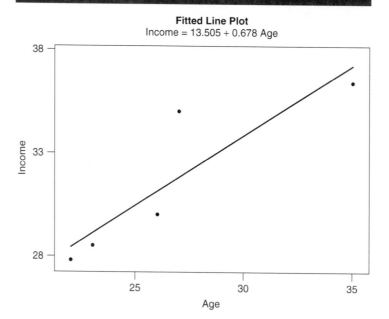

Fitted Line Plot
Income = 13.505 + 0.678 Age

The equation computed in Example 2.11, along with other values that can be calculated from the sample data, might be profitably used by managers to forecast future values of an important variable and to assess in advance just how accurate such forecasts might be. In a later chapter you will learn how to extract a great deal of information from sample data and use it to make forecasts using regression analysis.

The least squares slope coefficient is related to the sample correlation coefficient. Specifically,

$$b_1 = \left(\frac{\sqrt{\Sigma(Y - \bar{Y})^2}}{\sqrt{\Sigma(X - \bar{X})^2}} \right) r \qquad \textbf{(2.14)}$$

So, b_1 and r are proportional to one another and have the same sign.

Example 2.12

Using the results in Table 2-7 and Examples 2.10 and 2.11, we can verify Equation 2.14 numerically. Using Equation 2.14, we have

$$b_1 = \left(\frac{\sqrt{\Sigma(Y - \bar{Y})^2}}{\sqrt{\Sigma(X - \bar{X})^2}} \right) r = \frac{\sqrt{61.192}}{\sqrt{105.2}} .89 = (.763)(.89) = .679$$

This value, within rounding error, agrees with the value of the slope coefficient computed directly in Example 2.11 using Equation 2.12.

Example 2.13

Suppose the CEO of a large construction firm suspects that the estimated expenses of his company's construction projects are not very close to the actual expenses at project completion. The data shown in Table 2-8 are collected for the past few projects in order to analyze the relationship between estimated and actual costs. Since Minitab is available, the data are analyzed using this program.

Figure 2-16 shows that the correlation between estimated and actual construction costs, based on the sample data, is $r = .912$. The company CEO is surprised to learn that it is this high.

Figure 2-17 shows the data plotted as a scatter diagram and the line that best fits these data: $\hat{Y} = .683 + .922X$. The CEO can now forecast an actual construction cost (Y) after the estimate for the project (X) is prepared.

ASSESSING NORMALITY

Many statistical techniques, including some of those used in forecasting, require the assumption that a data set follows a normal distribution. For this reason statistical

---

FIGURE 2-16 Minitab Regression Output for Example 2.13

Correlations: Actual, Estimate

Pearson correlation of Actual and Estimate = 0.912

Regression Analysis: Actual versus Estimate

The regression equation is
Actual = 0.683 + 0.922 Estimate

TABLE 2-8	Estimated and Actual Construction Project Costs	
Row	Actual	Estimate
1	0.918	0.575
2	7.214	6.127
3	14.577	11.215
4	30.028	28.195
5	38.173	30.100
6	15.320	21.091
7	14.837	8.659
8	51.284	40.630
9	34.100	37.800
10	2.003	1.803
11	20.099	18.048
12	4.324	8.102
13	10.523	10.730
14	13.371	8.947
15	1.553	3.157
16	4.069	3.540
17	27.973	37.400
18	7.642	7.650
19	3.692	13.700
20	29.522	29.003
21	15.317	14.639
22	5.292	5.292
23	0.707	0.960
24	1.246	1.240
25	1.143	1.419
26	21.571	38.936

FIGURE 2-17   Fitted Line Plot for Example 2.13

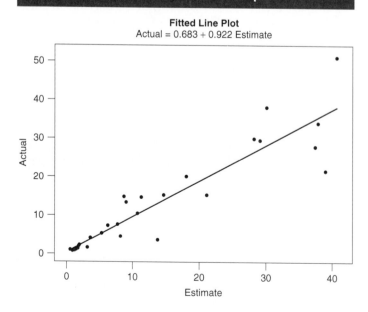

Fitted Line Plot
Actual = 0.683 + 0.922 Estimate

TABLE 2-9	Monthly Rates of Return (%) on the Standard & Poor 500 Index		

	Year			
	1	*2*	*3*	*4*
Jan.	—	6.87	−7.13	4.07
Feb.	4.10	−2.94	0.85	6.51
Mar.	−3.39	2.06	2.40	2.20
Apr.	0.94	4.89	−2.73	0.03
May	0.32	3.45	8.80	3.79
June	4.23	−0.80	−0.89	−4.91
July	−0.54	8.47	−0.52	4.39
Aug.	−3.94	1.54	−9.91	1.95
Sep.	3.90	−0.66	−5.25	−1.93
Oct.	2.56	−2.55	−0.67	1.18
Nov.	−1.91	1.64	5.82	−4.49
Dec.	1.46	2.12	2.45	10.58

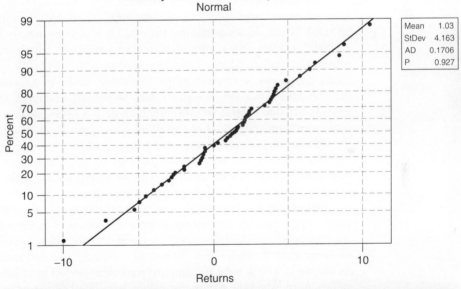

Probability Plot of S&P Monthly Returns
Normal

Mean	1.03
StDev	4.163
AD	0.1706
P	0.927

FIGURE 2-18   Normal Probability Plot for Monthly Return Rates

techniques have been developed that test the hypothesis that a collection of sample data was drawn from a normally distributed population.

Consider the monthly return rates on the S&P 500 stock market index shown in Table 2-9. Can it be assumed that these data follow a normal distribution? The answer, produced by Minitab, is contained in Figure 2-18.

The straight line displayed in Figure 2-18 shows what points from a perfect normal curve would look like if plotted using this special scale.[4] As shown, the data from Table 2-9 lie very close to this line, suggesting a good fit between the S&P data and a normal distribution.

The Minitab default normality test is the Anderson-Darling test, the results of which are shown in Figure 2-18. The details of this test need not concern us at present, but note the *p*-value (labeled P in the box in the upper right in the figure) of .927. In this case, the large *p*-value suggests the sample S&P data are consistent with the null hypothesis (certainly not unusual if the null hypothesis is true). To reject the null hypothesis of normality would result in almost certain error. Therefore, the null hypothesis should not be rejected and the assumption that the S&P data follow a normal distribution can safely be made.

APPLICATION TO MANAGEMENT

Many of the concepts in this review chapter may be considered background material necessary for understanding the more advanced forecasting techniques found throughout the remainder of this book. However, the concepts of this chapter also have value in many statistical applications by themselves. Although some of these applications might not logically fall under the heading "forecasting," they nonetheless involve using collected data to answer questions about the uncertainties of the business operation, especially the uncertain outcomes of the future.

The descriptive statistical procedures mentioned early in the chapter are widely used wherever large amounts of data must be cogently described so that they may be used in the decision-making process. It would be nearly impossible to think of a single area involving numerical measurements in which data collections are not routinely summarized using descriptive statistics. This fact applies particularly to the mean, commonly referred to as the "average," and—to a somewhat lesser extent—to the standard deviation. Averages are commonplace and have been used for many years to provide central measurements of data arrays. The recent emphasis on quality requires an understanding of variation; consequently, measures of dispersion, such as the standard deviation, are appearing more and more frequently in business practice.

The binomial and normal distributions are good examples of theoretical distributions that serve as models of many real-life situations. As such, their use is widespread in many applications, including forecasting.

Estimation and hypothesis testing are the two mainstays of basic statistical inference. Forecasting, or estimating, population values of interest from a random sample are routinely employed whenever time and cost constraints preclude an examination of all items under consideration. Sampling is especially widespread in auditing. Hypothesis testing is widely used to compare past-time-period population values with present values, to compare the parameter values associated with, say, two different branches or business locations, and to detect the changes in key parameters of production processes for the purpose of product improvement.

Correlation is widely used to examine the relationships between pairs of numerical variables. As will be seen in later chapters, these relationships are of great importance in forecasting because forecasting a variable often requires the values of relevant related variables. Both simple and multiple regression analysis are forecasting techniques that fall into this category.

---

[4]Other normal probability plots are available. One such plot, called a *normal scores plot*, is often used. In all of these plots, normality is indicated if the data plotted lie close to a straight line.

Glossary

Binomial distribution. The binomial distribution is a discrete probability distribution describing the likelihood of X successes in n trials of a binomial experiment.

Continuous random variable. A continuous random variable can assume any value within a specified range. These outcomes are represented numerically by an interval of values.

Correlation coefficient. The correlation coefficient measures the extent to which two variables are linearly related to each other.

Degrees of freedom. Degrees of freedom refers to the number of data items that are independent of one another and that carry unique pieces of information.

Discrete random variable. A discrete random variable can assume only values from a predetermined set. These outcomes are often represented numerically by integers.

Expected value. The expected value of a random variable is the mean value of the variable over many trials or observations.

Interval estimate. An interval estimate is a numerical interval within which a population parameter is likely to lie.

Method of least squares. The method of least squares is used to calculate the equation of a straight line such that the sum of the squared distances between the X–Y data points and the line, as measured in the vertical (Y) direction, is minimized.

Normal distribution. The normal distribution has a bell shape and is completely determined by its mean and standard deviation.

Point estimate. A point estimate is a single-valued estimate of a population parameter.

p-value. The p-value, or significance probability, is the probability of getting at least as extreme a sample result as the one actually observed if H_0 is true.

Sampling distribution. A sampling distribution is the array of all possible values of a sample statistic that can be drawn from a population for a given sample size.

Scatter diagram. A scatter diagram is a plot of X–Y data points on a two-dimensional graph.

Key Formulas

Sample mean

$$\bar{X} = \frac{\Sigma X}{n} \tag{2.1}$$

Sample standard deviation

$$S = \sqrt{\frac{\Sigma(X - \bar{X})^2}{n-1}} = \sqrt{\frac{\Sigma X^2 - \frac{(\Sigma X)^2}{n}}{n-1}} \tag{2.2}$$

Sample variance

$$S^2 = \frac{\Sigma(X - \bar{X})^2}{n-1} = \frac{\Sigma X^2 - \frac{(\Sigma X)^2}{n}}{n-1} \tag{2.3}$$

Expected value

$$E(X) = \Sigma[X \times P(X)] \tag{2.4}$$

Binomial probability distribution

$$P(X) = \binom{n}{X} p^X (1-p)^{n-X} \qquad \text{for } X = 0, 1, \ldots, n \tag{2.5}$$

Z-score

$$Z = \frac{X - \mu}{\sigma} \tag{2.6}$$

t-test statistic (Student's t distribution)

$$t = \frac{\bar{X} - \mu}{S/\sqrt{n}} \tag{2.7}$$

Interval estimate for population mean (large sample)

$$\bar{X} \pm Z \frac{S}{\sqrt{n}} \tag{2.9}$$

Sample correlation coefficient

$$r = \frac{1}{n-1} \Sigma Z_X Z_Y = \frac{\Sigma (X - \bar{X})(Y - \bar{Y})}{\sqrt{\Sigma \left(X - \bar{X}\right)^2} \sqrt{\Sigma \left(Y - \bar{Y}\right)^2}}$$

$$= \frac{n\Sigma XY - (\Sigma X)(\Sigma Y)}{\sqrt{n\Sigma X^2 - (\Sigma X)^2} \sqrt{n\Sigma Y^2 - (\Sigma Y)^2}} \tag{2.10}$$

Method of least squares minimizes this expression for b_0 and b_1

$$SSE = \Sigma (Y - \hat{Y})^2 = \Sigma (Y - b_0 - b_1 X)^2 \tag{2.11}$$

Fitted regression line slope equation

$$b_1 = \frac{\Sigma (X - \bar{X})(Y - \bar{Y})}{\Sigma (X - \bar{X})^2} = \frac{n\Sigma XY - \Sigma X \Sigma Y}{n\Sigma X^2 - (\Sigma X)^2} \tag{2.12}$$

Fitted regression line Y-intercept equation

$$b_0 = \bar{Y} - b_1 \bar{X} = \frac{\Sigma Y}{n} - \frac{b_1 \Sigma X}{n} \tag{2.13}$$

Alternative regression line slope equation

$$b_1 = \left(\frac{\sqrt{\Sigma \left(Y - \bar{Y}\right)^2}}{\sqrt{\Sigma \left(X - \bar{X}\right)^2}} \right) r \tag{2.14}$$

Problems

1. Dick Hoover, owner of Modern Office Equipment, is concerned about freight costs and clerical costs incurred on small orders. In an effort to reduce expenditures in this area, he has decided to introduce a discount policy rewarding orders over $40 in the hope that this will cause customers to consolidate a number of small orders into large orders. The following data show the amounts per transaction for a sample of 28 customers:

    10, 15, 20, 25, 15, 17, 41, 50, 5, 9,

    12, 14, 35, 18, 19, 17, 28, 29, 11, 11,

    43, 54, 7, 8, 16, 13, 37, 18

    a. Compute the sample mean.
    b. Compute the sample standard deviation.
    c. Compute the sample variance.
    d. If the policy is successful, will the mean of the distribution increase, decrease, or remain unaffected?
    e. If the policy is successful, will the standard deviation of the distribution increase, decrease, or remain unaffected?
    f. Given the data above, forecast the amount of the next customer order.

2. Sandy James thinks that housing prices have stabilized in the past few months. To persuade her boss, she intends to compare current prices with last year's prices. She collects 12 housing prices from the want ads and calculates the mean and standard deviation of the prices she has found. What are these two summary values?

    125,900 253,000 207,500 146,950 121,450 135,450

    175,000 200,000 210,950 166,700 185,000 191,950

3. A large construction company was trying to establish a useful way to view typical profits from jobs obtained from competitive bidding. Because the jobs vary substantially in size and the final amount of the successful bid, the company decided to express profits as percent earnings:

    $$Percent\ earnings = 100 \times \frac{Earnings}{Actual\ construction\ costs}$$

    When money is lost on a project, the earnings are negative and so is the resulting net profit. A sample of 30 jobs yielded the percent earnings:

15.9	21.3	−1.8	6.6	.4	53.6	19.7	−.5	6.7	−2.3
11.9	−.3	19.0	12.8	−9.6	26.8	21.0	32.0	−.4	10.9
6.9	−8.5	3.5	3.5	−1.9	4.0	13.0	15.1	9.7	33.9

    a. What is a plausible value for the mean percent earnings for the population of jobs or even all potential jobs?
    b. Construct a 95% confidence interval for the mean percent earnings for the population of jobs using a large-sample argument.
    c. Construct a 95% confidence interval for the mean percent earning for the population of jobs assuming 30 is a small sample size. What additional assumption do you need to make in this case?
    d. Compare the two intervals in b and c. Explain why a sample size of 30 is often taken as the cutoff between large and small samples.

4. From data on a large sample of sales transactions, a small business owner reports that a 95% confidence interval for the mean profit per transaction, μ, is (23.41, 102.59). Use these data to determine
   a. A point estimate (best guess) of the mean μ and its 95% error margin.
   b. A 90% confidence interval for the mean μ.

5. We want to forecast whether the mean number of absent days per year has increased for our large workforce. A year ago the mean was known to be 12.1. A recent sample of 100 employees reveals a sample mean of 13.5 with a sample standard deviation of 1.7 days. Test at the .05 significance level to determine if the population mean has increased, or if the difference between 13.5 and 12.1 simply represents sampling error.

6. New Horizons Airlines wants to forecast the mean number of unoccupied seats per flight to Germany next year. To develop this forecast, the records of 49 flights are randomly selected from the files for the past year, and the number of unoccupied seats is noted for each flight. The sample mean and standard deviation are 8.1 seats and 5.7 seats, respectively. Develop a point and 95% interval estimate of the mean number of unoccupied seats per flight during the past year. Forecast the mean number of unoccupied seats per flight to Germany next year. Discuss the accuracy of this forecast.

7. Over a period of years, a toothpaste has received a mean rating of 5.9, on a 7-point scale, for overall customer satisfaction with the product. Because of a minor unadvertised change in the product, there is concern that the customer satisfaction may have changed. Suppose the satisfaction ratings from a sample of 60 customers have a mean of 5.60 and a standard deviation of .87. Do these data indicate that the mean satisfaction rating is different from 5.9? Test with $\alpha = .05$. What is the p-value for the test?

8. The manager of a frozen yogurt store claims that a medium-size serving contains an average of more than 4 ounces of yogurt. From a random sample of 14 servings, she obtains a mean of 4.31 ounces and a standard deviation of .52 ounce. Test, with $\alpha = .05$, the manager's claim. Find the p-value for the test. Assume that the distribution of weight per serving is normal.

9. Based on past experience, the California Power Company forecasts that the mean residential electricity usage per household will be 700 kwh next January. In January the company selects a simple random sample of 50 households and computes a mean and standard deviation of 715 and 50, respectively. Test at the .05 significance level to determine whether California Power's forecast is reasonable. Calculate and interpret the p-value for the test.

10. Population experts indicate that family size has decreased in the last few years. Ten years ago the average family size was 2.9. Consider the population of 200 family sizes given in Table P-10. Randomly select a sample of 30 family sizes and test the hypothesis that the average family size has not changed in the last 10 years.

11. James Dobbins, maintenance supervisor for the Atlanta Transit Authority, would like to determine whether there is a positive relationship between the annual maintenance cost of a bus and its age. If a relationship exists, James feels that he can do a better job of predicting the annual bus maintenance budget. He collects the data shown in Table P-11.

TABLE P-10

(1) 3	(35) 1	(69) 2	(102) 1	(135) 5	(168) 6
(2) 2	(36) 2	(70) 4	(103) 2	(136) 2	(169) 3
(3) 7	(37) 4	(71) 3	(104) 5	(137) 1	(170) 2
(4) 3	(38) 1	(72) 7	(105) 3	(138) 4	(171) 3
(5) 4	(39) 4	(73) 2	(106) 2	(139) 2	(172) 4
(6) 2	(40) 2	(74) 6	(107) 1	(140) 4	(173) 2
(7) 3	(41) 1	(75) 2	(108) 2	(141) 1	(174) 2
(8) 1	(42) 3	(76) 7	(109) 2	(142) 2	(175) 1
(9) 5	(43) 5	(77) 3	(110) 1	(143) 4	(176) 5
(10) 3	(44) 2	(78) 6	(111) 4	(144) 1	(177) 3
(11) 2	(45) 1	(79) 4	(112) 1	(145) 2	(178) 2
(12) 3	(46) 4	(80) 2	(113) 1	(146) 2	(179) 4
(13) 4	(47) 3	(81) 3	(114) 2	(147) 5	(180) 3
(14) 1	(48) 5	(82) 5	(115) 2	(148) 3	(181) 5
(15) 2	(49) 2	(83) 2	(116) 1	(149) 1	(182) 3
(16) 2	(50) 4	(84) 1	(117) 4	(150) 2	(183) 1
(17) 4	(51) 1	(85) 3	(118) 2	(151) 6	(184) 2
(18) 4	(52) 6	(86) 3	(119) 1	(152) 2	(185) 4
(19) 3	(53) 2	(87) 2	(120) 3	(153) 5	(186) 3
(20) 2	(54) 5	(88) 4	(121) 5	(154) 1	(187) 2
(21) 1	(55) 4	(89) 1	(122) 1	(155) 2	(188) 5
(22) 5	(56) 1	(90) 2	(123) 2	(156) 1	(189) 3
(23) 2	(57) 2	(91) 3	(124) 3	(157) 4	(190) 4
(24) 1	(58) 1	(92) 3	(125) 4	(158) 2	(191) 3
(25) 4	(59) 5	(93) 2	(126) 3	(159) 2	(192) 2
(26) 3	(60) 2	(94) 4	(127) 2	(160) 7	(193) 3
(27) 2	(61) 7	(95) 1	(128) 1	(161) 4	(194) 2
(28) 3	(62) 1	(96) 2	(129) 6	(162) 2	(195) 5
(29) 6	(63) 2	(97) 4	(130) 1	(163) 1	(196) 3
(30) 1	(64) 6	(98) 3	(131) 2	(164) 7	(197) 3
(31) 2	(65) 4	(99) 2	(132) 5	(165) 2	(198) 2
(32) 4	(66) 1	(100) 6	(133) 2	(166) 7	(199) 5
(33) 3	(67) 2	(101) 4	(134) 1	(167) 4	(200) 1
(34) 2	(68) 1				

TABLE P-11

Bus	Maintenance Cost ($) Y	Age (years) X
1	859	8
2	682	5
3	471	3
4	708	9
5	1,094	11
6	224	2
7	320	1
8	651	8
9	1,049	12

TABLE P-12

Week	Books Sold Y	Shelf Space X
1	275	6.8
2	142	3.3
3	168	4.1
4	197	4.2
5	215	4.8
6	188	3.9
7	241	4.9
8	295	7.7
9	125	3.1
10	266	5.9
11	200	5.0

a. Plot a scatter diagram.
b. What kind of relationship exists between these two variables?
c. Compute the correlation coefficient.

12. Anna Sheehan is the manager of the Spendwise supermarket chain. She would like to be able to predict paperback book sales (books per week) based on the amount of shelf display space (feet) provided. Anna gathers data for a sample of 11 weeks as shown in Table P-12.
a. Plot a scatter diagram.
b. What kind of relationship exists between these two variables?
c. Compute the correlation coefficient. Determine the equation of the least squares line by calculating the slope and Y-intercept. Use this equation to forecast the number of books sold if 5.2 feet of shelf space are used (*i.e.*, $X = 5.2$).

13. Consider the population of 200 weekly observations that are presented in Table P-13. The independent variable X is the average weekly temperature of Spokane, Washington. The dependent variable Y is the number of shares of Sunshine Mining Stock traded on the Spokane exchange in a week. Randomly select data for 16 weeks and compute the coefficient of correlation. (Hint: Make sure your sample is randomly drawn from the population.) Then determine the least squares line and forecast Y for an average weekly temperature of 63.

14. A real estate investor collects the following data on a random sample of apartments on the west side of College Station, Texas.

Rent ($ per month)	Size (sq. ft)	Rent ($ per month)	Size (sq. ft)
720	1,000	650	800
595	900	748	960
915	1,200	685	650
760	810	755	970
1,000	1,210	815	1,000
790	860	745	1,000
880	1,135	715	1,000
845	960	885	1,180

TABLE P-13

OBS.	Y	X	OBS.	Y	X	OBS.	Y	X	OBS.	Y	X
(1)	50	37	(51)	54	86	(101)	22	43	(151)	79	85
(2)	90	77	(52)	76	48	(102)	32	5	(152)	79	27
(3)	46	55	(53)	55	48	(103)	24	13	(153)	48	61
(4)	47	27	(54)	12	15	(104)	63	3	(154)	5	7
(5)	12	49	(55)	5	70	(105)	16	58	(155)	24	79
(6)	23	23	(56)	2	9	(106)	4	13	(156)	47	49
(7)	65	18	(57)	77	52	(107)	79	18	(157)	65	71
(8)	37	1	(58)	6	71	(108)	5	5	(158)	56	27
(9)	87	41	(59)	67	38	(109)	59	26	(159)	52	15
(10)	83	73	(60)	30	69	(110)	99	9	(160)	17	88
(11)	87	61	(61)	3	13	(111)	76	96	(161)	45	38
(12)	39	85	(62)	6	63	(112)	15	94	(162)	45	31
(13)	28	16	(63)	70	65	(113)	10	30	(163)	90	35
(14)	97	46	(64)	33	87	(114)	20	41	(164)	69	78
(15)	69	88	(65)	13	18	(115)	37	1	(165)	62	93
(16)	87	87	(66)	10	4	(116)	56	27	(166)	0	51
(17)	52	82	(67)	21	29	(117)	6	73	(167)	8	68
(18)	52	56	(68)	56	21	(118)	86	19	(168)	47	30
(19)	15	22	(69)	74	9	(119)	27	94	(169)	7	81
(20)	85	49	(70)	47	8	(120)	67	5	(170)	48	30
(21)	41	44	(71)	34	18	(121)	22	31	(171)	59	46
(22)	82	33	(72)	38	84	(122)	32	13	(172)	76	99
(23)	98	77	(73)	75	64	(123)	90	11	(173)	54	98
(24)	99	87	(74)	0	81	(124)	88	50	(174)	95	11
(25)	23	54	(75)	51	98	(125)	35	40	(175)	7	6
(26)	77	8	(76)	47	55	(126)	57	80	(176)	24	83
(27)	42	64	(77)	63	40	(127)	73	44	(177)	55	49
(28)	60	24	(78)	7	14	(128)	13	63	(178)	41	39
(29)	22	29	(79)	6	11	(129)	18	74	(179)	14	16
(30)	91	40	(80)	68	42	(130)	70	40	(180)	24	13
(31)	68	35	(81)	72	43	(131)	9	53	(181)	36	31
(32)	36	37	(82)	95	73	(132)	93	79	(182)	62	44
(33)	22	28	(83)	82	45	(133)	41	9	(183)	77	11
(34)	92	56	(84)	91	16	(134)	17	52	(184)	32	60
(35)	34	33	(85)	83	21	(135)	10	82	(185)	12	82
(36)	34	82	(86)	27	85	(136)	69	37	(186)	85	7
(37)	63	89	(87)	13	37	(137)	5	57	(187)	90	68
(38)	30	78	(88)	6	89	(138)	18	62	(188)	78	10
(39)	31	24	(89)	76	76	(139)	88	21	(189)	60	27
(40)	84	53	(90)	55	71	(140)	99	94	(190)	96	90
(41)	56	61	(91)	13	53	(141)	86	99	(191)	51	6
(42)	48	18	(92)	50	13	(142)	95	45	(192)	9	62
(43)	0	45	(93)	60	12	(143)	78	19	(193)	93	78
(44)	58	4	(94)	61	30	(144)	3	76	(194)	61	22
(45)	27	23	(95)	73	57	(145)	38	81	(195)	5	99
(46)	78	68	(96)	20	66	(146)	57	95	(196)	88	51
(47)	78	79	(97)	36	27	(147)	77	30	(197)	45	44
(48)	72	66	(98)	85	41	(148)	25	59	(198)	34	86
(49)	21	80	(99)	49	20	(149)	99	93	(199)	28	47
(50)	73	99	(100)	83	66	(150)	9	28	(200)	44	49

a. Plot the data as a scatter diagram with $Y = $ rent and $X = $ size.
b. Determine the equation of the least squares line relating rent to size.
c. What is the estimated increase in rent for an additional square foot of space?
d. Forecast the monthly rent for an apartment with 750 square feet.

15. Abbott & Sons needs to forecast the mean age μ of its hourly workforce. A random sample of personnel files is pulled and give the results below. Prepare both a point estimate and a 98% confidence interval for the mean age of the entire workforce. Test the hypothesis $H_0: \mu = 44$ versus $H_1: \mu \neq 44$ at the 2% level. Are the results of the hypothesis test consistent with the confidence interval for μ? Would you expect them to be?

$$\bar{X} = 45.2 \qquad S = 10.3 \qquad n = 175$$

CASES

CASE 2-1   ALCOM ELECTRONICS

Jarrick Tilby recently received a degree in business administration from a small university and went to work for Alcam Electronics, a manufacturer of various electronic components for industry. After a few weeks on the job, he was called into the office of Alcam's owner and manager, McKennah Labrum, who asked him to investigate a question regarding a certain transistor manufactured by Alcam because a large TV company was interested in a major purchase.

McKennah wanted to forecast the average lifetime of the transistors, a matter of great concern to the TV company. Units currently in stock could represent those that would be produced over the lifetime of the new contract, should it be accepted.

Jarrick decided to take a random sample of the transistors in question and formulated a plan to accomplish this task. He numbered the storage bins holding the transistors, drew random numbers, and sampled all transistors in each selected bin for the sample. Since each bin contained about 20 transistors, he selected 10 random numbers, which gave him a final sample size of 205 transistors. Since he had selected 10 of 55 bins, he thought he had a good representative sample and could use the results of this sample to generalize to the entire population of transistors in inventory, as well as to units yet to be manufactured by the same process.

Jarrick then considered the question of the average lifetime of the units. Because these lifetimes can extend to several years, he realized that none of

the sampled units could be tested if a timely answer was desired. Therefore, he decided to contact several users of this component to determine if any lifetime records were available. Fortunately, he found three companies that had used the transistor in the past and that had limited records on component lifetimes. In total, he received data on 38 transistors whose failure times were known. Since these transistors were manufactured using the same process as the current process, he reasoned that the results of this sample could be used to make inferences about the units in inventory and those yet to be produced.

Following are the results of the computations Jarrick performed on the lifetime data of his sample:

$$n = 38$$

$$\text{Average lifetime } \bar{X} = 4,805 \text{ hours}$$

$$\text{Standard deviation of lifetimes } S = 675 \text{ hours}$$

After finding that the sample average lifetime was only 4,805 hours, Jarrick was concerned because he knew the other supplier of components was guaranteeing an average lifetime of 5,000 hours. Although his sample average was a bit below 5,000 hours, he realized that the sample size was only 38 and that this did not constitute positive proof that Alcam's quality was inferior to that of the other supplier.

He decided to test the hypothesis that the average lifetime of all Alcam transistors was 5,000 hours against the alternative that it was less. Following are the calculations he performed using $\alpha = .01$:

$$H_0: \mu = 5,000$$
$$H_1: \mu < 5,000$$

If $S = 675$, then

Decision Rule Point: $5,000 - 2.33\dfrac{675}{\sqrt{38}} = 4,744.9$

Decision Rule: If $\bar{X} < 4,744.9$, reject H_0

Since the sample mean (4,805) was not below the decision rule point for rejection (4,744.9), Jarrick failed to reject the hypothesis that the mean lifetime of all components was equal to 5,000 hours. He thought this would be good news to McKennah Labrum and included a summary of his findings in his final report. A few days after he gave his written and verbal report to her, McKennah called him into her office to compliment him on a good job and to share a concern she had regarding his findings. She said, "I am concerned about the very low significance level of your hypothesis test. You took only a 1% chance of rejecting the null hypothesis if it is true. This strikes me as very conservative. I am concerned that we will enter into a contract and then find that our quality level does not meet the desired 5,000-hour specification." ■

QUESTION

1. How would you respond to McKennah Labrum's comment?

CASE 2-2   MR. TUX

John Mosby, owner of several Mr. Tux rental stores, is interested in forecasting his monthly sales volume (see the Mr. Tux case at the end of Chapter 1). As a first step, John collects monthly sales data for the years 1989 through 1996 as shown in Table 2-10.

Next, John computes the average monthly sales value for each year (*e.g.*, he adds up the 12 values for 1989 and divides by 12). John also computes the standard deviation for the 12 monthly values for each year. The results are shown in Table 2-11. John also decides to construct a time series plot, given in Figure 2-19. He plots the mean monthly sales values on the *y* axis and time on the *x* axis. ■

TABLE 2-10	Mr. Tux Monthly Sales Data, Dollars							
	1989	*1990*	*1991*	*1992*	*1993*	*1994*	*1995*	*1996*
Jan.	6,028	16,850	15,395	27,773	31,416	51,604	58,843	71,043
Feb.	5,927	12,753	30,826	36,653	48,341	80,366	82,386	152,930
Mar.	10,515	26,901	25,589	51,157	85,651	208,938	224,803	250,559
Apr.	32,276	61,494	103,184	217,509	242,673	263,830	354,301	409,567
May	51,920	147,862	197,608	206,229	289,554	252,216	328,263	394,747
June	31,294	57,990	68,600	110,081	164,373	219,566	313,647	272,874
July	23,573	51,318	39,909	102,893	160,608	149,082	214,561	230,303
Aug.	36,465	53,599	91,368	128,857	176,096	213,888	337,192	375,402
Sep.	18,959	23,038	58,781	104,776	142,363	178,947	183,482	195,409
Oct.	13,918	41,396	59,679	111,036	114,907	133,650	144,618	173,518
Nov.	17,987	19,330	33,443	63,701	113,552	116,946	139,750	181,702
Dec.	15,294	22,707	53,719	82,657	127,042	164,154	184,546	258,713

TABLE 2-11	Mr. Tux Average Monthly Sales values	
Year	Average (Mean) $	Standard Deviation $
1989	22,013	13,165
1990	44,603	35,290
1991	64,841	47,217
1992	103,610	57,197
1993	141,381	70,625
1994	169,432	63,376
1995	213,866	96,387
1996	247,231	99,153

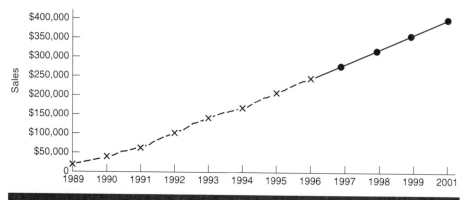

FIGURE 2-19   Mr. Tux Mean Monthly Sales

QUESTIONS

1. What forecasting ideas come to mind when you study John's mean monthly sales values for the years of his data?

2. Suppose John decides to draw a straight line through his scatter diagram freehand so that it "fits well" and then extends this line into the future, using points along the line as his monthly forecasts. How accurate do you think these forecasts will be? Use the standard deviation values John calculated in answering this question. Based on your analysis, would you encourage John to continue searching for a more accurate forecasting method? John has the latest version of Minitab on his computer. Do you think he should use the regression analysis feature of Minitab to calculate a least squares line? If he did, what X variable should be used to forecast monthly sales (Y)?

CASE 2-3   ALOMEGA FOOD STORES

In Example 1.1 the president of Alomega Food Stores, Julie Ruth, had collected data from her company's operations. She found several months of sales data along with several possible predictor variables, such as advertising dollars spent and seasonal effects (review this situation in Example 1.1). While her analysis team was working with the data in an attempt to forecast monthly sales, she became impatient and wondered which of the predictor variables was best for this purpose.

Because she had a statistical program on her desktop computer, she decided to have a look at the data herself. First, she found the correlation coefficients between the variable monthly sales and several of the potential predictor variables. Specifically, she was interested in the correlation between sales and the monthly newspaper ad dollars, monthly TV ad dollars, newspaper ad dollars lagged one and two months, TV ad dollars lagged one and two months, and her competitor's advertising rating. The r values (correlation coefficients) were:

Correlation coefficient (r) between variable sales and	
Monthly newspaper ad dollars	.45
Monthly TV ad dollars	.60
Newspaper ad dollars lagged one month	−.32
Newspaper ad dollars lagged two months	.21
TV ad dollars lagged one month	−.06
TV ad dollars lagged two months	.03
Competitor's advertising rating	−.18

Julie was not surprised to find that the highest correlation was between monthly sales and TV advertising dollars ($r = .60$) but she was hoping for a stronger correlation. She decided to use a regression feature to calculate the equation of the least squares line using sales as the dependent variable and monthly TV ads as the predictor variable. The results of this run were:

$$\text{sales} = 341{,}663 + .336 \text{ (monthly TV ads)}$$

$$r\text{-squared} = .36(36\%) \qquad p\text{-value} = .000$$

Julie had to dig out her college statistics textbook to interpret the r-squared and p-values from her printout. After reading, she recalled that r-squared (which is the square of the correlation coefficient, r) measures the percentage of the variability in sales that can be explained by the variability in monthly TV ads (this will be explained in Chapter 6). Also, the p-value indicates that the slope coefficient (.336) is significant; that is, the hypothesis that it is zero in the population from which the sample was drawn can be rejected with almost no chance of error.

Julie concluded that the regression equation she found was significant and can be used to forecast monthly sales if the TV ad budget is known. Since TV ad expenditures are under the company's control, she felt she had a good way to forecast future sales. In a brief conversation with the head of her data management department, Roger Jackson, she mentioned her findings. He replied, "Yeah, we found that, too. But realize that TV ads explain only about a third of sales variability. OK, 36%. We really don't think that is high enough and we're trying to use several variables together to try and get that r-squared value higher. Plus, we think we're onto a method that will do a better job than regression analysis anyway." ∎

QUESTIONS

1. What do you think of Julie Ruth's analysis?
2. Define the residuals (errors) to be the differences between the actual sales values and the values predicted by the straight line. How might you examine the residuals to decide if Julie's straight-line representation is adequate?

Minitab Applications

The problem. In Example 2.1 a collection of ages was analyzed using descriptive statistics.

Minitab Solution

1. Enter the variable name Ages below C1.
2. Enter the data in column C1.
3. Click on the menus shown below:

```
Stat>Basic Statistics>Graphical Summary
```

4. The Graphical Summary dialog box appears.
    a. Click on Variables and select Ages (C1) as shown in Figure 2-20.
    b. Click OK on the Graphical Summary dialog box and the summary shown in Figure 2-21 appears.
    c. To print this graph click the following menus:

    ```
    File>Print Graph
    ```

5. Click on the menus shown below:

    ```
    Stat>Basic Statistics>Display Descriptive Statistics
    ```

6. The Display Descriptive Statistics dialog box appears.
    a. Click on Variables and select Ages (C1).
    b. Click OK and the summary shown in Figure 2-1 appears in the Session window. (To get additional descriptive statistics, click on Statistics and select additional descriptive measures before clicking OK.)
    c. To print the session window that contains a summary of the descriptive statistics, click:

    ```
    File>Print Session Window
    ```

    The results are shown in Figure 2-1 (see p. 18).

7. The following commands will allow you to develop a histogram, dot plot, and box plot.

    ```
    Graph>Histogram
    Graph>Dotplot
    Graph>Boxplot
    ```

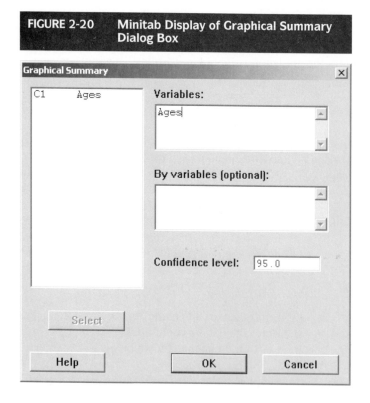

FIGURE 2-20   Minitab Display of Graphical Summary Dialog Box

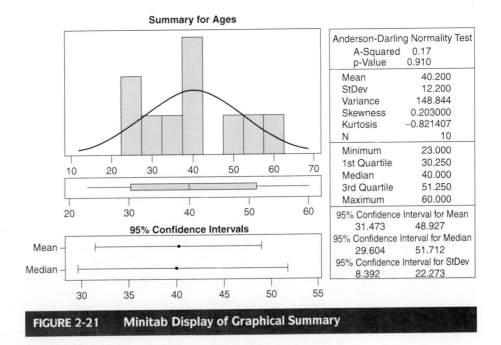

Summary for Ages

Anderson-Darling Normality Test	
A-Squared	0.17
p-Value	0.910
Mean	40.200
StDev	12.200
Variance	148.844
Skewness	0.203000
Kurtosis	−0.821407
N	10
Minimum	23.000
1st Quartile	30.250
Median	40.000
3rd Quartile	51.250
Maximum	60.000

95% Confidence Interval for Mean
31.473   48.927
95% Confidence Interval for Median
29.604   51.712
95% Confidence Interval for StDev
8.392   22.273

95% Confidence Intervals

Mean
Median

FIGURE 2-21	**Minitab Display of Graphical Summary**

Instructions on how to use Minitab to run correlation and regression analysis are presented at the end of Chapter 6.

Excel Applications

The problem. In Problem 1, Dick Hoover, owner of Modern Office Equipment, is concerned about freight costs and clerical costs incurred on small orders.

Excel Solution

1. The Excel program is entered and the spreadsheet screen shown in Figure 1-2 at the end of Chapter 1 appears. Move the cursor so that the highlighted cell is in the upper left corner of the spreadsheet, cell A1.
2. Enter the first value, 10, followed by the return key, then the next data value and so forth.
3. After all 28 data values are keyed into column A, the cursor is placed in a cell where the results of the first calculation are desired, A30.
4. The average of the data in cells A1 through A28 is computed by placing the formula in A30. In order to enter a formula, the = sign must precede it. The formula is =Average(A1:A28). Note: A30 is shown to the left of the formula bar and =Average(A1:A28) to the right above the spreadsheet.
5. The same approach is used to compute the standard deviation. The formula =Stdev(A1:A28) is entered into cell A31. The results are shown in Figure 2-22.

The average and standard deviation could also have been computed using either the Insert function or the Data Analysis tool. These approaches will be discussed in later chapters.

Instructions on how to use Excel to run correlation and regression analysis are presented at the end of Chapter 6.

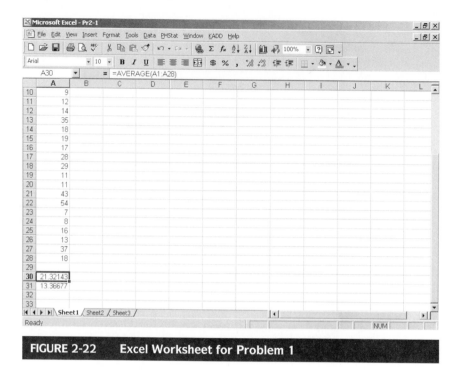

FIGURE 2-22   Excel Worksheet for Problem 1

If you are using the Excel or Minitab program, you are encouraged to try different data sets and statistical routines to familiarize yourself with these powerful programs. The skill you gain will be very useful as you learn about the forecasting procedures in this text.

References

Anderson, D. R., D. J. Sweeney, and T. A. Williams. *Modern Business Statistics with Microsoft Excel.* Cincinnati, OH: South-Western, 2003.

Cryer, J. D., and R. B. Miller. *Statistics for Business: Data Analysis and Modeling,* Second Edition. Belmont, CA: Duxbury Press, 1994.

Hanke, J., and A. Reitsch. *Understanding Business Statistics*, Second Edition. Homewood, IL: Richard D. Irwin, 1994.

Johnson, R. A., and D. W. Wichern. *Business Statistics: Decision Making with Data*. New York: John Wiley & Sons, 1997.

Keller, G., and B. Warrack. *Statistics for Management and Economics*, Sixth Edition. Pacific Grove, CA: Brooks/Cole, 2003.

CHAPTER

3

EXPLORING DATA PATTERNS AND CHOOSING A FORECASTING TECHNIQUE

One of the most time-consuming and difficult parts of forecasting is the collection of valid and reliable data. Data processing personnel are fond of using the expression "garbage in, garbage out" (GIGO). This expression also applies to forecasting. A forecast can be no more accurate than the data on which it is based. The most sophisticated forecasting model will fail if it is applied to unreliable data.

The advent of the computer has helped generate an incredible accumulation of data on almost all subjects. The difficult task facing most forecasters is how to find relevant data that will help solve their specific decision-making problems.

Four criteria can be applied to the determination of whether data will be useful:

1. Data should be reliable and accurate. Proper care must be taken that data are collected from a reliable source with proper attention given to accuracy.
2. Data should be relevant. The data must be representative of the circumstances for which they are being used.
3. Data should be consistent. When definitions change concerning how data are collected, adjustments need to be made to retain consistency in historical patterns. This can be a problem, for example, when government agencies change the mix or "market basket" used in determining a cost-of-living index. Thirty years ago personal computers were not part of the mix of products being purchased by consumers; now they are.
4. Data should be timely. Data collected, summarized, and published on a timely basis will be of greatest value to the forecaster. There can be too little data (not enough history on which to base future outcomes) or too much data (data from irrelevant historical periods far in the past).

Generally, two types of data are of interest to the forecaster. The first are data collected at a single point in time, be it an hour, a day, a week, a month, or a quarter. The second are observations of data made over time. When all observations are from the same time period, we call them *cross-sectional* data. The objective is to examine such data and then to extrapolate or extend the revealed relationships to the larger population. Drawing a random sample of personnel files to study the circumstances of the employees of a company is one example. Gathering data on the age and current maintenance cost of nine Spokane Transit Authority's buses is another. A scatter diagram such as Figure 3-1 helps us visualize the relationship and suggests age might be used to help in forecasting the annual maintenance budget.

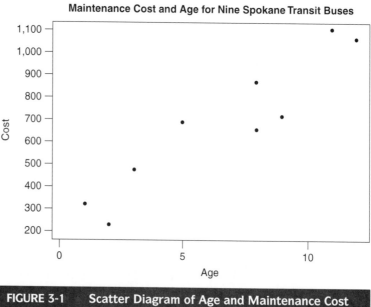

Maintenance Cost and Age for Nine Spokane Transit Buses

FIGURE 3-1	Scatter Diagram of Age and Maintenance Cost for Nine Spokane Transit Buses

Cross-sectional data are observations collected at a single point in time.

Any variable that consists of data that are collected, recorded, or observed over successive increments of time is called a *time series*. Monthly U.S. beer production is an example of a time series.

A *time series* consists of data that are collected, recorded, or observed over successive increments of time.

EXPLORING TIME SERIES DATA PATTERNS

One of the most important aspects in selecting an appropriate forecasting method for time series data is to consider the different types of data patterns. There are four general types: horizontal, trend, seasonal, and cyclical.

When data observations fluctuate around a constant level or mean, a *horizontal* pattern exists. This type of series is called *stationary* in its mean. Monthly sales for a product that do not increase or decrease consistently over time would be considered to have a horizontal pattern.

When data observations grow or decline over an extended period of time, a *trend* pattern exists. Figure 3-2 shows the long-term growth (trend) of a time series variable (such as housing costs) with data points 1 year apart. A linear trend line has been drawn to illustrate this growth. Although the variable housing costs have not increased every year, the movement of the variable has been generally upward between periods 1 and 20. Examples of the basic forces that affect and help explain the trend of a series are population growth, price inflation, technological change, consumer preferences, and productivity increases.

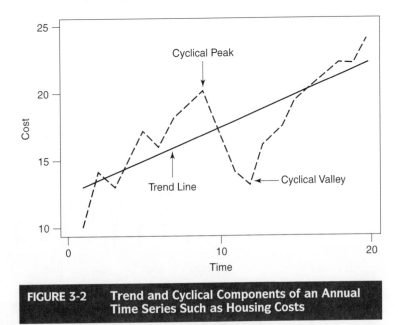

FIGURE 3-2   Trend and Cyclical Components of an Annual Time Series Such as Housing Costs

Many macroeconomic variables, such as the U.S. gross national product (GNP), employment, and industrial production exhibit trend-like behavior. Figure 3-10 (see p. 71) contains another example of a time series with a prevailing trend. This figure shows the growth of operating revenue for Sears from 1955 to 2000.

The *trend* is the long-term component that represents the growth or decline in the time series over an extended period of time.

When observations exhibit rises and falls that are not of a fixed period, a *cyclical* pattern exists. The cyclical component is the wavelike fluctuation around the trend that is usually affected by general economic conditions. Cyclical fluctuations are often influenced by changes in economic expansions and contractions, commonly referred to as the business cycle. Figure 3-2 shows a time series with a cyclical component. The cyclical peak at time period 9 illustrates an economic expansion and the cyclical valley at time period 12 an economic contraction.

The *cyclical component* is the wavelike fluctuation around the trend.

When observations are influenced by seasonal factors, a *seasonal* pattern exists. The seasonal component refers to a pattern of change that repeats itself year after year. For a monthly series, the seasonal component measures the variability of the series each January, each February, and so on. For a quarterly series, there are four seasonal elements, one for each quarter. Figure 3-3 shows that electrical usage for Washington Water Power residential customers is highest in the first quarter (winter months) of each year. Figure 3-14 (see p. 73) shows that the quarterly sales for Outboard Marine are typically low in the first quarter of each year. Seasonal variation may reflect weather conditions, holidays, or length of calendar months.

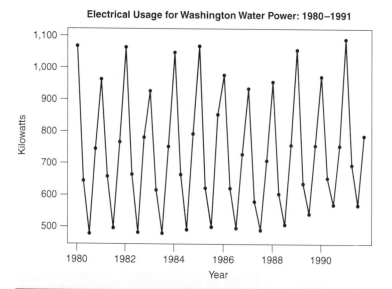

Electrical Usage for Washington Water Power: 1980–1991

FIGURE 3-3   **Electrical Usage for Washington Water Power Company, 1980–1991**

The *seasonal component* is a pattern of change that repeats itself year after year.

EXPLORING DATA PATTERNS WITH AUTOCORRELATION ANALYSIS

When a variable is measured over time, observations in different time periods are frequently related or correlated. This correlation is measured using the autocorrelation coefficient.

Autocorrelation is the correlation between a variable lagged one or more periods and itself.

Data patterns, including components such as trend and seasonality, can be studied using autocorrelations. Autocorrelation coefficients for different time lags of a variable are used to identify time series data patterns.

The concept of autocorrelation is illustrated by the data for Example 3.1 presented in Table 3-1. Note that variables Y_{t-1} and Y_{t-2} are actually the Y values that have been lagged by one and two periods, respectively. The values for March, which are shown on the row for time period 3, are March sales, $Y_t = 125$; February sales, $Y_{t-1} = 130$; and January sales, $Y_{t-2} = 123$.

Equation 3.1 contains the formula for computing the lag k autocorrelation coefficient (r_k) between observations Y_t and Y_{t-k}, which are k periods apart.

$$r_k = \frac{\sum_{t=k+1}^{n} (Y_t - \bar{Y})(Y_{t-k} - \bar{Y})}{\sum_{t=1}^{n} (Y_t - \bar{Y})^2} \qquad k = 0, 1, 2, \ldots \qquad (3.1)$$

TABLE 3-1	VCR Data for Example 3.1		
Time		*Original Data*	*Y Lagged One Period*	*Y Lagged Two Periods*
t	*Month*	Y_t	Y_{t-1}	Y_{t-2}
1	January	123		
2	February	130	123	
3	March	125	130	123
4	April	138	125	130
5	May	145	138	125
6	June	142	145	138
7	July	141	142	145
8	August	146	141	142
9	September	147	146	141
10	October	157	147	146
11	November	150	157	147
12	December	160	150	157

where

r_k = autocorrelation coefficient for a lag of k periods

$\bar{Y}$ = mean of the values of the series

Y_t = observation in time period t

Y_{t-k} = observation k time periods earlier or at time period $t - k$

Example 3.1

Harry Vernon has collected data on the number of VCRs sold last year for Vernon's Music Store. The data are presented in Table 3-1. Table 3-2 shows the computations that lead to the calculation of the lag 1 autocorrelation coefficient. Figure 3-4 contains a scatter plot of the pairs of observations (Y_{t-1}, Y_t). It is clear from the scatter diagram that the lag 1 correlation will be positive.

The lag 1 autocorrelation coefficient (r_1), or the autocorrelation between Y_t and Y_{t-1}, is computed using the totals from Table 3-2 and Equation 3.1. Thus,

$$r_1 = \frac{\sum_{t=1+1}^{n} (Y_t - \bar{Y})(Y_{t-1} - \bar{Y})}{\sum_{t=1}^{n} (Y_t - \bar{Y})^2} = \frac{843}{1{,}474} = .572$$

As suggested by the plot in Figure 3-4, positive lag 1 autocorrelation exists in this time series. The correlation between Y_t and Y_{t-1} or the autocorrelation for lag 1, is .572. This means that the successive monthly sales of VCRs are somewhat correlated with each other. This information may give Harry valuable insights about his time series, may help him prepare to use an advanced forecasting method, and may warn him about using regression analysis with his data. All of these ideas will be discussed in subsequent chapters.

The second-order autocorrelation coefficient (r_2), or the correlation between Y_t and Y_{t-2} for Harry's data, is also computed using Equation 3.1.

$$r_2 = \frac{\sum_{t=2+1}^{n} (Y_t - \bar{Y})(Y_{t-2} - \bar{Y})}{\sum_{t=1}^{n} (Y_t - \bar{Y})^2} = \frac{682}{1{,}474} = .463$$

TABLE 3-2	Computation of the Lag 1 Autocorrelation Coefficient for the Data in Table 3-1				
Time, t	Y_t	Y_{t-1}	$(Y_t - \bar{Y})$	$(Y_{t-1} - \bar{Y})$	$(Y_t - \bar{Y})^2$	$(Y_t - \bar{Y})(Y_{t-1} - \bar{Y})$
1	123	—	−19	—	361	—
2	130	123	−12	−19	144	228
3	125	130	−17	−12	289	204
4	138	125	−4	−17	16	68
5	145	138	3	−4	9	−12
6	142	145	0	3	0	0
7	141	142	−1	0	1	0
8	146	141	4	−1	16	−4
9	147	146	5	4	25	20
10	157	147	15	5	225	75
11	150	157	8	15	64	120
12	160	150	18	8	324	144
Total	1,704		0		1,474	843

$$\bar{Y} = \frac{1,704}{12} = 142$$

$$r_1 = \frac{843}{1,474} = .572$$

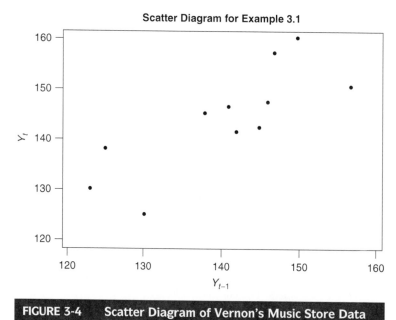

Scatter Diagram for Example 3.1

FIGURE 3-4	Scatter Diagram of Vernon's Music Store Data for Example 3.1

It appears that moderate autocorrelation exists in this time series lagged two time periods. The correlation between Y_t and Y_{t-2}, or the autocorrelation for lag 2, is .463. Notice that the autocorrelation coefficient at lag 2 (.463) is less than the autocorrelation coefficient at lag 1 (.572). Generally, as the number of time lags, k, increases, the magnitudes of the autocorrelation coefficients decrease.

Figure 3-5 shows a plot of the autocorrelations versus time lags for the Harry Vernon data used in Example 3.1. The horizontal scale on the bottom of the graph

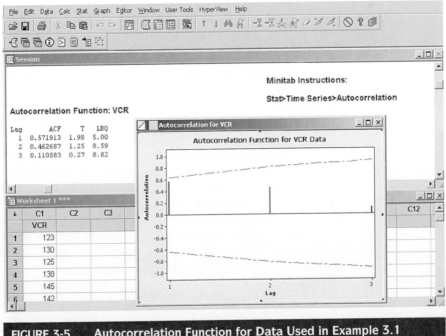

FIGURE 3-5   Autocorrelation Function for Data Used in Example 3.1

shows each time lag of interest, 1, 2, 3, and so on. The vertical scale on the left shows the possible range of an autocorrelation coefficient, -1 to $+1$. The horizontal line in the middle of the graph represents autocorrelations of zero. The vertical line that extends upward above time lag 1 shows an autocorrelation coefficient of .57, $r_1 = .57$. The vertical line that extends upward above time lag 2 shows an autocorrelation coefficient of .46, $r_2 = .46$. The dotted lines and the T and LBQ statistics displayed in the Session window will be discussed in Examples 3.2 and 3.3. Patterns in a correlogram are used to analyze key features of the data, a concept demonstrated in the next section. The Minitab computer package (see the "Minitab Applications" section at the end of the chapter for specific instructions) can be used to compute autocorrelations and develop correlograms.

> The *correlogram* or *autocorrelation function* is a graph of the autocorrelations for various lags of a time series.

With a display such as Figure 3-5, the data patterns, including trend and seasonality, can be studied. Autocorrelation coefficients for different time lags for a variable can be used to answer the following questions about a time series:

1. Are the data random?
2. Do the data have a trend (nonstationary)?
3. Are the data stationary?
4. Are the data seasonal?

If a series is random, the autocorrelations between Y_t and Y_{t-k} for any lag k are close to zero. The successive values of a time series are not related to each other.

If a series has a trend, successive observations are highly correlated, and the autocorrelation coefficients are typically significantly different from zero for the first several time lags and then gradually drop toward zero as the number of lags increases. The autocorrelation coefficient for time lag 1 is often very large (close to 1). The autocorrelation coefficient for time lag 2 will also be large. However, it will not be as large as for time lag 1.

If a series has a seasonal pattern, a significant autocorrelation coefficient will occur at the seasonal time lag or multiples of the seasonal lag. The seasonal lag is 4 for quarterly data and 12 for monthly data.

How does an analyst determine whether an autocorrelation coefficient is significantly different from zero for the data of Table 3-1? Quenouille (1949) and others have demonstrated that the autocorrelation coefficients of random data have a sampling distribution that can be approximated by a normal curve with mean zero and an approximate standard deviation of $1/\sqrt{n}$. Knowing this, the analyst can compare the sample autocorrelation coefficients with this theoretical sampling distribution and determine whether, for given time lags, they come from a population whose mean is zero.

Actually, some software packages use a slightly different formula, as shown in Equation 3.2, to compute the standard deviations (or standard errors) of the autocorrelation coefficients. This formula assumes any autocorrelation before lag k is different from zero and any autocorrelation at lags greater than or equal to k is zero. For an autocorrelation at lag 1, the standard error $1/\sqrt{n}$ is used.

$$SE(r_k) = \sqrt{\frac{1 + 2\sum_{i=1}^{k-1} r_i^2}{n}}$$ (3.2)

where

$SE(r_k)$ = standard error of the autocorrelation at lag k

r_i = autocorrelation at lag i

k = the time lag

n = number of observations in the time series

This computation will be demonstrated in Example 3.2. If the series is truly random, almost all of the sample autocorrelation coefficients should lie within a range specified by zero, plus or minus a certain number of standard errors. At a specified confidence level, a series can be considered random if the calculated autocorrelation coefficients are each within the interval about 0 given by:

$$0 \pm t \times SE(r_k)$$

where the multiplier t is an appropriate percentage point of a t distribution.

Although testing each of the r_k to see if they are individually significantly different from 0 is useful, it is also good practice to examine a set of consecutive r_k's as a group. We can use a portmanteau test to see whether the set, say, of the first 10 r_k values is significantly different from a set in which all 10 values are zero.

One common portmanteau test is the modified Box-Pierce Q statistic (Equation 3.3) developed by Ljung and Box. This test is usually applied to the residuals of a forecast model. If the autocorrelations are computed from a random (white noise) process, the statistic Q has a chi-square distribution with m (the number of time lags to be tested) degrees of freedom. For the residuals of a forecast model, however, the statistic Q has a chi-square distribution with the degrees of freedom equal to m minus the number of parameters estimated in the model. The value of the Q statistic can be compared with the chi-square table (Table C-4) to determine if it is larger than we would expect it to be under the null hypothesis that all the autocorrelations in the set are zero. Alternatively, the p-value generated by the test statistic Q can be computed and interpreted. The Q statistic is given in Equation 3.3. It will be demonstrated in Example 3.3.

$$Q = n(n+2) \sum_{k=1}^{m} \frac{r_k^2}{n-k} \tag{3.3}$$

where

n = the number of observations in the time series

k = the time lag

m = the number of time lags to be tested

r_k = sample autocorrelation function of the residuals lagged k time periods

Are the Data Random?

Equation 3.4 is a simple random model often called a *white noise model*. Observation Y_t is composed of two parts: c, the overall level, and ε_t, which is the random error component. It is important to note that the ε_t component is assumed to be uncorrelated from period to period.

$$Y_t = c + \varepsilon_t \tag{3.4}$$

Are the data in Table 3-1 consistent with this model? This issue will be explored in Examples 3.2 and 3.3.

Example 3.2
A hypothesis test is developed to determine whether a particular autocorrelation coefficient is significantly different from zero for the correlogram shown in Figure 3-5. The null and alternative hypotheses for testing the significance of the lag 1 population autocorrelation coefficient are

$$H_0: \rho_1 = 0$$
$$H_1: \rho_1 \neq 0$$

If the null hypothesis is true, the test statistic

$$t = \frac{r_1 - \rho_1}{SE(r_1)} = \frac{r_1 - 0}{SE(r_1)} = \frac{r_1}{SE(r_1)} \tag{3.5}$$

has a t distribution with df $= n - 1$. Here $n - 1 = 12 - 1 = 11$, so for a 5% significance level, the decision rule is:

Decision Rule: If $t < -2.2$ or $t > 2.2$, we reject H_0 and conclude the lag 1 autocorrelation is significantly different from 0.

The critical values ± 2.2 are the upper and lower .025 points of a t distribution with 11 degrees of freedom. The standard error of r_1 is $SE(r_1) = \sqrt{1/12} = \sqrt{.083} = .289$ and the value of the test statistic becomes

$$t = \frac{r_1}{SE(r_1)} = \frac{.572}{.289} = 1.98$$

and, using the decision rule above, $H_0: \rho_1 = 0$ cannot be rejected, because $-2.2 < 1.98 < 2.2$. Notice that the value of our test statistic, $t = 1.98$, is the same as the quantity in the lag 1 row under the heading T in the Minitab output in Figure 3-5. The T values in the Minitab output are simply the values of the test statistic for testing for 0 autocorrelation at the various lags.

To test for 0 autocorrelation at time lag 2, we consider

$$H_0: \rho_2 = 0$$
$$H_1: \rho_2 \neq 0$$

and the test statistic

$$t = \frac{r_2 - \rho_2}{SE(r_2)} = \frac{r_2 - 0}{SE(r_2)} = \frac{r_2}{SE(r_2)}$$

Using Equation (3.2),

$$SE(r_2) = \sqrt{\frac{1 + 2\sum_{i=1}^{k-1} r_i^2}{n}} = \sqrt{\frac{1 + 2\sum_{i=1}^{2-1} r_i^2}{n}} = \sqrt{\frac{1 + 2(.572)^2}{12}} = \sqrt{\frac{1.6544}{12}} = \sqrt{.138} = .371$$

and

$$t = \frac{.463}{.371} = 1.25$$

This result agrees with the T value for lag 2 in the Minitab output in Figure 3-5.

Using the decision rule above, $H_0: \rho_2 = 0$ cannot be rejected at the .05 level because $-2.2 < 1.25 < 2.2$. An alternative way to check for significant autocorrelation is to construct, say, 95% confidence limits centered at 0. These limits for lags 1 and 2 are given by

$$\text{lag 1: } 0 \pm t_{.025} \times SE(r_1) \qquad \text{or} \qquad 0 \pm 2.2(.289) \to (-.636, .636)$$

$$\text{lag 2: } 0 \pm t_{.025} \times SE(r_2) \qquad \text{or} \qquad 0 \pm 2.2(.371) \to (-.816, .816)$$

Autocorrelation significantly different from 0 is indicated whenever a value for r_k falls outside the corresponding confidence limits. The 95% confidence limits are shown in Figure 3-5 by the dashed lines in the graphical display of the autocorrelation function.

Example 3.3

Minitab was used to generate the time series of 40 pseudo-random three-digit numbers shown in Table 3-3. Figure 3-6 shows a time series graph of these data. Because these data are random (independent of one another and all from the same population), autocorrelations for all time lags should theoretically be equal to zero. Of course, the 40 values in Table 3-3 are only one set of a large number of possible samples of size 40. Each sample will produce different autocorrelations. Most of these samples will produce sample autocorrelation coefficients that are close to zero. However, it is possible that a sample will produce an autocorrelation coefficient that is significantly different from zero just by chance.

Next the autocorrelation function shown in Figure 3-7 (see p. 68) is constructed using Minitab. Note that the two dashed lines show the 95% confidence limits. Ten time lags are examined, and all the individual autocorrelation coefficients lie within these limits. There is no reason to doubt that each of the autocorrelations for the first 10 lags is zero. However, even though the individual sample autocorrelations are not significantly different from 0, are the magnitudes of the first 10 r_k as a group larger than one would expect under the hypothesis of no autocorrelation at any lag? This question is answered by the Ljung-Box Q (LBQ in Minitab) statistic.

If there is no autocorrelation at any lag, the Q statistic has a chi-square distribution with, in this case, df = 10. Consequently, a large value for Q (in the tail of the chi-square distribution) is evidence against the null hypothesis. From Figure 3-7, the value of Q (LBQ) for 10 time lags is 7.75. From Table C-4, the upper .05 point of a chi-square distribution with 10 degrees of freedom is 18.31. Because $7.75 < 18.31$, the null hypothesis cannot be rejected at the 5% significance level. These data are uncorrelated at any time lag, a result consistent with the model in Equation 3.4.

TABLE 3-3		Time Series of 40 Random Numbers for Example 3.3					
t	Y_t	t	Y_t	t	Y_t	t	Y_t
1	343	11	946	21	704	31	555
2	574	12	142	22	291	32	476
3	879	13	477	23	43	33	612
4	728	14	452	24	118	34	574
5	37	15	727	25	682	35	518
6	227	16	147	26	577	36	296
7	613	17	199	27	834	37	970
8	157	18	744	28	981	38	204
9	571	19	627	29	263	39	616
10	72	20	122	30	424	40	97

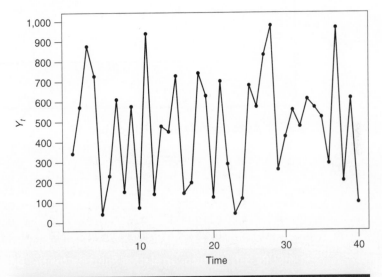

FIGURE 3-6   Time Series Plot of the Random Numbers Used in Example 3.3

Do the Data Have a Trend?

If a series has a trend, a significant relationship exists between successive time series values. The autocorrelation coefficients are typically large for the first several time lags and then gradually drop toward zero as the number of lags increases.

A *stationary* time series is one whose basic statistical properties, such as the mean and variance, remain constant over time. Consequently, a series that varies about a fixed level (no growth or decline) over time is said to be stationary. A series that contains a trend is said to be *nonstationary*. The autocorrelation coefficients for a stationary series decline to zero fairly rapidly, generally after the second or third time lag. On the other hand, sample autocorrelations remain fairly large for a nonstationary series for several time periods. Often, to analyze nonstationary series, the trend is removed before additional modeling occurs. The procedures discussed in Chapter 9 use this approach.

A method called *differencing* can often be used to remove the trend from a nonstationary series. The VCR data originally presented in Table 3-1 are shown again

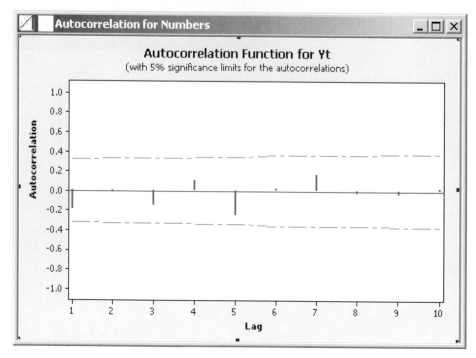

Autocorrelation Function: Yt

Lag	ACF	T	LBQ	Lag	ACF	T	LBQ
1	-0.191171	-1.21	1.57	6	0.028640	0.16	6.17
2	-0.006293	-0.04	1.58	7	0.169071	0.95	7.63
3	-0.145224	-0.89	2.53	8	-0.027390	-0.15	7.67
4	0.104475	0.63	3.04	9	-0.032551	-0.18	7.73
5	-0.253756	-1.50	6.13	10	0.021546	0.12	7.75

FIGURE 3-7   Autocorrelation Function for the Data Used in Example 3.3

in Figure 3-8, column A. The Y_t value lagged one period, Y_{t-1}, is shown in column B. The differences, $Y_t - Y_{t-1}$ (column A − column B), are shown in column C. For example, the first value for the differences is $Y_2 - Y_1 = 130 - 123 = 7$. Note the upward growth or trend of the VCR data shown in Figure 3-9, plot A. Now observe the stationary pattern of the differenced data in plot B. Differencing the data has removed the trend.

Example 3.4
Maggie Trymane, an analyst for Sears, is assigned the task of forecasting operating revenue for 2001. She gathers the data for the years 1955 to 2000, shown in Table 3-4. The data are plotted as a time series in Figure 3-10 (see p. 71). First, Maggie computes a 95% confidence interval for the autocorrelation coefficients at time lag 1 using $0 \pm Z_{.025}(1/\sqrt{n})$ where, for large samples, the standard normal .025 point has replaced the corresponding t distribution percentage point:

$$0 \pm 1.96(\sqrt{1/46})$$

$$0 \pm .289$$

Next Maggie runs the data on Minitab and produces the autocorrelation function shown in Figure 3-11. Upon examination, she notices that the autocorrelations for the first three

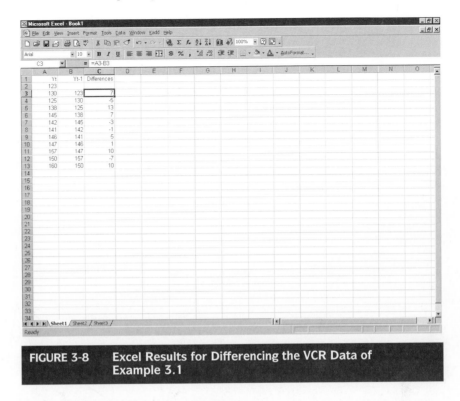

	A	B	C
	Yt	Yt-1	Differences
1	123		
2	130	123	7
3	125	130	-5
4	138	125	13
5	145	138	7
6	142	145	-3
7	141	142	-1
8	146	141	5
9	147	146	1
10	157	147	10
11	150	157	-7
12	160	150	10

FIGURE 3-8   **Excel Results for Differencing the VCR Data of Example 3.1**

time lags are significantly different from zero (.96, .92, and .87) and that the values then gradually drop to zero. As a final check, Maggie looks at the Q statistic for 10 time lags. The LBQ is 274.97, which is greater than the chi-square value 18.3 (the upper .05 point of a chi-square distribution with 10 degrees of freedom). She decides that the data are highly autocorrelated and exhibit trendlike behavior.

Maggie suspects that the series can be differenced to remove the trend and to create a stationary series. She differences the data (see "Minitab Applications" on p. 95), with the results shown in Figure 3-12. The differenced series shows no evidence of a trend, and the autocorrelation function, shown in Figure 3-13, appears to support this conclusion. Examining Figure 3-13, Maggie notes that the autocorrelation coefficient at time lag 3, .32, is significantly different from zero (tested at the .05 significance level). The autocorrelations at lags other than lag 3 are small, and Maggie wonders whether there is some pattern in these data that can be modeled by one of the more advanced forecasting techniques discussed in Chapter 9.

Are the Data Seasonal?

If a series is seasonal, a pattern related to the calendar repeats itself over a particular interval of time (usually a year). Observations in the same position for different seasonal periods tend to be related. If quarterly data with a seasonal pattern are analyzed, first quarters tend to look alike, second quarters tend to look alike, and so forth, and a significant autocorrelation coefficient will appear at time lag 4. If monthly data are analyzed, a significant autocorrelation coefficient will appear at time lag 12. That is, January will correlate with other Januarys, February will correlate with other Februarys, and so forth. Example 3.5 discusses a series that is seasonal.

Example 3.5

Perkin Kendell is an analyst for Outboard Marine Corporation. He has always felt that sales were seasonal. Perkin gathers the data shown in Table 3-5 (see p. 73) for the quarterly sales of Outboard Marine Corporation from 1984 to 1996 and plots them as the time series graph

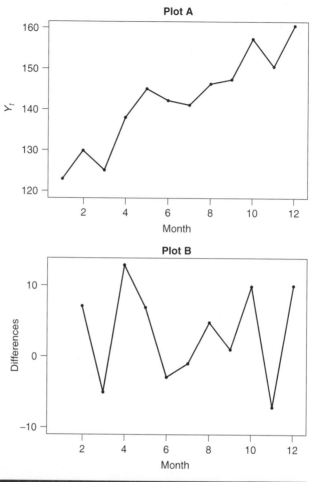

FIGURE 3-9   Time Series Plots of the VCR Data and the Differenced VCR Data

TABLE 3-4   Yearly Operating Revenue of Sears Roebuck & Co., 1955–2000, for Example 3.4

Year	Y_t	Year	Y_t	Year	Y_t	Year	Y_t
1955	3,307	1967	7,296	1979	17,514	1991	57,242
1956	3,556	1968	8,178	1980	25,195	1992	52,345
1957	3,601	1969	8,844	1981	27,357	1993	50,838
1958	3,721	1970	9,251	1982	30,020	1994	54,559
1959	4,036	1971	10,006	1983	35,883	1995	34,925
1960	4,134	1972	10,991	1984	38,828	1996	38,236
1961	4,268	1973	12,306	1985	40,715	1997	41,296
1962	4,578	1974	13,101	1986	44,282	1998	41,322
1963	5,093	1975	13,639	1987	48,440	1999	41,071
1964	5,716	1976	14,950	1988	50,251	2000	40,937
1965	6,357	1977	17,224	1989	53,794		
1966	6,769	1978	17,946	1990	55,972		

Source: Industry Surveys, various years.

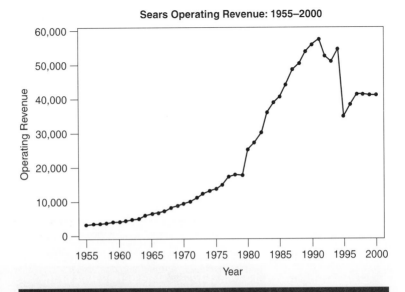

FIGURE 3-10   Time Series Plot of Sears Operating Revenue

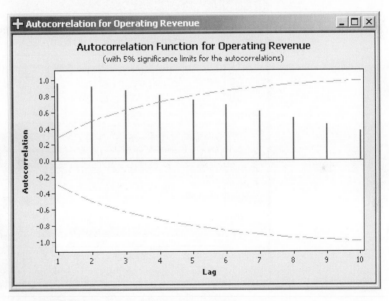

Autocorrelation Function: Revenue

Lag	ACF	T	LBQ	Lag	ACF	T	LBQ
1	0.957322	6.49	44.97	6	0.692167	1.61	217.26
2	0.915920	3.69	87.07	7	0.611867	1.35	238.45
3	0.870327	2.78	125.96	8	0.530836	1.13	254.83
4	0.810476	2.24	160.49	9	0.449109	0.93	266.86
5	0.750323	1.88	190.81	10	0.363433	0.74	274.97

FIGURE 3-11   Autocorrelation Function for Sears Operating Revenue

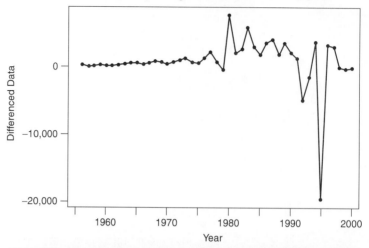

FIGURE 3-12   Time Series Plot of the First Differences of the Sears Operating Revenue

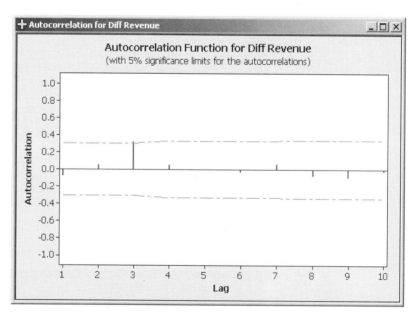

Autocorrelation Function: Diff Revenue

Lag	ACF	T	LBQ	Lag	ACF	T	LBQ
1	-0.082142	-0.55	0.32	6	-0.032326	-0.20	5.96
2	0.050143	0.33	0.45	7	0.060489	0.36	6.17
3	0.324999	2.16	5.77	8	-0.080592	-0.48	6.54
4	0.051342	0.31	5.90	9	-0.092040	-0.55	7.03
5	-0.006329	-0.04	5.91	10	-0.027916	-0.17	7.08

FIGURE 3-13   Autocorrelation Function for the First Differences of the Sears Operating Revenue

TABLE 3-5	Quarterly Sales for Outboard Marine, 1984–1996, for Example 3.5			
Fiscal Year Ends	*December 31*	*March 31*	*June 30*	*September 30*
1984	147.6	251.8	273.1	249.1
1985	139.3	221.2	260.2	259.5
1986	140.5	245.5	298.8	287.0
1987	168.8	322.6	393.5	404.3
1988	259.7	401.1	464.6	479.7
1989	264.4	402.6	411.3	385.9
1990	232.7	309.2	310.7	293.0
1991	205.1	234.4	285.4	258.7
1992	193.2	263.7	292.5	315.2
1993	178.3	274.5	295.4	286.4
1994	190.8	263.5	318.8	305.5
1995	242.6	318.8	329.6	338.2
1996	232.1	285.6	291.0	281.4

Source: The Value Line Investment Survey (New York: Value Line, 1988, 1992, 1996), p. 1773.

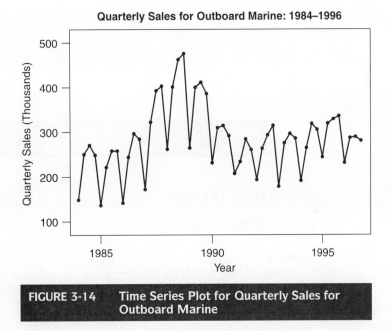

Quarterly Sales for Outboard Marine: 1984–1996

FIGURE 3-14	Time Series Plot for Quarterly Sales for Outboard Marine

shown in Figure 3-14. Next, he computes a large-sample 95% confidence interval for the autocorrelation coefficient at time lag 1:

$$0 \pm 1.96\sqrt{1/52}$$

$$0 \pm .272$$

Next, Perkin computes the autocorrelation coefficients shown in Figure 3-15. He notes that the autocorrelation coefficients at time lags 1 and 4 are significantly different from zero ($r_1 = .39 > .272$ and $r_4 = .74 > .333$). He concludes that Outboard Marine sales are seasonal on a quarterly basis.

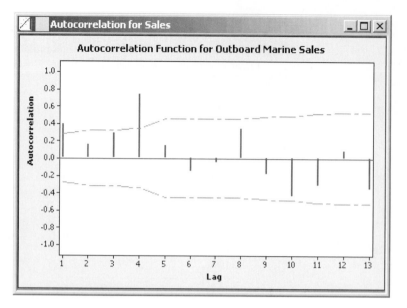

Autocorrelation Function: Sales

Lag	ACF	T	LBQ	Lag	ACF	T	LBQ
1	0.392861	2.83	8.50	8	0.346975	1.51	57.72
2	0.153945	0.97	9.83	9	-0.182601	-0.76	59.90
3	0.293782	1.82	14.77	10	-0.434729	-1.80	72.53
4	0.743520	4.34	47.11	11	-0.315031	-1.23	79.33
5	0.150655	0.67	48.47	12	0.091203	0.35	79.91
6	-0.153008	-0.67	49.90	13	-0.353274	-1.34	88.90
7	-0.046978	-0.21	50.04				

FIGURE 3-15   Autocorrelation Function for Quarterly Sales for Outboard Marine

CHOOSING A FORECASTING TECHNIQUE

This text is devoted mostly to explaining various forecasting techniques and demonstrating their usefulness. First, the important job of choosing the best forecasting techniques is addressed.

Some of the questions that must be considered before deciding on the most appropriate forecasting technique for a particular problem follow:

- Why is a forecast needed?
- Who will use the forecast?
- What are the characteristics of the available data?
- What time period is to be forecast?
- What are the minimum data requirements?
- How much accuracy is desired?
- What will the forecast cost?

To select the appropriate forecasting technique properly, the forecaster must be able to accomplish the following:

- Define the nature of the forecasting problem.
- Explain the nature of the data under investigation.

- Describe the capabilities and limitations of potentially useful forecasting techniques.
- Develop some predetermined criteria on which the selection decision can be made.

A major factor influencing the selection of a forecasting technique is the identification and understanding of historical patterns in the data. If trend, cyclical, or seasonal patterns can be recognized, techniques that are capable of effectively extrapolating these patterns can be selected.

Forecasting Techniques for Stationary Data

A stationary series was defined earlier as one whose mean value is not changing over time. Such situations arise when the demand patterns influencing the series are relatively stable. In its simplest form, forecasting a stationary series involves using the available history of the series to estimate its mean value, which then becomes the forecast for future periods. More sophisticated techniques involve updating the estimate as new information becomes available. These techniques are useful when initial estimates are unreliable or when the stability of the average is in question. In addition, updating techniques provide some degree of responsiveness to changes in the underlying structure of the series.

Stationary forecasting techniques are used whenever

- *The forces generating a series have stabilized and the environment in which the series exists is relatively unchanging.* Examples are the number of breakdowns per week on an assembly line having a uniform production rate, the unit sales of a product or service in the maturation stage of its life cycle, and the number of sales resulting from a constant level of effort.
- *A very simple model is needed because of a lack of data or for ease of explanation or implementation.* An example is when a business or organization is new and very little historical data are available.
- *Stability may be obtained by making simple corrections for factors such as population growth or inflation.* Examples are changing income to per capita income or changing dollar sales to constant dollar amounts.
- *The series may be transformed into a stable one.* Examples are transforming a series by taking logarithms, square roots, or differences.
- *The series is a set of forecast errors from a forecasting technique that is considered adequate.* (See Example 3.7 on p. 82.)

Techniques that should be considered when forecasting stationary series include naive methods, simple averaging methods, moving averages, and autoregressive moving average (ARMA) models (Box-Jenkins methods).

Forecasting Techniques for Data with a Trend

A *trending* series was defined earlier as a time series that contains a long-term component that represents the growth or decline in the series over an extended period of time. In other words, a time series is said to have a trend if its average value changes over time so that it is expected to increase or decrease during the period for which forecasts are desired. It is common for economic time series to contain a trend.

Forecasting techniques for trending data are used whenever

- *Increased productivity and new technology lead to changes in lifestyle.* Examples are the demand for electronic components, which increased with the advent of the computer, and railroad usage, which decreased with the advent of the airplane.

- *Increasing population causes increases in demand for goods and services.* Examples are the sales revenues of consumer goods, demand for energy consumption, and use of raw materials.
- *The purchasing power of the dollar affects economic variables due to inflation.* Examples are salaries, production costs, and prices.
- *Market acceptance increases.* An example is the growth period in the life cycle of a new product.

Techniques that should be considered when forecasting trending series include moving averages, Holt's linear exponential smoothing, simple regression, growth curves, exponential models, and autoregressive integrated moving average (ARIMA) models (Box-Jenkins methods).

Forecasting Techniques for Seasonal Data

A seasonal series was defined earlier as a time series with a pattern of change that repeats itself year after year. One way to develop seasonal forecasts involves selecting either a multiplicative or additive decomposition method and then estimating seasonal indexes from the history of the series. These indexes are then used to include seasonality in forecasts or to remove such effects from the observed values. The latter process is referred to as seasonally adjusting the data and is discussed in Chapter 5.

Forecasting techniques for seasonal data are used whenever

- *Weather influences the variable of interest.* Examples are electrical consumption, summer and winter activities (*e.g.*, sports such as skiing), clothing, and agricultural growing seasons.
- *The annual calendar influences the variable of interest.* Examples are retail sales influenced by holidays, three-day weekends, and school calendars.

Techniques that should be considered when forecasting seasonal series include classical decomposition, Census X-12, Winter's exponential smoothing, multiple regression, and ARIMA models (Box-Jenkins methods).

Forecasting Techniques for Cyclical Series

The cyclical effect was defined earlier as the wavelike fluctuation around the trend. Cyclical patterns are difficult to model because their patterns are typically not stable. The up–down wavelike fluctuations around the trend rarely repeat at fixed intervals of time, and the magnitude of the fluctuations also tends to vary. Decomposition methods (Chapter 5) can be extended to analyze cyclical data. However, because of the irregular behavior of cycles, analyzing the cyclical component of a series often requires finding coincidental or leading economic indicators.

Forecasting techniques for cyclical data are used whenever

- *The business cycle influences the variable of interest.* Examples are economic, market, and competitive factors.
- *Shifts in popular tastes occur.* Examples are fashions, music, and food.
- *Shifts in population occur.* Examples are wars, famines, epidemics, and natural disasters.
- *Shifts in product life cycle occur.* Examples are introduction, growth, maturation and market saturation, and decline.

Techniques that should be considered when forecasting cyclical series include classical decomposition, economic indicators, econometric models, multiple regression, and ARIMA models (Box-Jenkins methods).

Other Factors to Consider When Choosing a Forecasting Technique

The time horizon for a forecast has a direct bearing on the selection of a forecasting technique. For short- and intermediate-term forecasts, a variety of quantitative techniques can be applied. As the forecasting horizon increases, however, a number of these techniques become less applicable. For instance, moving averages, exponential smoothing, and ARIMA models are poor predictors of economic turning points, whereas econometric models can be more useful. Regression models are appropriate for the short, intermediate, and long terms. Means, moving averages, classical decomposition, and trend projections are quantitative techniques that are appropriate for the short and intermediate time horizons. The more complex Box-Jenkins and econometric techniques are also appropriate for short- and intermediate-term forecasts. Qualitative methods are frequently used for longer time horizons (see Chapter 10).

The applicability of forecasting techniques is generally something a forecaster bases on experience. Managers frequently need forecasts in a relatively short time. Exponential smoothing, trend projection, regression models, and classical decomposition methods have an advantage in this situation. (See Table 3-6.)

Computer costs are no longer a significant part of technique selection. Desktop computers (using microprocessors) and forecasting software packages are becoming commonplace for many organizations. Because of these developments, other criteria often overshadow computer cost considerations.

Ultimately, a forecast will be presented to management for approval and use in the decision-making process. Therefore, ease of understanding and interpreting the results is an important consideration. Regression models, trend projections, classical decomposition, and exponential smoothing techniques all rate highly on this criterion.

Empirical Evaluation of Forecasting Methods

Empirical research has found that the forecast accuracy of simple methods is at least as good as that of complex or statistically sophisticated techniques.[1] Results of the M3-IJF Competition, where different experts using their favorite forecasting methodology each generated forecasts for 3,003 different time series, tended to support this finding.[2] It would seem that the more statistically complex a technique the better it should predict time series patterns. Unfortunately, established time series patterns can and do change in the future. So, having a model that best represents the historical data (the thing complex methods do well) does not necessarily guarantee more accuracy in future predictions. Of course, the ability of the forecaster also plays an important role in the development of a good forecast.

The M3-IJF Competition was held in 1997. The forecasts produced by the various forecasting techniques were compared across the sample of 3,003 time series with the accuracy assessed using a range of measures on a holdout set. The aim of the 1997 study was to check the four major conclusions of the original M-Competition on a larger data set.[3] Makridakis and Hibon (2000) summarized the latest competition as follows:

1. As discussed previously, statistically sophisticated or complex methods do not necessarily produce more accurate forecasts than simpler methods.
2. Various accuracy measures (MAD, MSE, MAPE) produce consistent results when used to evaluate different forecasting methods.

---

[1] See Fildes *et al.* (1997), Makridakis *et al.* (1993), and Makridakis and Hibon (2000).
[2] See Makridakis and Hibon (2000).
[3] See Makridakis *et al.* (1982).

TABLE 3-6	Choosing a Forecasting Technique				

Method	Pattern of Data	Time Horizon	Type of Model	Minimal Data Requirements Nonseasonal	Seasonal
Naive	ST, T, S	S	TS	1	
Simple averages	ST	S	TS	30	
Moving averages	ST	S	TS	4–20	
Exponential smoothing	ST	S	TS	2	
Linear exponential smoothing	T	S	TS	3	
Quadratic exponential smoothing	T	S	TS	4	
Seasonal exponential smoothing	S	S	TS		2 × s
Adaptive filtering	S	S	TS		5 × s
Simple regression	T	I	C	10	
Multiple regression	C, S	I	C	10 × V	
Classical decomposition	S	S	TS		5 × s
Exponential trend models	T	I, L	TS	10	
S-curve fitting	T	I, L	TS	10	
Gompertz models	T	I, L	TS	10	
Growth curves	T	I, L	TS	10	
Census X-12	S	S	TS		6 × s
Box-Jenkins	ST, T, C, S	S	TS	24	3 × s
Leading indicators	C	S	C	24	
Econometric models	C	S	C	30	
Time series multiple regression	T, S	I, L	C		6 × s

Pattern of data: ST, stationary; T, trended; S, seasonal; C, cyclical.
Time horizon: S, short term (less than three months); I, intermediate; L, long term.
Type of model: TS, time series; C, causal.
Seasonal: s, length of seasonality.
Variable: V, number of variables.

3. The combination of three exponential smoothing methods outperforms, on average, the individual methods being combined and does well in comparison with other methods.

4. The performance of the various forecasting methods depends on the length of the forecasting horizon and the kind (yearly, quarterly, monthly) of data analyzed. Some methods perform more accurately for short horizons whereas others are more appropriate for longer ones. Some methods work better with yearly data and others are more appropriate for quarterly and monthly data.

As part of the final selection, each technique must be evaluated in terms of its reliability and applicability to the problem at hand, its cost effectiveness and accuracy compared with competing techniques, and its acceptance by management. Table 3-6 summarizes forecasting techniques appropriate for particular data patterns. This table represents a place to start, that is, it shows methods to consider for data with certain characteristics. Ultimately, any chosen method should be continuously monitored to be sure it is adequately doing the job for which it was intended.

MEASURING FORECASTING ERROR

Because quantitative forecasting techniques frequently involve time series data, a mathematical notation is developed to refer to each specific time period. The letter Y

will be used to denote a time series variable unless there is more than one variable involved. The time period associated with an observation is shown as a subscript. Thus Y_t refers to the value of the time series at time period t. The quarterly data for the Outboard Marine Corporation presented in Example 3.5 (see p. 73) would be denoted $Y_1 = 147.6$, $Y_2 = 251.8$, $Y_3 = 273.1, \ldots, Y_{52} = 281.4$.

Mathematical notation must also be developed for distinguishing between an actual value of time series and the forecast value. A ˆ (hat) will be placed above a value to indicate that it is being forecast. The forecast value for Y_t is $\hat{Y}_t$. The accuracy of a forecasting technique is frequently judged by comparing the original series $Y_1, Y_2, \ldots$ with the series of forecast values $\hat{Y}_1, \hat{Y}_2, \ldots$.

Basic Forecasting Notation

Basic forecasting notation is summarized as follows.

Y_t = value of a time series at period t
$\hat{Y}_t$ = forecast value of Y_t
$e_t = Y_t - \hat{Y}_t$ = residual, or forecast error

Several methods have been devised to summarize the errors generated by a particular forecasting technique. Most of these measures involve averaging some function of the difference between an actual value and its forecast value. These differences between observed values and forecast values are often referred to as *residuals*.

A *residual* is the difference between an actual value and its forecast value.

Equation 3.6 is used to compute the error, or residual, for each forecast period.

$$e_t = Y_t - \hat{Y}_t \tag{3.6}$$

where

e_t = forecast error in time period t
Y_t = actual value in time period t
$\hat{Y}_t$ = forecast value for time period t

One method for evaluating a forecasting technique uses the sum of the absolute errors. The mean absolute deviation (*MAD*) measures forecast accuracy by averaging the magnitudes of the forecast errors (absolute values of each error). *MAD* is most useful when the analyst wants to measure forecast error in the same units as the original series. Equation 3.7 shows how *MAD* is computed.

$$MAD = \frac{1}{n} \sum_{t=1}^{n} \left| Y_t - \hat{Y}_t \right| \tag{3.7}$$

The mean squared error (*MSE*) is another method for evaluating a forecasting technique. Each error or residual is squared; these are then summed and divided by the number of observations. This approach penalizes large forecasting errors because the errors are squared, which is important; a technique that produces moderate errors may well be preferable to one that usually has small errors but occasionally yields extremely large ones. The *MSE* is given by Equation 3.8.

$$MSE = \frac{1}{n} \sum_{t=1}^{n} (Y_t - \hat{Y}_t)^2 \tag{3.8}$$

Sometimes it is more useful to compute the forecasting errors in terms of percentages rather than amounts. The mean absolute percentage error (*MAPE*) is computed by finding the absolute error in each period, dividing this by the actual observed value for that period, and then averaging these absolute percentage errors. This approach is useful when the size or magnitude of the forecast variable is important in evaluating the accuracy of the forecast. *MAPE* provides an indication of how large the forecast errors are in comparison to the actual values of the series. The technique is especially useful when the Y_t values are large. *MAPE* can also be used to compare the accuracy of the same or different techniques on two entirely different series. Equation 3.9 shows how *MAPE* is computed.

$$MAPE = \frac{1}{n} \sum_{t=1}^{n} \frac{|Y_t - \hat{Y}_t|}{Y_t} \tag{3.9}$$

Sometimes it is necessary to determine whether a forecasting method is biased (consistently forecasting low or high). The mean percentage error (*MPE*) is used in these cases. It is computed by finding the error in each period, dividing this by the actual value for that period, and then averaging these percentage errors. If the forecasting approach is unbiased, *MPE* will produce a number that is close to zero. If the result is a large negative percentage, the forecasting method is consistently overestimating. If the result is a large positive percentage, the forecasting method is consistently underestimating. *MPE* is given by

$$MPE = \frac{1}{n} \sum_{t=1}^{n} \frac{(Y_t - \hat{Y}_t)}{Y_t} \tag{3.10}$$

Part of the decision to use a particular forecasting technique involves the determination of whether the technique will produce forecast errors that are judged to be sufficiently small. It is certainly realistic to expect a good forecasting technique to produce relatively small forecast errors on a consistent basis.

The four measures of forecast accuracy just described are used

- To compare the accuracy of two (or more) different techniques
- To measure a particular technique's usefulness or reliability
- To help search for an optimal technique

Example 3.6 illustrates how each of these error measurements is computed.

Example 3.6

Table 3-7 shows the data for the daily number of customers requiring repair work, Y_t, and a forecast of these data, $\hat{Y}_t$, for Gary's Chevron Station. The forecasting technique used the number of customers serviced in the previous period as the forecast for the current

TABLE 3-7	Computations for Forecasting Evaluation Methods for Example 3.6					
Time t	Customers Y_t	Forecast $\hat{Y}_t$	Error e_t	$\|e_t\|$	e_t^2	$\|e_t\|/Y_t$	e_t/Y_t
1	58	—	—	—	—	—	—
2	54	58	−4	4	16	.074	−.074
3	60	54	6	6	36	.100	.100
4	55	60	−5	5	25	.091	−.091
5	62	55	7	7	49	.113	.113
6	62	62	0	0	0	.000	.000
7	65	62	3	3	9	.046	.046
8	63	65	−2	2	4	.032	−.032
9	70	63	7	7	49	.100	.100
		Totals	12	34	188	.556	.162

period. This simple technique will be discussed in Chapter 4. The following computations were employed to evaluate this model using *MAD*, *MSE*, *MAPE*, and *MPE*.

$$MAD = \frac{1}{n}\sum_{t=1}^{n}\left|Y_t - \hat{Y}_t\right| = \frac{34}{8} = 4.3$$

$$MSE = \frac{1}{n}\sum_{t=1}^{n}(Y_t - \hat{Y}_t)^2 = \frac{188}{8} = 23.5$$

$$MAPE = \frac{1}{n}\sum_{t=1}^{n}\frac{\left|Y_t - \hat{Y}_t\right|}{Y_t} = \frac{.556}{8} = .0695 \ (6.95\%)$$

$$MPE = \frac{1}{n}\sum_{t=1}^{n}\frac{(Y_t - \hat{Y}_t)}{Y_t} = \frac{.162}{8} = .0203 \ (2.03\%)$$

MAD indicates that each forecast deviated by an average of 4.3 customers. The *MSE* of 23.5 and the *MAPE* of 6.95% would be compared to the *MSE* and *MAPE* for any other method used to forecast these data. Finally, the small *MPE* of 2.03% indicates that the technique is not biased: Because the value is close to zero, the technique does not consistently over- or underestimate the number of customers serviced daily.

DETERMINING THE ADEQUACY OF A FORECASTING TECHNIQUE

Before forecasting with a selected technique, the adequacy of the choice should be evaluated. The forecaster should answer the following questions:

- Are the autocorrelation coefficients of the residuals indicative of a random series? This question can be answered by examining the autocorrelation function for the residuals, such as the one demonstrated in Example 3.7.
- Are the residuals approximately normally distributed? This question can be answered by analyzing a histogram of the residuals or a normal probability plot.
- Do all parameter estimates have significant *t* ratios? The *t* distribution was reviewed in Chapter 2, and applications of *t* ratios are demonstrated in Example 3.2 (see pp. 65 and 66) and Chapters 6 to 9.
- Is the technique simple to use and easy to understand for decision makers?

The basic requirement that the residual pattern is random is verified by examining the autocorrelation coefficients of the residuals. There should be no significant autocorrelation coefficients. Example 3.2 illustrated how an autocorrelation function can be used to determine whether a series is random. The Ljung-Box Q statistic is also used to test that the autocorrelations for all lags up to lag m equal zero. Example 3.7 illustrates this procedure with the residuals from two fitted models.

Example 3.7

Maggie Trymane, the analyst for Sears, has been asked to forecast sales for 2001. The data are shown in Table 3-4 for 1955 to 2000. First, Maggie tries to forecast the data using a five-month moving average (see Chapter 4 for a description of this technique). The residuals, the difference between the actual values and the predicted values, are computed and stored. The autocorrelation coefficients for these residuals are shown in Figure 3-16. An examination of these autocorrelation coefficients indicates that two are significantly different from zero, $r_1 = .77$ and $r_2 = .63$. Significant autocorrelation coefficients indicate some association or pattern in the residuals. Furthermore, the autocorrelation function itself has a pattern of smoothly declining coefficients. Examining the first 10 autocorrelations as a group, the Q statistic for 10 lags is 72.26, much greater than the upper .05 value of a chi-square variable with 10 degrees of freedom, 18.3. The hypothesis that the first 10 autocorrelations are consistent with those for a random series is clearly rejected at the 5% level. Because one of the basic requirements for a forecasting technique is that it provide a residual or error series that is essentially random, Maggie judges the five-month moving average technique to be inadequate.

FIGURE 3-16   Autocorrelation Function for Residuals with a Pattern

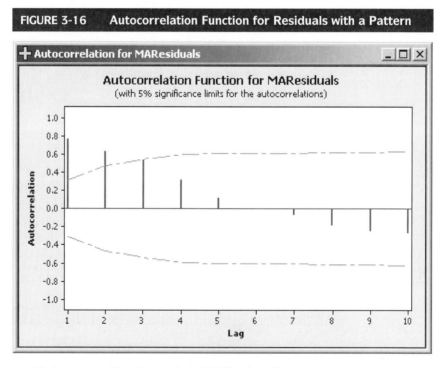

Autocorrelation Function: MAResiduals

Lag	ACF	T	LBQ	Lag	ACF	T	LBQ
1	0.768208	4.92	26.01	6	-0.000650	-0.00	62.36
2	0.628865	2.73	43.89	7	-0.076490	-0.25	62.66
3	0.531352	1.97	56.99	8	-0.184331	-0.61	64.48
4	0.313974	1.07	61.68	9	-0.248870	-0.81	67.89
5	0.117308	0.39	62.36	10	-0.277090	-0.89	72.26

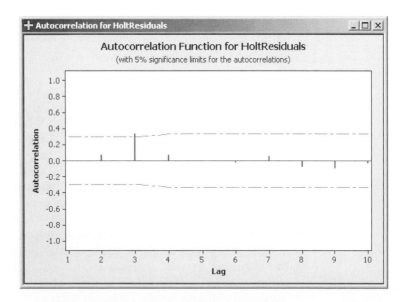

Autocorrelation Function: HoltResiduals

Lag	ACF	T	LBQ	Lag	ACF	T	LBQ
1	-0.010293	-0.07	0.01	6	-0.028641	-0.17	6.41
2	0.072582	0.49	0.27	7	0.055955	0.34	6.59
3	0.336058	2.27	6.07	8	-0.081304	-0.49	6.97
4	0.075102	0.46	6.37	9	-0.098068	-0.59	7.55
5	-0.001224	-0.01	6.37	10	-0.036649	-0.22	7.63

FIGURE 3-17   Autocorrelation Function for Residuals That Are Essentially Random

Maggie now tries Holt's linear exponential smoothing (see Chapter 4 for a description of this technique). The autocorrelation function for the residual series generated by this technique is shown in Figure 3-17. An examination of these autocorrelation coefficients indicates that only the lag 3 residual autocorrelation coefficient, .34, is significantly different from zero (at the 5% level). The Q statistic for 10 time lags is also examined. The LBQ value of 7.63 in the Minitab output is less than the upper .05 value of a chi-square variable with eight degrees of freedom, 15.5. (In this case the degrees of freedom are equal to the number of lags to be tested minus the number of parameters in the linear exponential smoothing model that have been fitted to the data.) Although the lag 3 residual autocorrelation is somewhat large, as a group the first 10 residual autocorrelations are not unlike those for a completely random series. Maggie decides to consider Holt's linear exponential smoothing technique as a possible model to forecast 2001 operating revenue for Sears.

APPLICATION TO MANAGEMENT

The concepts in this chapter provide a basis for selecting a proper forecasting technique in a given situation. Many of the most important forecasting techniques are discussed and applied to forecasting situations in the chapters that follow. It is important to note that in many practical situations, more than one forecasting method or model may produce acceptable and nearly indistinguishable forecasts. In fact, it is good practice to try several reasonable forecasting techniques. Often judgment, based on ease of use, cost, external environmental conditions and so forth, must be used to select a particular set of forecasts from, say, two sets of nearly indistinguishable values.

The following are a few examples of situations constantly arising in the business world for which a sound forecasting technique would help the decision-making process.

- A soft-drink company wants to project the demand for its major product over the next two years, by month.
- A major telecommunications company wants to forecast the quarterly dividend payments of its chief rival for the next three years.
- A university needs to forecast student credit hours by quarter for the next four years in order to develop budget projections for the state legislature.
- A public accounting firm needs monthly forecasts of dollar billings so it can plan for additional accounting positions and begin recruiting.
- The quality control manager of a factory that makes aluminum ingots needs a weekly forecast of production defects for top management of the company.
- A banker wants to see the projected monthly revenue of a small bicycle manufacturer that is seeking a large loan to triple its output capacity.
- A federal government agency needs annual projections of average miles per gallon of American-made cars over the next 10 years in order to make regulatory recommendations.
- A personnel manager needs a monthly forecast of absent days for the company workforce in order to plan overtime expenditures.
- A savings and loan company needs a forecast of delinquent loans over the next two years in an attempt to avoid bankruptcy.
- A company that makes computer chips needs an industry forecast for the number of personal computers sold over the next five years in order to plan its research and development budget.

Glossary

Autocorrelation.   Autocorrelation is the correlation between a variable lagged one or more periods and itself.

Correlogram or **autocorrelation function.**   The correlogram (autocorrelation function) is a graph of the autocorrelations for various lags of a time series.

Cross-sectional.   Cross-sectional data are observations collected at a single point in time.

Cyclical component.   The cyclical component is the wavelike fluctuation around the trend.

Residual.   A residual is the difference between an actual observed value and its forecast value.

Seasonal component.   The seasonal component is a pattern of change that repeats itself year after year.

Stationary series.   A stationary series is one whose basic statistical properties, such as the mean and variance, remain constant over time.

Time series.   A time series consists of data that are collected, recorded, or observed over successive increments of time.

Trend.   The trend is the long-term component that represents the growth or decline in the time series over an extended period of time.

Key Formulas

kth order autocorrelation coefficient

$$r_k = \frac{\sum\limits_{t=k+1}^{n} (Y_t - \bar{Y})(Y_{t-k} - \bar{Y})}{\sum\limits_{t=1}^{n} (Y_t - \bar{Y})^2} \tag{3.1}$$

Standard error of autocorrelation coefficient

$$SE(r_k) = \sqrt{\frac{1 + 2\sum_{i=1}^{k-1} r_i^2}{n}} \tag{3.2}$$

Ljung-Box Q statistic

$$Q = n(n+2)\sum_{k=1}^{m} \frac{r_k^2}{n-k} \tag{3.3}$$

Random model

$$Y_t = c + \varepsilon_t \tag{3.4}$$

t statistic for testing the significance of lag 1 autocorrelation

$$t = \frac{r_1}{SE(r_1)} \tag{3.5}$$

Forecast error, or residual

$$e_t = Y_t - \hat{Y}_t \tag{3.6}$$

Mean absolute deviation

$$MAD = \frac{1}{n}\sum_{t=1}^{n} \left| Y_t - \hat{Y}_t \right| \tag{3.7}$$

Mean squared error

$$MSE = \frac{1}{n}\sum_{t=1}^{n} (Y_t - \hat{Y}_t)^2 \tag{3.8}$$

Mean absolute percentage error

$$MAPE = \frac{1}{n}\sum_{t=1}^{n} \frac{\left| Y_t - \hat{Y}_t \right|}{Y_t} \tag{3.9}$$

Mean percentage error

$$MPE = \frac{1}{n}\sum_{t=1}^{n} \frac{(Y_t - \hat{Y}_t)}{Y_t} \tag{3.10}$$

Problems

1. Explain the differences between qualitative forecasting techniques and quantitative techniques.

2. What is a time series?

3. Describe each of the components in a time series.

4. What is autocorrelation?

5. What does an autocorrelation coefficient measure?

6. Describe how correlograms are used to analyze autocorrelations for various lags of a time series.

7. Each of the following statements describes either a stationary or nonstationary series. Indicate which.
   a. A series that has a trend.
   b. A series whose mean and variance remain constant over time.
   c. A series whose mean value is changing over time.
   d. A series that contains no growth or decline.

8. Descriptions are provided for several types of series: random, stationary, with a trend, or seasonal. Identify each type of series.
   a. A series having basic statistical properties, such as the mean and variance, that remain constant over time.
   b. The successive values of a time series are not related to each other.
   c. A high relationship exists between each successive value of a series.
   d. A significant autocorrelation coefficient appears at time lag 4 for quarterly data.
   e. A series that contains no growth or decline.
   f. The autocorrelation coefficients are typically significantly different from zero for the first several time lags and then gradually decrease toward zero as the number of lags increases.

9. List some of the forecasting techniques that should be considered when forecasting a stationary series. Give examples of situations in which these techniques would be applicable.

10. List some of the forecasting techniques that should be considered when forecasting a trending series. Give examples of situations in which these techniques would be applicable.

11. List some of the forecasting techniques that should be considered when forecasting a seasonal series. Give examples of situations in which these techniques would be applicable.

12. List some of the forecasting techniques that should be considered when forecasting a cyclical series. Give examples of situations in which these techniques would be applicable.

13. The number of marriages in the United States is given in Table P-13. Compute the first differences for these data. Plot the original data and the difference data as a time series. Is there a trend in either of these series? Discuss.

TABLE P-13			
Year	Marriages	Year	Marriages
1985	2413	1992	2362
1986	2407	1993	2334
1987	2403	1994	2362
1988	2396	1995	2336
1989	2403	1996	2344
1990	2443	1997	2384
1991	2371	1998	2244

Source: Statistical Abstract of the United States, 2002.

14. Compute the 95% confidence interval for the autocorrelation coefficient for time lag 1 for a series that contains 80 terms.

15. Which measure of forecast accuracy should be used in each of the following situations?
    a. The analyst needs to determine whether a forecasting method is biased.
    b. The analyst feels that the size, or magnitude, of the forecast variable is important in evaluating the accuracy of the forecast.
    c. The analyst needs to penalize large forecasting errors.

16. Which of the following statements is true concerning the accuracy measures used to evaluate forecasts?
    a. The *MAPE* takes into consideration the magnitude of the values being forecast.
    b. The *MSE* penalizes large errors.
    c. The *MPE* is used to determine whether a model is systematically predicting too high or too low.
    d. The advantage of the *MAD* method is that it relates the size of error to the actual observation.

17. Allie White, the chief loan officer for Dominion Bank, would like to analyze the bank's loan portfolio for the years 1998 to 2003. The data are shown in Table P-17.
    a. Compute the autocorrelations for time lags 1 and 2. Test to determine whether these autocorrelation coefficients are significantly different from zero at the .05 significance level.
    b. Use a computer program to plot the data and compute the autocorrelations for the first six time lags. Is this time series stationary?

18. This question refers to Problem 17. Compute the first differences of the quarterly loan data for Dominion Bank.
    a. Compute the autocorrelation coefficient for time lag 1 using the differenced data.
    b. Use a computer program to plot the differenced data and compute the autocorrelations for the differenced data for the first six time lags. Is this time series stationary?

19. Analyze the autocorrelation coefficients for the series shown in Figures 3-18 through 3-21. Briefly describe each series.

20. An analyst would like to determine whether there is a pattern to earnings per share for the Price Company, which operates a wholesale/retail cash-and-carry business in several states under the name Price Club. The data are shown in Table P-20.
    Describe any patterns that exist in these data.

TABLE P-17	Quarterly Loans for Dominion Bank, 1998–2003 ($ million)			
Calendar	*Mar. 31*	*June 30*	*Sep. 30*	*Dec. 31*
1998	2313	2495	2609	2792
1999	2860	3099	3202	3161
2000	3399	3471	3545	3851
2001	4458	4850	5093	5318
2002	5756	6013	6158	6289
2003	6369	6568	6646	6861

Source: Dominion Bank records.

a. Find the forecast value of the quarterly earnings per share of Price Club for each quarter by using the naive approach (*e.g.*, the forecast for first-quarter 1987 is the value for fourth-quarter 1986, .32).
b. Evaluate the naive forecast using *MAD*.
c. Evaluate the naive forecast using *MSE*.
d. Evaluate the naive forecast using *MAPE*.
e. Evaluate the naive forecast using *MPE*.
f. Write a memo summarizing your findings.

FIGURE 3-18   Autocorrelation Function for Problem 19

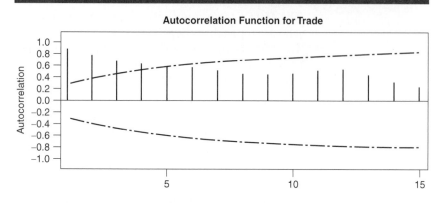

FIGURE 3-19   Autocorrelation Function for Problem 19

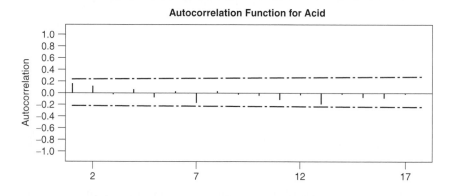

FIGURE 3-20   Autocorrelation Function for Problem 19

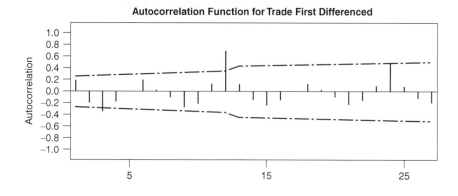

Autocorrelation Function for Fuel

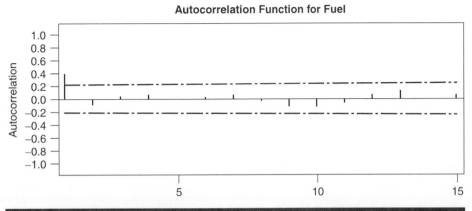

FIGURE 3-21	Autocorrelation Function for Problem 19

TABLE P-20	Quarterly Earnings Per Share for Price Company: 1986–1993 Quarters			
Calendar	*1st*	*2nd*	*3rd*	*4th*
1986	.40	.29	.24	.32
1987	.47	.34	.30	.39
1988	.63	.43	.38	.49
1989	.76	.51	.42	.61
1990	.86	.51	.47	.63
1991	.94	.56	.50	.65
1992	.95	.42	.57	.60
1993	.93	.38	.37	.57

Source: The Value Line Investment Survey (New York: Value Line, 1994), p. 1646.

TABLE P-21	Weekly Sales of a Food Item

(Read across)

2649.9	2898.7	2897.8	3054.3	3888.1	3963.6	3258.9	3199.6
3504.3	2445.9	1833.9	2185.4	3367.4	1374.1	497.5	1699.0
1425.4	1946.2	1809.9	2339.9	1717.9	2420.3	1396.5	1612.1
1367.9	2176.8	2725.0	3723.7	2016.0	862.2	1234.6	1166.5
1759.5	1039.4	2404.8	2047.8	4072.6	4600.5	2370.1	3542.3
2273.0	3596.6	2615.8	2253.3	1779.4	3917.9	3329.3	1864.4
3318.9	3342.6	2131.9	3003.2				

21. Table P-21 contains the weekly sales of a food item for 52 consecutive weeks.
    a. Use a computer to plot the sales data as a time series.
    b. Do you think this series is stationary or nonstationary?
    c. Using Minitab or a similar program, compute the autocorrelations of the sales series for the first 10 time lags. Is the behavior of the autocorrelations consistent with your choice in part b? Explain.

22. This question refers to Problem 21.
    a. Fit the random model given by Equation 3.4 to the data in Table P-21 by estimating c with the sample mean $\bar{Y}$ so $\hat{Y}_t = \bar{Y}$. Compute the residuals

$$e_t = Y_t - \hat{Y}_t = Y_t - \bar{Y}.$$

    b. Using Minitab or a similar program, compute the autocorrelations of the residuals for the first 10 time lags. Is the random model adequate for the sales data? Explain.

CASES

CASE 3-1A   MURPHY BROTHERS FURNITURE

In 1958 the Murphy brothers established a furniture store in downtown Dallas. Over the years they were quite successful and extended their retail coverage throughout the West and Midwest. By 1996, their chain of furniture stores had become well established in 36 states.

Julie Murphy, the daughter of one of the founders, recently joined the firm. Her father and uncle were sophisticated in many ways but not in the area of quantitative skills. In particular, they both felt that they could not accurately forecast the future sales of Murphy Brothers using modern computer techniques. For this reason, they appealed to Julie for help as part of her new job.

Julie first considered using Murphy sales dollars as her variable but found that several years of history were missing. She asked her father, Glen, about this and he told her that at the time he "didn't think it was that important." Julie explained the importance of past data to Glen and he indicated that he would save future data.

Julie decided that Murphy sales were probably closely related to national sales figures and decided to search for an appropriate variable in one of the many federal publications. After looking through a recent copy of the *Survey of Current Business*, she found the history on monthly sales for all retail stores in the United States and decided to use this variable as a substitute for her variable of interest, Murphy Brothers sales dollars. She reasoned that if she could establish accurate forecasts for national sales she could relate these forecasts to Murphy's own sales and come up with the forecasts she wanted.

Table 3-8 shows the data that Julie collected, and Figure 3-22 shows a data plot provided by Julie's computer program. Julie began her analysis by using the computer to develop a plot of the autocorrelation coefficients.

After examining the autocorrelation function produced in Figure 3-23, it was obvious to Julie that her data contained a trend. The early autocorrelation coefficients are very large, and they drop toward zero very slowly with time. To make the series stationary, so that various forecasting methods could be considered, Julie decided to first difference her data to see if the trend could be removed. The autocorrelation function for the first differenced data is shown in Figure 3-24. ∎

QUESTIONS

1. What should Julie conclude about the retail sales series?
2. Has Julie made good progress toward finding a forecasting technique?
3. What forecasting techniques should Julie try?
4. How will Julie know which technique works best?

TABLE 3-8	Monthly Sales ($ Billions) for All Retail Stores, 1983–1995, for Case 3-1A											
	1983	*1984*	*1985*	*1986*	*1987*	*1988*	*1989*	*1990*	*1991*	*1992*	*1993*	*1994*	*1995*
Jan.	81.3	93.1	98.8	105.6	106.4	113.6	122.5	132.6	130.9	142.1	148.4	154.6	167.0
Feb.	78.9	93.7	95.6	99.7	105.8	115.0	118.9	127.3	128.6	143.1	145.0	155.8	164.0
Mar.	93.8	103.3	110.2	114.2	120.4	131.6	141.3	148.3	149.3	154.7	164.6	184.2	192.1
Apr.	93.8	103.9	113.1	115.7	125.4	130.9	139.8	145.0	148.5	159.1	170.3	181.8	187.5
May	97.8	111.8	120.3	125.4	129.1	136.0	150.3	154.1	159.8	165.8	176.1	187.2	201.4
Jun.	100.6	112.3	115.0	120.4	129.0	137.5	149.0	153.5	153.9	164.6	175.7	190.1	202.6
Jul.	99.4	106.9	115.5	120.7	129.3	134.1	144.6	148.9	154.6	166.0	177.7	185.8	194.9
Aug.	100.1	111.2	121.1	124.1	131.5	138.7	153.0	157.4	159.9	166.3	177.1	193.8	204.2
Sep.	97.9	104.0	113.8	124.4	124.5	131.9	144.1	145.6	146.7	160.6	171.1	185.9	192.8
Oct.	100.7	109.6	115.8	123.8	128.3	133.8	142.3	151.5	152.1	168.7	176.4	189.7	194.0
Nov.	103.9	113.5	118.1	121.4	126.9	140.2	148.8	156.1	155.6	167.2	180.9	194.7	202.4
Dec.	125.8	132.3	138.6	152.1	157.2	171.0	176.5	179.7	181.0	204.1	218.3	233.3	238.0

Source: Survey of Current Business, various years.

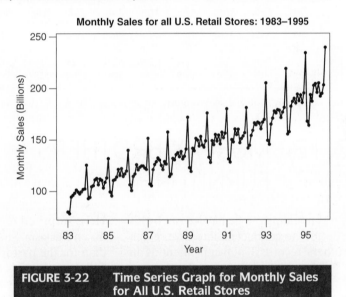

Monthly Sales for all U.S. Retail Stores: 1983–1995

FIGURE 3-22	Time Series Graph for Monthly Sales for All U.S. Retail Stores

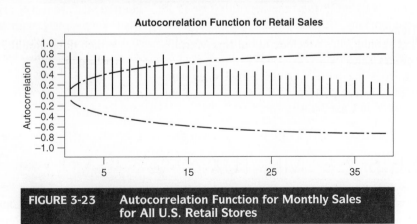

Autocorrelation Function for Retail Sales

FIGURE 3-23	Autocorrelation Function for Monthly Sales for All U.S. Retail Stores

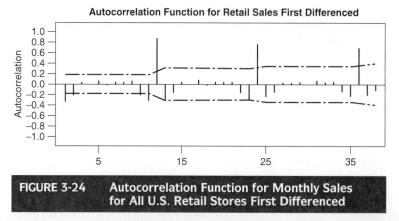

FIGURE 3-24 **Autocorrelation Function for Monthly Sales for All U.S. Retail Stores First Differenced**

TABLE 3-9 **Monthly Sales for Murphy Brothers Furniture, 1992–1995, for Case 3-1B**

	Jan.	*Feb.*	*Mar.*	*Apr.*	*May*	*Jun.*	*Jul.*	*Aug.*	*Sep.*	*Oct.*	*Nov.*	*Dec.*
1992	4906	5068	4710	4792	4638	4670	4574	4477	4571	4370	4293	3911
1993	5389	5507	4727	5030	4926	4847	4814	4744	4844	4769	4483	4120
1994	5270	5835	5147	5354	5290	5271	5328	5164	5372	5313	4924	4552
1995	6283	6051	5298	5659	5343	5461	5568	5287	5555	5501	5201	4826

Source: Murphy Brothers' sales records.

CASE 3-1B   MURPHY BROTHERS FURNITURE

Glen Murphy was not happy to be bawled out by his daughter. He decides to conduct an intensive search of Murphy Brothers' records. Upon implementing an investigation, he is excited to discover sales data for the years 1992 through 1995 as shown in Table 3-9.

He is surprised to find out that Julie does not share his enthusiasm. She knows that acquiring actual sales data for the past four years is a positive occurrence. Julie's problem is that she is not quite sure what to do with the newly acquired data. ■

QUESTIONS
1. What should Julie conclude about this Murphy Brothers' sales data?
2. How does the pattern of the actual sales data compare to the pattern of the retail sales data presented in Case 3-1A?
3. Which data should Julie use to develop a forecasting model?

CASE 3-2   MR. TUX

John Mosby, owner of several Mr. Tux rental stores, is beginning to forecast his most important business variable, monthly dollar sales (see the Mr. Tux

cases at the ends of Chapters 1 and 2). One of his employees, Virginia Perot, gathered the sales data shown in the Chapter 2 case. John decides to use all

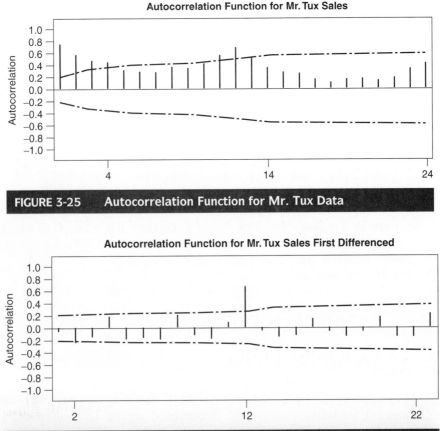

FIGURE 3-25   Autocorrelation Function for Mr. Tux Data

FIGURE 3-26   Autocorrelation Function for Mr. Tux Data First Differenced

96 months of data he has collected. He runs the data on Minitab and obtains the autocorrelation coefficient pattern shown in Figure 3-25. Because all the autocorrelation coefficients are positive and they are trailing off very slowly, John concludes that his data have a trend.

Next, John asks the program to compute the first differences of the data. Figure 3-26 shows the autocorrelation coefficients for the differenced data. The autocorrelation coefficient for time lag 12, $r_{12} = .68$, is significantly different from zero.

Finally, John uses another computer program to calculate the percentage of the variance in the original data explained by the trend, seasonal, and random components. The program calculates the percentage of the variance in the original data explained by the factors in the analysis:

FACTOR	% EXPLAINED
Data	100
Trend	6
Seasonal	45
Random	49

QUESTIONS

1. Summarize the results of John's analysis in one paragraph that a manager, not a forecaster, can understand.

2. Describe the trend and seasonal effects that appear to be present in the sales data for Mr. Tux.

TABLE 3-10	Number of New Clients Seen by CCC from January 1985 through March 1993											
	Jan.	*Feb.*	*Mar.*	*Apr.*	*May*	*Jun.*	*Jul.*	*Aug.*	*Sep.*	*Oct.*	*Nov.*	*Dec.*
1985	182	136	99	77	75	63	87	73	83	82	74	75
1986	102	121	128	128	112	122	104	108	97	141	97	87
1987	145	103	113	150	100	131	96	92	88	118	102	98
1988	101	153	138	107	100	115	78	106	94	93	103	104
1989	150	102	151	100	100	98	97	120	98	135	141	67
1990	127	146	175	110	153	117	121	121	131	147	121	110
1991	171	185	172	168	142	152	151	141	128	151	121	126
1992	166	138	175	108	112	147	168	149	145	149	169	138
1993	152	151	199									

3. How would you explain the line "Random 49%."

4. Suppose that autocorrelations r_{24} and r_{36} are significant. Would you conclude that the seasonality has a trend? If so, explain what is meant by a trend in the seasonality.

CASE 3-3   CONSUMER CREDIT COUNSELING

The Consumer Credit Counseling (CCC) operation was described in Chapter 1 (Case 1-2).

Marv Harnishfeger, executive director, was concerned about the size and scheduling of staff for the remainder of 1993. He explained the problem to Dorothy Mercer, recently elected president of the Executive Committee. Dorothy thought about the problem and concluded that CCC needed to analyze the number of new clients it acquired each month. Dorothy, who worked for a local utility and was familiar with various data exploration techniques, agreed to analyze the problem. She asked Marv to provide monthly data for the number of new clients seen. Marv provided the monthly data shown in Table 3-10 for the number of new clients seen by CCC for the period January 1985 through March 1993.

Dorothy analyzed these data using a time series plot and autocorrelation analysis. ■

QUESTIONS

1. Explain how Dorothy used autocorrelation analysis to explore the data pattern for the number of new clients seen by CCC.

2. What did she conclude after she completed this analysis?

3. What type of forecasting technique did Dorothy recommend for this data set?

CASE 3-4   ALOMEGA FOOD STORES

In Example 1.1 the president of Alomega, Julie Ruth, had collected data from her company's operations. She found several months of sales data along with several possible predictor variables (review this situation in Example 1.1). While her analysis team was working with the data in an

TABLE 3-11	Monthly Sales for 27 Alomega Food Stores, 1999–2002, for Case 3-4			
Month	*1999*	*2000*	*2001*	*2002*
Jan.	425,075	629,404	655,748	455,136
Feb.	315,305	263,467	270,483	247,570
Mar.	432,101	468,612	429,480	732,005
Apr.	357,191	313,221	260,458	357,107
May	347,874	444,404	528,210	453,156
Jun.	435,529	386,986	379,856	320,103
Jul.	299,403	414,314	472,058	451,779
Aug.	296,505	253,493	254,516	249,482
Sep.	426,701	484,365	551,354	744,583
Oct.	329,722	305,989	335,826	421,186
Nov.	281,783	315,407	320,408	397,367
Dec.	166,391	182,784	276,901	269,096

attempt to forecast monthly sales, she became impatient and wondered which of the predictor variables was best for this purpose.

In Case 2-3 Julie investigated the relationships between sales and the possible predictor variables. She now realizes that this step was premature because she doesn't even know the data pattern of her sales. (See Table 3-11.) ∎

QUESTION

1.   What did Julie conclude about the data pattern of Alomega Sales?

Minitab Applications

The problem.   In Example 3.4 Maggie Trymane, an analyst for Sears, wants to forecast sales for 2001. She needs to determine the pattern for the sales data for the years from 1955 to 2000.

Minitab Solution

1.   Enter the Sears data shown in Table 3-4 into column C1. Because the data are already stored in a file called Tab3-4.MTW, click on

```
File>Open Worksheet
```

and you will obtain the dialog box shown in Figure 3-27. Locate the file you want to open and enter the name, in this case Tab3-4.MTW, to the right of File name and click Open. The Sears data will appear in C1.

2.   To construct an autocorrelation function, click on the following menus as shown in Figure 3-28:

```
Stat>Time Series>Autocorrelation
```

3.   The Autocorrelation Function dialog box shown in Figure 3-29 appears.

   a.   Double-click on the variable Revenue and it will appear to the right of Series.

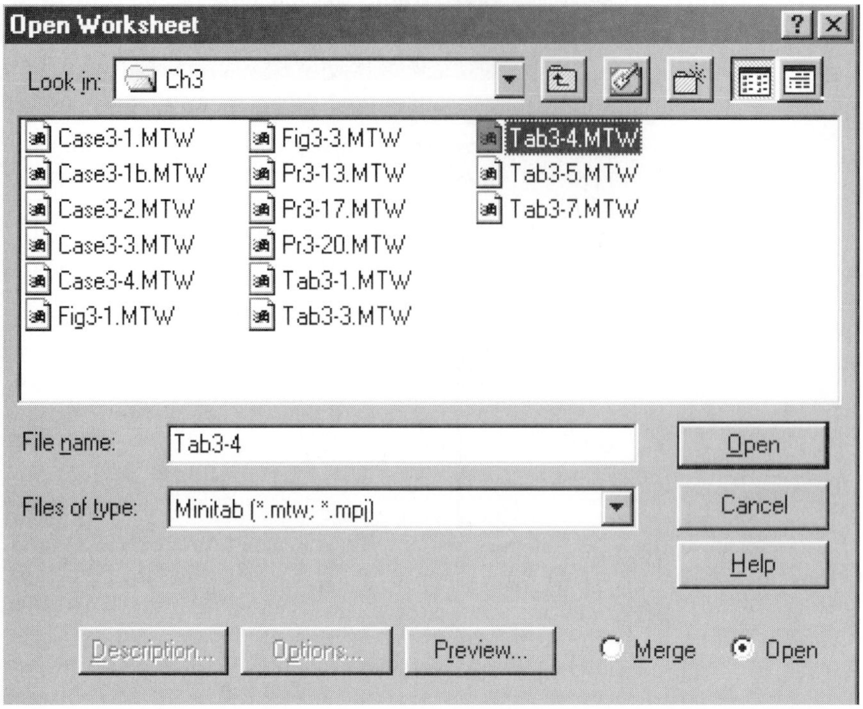

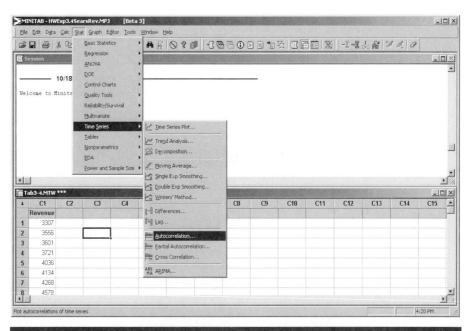

FIGURE 3-27   Open Worksheet Menu

FIGURE 3-28   Minitab Autocorrelation Menu

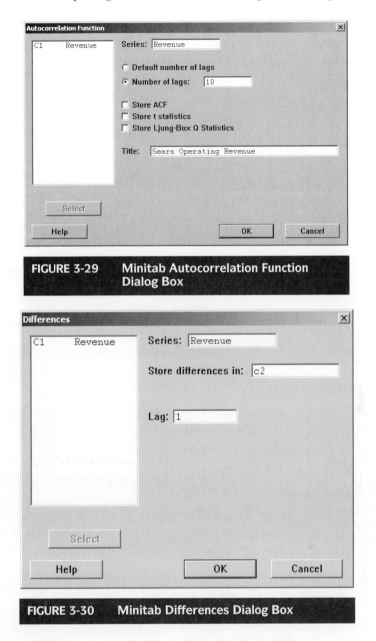

FIGURE 3-29   Minitab Autocorrelation Function Dialog Box

FIGURE 3-30   Minitab Differences Dialog Box

   b.   Click on Number of lags and enter 10 in the box to the right.

   c.   Enter a Title in the appropriate space and click OK. The resulting autocorrelation function is shown in Figure 3-11 on page 71.

4.   In order to difference the data, click on the following menus:

```
Stat>Time Series>Differences
```

The Differences option is above the Autocorrelation option shown in Figure 3-28.

5.   The Differences dialog box shown in Figure 3-30 appears.

   a.   Double-click on the variable Revenue and it will appear to the right of Series.

   b.   Tab to Store differences in: and enter C2. The differenced data will now appear in the worksheet in column C2.

Excel Applications

The problem. Harry Vernon wants to use Excel to compute the autocorrelation coefficients and a correlogram for the data presented in Table 3-1 (see p. 61).

Excel Solution

The best method for solving this problem would be to use a statistical analysis add-in to Excel like CB Predictor. The add-in approach will be presented at the end of Chapter 9. The following commands solve the problem without CB Predictor.

1. Create a new file by clicking on the following menus:

```
File>New
```

2. Position the mouse at A1. Notice that whenever you position the mouse on a cell it is highlighted. Type the heading VERNON'S MUSIC STORE. Position the mouse at A2 and type NUMBER OF VCRS SOLD.
3. Position the mouse at A4 and type Month. Press <enter> and the A5 cell is highlighted. Now enter each month starting with January and ending with December in A16.
4. Position the mouse at B4 and type Y. Enter the data from Table 3-1 beginning in cell B5. Position the mouse at C4 and type Z.
5. Highlight cells B4:C16 and click on the following menus:

```
Insert>Name>Create
```

In the Create Names dialog box, click on the Top row check box, and click OK. This step creates the name Y for the range B5:B16 and the name Z for the range C5:C16.
6. Highlight C5 and enter the formula

```
=(B5-AVERAGE(Y))/STDEV(Y)
```

Copy C5 to the rest of the column by highlighting it; then click the Fill handle in the lower-right corner and drag it down to cell C16. With cells C5:C16 still highlighted, click the Decrease Decimal button (shown in Figure 3-31 toward the upper right) until three decimal places are displayed. The Decrease Decimal button is on the Formatting taskbar. This taskbar can be displayed by right-clicking File and then left-clicking Formatting.
7. Enter the labels LAG and ACF in cells E4 and F4. In order to examine the first six time lags, enter the digits 1 through 6 in cells E5:E10.
8. Highlight F5 and enter the formula

```
=SUMPRODUCT(OFFSET(Z,E5,0,12-E5),OFFSET(Z,0,0,12-E5))/11
```

Highlight F5, click the Fill handle in the lower-right corner, and drag down to cell F10. With cells F5:F10 still highlighted, click the Decrease Decimal button until three decimal places are displayed. The results are shown in Figure 3-31.
9. To develop the autocorrelation function, highlight cells F5:F10. Click on the ChartWizard tool (shown in Figure 3-32 toward the upper right).
10. The ChartWizard—Step 1 to 4 dialog box appears. In step 1, select a chart type by clicking Column, then click Next. In the dialog box for step 2, click on the Series dialog box. In the blank next to Name type Corr.. Click Next and the step 3 dialog box appears. Under Chart title delete Corr.. Under Category (X) axis,

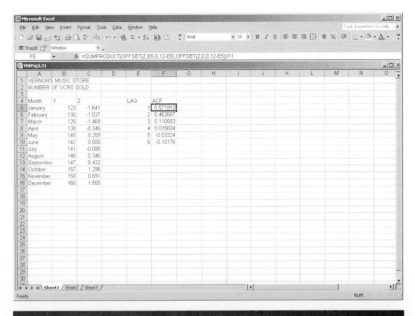

FIGURE 3-31   Excel Spreadsheet for VCR Data

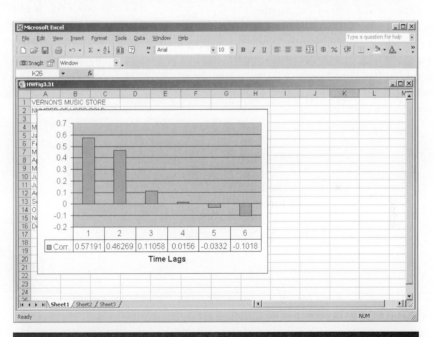

FIGURE 3-32   Excel Output for Autocorrelation Function

type Time Lags. Now click on the Data Table dialog box and click the box next to
Show data table. Click Next to obtain the step 4 dialog box and then click Finish
to produce the autocorrelation function shown in Figure 3-31. Click on one of the
corners of the chart and move it outward in order to enlarge the autocorrelation
function.

11. In order to save the data for use in Chapter 9, click

```
File>Save As
```

In the Save As dialog box, type Tab3-1 in the space to the right of File name:. Click on Save and the file will be saved as Tab3-1.xls.

References

Armstrong, J. S., Ed. *Principles of Forecasting: A Handbook for Researchers and Practitioners.* Norwell, MA: Kluwer Academic Publishers, 2001.

Diebold, F. X. *Elements of Forecasting*, Third Edition. Cincinnati, OH: South-Western, 2004.

Ermer, C. M. "Cost of Error Affects the Forecasting Model Selection." *Journal of Business Forecasting* (Spring 1991): 10–12.

Fildes, R., M. Hibon, S. Makridakis, and N. Meade. "The Accuracy of Extrapolative Forecasting Methods: Additional Empirical Evidence." *International Journal of Forecasting* (1997):13.

Makridakis, S., A. Andersen, R. Carbone, R. Fildes, M. Hibon, R. Lewandowski, J. Newton, E. Parzen, and R. Winkler. "The Accuracy of Extrapolation (Time Series) Methods: Results of a Forecasting Competition." *Journal of Forecasting* 1 (1982):111–153.

Makridakis, S., C. Chatfield, M. Hibon, M. Lawrence, T. Mills, K. Ord, and L. F. Simmons. "The M2-Competition: A Real Time Judgmentally Based Forecasting Study." *International Journal of Forecasting* 9 (1993):5–30.

Makridakis, S., and M. Hibon. "The M3-Competition: Results, Conclusions and Implications." *International Journal of Forecasting* 16 (2000):451–476.

Newbold, P., and T. Bos. *Introductory Business and Economic Forecasting*, Second Edition. Cincinnati, OH: South-Western, 1994.

Quenouille, M. H. "The Joint Distribution of Serial Correlation Coefficients." *Annals of Mathematical Statistics* 20 (1949):561–571.

Wilkinson, G. F. "How a Forecasting Model Is Chosen." *Journal of Business Forecasting* (Summer 1989): 7–8.

CHAPTER 4

MOVING AVERAGES AND SMOOTHING METHODS

This chapter will describe three simple approaches to forecasting a time series: naive, averaging, and smoothing. *Naive* methods are used to develop simple models that assume that very recent data provide the best predictors of the future. *Averaging* methods generate forecasts based on an average of past observations. *Smoothing* methods produce forecasts by averaging past values of a series with a decreasing (exponential) series of weights.

Figure 4-1 shows an outline of the forecasting procedure for the methods discussed in this chapter. Visualize yourself on a time scale. You are at point t in Figure 4-1 and can look backward over past observations of the variable of interest (Y_t) or forward into the future. Once a forecasting technique has been selected, it is adjusted to the known data, and forecast values ($\hat{Y}_t$) are obtained. When forecast values are available, they can be compared to the known observations, and the forecast error (e_t) can be calculated.

A good strategy for evaluating forecasting methods involves the following steps:

1. A forecasting method is selected based on the forecaster's analysis and intuition about the nature of the data.
2. The data set is divided into two sections—an initialization, or fitting, section and a test, or forecasting, section.
3. The selected forecasting technique is used to develop fitted values for the initialization part of the data.
4. The technique is used to forecast the test part of the data, and the forecasting error is determined and evaluated (refer to Chapter 3 for a review of measures of forecasting accuracy).
5. A decision is made. The decision might be to use the technique in its present form, to modify the technique, or to develop a forecast using another technique and compare the results.

FIGURE 4-1	Forecasting Outline		
		You are here	
	Past data	t	Periods to be forecast
	$Y_{t-3}, Y_{t-2}, Y_{t-1},$	$Y_t,$	$\hat{Y}_{t+1}, \hat{Y}_{t+2}, \hat{Y}_{t+3}, \ldots$
where	Y_t	is the most recent observation of a variable	
	$\hat{Y}_{t+1}$	is the forecast for one period in the future	

NAIVE MODELS

Often young businesses face the dilemma of trying to forecast with very small data sets. This situation creates a real problem because many forecasting techniques require large amounts of data. Naive forecasts are one possible solution as they are based solely on the most recent information available.

Naive forecasts assume that recent periods are the best predictors of the future. The simplest model is

$$\hat{Y}_{t+1} = Y_t \tag{4.1}$$

where $\hat{Y}_{t+1}$ is the forecast made at time t (the forecast origin) for time $t + 1$. The naive forecast for each period is the immediately preceding observation. One hundred percent of the weight is given to the current value of the series. The naive forecast is sometimes called the "no change" forecast.

Since the naive forecast (Equation 4.1) discards all other observations, this scheme tracks changes very rapidly. The problem with this approach is that random fluctuations are tracked as faithfully as other fundamental changes.

Example 4.1

Figure 4-2 shows the quarterly sales of saws for the Acme Tool Company. The naive technique forecasts that sales for the next quarter will be the same as the previous quarter. Table 4-1 shows the data from 1996 to 2002. If the data from 1996 to 2001 are used as the initialization part and 2002 as the test part, the forecast for the first quarter of 2002 is

$$\hat{Y}_{24+1} = Y_{24}$$
$$\hat{Y}_{25} = 650$$

The forecasting error is determined using Equation 3.6. The error for period 25 is

$$e_{25} = Y_{25} - \hat{Y}_{25} = 850 - 650 = 200$$

In a similar fashion, the forecast for period 26 is 850 with an error of −250. Figure 4-2 shows that these data have an upward trend and there appears to be a seasonal pattern (first and fourth quarters are relatively high), so a decision is made to modify the naive model.

FIGURE 4-2   Time Series Plot for Sales of Saws for Acme Tool Company

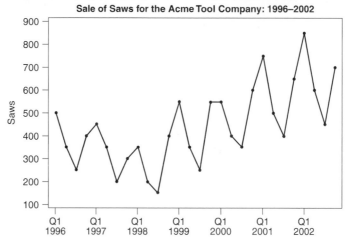

Sale of Saws for the Acme Tool Company: 1996–2002

TABLE 4-1	Sales of Saws for Acme Tool Company, 1996–2002		
Year	Quarter	t	Sales
1996	1	1	500
	2	2	350
	3	3	250
	4	4	400
1997	1	5	450
	2	6	350
	3	7	200
	4	8	300
1998	1	9	350
	2	10	200
	3	11	150
	4	12	400
1999	1	13	550
	2	14	350
	3	15	250
	4	16	550
2000	1	17	550
	2	18	400
	3	19	350
	4	20	600
2001	1	21	750
	2	22	500
	3	23	400
	4	24	650
2002	1	25	850
	2	26	600
	3	27	450
	4	28	700

Examination of the data in Example 4.1 leads us to conclude that the values are increasing over time. When data values increase over time, they are said to be *nonstationary* in level or to have a *trend*. If Equation 4.1 is used, the projections are consistently low. However, the technique can be adjusted to take trend into consideration by adding the difference between this period and the last period. The forecast equation is

$$\hat{Y}_{t+1} = Y_t + (Y_t - Y_{t-1}) \tag{4.2}$$

Equation 4.2 takes into account the amount of change that occurred between quarters.

Example 4.1 (cont.)
Using Equation 4.2, the forecast for the first quarter of 2002 is

$$\hat{Y}_{24+1} = Y_{24} + (Y_{24} - Y_{24-1})$$
$$\hat{Y}_{25} = Y_{24} + (Y_{24} - Y_{23})$$
$$\hat{Y}_{25} = 650 + (650 - 400)$$
$$\hat{Y}_{25} = 650 + 250 = 900$$

The forecast error of this model is

$$e_{25} = Y_{25} - \hat{Y}_{25} = 850 - 900 = -50$$

For some purposes, the rate of change might be more appropriate than the absolute amount of change. If so, it is reasonable to generate forecasts according to

$$\hat{Y}_{t+1} = Y_t \frac{Y_t}{Y_{t-1}} \tag{4.3}$$

Visual inspection of the data in Table 4-1 indicates that seasonal variation seems to exist. Sales in the first and fourth quarters are typically larger than those in any of the other quarters. If the seasonal pattern is strong, an appropriate forecast equation for quarterly data might be

$$\hat{Y}_{t+1} = Y_{t-3} \tag{4.4}$$

Equation 4.4 says that next quarter the variable will take on the same value that it did in the corresponding quarter one year ago.

The major weakness of this approach is that it ignores everything that has occurred since last year and also any trend. There are several ways of introducing more recent information. For example, the analyst can combine seasonal and trend estimates and forecast the next quarter using

$$\hat{Y}_{t+1} = Y_{t-3} + \frac{(Y_t - Y_{t-1}) + \cdots + (Y_{t-3} - Y_{t-4})}{4} = Y_{t-3} + \frac{Y_t - Y_{t-4}}{4} \tag{4.5}$$

where the Y_{t-3} term forecasts the seasonal pattern, and the remaining term averages the amount of change for the past four quarters and provides an estimate of the trend.

The naive forecasting models in Equations 4.4 and 4.5 are given for quarterly data. Adjustments can be made for data collected over different time periods. For monthly data, for example, the seasonal period is 12, not 4, and the forecast for the next period (month) given by Equation 4.4 is $\hat{Y}_{t+1} = Y_{t-11}$.

It is apparent that the number and complexity of possible naive models are limited only by the ingenuity of the analyst, but use of these techniques should be guided by sound judgment.

Naive methods are also used as the basis for making comparisons against which the performance of more sophisticated methods are judged.

Example 4.1 (cont.)
The forecasts for the first quarter of 2002 using Equations 4.3, 4.4, and 4.5 are

$$\hat{Y}_{24+1} = Y_{24} \frac{Y_{24}}{Y_{24-1}} = Y_{24} \frac{Y_{24}}{Y_{23}}$$

$$\hat{Y}_{25} = 650 \frac{650}{400} = 1,056 \qquad \text{(Equation 4.3)}$$

$$\hat{Y}_{24+1} = Y_{24-3} = Y_{21}$$

$$\hat{Y}_{25} = Y_{21} = 750 \qquad \text{(Equation 4.4)}$$

$$\hat{Y}_{24+1} = Y_{24-3} + \frac{(Y_{24} - Y_{24-1}) + \cdots + (Y_{24-3} - Y_{24-4})}{4} \qquad \text{(Equation 4.5)}$$

$$\hat{Y}_{25} = Y_{24-3} + \frac{Y_{24} - Y_{24-4}}{4}$$

$$\hat{Y}_{25} = Y_{21} + \frac{Y_{24} - Y_{20}}{4} = 750 + \frac{650 - 600}{4}$$

$$\hat{Y}_{25} = 750 + 12.5 = 762.5$$

FORECASTING METHODS BASED ON AVERAGING

Frequently, management faces the situation in which forecasts need to be updated daily, weekly, or monthly for inventories containing hundreds or thousands of items. Often it is not possible to develop sophisticated forecasting techniques for each item. Instead, some quick, inexpensive, very simple short-term forecasting tools are needed to accomplish this task.

A manager facing such a situation is likely to use an averaging or smoothing technique. These types of techniques use a form of weighted average of past observations to smooth short-term fluctuations. The assumption underlying these techniques is that the fluctuations in past values represent random departures from some underlying structure. Once this structure is identified, it can be projected into the future to produce a forecast.

Simple Averages

Historical data can be smoothed in many ways. The objective is to use past data to develop a forecasting model for future periods. In this section the method of simple averages is considered. As with the naive methods, a decision is made to use the first t data points as the initialization part and the remaining data as a test part. Next, Equation 4.6 is used to average (compute the mean of) the initialization part of the data and to forecast the next period.

$$\hat{Y}_{t+1} = \frac{1}{t} \sum_{i=1}^{t} Y_i \qquad \textbf{(4.6)}$$

When a new observation becomes available, the forecast for the next period, $\hat{Y}_{t+2}$, is the average, or mean, computed using Equation 4.6 and this new observation.

When forecasting a large number of series simultaneously (e.g., inventory management), data storage may be an issue. Equation 4.7 solves this potential problem. Only the most recent forecast and the most recent observation need be stored as time moves forward.

$$\hat{Y}_{t+2} = \frac{t\hat{Y}_{t+1} + Y_{t+1}}{t + 1} \qquad \textbf{(4.7)}$$

The method of *simple averages* is an appropriate technique when the forces generating the series to be forecast have stabilized, and the environment in which the series exists is generally unchanging. Examples of this type of series are the quantity of sales resulting from a consistent level of salesperson effort; the quantity of sales of a product in the mature stage of its life cycle; and the number of appointments per week requested of a dentist, doctor, or lawyer whose patient or client base is fairly constant.

A *simple average* uses the mean of all relevant historical observations as the forecast of the next period.

Example 4.2
The Spokane Transit Authority (STA) operates a fleet of vans used to transport both the disabled and elderly. A record of the gasoline purchased for this fleet of vans is shown in Table 4-2. The actual amount of gasoline consumed by a van on a given day is determined by the random nature of the calls and the destinations. Examination of the gasoline purchases plotted in Figure 4-3 shows the data are very stable. Since the data seem stationary, the

TABLE 4-2	Gasoline Purchases for Spokane Transit Authority				
Week t	Gallons Y_t	Week t	Gallons Y_t	Week t	Gallons Y_t
1	275	11	302	21	310
2	291	12	287	22	299
3	307	13	290	23	285
4	281	14	311	24	250
5	295	15	277	25	260
6	268	16	245	26	245
7	252	17	282	27	271
8	279	18	277	28	282
9	264	19	298	29	302
10	288	20	303	30	285

FIGURE 4-3   Time Series Plot for Weekly Gasoline Purchases for the Spokane Transit Authority

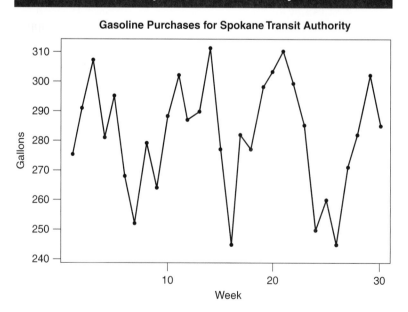

Gasoline Purchases for Spokane Transit Authority

method of simple averages is used for weeks 1 to 28 to forecast gasoline purchases for weeks 29 and 30. The forecast for week 29 is

$$\hat{Y}_{28+1} = \frac{1}{28} \sum_{i=1}^{28} Y_i$$

$$\hat{Y}_{29} = \frac{7,874}{28} = 281.2$$

The forecast error is

$$e_{29} = Y_{29} - \hat{Y}_{29} = 302 - 281.2 = 20.8$$

The forecast for week 30 includes one more data point (302) added to the initialization period. The forecast using Equation 4.7 is

$$\hat{Y}_{28+2} = \frac{28\hat{Y}_{28+1} + Y_{28+1}}{28 + 1} = \frac{28\hat{Y}_{29} + Y_{29}}{29}$$

$$\hat{Y}_{30} = \frac{28(281.2) + 302}{29} = 281.9$$

The forecast error is

$$e_{30} = Y_{30} - \hat{Y}_{30} = 285 - 281.9 = 3.1$$

Using the method of simple averages, the forecast of gallons of gasoline purchased for week 31 is

$$\hat{Y}_{30+1} = \frac{1}{30} \sum_{i=1}^{30} Y_i = \frac{8,461}{30} = 282$$

Moving Averages

The method of simple averages uses the mean of all the data to forecast. What if the analyst is more concerned with recent observations? A constant number of data points can be specified at the outset and a mean computed for the most recent observations. The term *moving average* is used to describe this approach. As each new observation becomes available, a new mean is computed by adding the newest value and dropping the oldest. This moving average is then used to forecast the next period. Equation 4.8 gives the simple moving average forecast. A moving average of order k, MA(k), is computed by

$$\hat{Y}_{t+1} = \frac{Y_t + Y_{t-1} + \cdots + Y_{t-k+1}}{k} \tag{4.8}$$

where

$\hat{Y}_{t+1}$ = forecast value for next period
Y_t = actual value at period t
k = number of terms in the moving average

The moving average for time period t is the arithmetic mean of the k most recent observations. In a moving average, equal weights are assigned to each observation. Each new data point is included in the average as it becomes available, and the earliest data point is discarded. The rate of response to changes in the underlying data pattern depends on the number of periods, k, included in the moving average.

Note that the moving average technique deals only with the latest k periods of known data; the number of data points in each average does not change as time advances. The moving average model does not handle trend or seasonality very well, although it does better than the simple average method.

The analyst must choose the number of periods, k, in a moving average. A moving average of order 1, MA(1), would use the current observation, Y_t, to forecast Y for the next period. This is simply the naive forecasting approach of Equation 4.1.

A *moving average* of order k is the mean value of k consecutive observations. The most recent moving average value provides a forecast for the next period.

TABLE 4-3	Gasoline Purchases for Spokane Transit Authority		
t	*Gallons*	$\hat{Y}_t$	e_t
1	275	—	—
2	291	—	—
3	307	—	—
4	281	—	—
5	295	—	—
6	268	289.8	−21.8
7	252	288.4	−36.4
8	279	280.6	−1.6
9	264	275.0	−11.0
10	288	271.6	16.4
11	302	270.2	31.8
12	287	277.0	10.0
13	290	284.0	6.0
14	311	286.2	24.8
15	277	295.6	−18.6
16	245	293.4	−48.4
17	282	282.0	0.0
18	277	281.0	−4.0
19	298	278.4	19.6
20	303	275.8	27.2
21	310	281.0	29.0
22	299	294.0	5.0
23	285	297.4	−12.4
24	250	299.0	−49.0
25	260	289.4	−29.4
26	245	280.8	−35.8
27	271	267.8	3.2
28	282	262.2	19.8
29	302	261.6	40.4
30	285	272.0	13.0

Example 4.3

Table 4-3 demonstrates the moving average forecasting technique with the Spokane Transit Authority data, using a five-week moving average. The moving average forecast for week 29 is

$$\hat{Y}_{28+1} = \frac{Y_{28} + Y_{28-1} + \cdots + Y_{28-5+1}}{5}$$

$$\hat{Y}_{29} = \frac{Y_{28} + Y_{27} + Y_{26} + Y_{25} + Y_{24}}{5}$$

$$\hat{Y}_{29} = \frac{282 + 271 + 245 + 260 + 250}{5} = \frac{1,308}{5} = 261.6$$

When the actual value for week 29 is known, the forecast error is calculated:

$$e_{29} = Y_{29} - \hat{Y}_{29} = 302 - 261.6 = 40.4$$

The forecast for week 31 is

$$\hat{Y}_{30+1} = \frac{Y_{30} + Y_{30-1} + \cdots + Y_{30-5+1}}{5}$$

$$\hat{Y}_{31} = \frac{Y_{30} + Y_{29} + Y_{28} + Y_{27} + Y_{26}}{5}$$

$$\hat{Y}_{31} = \frac{285 + 302 + 282 + 271 + 245}{5} = \frac{1,385}{5} = 277$$

Minitab can be used to compute a five-week moving average (see "Minitab Applications" at the end of the chapter for instructions). Figure 4-4 shows the five-week moving average plotted against the actual data, the *MAPE*, *MAD*, *MSD*, and the basic Minitab instructions. Note that Minitab calls the mean squared error *MSD* (mean squared deviation).

Figure 4-5 shows the autocorrelation function for the residuals from the five-week moving average method. Error limits for the individual autocorrelations centered at 0, and the Ljung-Box *Q* statistic, indicate that significant residual autocorrelation exists, that is, the residuals are not random. The association contained in the residuals at certain time lags can be used to improve the forecasting model.

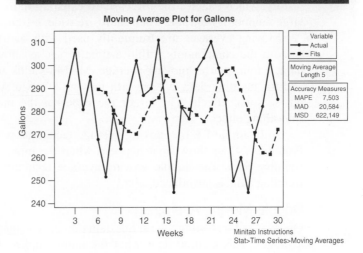

FIGURE 4-4   Five-Week Moving Average Applied to Weekly Gasoline Purchases for the Spokane Transit Authority

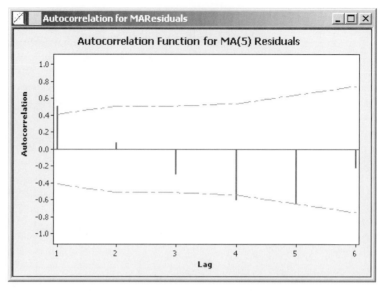

Autocorrelation Function: MAResiduals

Lag	ACF	T	LBQ	Lag	ACF	T	LBQ
1	0.506290	2.53	7.21	4	-0.602830	-2.31	21.81
2	0.078551	0.32	7.39	5	-0.642632	-2.06	35.74
3	-0.298611	-1.21	10.13	6	-0.219452	-0.61	37.46

FIGURE 4-5   Autocorrelation Function for the Residuals When a Five-Week Moving Average Method Was Used with the Spokane Transit Authority Data

The analyst must use judgment when determining how many days, weeks, months, or quarters on which to base the moving average. The smaller the number, the more weight is given to recent periods. Conversely, the greater the number, the less weight is given to more recent periods. A small number is most desirable when there are sudden shifts in the level of the series. A small number places heavy weight on recent history, which enables the forecasts to catch up more rapidly to the current level. A large number is desirable when there are wide, infrequent fluctuations in the series.

Moving averages are frequently used with quarterly or monthly data to help smooth the components within a time series, as shown in Chapter 5. For quarterly data, a four-quarter moving average, MA(4), yields an average of the four quarters, and for monthly data, a 12-month moving average, MA(12), eliminates or averages out seasonal effects. The larger the order of the moving average, the greater the smoothing effect.

In Example 4.3, the moving average technique was used with stationary data. In Example 4.4, we show what happens when the moving average method is used with trending data. The double moving average technique, which is designed to handle trending data, is introduced next.

Double Moving Averages

One way of forecasting time series data that have a linear trend is to use double moving averages. This method does what the name implies: One set of moving averages is computed, and a second set is then computed as a moving average of the first set.

	TABLE 4-4	Weekly Rentals for the Movie Video Store for Example 4.4		
	Weekly Units Rented	*Three-Week Moving*	*Moving Average Forecast*	
t	Y_t	*Total*	$\hat{Y}_{t+1}$	e_t
1	654	—	—	—
2	658	—	—	—
3	665	1,977	—	—
4	672	1,995	659	13
5	673	2,010	665	8
6	671	2,016	670	1
7	693	2,037	672	21
8	694	2,058	679	15
9	701	2,088	686	15
10	703	2,098	696	7
11	702	2,106	699	3
12	710	2,115	702	8
13	712	2,124	705	7
14	711	2,133	708	3
15	728	2,151	711	17
16	—	—	717	—

MSE = 133.

Table 4-4 shows the weekly rentals data for the Movie Video Store along with the results of using a three-week moving average to forecast future sales. Examination of the error column in Table 4-4 shows that every entry is positive, signifying that the forecasts do not catch up to the trend. The three-week moving average and the double moving average for these data are shown in Figure 4-6. Note how the three-week moving averages lag behind the actual values for comparable periods, illustrating what happens when the moving average technique is used with trending data. Note also that the double moving averages lag behind the first set about as much as the first set lags behind the actual values. The difference between the two sets of moving averages is added to the three-week moving average to forecast the actual values.

Equations 4.9 through 4.12 summarize double moving average construction. First, Equation 4.8 is used to compute the moving average of order *k*.

$$M_t = \hat{Y}_{t+1} = \frac{Y_t + Y_{t-1} + Y_{t-2} + \cdots + Y_{t-k+1}}{k}$$

Then Equation 4.9 is used to compute the second moving average.

$$M_t' = \frac{M_t + M_{t-1} + M_{t-2} + \cdots + M_{t-k+1}}{k} \tag{4.9}$$

Equation 4.10 is used to develop a forecast by adding the difference between the single and second moving averages to the single moving average.

$$a_t = M_t + (M_t - M_t') = 2M_t - M_t' \tag{4.10}$$

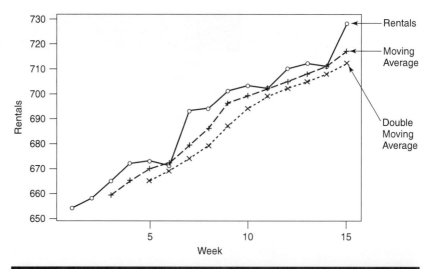

FIGURE 4-6 **Three-Week Single and Double Moving Averages for the Movie Video Store Data**

Equation 4.11 is an additional adjustment factor, which is similar to a slope measure that can change over the series.

$$b_t = \frac{2}{k-1}(M_t - M'_t) \tag{4.11}$$

Finally, Equation 4.12 is used to make the forecast p periods into the future.

$$\hat{Y}_{t+p} = a_t + b_t p \tag{4.12}$$

where

$k =$ number of periods in the moving average

$p =$ number of periods ahead to be forecast

Example 4.4

The Movie Video Store operates several videotape rental outlets in Denver, Colorado. The company is growing and needs to expand its inventory to accommodate the increasing demand for its services. The president of the company assigns Jill Ottenbreit to forecast rentals for the next month. Rental data for the last 15 weeks are available and are presented in Table 4-5. At first, Jill attempts to develop a forecast using a three-week moving average. The *MSE* for this model is 133. Because the data are obviously trending, she finds that her forecasts are consistently underestimating actual rentals. For this reason, she decides to try a double moving average. The results are presented in Table 4-5. To understand the forecast for week 16, the computations are presented next. Equation 4.8 is used to compute the three-week moving average (column 3).

$$M_{15} = \hat{Y}_{15+1} = \frac{Y_{15} + Y_{15-1} + Y_{15-3+1}}{3}$$

$$M_{15} = \hat{Y}_{16} = \frac{728 + 711 + 712}{3} = 717$$

TABLE 4-5	Double Moving Average Forecast for the Movie Video Store for Example 4.4						
(1)	*(2)*	*(3)*	*(4)*	*(5)*	*(6)*	*(7)*	*(8)*
	Weekly	*Three-Week*	*Double*			*Forecast*	
	Sales	*Moving Average*	*Moving*			*a + bp*	
Time			*Average, M'_t*	*Value of a*	*Value of b*		
t	Y_t	M_t				*(p = 1)*	e_t
1	654	—	—	—	—	—	—
2	658	—	—	—	—	—	—
3	665	659	—	—	—	—	—
4	672	665	—	—	—	—	—
5	673	670	665	675	5	—	—
6	671	672	669	675	3	680	−9
7	693	679	674	684	5	678	15
8	694	686	679	693	7	689	5
9	701	696	687	705	9	700	1
10	703	699	694	704	5	714	−11
11	702	702	699	705	3	709	−7
12	710	705	702	708	3	708	2
13	712	708	705	711	3	711	1
14	711	711	708	714	3	714	−3
15	728	717	712	722	5	717	11
16	—	—	—	—	—	727	—

$MSE = 63.7$.

Then Equation 4.9 is used to compute the double moving average (column 4).

$$M'_{15} = \frac{M_{15} + M_{15-1} + M_{15-3+1}}{3}$$

$$M'_{15} = \frac{717 + 711 + 708}{3} = 712$$

Equation 4.10 is used to compute the difference between the two moving averages (column 5).

$$a_{15} = 2M_{15} - M'_{15} = 2(717) - 712 = 722$$

Equation 4.11 adjusts the slope (column 6).

$$b_{15} = \frac{2}{3-1}(M_{15} - M'_{15}) = \frac{2}{2}(717 - 712) = 5$$

Equation 4.12 is used to make the forecast one period into the future (column 7).

$$\hat{Y}_{15+1} = a_{15} + b_{15}p = 722 + 5(1) = 727$$

The forecast four weeks into the future is

$$\hat{Y}_{15+4} = a_{15} + b_{15}p = 722 + 5(4) = 742$$

Note that the *MSE* has been reduced from 133 to 63.7.

It seems reasonable that more recent observations are likely to contain more important information. A procedure is introduced in the next section that gives more emphasis to the most recent observations.

EXPONENTIAL SMOOTHING METHODS

Whereas the method of moving averages only takes into account the most recent observations, simple exponential smoothing provides an exponentially weighted moving average of all previously observed values. The model is often appropriate for data with no predictable upward or downward trend. The aim is to estimate the current level. This level estimate is then used as the forecast of future values.

Exponential smoothing continually revises an estimate in the light of more recent experiences. This method is based on averaging (smoothing) past values of a series in an exponentially decreasing manner. The most recent observation receives the largest weight α (where $0 < \alpha < 1$), the next most recent observation receives less weight, $\alpha(1 - \alpha)$, the observation two time periods in the past even less weight, $\alpha(1 - \alpha)^2$, and so forth.

In one representation of exponentially smoothing, the new forecast (for time $t + 1$) may be thought of as a weighted sum of the new observation (at time t) and the old forecast (for time t). The weight α (where $0 < \alpha < 1$) is given to the newly observed value, and weight $(1 - \alpha)$ is given to the old forecast. Thus,

$$\text{New forecast} = [\alpha \times (\text{new observation})] + [(1 - \alpha) \times (\text{old forecast})]$$

More formally, the exponential smoothing equation is

$$\hat{Y}_{t+1} = \alpha Y_t + (1 - \alpha)\hat{Y}_t \tag{4.13}$$

where

$\hat{Y}_{t+1}$ = new smoothed value or the forecast value for the next period
α = smoothing constant $(0 < \alpha < 1)$
Y_t = new observation or actual value of series in period t
$\hat{Y}_t$ = old smoothed value or forecast for period t

Equation 4.13 can be written as

$$\hat{Y}_{t+1} = \alpha Y_t + (1 - \alpha)\hat{Y}_t = \alpha Y_t + \hat{Y}_t - \alpha \hat{Y}_t$$
$$\hat{Y}_{t+1} = \hat{Y}_t + \alpha(Y_t - \hat{Y}_t)$$

In this form, the new forecast ($\hat{Y}_{t+1}$) is the old forecast ($\hat{Y}_t$) adjusted by α times the error ($Y_t - \hat{Y}_t$) in the old forecast.

In Equation 4.13, the smoothing constant α serves as the weighting factor. The value of α determines the extent to which the current observation influences the forecast of the next observation. When α is close to one, the new forecast will be essentially the current observation. (Equivalently, the new forecast will be the old forecast plus a substantial adjustment for any error that occurred in the preceding forecast.) Conversely, when α is close to zero, the new forecast will be very similar to the old forecast and the current observation will have very little impact.

Exponential smoothing is a procedure for continually revising a forecast in the light of more recent experience.

Finally, Equation 4.13 implies, for time t, that $\hat{Y}_t = \alpha Y_{t-1} + (1 - \alpha)\hat{Y}_{t-1}$ and substitution for $\hat{Y}_t$ in Equation 4.13 gives

$$\hat{Y}_{t+1} = \alpha Y_t + (1 - \alpha)\hat{Y}_t = \alpha Y_t + (1 - \alpha)[\alpha Y_{t-1} + (1 - \alpha)\hat{Y}_{t-1}]$$

$$\hat{Y}_{t+1} = \alpha Y_t + \alpha(1 - \alpha)Y_{t-1} + (1 - \alpha)^2\hat{Y}_{t-1}$$

Continued substitution (next, substitute for $\hat{Y}_{t-1}$ and so forth) shows $\hat{Y}_{t+1}$ can be written as a sum of current and previous Y's with exponentially declining weights, or

$$\hat{Y}_{t+1} = \alpha Y_t + \alpha(1 - \alpha)Y_{t-1} + \alpha(1 - \alpha)^2 Y_{t-2} + \alpha(1 - \alpha)^3 Y_{t-3} + \cdots \qquad \textbf{(4.14)}$$

That is, $\hat{Y}_{t+1}$ is an exponentially smoothed value. The speed at which past observations lose their impact depends on the value of α as demonstrated in Table 4-6.

Equations 4.13 and 4.14 are equivalent, but Equation 4.13 is typically used to calculate the forecast $\hat{Y}_{t+1}$ because it requires less data storage and is easily implemented.

The value assigned to α is the key to the analysis. If it is desired that predictions be stable and random variations smoothed, a small value of α is required. If a rapid response to a real change in the pattern of observations is desired, a larger value of α is appropriate. One method of estimating α is an iterative procedure that minimizes the mean squared error (*MSE*) given by Equation 3.8. Forecasts are computed for, say, α equal to .1, .2, ..., .9, and the sum of the squared forecast errors is computed for each. The value of α producing the smallest error is chosen for use in generating future forecasts.

To start the algorithm for Equation 4.13, an initial value for the old smoothed series must be set. One approach is to set the first smoothed value equal to the first observation. Example 4.5 will illustrate this approach. Another method is to use the average of the first five or six observations for the initial smoothed value.

Example 4.5
The exponential smoothing technique is demonstrated in Table 4-7 and Figure 4-7 for Acme Tool Company for the years 1996 to 2002, using smoothing constants of .1 and .6. The data for the first quarter of 2002 will be used as test data to help determine the best value of α (among the two considered). The exponentially smoothed series is computed by initially setting $\hat{Y}_1$ equal to 500. If earlier data are available, it might be possible to use them to develop a smoothed series up to 1996 and use this experience as the initial value for the smoothed series. The computations leading to the forecast for periods 3 and 4 are demonstrated next.

TABLE 4-6	Comparison of Smoothing Constants				
	$\alpha = .1$			$\alpha = .6$	
Period	*Calculations*	*Weight*		*Calculations*	*Weight*
t		.100			.600
$t - 1$	$.9 \times .1$	.090		$.4 \times .6$	.240
$t - 2$	$.9 \times .9 \times .1$	.081		$.4 \times .4 \times .6$	.096
$t - 3$	$.9 \times .9 \times .9 \times .1$	.073		$.4 \times .4 \times .4 \times .6$	.038
$t - 4$	$.9 \times .9 \times .9 \times .9 \times .1$	.066		$.4 \times .4 \times .4 \times .4 \times .6$	.015
All others		.590			.011
	Totals	1.000			1.000

TABLE 4-7	Exponentially Smoothed Values for Acme Tool Company Sales for Example 4.5				
Time		**Actual Value**	**Smoothed Value**	**Forecast Error**	**Smoothed Value**	**Forecast Error**
Year	**Quarters**	Y_t	$\hat{Y}_t (\alpha = .1)$	e_t	$\hat{Y}_t (\alpha = .6)$	e_t
1996	1	500	500.0	0.0	500.0	0.0
	2	350	500.0	−150.0	500.0	−150.0
	3	250	485.0 (1)	−235.0 (2)	410.0	−160.0
	4	400	461.5 (3)	−61.5	314.0	86.0
1997	5	450	455.4	−5.4	365.6	84.4
	6	350	454.8	−104.8	416.2	−66.2
	7	200	444.3	−244.3	376.5	−176.5
	8	300	419.9	−119.9	270.6	29.4
1998	9	350	407.9	−57.9	288.2	61.8
	10	200	402.1	−202.1	325.3	−125.3
	11	150	381.9	−231.9	250.1	−100.1
	12	400	358.7	41.3	190.0	210.0
1999	13	550	362.8	187.2	316.0	234.0
	14	350	381.6	−31.5	456.4	−106.4
	15	250	378.4	−128.4	392.6	−142.6
	16	550	365.6	184.4	307.0	243.0
2000	17	550	384.0	166.0	452.8	97.2
	18	400	400.6	−0.6	511.1	−111.1
	19	350	400.5	−50.5	444.5	−94.5
	20	600	395.5	204.5	387.8	212.2
2001	21	750	415.9	334.1	515.1	234.9
	22	500	449.3	−50.7	656.0	−156.0
	23	400	454.4	−54.4	562.4	−162.4
	24	650	449.0	201.0	465.0	185.0
2002	25	850	469.0	381.0	576.0	274.0

The numbers in parentheses refer to the explanations given in the text in Example 4.5.

1. Using Equation 4.13, at time period 2, the forecast for period 3 with $\alpha = .1$ is

$$\hat{Y}_{2+1} = \alpha Y_2 + (1 - \alpha)\hat{Y}_2$$
$$\hat{Y}_3 = .1(350) + .9(500) = 485$$

2. The error in this forecast is

$$e_3 = Y_3 - \hat{Y}_3 = 250 - 485 = -235$$

3. The forecast for period 4 is

$$\hat{Y}_{3+1} = \alpha Y_3 + (1 - \alpha)\hat{Y}_3$$
$$\hat{Y}_4 = .1(250) + .9(485) = 461.5$$

From Table 4-7, when the smoothing constant is .1, the forecast for the first quarter of 2002 is 469 with a squared error of 145,161. When the smoothing constant is .6, the forecast for the first quarter of 2002 is 576 with a squared error of 75,076. On the basis of this limited evidence, exponential smoothing with $\alpha = .6$ performs better than exponential smoothing with $\alpha = .1$.

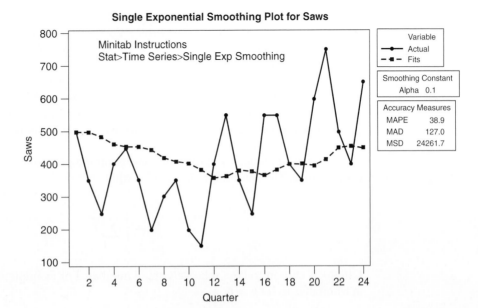

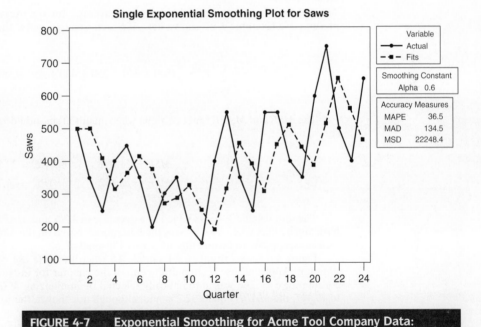

FIGURE 4-7 **Exponential Smoothing for Acme Tool Company Data:** $\alpha = .1$ **(Top) and** $\alpha = .6$ **(Bottom)**

In Figure 4-7, note how stable the smoothed values are for the .1 smoothing constant. On the basis of minimizing the mean squared error *MSE* (*MSE* is called *MSD* on the Minitab output) over the first 24 quarters, the .6 smoothing constant is better. If the mean absolute percentage errors (*MAPE*) are compared, the .6 smoothing constant is also better. To summarize:

$$\alpha = .1 \qquad MSE = 24{,}262 \qquad MAPE = 38.9\%$$
$$\alpha = .6 \qquad MSE = 22{,}248 \qquad MAPE = 36.5\%$$

However, *MSE* and *MAPE* are both large and, on the basis of these summary statistics, it is apparent that exponential smoothing does not represent these data well. As we shall see, a smoothing method that allows for seasonality does a better job of predicting the Acme Tool Company saw sales.

A factor, other than the choice of α, that affects the values of subsequent forecasts is the choice of the initial value, $\hat{Y}_1$, for the smoothed series. In Table 4-7 (see Example 4.5), $\hat{Y}_1 = Y_1$ was used as the initial smoothed value. This choice tends to give Y_1 too much weight in later forecasts. Fortunately, the influence of the initial forecast diminishes greatly as t increases.

Another approach to initializing the smoothing procedure is to average the first k observations. The smoothing then begins with

$$\hat{Y}_1 = \frac{1}{k} \sum_{t=1}^{k} Y_t$$

Often k is chosen to be a relatively small number. For example, the default approach in Minitab is to set $k = 6$.

Example 4.6

The computation of the initial value as an average for the Acme Tool Company data presented in Example 4.5 is shown next. If k is chosen to equal 6, then the initial value is

$$\hat{Y}_1 = \frac{1}{6} \sum_{t=1}^{6} Y_t = \frac{1}{6}(500 + 350 + 250 + 400 + 450 + 350) = 383.3$$

The *MSE* and *MAPE* for each alpha when an initial smoothed value of 383.3 is used are shown next.

$$\alpha = .1 \qquad MSE = 21{,}091 \qquad MAPE = 32.1\%$$
$$\alpha = .6 \qquad MSE = 22{,}152 \qquad MAPE = 36.7\%$$

The initial value $\hat{Y}_1 = 383.3$ led to a decrease in *MSE* and *MAPE* for $\alpha = .1$ but did not have much effect when $\alpha = .6$. Now the best model, based on the *MSE* and *MAPE* summary measures, appears to be one that uses $\alpha = .1$ instead of .6.

Figure 4-8 shows results for Example 4.5 when the data are run on Minitab (see the "Minitab Applications" section at the end of the chapter for instructions). The smoothing constant of $\alpha = .266$ was automatically selected by minimizing *MSE*. The *MSE* is reduced to 19,447, the *MAPE* equals 32.2% and, although not shown, the *MPE* equals -6.4%. The forecast for the first quarter of 2002 is 534.

Figure 4-9 shows the autocorrelation function for the residuals of the exponential smoothing method using an alpha of .266. When the Ljung-Box test is conducted for six time lags, the large value of LBQ (33.86) shows that the first six residual autocorrelations as a group are larger than would be expected if the residuals were random. In particular, the significantly large residual autocorrelations at lags 2 and 4 indicate that the seasonal variation in the data is not accounted for by simple exponential smoothing.

Exponential smoothing is often a good forecasting procedure when a nonrandom time series exhibits trending behavior. It is useful to develop a measure that can be used to determine when the basic pattern of a time series has changed. A *tracking signal* is one way to monitor change. A tracking signal involves computing a measure of forecast errors over time and setting limits so that, when the errors go outside those limits, the forecaster is alerted.

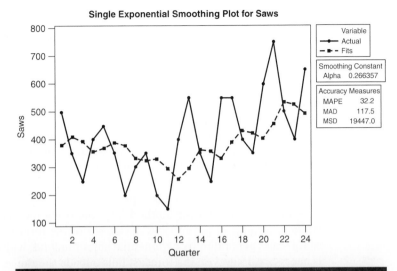

FIGURE 4-8 Exponential Smoothing with $\alpha = .266$: Acme Tool Company Data

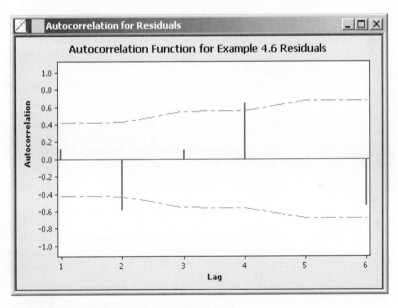

Autocorrelation Function: Residuals

Lag	ACF	T	LBQ	Lag	ACF	T	LBQ
1	0.121421	0.59	0.40	4	0.646967	2.40	23.65
2	-0.588941	-2.84	10.24	5	-0.006908	-0.02	23.65
3	0.109122	0.41	10.59	6	-0.542625	-1.65	33.86

FIGURE 4-9 Autocorrelation Function for the Residuals When Exponential Smoothing with $\alpha = .266$ Was Used with Acme Tool Company Data

> A *tracking signal* involves computing a measure of forecast errors over time and setting limits so that, when the cumulative error goes outside those limits, the forecaster is alerted.

For example, a tracking signal might be used to determine when the size of the smoothing constant alpha (α) should be changed. Since a large number of items are usually being forecast, common practice is to continue with the same value of α for many periods before attempting to determine if a revision is necessary. Unfortunately, the simplicity of using an established exponential smoothing model is a strong motivator for not making a change. But at some point it may be necessary to update α or abandon exponential smoothing altogether. When the model produces forecasts containing a great deal of error, a change is appropriate.

A tracking system is a method for monitoring the need for change. Such a system contains a range of permissible deviations of the forecast from actual values. So long as forecasts generated by exponential smoothing fall within this range, no change in α is necessary. However, if a forecast falls outside the range, the system signals a need to update α.

For instance, if things are going well, the forecasting technique should over- and underestimate equally often. A tracking signal based on this rationale can be developed.

Let U equal the number of underestimates out of the last k forecasts. In other words, U is the number of errors out of the last k that are positive. If the process is in control, the expected value of U is $k/2$ but sampling variability is involved, so values close to $k/2$ would not be unusual. On the other hand, values that are not close to $k/2$ would indicate that the technique is producing biased forecasts.

Example 4.7

Suppose that Acme Tool Company has decided to use the exponential smoothing technique with α equal to .1, as shown in Example 4.5 (see p. 115). If the process is in control and the analyst decides to monitor the last 10 error values, U has an expected value of 5. Actually, U values of 2, 3, 4, 6, 7, or 8 would not be unduly alarming. However, values of 0, 1, 9, or 10 would be of concern since the probability of obtaining such values by chance alone would be .022 (based on the binomial distribution). With this information a tracking system can be developed based on the following rules.

If $2 \leq U \leq 8$ then the process is in control.

If $U < 2$ or $U > 8$ then the process is out of control.

Assume that, out of the next 10 forecasts using this technique, only one has a positive error. Because the probability of obtaining only one positive error out of 10 is quite low, .011, the process is considered to be out of control (overestimating), and the value of α should be changed.

Another way of tracking a forecasting technique is to determine a range that should contain the forecasting errors, which can be accomplished by using the *MSE* that was established when the optimally sized α was determined. If the exponential smoothing technique is reasonably accurate, the forecast error should be approximately normally distributed about a mean of zero. Under this condition, there is about a 95% chance that the actual observation will fall within approximately 2 standard deviations of the forecast. Using $\sqrt{MSE}$ as an estimate of the standard deviation of the forecast error, approximate 95% error limits can be determined. Forecast errors falling within these limits indicate no cause for alarm. Errors (particularly a sequence of errors) outside the limits suggest a change. Example 4.8 illustrates this approach.

Example 4.8

In the Acme Tool Company example, the optimal alpha was determined to be $\alpha = .266$ with $MSE = 19{,}447$. An estimate of the standard deviation of the forecast errors is $\sqrt{MSE} = \sqrt{19{,}447} = 139.5$. If the forecast errors are approximately normally distributed about a mean of zero, there is about a 95% chance that the actual observation will fall within 2 standard deviations of the forecast or within

$$\pm 2\sqrt{MSE} = \pm 2\sqrt{19{,}447} = \pm 2(139.5) = \pm 279$$

For this example, the permissible absolute error is 279. If for any future forecast the magnitude of the error is greater than 279, there is reason to believe that the optimal smoothing constant alpha should be updated or a different forecasting method considered.

The preceding discussion on tracking signals also applies to the smoothing methods yet to be discussed in the rest of the chapter.

Simple exponential smoothing works well when the data vary about a level that changes infrequently. Whenever a sustained trend exists, exponential smoothing will lag behind the actual values over time. Holt's linear exponential smoothing technique, which is designed to handle data with a well-defined trend, addresses this problem and is introduced next.

Exponential Smoothing Adjusted for Trend: Holt's Method

In simple exponential smoothing the level of the time series is assumed to be changing occasionally, and an estimate of the current level is required. In some situations, the observed data will be clearly trending and will contain information that allows the anticipation of future upward movements. When this is the case, a linear trend forecast function is needed. Because business and economic series rarely exhibit a fixed linear trend, we consider the possibility of modeling evolving local linear trends over time. Holt (1957) developed an exponential smoothing method, *Holt's linear exponential smoothing*,[1] that allows for evolving local linear trends in a time series and can be used to generate forecasts.

When a trend in the time series is anticipated, an estimate of the current slope as well as the current level is required. Holt's technique smoothes the level and slope directly by using different smoothing constants for each. These smoothing constants provide estimates of level and slope that adapt over time as new observations become available. One of the advantages of Holt's technique is that it provides a great deal of flexibility in selecting the rates at which the level and trend are tracked.

The three equations used in Holt's method are:

1. The exponentially smoothed series, or current level estimate:

$$L_t = \alpha Y_t + (1 - \alpha)(L_{t-1} + T_{t-1}) \tag{4.15}$$

2. The trend estimate:

$$T_t = \beta(L_t - L_{t-1}) + (1 - \beta)T_{t-1} \tag{4.16}$$

3. Forecast p periods into the future:

$$\hat{Y}_{t+p} = L_t + pT_t \tag{4.17}$$

---

[1] Holt's linear exponential smoothing is sometimes called *double exponential smoothing*.

where

L_t = new smoothed value (estimate of current level)

α = smoothing constant for the level $(0 < \alpha < 1)$

Y_t = new observation or actual value of series in period t

β = smoothing constant for trend estimate $(0 < \beta < 1)$

T_t = trend estimate

p = periods to be forecast into the future

$\hat{Y}_{t+p}$ = forecast for p periods into the future

Equation 4.15 is very similar to the equation for simple exponential smoothing, Equation 4.13, except that a term (T_{t-1}) has been incorporated to properly update the level when a trend exists. That is, the current level (L_t) is calculated by taking a weighted average of two estimates of level—one estimate is given by the current observation (Y_t), and the other estimate is given by adding the previous trend (T_{t-1}) to the previously smoothed level (L_{t-1}). If there is no trend in the data, there is no need for the term T_{t-1} in Equation 4.15, effectively reducing it to Equation 4.13. There is also no need for Equation 4.16.

A second smoothing constant, β, is used to create the trend estimate. Equation 4.16 shows that the current trend (T_t) is a weighted average (with weights β and $1 - \beta$) of two trend estimates—one estimate is given by the change in level from time $t - 1$ to t $(L_t - L_{t-1})$, and the other estimate is the previously smoothed trend (T_{t-1}). Equation 4.16 is similar to Equation 4.15, except that the smoothing is done for the trend rather than the actual data.

Equation 4.17 shows the forecast for p periods into the future. For a forecast made at time t, the current trend estimate (T_t) is multiplied by the number of periods to be forecast (p), and the product is then added to the current level (L_t). Note that the forecasts for future periods lie along a straight line with slope T_t and intercept L_t.

As with simple exponential smoothing, the smoothing constants α and β can be selected subjectively or by minimizing a measure of forecast error such as the *MSE*. Large weights result in more rapid changes in the component; small weights result in less rapid changes. Therefore, the larger the weights, the more the smoothed values follow the data; the smaller the weights, the smoother the pattern in the smoothed values.

We could develop a grid of values of α and β (e.g., each combination of $\alpha = 0.1, 0.2, \ldots, 0.9$ and $\beta = 0.1, 0.2, \ldots, 0.9$) and then select the combination that provides the lowest *MSE*. Most forecasting software packages use an optimization algorithm to minimize *MSE*. We might insist that $\alpha = \beta$, thus providing equal amounts of smoothing for the level and the trend. In the special case where $\alpha = \beta$, Holt's approach is the same as Brown's double exponential smoothing.

To get started, initial values for L and T in Equations 4.15 and 4.16 must be determined. One approach is to set the first estimate of the smoothed level equal to the first observation. The trend is then estimated to be zero. A second approach is to use the average of the first five or six observations as the initial smoothed value L. The trend is then estimated using the slope of a line that is fit to these five or six observations. Minitab develops a regression equation using the variable of interest as Y and time as the independent variable X. The constant from this equation is the initial estimate of the level component, and the slope or regression coefficient is the initial estimate of the trend component.

Example 4.9

In Example 4.6 simple exponential smoothing did not produce successful forecasts of Acme Tool Company saw sales. Because Figure 4-8 suggests that there might be a trend in these data, Holt's linear exponential smoothing is used to develop forecasts. To begin the computations shown in Table 4-8, two estimated initial values are needed, namely, the initial level and the initial trend value. The estimate of the level was set equal to the first observation. The trend was estimated to equal zero. The technique is demonstrated in Table 4-8 for $\alpha = .3$ and $\beta = .1$.

The value for α used here is close to the optimal alpha ($\alpha = .266$) for simple exponential smoothing in Example 4.6. Alpha is used to smooth the data to eliminate randomness and estimate level. The smoothing constant β is like α except that it is used to smooth the trend in the data. Both smoothing constants are used to average past values and thus remove randomness. The computations leading to the forecast for period 3 are shown next.

1. Update the exponentially smoothed series or level:

$$L_t = \alpha Y_t + (1 - \alpha)(L_{t-1} + T_{t-1})$$

$$L_2 = .3Y_2 + (1 - .3)(L_{2-1} + T_{2-1})$$

$$L_2 = .3(350) + .7(500 + 0) = 455$$

TABLE 4-8   Exponentially Smoothed Values for Acme Tool Company Sales, Holt's Method, for Example 4.9

(1) Year	(2) t	(3) Y_t	(4) L_t	(5) T_t	(6) $\hat{Y}_{t+p}$	e_t
1996	1	500	500.0	0.0	500.0	0.0
	2	350	455.0	−4.5	500.0	−150.0
	3	250	390.4	−10.5	450.5	−200.5
	4	400	385.9	−9.9	379.8	20.2
1997	5	450	398.2	−7.7	376.0	74.0
	6	350	378.3	−8.9	390.5	−40.5
	7	200	318.6	−14.0	369.4	−169.4
	8	300	303.2	−14.1	304.6	−4.6
1998	9	350	307.4	−12.3	289.1	60.9
	10	200	266.6	−15.2	295.1	−95.0
	11	150	221.0	−18.2	251.4	−101.4
	12	400	262.0	−12.3	202.8	197.2
1999	13	550	339.8	−3.3	249.7	300.3
	14	350	340.6	−2.9	336.5	13.5
	15	250	311.4	−5.5	337.7	−287.7
	16	550	379.1	1.8	305.9	244.1
2000	17	550	431.7	6.9	381.0	169.0
	18	400	427.0	5.7	438.6	−38.6
	19	350	407.9	3.3	432.7	−82.7
	20	600	467.8	8.9	411.2	188.8
2001	21	750	558.7	17.1	476.8	273.2
	22	500	553.1	14.8	575.9	−75.9
	23	400	517.6	9.8	567.9	−167.9
	24	650	564.2	13.5	527.4	122.6
2002	25	850	—	—	577.7	273.3

$MSE = 20,515.5$.

2. Update the trend estimate:

$$T_t = \beta(L_t - L_{t-1}) + (1 - \beta)T_{t-1}$$
$$T_2 = .1(L_2 - L_{2-1}) + (1 - .1)T_{2-1}$$
$$T_2 = .1(455 - 500) + .9(0) = -4.5$$

3. Forecast one period into the future:

$$\hat{Y}_{t+p} = L_t + pT_t$$
$$\hat{Y}_{2+1} = L_2 + 1T_2 = 455 + 1(-4.5) = 450.5$$

4. Determine the forecast error:

$$e_3 = Y_3 - \hat{Y}_3 = 250 - 450.5 = -200.5$$

The forecast for period 25 is computed as follows:

1. Update the exponentially smoothed series or level:

$$L_{24} = .3Y_{24} + (1 - .3)(L_{24-1} + T_{24-1})$$
$$L_{24} = .3(650) + .7(517.6 + 9.8) = 564.2$$

2. Update the trend estimate:

$$T_{24} = .1(L_{24} - L_{24-1}) + (1 - .1)T_{24-1}$$
$$T_{24} = .1(564.2 - 517.6) + .9(9.8) = 13.5$$

3. Forecast one period into the future:

$$\hat{Y}_{24+1} = L_{24} + 1T_{24}$$
$$\hat{Y}_{25} = 564.2 + 1(13.5) = 577.7$$

On the basis of minimizing the *MSE* over the period 1996 to 2002, Holt's linear smoothing (with $\alpha = .3$ and $\beta = .1$) does not reproduce the data any better than simple exponential smoothing that used a smoothing constant of .266. A comparison of the *MAPEs* shows them to be about the same. When the forecasts for the actual sales for the first quarter of 2002 are compared, again, Holt's smoothing and simple exponential smoothing are similar. To summarize:

$\alpha = .266$	$MSE = 19{,}447$	$MAPE = 32.2\%$
$\alpha = .3, \beta = .1$	$MSE = 20{,}516$	$MAPE = 35.4\%$

Figure 4-10 shows the results when Holt's method using $\alpha = .3$ and $\beta = .1$ is run on Minitab.[2] The autocorrelation function for the residuals from Holt's linear exponential smoothing is given in Figure 4-11. The autocorrelation coefficients at time lags 2 and 4 appear to be significant. In addition, when the Ljung-Box Q statistic is computed for six time lags, the large value of LBQ (36.33) shows that the residuals contain extensive

---

[2] In the Minitab program the trend parameter gamma (γ) is identical to our beta (β).

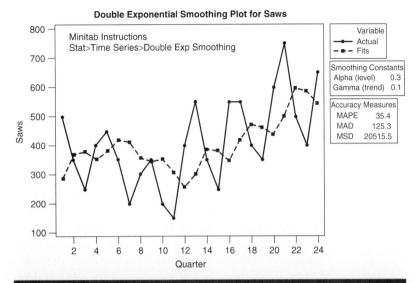

FIGURE 4-10   Holt's Linear Exponential Smoothing: Acme Tool Company Data

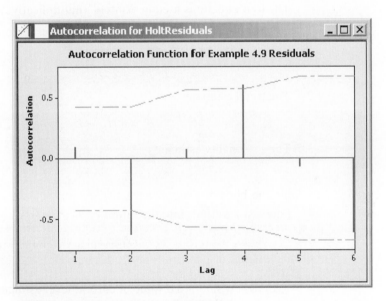

Autocorrelation Function: Residuals

Lag	ACF	T	LBQ	Lag	ACF	T	LBQ
1	0.092547	0.45	0.23	4	0.601371	2.18	22.92
2	-0.629408	-3.06	11.47	5	-0.070132	-0.22	23.08
3	0.074355	0.27	11.63	6	-0.618267	-1.90	36.33

FIGURE 4-11   Autocorrelation Function for the Residuals from Holt's Linear Exponential Smoothing: Acme Tool Company Data

autocorrelation; they are not random. The large residual autocorrelations at lags 2 and 4 suggest that a seasonal component may be present in Acme Tool Company data.

The results in Examples 4.6 and 4.9 (see Figures 4-8 and 4-10) are not much different because the smoothing constant α is about the same in both cases, and the smoothing constant β in Example 4.9 is small. (For $\beta = 0$, Holt's linear smoothing reduces to simple exponential smoothing.)

Exponential Smoothing Adjusted for Trend and Seasonal Variation: Winters' Method

Examination of the data for Acme Tool Company in Table 4-8 indicates that sales are consistently higher during the first and fourth quarters and lower during the third quarter. A seasonal pattern appears to exist. Winters' three-parameter linear and seasonal exponential smoothing method, an extension of Holt's method, might represent the data better and reduce forecast error. In Winters' method, one additional equation is used to estimate seasonality. In the multiplicative version of Winters' method, the seasonality estimate is given as a seasonal index and is calculated with Equation 4.20. Equation 4.20 shows that the current seasonal component, S_t, is computed as γ times an estimate of the seasonal index given by Y_t/L_t added to $(1 - \gamma)$ times the previous seasonal component S_{t-s}. This procedure is equivalent to smoothing current and previous values of Y_t/L_t. The reason Y_t is divided by the current level estimate L_t is to create an index (ratio) that can be used in a multiplicative fashion to adjust a forecast to account for seasonal peaks and valleys.

The four equations used in Winters' (multiplicative) smoothing are:

1. The exponentially smoothed series or level estimate:

$$L_t = \alpha \frac{Y_t}{S_{t-s}} + (1 - \alpha)(L_{t-1} + T_{t-1}) \tag{4.18}$$

2. The trend estimate:

$$T_t = \beta(L_t - L_{t-1}) + (1 - \beta)T_{t-1} \tag{4.19}$$

3. The seasonality estimate:

$$S_t = \gamma \frac{Y_t}{L_t} + (1 - \gamma)S_{t-s} \tag{4.20}$$

4. Forecast p periods into the future:

$$\hat{Y}_{t+p} = (L_t + pT_t)S_{t-s+p} \tag{4.21}$$

where

L_t = new smoothed value or current level estimate
α = smoothing constant for the level
Y_t = new observation or actual value in period t
β = smoothing constant for trend estimate
T_t = trend estimate
γ = smoothing constant for seasonality estimate
S_t = seasonal estimate
p = periods to be forecast into the future
s = length of seasonality
$\hat{Y}_{t+p}$ = forecast for p periods into the future

Equation 4.18 updates the smoothed series. A slight difference in this equation distinguishes it from the corresponding one in Holt's procedure, Equation 4.15. In Equation 4.18, Y_t is divided by S_{t-s}, which adjusts Y_t for seasonality, thus removing the seasonal effects that might exist in the original data Y_t.

After the trend estimate and seasonal estimate have been smoothed in Equations 4.19 and 4.20, a forecast is obtained with Equation 4.21. It is almost the same as the corresponding formula, Equation 4.17, used to obtain a forecast using Holt's smoothing. The difference is that this estimate for future periods, $t + p$, is multiplied by S_{t-s+p}. This seasonal index is the last one available and is, therefore, used to adjust the forecast for seasonality.

As with Holt's linear exponential smoothing, the weights α, β, and γ can be selected subjectively or by minimizing a measure of forecast error such as *MSE*. The most common approach for determining these values is to use an optimization algorithm to find the optimal smoothing constants.

To begin the algorithm for Equation 4.18, the initial values for the smoothed series L_t, the trend T_t, and the seasonal indices S_t must be set. One approach is to set the first estimate of the smoothed series (level) equal to the first observation. The trend is then estimated to equal zero and the seasonal indices are each set to 1.0. Other approaches for initializing the level, trend, and seasonal estimates are available. Minitab, for example, develops a regression equation using the variable of interest as Y and time as the independent variable X. The constant from this equation is the initial estimate of the smoothed series or level component, and the slope, or regression coefficient, is the initial estimate of the trend component. Initial values for the seasonal components are obtained from a dummy variable regression using detrended data (see Chapter 8).

Example 4.10

Winters' technique is demonstrated in Table 4-9 for $\alpha = .4$, $\beta = .1$, and $\gamma = .3$ for the Acme Tool Company data. The value for alpha is similar to the one used for simple exponential smoothing in Example 4.6 and is used to smooth the data to create a level estimate. The smoothing constant beta (β) is used to create a smoothed estimate of trend. The smoothing constant gamma (γ) is used to create a smoothed estimate of the seasonal component in the data.

Minitab can be used to solve this example (see the "Minitab Applications" section at the end of the chapter for the instructions).[3] The results are shown in Table 4-9 and Figure 4-12. The forecast for the first quarter of 2002 is 778.2. The computations leading to the forecast value for the first quarter of 2002, or period 25, are shown next.

1. The exponentially smoothed series or level estimate:

$$L_t = \alpha \frac{Y_t}{S_{t-s}} + (1-\alpha)(L_{t-1} + T_{t-1})$$

$$L_{24} = .4 \frac{Y_{24}}{S_{24-4}} + (1 - .4)(L_{24-1} + T_{24-1})$$

$$L_{24} = .4 \frac{650}{1.39628} + (1 - .4)(501.286 + 9.148)$$

$$L_{24} = .4(465.52) + .6(510.434) = 492.469$$

---

[3] In the Minitab program, the trend parameter gamma (γ) is identical to our beta (β), and the seasonal parameter delta (δ) is identical to our gamma (γ) in Equations 4.19 and 4.20, respectively.

| TABLE 4-9 | | Exponentially Smoothed Values for Acme Tool Company Sales, Winters' Method, for Example 4.10 | | | | | |

	(1)	(2)	(3)	(4)	(5)	(6)	(7)
Year	*t*	Y_t	L_t	T_t	S_t	$\hat{Y}_{t+p}$	e_t
1996	1	500	415.459	−41.9541	1.26744	563.257	−63.257
	2	350	383.109	−40.9937	0.89040	328.859	21.141
	3	250	358.984	−39.3068	0.66431	222.565	27.435
	4	400	328.077	−38.4668	1.18766	375.344	24.656
1997	5	450	315.785	−35.8494	1.31471	367.063	82.937
	6	350	325.194	−31.3235	0.94617	249.255	100.745
	7	200	296.748	−31.0358	0.66721	195.221	4.779
	8	300	260.466	−31.5604	1.17690	315.576	−15.576
1998	9	350	243.831	−30.0679	1.35093	300.945	49.055
	10	200	212.809	−30.1632	0.94426	202.255	−2.255
	11	150	199.515	−28.4764	0.69259	121.863	28.137
	12	400	238.574	−21.7228	1.32682	201.294	198.706
1999	13	550	292.962	−14.1117	1.50886	292.949	257.051
	14	350	315.575	−10.4393	0.99371	263.306	86.694
	15	250	327.466	−8.2062	0.71385	211.335	38.665
	16	550	357.366	−4.3956	1.39048	423.599	126.401
2000	17	550	357.588	−3.9339	1.51763	532.584	17.416
	18	400	373.206	−1.9787	1.01713	351.428	48.572
	19	350	418.856	2.7843	0.75038	264.999	85.001
	20	600	425.586	3.1788	1.39628	586.284	13.716
2001	21	750	454.936	5.7959	1.55691	650.706	99.294
	22	500	473.070	7.0297	1.02907	468.626	31.374
	23	400	501.286	9.1484	0.76465	360.255	39.745
	24	650	492.469	7.3518	1.37336	712.712	−62.712
2002	25	850	—	—	—	778.179	—
	26	600	—	—	—	521.917	—
	27	450	—	—	—	393.430	—
	28	700	—	—	—	716.726	—

$MSE = 7,636.86.$

2. The trend estimate:

$$T_t = \beta(L_t - L_{t-1}) + (1 - \beta)T_{t-1}$$

$$T_{24} = .1(L_{24} - L_{24-1}) + (1 - .1)T_{24-1}$$

$$T_{24} = .1(492.469 - 501.286) + .9(9.148)$$

$$T_{24} = .1(-8.817) + .9(9.148) = 7.352$$

3. The seasonality estimate:

$$S_t = \gamma\frac{Y_t}{L_t} + (1 - \gamma)S_{t-s}$$

$$S_{24} = .3\frac{Y_{24}}{L_{24}} + (1 - .3)S_{24-4}$$

$$S_{24} = .3\frac{650}{492.469} + .7(1.39628)$$

$$S_{24} = .3(1.3199) + .9774 = 1.3734$$

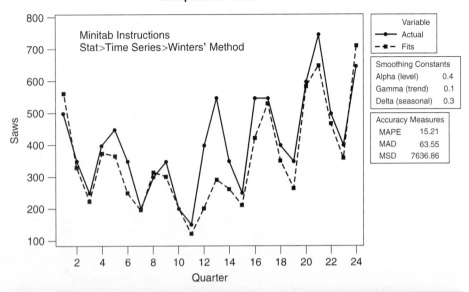

Winters' Model Plot for Saws
Multiplicative Model

FIGURE 4-12   Winters' Exponential Smoothing: Acme Tools Company Data

4.   Forecast $p = 1$ period into the future:

$$\hat{Y}_{24+1} = (L_{24} + 1T_{24})S_{24-4+1}$$

$$\hat{Y}_{25} = (492.469 + 1(7.352))1.5569 = 778.17$$

For the parameter values considered, the Winters' technique is better than both of the previous smoothing procedures in terms of minimizing *MSE*. When the forecasts for the actual sales for the first quarter of 2002 are compared, the Winters' technique also appears to do a better job. Figure 4-13 shows the autocorrelation function for the Winters' exponential smoothing residuals. None of the residual autocorrelation coefficients appear to be significantly larger than zero. When the Ljung-Box Q statistic is calculated for six time lags, the small value of LBQ (5.01) shows that the residual series is random. Winters' exponential smoothing method seems to provide adequate forecasts for the Acme Tool Company data.

Winters' method provides an easy way to account for seasonality when data have a seasonal pattern. An alternative method consists of first deseasonalizing or seasonally adjusting the data. Deseasonalizing is a process that removes the effects of seasonality from the raw data and will be demonstrated in Chapter 5. The forecasting model is applied to the deseasonalized data and, if required, the seasonal component is reinserted to provide accurate forecasts.

Exponential smoothing is a popular technique for short-run forecasting. Its major advantages are low cost and simplicity. When forecasts are needed for inventory systems containing thousands of items, smoothing methods are often the only acceptable approach.

Simple moving averages and exponential smoothing base forecasts on weighted averages of past measurements. The rationale is that past values contain information about what will occur in the future. Because past values include random fluctuations as well as information concerning the underlying pattern of a variable, an attempt is

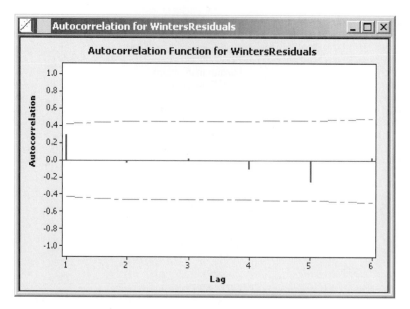

Autocorrelation Function: Residuals

Lag	ACF	T	LBQ	Lag	ACF	T	LBQ
1	0.297749	1.46	2.41	4	-0.107084	-0.48	2.80
2	-0.031543	-0.14	2.43	5	-0.257066	-1.15	4.97
3	0.017610	0.08	2.44	6	0.033280	0.14	5.01

FIGURE 4-13   Autocorrelation Function for the Residuals from Winters' Multiplicative Exponential Smoothing Method: Acme Tool Company Data

made to smooth the values. This approach assumes that extreme fluctuations represent randomness in a series of historical observations.

Moving averages, on the other hand, are the means of a certain number, k, of values of a variable. The most recent average is then the forecast for the next period. This approach assigns an equal weight to each past value involved in the average. However, a convincing argument can be made for using all the data but emphasizing the most recent values. Exponential smoothing methods are attractive because they generate forecasts by assigning weights that decline exponentially as the observations get older.

APPLICATION TO MANAGEMENT

Forecasts are one of the most important inputs managers have to aid them in the decision-making process. Virtually every important operating decision depends to some extent on a forecast. The production department has to schedule employment needs and raw material orders for the next month or two; the finance department must determine the best investment opportunities; marketing must forecast the demand for a new product. The list of forecasting applications is lengthy.

Executives are keenly aware of the importance of forecasting. Indeed, a great deal of time is spent studying trends in economic and political affairs and how events might affect demand for products or services. One issue of interest is the importance executives place on quantitative forecasting methods compared to their own opinions. This issue is especially sensitive when events that have a significant impact on demand are involved. One problem with quantitative forecasting methods is that they depend on historical data. For this reason they are relatively ineffective in anticipating a dramatic change that often results in sharply higher or lower demand.

The averaging and smoothing forecasting methods discussed in this chapter are useful because of their relative simplicity. These simple methods tend to be less costly, easier to implement, and easier to understand than complex methods. Frequently, the cost and difficulties of more sophisticated models outweigh any gains in accuracy. For these reasons, small businesses find simple methods practical. Businesses without computers and/or personnel capable of handling statistical models also turn to simple methods. Business managers frequently face the need to prepare short-term forecasts for a number of different items. A typical example is the manager who must schedule production on the basis of some forecast of demand for several hundred different products in a product line. Finally, new businesses without lengthy historical databases find these approaches helpful.

With a judicious choice of order k, the moving average method can do a good job of adjusting to shifts in levels. It is economical to update, and it does not require much data storage. The moving average methods are most frequently used when repeated forecasts are necessary.

Exponential smoothing is a popular technique, the strength of which lies in good short-term accuracy combined with quick, low-cost updating. The technique is widely used when regular monthly or weekly forecasts are needed for a large number, perhaps thousands, of items. Inventory control is one example where exponential smoothing methods are routinely used.

Glossary

Exponential smoothing. Exponential smoothing is a procedure for continually revising a forecast in the light of more recent experience.

Moving average. A moving average of order k is the mean value of k consecutive observations. The most recent moving average value provides a forecast for the next period.

Simple average. A simple average uses the mean of all relevant historical observations as the forecast for the next period.

Tracking signal. A tracking signal involves computing a measure of forecast errors over time and setting limits so that, when the cumulative error goes outside those limits, the forecaster is alerted.

Key Formulas

Naive model

$$\hat{Y}_{t+1} = Y_t \tag{4.1}$$

Naive trend model

$$\hat{Y}_{t+1} = Y_t + (Y_t - Y_{t-1}) \tag{4.2}$$

Naive rate of change model

$$\hat{Y}_{t+1} = Y_t \frac{Y_t}{Y_{t-1}} \tag{4.3}$$

Naive seasonal model for quarterly data

$$\hat{Y}_{t+1} = Y_{t-3} \tag{4.4}$$

Naive trend and seasonal model for quarterly data

$$\hat{Y}_{t+1} = Y_{t-3} + \frac{Y_t - Y_{t-4}}{4} \tag{4.5}$$

Simple average model

$$\hat{Y}_{t+1} = \frac{1}{t} \sum_{i=1}^{t} Y_i \tag{4.6}$$

Updated simple average, new period

$$\hat{Y}_{t+2} = \frac{t\hat{Y}_{t+1} + Y_{t+1}}{t+1} \tag{4.7}$$

Moving average model for *k* time periods

$$\hat{Y}_{t+1} = \frac{Y_t + Y_{t-1} + \cdots + Y_{t-k+1}}{k} \tag{4.8}$$

Double moving average

$$M'_t = \frac{M_t + M_{t-1} + M_{t-2} + \cdots + M_{t-k+1}}{k} \tag{4.9}$$

$$a_t = 2M_t - M'_t \tag{4.10}$$

$$b_t = \frac{2}{k-1}(M_t - M'_t) \tag{4.11}$$

$$\hat{Y}_{t+p} = a_t + b_t p \tag{4.12}$$

Simple exponential smoothing

$$\hat{Y}_{t+1} = \alpha Y_t + (1-\alpha)\hat{Y}_t \tag{4.13}$$

Equivalent alternative expression:

$$\hat{Y}_{t+1} = \alpha Y_t + \alpha(1-\alpha)Y_{t-1} + \alpha(1-\alpha)^2 Y_{t-2} + \alpha(1-\alpha)^3 Y_{t-3} + \cdots \tag{4.14}$$

Holt's linear smoothing
The exponentially smoothed series, or current level estimate:

$$L_t = \alpha Y_t + (1-\alpha)(L_{t-1} + T_{t-1}) \tag{4.15}$$

The trend estimate:

$$T_t = \beta(L_t - L_{t-1}) + (1-\beta)T_{t-1} \tag{4.16}$$

Forecast p periods into the future:

$$\hat{Y}_{t+p} = L_t + pT_t \tag{4.17}$$

Winters' multiplicative smoothing

The exponentially smoothed series, or level estimate:

$$L_t = \alpha \frac{Y_t}{S_{t-s}} + (1 - \alpha)(L_{t-1} + T_{t-1}) \tag{4.18}$$

The trend estimate:

$$T_t = \beta(L_t - L_{t-1}) + (1 - \beta)T_{t-1} \tag{4.19}$$

The seasonality estimate:

$$S_t = \gamma \frac{Y_t}{L_t} + (1 - \gamma)S_{t-s} \tag{4.20}$$

Forecast p periods into the future:

$$\hat{Y}_{t+p} = (L_t + pT_t)S_{t-s+p} \tag{4.21}$$

Problems

1. Which forecasting technique continually revises an estimate in the light of more recent experiences?

2. Which forecasting technique uses the value for the current period as the forecast for the next period?

3. Which forecasting technique assigns equal weights to each observation?

4. Which forecasting technique(s) should be tried if the data are trending?

5. Which forecasting techniques should be tried if the data are seasonal?

6. Apex Mutual Fund invests primarily in technology stocks. The prices of the fund at the end of each month for the 12 months of 2003 are given in Table P-6:
   a. Find the forecast value of the mutual fund for each month by using a naive model. The value for December 2002 was 19.00.

TABLE P-6	
Month	*Mutual Fund Price*
January	19.39
February	18.96
March	18.20
April	17.89
May	18.43
June	19.98
July	19.51
August	20.63
September	19.78
October	21.25
November	21.18
December	22.14

    b. Evaluate this forecasting method using *MAD*.
    c. Evaluate this forecasting method using *MSE*.
    d. Evaluate this forecasting method using *MAPE*.
    e. Evaluate this forecasting method using *MPE*.
    f. Using a naive model, forecast the mutual fund price for January 2004.
    g. Write a memo summarizing your findings.

7. Refer to Problem 6. Use a three-month moving average to forecast the mutual fund price for January 2004. Is this forecast better than the forecast made using the naive model? Explain.

8. Given the series Y_t in Table P-8:
    a. What is the forecast for period 9 using a five-period moving average?
    b. If simple exponential smoothing with a smoothing constant of .4 is used, what is the forecast for period 4?
    c. In part b, what is the forecast error for time period 3?

9. The yield on a general obligation bond for the city of Davenport fluctuates with the market. The monthly quotations for 2002 are given in Table P-9:
    a. Find the forecast value of the yield on the obligation bonds for each month, starting with April, by using a three-month moving average.
    b. Find the forecast value of the yield on the obligation bonds for each month, starting with June, by using a five-month moving average.
    c. Evaluate these forecasting methods using *MAD*.

TABLE P-8

Time Period	Y_t	$\hat{Y}_t$	e_t
1	200	200	—
2	210	—	—
3	215	—	—
4	216	—	—
5	219	—	—
6	220	—	—
7	225	—	—
8	226	—	—

TABLE P-9

Month	Yield
January	9.29
February	9.99
March	10.16
April	10.25
May	10.61
June	11.07
July	11.52
August	11.09
September	10.80
October	10.50
November	10.86
December	9.97

d. Evaluate these forecasting methods using *MSE*.

e. Evaluate these forecasting methods using *MAPE*.

f. Evaluate these forecasting methods using *MPE*.

g. Forecast the yield for January 2003 using the best technique.

h. Write a memo summarizing your findings.

10. This question refers to Problem 9. Use exponential smoothing with a smoothing constant of .2 and an initial value of 9.29 to forecast the yield for January 2003. Is this forecast better than the forecast made using the best moving average model? Explain.

11. The Hughes Supply Company uses an inventory management method to determine the monthly demands for various products. The demand values for the last 12 months of each product have been recorded and are available for future forecasting. The demand values for the 12 months of 2002 for one electrical fixture are presented in Table P-11.

   Use exponential smoothing with a smoothing constant of .5 and an initial value of 205 to forecast the demand for January 2003.

12. General American Investors Co., a closed-end regulated investment management company, invests primarily in medium- and high-quality stocks. Jim Campbell is studying the asset value per share for this company and would like to forecast this variable for the remaining quarters of 1996. The data are presented in Table P-12.

   Evaluate the ability to forecast the asset value per share variable using the following forecasting methods: naive, moving average, and exponential smoothing. When you compare techniques, take into consideration that the actual asset value per share for the second quarter of 1996 was 26.47. Write a report for Jim indicating which method he should use and why.

13. Southdown, Inc., one of the nation's largest cement producers, is pushing ahead with a waste fuel burning program. The cost for Southdown will total about $37 million. For this reason, it is extremely important for the company to have an accurate forecast of revenues for the first quarter of 2000. The data are presented in Table P-13.

TABLE P-11	
Month	*Demand*
January	205
February	251
March	304
April	284
May	352
June	300
July	241
August	284
September	312
October	289
November	385
December	256

Source: Hughes Supply Company records.

TABLE P-12				
		Quarter		
Year	*1*	*2*	*3*	*4*
1985	16.98	18.47	17.63	20.65
1986	21.95	23.85	20.44	19.29
1987	22.75	23.94	24.84	16.70
1988	18.04	19.19	18.97	17.03
1989	18.23	19.80	22.89	21.41
1990	21.50	25.05	20.33	20.60
1991	25.33	26.06	28.89	30.60
1992	27.44	26.69	28.71	28.56
1993	25.87	24.96	27.61	24.75
1994	23.32	22.61	24.08	22.31
1995	22.67	23.52	25.41	23.94
1996	25.68	—	—	—

Source: The Value Line Investment Survey (New York: Value Line, 1990, 1993, 1996), p. 2187.

TABLE P-13	Southdown Revenues, 1986–1999			
		Quarter		
Year	*1*	*2*	*3*	*4*
1986	77.4	88.8	92.1	79.8
1987	77.5	89.1	92.4	80.1
1988	74.4	185.2	162.4	178.1
1989	129.1	158.4	160.6	138.7
1990	127.2	149.8	151.7	132.9
1991	103.0	136.8	141.3	123.5
1992	107.3	136.1	138.6	123.7
1993	106.1	144.4	156.1	138.2
1994	111.8	149.8	158.5	141.8
1995	119.1	158.0	170.4	151.8
1996	127.4	178.2	189.3	169.5
1997	151.4	187.2	199.2	181.4
1998	224.9	317.7	341.4	300.7
1999	244.9	333.4	370.0	326.7

Source: The Value Line Investment Survey (New York: Value Line, 1990, 1993, 1996, 1999), p. 896.

a. Use exponential smoothing with a smoothing constant of .4 and an initial value of 77.4 to forecast the quarterly revenues for the first quarter of 2000.
b. Now use a smoothing constant of .6 and an initial value of 77.4 to forecast the quarterly revenues for the first quarter of 2000.
c. Which smoothing constant provides the best forecast?
d. Refer to part c. Examine the residual autocorrelations. Are you happy with simple exponential smoothing for this example? Explain.

TABLE P-14	Triton Sales per Share, 1974–1999		
Year	Sales per Share	Year	Sales per Share
1974	.93	1987	5.33
1975	1.35	1988	8.12
1976	1.48	1989	10.65
1977	2.36	1990	12.06
1978	2.45	1991	11.63
1979	2.52	1992	6.58
1980	2.81	1993	2.96
1981	3.82	1994	1.58
1982	5.54	1995	2.99
1983	7.16	1996	3.69
1984	1.93	1997	3.98
1985	5.17	1998	4.39
1986	7.72	1999	6.85

Source: The Value Line Investment Survey (New York: Value Line, 1990, 1993, 1996, 1999), p. 1872.

14. The Triton Energy Corporation explores for and produces oil and gas. Company president Gail Freeman wants to have her company's analyst forecast the company's sales per share for 2000. This will be an important forecast because Triton's restructuring plans have hit a snag. The data are presented in Table P-14.

    Determine the best forecasting method and forecast sales per share for 2000.

15. The Consolidated Edison Company sells electricity (82% of revenues), gas (13%), and steam (5%) in New York City and Westchester County. Bart Thomas, company forecaster, is assigned the task of forecasting the company's quarterly revenues for the rest of 2002 and all of 2003. He collects the data shown in Table P-15.

    Determine the best forecasting technique and forecast quarterly revenue for the rest of 2002 and all of 2003.

16. A job shop manufacturer that specializes in replacement parts has no forecasting system in place, and manufactures products based on last month's sales. Twenty-four months of sales data are available and are given in Table P-16.
    a. Plot the sales data as a time series. Are the data seasonal?

    Hint: For monthly data, the seasonal period is $s = 12$. Is there a pattern (e.g., summer sales relatively low, fall sales relatively high) that tends to repeat itself every 12 months?
    b. Use a naive model to generate monthly sales forecasts (e.g., the February 2001 forecast is given by the January 2001 value and so forth). Compute the *MAPE*.
    c. Use simple exponential smoothing with a smoothing constant of .5 and an initial smoothed value of 430 to generate sales forecasts for each month. Compute the *MAPE*.
    d. Do you think either of the models in parts b or c is likely to generate accurate forecasts for future monthly sales? Explain.

TABLE P-15	Quarterly Revenues for Consolidated Edison ($ million), 1985–2002			
Year	Mar. 31	Jun. 30	Sept. 30	Dec. 31
1985	1,441	1,209	1,526	1,321
1986	1,414	1,187	1,411	1,185
1987	1,284	1,125	1,493	1,192
1988	1,327	1,102	1,469	1,213
1989	1,387	1,218	1,575	1,371
1990	1,494	1,263	1,613	1,369
1991	1,479	1,330	1,720	1,344
1992	1,456	1,280	1,717	1,480
1993	1,586	1,396	1,800	1,483
1994	1,697	1,392	1,822	1,461
1995	1,669	1,460	1,880	1,528
1996	1,867	1,540	1,920	1,632
1997	1,886	1,504	2,011	1,720
1998	1,853	1,561	2,062	1,617
1999	1,777	1,479	2,346	1,889
2000	2,318	2,042	2,821	2,250
2001	2,886	2,112	2,693	1,943
2002	2,099	1,900	—	—

Source: The Value Line Investment Survey (New York: Value Line, 1990, 1993, 1996, 1999, 2001).

TABLE P-16			
Month	Sales	Month	Sales
January 2001	430	January 2002	442
February	420	February	449
March	436	March	458
April	452	April	472
May	477	May	463
June	420	June	431
July	398	July	400
August	501	August	487
September	514	September	503
October	532	October	503
November	512	November	548
December	410	December	432

e. Using either Minitab or CB Predictor (see "Excel Applications: CB Predictor" at the end of this chapter), use Winters' multiplicative smoothing method with smoothing constants $\alpha = \beta = \gamma = .5$ to generate a forecast for January 2003. Save the residuals.

f. Refer to part e. Compare the *MAPE* for Winters' method from the computer printout with the *MAPE*s in parts b and c. Which of the three forecasting procedures do you prefer?

g. Refer to part e. Compute the autocorrelations (for six lags) for the residuals from Winters' multiplicative procedure. Do the residual autocorrelations suggest that Winters' procedure works well for these data? Explain.

CASES

CASE 4-1   THE SOLAR ALTERNATIVE COMPANY[4]

The Solar Alternative Company is about to enter its third year of operation. Bob and Mary Johnson, who both teach science in the local high school, founded the company. The Johnsons started the Solar Alternative Company to supplement their teaching income. Based on their research into solar energy systems, they were able to put together a solar system for heating domestic hot water. The system consists of a 100-gallon fiberglass storage tank, two 36-foot solar panels, electronic controls, PVC pipe, and miscellaneous fittings.

The payback period on the system is 10 years. Although this situation does not present an attractive investment opportunity from a financial point of view, there is sufficient interest in the novelty of the concept to provide a moderate level of sales. The Johnsons clear about $75 on the $2,000 price of an installed system, after costs and expenses. Material and equipment costs account for 75% of the installed system cost. An advantage that helps to offset the low profit margin is that the product is not profitable enough to generate any significant competition from heating contractors. The Johnsons operate the business out of their home. There is an office in the basement, and their one-car garage is used exclusively to store the system components and materials. As a result, overhead is at a minimum. The Johnsons enjoy a modest supplemental income from the company's operation. The business also provides a number of tax advantages.

Bob and Mary are pleased with the growth of the business. Although sales vary from month to month, overall the second year was much better than the first. Many of the second-year customers are neighbors of people who had purchased the system in the first year. Apparently, after seeing the system operate successfully for a year, others were willing to try the solar concept. Sales occur throughout the year. Demand for the system is greatest in late summer and early fall, when homeowners typically make plans to winterize their homes for the upcoming heating season.

With the anticipated growth in the business, the Johnsons felt that they needed a sales forecast to manage effectively in the coming year. It usually takes 60 to 90 days to receive storage tanks after placing the order. The solar panels are available off the shelf most of the year. However, in the late summer and throughout the fall, the lead time can be as great as 90 to 100 days. Although there is limited competition, lost sales are nevertheless a real possibility if potential customers are asked to wait several months for installation. Perhaps more important is the need to make accurate sales projections to take advantage of quantity discount buying. These factors, when combined with the high cost of system components and the limited storage space available in their garage, make it necessary to develop a reliable forecast. The sales history for the company's first two years is given in Table 4-10. ∎

TABLE 4-10					
Month	*2001*	*2002*	*Month*	*2001*	*2002*
January	5	17	July	23	44
February	6	14	August	26	41
March	10	20	September	21	33
April	13	23	October	15	23
May	18	30	November	12	26
June	15	38	December	14	17

[4]This case was contributed by William P. Darrow of Towson State University, Towson, Maryland.

QUESTIONS

1. Identify the model Bob and Mary should use as the basis for their business planning in 2003, and discuss why you selected this model.

2. Forecast sales for 2003.

CASE 4-2   MR. TUX

John Mosby, owner of several Mr. Tux rental stores, is beginning to forecast his most important business variable, monthly dollar sales (see the Mr. Tux cases in previous chapters). One of his employees, Virginia Perot, gathered the sales data shown in Case 2-2. John now wants to forecast these sales data using moving average and exponential smoothing techniques.

John used Minitab in Case 3-2 to determine that these data are both trending and seasonal. He has been told that simple moving averages and exponential smoothing techniques will not work with these data but decides to find out for himself.

He begins by trying a three-month moving average. The program calculates several summary forecast error measurements. These values summarize the errors found in predicting actual historical data values using a three-month moving average. John decides to record three of these error measurements:

$$MAD = 54,373$$
$$MPE = -16.5\%$$
$$MAPE = 47.0\%$$

MAD (mean absolute deviation) is the average absolute error made in forecasting past values. Each forecast using the three-month moving average method is off by an average of 54,373. *MPE* (mean percentage error) measures bias. The -16.5% indicates that the forecasting technique is consistently overestimating. The forecasts are larger than the actual values. *MAPE* (mean absolute percentage error) shows the error as a percentage of the actual value to be forecast. The average error using the three-month moving average technique is 47%, or almost half as large as the value to be forecast.

Next, John tries simple exponential smoothing. The program asks him to input the smoothing constant (α) to be used, or else ask for the optimum value to be calculated. John does the latter and the program finds the optimum α value to be .867. Again he records the appropriate error measurements:

$$MAD = 46,562$$
$$MPE = -11.8\%$$
$$MAPE = 44.0\%$$

John asks the program to use Holt's linear exponential smoothing on his data. This program uses the exponential smoothing method but can account for a trend in the data as well. John has the program use a smoothing constant of .4 for both α and β. The three summary error measurements for Holt's method are:

$$MAD = 63,579$$
$$MPE = -15.3\%$$
$$MAPE = 59.0\%$$

John is surprised to find larger measurement errors for this technique. He decides that the seasonal aspect of the data is the problem. Winters' multiplicative exponential smoothing is the next method John tries. This method can account for seasonal factors as well as trend. John uses smoothing constants of $\alpha = .2$, $\beta = .2$, and $\gamma = .2$. Error measurements are:

$$MAD = 25,825$$
$$MPE = -4.9\%$$
$$MAPE = 22.0\%$$

When John sits down and begins studying the results of his analysis, he is disappointed. The Winters' method is a big improvement; however, the *MAPE* is still 22%. He had hoped that one of the methods he used would result in accurate forecasts of past periods; he could then use this method to forecast the sales levels for coming months over the next year. But the average absolute errors (*MAD*) and percentage errors (*MAPE*) for the methods lead him to look for another way of forecasting. ∎

QUESTIONS

1. Summarize the forecast error level for the best method John has found using Minitab.
2. What is the ideal value for *MPE* when using any exponential smoothing method?
3. What is the implication of the negative sign on *MPE*?
4. Do you agree with John regarding his disappointment in his results?
5. What should John do in order to determine the adequacy of the Winters' forecasting technique?

CASE 4-3   CONSUMER CREDIT COUNSELING

The Consumer Credit Counseling (CCC) operation was described in Chapter 1 (Case 1-2). The executive director, Marv Harnishfeger, concluded that the most important variable that CCC needed to forecast was the number of new clients that would be seen in the rest of 1993. Marv provided Dorothy Mercer monthly data for the number of new clients seen by CCC for the period January 1985 through March 1993 (see Case 3-3 on p. 94). In that case study, Dorothy used autocorrelation analysis to explore the data pattern. Use the results of this investigation to answer the following questions. ∎

QUESTIONS

1. Develop a naive model to forecast the number of new clients seen by CCC for the rest of 1993.
2. Develop a moving average model to forecast the number of new clients seen by CCC for the rest of 1993.
3. Develop an exponential smoothing procedure to forecast the number of new clients seen by CCC for the rest of 1993.
4. Evaluate these forecasting methods using the forecast error summary measures presented in Chapter 3.
5. Choose the best model and forecast new clients for the rest of 1993.
6. Determine the adequacy of the forecasting model you have chosen.

CASE 4-4   MURPHY BROTHERS FURNITURE

Julie Murphy knows that most important operating decisions depend, to some extent, on a forecast. For Murphy Brothers Furniture, sales forecasts influence adding new furniture lines or dropping old ones, purchase planning, setting sales quotas, and making personnel, advertising, and financial decisions. Specifically, Julie is aware of several current forecasting needs. She knows that the production department has to schedule employees and determine raw material orders for the next month or two. She also knows that her dad, Glen Murphy, needs to determine the best investment opportunities and must forecast the demand for a new furniture line.

In Case 3-1A Julie Murphy used national monthly sales for all retail stores from 1983 through 1995 (see Table 3-8) to develop a pattern for Murphy Brothers Furniture sales. In Case 3-1B, Glen Murphy discovered actual sales data for the past four years, 1992 through 1995 (see Table 3-9). Julie was not excited about her father's discovery because she was not sure which set of data to use to develop a forecast for 1996. She determined that sales for all retail stores had somewhat the same pattern as actual Murphy Brothers' sales data. ∎

QUESTIONS

1. Do any of the forecasting models studied in this chapter work with the national sales data?
2. Do any of the forecasting models studied in this chapter work with the actual Murphy Brothers' sales data?
3. Which data set and forecasting model should Julie use to forecast sales for 1996?

CASE 4-5   FIVE-YEAR REVENUE PROJECTION FOR DOWNTOWN RADIOLOGY

Some years ago, Downtown Radiology developed a medical imaging center more complete and technologically advanced than any located in an area of eastern Washington and northern Idaho called the Inland Empire. The equipment planned for the center equaled or surpassed the imaging facilities of all medical centers in the region. The center initially contained a 9800 series CT scanner and nuclear magnetic resonance imaging (MRI) equipment. The center also included ultrasound, nuclear medicine, digital subtraction angiography (DSA), mammography equipment, and conventional radiology and fluoroscopy equipment. Ownership interest was made available in a type of public offering, and Downtown Radiology used an independent evaluation of the market. Professional Marketing Associates, Inc. evaluated the market and completed a five-year projection of revenue.

STATEMENT OF THE PROBLEM

The purpose of this study is to forecast revenue for the next five years for the proposed medical imaging center assuming you are employed by Professional Marketing Associates, Inc. in the year 1984.

Objectives

The objectives of this study then are to

- Identify market areas for each type of medical procedure to be offered by the new facility.

- Gather and analyze existing data on market area revenue for each type of procedure to be offered by the new facility.

- Identify trends in the health care industry that will positively or negatively affect revenue of procedures to be provided by the proposed facility.

- Identify factors in the business, marketing, and facilities planning of the new venture that will positively or negatively affect revenue projections.

- Analyze past procedures of Downtown Radiology as a database for the forecasting model to be developed.

- Utilize the appropriate quantitative forecasting model to arrive at five-year revenue projections for the proposed center.

METHODOLOGY
Medical Procedures
The following steps were implemented in order to complete the five-year projection of revenue. An analysis of the past number of procedures was performed. The appropriate forecasting model was developed and used to determine a starting point for the projection of each procedure.

1. The market area was determined for each type of procedure, and population forecasts were obtained for 1986 and 1990.
2. Doctor referral patterns were studied to determine the percentage of doctors who refer to Downtown Radiology and the average number of referrals per doctor.
3. National rates were acquired from the National Center for Health Statistics. These rates were compared with actual numbers obtained from the Hospital Commission.
4. Downtown Radiology's market share was calculated based on actual CT scans in the market area. (Market share for other procedures was determined based on Downtown Radiology's share compared with rates provided by the National Center for Health Statistics.)

Assumptions
Certain assumptions were necessary to develop a quantitative forecast. The following assumptions were made:

- The new imaging center will be operational, with all equipment functional except the MRI, on January 1, 1985.
- The nuclear magnetic resonance imaging equipment will be functional in April 1985.
- The offering of the limited partnership will be successfully marketed to at least 50 physicians in the service area.
- Physicians who have a financial interest in the new imaging center will increase their referrals to the center.
- There will be no other MRIs in the market area before 1987.
- The new imaging center will offer services at lower prices than the competition.

- An effective marketing effort will take place, especially concentrating on large employers, insurance groups, and unions.
- The MRI will replace approximately 60% of the head scans that are presently done with the CT scanner during the first six months of operation, and 70% during the next 12 months.
- The general public will continue to pressure the health care industry to hold down costs.
- Costs of outlays in the health care industry rose 13.2% annually from 1971 to 1981. The Health Care Financing Administration estimates that the average annual rate of increase will be reduced to approximately 11% to 12% between 1981 and 1990 (*Industry Surveys*, April 1984).
- Insurance firms will reimburse patients for (at worst) 0% up to 100% of the cost of magnetic resonance imaging (*Imaging News*, February 1984).

Models
A forecast was developed for each procedure based on past experience, industry rates, and reasonable assumptions. Because the models were developed based on the preceding assumptions, if the assumptions are not valid, the models will not be accurate.

ANALYSIS OF PAST DATA
Office X-Rays
The number of X-ray procedures performed was analyzed from July 1981 to May 1984. The data included diagnostic X-rays, gastrointestinal X-rays, breast imaging, injections, and special procedures. Examination of these data indicates that no trend or seasonal or cyclical pattern was present. For this reason simple exponential smoothing was chosen as the appropriate forecasting method. Various smoothing constants were examined, and a smoothing constant of .3 was found to provide the best model. The results are presented in Figure 4-14. The forecast for June 1984 is 855 X-ray procedures.

Office Ultrasound
The number of ultrasound procedures performed was analyzed from July 1981 to May 1984. Figure 4-15 shows the data pattern. Again, no trend or seasonal or cyclical pattern was present. Exponential smoothing with a smoothing constant of $\alpha = .5$ was determined to provide the best model. The forecast for June 1984 is 127 ultrasound procedures.

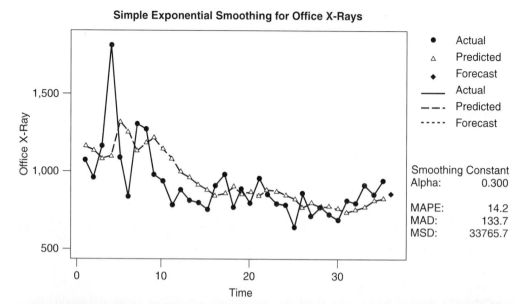

FIGURE 4-14   Simple Exponential Smoothing: Downtown Radiology X-Rays

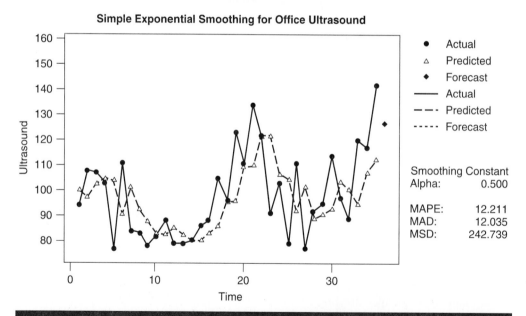

FIGURE 4-15   Simple Exponential Smoothing: Downtown Radiology Ultrasound

The number of ultrasound procedures performed by the two mobile units owned by Downtown Radiology was analyzed from July 1981 to May 1984. Figure 4-16 shows the data pattern. An increasing trend is apparent and can be modeled using Holt's two-parameter linear exponential smoothing. Smoothing constants of $\alpha = .5$ and $\beta = .1$ are used, and the forecast for June 1984 is 227.

Nuclear Medicine Procedures

The number of nuclear medicine procedures performed by the two mobile units owned by Downtown Radiology was analyzed from August 1982 to May 1984. Figure 4-17 shows the data pattern. The data were not seasonal and had no trend or cyclical pattern. For this reason simple exponential smoothing was chosen as the appropriate forecasting

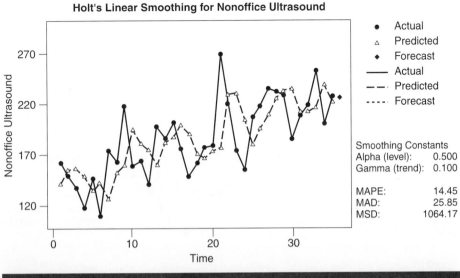

FIGURE 4-16   **Holt's Linear Exponential Smoothing: Downtown Radiology Ultrasound**

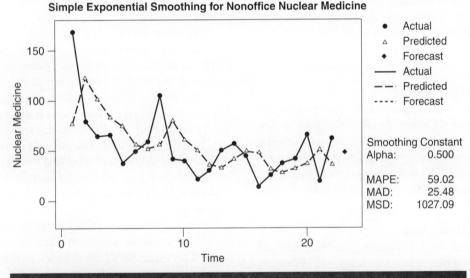

FIGURE 4-17   **Simple Exponential Smoothing: Downtown Radiology Nuclear Medicine**

method. A smoothing factor of $\alpha = .5$ was found to provide the best model. The forecast for June 1984 is 48 nuclear medicine procedures.

Office CT Scans

The number of CT scans performed was also analyzed from July 1981 to May 1984. Seasonality was not found, and the number of CT scans did not seem to have a trend. However, a cyclical pattern seemed to be present. Knowledge of how many scans were performed last month would be important in the forecast of what is going to happen this month. An autoregressive model (see Chapters 8 and 9) was examined and compared to an exponential smoothing model with a smoothing constant of $\alpha = .461$. The larger smoothing constant gives the most recent observation more weight in the forecast.

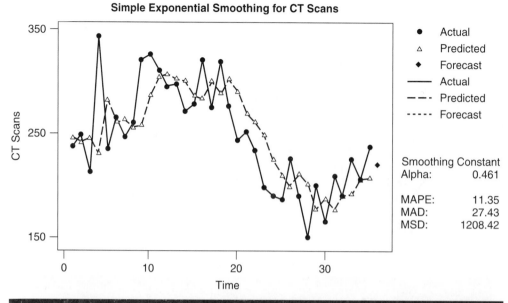

FIGURE 4-18   Simple Exponential Smoothing: Downtown Radiology CT Scans

The exponential smoothing model was determined to be better than the autoregressive model, and Figure 4-18 shows the projection of the number of CT scans for June 1984 to be 221.

MARKET AREA ANALYSIS

Market areas were determined for procedures currently done by Downtown Radiology by examining patient records and doctor referral patterns. Market areas were determined for procedures *not* currently done by Downtown by investigating the competition and analyzing the geographical areas they served.

CT Scanner Market Area

The market area for CT scanning for the proposed medical imaging center includes Spokane, Whitman, Adams, Lincoln, Stevens, and Pend Oreille counties in Washington and Bonner, Boundary, Kootenai, Benewah, and Shoshone counties in Idaho. Based on the appropriate percentage projections, the CT scanning market area will have a population of 630,655 in 1985 and 696,018 in 1990.

Quantitative Estimates

To project revenue, it is necessary to determine certain quantitative estimates. The most important estimate involves the number of doctors who will participate in the limited partnership. The estimate used in computations for the future is that at least 8% of the doctor population of Spokane County will participate.

The next uncertainty that must be quantified involves the determination of how the referral pattern will be affected by the participation of 50 doctors in the limited partnership. It is assumed that 30 of the doctors who presently refer to Downtown will join the limited partnership. Of the 30 who join, it is assumed that 10 will not increase their referrals and the other 20 will double their referrals. It is also assumed that 20 doctors who had never referred to Downtown will join the limited partnership and will begin to refer at least half of their work to Downtown Radiology.

The quantification of additional doctor referrals should be clarified with some qualitative observations. The estimate of 50 doctors joining the proposed limited partnership is conservative. There is a strong possibility that doctors from areas outside of Spokane County may join. Traditionally, the doctor referral pattern changes very slowly. However, the sudden competitive nature of the marketplace will probably have an impact on doctor referrals. If the limited partnership is marketed to doctors in specialties with high radiology referral potential, the number of referrals should increase more than projected. The variability in the number of doctor referrals per procedure is extremely large. A few doctors referred an extremely large percentage of the procedures done by Downtown Radiology. If a few new many-referral doctors are recruited, they can have a major effect on the total number of procedures done for any individual service provided by Downtown.

Finally, the effect that a new imaging center will have on Downtown Radiology's market share must be estimated. The new imaging center will have the best equipment and will be prepared to do the total spectrum of procedures at a lower cost. The number of new doctors referring should increase on the basis of word of mouth from the new investing doctors. If insurance companies, large employers, and/or unions enter into agreements with the new imaging center, Downtown should be able to increase its share of the market by at least 4% in 1985, 2% in 1986, and 1% in 1987 and retain this market share in 1988 and 1989. This market share increase will be referred to as the *total imaging effect* in the rest of this revenue projection report.

Revenue Projections

Revenue projections were completed for every procedure. Only the projections for the CT scanner are shown in this case.

CT Scan Projections

Based on the exponential smoothing model and what has already taken place in the first five months of 1984, the forecast of CT scans for 1984 (January 1984 to January 1985) is 2,600.

The National Center for Health Statistics reports a rate of 261 CT scans per 100,000 population per month. Using the population of 630,655 projected for the CT scan market area, the market should be 19,752 procedures for all of 1985. The actual number of CT scans performed in the market area during 1983 was estimated to be 21,600. This estimate was based on actual known procedures for Downtown Radiology (2,260), Sacred Heart (4,970), Deaconess (3,850), Valley (2,300), and Kootenai (1,820) and estimates for Radiation Therapy (2,400) and Northwest Imaging (4,000). If the estimates are accurate, Downtown Radiology had a market share of approximately 10.5% in 1983. The actual values were also analyzed for 1982, and Downtown was projected to have approximately 15.5% of the CT scan market during that year. Therefore, Downtown Radiology is forecast to average about 13% of the market.

Based on the increased referrals from doctors belonging to the limited partnership and an analysis of the average number of referrals of CT scans, an increase of 320 CT scans is projected for 1985 from this source. If actual values for 1983 are used, the rate for the Inland Empire CT scan market area is 3,568 (21,600/6.054) per 100,000 population. If this pattern continues, the number of CT scans in the market area will increase to 22,514 (3,568 × 6.31) in 1985. Therefore, Downtown Radiology's market share is projected to be 13% (2,920/22,514). When the 4% increase in market share based on total imaging is added, Downtown Radiology's market share increases to 17.0%, and its projected number of CT scans is 3,827 (22,514 × .17).

However, research seems to indicate that MRIs will eventually replace a large number of CT head scans (*Applied Radiology,* May/June 1983, and *Diagnostic Imaging,* February 1984). The National Center for Health Statistics indicated that 60% of all CT scans were of the head. Downtown Radiology records showed that 59% of its CT scans in 1982 were head scans, and 54% in 1983. If 60% of Downtown's CT scans are of the head and the MRI approach replaces approximately 60% of them, new projections for CT scans in 1985 are necessary. Since the MRI will operate for only half the year, a reduction of 689 (3,827/2 × .60 × .60) CT scans is forecast.

The projected number of CT scans for 1985 is 3,138. The average cost of a CT scan is $360, and the projected revenue from CT scans is $1,129,680. Table 4-11 shows the projected revenue from CT scans for the next five years. The cost of procedures is estimated to increase approximately 11% per year.

Without the effect of the MRI, the projection for CT scans in 1986 is estimated to be 4,363 (6.31 × 1.02 × 3,568 × .19). However, if 60% are CT head scans and the MRI replaces 70% of the head scans, the projected number of CT scans should drop to 2,531 [4, 363 − (4,363 × .60 × .70)].

The projection of CT scans without the MRI effect for 1987 is 4,683 (6.31 × 1.04 × 3,568 × .20). The forecast with the MRI effect is 2,716 [4, 683 − (4,683 × .60 × .70)].

TABLE 4-11	Five-Year Projected Revenue for CT Scans	
Year	*Procedures*	*Revenue*
1985	3,138	$1,129,680
1986	2,531	1,012,400
1987	2,716	1,205,904
1988	2,482	1,223,626
1989	2,529	1,383,363

The projection of CT scans without the MRI effect for 1988 is 4,773 (6.31 × 1.06 × 3,568 × .20). The forecast with the MRI effect is 2,482 [4,773 − (4,773 × .60 × .80)].

The projection of CT scans without the MRI effect for 1989 is 4,863 (6.31 × 1.08 × 3,568 × .20). The forecast with the MRI effect is 2,529 [4,863 − (4,863 × .60 × .80)]. ■

QUESTION

1. Downtown Radiology's accountant projected that revenue would be considerably higher. Since ownership interest will be made available in some type of public offering, Downtown Radiology's management must make a decision concerning the accuracy of Professional Marketing Associates' projections. You are asked to analyze the report. What recommendations would you make?

Minitab Applications

The problem. In Example 4.3 the Spokane Transit Authority data need to be forecast using a five-week moving average.

Minitab Solution

1. Enter the Spokane Transit Authority data shown in Table 4-2 (see p. 106) into column C1 or open the Tab4-2 worksheet. Click on the following menus:

   ```
   Stat>Time Series>Moving Average
   ```

2. The Moving Average dialog box appears.
   a. Double-click on the variable Gallons and it will appear to the right of Variable.
   b. Since we want a five-month moving average, indicate 5 for MA length.
   c. Do not click the Center moving average box. We will use a centered moving average to smooth data in Chapter 5.
   d. Click Generate forecasts and indicate 1 to the right of Number of forecasts.
   e. Click OK and Figure 4-4 will appear.

The problem. In Example 4.6 the Acme Tool Company data need to be forecast using single exponential smoothing.

Minitab Solution

1. Enter the Acme Tool Company data shown in Table 4-1 (see p. 103) for the years 1996 through 2001 into column C1. Click on the following menus:

   ```
   Stat>Time Series>Single Exponential Smoothing
   ```

2. The Simple Exponential Smoothing dialog box appears.
   a. Double-click on the variable Saws and it will appear to the right of Variable.
   b. Under Weight to Use in Smoothing choose Optimal ARIMA, then click OK. The result is shown in Figure 4-8 (see p. 119).

The problem. In Example 4.10 the Acme Tool Company data need to be forecast using exponential smoothing adjusted for trend and seasonality.

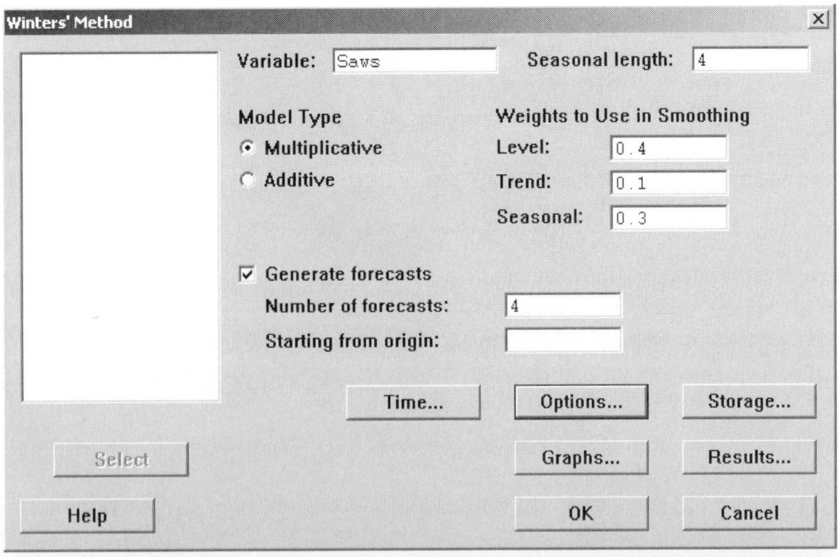

Winters' Method ☒

| Variable: | Saws | Seasonal length: | 4 |

Model Type
⦿ Multiplicative
○ Additive

Weights to Use in Smoothing
Level: [0.4]
Trend: [0.1]
Seasonal: [0.3]

☑ Generate forecasts
Number of forecasts: [4]
Starting from origin: [ ]

Time...   Options...   Storage...

Select   Graphs...   Results...

Help   OK   Cancel

FIGURE 4-19   Minitab Winters' Method Dialog Box

Minitab Solution

1. Enter the Acme Tool Company data shown in Table 4-1 (see p. 103) for the years 1996 through 2001 in column C1. Click on the following menus:

   ```
   Stat>Time Series>Winters' Method
   ```

2. The Winters' Method dialog box appears as shown in Figure 4-19.

   a. The variable of interest is Saws.
   b. Because the data are quarterly, indicate 4 for Seasonal length.
   c. The Weights to Use in Smoothing are Level: 0.4; Trend: 0.1; and Seasonal, 0.3.
   d. Click Generate forecasts, and for Number of forecasts, indicate 4.
   e. Click Storage.

3. The Winters' Method Storage dialog box appears.

   a. Click Level estimates, Trend estimates, Seasonal estimates, Fits (one-period-ahead forecasts), and Residuals.
   b. Click OK on both the Winters' Method Storage dialog box and the Winters' Method dialog box. The results are shown in Table 4-9 and Figure 4-12. The forecast for the first quarter of 2002 is 778.2.

4. To store the data for further use click on the following menus:

   ```
   File>Save Worksheet As
   ```

5. The Save Worksheet As dialog box appears.

   a. Type a name in the File Name space such as Saws.
   b. The Save as Type space allows you to choose how you want to save your file. Most of the time you will select Minitab. However, you can save your file so several software programs can use it. As an example, you could choose to save

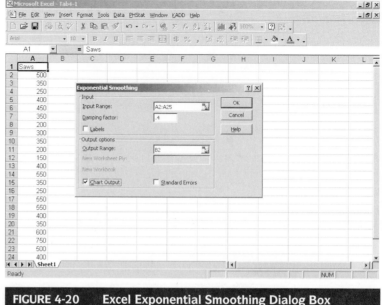

FIGURE 4-20   Excel Exponential Smoothing Dialog Box

the file as an Excel file. The file is saved as Saws.xls and will be used in the following "Excel Applications" section.

Excel Applications

The problem. In Example 4.5 the Acme Tool Company data were forecast using single exponential smoothing with a smoothing constant equal to .6.

Excel Solution

1. Open the file containing the data presented in Table 4-1 (see p. 103) by clicking on the following menus:

    `File>Open`

    Look for the file called Saws.xls.
2. Click on the following menus:

    `Tools>Data Analysis`

    The Data Analysis dialog box appears. Under Analysis Tools choose Exponential Smoothing and click OK. The Exponential Smoothing dialog box shown in Figure 4-20 appears.
3. a. Enter A2:A25 in the Input Range edit box.
    b. Enter .4 in the Damping factor edit box since the Damping factor $(1 - \alpha)$ is defined as the complement of the smoothing constant.
    c. Select the Labels check box.
    d. Enter B2 in the Output Range edit box.
    e. Check the Chart Output box.
    f. Now click OK.
4. The results (column B) and the graph are shown in Figure 4-21. Note that the Exponential Smoothing analysis tool puts formulas in the worksheet. Cell B4 is highlighted and the formula $= 0.6 * A3 + 0.4 * B3$ is shown on the formula toolbar.

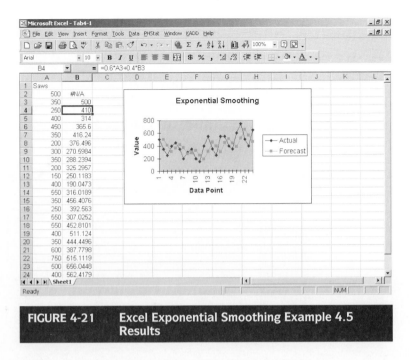

FIGURE 4-21   Excel Exponential Smoothing Example 4.5 Results

Excel Applications: CB Predictor

The problem. In Example 4.10 the Acme Tool Company data need to be forecast using exponential smoothing adjusted for trend and seasonality.

CB Predictor Solution

1. Open the Excel Add-In Crystal Ball.
2. Open the file containing the data given in Table 4-1 by clicking on the menus:

   `File>Open` (look for the Saws.xls file)

3. Click on the following menus and the dialog box shown in Figure 4-22 will appear:

   `CBTools > CB Predictor`

4. a. In **Step 1**, enter A1:A25 in the Range edit box.
   b. In **Step 2**, select the First row has headers check box.
   c. In **Step 3** (Optional), click on View Data for a time series plot of saw sales.
   d. Select Next (or the Data Attributes tab) and the dialog box shown in Figure 4-23 appears.
5. a. In **Step 4**, enter quarters in Data is in edit box. Click seasonality of and enter 4 in the edit box.
   b. Omit **Step 5**.
   c. Select Next (or the Method Gallery tab) and the dialog box shown in Figure 4-24 appears.
6. a. In **Step 6**, click on Holt-Winters' Multiplicative.
   b. Put cursor over words "Holt-Winters' Multiplicative" and double-click. The window shown in Figure 4-25 (see p. 153) appears.
   c. Select User defined and enter .4 in Alpha box, .1 in Beta box, and .3 in Gamma box. Click OK.

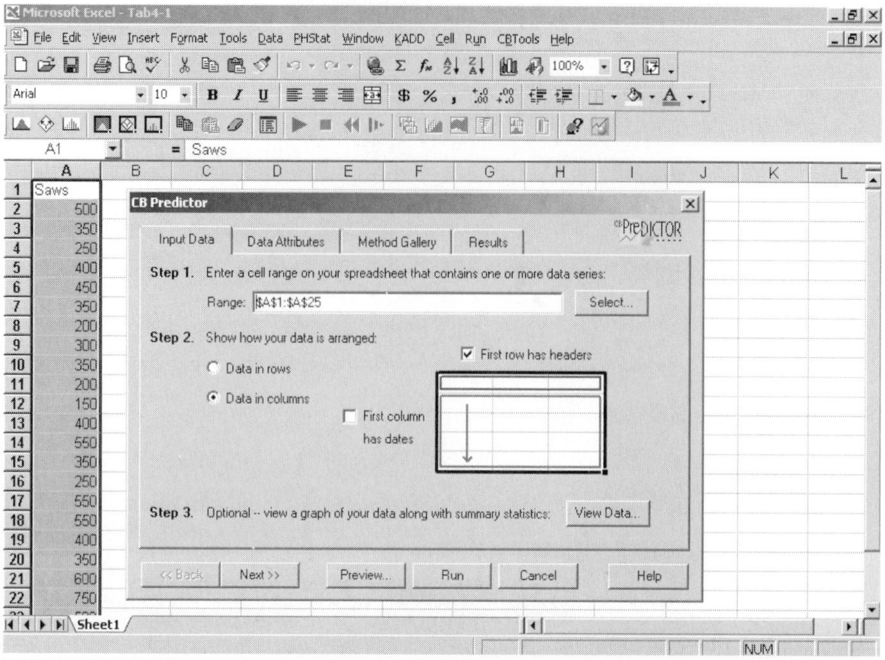

FIGURE 4-22 **CB Predictor Input Data Dialog Box: Acme Tool Company Data**

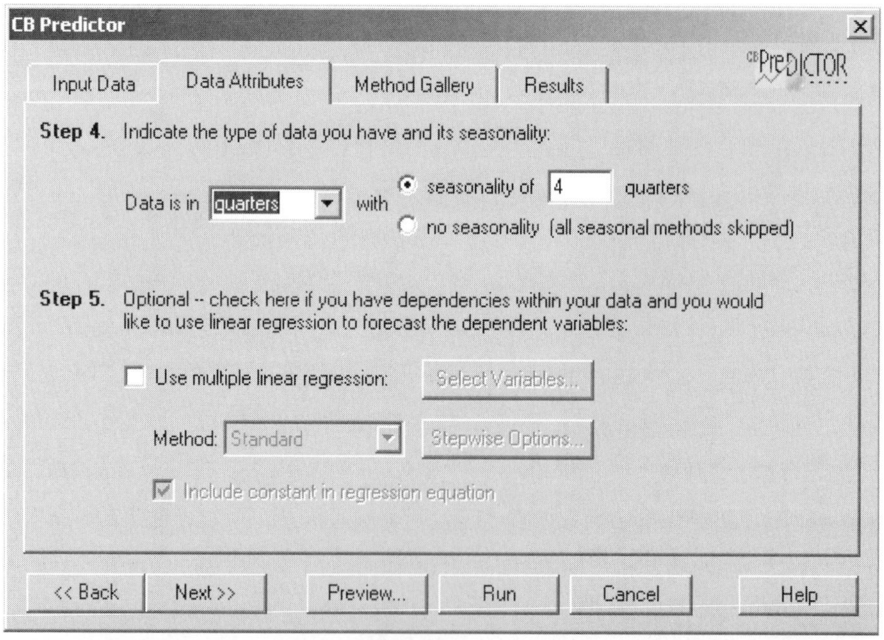

FIGURE 4-23 **CB Predictor Data Attributes Dialog Box: Acme Tool Company Data**

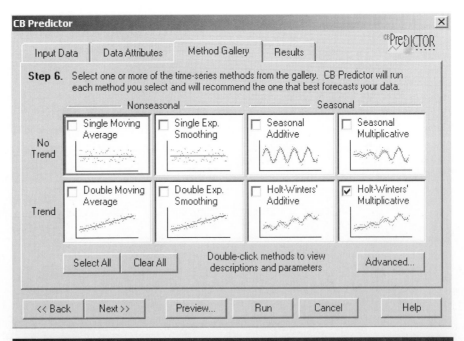

FIGURE 4-24 **CB Predictor Method Gallery Dialog Box: Acme Tool Company Data**

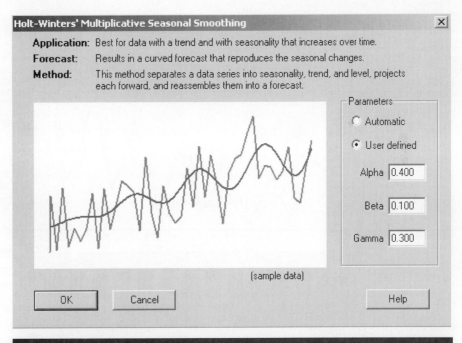

FIGURE 4-25 **CB Predictor Holt-Winters' Multiplicative Smoothing Window**

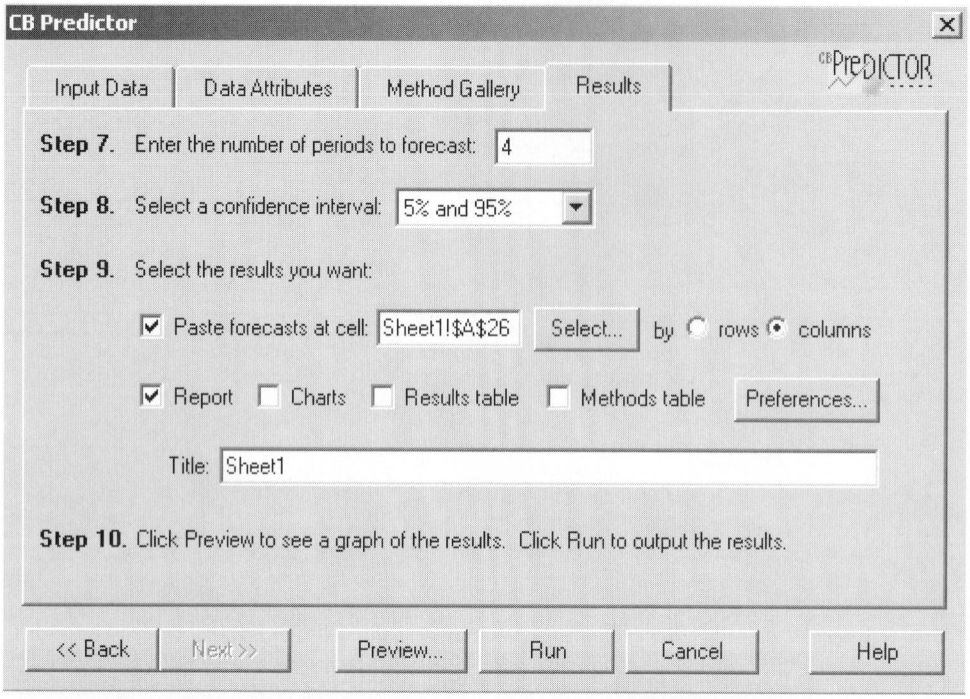

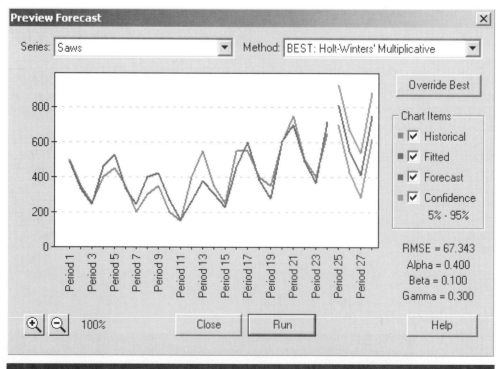

FIGURE 4-26   CB Predictor Results Dialog Box: Acme Tool Company Data

FIGURE 4-27   CB Predictor Preview Forecast Screen

    d.   Select Next (or the Results tab) and the dialog box shown in Figure 4-26 (see p. 154) appears.

7.   a.   In **Step 7**, enter 4 in the Enter the number of periods to forecast edit box.

    b.   In **Step 8**, use the default 5% and 95% values in the Select a confidence interval edit box.

    c.   In **Step 9**, check Paste forecasts at cell and use the default or enter, say, A26 to append forecasts to data values. Select columns. Check Report for comprehensive summary of results including data and forecast plot. If desired, type a heading in the Title edit box.

    d.   In **Step 10** (Optional), click Preview to see an initial graph of data, smoothed values, and forecasts. See Figure 4-27. (Note: $RMSE = \sqrt{MSE}$.)

    e.   Click Run and model results will appear on separate Report sheet. Forecasts for the next 4 quarters will appear in cells A26 to A29 on data sheet.

References

Aaker, D. A., and R. Jacobson. "The Sophistication of 'Naive' Modeling." *International Journal of Forecasting* 3, No. 314 (1987):449–452.

Dalrymple, D. J., and B. E. King. "Selecting Parameters for Short-Term Forecasting Techniques." *Decision Sciences* 12 (1981):661–669.

Gardner, E. S. Jr., and D. G. Dannenbring. "Forecasting with Exponential Smoothing: Some Guidelines for Model Selection." *Decision Sciences* 11 (1980):370–383.

Holt, C. C. "Forecasting Seasonal and Trends by Exponentially Weighted Moving Averages." Office of Naval Research, Memorandum No. 52 (1957).

Holt, C. C., F. Modigliani, J. F. Muth, and H. A. Simon. *Planning Production Inventories and Work Force.* Upper Saddle River, NJ: Prentice Hall, 1960.

Ledolter, J., and B. Abraham. "Some Comments on the Initialization of Exponential Smoothing." *Journal of Forecasting* 3, No. 1 (1984):79–84.

Makridakis, S., S. C. Wheelwright, and R. Hyndman. *Forecasting Methods and Applications.* New York: John Wiley & Sons, 1998.

McKenzie, E. "An Analysis of General Exponential Smoothing." *Operations Research* 24 (1976):131–140.

Newbold, P., and T. Bos. *Introductory Business and Economic Forecasting*, Second Edition. Cincinnati, OH: South-Western, 1994.

Winters, P. R. "Forecasting Sales by Exponentially Weighted Moving Averages." *Management Science* 6 (1960):324–342.

CHAPTER

5

TIME SERIES AND THEIR COMPONENTS

As we have pointed out in earlier chapters, observations of a variable Y that become available over time are called *time series data*, or, more simply, a *time series*. These observations are often recorded at fixed time intervals. So, for example, Y might represent sales, and the associated time series could be a sequence of annual sales figures. Other examples of time series include quarterly earnings, monthly inventory levels, and weekly exchange rates. In general, time series do not behave like a random sample and require special methods for their analysis. Observations of a time series are typically related to one another (autocorrelated). This dependence produces patterns of variability that can be used to forecast future values and assist in the management of business operations. Consider these situations.

American Airlines (AA) compares current reservations with forecasts based on projections of historical patterns. Depending on whether current reservations are lagging behind or exceeding the projections, AA adjusts the proportion of discounted seats accordingly. The adjustments are made for each flight segment in the AA system.

A Canadian importer of cut flowers buys from growers in the United States, Mexico, Central America, and South America. However, because these sources purchase their growing stock and chemicals from the United States, all the selling prices are quoted in U.S. dollars at the time of the sale. An invoice is not paid immediately, and because the Canadian–U.S. exchange rate fluctuates, the cost to the importer in Canadian dollars is not known at the time of purchase. If the exchange rate does not change before the invoice is paid, there is no monetary risk to the importer. If the index rises, the importer loses money for each U.S. dollar of purchase. If the index drops, the importer gains. The importer uses forecasts of the weekly Canadian dollar to U.S. dollar exchange rate to manage the inventory of cut flowers.

Although time series are often generated internally and are unique to the organization, many time series of interest in business can be obtained from external sources. Publications such as *Statistical Abstract of the United States, Survey of Current Business, Monthly Labor Review,* and *Federal Reserve Bulletin* contain time series of all types. These and other publications provide time series data on prices, production, sales, employment, unemployment, hours worked, fuel used, energy produced, earnings, and so forth, reported on a monthly, quarterly, or annual basis. Today, extensive collections of time series are available on World Wide Web sites maintained by U.S. government agencies, statistical organizations, universities, and individuals.

It is important that managers understand the past and use historical data and sound judgment to make intelligent plans to meet the demands of the future. Properly constructed time series forecasts help eliminate some of the uncertainty associated with the future and can assist management in determining alternative strategies.

The alternative, of course, is not to plan ahead. In a dynamic business environment, however, this lack of planning might be disastrous. A mainframe computer manufacturer that some years ago ignored the trend to personal computers and workstations would have lost a large part of its market share rather quickly.

Although we will focus our attention on a model-based approach to time series analysis that relies primarily on the data, a subjective review of the forecasting effort is very important. Whenever the past is examined to obtain clues about the future, it is relevant only to the extent that causal conditions previously in effect continue to hold in the period ahead. In economic and business activity, causal conditions seldom remain constant. The multitude of causal factors at work tends to be constantly shifting, so the connection between the past, the present, and the future must be continually reevaluated.

The techniques of time series provide a conceptual approach to forecasting that has proved to be very useful. Forecasts are made with the aid of a set of specific, formal procedures, and the judgments that follow are indicated explicitly.

DECOMPOSITION

One approach to the analysis of time series data involves an attempt to identify the component factors that influence each of the values in a series. This identification procedure is called *decomposition*. Each component is identified separately. Projections of each of the components can then be combined to produce forecasts of future values of the time series. Decomposition methods are used for both short-run and long-run forecasting. They are also used to simply display the underlying growth or decline of a series, or to adjust the series by eliminating one or more of the components.

Analyzing a time series by decomposing it into its component parts has a long history. Recently, however, decomposition methods of forecasting have lost some of their luster. Projecting the individual components into the future and recombining these projections to form a forecast of the underlying series often does not work very well in practice. The difficulty lies in getting accurate forecasts of the components. The development of more flexible, model-based forecasting procedures (some of which we discuss in later chapters) has made decomposition primarily a tool for understanding a time series rather than a forecasting method in its own right.

To understand decomposition, we start with the four components of a time series that were introduced in Chapter 3. These are the trend component, the cyclical component, the seasonal component, and the irregular or random component.

1. *Trend.* The trend is the component that represents the underlying growth (or decline) in a time series. The trend may be produced, for example, by consistent population change, inflation, technological change, and productivity increases. The trend is denoted by T.
2. *Cyclical.* The cyclical component is a series of wavelike fluctuations or cycles of more than one year's duration. Changing economic conditions generally produce cycles. C denotes the cyclical component.

    In practice, cycles are often difficult to identify and are frequently regarded as part of the trend. In this case, the underlying general growth (or decline) component is called the *trend-cycle* and denoted by T. We use the notation for the trend because the cyclical component often cannot be separated from the trend.
3. *Seasonal.* Seasonal fluctuations are typically found in quarterly, monthly, or weekly data. Seasonal variation refers to a more or less stable pattern of

change that appears annually and repeats itself year after year. Seasonal patterns occur because of the influence of the weather, or because of calendar-related events such as school vacations and national holidays. S denotes the seasonal component.

4. *Irregular.* The irregular component consists of unpredictable or random fluctuations. These fluctuations are the result of a myriad of events that individually may not be particularly important but whose combined effect could be large. I denotes the irregular component.

To study the components of a time series, the analyst must consider how the components relate to the original series. This task is accomplished by specifying a *model* (mathematical relationship) that expresses the time-series variable Y in terms of the components T, C, S, and I. A model that treats the time-series values as a sum of the components is called an *additive components model*. A model that treats the time-series values as the product of the components is called a *multiplicative components model*. Both models are sometimes referred to as *unobserved components models* because, in practice, although we observe the values of the time series, the values of the components are not observed. The approach to time-series analysis described in this chapter involves an attempt, given the observed series, to estimate the values of the components. These estimates can then be used for forecasting or to display the series unencumbered by seasonal fluctuations. The latter process is called *seasonal adjustment*.

It is difficult to deal with the cyclical component of a time series. To the extent that cycles can be determined from historical data, both their lengths (measured in years) and magnitudes (differences between highs and lows) are far from constant. This lack of a consistent wavelike pattern makes distinguishing cycles from smoothly evolving trends difficult. Consequently, to keep things relatively simple we will assume any cycle in the data is part of the trend. Initially, then, we only consider the three components, T, S, and I. A brief discussion of one way to handle cyclical fluctuations in the decomposition approach to time series analysis is available in the "Cyclical and Irregular Variations" section of this chapter (see p. 172).

The two simplest models relating the observed value (Y_t) of a time series to the trend (T_t), seasonal (S_t), and irregular (I_t) components are the additive components model

$$Y_t = T_t + S_t + I_t \tag{5.1}$$

and the multiplicative components model

$$Y_t = T_t \times S_t \times I_t \tag{5.2}$$

The additive components model works best when the time series being analyzed has roughly the same variability throughout the length of the series. That is, all the values of the series fall essentially within a band of constant width centered on the trend.

The multiplicative components model works best when the variability of the time series increases with the level.[1] That is, the values of the series spread out as the trend increases, and the set of observations have the appearance of a megaphone, or funnel. A time series with constant variability and a time series with variability increasing with

---

[1] It is possible to convert a multiplicative decomposition to an additive decomposition by working with the logarithms of the data. Using Equation 5.2 and the properties of logarithms we have $\log Y = \log(T \times S \times I) = \log T + \log S + \log I$. Decomposition of logged data is explored in Problem 5.15.

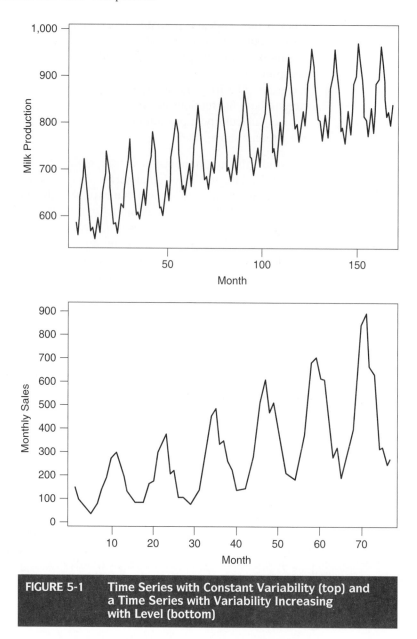

FIGURE 5-1   Time Series with Constant Variability (top) and a Time Series with Variability Increasing with Level (bottom)

level are shown in Figure 5-1. Both of these monthly series have an increasing trend and a clearly defined seasonal pattern.[2]

TREND

Trends are long-term movements in a time series that can sometimes be described by a straight line or a smooth curve. Examples of the basic forces producing or

---

[2] Variants of the decomposition models (see Equations 5.1 and 5.2) exist that contain both multiplicative and additive terms. For example, some software packages do "multiplicative" decomposition using the model $Y = T \times S + I$.

affecting the trend of a series are population change, price change, technological change, productivity increases, and product life cycles.

A population increase may cause retail sales of a community to rise each year for several years. Moreover, the sales in current dollars may have been pushed upward during the same period because of general increases in the prices of retail goods—even though the physical volume of goods sold did not change.

Technological change may cause a time series to move upward or downward. The development of high-speed computer chips, enhanced memory devices, and improved display panels, accompanied by improvements in telecommunications technology, has resulted in dramatic increases in the use of personal computers and cellular telephones. Of course, the same technological developments have led to a downward trend in the production of mechanical calculators and rotary telephones.

Productivity increases—which, in turn, may be due to technological change—give an upward slope to many time series. Any measure of total output, such as manufacturers' sales, is affected by changes in productivity.

For business and economic time series, it is best to view the trend (or trend-cycle) as smoothly changing over time. Rarely can we realistically assume that the trend can be represented by some simple function such as a straight line over the whole period for which the time series is observed. However, it is often convenient to fit a trend curve to a time series for two reasons: (1) It provides some indication of the general direction of the observed series, and (2) it can be removed from the original series to get a clearer picture of the seasonality.

If the trend appears to be roughly linear, that is, if it increases or decreases like a straight line, then it is represented by the equation

$$\hat{T}_t = b_0 + b_1 t \qquad (5.3)$$

Here $\hat{T}_t$ is the predicted value for the trend at time t. The symbol t used for the independent variable represents time and ordinarily assumes integer values $1, 2, 3, \ldots$ corresponding to consecutive time periods. The slope coefficient b_1 is the average increase or decrease in T for each one-period increase in time.

Time trend equations, including the straight-line trend, can be fit to the data using the *method of least squares*. Recall that this method selects the values of the coefficients in the trend equation (b_0 and b_1 in the straight-line case) so that the estimated trend values $\hat{T}_t$ are close to the actual values Y_t as measured by the sum of squared errors criterion

$$SSE = \Sigma(Y_t - \hat{T}_t)^2 \qquad (5.4)$$

Example 5.1
Data on annual registrations of new passenger cars in the United States from 1960 to 1992 are shown in Table 5-1 and plotted in Figure 5-2. The values from 1960 to 1992 are used to develop the trend equation. Registrations is the dependent variable, and the independent variable is time t coded as $1960 = 1$, $1961 = 2$, and so on.

The fitted trend line has the equation

$$\hat{T}_t = 7.988 + .0687t$$

The slope of the trend equation indicates that registrations are estimated to increase an average of 68,700 each year. Figure 5-3 shows the straight-line trend fitted to the actual data. Figure 5-3 also shows forecasts of new car registrations for the years 1993 and 1994 ($t = 34$ and $t = 35$) obtained by extrapolating the trend line. We will say more about forecasting a trend shortly.

TABLE 5-1	Registration of New Passenger Cars in the United States, 1960–1992, for Example 5.1			
Year	Registrations (millions) Y	Time t	Trend Estimates (millions) $\hat{T}$	Error (millions) $Y - \hat{T}$
1960	6.577	1	8.0568	−1.4798
1961	5.855	2	8.1255	−2.2705
1962	6.939	3	8.1942	−1.2552
1963	7.557	4	8.2629	−0.7059
1964	8.065	5	8.3316	−0.2666
1965	9.314	6	8.4003	0.9138
1966	9.009	7	8.4690	0.5401
1967	8.357	8	8.5376	−0.1807
1968	9.404	9	8.6063	0.7977
1969	9.447	10	8.6750	0.7720
1970	8.388	11	8.7437	−0.3557
1971	9.831	12	8.8124	1.0186
1972	10.409	13	8.8811	1.5279
1973	11.351	14	8.9498	2.4012
1974	8.701	15	9.0185	−0.3175
1975	8.168	16	9.0872	−0.9192
1976	9.752	17	9.1559	0.5961
1977	10.826	18	9.2246	1.6014
1978	10.946	19	9.2933	1.6527
1979	10.357	20	9.3620	0.9950
1980	8.761	21	9.4307	−0.6697
1981	8.444	22	9.4994	−1.0554
1982	7.754	23	9.5681	−1.8141
1983	8.924	24	9.6368	−0.7128
1984	10.118	25	9.7055	0.4125
1985	10.889	26	9.7742	1.1148
1986	11.140	27	9.8429	1.2971
1987	10.183	28	9.9116	0.2714
1988	10.398	29	9.9803	0.4177
1989	9.833	30	10.0490	−0.2160
1990	9.160	31	10.1177	−0.9577
1991	9.234	32	10.1863	−0.9524
1992	8.054	33	10.2550	−2.2010

Source: Data from U.S. Department of Commerce, *Survey of Current Business* (various years).

The estimated trend values for passenger car registrations from 1960 to 1992 are shown in Table 5-1 under $\hat{T}$. For example, the trend equation estimates registrations in 1992 ($t = 33$) to be

$$\hat{T}_{33} = 7.988 + .0687(33) = 10.225$$

or 10,255,000 registrations. Registrations of new passenger cars were actually 8,054,000 in 1992. For 1992, the trend equation overestimates registrations by approximately 2.2 million. This error and the remaining estimation errors are listed in Table 5-1 under $Y - \hat{T}$. The estimation errors were used to compute the measures of fit, *MAD*, *MSD*, and *MAPE* shown in Figure 5-3. These are the same measures of forecast accuracy that are given

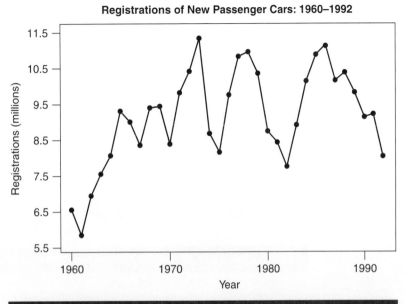

FIGURE 5-2   Car Registrations Time Series for Example 5.1

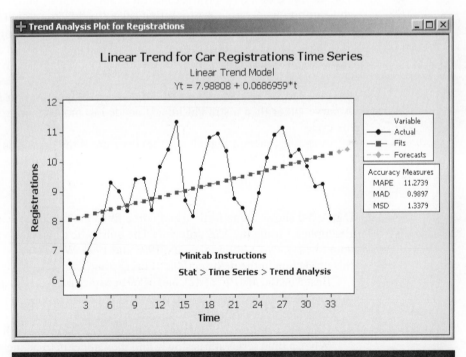

FIGURE 5-3   Trend Line for the Car Registrations Time Series of Example 5.1

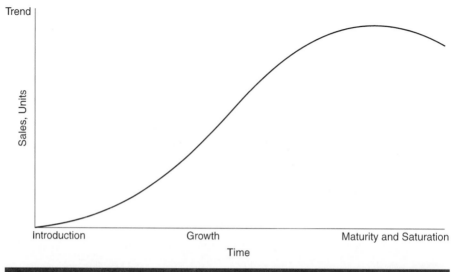

FIGURE 5-4   Life Cycle of a Typical New Product

by equations (3.7), (3.8), and (3.9), respectively, in Chapter 3. (Minitab commands used to produce the results in Example 5.1 are given at the end of this chapter.)

Additional Trend Curves

The life cycle of a new product has three stages: introduction, growth, and maturity and saturation. A curve representing sales (in dollars or units) over a new-product life cycle is shown in Figure 5-4. Time, shown on the horizontal axis, can vary from days to years depending on the nature of the market. A straight-line trend would not work for these data. Linear models assume that a variable is increasing (or decreasing) by a constant amount each time period. The increases per time period in the product life cycle curve are quite different depending on the stage of the cycle. A curve, other than a straight line, is needed to model the trend over a new-product life cycle.

A simple function that allows for curvature is the quadratic trend

$$\hat{T}_t = b_0 + b_1 t + b_2 t^2 \tag{5.5}$$

Figure 5-5 shows a quadratic trend curve fit to the passenger car registrations data of Example 5.1 using the *SSE* criterion. The quadratic trend can be projected beyond the data for, say, two additional years, 1993 and 1994. We will consider the implications of this projection in the next section, "Forecasting Trend."

Based on the *MAPE*, *MAD*, and *MSD* accuracy measures, a quadratic trend appears to be a better representation of the general direction of the car registrations series than the linear trend in Figure 5-3. Which trend model is appropriate? Before considering this issue, we will introduce a few additional trend curves that have proved useful.

When a time series starts slowly and then appears to be increasing at an increasing rate (see Fig. 5-4) such that the percentage difference from observation to observation is constant, an exponential trend can be fitted. The exponential trend is given by

$$\hat{T}_t = b_0 \, b_1^t \tag{5.6}$$

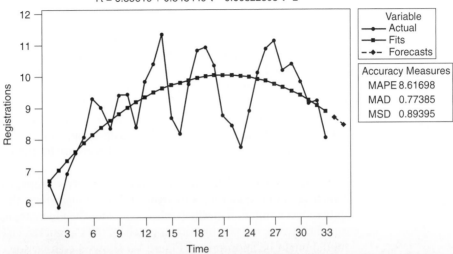

Quadratic Trend for Car Registrations Time Series
Quadratic Trend Model
$Y_t = 6.35619 + 0.348449 \cdot t - 0.00822803 \cdot t^{**}2$

FIGURE 5-5 **Quadratic Trend Curve for the Car Registrations Time Series of Example 5.1**

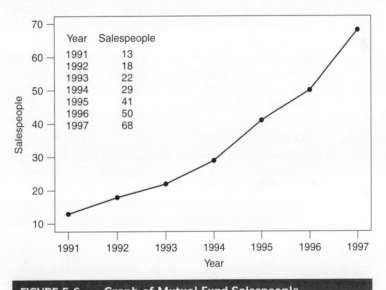

FIGURE 5-6 **Graph of Mutual Fund Salespeople**

The coefficient b_1 is related to the growth rate. If the exponential trend is fit to annual data, the annual growth rate is estimated to be $100(b_1 - 1)\%$.

Figure 5-6 contains the number of mutual fund salespeople for a particular company for several consecutive years. The increase in the number of salespeople is not constant. It appears as if increasingly larger numbers of people are being added in the later years.

An exponential trend curve fit to the salespeople data has the equation

$$\hat{T}_t = 10.016(1.313)^t$$

implying an annual growth rate of about 31%. Consequently, if the model estimates 51 salespeople for 1996, the increase for 1997 would be $16(51 \times .31)$ for an estimated total of 67. This can be compared to the actual value of 68 salespeople.

A linear trend fit to the salespeople data would indicate a constant average increase of about nine salespeople per year. This trend overestimates the actual increase in the earlier years and underestimates the increase in the last year. It does not model the apparent trend in the data as well as the exponential curve.

It is clear that extrapolating an exponential trend with a 31% growth rate will quickly result in some very big numbers. This is a potential problem with an exponential trend model. What happens when the economy cools off and stock prices begin to retreat? The demand for mutual fund salespeople will decrease and the number of salespeople could even decline. The trend forecast by the exponential curve will be much too high.

Growth curves of the Gompertz and logistic types represent the tendency of many industries and product lines to grow at a declining rate as they mature. If the plotted data reflect a situation in which sales begin low, then increase as the product catches on, and finally ease off as saturation is reached, the Gompertz curve or Pearl-Reed logistic model might be appropriate. Figure 5-7 shows a comparison of the general shapes of the Gompertz curve (a) and the Pearl-Reed logistic model (b). Note that the logistic curve is a very similar curve to the Gompertz, with a slightly gentler slope. Figure 5-7 shows how the Y-intercepts and maximum values for these curves are related to some of the coefficients in their functional forms. The formulas for these trend curves are complex and not within the scope of this text. Many statistical software packages, including Minitab, allow one to fit several of the trend models discussed in this section.

Although there are some objective criteria for selecting an appropriate trend, in general the correct choice is a matter of judgment and thus requires experience and common sense on the part of the analyst. As we will discuss in the next section, the line or curve that best fits a set of data points might not make sense when projected as the trend of the future.

Forecasting Trend

Suppose we are presently at time $t = n$ (end of series) and we want to use a trend model to forecast the value of Y, p steps ahead. The time period at which we make the forecast,

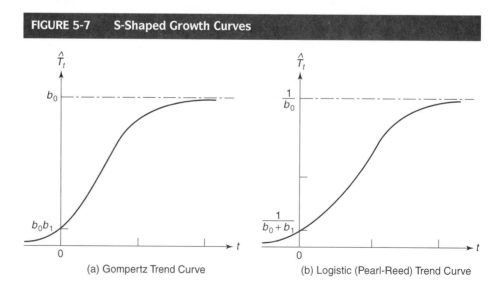

FIGURE 5-7   S-Shaped Growth Curves

(a) Gompertz Trend Curve

(b) Logistic (Pearl-Reed) Trend Curve

n in this case, is called the *forecast origin*. The value p is called the *lead time*. For the linear trend model, we can produce a forecast by evaluating $\hat{T}_{n+p} = b_0 + b_1(n + p)$.

Using the trend line fitted to the car registration data in Example 5.1, a forecast of the trend for 1993 ($t = 34$) made in 1992 ($t = n = 33$) would be the $p = 1$ step ahead forecast

$$\hat{T}_{33+1} = 7.988 + .0687(33 + 1) = 7.988 + .0687(34) = 10.324$$

Similarly, the $p = 2$ step ahead forecast (1994) is given by

$$\hat{T}_{33+2} = 7.988 + .0687(33 + 2) = 7.988 + .0687(35) = 10.393$$

These two forecasts are shown in Figure 5-3 as extrapolations of the fitted trend line.

Figure 5-5 shows the fitted quadratic trend curve for the car registration data. Using the equation shown in the figure, we can calculate forecasts of the trend for 1993 and 1994 by setting $t = 33 + 1 = 34$ and $t = 33 + 2 = 35$. The reader may verify that $\hat{T}_{33+1} = 8.690$ and $\hat{T}_{33+2} = 8.470$. These numbers were plotted in Figure 5-5 as extrapolations of the quadratic trend curve.

Recalling that car registrations are measured in millions, the two forecasts of trend produced from the quadratic curve are quite different from the forecasts produced by the linear trend equation. Moreover, they are headed in the opposite direction. If we were to extrapolate the linear and quadratic trends for additional time periods, their differences would be magnified.

The car registration example illustrates why great care must be exercised in using fitted trend curves for the purpose of forecasting future trends. Two equations, both of which may reasonably represent the observed time series, can give very different results when projected over future time periods. These differences can be substantial for large lead times (long-run forecasting).

Trend curve models are based on the following assumptions:

1. The correct trend curve has been selected.
2. The curve that fits the past is indicative of the future.

These assumptions suggest that judgment and expertise play a substantial role in the selection and use of a trend curve. To use a trend curve for forecasting, we must be able to argue that the correct trend has been selected, and that, in all likelihood, the future will be like the past.

There are objective criteria for selecting a trend curve. We will discuss two of these criteria, the Akaike Information Criterion (AIC) and the Bayesian Information Criterion (BIC), in later chapters. However, although these and other criteria help to determine an appropriate model, they do not replace good judgment.

Seasonality

A seasonal pattern is one that repeats itself year after year. For annual data, seasonality is not an issue because there is no chance to model a within-year pattern with data recorded once per year. However, time series consisting of weekly, monthly, or quarterly observations often exhibit seasonality.

The analysis of the seasonal component of a time series has immediate short-term implications and is of greatest importance to mid- and lower-level management. Marketing plans, for example, have to take into consideration expected seasonal patterns in consumer purchases.

Several methods for measuring seasonal variation have been developed. The basic idea in all of these methods is to first estimate and remove the trend from the original series and then smooth out the irregular component. Keeping in mind our decomposition models, this leaves data containing only seasonal variation. The seasonal values are collected and summarized to produce a number (generally an *index number*) for each observed interval of the year (week, month, quarter, and so on).

Thus the identification of the seasonal component in a time series differs from trend analysis in at least two ways:

1. The trend is determined directly from the original data, but the seasonal component is determined indirectly after eliminating the other components from the data so that only the seasonality remains.
2. The trend is represented by one best-fitting curve, or equation, but a separate seasonal value has to be computed for each observed interval (week, month, quarter) of the year and is often in the form of an index number.

If an additive decomposition is employed, estimates of the trend, seasonal, and irregular components are added together to produce the original series. If a multiplicative decomposition is used, the individual components must be multiplied together to reconstruct the original series, and in this formulation, the seasonal component is represented by a collection of index numbers. These numbers show which periods within the year are relatively low and which periods are relatively high. The seasonal indices trace out the seasonal pattern.

Index numbers are percentages that show changes over time.

With monthly data, for example, a seasonal index of 1.0 for a particular month means the expected value for that month is 1/12 the total for the year. An index of 1.25 for a different month implies the observation for that month is expected to be 25% more than 1/12 of the annual total. A monthly index of 0.80 indicates that the expected level of activity that month is 20% less than 1/12 of the total for the year, and so forth. The index numbers indicate the expected ups and downs in levels of activity over the course of a year after the effects due to the trend (or trend-cycle) and irregular components have been removed.

To highlight seasonality, we must first estimate and remove the trend. The trend can be estimated with one of the trend curves we discussed previously, or it can be estimated using a moving average as discussed in Chapter 4.

Assuming a multiplicative decomposition model, the *ratio to moving average* is a popular method for measuring seasonal variation. In this method the trend is estimated using a centered moving average. We illustrate the ratio-to-moving-average method using the monthly sales of the Cavanaugh Company shown in Figure 5-1 in the next example.

Example 5.2

To illustrate the ratio-to-moving-average method, we use two years of the monthly sales of the Cavanaugh Company.[3] Table 5-2 gives the monthly sales from January 2000 to December 2001 to illustrate the beginning of the computations. The first step for monthly data is to compute a 12-month moving average (for quarterly data, a four-month moving average would be computed). Because all of the months of the year are included in the calculation of this moving average, effects due to the seasonal component are removed, and the moving average itself contains only the trend and irregular components.

---

[3]The units have been omitted and the dates and name have been changed to protect the identity of the company.

TABLE 5-2 Sales of the Cavanaugh Company, 2000–2001, for Example 5.2

Period	*Sales*	*12-Month Moving Total*	*Two-Year Moving Total*	*12-Month Centered Moving Average*	*Seasonal Index*
2000					
January	518				
February	404				
March	300				
April	210				
May	196				
June	186				
	} 1				
July	247	4,869 } 2	9,833} 3	409.7} 4	0.60} 5
August	343	4,964	9,916	413.2	0.83
September	464	4,952	9,877	411.5	1.13
October	680	4,925	9,962	415.1	1.64
November	711	5,037	10,067	419.5	1.69
December	610	5,030	10,131	422.1	1.45
2001					
January	613	5,101	10,279	428.3	1.43
February	392	5,178	10,417	434.0	0.90
March	273	5,239	10,691	445.5	0.61
April	322	5,452	11,082	461.8	0.70
May	189	5,630	11,444	476.8	0.40
June	257	5,814	11,682	486.8	0.53
July	324	5,868			
August	404				
September	677				
October	858				
November	895				
December	664				

The steps (identified in Table 5-2) for computing seasonal indices by the ratio-to-moving-average method follow.

Step 1 Starting at the beginning of the series, compute the 12-month moving total and place the total for January 2000 through December 2000 between June and July 2000.

Step 2 Compute a two-year moving total so that the subsequent averages are centered on July rather than between months.

Step 3 Because the two-year total contains the data for 24 months (January 2000 once, February 2000 to December 2000 twice, and January 2001 once), this total is centered (opposite) July 2000.

Step 4 Divide the two-year moving total by 24 in order to obtain the 12-month centered moving average.

Step 5 The seasonal index for July is calculated by dividing the actual value for July by the 12-month centered moving average.[4]

Repeat Steps 1 to 5 beginning with the second month of the series, August 2000, and so forth. The process ends when a full 12-month moving total can no longer be calculated.

Because there are several estimates (corresponding to different years) of the seasonal index for each month, they must be summarized to produce a single number. The median,

[4] This is the ratio-to-moving-average operation that gives the procedure its name.

									Adjusted Seasonal Index (Median
Month	1996	1997	1998	1999	2000	2001	2002	Median	× 1.0044)
January	—	1.208	1.202	1.272	1.411	1.431	—	1.272	1.278
February	—	0.700	0.559	0.938	1.089	0.903	—	0.903	0.907
March	—	0.524	0.564	0.785	0.800	0.613	—	0.613	0.616
April	—	0.444	0.433	0.480	0.552	0.697	—	0.480	0.482
May	—	0.424	0.365	0.488	0.503	0.396	—	0.424	0.426
June	—	0.490	0.459	0.461	0.465	0.528		0.465	0.467
July	0.639	0.904	0.598	0.681	0.603	0.662		0.651	0.654
August	1.115	0.913	0.889	0.799	0.830	0.830		0.860	0.864
September	1.371	1.560	1.346	1.272	1.128	1.395		1.359	1.365
October	1.792	1.863	1.796	1.574	1.638	1.771		1.782	1.790
November	1.884	2.012	1.867	1.697	1.695	1.846		1.857	1.865
December	1.519	1.088	1.224	1.282	1.445	—		1.282	1.288
								11.948	12.002

TABLE 5-3   A Summary of the Monthly Seasonal Indices for the Cavanaugh Company for Example 5.2

rather than the mean, is used as the summary measure. Using the median eliminates the influence of data for a month in a particular year that is unusually large or small. A summary of the seasonal ratios along with the median value for each month is contained in Table 5-3.

The monthly seasonal indices for each year must sum to 12, so the medians for each month must be adjusted to get the final set of seasonal indices.[5] Because this multiplier should be greater than 1 if the total of the median ratios before adjustment is less than 12, and smaller than 1 if the total is greater than 12, the multiplier is defined as

$$Multiplier = \frac{12}{Actual\ total}$$

Using the information in Table 5-3,

$$Multiplier = \frac{12}{11.948} = 1.0044$$

The final column in Table 5-3 contains the final seasonal indices for each month, determined by making the adjustment (multiplying by 1.0044) to each of the median ratios.[6] The final seasonal indices, shown in Figure 5-8, represent the seasonal component in a multiplicative decomposition of the sales of the Cavanaugh Company time series.

The seasonality in sales is evident from Figure 5-8. Sales for this company are periodic with relatively low sales in the late spring and relatively high sales in the late fall.

Our analysis of the sales series in Example 5.2 assumed the seasonal pattern remained constant from year to year. If the seasonal pattern appears to change over time, then estimating the seasonal component with the entire data set can produce misleading results. It is better, in this case, to either (1) use only recent (last few years) data to estimate the seasonal component, or (2) to use a time series model that allows for evolving seasonality. We will discuss models that allow for evolving seasonality in a later chapter.

[5]The monthly indices must sum to 12 so that the expected annual total equals the actual total for the year.
[6]The seasonal indices are sometimes multiplied by 100 and expressed as percentages.

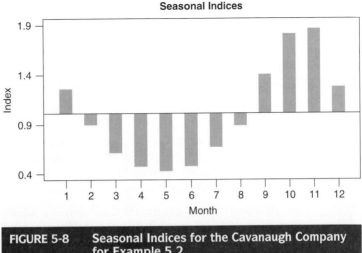

FIGURE 5-8   Seasonal Indices for the Cavanaugh Company for Example 5.2

The seasonal analysis illustrated in Example 5.2 is appropriate for a multiplicative decomposition model. However, the general approach outlined in Steps 1 to 5 works for an additive decomposition if, in Step 5, the seasonality is estimated by subtracting the trend from the original series rather than dividing by the trend (moving average) to get an index. In an additive decomposition, the seasonal component is expressed in the same units as the original series.

In addition, it is apparent from our sales example that determining trend by using a centered moving average results in some missing values at the ends of the series. This is particularly problematic if forecasting is the objective. To forecast future values using a decomposition approach, alternative methods for estimating the trend must be used.

The results of a seasonal analysis can be used to (1) eliminate the seasonality in data, (2) forecast future values, (3) evaluate current positions in, for example, sales, inventory, and shipments, and (4) schedule production.

SEASONALLY ADJUSTED DATA

After the seasonal component has been isolated, it can be used to calculate *seasonally adjusted data*. For an additive decomposition, the seasonally adjusted data are computed by subtracting the seasonal component

$$Y_t - S_t = T_t + I_t$$

For a multiplicative decomposition, the seasonally adjusted data are computed by dividing the original observations by the seasonal component

$$\frac{Y_t}{S_t} = T_t \times I_t \qquad (5.7)$$

Most economic series published by government agencies are seasonally adjusted because seasonal variation is not of primary interest. Rather, it is the general pattern of economic activity, independent of the normal seasonal fluctuations, that is of interest. For example, new car registrations might increase by 10% from May to June, but is this increase an indication that new car sales are completing a banner quarter? The answer is "no" if the 10% increase is typical at this time of year largely due to seasonal factors.

In a survey concerned with the acquisition of seasonally adjusted data, Bell and Hillmer (1984) found that a wide variety of users value seasonal adjustment. They identified three motives for seasonal adjustment:

1. Seasonal adjustment allows reliable comparison of values at different points in time.
2. It is easier to understand the relationships among economic or business variables after the complicating factor of seasonality has been removed from the data.
3. Seasonal adjustment may be a useful element in the production of short-term forecasts of future values of a time series.

Bell and Hillmer concluded that "seasonal adjustment is done to simplify data so that they may be more easily interpreted by statistically unsophisticated users without a significant loss of information" (p. 301).

Cyclical and Irregular Variations

Cycles are long-run, wavelike fluctuations that occur most frequently in macro indicators of economic activity. As we have discussed, to the extent that they can be measured, cycles do not have a consistent pattern. However, some insight into the cyclical behavior of a time series can be obtained by eliminating the trend and seasonal components to give, using a multiplicative decomposition,[7]

$$\frac{Y_t}{T_t \times S_t} = \frac{T_t \times C_t \times S_t \times I_t}{T_t \times S_t} = C_t \times I_t \qquad (5.8)$$

A moving average can be used to smooth out the irregularities, I_t, leaving the cyclical component, C_t. To eliminate the centering problem encountered when a moving average with an even number of time periods is used, the irregularities are smoothed using a moving average with an odd number of time periods. For monthly data, a 5-, 7-, 9-, or even an 11-period moving average will work. For quarterly data, an estimate of C can be computed using a three-period moving average of the values.[8]

Finally, the irregular component is estimated by

$$I_t = \frac{C_t \times I_t}{C_t} \qquad (5.9)$$

The irregular component represents the variability in the time series after the other components have been removed. It is sometimes called the *residual*, or *error*. With a multiplicative decomposition, both the cyclical and irregular components are expressed as indices.

One reason for decomposing a time series is to isolate and examine the components of the series. After the analyst is able to look at the trend, seasonal, cyclical, and irregular components of a series one at a time, insights into the patterns in the original data values may be gained. Also, once the components have been isolated, they may be recombined or synthesized to produce forecasts of future values of the time series.

---

[7] Notice that we have added the cyclical component C to the multiplicative decomposition shown in Equation 5.2.

[8] For annual data, there is no seasonal component and the cyclical $\times$ irregular component is obtained by simply removing the trend from the original series.

TABLE 5-4			**Multiplicative Decomposition for Outboard Marine Sales**						
t	*Year*	*Quarter*	*Sales*	*T*	*SCI*	*S*	*TCI*	*CI*	*C*	*I*

t	*Year*	*Quarter*	*Sales*	*T*	*SCI*	*S*	*TCI*	*CI*	*C*	*I*
1	1990	1	232.7	255.026	0.912	0.780	298.486	1.170	—	—
2		2	309.2	256.310	1.206	1.016	304.297	1.187	1.146	1.036
3		3	310.7	257.594	1.206	1.117	278.175	1.080	1.103	0.979
4		4	293.0	258.878	1.132	1.087	269.459	1.041	1.044	0.997
5	1991	1	205.1	260.162	0.788	0.780	263.084	1.011	0.978	1.034
6		2	234.4	261.446	0.897	1.016	230.683	0.882	0.955	0.924
7		3	285.4	262.730	1.086	1.117	255.524	0.973	0.919	1.059
8		4	258.7	264.014	0.980	1.087	237.914	0.901	0.936	0.963
9	1992	1	193.2	265.298	0.728	0.780	247.820	0.934	0.936	0.998
10		2	263.7	266.583	0.989	1.016	259.518	0.974	0.962	1.013
11		3	292.5	267.867	1.092	1.117	261.880	0.978	1.009	0.969
12		4	315.2	269.151	1.171	1.087	289.875	1.077	0.967	1.114
13	1993	1	178.3	270.435	0.659	0.780	228.708	0.846	0.972	0.870
14		2	274.5	271.719	1.010	1.016	270.147	0.994	0.936	1.062
15		3	295.4	273.003	1.082	1.117	264.477	0.969	0.974	0.995
16		4	286.4	274.287	1.044	1.087	263.389	0.960	0.939	1.022
17	1994	1	190.8	275.571	0.692	0.780	244.742	0.888	0.928	0.957
18		2	263.5	276.855	0.952	1.016	259.321	0.937	0.950	0.986
19		3	318.8	278.139	1.146	1.117	285.427	1.026	0.989	1.037
20		4	305.3	279.423	1.093	1.087	280.770	1.005	1.047	0.960
21	1995	1	242.6	280.707	0.864	0.780	311.186	1.109	1.075	1.032
22		2	318.8	281.991	1.131	1.016	313.744	1.113	1.088	1.023
23		3	329.6	283.275	1.164	1.117	295.097	1.042	1.082	0.963
24		4	338.2	284.559	1.189	1.087	311.027	1.093	1.059	1.032
25	1996	1	232.1	285.843	0.812	0.780	297.718	1.042	1.038	1.004
26		2	285.6	287.127	0.995	1.016	281.071	0.979	0.975	1.004
27		3	291.0	288.411	1.009	1.117	260.537	0.903	0.925	0.976
28		4	281.4	289.695	0.971	1.087	258.791	0.893	—	—

Example 5.3

In Example 3.5 (see p. 69), Perkin Kendell, the analyst for the Outboard Marine Corporation, used autocorrelation analysis to determine that sales were seasonal on a quarterly basis. Now, he uses decomposition to understand the quarterly sales variable. Perkin uses Minitab (see "Minitab Applications" at the end of the chapter) to produce Table 5-4 and Figure 5-9. To keep the seasonal pattern current, only the last seven years (1990 to 1996) of sales data (Y), were analyzed.

The original data are shown at the chart at the upper left of Figure 5-10. The trend is computed using the linear model: $\hat{T}_t = 253.742 + 1.284t$. Because 1 represented the first quarter of 1990, Table 5-4 shows the trend value equal to 255.026 for this time period and estimated sales (the T column) increased by 1.284 each quarter.

The chart at the upper right of Figure 5-10 shows the detrended data. These data are also shown in the *SCI* column of Table 5-4. The detrended value for the first quarter of 1990 was[9]

$$SCI = \frac{Y}{T} = \frac{232.7}{255.026} = .912$$

---

[9]To simplify the notation in this example, we omit the subscript t on the original data Y and each of its components $T, S, C,$ and I. We also omit the multiplication sign, ×, between components, since it is clear we are considering a multiplicative decomposition.

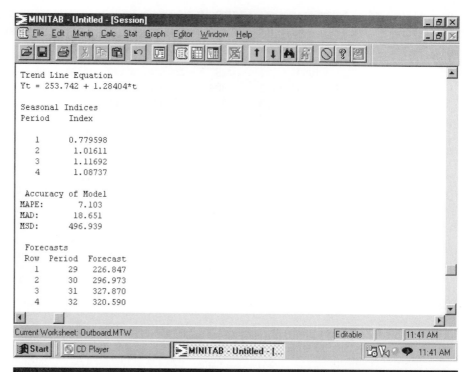

FIGURE 5-9   Minitab Output for Decomposition of Outboard Marine Quarterly Sales for Example 5.3

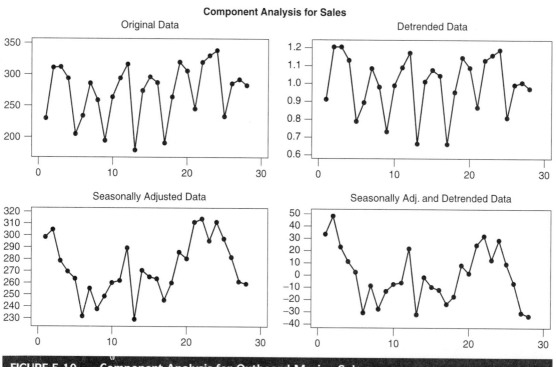

FIGURE 5-10   Component Analysis for Outboard Marine Sales

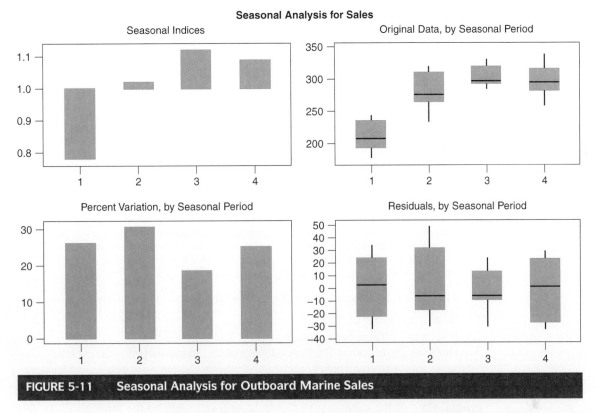

FIGURE 5-11   Seasonal Analysis for Outboard Marine Sales

The seasonally adjusted data are shown in the *TCI* column in Table 5-4 and in the chart at the lower left of Figure 5-10. The seasonally adjusted value for the first quarter of 1990 was

$$TCI = \frac{232.7}{.7796} = 298.486$$

Sales in the first quarter of 1995 were 242.6. However, examination of the seasonally adjusted column shows that the sales for this quarter were actually high when the data were adjusted for the fact that the first quarter is typically a very weak quarter.

The seasonal indices in Figure 5-9 were

First quarter $= .77960 \rightarrow 78.0\%$

Second quarter $= 1.01611 \rightarrow 101.6\%$

Third quarter $= 1.11692 \rightarrow 111.7\%$

Fourth quarter $= 1.08737 \rightarrow 108.7\%$

The chart on the upper left of Figure 5-11 shows the seasonal components relative to 1.0. We see that first-quarter sales are 22% below average, second-quarter sales are about as expected, third-quarter sales are almost 12% above average, and fourth-quarter sales are almost 9% above normal.

The cyclical-irregular value for first quarter 1990 was[10]

$$CI = \frac{Y}{TS} = \frac{232.7}{(255.026)(.7796)} = 1.170$$

---

[10] Minitab calculates the cyclical × irregular component (or simply the irregular component if no cyclical component is contemplated) by subtracting the trend × seasonal component from the original data. In symbols, Minitab sets $CI = Y - TS$. The Minitab *CI* component is shown in the lower right-hand chart of Figure 5-10, and as boxplots by quarter in the lower right-hand chart of Figure 5-11.

In order to calculate the cyclical column, a three-period moving average was computed. The value for the second quarter 1990 was

$$
\begin{array}{r}
1.170 \\
1.187 \\
\underline{1.080} \\
3.437
\end{array}
\qquad 3.437/3 = 1.146
$$

Notice how smooth the *C* column is compared to the *CI* column. The reason is that using the moving average has smoothed out the irregularities. Finally, the *I* column was computed. For example, for the second quarter of 1990,

$$
I = \frac{CI}{C} = \frac{1.187}{1.146} = 1.036
$$

Examination of the *I* column shows that there were some large changes in the irregular component. The irregular index dropped from 111.4% in the fourth quarter of 1992 to 87% in the first quarter of 1993 and then increased to 106.2% in the second quarter of 1993. This behavior results from the unusually low sales in the first quarter of 1993.

The cyclical indices can be used to answer the following questions:

1. Does the series cycle?
2. If so, how extreme is the cycle?
3. Does the series follow the general state of the economy (business cycle)?

One way to investigate cyclical patterns is through the study of business indicators. A *business indicator* is a business-related time series that is used to help assess the general state of the economy, particularly with reference to the business cycle. Many businesspeople and economists systematically follow the movements of such statistical series to obtain economic and business information in the form of an unfolding picture that is up-to-date, comprehensive, relatively objective, and capable of being read and understood with a minimum expenditure of time.

> *Business indicators* are business-related time series that are used to help assess the general state of the economy.

The most important list of statistical indicators originated during the sharp business setback of 1937 to 1938. Secretary of the Treasury Henry Morgenthau requested that the National Bureau of Economic Research (NBER) devise a system that would signal when the setback was nearing an end. Under the leadership of Wesley Mitchell and Arthur F. Burns, NBER economists selected 21 series that, from past performance, promised to be fairly reliable indicators of business revival. Since then the bureau has revised the list several times. The current list consists of 22 indicators—11 classified as leading, 4 as coincident, and 7 as lagging.

1. *Leading indicators.* In practice, components of the leading series are studied to help anticipate turning points in the economy. The *Survey of Current Business* publishes this list each month along with the actual values of each series for the past several months and the most recent year. Also, a composite index of leading indicators is computed for each month and year; the most recent monthly value is frequently reported in the popular press to indicate the general direction of the future economy. Examples of leading indicators are manufacturers' new orders and an index of stock prices.

2. *Coincident indicators.* The four coincident indicators provide a measure of how the U.S. economy is currently performing. An index of these four series is computed each month. Examples of coincident indicators are personal income and sales.
3. *Lagging indicators.* The lagging indicators tend to lag behind the general state of the economy, both on the upswing and on the downswing. A composite index is also computed for this list. Examples of lagging indicators are the prime interest rate and commercial loans outstanding.

Cycles imply turning points. That is, turning points come into existence only as a consequence of a following decline or gain in the business cycle. Leading indicators change direction ahead of turns in general business activity, coincident indicators turn at about the same time as the general economy, and turns in the lagging indicators follow those of the general economy. However, it is difficult to identify cyclical turning points at the time they occur because all areas of the economy do not expand at the same time during periods of expansion, nor do all contract concurrently during periods of contraction. Hence, several months may go by before a genuine cyclical upturn or downturn is finally identified with any assurance.

In their article entitled "Early Warning Signals for the Economy," Geoffrey H. Moore and Julius Shiskin (1976) have the following to say on the usefulness of business cycle indicators:

> It seems clear from the record that business cycle indicators are helpful in judging the tone of current business and short-term prospects. But because of their limitations, the indicators must be used together with other data and with full awareness of the background of business and consumer confidence and expectations, governmental policies, and international events. We also must anticipate that the indicators will often be difficult to interpret, that interpretations will sometimes vary among analysts, and that the signals they give will not be correctly interpreted. Indicators provide a sensitive and revealing picture of the ebb and flow of economic tides that a skillful analyst of the economic, political, and international scene can use to improve his chances of making a valid forecast of short-run economic trends. If the analyst is aware of their limitations and alert to the world around him, he will find the indicators useful guideposts for taking stock of the economy and its needs. (p. 81)

Cyclical components of individual time series generally conform only loosely—and sometimes not at all—to the business cycle as identified by the NBER indicators. However, if a cyclical component for a given time series is estimated, it should always be plotted over time to get some indication of the magnitudes and lengths of any cycles that appear to exist. In addition, the plot can be examined for any relation to the ups and downs of general economic activity.

The discussion so far shows how the factors that create variation in a time series can be separated and studied individually. *Analysis* is the process for taking the time series apart; *synthesis* is the process for putting it back together. We shall put the components of the time series back together to do forecasting.

FORECASTING A SEASONAL TIME SERIES

In forecasting a seasonal time series, the decomposition process is reversed. Instead of separating the series into individual components for examination, the components are recombined to develop the forecasts for future periods. We will use the multiplicative

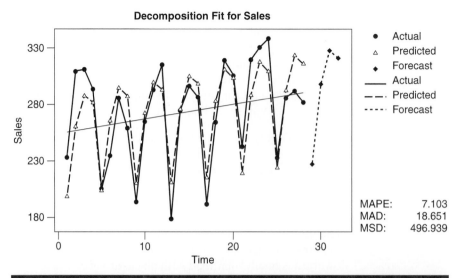

FIGURE 5-12   Decomposition Fit and Forecasts for Outboard Marine Sales

model and the results of Example 5.3 to develop forecasts for Outboard Marine Corporation sales.

Example 5.4

Forecasts of Outboard Marine Corporation sales for the four quarters of 1997 can be developed using Table 5-4.

1. *Trend.* The quarterly trend equation is: $\hat{T}_t = 253.742 + 1.284t$. The forecast origin is the fourth quarter of 1996, or time period $t = n = 28$. Sales for the first quarter of 1997 occurred in time period $t = 28 + 1 = 29$. This notation shows we are forecasting $p = 1$ period ahead from the end of the time series. Setting $t = 29$, the trend projection is then

$$\hat{T}_{29} = 253.742 + 1.284(29) = 290.978$$

2. *Seasonal.* The seasonal index for the first quarter, .7796, is given in Figure 5-9.
3. *Cyclical.* The cyclical projection must be determined from the estimated cyclical pattern (if any) and any other information generated by indicators of the general economy for 1997. Projecting the cyclical pattern for future time periods is fraught with uncertainty, and as we indicated earlier, is generally assumed for forecasting purposes to be included in the trend. To demonstrate the completion of this example, we set the cyclical index to 1.0.
4. *Irregular.* Irregular fluctuations represent random variation that can't be explained by the other components. For forecasting, the irregular component is set to the average value 1.0.[11]

The forecast for the first quarter of 1997 is

$$\hat{Y}_{29} = T_{29} \times S_{29} \times C_{29} \times I_{29} = (290.978)(.7796)(1.0)(1.0) = 226.846$$

The forecasts for the rest of 1997 are

$$\text{Second quarter} = 296.973$$
$$\text{Third quarter} = 327.870$$
$$\text{Fourth quarter} = 320.590$$

---

[11] For forecasts generated from an additive model, the irregular index is set to the average value 0.

The multiplicative decomposition fit for Outboard Marine Corporation sales along with the forecasts for 1997 are shown in Figure 5-12. We can see from the figure that the fit, constructed from the trend and seasonal components, represents the actual data reasonably well. However, the fit is not good for the last two quarters of 1996. The forecasts for 1997 mimic the pattern of the fit.

Forecasts produced by an additive or multiplicative decomposition model reflect the importance of the individual components. If a variable is highly seasonal, the forecasts will have a strong seasonal pattern. In addition, if there is a trend, the forecasts will follow the seasonal pattern superimposed on the extrapolated trend. If one component dominates the analysis, it alone might provide a practical, accurate, short-term forecast.

THE CENSUS II DECOMPOSITION METHOD

Time series decomposition methods have a long history. In the 1920s and early 1930s, the Federal Reserve Board and the National Bureau of Economic Research were heavily involved in seasonal adjustment and smoothing of economic time series. However, before the development of computers the decomposition calculations were laborious, and practical application of the methods was limited. In the early 1950s, Julius Shiskin, chief economic statistician at the Bureau of the Census, developed a large-scale computer program to decompose time series. The first computer program essentially approximated the hand methods that were used up to that time, and was replaced a year later by an improved program known as Method II. Over the years, improved variants of Method II followed. The current variant of the Census Bureau time series decomposition program is known as X-12-ARIMA. This program is available from the Census Bureau at no charge and is widely used by government agencies and private companies.[12]

Census II decomposition is usually multiplicative because most economic time series have seasonal variation that increases with the level of the series. The decomposition also assumes three components: trend-cycle, seasonal, and irregular.

The Census II method iterates through a series of steps until the components are successfully isolated. Many of the steps involve the application of weighted moving averages to the data, which results in inevitable loss of data at the beginning and end of the series because of the averaging. The ARIMA part of X-12-ARIMA provides the facility to extend the original series in both directions with forecasts so that more of the observations are adjusted using the full weighted moving averages. These forecasts are generated from an ARIMA time series model (see Chapter 9).

The steps for each iteration of the Census II method as implemented in X-12-ARIMA are outlined next. It may seem that the method is complicated because of the many steps involved. However, the basic idea is quite simple—to isolate the trend-cycle, seasonal, and irregular components one by one. The various iterations are designed to improve the estimate of each component. Good references for additional study are *Forecasting: Methods and Applications* (Third Edition) by Makridakis, Wheelwright, and Hyndman (1998), and Findley *et al*. (1998), "New Capabilities and Methods of the X-12-ARIMA Seasonal-Adjustment Program."

Step 1   An s-period moving average is applied to the original data to get a rough estimate of the trend-cycle. (For monthly data, $s = 12$; for quarterly data, $s = 4$; and so forth.)

---

[12] The PC version of the X-12-ARIMA program can be downloaded from the U.S. Census Bureau Web site. At the time this book was written, the Web address for the download page was: *www.census. gov/srd/www/x12a/x12down_pc.html*

Step 2   The ratios of the original data to these moving average values are calculated as in classical multiplicative decomposition illustrated in Example 5.2.

Step 3   The ratios from Step 2 contain both the seasonal and irregular components. They also include extreme values resulting from unusual events such as strikes or wars. The ratios are divided by a rough estimate of the seasonal component to give an estimate of the irregular component. A large value for an irregular term indicates an extreme value in the original data. These extreme values are identified and the ratios in Step 2 adjusted accordingly. This effectively eliminates values that do not fit the pattern of the remaining data. Missing values at the beginning and end of the series are also replaced by estimates at this stage.

Step 4   The ratios created from the modified data (with extreme values replaced and estimates for missing values) are smoothed using a moving average to eliminate irregular variation. This creates a preliminary estimate of the seasonal component.

Step 5   The original data are then divided by the preliminary seasonal component from Step 4 to get the preliminary seasonally adjusted series. This seasonally adjusted series contains the trend-cycle and irregular components, expressed mathematically as

$$\frac{Y_t}{S_t} = \frac{T_t \times S_t \times I_t}{S_t} = T_t \times I_t$$

Step 6   The trend-cycle is estimated by applying a weighted moving average to the preliminary seasonally adjusted series. This moving average eliminates irregular variation and gives a smooth curve that indicates the preliminary trend-cycle in the data.

Step 7   Repeat Step 2 with this new estimate of the trend-cycle. That is, new ratios, containing only the seasonal and irregular components, are obtained by dividing the original observations by the trend-cycle from Step 6. These are the final seasonal-irregular ratios;
Mathematically,

$$\frac{Y_t}{T_t} = \frac{T_t \times S_t \times I_t}{T_t} = S_t \times I_t$$

Step 8   Repeat Step 3 using the new ratios computed in Step 7.

Step 9   Repeat Step 4 to get a new estimate of the seasonal component.

Step 10   Repeat Step 5 with the seasonal component from Step 9.

Step 11   Divide the seasonally adjusted data from Step 10 by the trend-cycle obtained in Step 6 to get the estimated irregular component.

Step 12   Extreme values of the irregular component are replaced as in Step 3. A series of modified data is obtained by multiplying the trend-cycle, seasonal component, and adjusted irregular component together. These data reproduce the original data except for the extreme values.

The preceding 12 steps are repeated, beginning with the modified data from Step 12 rather than the original data. Some of the lengths of the moving averages used in the various steps are changed depending on the variability in the data.

The final seasonally adjusted series is determined by dividing the final seasonal component into the original data. The result contains only the product of the trend-cycle and irregular components.

The values of each of the final components are printed out and plotted. A series of diagnostic tests is available to determine if the decomposition was successful.

The X-12-ARIMA program contains many additional features that we have not described. For example, adjustments can be made for different numbers of trading days and for holiday effects, missing values within the series can be estimated and replaced, the effects of outliers can be removed before decomposition, and other changes in trend such as shifts in level or temporary ramp effects can be modeled.

APPLICATION TO MANAGEMENT

Time series analysis is a widely used statistical tool for forecasting future events that are intertwined with the economy in some fashion. Manufacturers are extremely interested in the boom-bust cycles of our economy as well as those of foreign economies so that they can better predict demand for their products, which in turn affects their inventory levels, employment needs, cash flows, and almost all other business activities within the firm.

The complexity of these problems is enormous. Take, for example, the problem of predicting demand for oil and its by-products. In the late 1960s the price of oil per barrel was very low, and there seemed to be an insatiable worldwide demand for gas and oil. Then came the oil price shocks of the early and mid-1970s. What would the future demand for oil be? What about prices? Firms such as Shell and General Motors were obviously very interested in these questions. If oil prices continued to escalate, would the demand for large cars diminish? What would be the demand for electricity? By and large, analysts predicted that the demand for energy and, therefore, oil would be very inelastic; thus prices would continue to outstrip inflation. However, these predictions did not take into account a major downswing in the business cycle of the early 1980s and a greater elasticity of consumer demand for energy than predicted. By 1980 the world began to see a glut of oil on the market and radically falling prices. At the time, it seemed hard to believe that consumers were actually benefiting once again from gasoline price wars.

Oil demand is affected not only by long-term cyclical events but also by seasonal and random events, as are most other forecasts of demand for any type of product or service. For instance, consider the service and retail industries. We have witnessed a continued movement of employment away from manufacturing to the retail and service fields. Thus, because retailing (in store, catalog, Web-based) is an extremely seasonal and cyclical business, and demand and inventory projections are critical to retailers, time series analysis will be used more widely by increasingly sophisticated retailers.

Manufacturers will have a continued need for statistical projections of future events. Witness the explosive growth in the technology and telecommunications fields during the 1990s and the substantial contraction of these industries in the early 2000s. This growth and contraction was a result, to a large extent, of projections of demand that never completely materialized. Questions that all manufacturers must address include: What will the future inflation rate be? How will it affect the cost-of-living adjustments that may be built into a company's labor contract? How will these adjustments affect prices and demand? What is the projected pool of managerial skills for 2020? What will be the effect of the government's boom-bust spending and taxing strategies?

What will the future population of young people look like? What will the ethnic mix be? These issues affect almost all segments of our economy. Demographers are closely watching the current fertility rate and using almost every available time series forecasting technique to try and project population variables. Very minor miscalculations will have major impacts on everything from the production of babies' toys to the financial soundness of the Social Security system. Interestingly, demographers are looking at very long-term business cycles (20 years or more per cycle) in trying to predict what this generation's population of women of childbearing age will do about having children. Will they have one or two children, as did families in the 1960s and 1970s, or will they return to having two or three, as did preceding generations? These decisions will determine the age composition of our population for the next 50 to 75 years.

Political scientists are interested in using time series analysis to study the changing patterns of government spending on defense and social welfare programs. Obviously, these trends have great impact on the future of whole industries.

Finally, one interesting microcosm of applications of time series analysis has shown up in the legal fields. Lawyers are making increasing use of expert witnesses to testify about the present value of a person's or a firm's future income, the cost incurred from the loss of a job due to discrimination, or the effect of an illegal strike on a market. These questions can often be best answered through the judicious use of time series analysis.

Satellite technology and the World Wide Web have made the transmission and accumulation of information almost instantaneous. The proliferation of personal computers, easy-to-use statistical software programs, and access to databases has brought information processing to the desktop. Business survival during periods of major competitive change requires quick, data-driven decision making. Time series analysis and forecasting play a major role in these decision-making processes.

APPENDIX: PRICE INDEX

Several of the series on production, sales, and other economic situations contain data available only in dollar values. These data are affected by both the physical quantity of goods sold and their prices. Inflation and widely varying prices over time can cause analysis problems. For instance, an increased dollar volume may hide decreased sales in units caused by inflated prices. Thus it is frequently necessary to know how much of the change in dollar values represents a real change in physical quantity and how much is due to change in price because of inflation. It is desirable in these instances to express dollar values in terms of constant dollars.

The concept of *purchasing power* is important. The current purchasing power of $1 is defined as

$$\text{Current purchasing power of \$1} = \frac{100}{\text{Consumer Price Index}} \qquad \textbf{(5.10)}$$

Thus, if in November 2001 the Consumer Price Index (with 1997 as 100) reaches 150, the current purchasing power of the November 2001 consumer dollar is

$$\text{Current purchasing power of \$1} = \frac{100}{150} = .67$$

The 2001 dollar purchased only two-thirds of the goods and services that could have been purchased with a base period (1997) dollar.

To express dollar values in terms of *constant dollars*, Equation 5.11 is used.

$$\text{Deflated dollar value} = (\text{Dollar value}) \times (\text{Purchasing power of \$1}) \qquad \textbf{(5.11)}$$

Suppose that car sales rose from \$300,000 in 2000 to \$350,000 in 2001, while the new-car price index (1997 as base) rose from 135 to 155. Deflated sales for 2000 and 2001 would be

$$\text{Deflated 2000 sales} = (\$300,000)\left(\frac{100}{135}\right) = \$222,222$$

$$\text{Deflated 2001 sales} = (\$350,000)\left(\frac{100}{155}\right) = \$225,806$$

Note that actual dollar sales had a sizable increase of \$350,000 − \$300,000 = \$50,000. However, deflated sales only increased by \$225,806 − \$222,222 = \$3,584.

The purpose of deflating dollar values is to remove the effect of price changes. This adjustment is called *price deflation* or is referred to as expressing a series in constant dollars.

Price deflation is the process of expressing terms in a series in constant dollars.

The deflation process is relatively simple. To adjust prices to constant dollars, an index number computed from the prices of commodities the values of which are to be deflated is used. For example, shoe store sales should be deflated by an index of shoe prices, not by a general price index. For deflated dollar values that represent more than one type of commodity, the analyst should develop a price index by combining the appropriate price indices together in the proper mix.

Example 5.5

Mr. Burnham wishes to study the long-term growth of the Burnham Furniture Store. The long-term trend of his business should be evaluated by using the physical volume of sales. If this evaluation cannot be done, price changes reflected in dollar sales will follow no consistent pattern and will merely obscure the real growth pattern. If sales dollars are to be used, actual dollar sales need to be divided by an appropriate price index to obtain sales that are measured in constant dollars.

The Consumer Price Index (CPI) is not suitable for Burnham because it contains elements such as rents, food, and personal services not sold by the store; however, some components of this index may be appropriate. Burnham is aware that 70% of sales are from furniture and 30% from appliances. He can, therefore, multiply the CPI retail furniture component

	Burnham Sales (thousands)	Retail Furniture Price Index (1997 = 100)	Retail Appliance Price Index (1997 = 100)	Price Index[a] (1997 = 100)	Deflated Sales[b] (thousands of 1997 dollars)
TABLE 5-5	**Burnham Furniture Sales Data, 1994–2001, for Example 5.5**				
Year					
1994	42.1	90.1	94.6	91.45	46.0
1995	47.2	95.4	97.2	95.94	49.2
1996	48.4	97.2	98.4	97.56	49.6
1997	50.6	100.0	100.0	100.00	50.6
1998	55.2	104.5	101.1	103.48	53.3
1999	57.9	108.6	103.2	106.98	54.1
2000	59.8	112.4	104.3	109.97	54.4
2001	60.7	114.0	105.6	111.48	54.4

[a]Constructed for furniture (weight 70%) and appliance (weight 30%).
[b]Sales divided by price index times 100.

by .70, multiply the appliance component by .30, and then add to obtain a combined price index. Table 5-5 illustrates this approach in which the computations for 1994 are

$$90.1(.70) + 94.6(.30) = 91.45$$

The sales are deflated for 1994 in terms of 1997 purchasing power so that

$$\text{Deflated 1994 sales} = (42.1)\left(\frac{100}{91.45}\right) = 46.0$$

Table 5-5 shows that although actual sales gained steadily from 1992 to 1999, physical volume remained rather stable from 1999 to 2001. Evidently, the sales increases were due to price markups that were generated, in turn, by the inflationary tendency of the economy.

Glossary

Business indicators. Business indicators are business-related time series that are used to help assess the general state of the economy.

Index numbers. Index numbers are percentages that show changes over time.

Price deflation. Price deflation is the process of expressing terms in a series in constant dollars.

Key Formulas

Time series additive decomposition

$$Y_t = T_t + S_t + I_t \tag{5.1}$$

Time series multiplicative decomposition

$$Y_t = T_t \times S_t \times I_t \tag{5.2}$$

Linear trend

$$\hat{T}_t = b_0 + b_1 t \tag{5.3}$$

Quadratic trend

$$\hat{T}_t = b_0 + b_1 t + b_2 t^2 \tag{5.5}$$

Exponential trend

$$\hat{T}_t = b_0\, b_1^t \tag{5.6}$$

Seasonally adjusted data (multiplicative decomposition)

$$\frac{Y_t}{S_t} = T_t \times I_t \tag{5.7}$$

Cyclical-irregular component (multiplicative decomposition)

$$C_t \times I_t = \frac{Y_t}{T_t \times S_t} \tag{5.8}$$

Irregular component (multiplicative decomposition)

$$I_t = \frac{C_t \times I_t}{C_t} \tag{5.9}$$

Current purchasing power of \$1

$$\frac{100}{\text{Consumer Price Index}} \qquad \textbf{(5.10)}$$

Deflated dollar value

$$(\text{Dollar value}) \times (\text{Purchasing power of \$1}) \qquad \textbf{(5.11)}$$

Problems

1. Explain the concept of decomposing a time series.

2. Explain when a multiplicative decomposition may be more appropriate than an additive decomposition.

3. What are some basic forces that affect the trend-cycle of most variables?

4. What kind of trend model should be used in each of the following cases?
   a. The variable is increasing by a constant rate.
   b. The variable is increasing by a constant rate until it reaches saturation and levels out.
   c. The variable is increasing by a constant amount.

5. What are some basic forces that affect the seasonal component of most variables?

6. Value Line estimates of sales and earnings growth for individual companies are derived by correlating sales, earnings, and dividends to appropriate components of the National Income Accounts such as capital spending. Jason Black, an analyst for Value Line, is examining the trend of the capital spending variable from 1977 to 1993. The data are given in Table P-6.
   a. Plot the data.
   b. Determine the appropriate trend model for the years 1977 to 1993.
   c. If the appropriate model is linear, compute the linear trend model for the years 1977 to 1993.
   d. What has the average increase in capital spending per year been since 1977?
   e. Estimate the trend value for capital spending in 1994.
   f. Compare your trend estimate with Value Line's.
   g. What factor(s) influence the trend of capital spending?

7. A large company is considering cutting back on its TV advertising in favor of business videos to be given to its customers. This action is being considered after

TABLE P-6	Capital Spending (\$ billions), 1977–1993				
Year	\$ Billions	Year	\$ Billions	Year	\$ Billions
1977	214	1983	357	1989	571
1978	259	1984	416	1990	578
1979	303	1985	443	1991	556
1980	323	1986	437	1992	566
1981	369	1987	443	1993	623
1982	367	1988	545	1994	680[a]

[a]Value Line estimate 1994.

Source: The Value Line Investment Survey (New York: Value Line, 1988, 1990, 1994), p. 175.

TABLE P-7			
Year	Y	Year	Y
1980	11,424	1989	26,891
1981	12,811	1990	29,073
1982	14,566	1991	28,189
1983	16,542	1992	30,450
1984	19,670	1993	31,698
1985	20,770	1994	35,435
1986	22,585	1995	37,828
1987	23,904	1996	42,484
1988	25,686	1997	44,580

Source: *Statistical Abstract of the United States*, various years.

the company president read a recent article in the popular press touting business videos as today's "hot sales weapon." One thing the president would like to investigate before taking this action is the history of TV advertising in this country, especially the trend-cycle.

Table P-7 contains the total dollars spent on U.S. TV advertising, in millions.

a. Plot the time series of U.S. TV advertising expenditures.
b. Fit a linear trend to the advertising data and plot the fitted line on the time series graph.
c. Forecast TV advertising dollars for 1998.
d. Given the results in part b, do you think there may be a cyclical component in TV advertising dollars? Explain.

8. Assume the following specific percentage seasonal indices for March based on the ratio-to-moving-average method:

$$102.2 \quad 105.9 \quad 114.3 \quad 122.4 \quad 109.8 \quad 98.9$$

What is the seasonal index for March using the median?

9. The expected trend value for October is $850. Assuming an October seasonal index of 1.12 (112%) and the multiplicative model given by Equation 5.2, what would be the forecast for October?

10. The following specific percentage seasonal indices are given for the month of December:

$$75.4 \quad 86.8 \quad 96.9 \quad 72.6 \quad 80.0 \quad 85.4$$

Assume a multiplicative decomposition model. If the expected trend for December is $900, and the median seasonal adjustment is used, what is the forecast for December?

11. A large resort near Portland, Maine, has been tracking its monthly sales for several years but has never analyzed these data. The resort computes the seasonal indices for its monthly sales. Which of the following statements about the index are correct?

a. The sum of the 12 monthly index numbers, expressed as percentages, should be 1,200.

TABLE P-12

Month	Sales ($ thousands)	Adjusted Seasonal Index (%)
January	125	51
February	113	50
March	189	87
April	201	93
May	206	95
June	241	99
July	230	96
August	245	89
September	271	103
October	291	120
November	320	131
December	419	189

Source: Kula Department Store records.

b. An index of 85 for May indicates that sales are 15% lower than the average monthly sales.

c. An index of 130 for January indicates that sales are 30% above the average monthly sales.

d. The index for any month must be between zero and 200.

e. The average percent index for each of the 12 months should be 100.

12. In preparing a report for June Bancock, manager of the Kula Department Store, you include the following statistics (Table P-12) from last year's sales. Upon seeing them, Ms. Bancock says, "This report confirms what I've been telling you: Business is getting better and better." Is this statement accurate? Why or why not?

13. The quarterly sales levels measured in millions of dollars for Goodyear Tire are shown in Table P-13. Does there appear to be a significant seasonal effect in these

TABLE P-13

Year	Quarter 1	2	3	4
1985	2292	2450	2363	2477
1986	2063	2358	2316	2366
1987	2268	2533	2479	2625
1988	2616	2793	2656	2746
1989	2643	2811	2679	2736
1990	2692	2871	2900	2811
1991	2497	2792	2838	2780
1992	2778	3066	3213	2928
1993	2874	3000	2913	2916
1994	2910	3052	3116	3210
1995	3243	3351	3305	3267
1996	3246	3330	3340[a]	3300[a]

[a]Value Line Estimates 1996.

Source: The Value Line Investment Survey (New York: Value Line, 1988, 1989, 1993, 1994, 1996), p. 126.

| TABLE P-14 | | | | | | | |
Month	1996	1997	1998	1999	2000	2001	2002
January	154	200	223	346	518	613	628
February	96	118	104	261	404	392	308
March	73	90	107	224	300	273	324
April	49	79	85	141	210	322	248
May	36	78	75	148	196	189	272
June	59	91	99	145	186	257	
July	95	167	135	223	247	324	
August	169	169	211	272	343	404	
September	210	289	335	445	464	677	
October	278	347	460	560	680	858	
November	298	375	488	612	711	895	
December	245	203	326	467	610	664	

sales levels? Analyze this time series to get the four seasonal indices, and determine the extent of the seasonal component in Goodyear's sales.
a. Would you use the trend, seasonal, or both components to forecast?
b. Forecast for the third and fourth quarters of 1996.
c. Compare your forecasts to Value Line's.

14. The monthly sales of the Cavanaugh Company, listed in Table P-14 and pictured in Figure 5-1, are given next.
a. Perform a multiplicative decomposition of the Cavanaugh Company sales time series assuming trend, seasonal, and irregular components.
b. Would you use the trend, seasonal, or both components to forecast?
c. Provide forecasts for the rest of 2002.

15. Construct a table similar to Table P-14 with the natural logarithms of monthly sales. For example, the value for January 1996 is ln(154) = 5.037.
a. Perform an additive decomposition of ln(sales) assuming the model

$$Y = T + S + I.$$

b. Would you use the trend, seasonal, or both components to forecast?
c. Provide forecasts of ln(sales) for the remaining months of 2002.
d. Take the antilogs of the forecasts calculated in part c to get forecasts of the actual sales for the remainder of 2002.
e. Compare the forecasts in part d with those in Problem 14c. Which set of forecasts do you prefer? Why?

16. Table P-16 contains the quarterly sales ($ millions) for the Disney Company from January 1980 to March 1995.
a. Perform a multiplicative decomposition of the time series consisting of Disney's quarterly sales.
b. Does there appear to be a significant trend? Discuss the nature of the seasonal component.
c. Would you use both trend and seasonal components to forecast?
d. Forecast sales for the last quarter of 1995 and the four quarters of 1996.

17. The monthly gasoline demand (thousands of barrels/day) for Yukong Oil Company of South Korea for the period January 1986 to September 1996 is contained in Table P-17.

TABLE P-16

	Quarter			
Year	1	2	3	4
1980	218.1	245.4	265.5	203.5
1981	235.1	258.0	308.4	211.8
1982	247.7	275.8	295.0	270.1
1983	315.7	358.5	363.0	302.2
1984	407.3	483.3	463.2	426.5
1985	451.5	546.9	590.4	504.2
1986	592.4	647.9	726.4	755.5
1987	766.4	819.4	630.1	734.6
1988	774.5	915.7	1013.4	1043.6
1989	1037.9	1167.6	1345.1	1288.2
1990	1303.8	1539.5	1712.2	1492.4
1991	1439.0	1511.6	1739.4	1936.6
1992	1655.1	1853.5	2079.1	2391.4
1993	2026.5	1936.8	2174.5	2727.3
1994	2275.8	2353.6	2698.4	3301.7
1995	2922.8	2764.0	3123.6	

TABLE P-17

Month	1986	1987	1988	1989	1990	1991	1992	1993	1994	1995	1996
January	15.5	20.4	26.9	36.0	52.1	64.4	82.3	102.7	122.2	145.8	170.0
February	17.8	20.8	29.4	39.0	53.1	68.1	83.6	102.2	121.4	144.4	176.3
March	18.1	22.2	29.9	42.2	56.5	68.5	85.5	104.7	125.6	145.2	174.2
April	20.5	24.1	32.4	44.3	58.4	72.3	91.0	108.9	129.7	148.6	176.1
May	21.3	25.5	33.3	46.6	61.7	74.1	92.1	112.2	133.6	153.7	185.3
June	19.8	25.9	34.5	46.1	61.0	77.6	95.8	109.7	137.5	157.9	182.7
July	20.5	26.1	34.8	48.5	65.5	79.9	98.3	113.5	143.0	169.7	197.0
August	22.3	27.5	39.1	52.6	71.0	86.7	102.2	120.4	149.0	184.2	216.1
September	22.9	25.8	39.0	52.2	68.1	84.4	101.5	124.6	149.9	163.2	192.2
October	21.1	29.8	36.5	50.8	67.5	81.4	98.5	116.7	139.5	155.4	
November	22.0	27.4	37.5	51.9	68.8	85.1	101.1	120.6	147.7	168.9	
December	22.8	29.7	39.7	55.1	68.1	81.7	102.5	124.9	154.7	178.3	

a. Plot the gasoline demand time series. Do you think an additive or multiplicative decomposition would be appropriate for this time series? Explain.

b. Perform a decomposition analysis of gasoline demand.

c. Interpret the seasonal indices.

d. Forecast gasoline demand for the last three months of 1996.

18. Table P-18 contains data values that represent the monthly sales of all retail stores in the United States in billions of dollars. Using the data through 1994, perform a decomposition analysis of this series. Comment on all three components of the series. Forecast retail sales for 1995 and compare your results with the actual values provided in the table.

19. The adjusted seasonal indices presented in Table P-19 reflect the changing volume of business of the Mt. Spokane Resort Hotel, which caters to family tourists in the summer and skiing enthusiasts during the winter months. No sharp cyclical variations are expected during 2003.

TABLE P-18

Month	1988	1989	1990	1991	1992	1993	1994	1995
January	113.6	122.5	132.6	130.9	142.1	148.4	154.6	167.0
February	115.0	118.9	127.3	128.6	143.1	145.0	155.8	164.0
March	131.6	141.3	148.3	149.3	154.7	164.6	184.2	192.1
April	130.9	139.8	145.0	148.5	159.1	170.3	181.8	187.5
May	136.0	150.3	154.1	159.8	165.8	176.1	187.2	201.4
June	137.5	149.0	153.5	153.9	164.6	175.7	190.1	202.6
July	134.1	144.6	148.9	154.6	166.0	177.7	185.8	194.9
August	138.7	153.0	157.4	159.9	166.3	177.1	193.8	204.2
September	131.9	144.1	145.6	146.7	160.6	171.1	185.9	192.8
October	133.8	142.3	151.5	152.1	168.7	176.4	189.7	194.0
November	140.2	148.8	156.1	155.6	167.2	180.9	194.7	202.4
December	171.0	176.5	179.7	181.0	204.1	218.3	233.3	238.0

Source: Survey of Current Business, 1989, 1993, 1996.

TABLE P-19

Month	Adjusted Seasonal Index	Month	Adjusted Seasonal Index
January	120	July	153
February	137	August	151
March	100	September	95
April	33	October	60
May	47	November	82
June	125	December	97

Source: Mt. Spokane Resort Hotel records.

TABLE P-24

		Sales Volume (dollars)	Commodity Price Index (1992 = 100)
1996	January	358,235	118.0
	February	297,485	118.4
	March	360,321	118.7
	April	378,904	119.2
	May	394,472	119.7
	June	312,589	119.6
	July	401,345	119.3

Source: Survey of Current Business.

a. If 600 tourists were at the resort in January 2003, what is a reasonable estimate for February?

b. The monthly trend equation is $\hat{T} = 140 + 5t$ where $t = 0$ represents January 15, 1997. What is the forecast for each month of 2003?

c. What is the average number of new tourists per month?

20. Discuss the performance of the composite index of leading indicators as a barometer of business activity in recent years.

21. What is the present position of the business cycle? Is it expanding or contracting? When will the next turning point occur?

22. What is the purpose of deflating a time series that is measured in dollars?

23. In the base period of June, the price of a selected quantity of goods was $1,289.73. In the most recent month, the price index for these goods was 284.7. How much would the selected goods cost if purchased in the most recent month?

24. Deflate the dollar sales volumes using the commodity price index values, shown in Table P-24. These indices are for all commodities with 1992 = 100.

CASES

CASE 5-1   THE SMALL ENGINE DOCTOR[13]

The Small Engine Doctor was the name of a business developed by Thomas Brown, who was a mail carrier for the U.S. Postal Service. He had been a tinkerer since childhood, always taking discarded household gadgets apart in order to understand "what made them tick." As Tom grew up and became a typical suburbanite, he acquired numerous items of lawn and garden equipment. When Tom found out about a course in small engine repair offered at a local community college, he jumped at the opportunity. Tom started small engine repair by dismantling his own equipment, overhauling it, and then reassembling it. Soon after completing the course in engine repair, he began to repair lawn mowers, rototillers, snowblowers, and other lawn and garden equipment for friends and neighbors. In the process he acquired various equipment manuals and special tools.

It was not long before Tom decided to turn his hobby into a part-time business. He placed an advertisement in a suburban shopping circular under the name of The Small Engine Doctor. Over the last two years the business had grown enough to provide a nice supplement to his regular salary. Although the growth was welcomed, as the business was about to enter its third year of operation there were a number of concerns. The business was operated out of Tom's home. The basement was partitioned into a family room, a workshop, and an office. Originally the office area was used to handle the advertising, order processing, and bookkeeping. The entire engine repair was done in the workshop. Tom's policy is to stock only a limited number of parts, ordering replacement parts as they are needed. This seemed to be the only practical way of dealing with the large variety of parts involved in repairing engines made by the dozen or so manufacturers of lawn and garden equipment.

Spare parts had proved to be the most aggravating problem in running the business. Tom started his business by buying parts from equipment dealers. This practice had several disadvantages. First, he had to pay retail for the parts. Second, most of the time the dealer had to back-order one or more parts for any given repair job. Parts ordered from the manufacturer had lead times of anywhere from 30 to 120 days. As a result, Tom changed his policy and began to order parts directly from the factory. He found that shipping and handling charges ate into his profits, even though the part price was only 60% of retail. However, the two most important problems created by the replacement parts were lost sales and storage space. Tom attracted customers because of his quality service and reasonable repair charges, which were possible because of his low overhead. Unfortunately, many potential customers would go to equipment dealers rather than wait several months for repair. The most pressing problem was storage space. While a piece of equipment was waiting for spare parts, it had to be stored on the premises. It did not take long for both his workshop and his one-car garage to overflow with equipment while he was

---

[13] This case was contributed by William P. Darrow of Towson State University, Towson, Maryland.

TABLE 5-6	The Small Engine Doctor Sales History for Case 5-1					
Month	2002 (units)	2003 (units)	Month	2002 (units)	2003 (units)
January	5	21	July	28	46
February	8	20	August	20	32
March	10	29	September	14	27
April	18	32	October	8	13
May	26	44	November	6	11
June	35	58	December	26	52

waiting for spare parts. In the second year of operation Tom actually had to suspend advertising as a tactic to limit customers due to lack of storage space.

Tom has considered stocking inventory for his third year of operation. This practice will reduce purchasing costs by making it possible to obtain quantity discounts and more favorable shipping terms. He also hopes that it will provide much better turnaround time for the customers, improving both cash flow and sales. The risks in this strategy are uncontrolled inventory carrying costs and part obsolescence.

Before committing himself to stocking spare parts, Tom wants to have a reliable forecast for business activity in the forthcoming year. He is confident enough in his knowledge of product mix to use an aggregate forecast of customer repair orders as a basis for selectively ordering spare parts. The forecast is complicated by seasonal demand patterns and a trend toward increasing sales.

Tom plans to develop a sales forecast for the third year of operation. A sales history for the first two years is given in Table 5-6. ■

QUESTIONS

1. Plot the data on a 2-year time horizon from 2002 through 2003. Connect the data points to make a time series plot.
2. Develop a trend-line equation using linear regression and plot the results.
3. Estimate the seasonal adjustment factors for each month by dividing the average demand for corresponding months by the average of the corresponding trend-line forecasts. Plot a seasonally adjusted trend line.
4. Smooth the time series using trend-adjusted exponential smoothing with three sets of smoothing constants: ($\alpha = .1, \beta = .1$), ($\alpha =$ .25, $\beta = .25$), and ($\alpha = .5, \beta = .5$). Plot the three sets of smoothed values on the time series graph. Generate forecasts through the end of the third year for each of the trend-adjusted exponential smoothing possibilities considered.
5. Calculate *MAD* values for the two models that visually appear to give the best fits (most accurate one-step-ahead forecasts).
6. If you had to limit your choice to one of the models in questions 2 and 4, identify the model you would use for your business planning in 2004, and discuss why you selected that model over the others.

CASE 5-2   MR. TUX

John Mosby has been looking forward to the decomposition of his monthly time series, monthly sales dollars. He knows that the series has a strong seasonal effect and would like it measured for two reasons. First, his banker is reluctant to allow him to make variable monthly payments on his loan. John

has explained that, because of the seasonality of his sales and monthly cash flow, he would like to make extra payments in some months and reduced, even zero, payments in others. His banker wants to see some verification of John's assertion that his sales have a strong seasonal effect.

Second, John wants to be able to forecast his monthly sales. He needs such forecasts for planning purposes, especially because his business is growing. Both bankers and venture capitalists want some solid forecasts on which to base their investment decisions. John knows his business is improving and that future prospects look bright, but investors want documentation.

The monthly sales volumes for Mr. Tux for the years 1990 through 1996 are entered into Minitab. Since 1989 was the first year of business, the sales volumes were extremely low compared to the rest of the years. For this reason, John decides to eliminate these values from the analysis. The seasonal indices are shown in Table 5-7. The rest of the computer printout is shown in Table 5-8.

John is not surprised to see the seasonal indices shown in this printout, but he is pleased to have some hard numbers to show his banker. After reviewing these figures with him, it is agreed that John will make double payments in April, May, June, and August and make no payments at all on his loan in January, February, November, and December. His

banker asks for a copy of the seasonal indices to show his boss and include in John's loan file.

Turning to a forecast for the first six months of 1997, John begins by projecting trend values using the trend equation $\hat{T}_t = 19{,}092.3 + 2{,}861.58t$. The trend estimate for January 1997 is

$$\hat{T}_{85} = 19{,}092.3 + 2{,}861.58(85) = 262{,}326.6$$

Next, John obtains the seasonal index from Table 5-7. The index for January is 31.73%. John has been reading the *Wall Street Journal* and watching the business news talk shows on a regular basis, so he already has an idea of the overall nature of the economy and its future course. He also belongs to a business service club that features talks by local economic experts on a regular basis. As he studies the C column of his computer output, showing the cyclical history of his series, he thinks about how he will forecast this value for the first six months of 1997. Since the forecasts of national and local experts call for a slow improvement in business in 1997, and since the last C value for October 1996 has turned up

TABLE 5-7	Summary of the Monthly Seasonal Indices for Mr. Tux for Case 5-2

Time Series Decomposition

Trend-Line Equation
$\hat{T}_t = 19092.3 + 2861.58t$

Seasonal Index

Period	Index
1	0.3173
2	0.4817
3	0.9013
4	1.8194
5	1.9409
6	1.1913
7	1.0229
8	1.2616
9	0.9016
10	0.7806
11	0.6035
12	0.7780

Accuracy of Model

MAPE:	19
MAD:	20672
MSD:	8.56E + 08

			TABLE 5-8	Calculations for the Short-Term Components for Mr. Tux for Case 5-2					
t	*Year*	*Month*	*Sales*	*T*	*SCI*	*TCI*	*CI*	*C*	*I*
1	1990	January	16,850	21,954	0.7675	53,106	2.4190	—	—
2		February	12,753	24,815	0.5139	26,476	1.0669	—	—
3		March	26,901	27,677	0.9720	29,848	1.0784	1.5904	0.6781
4		April	61,494	30,539	2.0137	33,799	1.1068	1.3751	0.8049
5		May	147,862	33,400	4.4270	76,183	2.2809	1.4182	1.6084
6		June	57,990	36,262	1.5992	48,676	1.3424	1.4049	0.9555
7		July	51,318	39,123	1.3117	50,168	1.2823	1.2975	0.9883
8		August	53,599	41,985	1.2766	42,486	1.0120	1.0636	0.9514
9		September	23,038	44,846	0.5137	25,553	0.5698	0.9218	0.6181
10		October	41,396	47,708	0.8677	53,028	1.1115	0.7746	1.4350
11		November	19,330	50,570	0.3823	32,032	0.6334	0.7446	0.8507
12		December	22,707	53,431	0.4250	29,188	0.5463	0.8470	0.6449
13	1991	January	15,395	56,293	0.2735	48,521	0.8619	0.7163	1.2034
14		February	30,826	59,154	0.5211	63,996	1.0819	0.7644	1.4153
15		March	25,589	62,016	0.4126	28,392	0.4578	0.9558	0.4790
16		April	103,184	64,878	1.5904	56,712	0.8742	0.9465	0.9236
17		May	197,608	67,739	2.9172	10,181	1.5030	0.8363	1.7971
18		June	68,600	70,601	0.9717	57,582	0.8156	0.9346	0.8727
19		July	39,909	73,462	0.5433	39,015	0.5311	0.9244	0.5745
20		August	91,368	76,324	1.1971	72,425	0.9489	0.8102	1.1713
21		September	58,781	79,185	0.7423	65,198	0.8234	0.7776	1.0589
22		October	59,679	82,047	0.7274	76,449	0.9318	0.8287	1.1244
23		November	33,443	84,909	0.3939	55,420	0.6527	0.8321	0.7844
24		December	53,719	87,770	0.6120	69,051	0.7867	0.8302	0.9477
25	1992	January	27,773	90,632	0.3064	87,532	0.9658	0.7616	1.2681
26		February	36,653	93,493	0.3920	76,093	0.8139	0.8721	0.9333
27		March	51,157	96,355	0.5309	56,761	0.5891	0.9229	0.6383
28		April	217,509	99,216	2.1923	11,955	1.2049	0.9059	1.3301
29		May	206,229	102,078	2.0203	106,255	1.0409	0.9297	1.1196
30		June	110,081	104,940	1.0490	92,401	0.8805	0.9965	0.8836
31		July	102,893	107,801	0.9545	100,588	0.9331	0.9602	0.9717
32		August	128,857	110,663	1.1644	102,141	0.9230	0.9965	0.9263
33		September	104,776	113,524	0.9229	116,215	1.0237	0.9974	1.0263
34		October	111,036	116,386	0.9540	142,237	1.2221	0.9848	1.2409
35		November	63,701	119,247	0.5342	105,561	0.8852	0.9587	0.9234
36		December	82,657	122,109	0.6769	106,248	0.8701	0.9110	0.9551
37	1993	January	31,416	124,971	0.2514	99,014	0.7923	0.8120	0.9758
38		February	48,341	127,832	0.3782	100,358	0.7851	0.8347	0.9406
39		March	85,651	130,694	0.6554	95,033	0.7272	0.8794	0.8269
40		April	242,673	133,555	1.8170	133,379	0.9987	0.9190	1.0867
41		May	289,554	136,417	2.1226	149,186	1.0936	0.9829	1.1126
42		June	164,373	139,279	1.1802	137,973	0.9906	1.0300	0.9617
43		July	160,608	142,140	1.1299	157,010	1.1046	1.0439	1.0582
44		August	176,096	145,002	1.2144	139,586	0.9627	1.0205	0.9433
45		September	142,363	147,863	0.9628	157,905	1.0679	1.0674	1.0005
46		October	114,907	150,725	0.7624	147,196	0.9766	1.0552	0.9255
47		November	113,552	153,586	0.7393	188,171	1.2252	1.0669	1.1484
48		December	127,042	156,448	0.8120	163,300	1.0438	1.0591	0.9856

t	Year	Month	Sales	T	SCI	TCI	CI	C	I

TABLE 5-8   (Continued)

t	Year	Month	Sales	T	SCI	TCI	CI	C	I
49	1994	January	51,604	159,310	0.3239	162,641	1.0209	1.1447	0.8919
50		February	80,366	162,171	0.4956	166,844	1.0288	1.0724	0.9594
51		March	208,938	165,033	1.2660	231,826	1.4047	1.0158	1.3828
52		April	263,830	167,894	1.5714	145,007	0.8637	1.0240	0.8435
53		May	252,216	170,756	1.4771	129,949	0.7610	0.9834	0.7739
54		June	219,566	173,617	1.2647	184,302	1.0615	0.8915	1.1908
55		July	149,082	176,479	0.8448	145,742	0.8258	0.9366	0.8817
56		August	213,888	179,341	1.1926	169,543	0.9454	0.9694	0.9752
57		September	178,947	182,202	0.9821	198,483	1.0894	0.9634	1.1308
58		October	133,650	185,064	0.7222	171,206	0.9251	1.0194	0.9075
59		November	116,946	187,925	0.6223	193,796	1.0312	1.0219	1.0092
60		December	164,154	190,787	0.8604	211,004	1.1060	0.9781	1.1308
61	1995	January	58,843	193,649	0.3039	185,456	0.9577	1.0433	0.9180
62		February	82,386	196,510	0.4193	171,037	0.8704	1.0296	0.8454
63		March	224,803	199,372	1.1276	249,429	1.2511	0.9733	1.2853
64		April	354,301	202,233	1.7519	194,732	0.9629	1.0350	0.9304
65		May	328,263	205,095	1.6005	169,130	0.8246	1.0599	0.7780
66		June	313,647	207,956	1.5082	263,273	1.2660	1.0599	1.1945
67		July	214,561	210,818	1.0178	209,754	0.9950	1.0553	0.9429
68		August	337,192	213,680	1.5780	267,283	1.2509	1.0592	1.1810
69		September	183,482	216,541	0.8473	203,513	0.9398	1.0144	0.9265
70		October	144,618	219,403	0.6591	185,256	0.8444	1.0261	0.8229
71		November	139,750	222,264	0.6288	231,585	1.0419	0.9724	1.0715
72		December	184,546	225,126	0.8198	237,216	1.0537	1.0595	0.9946
73	1996	January	71,043	227,987	0.3116	223,907	0.9821	1.1285	0.8703
74		February	152,930	230,849	0.6625	317,490	1.3753	1.1104	1.2385
75		March	250,559	233,711	1.0721	278,006	1.1895	1.0696	1.1121
76		April	409,567	236,572	1.7313	225,108	0.9515	1.0622	0.8958
77		May	394,747	239,434	1.6487	203,385	0.8494	0.9708	0.8750
78		June	272,874	242,295	1.1262	229,048	0.9453	0.9729	0.9717
79		July	230,303	245,157	0.9394	225,144	0.9184	0.9554	0.9613
80		August	375,402	248,018	1.5136	297,571	1.1998	0.9607	1.2489
81		September	195,409	250,880	0.7789	216,742	0.8639	1.0063	0.8585
82		October	173,518	253,742	0.6838	222,276	0.8760	1.0790	0.8119
83		November	181,702	256,603	0.7081	301,105	1.1734	—	—
84		December	258,713	259,465	0.9971	332,551	1.2817	—	—

(107.9%), he decides to use the following *C* values for his forecasts:

1996	November	108
	December	109
1997	January	109
	February	110
	March	111
	April	113
	May	114
	June	115

Turning to the irregular (*I*) value for these months, John does not foresee any unusual events

except for March 1997. In that month he plans to hold an open house along with reduced rates in one of his stores that he is finishing remodeling. Because of this promotion, to be accompanied by radio and TV advertising, he expects sales in that store to be 50% higher than normal. For his overall monthly sales, he thinks this effect will result in about 15% higher sales overall.

Using all the figures John has estimated, along with his computer output, he makes the forecasts for Mr. Tux sales for the first six months of 1997 as shown in Table 5-9.

TABLE 5-9	Forecasts for Mr. Tux for Case 5-2							
	Sales Forecast	=	*T*	×	*S*	×	*C*	× *I*
January	90,727	=	262,326.6		.3173		1.09	1.00
February	140,515	=	265,188.2		.4817		1.10	1.00
March	308,393	=	268,049.8		.9013		1.11	1.15
April	556,972	=	270,911.4		1.8194		1.13	1.00
May	605,757	=	273,773.0		1.9409		1.14	1.00
June	378,988	=	276,634.5		1.1913		1.15	1.00

After studying the 1997 forecasts, John is disturbed to see the wide range of monthly sales projections—from $90,727 to $605,757. Although he knew his monthly volume had considerable variability, he is concerned about such wide fluctuations. John has been thinking about expanding from his current Spokane location into the Seattle area. He has recently discovered that there are several "dress up" events in Seattle that are different from his present Spokane market. Formal homecoming dances, in particular, are big in Seattle but not in Spokane. Since these dances take place in the fall, when his Spokane business is slower (see the seasonal indices for October and November), he sees the advantage of leveling his business by entering the Seattle market.

His real concern, however, is focused on his worst months, January and February. He has recently been considering buying a tuxedo-shirt-making machine that he saw at a trade show, thinking that he might be able to concentrate on that activity during the winter months. If he receives a positive reaction from potential buyers of shirts for this period of time, he might be willing to give it a try. As it is, the seasonal indices on his computer output have focused his attention on the extreme swings in his monthly sales levels. ■

QUESTIONS

1. Suppose John's banker asked for two sentences to show his boss that would justify John's request to make extra loan payments in some months and no payments in others. Write these two sentences.
2. Assume that John will do exactly twice as much business in Seattle as in Spokane next year. Determine the Seattle seasonal indices that would be ideal to balance out the monthly revenues for Mr. Tux.
3. Disregarding Seattle, how much volume would John have to realize from his shirt-making machine to make both January and February "average"?

CASE 5-3   CONSUMER CREDIT COUNSELING

The Consumer Credit Counseling (CCC) operation was described in Chapter 1 (Case 1-2). The executive director, Marv Harnishfeger, concluded that the most important variable that CCC needed to forecast was the number of new clients that would be seen for the rest of 1993. Marv provided Dorothy Mercer monthly data for the number of new clients seen by CCC for the period January 1985 through March 1993 (see Case 3-3).

Dorothy gave you these data and asked you to complete a time series decomposition analysis. She emphasized that she wanted to completely understand the trend and seasonality components. Dorothy wanted to know the importance of each component. She also wanted to know if any unusual irregularities appeared in the data. Her final instruction required you to forecast for the rest of 1993.

Assignment

Write a report that provides Dorothy with the information she has requested. ■

CASE 5-4   MURPHY BROTHERS FURNITURE

In Case 4-4 Julie Murphy developed a naive model that combined seasonal and trend estimates (similar to Equation 4.5). One of the major reasons why she chose this naive model was its simplicity. Julie knew that her father, Glen, would need to understand the forecasting model used by the company.

It is now October of 2002 and a lot has changed. Glen Murphy has retired. Julie has completed several business courses including business forecasting at the local university. Murphy Brothers Furniture built a factory in Dallas and began to manufacture its own line of furniture in October 1995.

Monthly sales data for Murphy Brothers Furniture from 1996 to the present are shown in Table 5-10. As indicated by the pattern of these data demonstrated in Figure 5-13, sales have grown dramatically since 1996. Unfortunately, Figure 5-13 also demonstrates that one of the problems with demand is that it is somewhat seasonal. The company's general policy was to employ two shifts during the summer and early fall months and then work a single shift through the remainder of the year; substantial inventories were thus developed in the late summer and fall months until demand began to pick

up in November and December. Because of these production requirements, Julie was very anxious to prepare short-term forecasts for the company that would be based on the best available information concerning demand.

For forecasting purposes, Julie has decided to use only the data gathered since Murphy Brothers began to manufacture its own line of furniture in 1996 (Table 5-10). Julie can see (Figure 5-13) that her data have both trend and seasonality. For this reason she decides to use a time series decomposition approach to analyze her sales variable.

Because Figure 5-13 shows that the time series she is analyzing has roughly the same variability throughout the length of the series, Julie decides to use an additive components model to forecast. She runs the model, $Y_t = T_t + S_t + I_t$. A summary of the results is shown in Table 5-11. Julie checks the autocorrelation pattern of the residuals (see Figure 5-14) for randomness. The residuals are not random and the model does not appear to be adequate.

Julie is stuck. She has tried a naive model that combined seasonal and trend estimates, Winter's

TABLE 5-10		Monthly Sales for Murphy Brothers Furniture, 1996–2002 for Case 5-4										
	Jan.	*Feb.*	*Mar.*	*Apr.*	*May*	*Jun.*	*Jul.*	*Aug.*	*Sep.*	*Oct.*	*Nov.*	*Dec.*
1996	4946	4968	5601	5454	5721	5690	5804	6040	5843	6087	6469	7002
1997	5416	5393	5907	5768	6107	6016	6131	6499	6249	6472	6946	7615
1998	5876	5818	6342	6143	6442	6407	6545	6758	6485	6805	7361	8079
1999	6061	6187	6792	6587	6918	6920	7030	7491	7305	7571	8013	8727
2000	6776	6847	7531	7333	7685	7518	7672	7992	7645	7923	8297	8537
2001	7005	6855	7420	7183	7554	7475	7687	7922	7426	7736	8483	9329
2002	7120	7124	7817	7538	7921	7757	7816	8208	7828			

Murphy Brothers Furniture sales records.

FIGURE 5-13   Murphy Brothers Furniture Monthly Sales, 1996–2002

TABLE 5-11   Summary of the Decomposition Model for Murphy Brothers Furniture for Case 5-4

Time Series Decomposition

Trend-Line Equation
$$\hat{T}_t = 5604.8 + 32.45t$$

Seasonal Index

Period	Index
1	−674.60
2	−702.56
3	−143.72
4	−366.64
5	−53.52
6	−173.27
7	−42.74
8	222.32
9	−57.95
10	145.76
11	612.30
12	1234.63

Accuracy Measures

MAPE:	1.8
MAD:	131.6
MSD:	32160.2

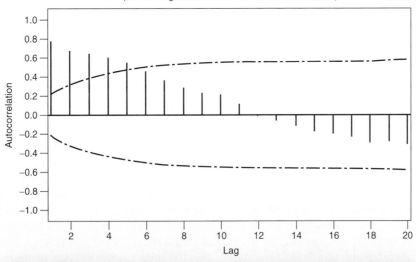

Autocorrelation Function for Residuals
(with 5% significance limits for the autocorrelations)

FIGURE 5-14	Autocorrelation Function for Residuals Using an Additive Time Series Decomposition Model

TABLE 5-12	Seasonally Adjusted Monthly Sales for Murphy Brothers Furniture, 1996–2002

	Jan.	Feb.	Mar.	Apr.	May	Jun.	Jul.	Aug.	Sep.	Oct.	Nov.	Dec.
1996	5621	5671	5745	5821	5775	5863	5847	5818	5901	5941	5857	5767
1997	6091	6096	6051	6135	6161	6189	6741	6277	6307	6326	6334	6380
1998	6551	6521	6486	6510	6496	6580	6588	6536	6543	6659	6749	6844
1999	6736	6890	6936	6954	6972	7093	7073	7269	7363	7425	7401	7492
2000	7451	7550	7675	7700	7739	7691	7715	7770	7703	7777	7685	7302
2001	7680	7558	7564	7550	7608	7648	7730	7700	7484	7590	7871	8094
2002	7795	7827	7961	7905	7975	7930	7859	7986	7886			

exponential smoothing, and classical decomposition. Julie finally decides to adjust seasonality out of the data so that forecasting techniques that cannot handle seasonal data can be applied. Julie deseasonalizes the data by adding or subtracting the seasonal index for the appropriate month. For example, she adds 674.60 to the data for each January and subtracts 1234.63 from each December. Table 5-12 shows the seasonally adjusted data.

Assignment

1. Develop a model to forecast the seasonally adjusted sales data.

2. Although all the data were involved in the decomposition, using the forecast origin of December 2001, forecast sales for the first nine months of 2002. Is this forecast accurate when compared to the actual data?

3. Forecast sales for October 2002.

4. Compare the pattern of the retail sales data presented in Case 3-1A with the pattern of the actual sales data from 1992 through 1995 presented in Case 4-4 with the pattern of the actual sales data from 1996 through 2001 presented in this case. ■

CASE 5-5   AAA WASHINGTON[14]

AAA Washington is one of the two regional automobile clubs affiliated with the American Automobile Association (AAA, or Triple A) operating in Washington State. In 1993, 69% of all people belonging to automobile clubs were members of the American Automobile Association, making it the largest automobile club in North America. AAA is a national association that services its individual members through a federation of approximately 150 regional clubs that have chosen to be affiliated with the national association. The national association sets a certain number of minimum standards with which the affiliated clubs must comply in order to retain their affiliation with the association. Its own board of trustees and management administer each regional club locally. The local management and trustees are responsible for recruiting and retaining members within their assigned territories and for ensuring the financial health of the regional club. Beyond compliance with the minimum standards set by the AAA, each regional club is free to determine what additional products and services it will offer and how it will price these products and services.

AAA Washington was founded in 1904. Its service territory comprises the 26 Washington counties west of the Columbia River. The club offers its members a variety of automobile and automobile-travel-related services. Member benefits provided in cooperation with the national association include emergency road services; a rating service for lodging, restaurants, and automotive repair shops; tour guides to AAA-approved lodging, restaurants, camping, and points of interest; and advocacy for legislation and public spending in the best interests of the motoring public. In addition to these services, AAA Washington offers its members expanded protection plans for emergency road service; financial services, including affinity credit cards, personal lines of credit, checking and savings accounts, time deposits, and no-fee American Express traveler's checks; access to a fleet of mobile diagnostic vans for determining the "health" of a member's vehicle; a travel agency; and an insurance agency. The club provides these services through a network of offices located in Bellevue, Bellingham, Bremerton, Everett, Lynnwood, Olympia, Renton, Seattle, Tacoma, the Tri-Cities (Pasco, Richland, and Kennewick), Vancouver, Wenatchee, and Yakima.

Club research has consistently shown that the emergency road service benefit is the primary reason that people join AAA. The importance of emergency road service in securing members is reflected in the three types of memberships offered by AAA Washington: Basic, AAA Plus, and AAA Plus RV. Basic membership provides members 5 miles of towing from the point at which their vehicle is disabled. AAA Plus provides members with 100 miles of towing from the disabled point. AAA Plus RV provides the 100-mile towing service to members who own recreational vehicles in addition to passenger cars and light trucks. Providing emergency road service is also the club's single largest operating expense. It is projected that delivering emergency road service will cost $9.5 million in the next fiscal year, 37% of the club's annual operating budget.

Michael DeCoria, a CPA and M.B.A. graduate of Eastern Washington University, had recently joined the club's management team as vice president of operations. One of the responsibilities Mr. DeCoria assumed was the management of emergency road services. Early in his assessment of the emergency road service operation, Mr. DeCoria discovered that emergency road service costs had increased at a rate faster than could be justified by the rate of inflation and the growth in club membership. Mr. DeCoria began by analyzing the way the club delivers emergency road service to determine if costs could be controlled more tightly in this area.

Emergency road service is delivered in one of four ways: AAA Washington service fleet, contracting companies, reciprocal reimbursement, and direct reimbursement. AAA Washington's fleet of service vehicles responds to emergency road service calls from members who become disabled in the downtown Seattle area. Within AAA Washington's service area, but outside of downtown Seattle, commercial towing companies that have contracted with AAA Washington to provide this service

---

[14]This case was provided by Steve Branton, former student and M.B.A. graduate, Eastern Washington University.

respond to emergency road service calls. Members arrange for both of these types of emergency road service by calling the club's dispatch center. Should a member become disabled outside of AAA Washington's service area, the member can call the local AAA-affiliated club to receive emergency road service. The affiliate club pays for this service and then bills AAA Washington for reciprocal reimbursement through a clearing service provided by the national association. Finally, members may contact a towing company of their choice directly, paying for the towing service and then submitting a request for reimbursement to the club. AAA Washington reimburses the actual cost of the towing

or $50, whichever is less, directly to the member. After a careful examination of the club's four service delivery methods, Mr. DeCoria concluded that the club was controlling the cost of service delivery as tightly as was practical.

Another possible source of increasing costs was a rise in the use of emergency road service. Membership had been growing steadily for several years, but the increased cost was more than what could be attributed to simple membership growth. Mr. DeCoria then checked to see if there was a growth in emergency road service use on a per-member basis. He discovered that between fiscal year 1990 and fiscal year 1991 the average number

TABLE 5-13		Emergency Road Call Volume by Month for Case 5-5			
Year	Month	Calls	Year	Month	Calls
1988	May	20,002	1991	January	23,441
	June	21,591		February	19,205
	July	22,696		March	20,386
	August	21,509		April	19,988
	September	22,123		May	19,077
	October	21,449		June	19,141
	November	23,475		July	20,883
	December	23,529		August	20,709
1989	January	23,327		September	19,647
	February	24,050		October	22,013
	March	24,010		November	22,375
	April	19,735		December	22,727
	May	20,153	1992	January	22,367
	June	19,512		February	21,155
	July	19,892		March	21,209
	August	20,326		April	19,286
	September	19,378		May	19,725
	October	21,263		June	20,276
	November	21,443		July	20,795
	December	23,366		August	21,126
1990	January	23,836		September	20,251
	February	23,336		October	22,069
	March	22,003		November	23,268
	April	20,155		December	26,039
	May	20,070	1993	January	26,127
	June	19,588		February	20,067
	July	20,804		March	19,673
	August	19,644		April	19,142
	September	17,424			
	October	20,833			
	November	22,490			
	December	24,861			

of emergency road service calls per member grew by 3.28%, from an average of 0.61 calls per member to 0.63 calls (AAA Washington's fiscal year begins July 1). Concerned that a continuation of this trend will have a negative impact on the club financially, Mr. DeCoria has gathered the data on emergency road service call volume as presented in Table 5-13. ∎

QUESTIONS

1. Perform a time series decomposition on the AAA emergency road service calls data.
2. Write a memo to Mr. DeCoria summarizing the important insights into changes in emergency road service call volume that you discovered from your time series decomposition analysis.

CASE 5-6   ALOMEGA FOOD STORES

In Example 1.1 Julie Ruth, Alomega Food Stores president, had collected data on her company's monthly sales along with several other variables she thought might be related to sales (review Example 1.1 in Chapter 1). Case Study 2-3 in Chapter 2 explained how Julie used her Minitab program to calculate a simple regression equation using the best predictor for monthly sales (see pp. 52–53).

After reviewing the results of this regression analysis including the low *r*-squared value (36%), she decided to try time series decomposition on the single variable, monthly sales. Figure 5-15 shows the plot of sales data (see Case 3-4) that she obtained. It looked like sales were too widely scattered around the trend line for accurate forecasts. This impression was confirmed when she looked at the *MAPE* value of 28. She interpreted this to mean that the average percentage error between the actual values and the trend line was 28%, a value she considered too high. She next tried a multiplicative decomposition of the data. The results are shown in Figure 5-16.

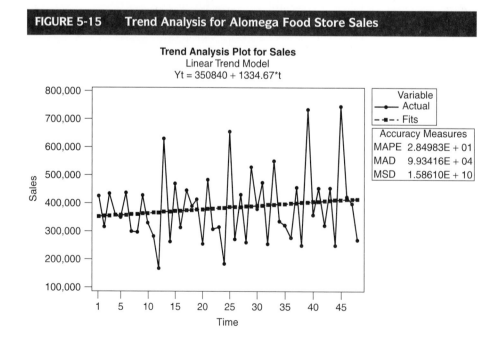

FIGURE 5-15   Trend Analysis for Alomega Food Store Sales

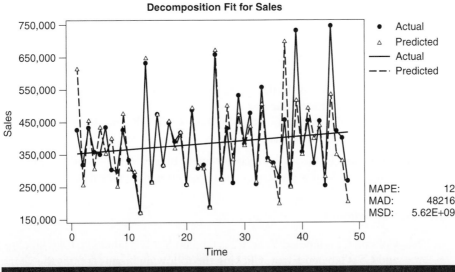

Decomposition Fit for Sales

MAPE:	12
MAD:	48216
MSD:	5.62E+09

FIGURE 5-16   Decomposition Fit for Alomega Food Store Sales

In addition to the trend equation shown on the printout, Julie was interested in the seasonal (monthly) indices that the program calculated. She noted that the lowest sales month was December (month 12, index = 0.49) and the highest was January (month 1, index = 1.74). She was aware of the wide swing between December and January but didn't realize how extreme it was.

She also noted that the *MAPE* had dropped to 12%, a definite improvement over the value obtained using the trend equation alone.

Finally, she had the program provide forecasts for the next 12 months, using the trend equation projections modified by the seasonal indices. She thought she might use these as forecasts for her planning purposes but wondered if another forecasting method might produce better forecasts. She was also concerned about what her production manager, Jackson Tilson, might say about her forecasts, especially since he had expressed concern about using the computer to make predictions (see his remarks at the end of Example 1.1 on page 8). ■

QUESTION

What might Jackson Tilson say about her forecasts?

Minitab Applications

The problem. In Example 5.1 a trend equation was developed for annual registration of new passenger cars in the United States from 1960 to 1992.

Minitab Solution

1. After the new passenger car registration data are entered into C1 of the worksheet, click on the following menus to run the trend analysis:

```
Stat>Time Series>Trend Analysis
```

2. The Trend Analysis dialog box appears.

   a. The Variable is Registrations.
   b. Click Linear for Model Type.
   c. Click Generate forecasts, and place a 1 in the number of forecasts box in order to forecast 1993.
   d. Click Options. In the space provided for a TITLE place Linear Trend for Car Registrations Time Series.
   e. Click OK for Options dialog box. Click OK and the graph that was shown in Figure 5-3 appears.

The problem. Table 5-1 was constructed to show the trend estimates and errors computed for the new passenger car registration data (see p. 162).

Minitab Solution

1. Column C1 is labeled Year, C2 is labeled Y, C3 is labeled t, C4 is labeled Estimates, and C5 is labeled Error. Clicking the following menus creates the years:

```
Calc>Make Patterned Data>Simple Set of Numbers
```

2. The Simple Set of Numbers dialog box appears.

   a. The following responses are given:
   Store patterned data in: C1
   From first value: 1960
   To last value: 1992
   In steps of: 1
   b. Click OK and the years appear in column 1.
   c. The new passenger car registration data are entered into C2.

3. The time-coded data *t* are entered into C3 using the Simple Set of Numbers dialog box.
4. The trend estimates are entered into C4 by clicking the same menus for the trend analysis used to solve Example 5.1, with one additional step.
5. Click on the Storage menu and obtain the Trend Analysis-Storage dialog box.

   a. Under Storage click on Fits (trend line) and Residuals (detrended data).
   b. Click OK for this dialog box and then the Trend Analysis dialog box. The trend estimates will appear in C4 and the errors (residuals) will appear in C5.

The problem. In Examples 5.3 and 5.4 Perkin Kendell, the analyst for the Outboard Marine Corporation, wanted to forecast quarterly sales for 1997.

Minitab Solution

1. Enter the appropriate years into C1, quarters into C2, and the data into C3. To run a decomposition model click on the following menus:

```
Stat>Time Series>Decomposition
```

2. The Decomposition dialog box shown in Figure 5-17 appears.

   a. The Variable is C3 or Sales.
   b. Since the data are quarterly, the Seasonal length is 4.

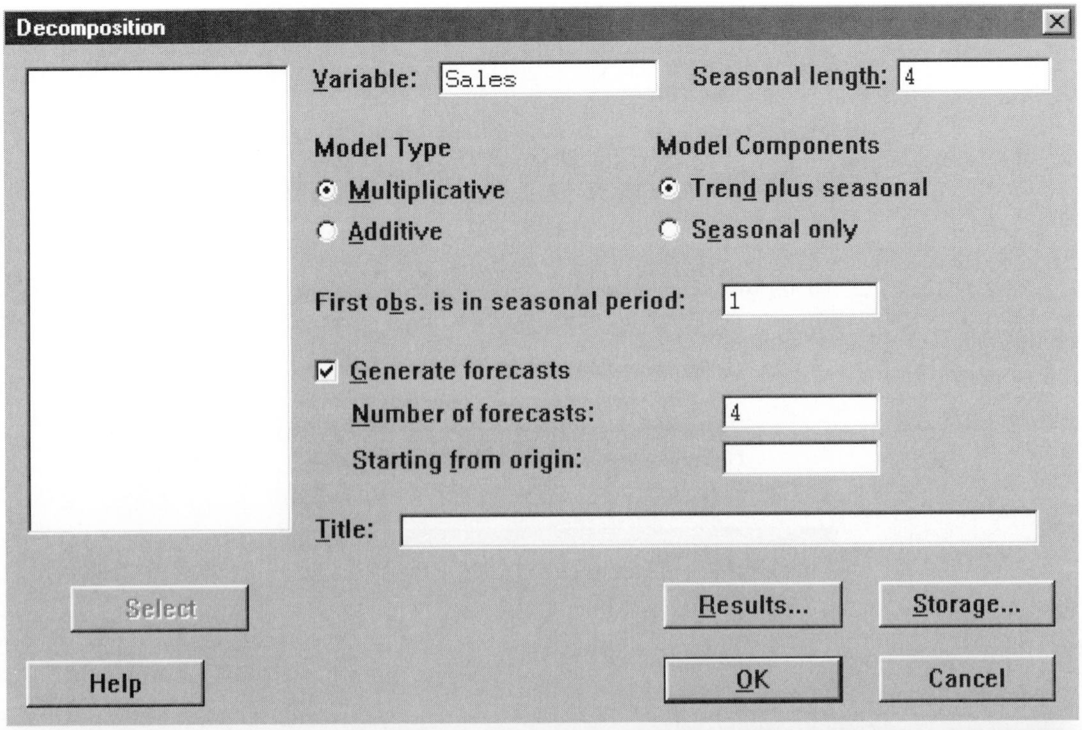

FIGURE 5-17   Minitab Decomposition Dialog Box

      c. The Model type is Multiplicative and the Model Components are Trend plus seasonal.

      d. Click on Options. The initial seasonal period is 1. Click OK.

      e. Click Generate forecasts and enter 4 for the Number of forecasts.

3. Click on the Storage menu and obtain the Decomposition—Storage dialog box shown in Figure 5-18.

      a. Under Storage click on Trend line, Detrended data, Seasonals, and Seasonally adjusted data.

      b. Click OK for both this dialog box and the Decomposition dialog box. Table 5-4 shows the trend estimates in C4 (labeled T), the detrended data in C5 (labeled SCI), the seasonals in C6 (labeled S), and the seasonally adjusted data in C7 (labeled TCI).

4. Figures 5-10 and 5-11 appear on the screen and can be printed one at a time using the following menus:

```
File>Print Graph
```

5. After the graphs have been printed, click

```
File>Print Session Window
```

and the forecasts shown in Figure 5-9 will print.

The CI, C, and I columns could be computed using Minitab but will be demonstrated in the next section, "Excel Applications."

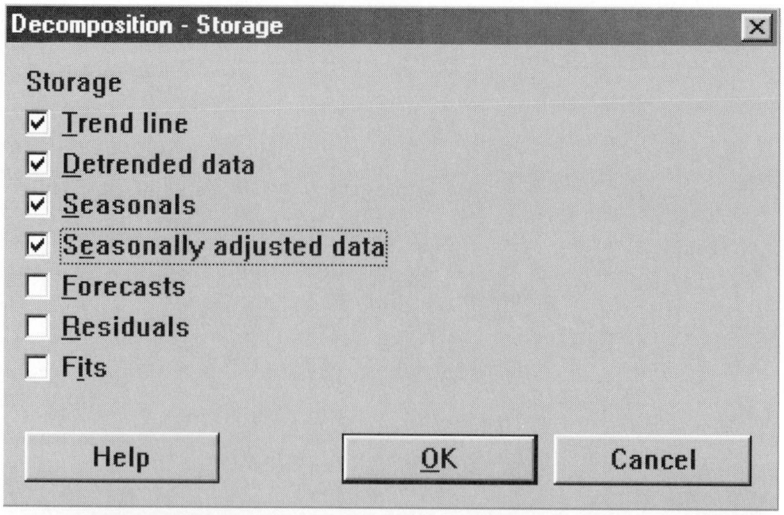

FIGURE 5-18   Minitab Decomposition—Storage Dialog Box

Excel Applications

The problem. Figure 5-6 shows data and a graph for mutual fund salespeople (see p. 165). An exponential trend model is needed to fit these data.

Excel Solution

1. Enter Y in A1 and the salespeople data in A2:A8.
2. Enter X in B1 and the X-coded variable (1, 2, 3, 4, 5, 6, 7) in B2:B8.
3. Enter Log Y in C1 and create the logarithms (to the base 10) of the Y variable by entering the formula =LOG10(A2) in cell C2. Copy this formula to the rest of the column.
4. Click on the following menus to compute the exponential trend.

   ```
   Tools>Data Analysis
   ```

5. The Data Analysis dialog box appears. Under Analysis Tools choose Regression and click OK. The Regression dialog box shown in Figure 5-19 appears.
   a. Enter C1:C8 as the Input Y Range.
   b. Enter B1:B8 as the Input X Range.
   c. Select the Labels check box.
   d. Enter Figure 5-20 as the name of the New Worksheet Ply. Click OK.

   Figure 5-20 represents Excel output for an exponential model of mutual fund salespeople. The equation is

$$\log \hat{T} = 1.00069 + 0.11834t$$

The antilogs of the regression coefficients in this equation are

$$b_0 = antilog\,1.000692 = 10.016$$
$$b_1 = antilog\,0.118338 = 1.313$$

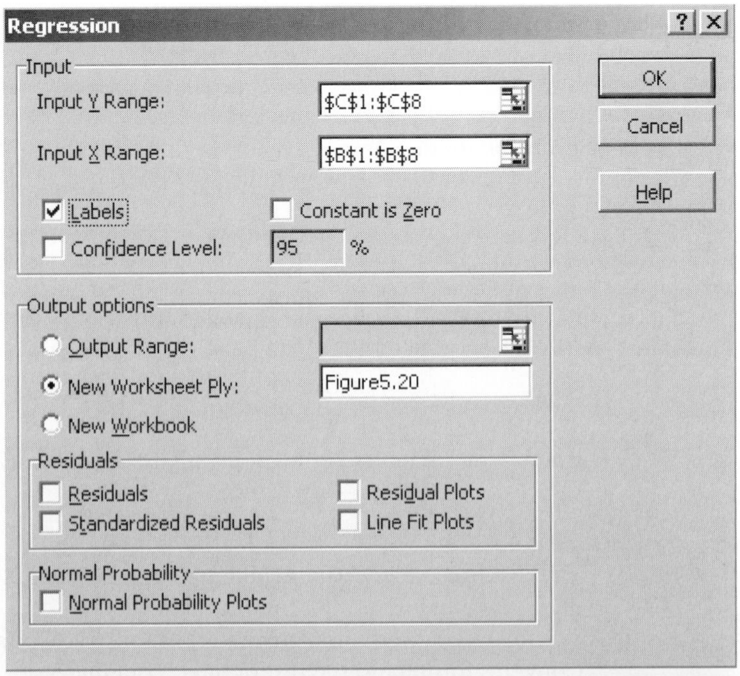

FIGURE 5-19 **Excel Regression Dialog Box**

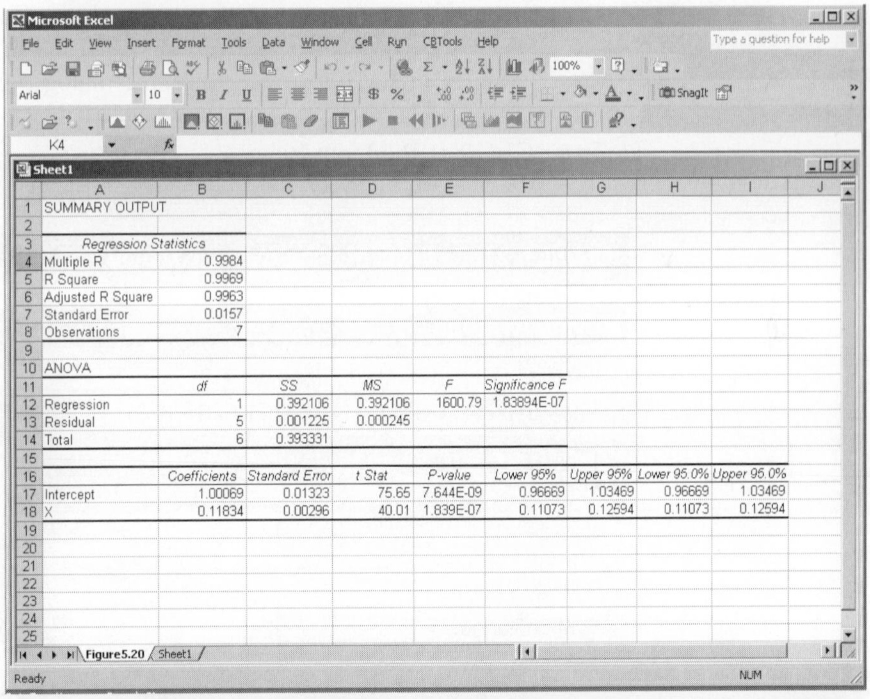

	A	B	C	D	E	F	G	H	I
1	SUMMARY OUTPUT								
2									
3	*Regression Statistics*								
4	Multiple R	0.9984							
5	R Square	0.9969							
6	Adjusted R Square	0.9963							
7	Standard Error	0.0157							
8	Observations	7							
9									
10	ANOVA								
11		*df*	*SS*	*MS*	*F*	*Significance F*			
12	Regression	1	0.392106	0.392106	1600.79	1.83894E-07			
13	Residual	5	0.001225	0.000245					
14	Total	6	0.393331						
15									
16		*Coefficients*	*Standard Error*	*t Stat*	*P-value*	*Lower 95%*	*Upper 95%*	*Lower 95.0%*	*Upper 95.0%*
17	Intercept	1.00069	0.01323	75.65	7.644E-09	0.96669	1.03469	0.96669	1.03469
18	X	0.11834	0.00296	40.01	1.839E-07	0.11073	0.12594	0.11073	0.12594

FIGURE 5-20 **Excel Regression Output for the Mutual Fund Salespeople Example**

Thus the fitted exponential trend equation is

$$\hat{T} = (10.016)(1.313)^t$$

The problem. In the Outboard Marine situation, Examples 5.3 and 5.4, the *CI* column, the *C* column (a three-period moving average), and the *I* column are computed for Table 5-4.

Excel Solution

1. Enter the Minitab file that contains the data for Table 5-4 and highlight the *T* column, C4. Click on the following menus:

   ```
   Edit>Copy Cells
   ```

2. Enter your Excel spreadsheet, highlight A1, and click the following menus:

   ```
   Edit>Paste
   ```

3. The data for the *T* column will appear in column A. Repeat the process copying the *TCI* column C7 to B1 on the worksheet.
4. To create the *CI* column, position the mouse at C1 and enter the formula =B1/A1. Copy this formula to the rest of the C column.
5. Click on the following menus to compute the *C* column using a three-period moving average.

   ```
   Tools>Data Analysis
   ```

6. The Data Analysis dialog box appears. Under Analysis Tools choose Moving Average and click OK. The Moving Average dialog box shown in Figure 5-21 appears.

   a. Enter C1:C28 in the Input Range.
   b. The Interval is equal to 3.

FIGURE 5-21   Excel Moving Average Dialog Box

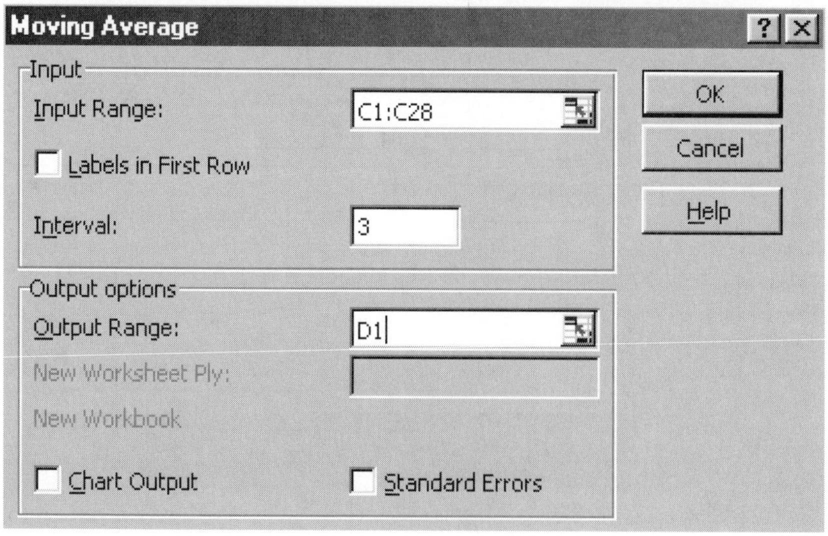

c. Enter D1 in the Output Range. Excel has improperly placed the first moving average in D3 instead of D2.
d. Highlight the first cell of the output range, D1.
e. Click on

```
Edit>Delete
```

and in the Delete dialog box select the Shift Cells Up option.
f. Click OK.

7. To create the *I* column, position the mouse at E2 and enter the formula =C2/D2. Copy this formula to the rest of the E column.

8. In order to transfer the *CI*, *C*, and *I* columns to the Minitab worksheet, position the mouse at C1 and highlight through E28. Click the following menus:

```
Edit>Copy
```

9. Enter the Minitab worksheet that contains Table 5-4 and highlight row 1 of C8. Click:

```
Edit>Paste>Insert Cells
```

Table 5-4 is complete.

References

Bell, W. R., and S. C. Hillmer. "Issues Involved with the Seasonal Adjustment of Economic Time Series." *Journal of Business and Economic Statistics* (1984):291–320.

Diebold, F. X. *Elements of Forecasting*, Third Edition. Cincinnati, OH: South-Western, 2004.

Findley, D. F., B. C. Monsell, W. R. Bell, M. C. Otto, and B. Chen. "New Capabilities and Methods of the X-12-ARIMA Seasonal-Adjustment Program." *Journal of Business and Economic Statistics* (1998):127–152.

Johnson, R. A., and D. W. Wichern. *Business Statistics: Decision Making with Data.* New York: John Wiley & Sons, 1997.

Makridakis, S., S. C. Wheelwright, and R. J. Hyndman. *Forecasting Methods and Applications,* Third Edition. New York: John Wiley & Sons, 1998.

Moore, G. H., and J. Shiskin. "Early Warning Signals for the Economy." In *Statistics: A Guide to Business and Economics,* J. M. Tanur *et al.,* Eds. San Francisco: Holden-Day, 1976.

Wichern, D. W. "Lagging Indicators." In *Encyclopedia of Statistical Sciences,* S. Kotz *et al.,* Eds., Vol. 4. New York: John Wiley & Sons, 1983:439–440.

Wichern, D. W. "Leading Indicators." In *Encyclopedia of Statistical Sciences,* S. Kotz *et al.,* Eds., Vol. 4. New York: John Wiley & Sons, 1983:582–585.

CHAPTER

6

SIMPLE LINEAR REGRESSION

In Chapter 2, the linear association between two numerical variables (correlation) was discussed. Linear association implies a straight-line relationship, and we showed how to fit a straight line to pairs of observations on the two variables using the method of least squares. In this chapter, simple linear regression (straight-line) models are discussed in some detail. Once a linear relationship is established, knowledge of the independent variable can be used to forecast the dependent variable.

To review the analysis of the relationship between two variables discussed in Chapter 2, consider the following example.

Example 6.1

Suppose Mr. Bump observes the selling price and sales volume gallons of milk for 10 randomly selected weeks. The data he has collected are presented in Table 6-1.

First he constructs a scatter diagram of the data, shown in Figure 6-1. It appears from this scatter diagram that a negative linear relationship exists between Y, the number of milk gallons sold, and X, the price of each gallon. It seems that as price goes up, volume goes down.

Bump now wishes to measure the degree of this apparent relationship by calculating the sample correlation coefficient r. Using Equation 2.9 and the calculations in Table 6-2, he finds

$$r = \frac{n\Sigma XY - (\Sigma X)(\Sigma Y)}{\sqrt{n\Sigma X^2 - (\Sigma X)^2}\sqrt{n\Sigma Y^2 - (\Sigma Y)^2}}$$

$$= \frac{10(149.3) - (14.4)(112)}{\sqrt{10(21.56) - (14.4)^2}\sqrt{10(1,488) - (112)^2}}$$

$$= \frac{-119.8}{138.7} = -.86$$

TABLE 6-1	Data for Milk Gallons for Example 6.1	
Week	Weekly Sales Level, Y (thousands of gallons)	Selling Price X
1	10	$1.30
2	6	2.00
3	5	1.70
4	12	1.50
5	10	1.60
6	15	1.20
7	5	1.60
8	12	1.40
9	17	1.00
10	20	1.10

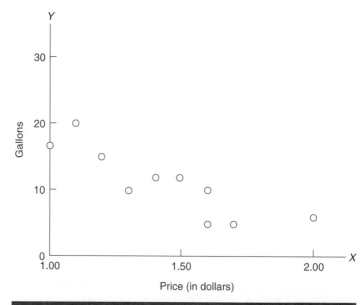

FIGURE 6-1   Scatter Diagram for Example 6.1

TABLE 6-2   Computations Needed for Example 6.1

	Y	X	XY	X^2	Y^2
$n = 10$	10	1.30	13.0	1.69	100
	6	2.00	12.0	4.00	36
	5	1.70	8.5	2.89	25
	12	1.50	18.0	2.25	144
	10	1.60	16.0	2.56	100
	15	1.20	18.0	1.44	225
	5	1.60	8.0	2.56	25
	12	1.40	16.8	1.96	144
	17	1.00	17.0	1.00	289
	20	1.10	22.0	1.21	400
Totals	112	14.40	149.3	21.56	1,488

The sample correlation coefficient of −.86 indicates a fairly strong negative relationship between Y and X—as the price of a gallon of milk goes up, the number of gallons sold goes down.

The question that may occur next is: How much does the volume drop as price is raised? This question suggests drawing a straight line through the data points displayed on the scatter diagram. After this line has been drawn, the slope of the line will show the average decrease in volume Y for each dollar increase in X.

REGRESSION LINE

Mr. Bump might visually draw a straight line through the data points, attempting to fit the line to the points as closely as possible. However, someone else might draw a different line. A better procedure is to find the best straight line using a criterion that, for a given set of data, produces the same line regardless of the person doing the fitting.

As we pointed out in Chapter 2, one popular criterion for determining the best-fitting straight line is the *least squares criterion*.

> The *line that best fits* a collection of *X–Y* data points is that line minimizing the sum of squared distances from the points to the line as measured in the vertical, or *Y*, direction. This line is known as the *least squares line* or *fitted regression line*, and its equation is called the *fitted regression equation*.

The fitted straight line is of the form $\hat{Y} = b_0 + b_1 X$. The first term, b_0, is the *Y intercept*, and the second term, b_1, is the *slope*. Recall that the slope represents the amount of change in *Y* when *X* increases by one unit. The immediate objective is to determine the values of b_0 and b_1.

The *method of least squares* chooses the values for b_0 and b_1 to minimize the sum of squared errors (distances):

$$SSE = \Sigma(Y - \hat{Y})^2 = \Sigma(Y - b_0 - b_1 X)^2 \qquad (6.1)$$

Using a little calculus (see Appendix A), specific algebraic expressions can be derived for the least squares values. In particular,

$$b_1 = \frac{n\Sigma XY - \Sigma X \Sigma Y}{n\Sigma X^2 - (\Sigma X)^2} = \frac{\Sigma(X - \bar{X})(Y - \bar{Y})}{\Sigma(X - \bar{X})^2} \qquad (6.2)$$

$$b_0 = \frac{\Sigma Y}{n} - \frac{b_1 \Sigma X}{n} = \bar{Y} - b_1 \bar{X} \qquad (6.3)$$

As you might guess, the least squares slope coefficient is related to the sample correlation coefficient. Specifically,

$$b_1 = \frac{\sqrt{\Sigma(Y - \bar{Y})^2}}{\sqrt{\Sigma(X - \bar{X})^2}} r \qquad (6.4)$$

So b_1 and r are proportional to one another and have the same sign.

The difference between the *Y* values actually observed and the corresponding fitted *Y* values, the $\hat{Y}$'s, are called the *residuals*. The residuals are the vertical distances (positive or negative) of the data points from the least squares line.

We have the identity

$$\text{Observation} = \text{Fit} + \text{Residual}$$

or, in symbols,

$$Y = \hat{Y} + (Y - \hat{Y}) \qquad (6.5)$$

In this context, the fit represents the overall pattern in the data and the residuals represent the deviations from this pattern. The split into fit plus residual applies to patterns other than straight lines, and we will make use of it repeatedly in later chapters.

Example 6.2

The least squares coefficients for a straight line fit to Mr. Bump's data (see Figure 6-1) are easily computed using Equations 6.2 and 6.3 and the information in Table 6-2. We have

$$b_1 = \frac{10(149.3) - (14.4)(112)}{10(21.56) - (14.4)^2} = \frac{-119.8}{8.24} = -14.54$$

$$b_0 = \frac{112}{10} - (-14.54)\frac{14.4}{10} = 11.2 + 14.54(1.44) = 32.14$$

The fitted least squares line has the equation

$$\hat{Y} = b_0 + b_1 X \qquad\qquad\qquad (6.6)$$

$$\hat{Y} = 32.14 - 14.54X$$

This equation is called the *fitted regression equation*.

Mr. Bump may now wish to interpret the values in this equation. The Y intercept, b_0, is the value Y when X is equal to zero. A strict interpretation would suggest that the average number of gallons sold when $X = 0$ (that is, if the price of a gallon of milk were zero) is 32,140 gallons. This interpretation does not agree with common sense because one would expect more milk to be "sold" if it were free. The problem illustrated here involves predicting a value for Y based on an X value about which no sample evidence has been collected. That is, none of the sample points have an X value at or near zero. In this case, as in many regression analysis cases, a useful interpretation of the Y intercept is not possible.

In more general terms, it is often not wise to predict Y values for any X beyond the range of the X's collected in the sample data. A regression function should be interpreted as a useful approximation to real-world behavior *over the region for which there is data*. Extrapolation beyond the data requires the strong assumption that the nature of the relation between Y and X does not change.[1]

The slope coefficient, b_1, may be interpreted as the average change in Y that occurs when X increases by 1 unit. In this example Y decreases by an average of 14.54 (that is, 14,540 fewer gallons are sold) when X increases by 1 (the cost of a gallon of milk is raised by $1). Each dollar increase in a gallon of milk reduces the quantity purchased by an average of 14,540 gallons, or, to put this statement in more meaningful units, the sample evidence indicates that each increase of 1 cent in a gallon of milk reduces the quantity purchased by an average of 145.4 gallons.

The X–Y relationship can be illustrated by drawing the straight line that best fits the data points on the scatter diagram. The result is shown in Figure 6-2. Notice that the vertical distances from the points to the line have been shown as dotted lines. If these distances were squared and added, the resulting sum would be smaller than that of any other line that could be drawn through the points.[2] In accordance with the least squares procedure, then, this line represents the best possible fit to the 10 sample data points.

Statistical ideas must be introduced in the study of the relation between two variables when the points in the scatterplot do not lie exactly on a line, as in Figure 6-2. We think of the data in the scatterplot as a sample of observations on an underlying relation that holds in the population of X–Y values. The statistical model for simple linear regression assumes that for each value of X, the observed values of the dependent variable Y are normally distributed about a mean, $\mu_y = \beta_0 + \beta_1 X$, that depends linearly on X. That is, as X changes, the means of the distributions

---

[1] We encountered a similar situation when we discussed the usefulness of extrapolating trend curves to forecast future values of a time series in Chapter 5.

[2] For Bump's data, this smallest sum of squared distances is $SSE = 59.14$.

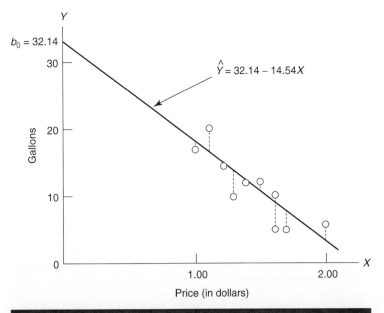

FIGURE 6-2   Fitted Regression Line for Bump's Data

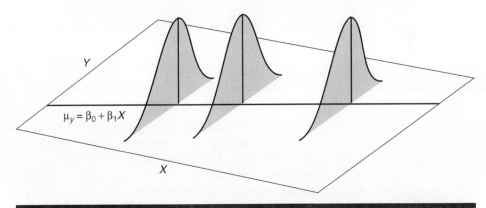

FIGURE 6-3   The Statistical Model for Simple Linear Regression

of possible Y values lie along a straight line. This line is known as the *population regression line*. Observed Y's will vary about these means because of the influence of unmeasured factors. The model assumes that this variation, measured by the standard deviation σ, is the same for all values of X. Finally, the deviation (distance) between a Y value and its mean is known as *error* and is represented by ε, the Greek letter epsilon.

In the simple linear regression model, a response Y is the sum of its mean and a random deviation ε from the mean. The deviations ε represent variation in Y due to other unobserved factors that prevent the X–Y values from lying exactly on a straight line in the scatterplot.

The statistical model for simple linear regression is illustrated schematically in Figure 6-3.

Statistical Model for Straight-Line Regression

The response, or dependent variable Y, is related to the controlled, or independent, variable X by

$$Y = \beta_0 + \beta_1 X + \varepsilon$$

Here $\beta_0 + \beta_1 X$ is the mean response for a given X. The deviations ε are assumed to be independent and normally distributed with mean 0 and standard deviation σ. The unknown constants are β_0, β_1, and σ.

The fitted (sample) regression line $\hat{Y} = b_0 + b_1 X$ may be regarded as an estimate of the population regression line $\mu_y = \beta_0 + \beta_1 X$ and the residuals $e = Y - \hat{Y}$ may be regarded as estimates of the error components ε. This implies the following correspondence

$$\text{Population:} \quad Y = \beta_0 + \beta_1 X + \varepsilon$$
$$\text{Sample:} \quad Y = b_0 + b_1 X + e$$

Most computer software packages perform correlation and regression analysis. The instructions for using Excel to run Examples 6.1 and 6.2 are presented in the "Excel Applications" section at the end of this chapter.

STANDARD ERROR OF THE ESTIMATE

Having computed the fitted straight line, Mr. Bump might next be interested in measuring the extent to which the sample data points are spread around the fitted regression function. A measure of dispersion analogous to the sample standard deviation can be developed. This measure, called the *standard error of the estimate*, measures the spread of the data points about the fitted line in the Y direction. The standard error of the estimate is denoted by $s_{y \cdot x}$ and is given by

$$s_{y \cdot x} = \sqrt{\frac{\Sigma(Y - \hat{Y})^2}{n - 2}} \tag{6.7}$$

The *standard error of the estimate* measures the amount by which the actual Y values differ from the estimated values $\hat{Y}$. For relatively large samples, we would expect about 67% of the differences $Y - \hat{Y}$ to be within $s_{y \cdot x}$ of 0 and about 95% of these differences to be within $2s_{y \cdot x}$ of 0.

The standard error of the estimate is similar to the sample standard deviation introduced in Chapter 2. It can be used to estimate a population standard deviation. In fact, $s_{y \cdot x}$ estimates the standard deviation σ of the error term ε in the statistical model for simple linear regression. Equivalently, $s_{y \cdot x}$ estimates the common standard deviation σ of the normal distribution of Y values about the population regression line $\mu_y = \beta_0 + \beta_1 X$ at each X (see Figure 6-3).

A regression analysis with a small standard error of the estimate means that all the data points lie very close to the fitted regression line.[3] If the standard error of the estimate is large, the data points are widely dispersed about the fitted line.

For computational purposes, Equation 6.7 can be converted to

$$s_{y \cdot x} = \sqrt{\frac{\Sigma Y^2 - b_0 \Sigma Y - b_1 \Sigma XY}{n - 2}} \qquad \textbf{(6.8)}$$

For the Bump example, the standard error of the estimate is

$$s_{y \cdot x} = \sqrt{\frac{1{,}488 - (32.14)(112) - (-14.54)(149.3)}{10 - 2}}$$

$$= \sqrt{\frac{59.14}{8}} = \sqrt{7.39} = 2.72$$

With $\hat{Y}$ values in the 3–18 range (see Figure 6-2), $s_{y \cdot x}$ is moderately large and indicates that an appreciable amount of the variation in Y (gallons sold) is not explained by X (price). We investigate this assertion further in the section on "Coefficient of Determination" later.

FORECASTING *Y*

Next, the fitted regression line can be used to estimate the value of Y for a given value of X. To obtain a *point prediction*, or forecast, for a given value of X, simply evaluate the estimated regression function at X.

Example 6.3
Suppose Mr. Bump wished to forecast the quantity of milk sold if the price per gallon were set at \$1.63. From Equation 6.6 the forecast is

$$\hat{Y} = 32.14 - 14.54X$$
$$\hat{Y} = 32.14 - 14.54(1.63) = 8.440$$

or 8,440 gallons. Note that this forecast is a value of $\hat{Y}$; that is, the forecast is the Y coordinate of the point on the fitted regression line where $X = 1.63$.

Of course, Mr. Bump realizes that the actual Y values corresponding to settings of the X's are unlikely to lie exactly on the regression line. In fact, they will be spread about the line as measured by $s_{y \cdot x}$. Moreover, the sample (fitted) regression line is an estimate of the population regression line based on a sample of 10 data points. Other random samples of 10 would produce different fitted regression lines, similar to the case in which many samples drawn from the same population have different sample means.

There are two sources of uncertainty then associated with a point prediction generated by the fitted regression equation:

1. Uncertainty due to the dispersion of the data points about the sample regression line.
2. Uncertainty due to the dispersion of the sample regression line about the population regression line.

---

[3] If all the data points lie exactly on the fitted line, $Y = \hat{Y}$ for all X, and $s_{y \cdot x} = 0$.

An *interval prediction* of Y can be constructed that takes these two sources of uncertainty into account.

The *standard error of the forecast*, s_f, measures the variability of the predicted Y about the actual Y for a given value of X. The standard error of the forecast is

$$s_f = \sqrt{s_{y\cdot x}^2 + s_{y\cdot x}^2 \left(\frac{1}{n} + \frac{(X - \bar{X})^2}{\Sigma(X - \bar{X})^2}\right)}$$

$$s_f = s_{y\cdot x}\sqrt{1 + \frac{1}{n} + \frac{(X - \bar{X})^2}{\Sigma(X - \bar{X})^2}} \tag{6.9}$$

The first term, $s_{y\cdot x}^2$, under the first radical sign in Equation 6.9 measures the dispersion of the data points about the sample regression line (first source of uncertainty). The second term under the radical sign measures the dispersion of the sample regression line about the population regression line (second source of uncertainty). Notice that the standard error of the forecast depends on X, the value of X for which a forecast of Y is desired. Also notice that s_f is smallest when $X = \bar{X}$ because then the numerator in the third term under the radical in Equation 6.9 will be $(\bar{X} - \bar{X})^2 = 0$.[4] All things equal, the farther X is from $\bar{X}$, the larger the standard error of the forecast.

If the statistical model for simple linear regression is appropriate, a prediction interval for Y is given by

$$\hat{Y} \pm t s_f \tag{6.10}$$

where t is a percentage point of Student's t distribution with $df = n - 2$. If the sample size is large ($n \geq 30$), the t percentage point can be replaced with the corresponding percentage point Z of the standard normal distribution. For example, a large-sample 95% prediction interval for Y is essentially

$$\hat{Y} \pm 2 s_f \tag{6.11}$$

Example 6.4

Pictorially, Mr. Bump's 95% prediction interval for Y at various values of X would look as pictured in Figure 6-4.

Using the results in Table 6-3, and Equation 6.9 with $\bar{X} = 1.44$, the standard error of the forecast at $X = 1.63$ is

$$s_f = 2.72\sqrt{1 + \frac{1}{10} + \frac{(1.63 - 1.44)^2}{.824}} = 2.72(1.069) = 2.91$$

From Example 6.3, $\hat{Y} = 8.440$ when $X = 1.63$ and, using Equation 6.10, a 95% prediction interval for Y is

$$\hat{Y} \pm t s_f = 8.44 \pm 2.306(2.91) = 8.44 \pm 6.71$$

or (1.73, 15.15); that is, 1,730 gallons to 15,150 gallons. Here $2.306 = t_{.025}$ is the upper 2.5% point of a t distribution with $df = 8$.

The prediction interval is very wide—so wide as to be virtually worthless in forecasting Y, and occurs because of the small sample size and the relatively large value for s_f. The amount of uncertainty reflected by the wide prediction interval is not apparent in the point

---

[4] For the choice, $X = \bar{X}$, the predicted Y is $\hat{Y} = \bar{Y}$.

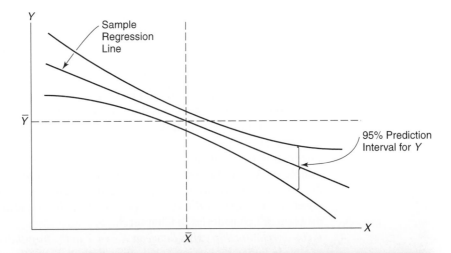

FIGURE 6-4   Prediction Interval for Bump's Data

TABLE 6-3	Calculation of $\Sigma(X - \overline{X})^2$ for Example 6.4
X	$(X - \overline{X})^2$
1.30	.0196
2.00	.3136
1.70	.0676
1.50	.0036
1.60	.0256
1.20	.0576
1.60	.0256
1.40	.0016
1.00	.1936
1.10	.1156
	$\Sigma(X - \overline{X})^2 = .8240$

forecast computed from the fitted regression function. The major advantage of the interval estimate is that it explicitly accounts for the uncertainty associated with the forecast.

In general, it is dangerous to use the fitted regression function to predict Y values beyond the range of the available data. Mr. Bump is justified in trying to forecast Y when $X = 1.63$ because some of the original X values are near 1.63. On the other hand, it may not be wise to forecast Y when $X = 3.00$. No data have been collected for X values this large, and for this reason any prediction involving such an X value would be highly suspect.[5] To estimate the quantity of milk sold when the price per gallon is $3.00, Mr. Bump has to assume the straight-line model is still valid. He may have good reason to make this assumption, but he has no direct evidence to support it.

It is useful to end this section by reviewing the assumptions underlying the statistical model for linear regression.

---

[5] Moreover, the standard error of the forecast would be large because the quantity $(X - \overline{X})^2$ would be relatively large.

1. *For a given value of X, the population of Y values is normally distributed about the population regression line.* This condition is shown in Figure 6-3. In practice, reasonably accurate results are obtained so long as the Y values are approximately normally distributed.
2. *The dispersion of population data points around the population regression line remains constant everywhere along the line.* That is, the population variance does not become larger or smaller as the X values of the data points increase. A violation of this assumption is called *heteroscedasticity*; an example of this condition and its cure appear in Chapter 8.
3. *The error terms (ε) are independent of each other.* This assumption implies a random sample of X–Y data points. When the X–Y data points are recorded over time, this assumption is often violated. Rather than being independent, consecutive observations are *serially correlated*. Methods for handling the serial correlation problem are considered in Chapter 8.
4. *A linear relationship exists between X and Y in the population.* There are extensions of simple linear regression for dealing with X–Y relationships that are nonlinear; some of these are discussed later in this chapter.

DECOMPOSITION OF VARIANCE

From Equation 6.5,

$$Y = \hat{Y} + (Y - \hat{Y})$$

or

$$Y = b_0 + b_1 X + (Y - b_0 - b_1 X)$$

Observed Y value   Explained by linear relation   Residual or deviation from linear relation

In an ideal situation in which all the points lie exactly on the fitted line, the residuals are all zero and the Y values are completely accounted for or explained by the linear relation with X.

Subtracting $\bar{Y}$ from both sides of the previous expression,

$$(Y - \bar{Y}) = (\hat{Y} - \bar{Y}) + (Y - \hat{Y})$$

It can be shown with a little algebra that the sums of squares add:

$$\Sigma(Y - \bar{Y})^2 = \Sigma(\hat{Y} - \bar{Y})^2 + \Sigma(Y - \hat{Y})^2 \tag{6.12}$$

or

$$SST = SSR + SSE$$

where

$$SST = \Sigma(Y - \bar{Y})^2$$
$$SSR = \Sigma(\hat{Y} - \bar{Y})^2$$
$$SSE = \Sigma(Y - \hat{Y})^2$$

Here *SS* stands for *sum of squares* and *T*, *R*, and *E* represent *total, regression*, and *error*, respectively. These sums of squares have associated degrees of freedom

$$df(SST) = n - 1$$
$$df(SSR) = 1$$
$$df(SSE) = n - 2$$

Corresponding to the sums of squares, the degrees of freedom are related by

$$n - 1 = 1 + (n - 2) \qquad \textbf{(6.13)}$$

If there is no linear relation, *Y* does not depend on *X* and the variation in *Y* is described by the sample variance

$$s_y^2 = \frac{1}{n-1} \Sigma (Y - \bar{Y})^2$$

If, on the other hand, *Y* is related to *X*, some of the differences in the *Y* values are due to this relationship.

The regression sum of squares, *SSR*, measures that part of the variation in *Y* explained by the linear relation. The error sum of squares, *SSE*, is the remaining variation in *Y*, or the variation in *Y* not explained by the linear relation.

Decomposition of Variability

SST	=	*SSR*	+	*SSE*
Total variability of *Y*		Variability explained by linear relation		Residual or unexplained variability

---

The sums of squares associated with the decomposition of the variability of *Y* and their corresponding degrees of freedom can be set out as shown in Table 6-4, which is known as an *analysis of variance*, or *ANOVA*, table.

The final column in the ANOVA table is the *mean square* column. The mean square regression, *MSR*, is the regression sum of squares divided by its degrees of freedom. Similarly, the mean square error, *MSE*, is the error sum of squares divided by its degrees of freedom.

TABLE 6-4   ANOVA Table for Straight-Line Regression

Source	Sum of Squares	df	Mean Square
Regression	SSR	1	$MSR = SSR/1$
Error	SSE	$n - 2$	$MSE = SSE/(n - 2)$
Total	SST	$n - 1$	

TABLE 6-5	Residuals for Bump's Data with Predictor $\overline{Y}$		
Actual Y	Predicted Y ($\overline{Y}$)	Residual (Y − $\overline{Y}$)	(Y − $\overline{Y}$)²
10	11.2	−1.2	1.44
6	11.2	−5.2	27.04
5	11.2	−6.2	38.44
12	11.2	.8	.64
10	11.2	−1.2	1.44
15	11.2	3.8	14.44
5	11.2	−6.2	38.44
12	11.2	.8	.64
17	11.2	5.8	33.64
20	11.2	8.8	77.44
		Totals 0.0	233.60

Notice from Equation 6.7 that the mean square error is

$$MSE = \frac{SSE}{n-2} = \frac{\Sigma(Y - \hat{Y})^2}{n-2} = s_{y \cdot x}^2$$

the square of the standard error of the estimate. The mean square ratios will be used for another purpose later in this chapter.

Example 6.5

Mr. Bump's analysis began with knowledge of only 10 weekly sales volume quantities (the Y variable). If no further information were available, Mr. Bump might employ the sample average $\overline{Y} = 11.2$ as a predictor of gallons of milk sold for each week. The errors, or residuals, associated with this forecast are $Y - \overline{Y}$ and the sum of the squared errors is $\Sigma(Y - \overline{Y})^2$. Notice that this latter quantity, $\Sigma(Y - \overline{Y})^2$, is exactly *SST*, the total sum of squares introduced in Equation 6.12. Thus *SST* measures the variability of Y about a predictor that uses only the Y values in its calculation.[6] The predictions $\overline{Y}$, the residuals $Y - \overline{Y}$, and the total sum of squares $SST = \Sigma(Y - \overline{Y})^2$ are shown in Table 6-5.[7]

Mr. Bump also has information about a variable X, the price per gallon of milk, that is related to Y, the weekly volume of milk sold. (Recall, from Example 6.1, $r = -.86$.) With this additional variable, he expects to be able to explain some of the variation (differences) in the Y values beyond that explained by the predictor $\overline{Y}$.

From Example 6.2, the line fit to the scatterplot of X–Y observations has the equation $\hat{Y} = 32.14 - 14.54X$. A table similar to Table 6-5 can be constructed if $\hat{Y}$ is used to predict Y. The result is Table 6-6.[8]

A comparison of Tables 6-5 and 6-6 shows that the use of $\hat{Y}$ as a predictor of Y has resulted in generally smaller residuals (in absolute value) and a considerably smaller residual (error) sum of squares than when $\overline{Y}$ is used as a predictor. Use of the related variable X reduces the prediction, or forecast, errors. That is, knowledge of X helps to further explain the differences in the Y's. How much does X help? The decomposition of variability provides an answer to this question.

Using Table 6-5, Table 6-6, and Equation 6.12,

$$SST = \Sigma(Y - \overline{Y})^2 = 233.60$$
$$SSE = \Sigma(Y - \hat{Y})^2 = 59.41$$

---

[6] If the analysis were to stop at this point, the variability in Y would be measured by the sample variance $s_y^2 = \Sigma(Y - \overline{Y})^2/(n-1)$ rather than $SST = \Sigma(Y - \overline{Y})^2$. The sample variance is the usual measure of variability for measurements on a single variable.

[7] The residuals $Y - \overline{Y}$ always sum to zero because the average $\overline{Y}$ is the mathematical center of the Y values.

[8] If an intercept term is included in the regression equation, the sum of the residuals $\Sigma(Y - \hat{Y})$ is always zero.

TABLE 6-6	Residuals for Bump's Data with Predictor $\hat{Y}$			
X	Y	Predicted $Y\,(\hat{Y})$ Using $\hat{Y} = 32.14 - 14.54X$	Residual $(Y - \hat{Y})$	$(Y - \hat{Y})^2$
1.30	10	13.238	−3.238	10.48
2.00	6	3.060	2.940	8.64
1.70	5	7.422	−2.422	5.87
1.50	12	10.330	1.670	2.79
1.60	10	8.876	1.124	1.26
1.20	15	14.692	.308	.09
1.60	5	8.876	−3.876	15.02
1.40	12	11.784	.216	.05
1.00	17	17.600	−.600	.36
1.10	20	16.146	3.854	14.85
		Totals	0.000	59.41

and, consequently,

$$SSR = \Sigma(\hat{Y} - \bar{Y})^2 = 233.60 - 59.41 = 174.19$$

The decomposition of variability is

$$
\begin{array}{ccccc}
SST & = & SSR & + & SSE \\
233.60 & = & 174.19 & + & 59.41 \\
\text{Total} & & \text{Explained} & & \text{Unexplained} \\
\text{variation} & & \text{variation} & & \text{variation}
\end{array}
$$

Of the variability remaining after predicting Y with $\bar{Y}$, Mr. Bump sees that a proportion

$$\frac{SSR}{SST} = \frac{174.19}{233.60} = .75$$

of it has been explained by the relationship of Y with X. A proportion $1 - .75 = .25$ of the variation in Y about $\bar{Y}$ remains unexplained. From this perspective, knowledge of the related variable X results in better predictions of Y than can be obtained from $\bar{Y}$, a quantity that doesn't depend on X.

The decomposition of variability for Mr. Bump's data can be set out in an analysis of variance table, as the next example demonstrates.

Example 6.6
Mr. Bump constructs an analysis of variance (ANOVA) table for his data using the format in Table 6-4 and the sums of squares calculations from Example 6.5, as shown in Table 6-7.

The decomposition of variability is clearly shown in the sum of squares column. Notice that, within rounding error,

$$MSE = 7.43 = (2.72)^2 = s_{y \cdot x}^2.$$

TABLE 6-7	ANOVA Table for Bump's Data		
Source	Sum of Squares	df	Mean Square
Regression	174.19	1	174.19
Error	59.41	8	7.43
Total	233.60	9	

COEFFICIENT OF DETERMINATION

The identity

$$(Y - \bar{Y}) = (\hat{Y} - \bar{Y}) + (Y - \hat{Y})$$

leading to the decomposition of variance given by Equation 6.12 is shown graphically for Mr. Bump's fitted regression line and a hypothetical data point in Figure 6-5.

If Y did not depend on X, Mr. Bump would expect Y to be close to $\bar{Y}$ and the deviation $Y - \bar{Y}$ to simply reflect random variation. However, Y does depend on X in a manner suggested by the fitted regression function. In the figure, the observed X value is greater than $\bar{X}$, and it is known that X and Y have a fairly strong negative correlation ($r = -.86$). Of the total vertical distance $Y - \bar{Y}$, an amount $\hat{Y} - \bar{Y}$ is, therefore, "explained" by the movement in X, whereas the remaining vertical distance $Y - \hat{Y}$ is "unexplained" by movement in X.

As indicated in the previous section, SST measures the total variation about $\bar{Y}$, and that part of the total that is explained by movement in X is SSR. The remaining or unexplained variation is SSE. The ratio of the explained to total variation is called the sample *coefficient of determination* and is denoted by r^2.

$$r^2 = \frac{Explained\ variation}{Total\ variation} = \frac{SSR}{SST} = \frac{\Sigma(\hat{Y} - \bar{Y})^2}{\Sigma(Y - \bar{Y})^2}$$

$$= 1 - \frac{Unexplained\ variation}{Total\ variation} = 1 - \frac{SSE}{SST} = 1 - \frac{\Sigma(Y - \hat{Y})^2}{\Sigma(Y - \bar{Y})^2} \qquad \textbf{(6.14)}$$

The *coefficient of determination* measures the percentage of variability in Y that can be explained through knowledge of the variability (differences) in the independent variable X.

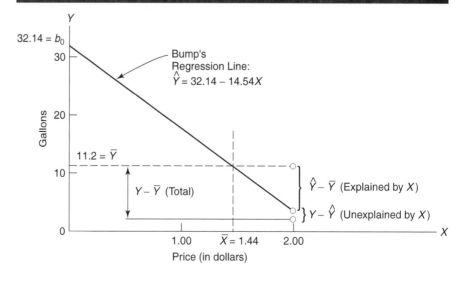

FIGURE 6-5   Explained and Unexplained Variation in Bump's Data

Example 6.7

The coefficient of determination r^2 for Mr. Bump's data was calculated in Example 6.5, although, at that point, it was not labeled as such. The coefficient of determination is also readily available for the ANOVA table, Table 6-7, in Example 6.6. Recall

$$SST = \Sigma(Y - \bar{Y})^2 = 233.60$$
$$SSR = \Sigma(\hat{Y} - \bar{Y})^2 = 174.19$$
$$SSE = \Sigma(Y - \hat{Y})^2 = 59.41$$

and

$$r^2 = \frac{174.19}{233.60} = .746$$

Alternatively, r^2 may be calculated as

$$r^2 = 1 - \frac{59.41}{233.60} = 1 - .254 = .746$$

About 75% of the variability in gallons of milk sold (Y) can be explained by differences in price per gallon (X). About 25% of the variability in quantity of milk sold *cannot* be explained by price. This portion of the variability must be explained by factors that have not been considered in this regression analysis (for example, amount of advertising, availability of substitute products, quality of milk).

For straight-line regression, r^2 is the square of r, the coefficient of correlation.

$$\text{Coefficient of determination} = (\text{Coefficient of correlation})^2$$
$$r^2 = (r)^2$$

Thus, for Mr. Bump's data and ignoring rounding error,

$$.746 = (-.863)^2$$

Why is it necessary to specifically identify both r and r^2 in a regression analysis? The answer is that they convey different information.

The correlation coefficient reveals the strength and the direction of the linear relation. In the case of the data that Mr. Bump has collected, a negative relationship exists ($r = -.86$). In other cases, a positive relationship might be indicated by the value for r. As will be seen in the next chapter, it is useful to identify the nature of the relationships that exist between certain pairs of variables when dealing with a large collection of variables. Note that when the coefficient of correlation is squared, the value is always positive, and so the nature of the relationship is lost.

The coefficient of determination r^2 measures the strength of the relationship between Y and X in a different way than r. The value for r^2 measures the *percentage* of the variability in Y that is explained by differences in X. This useful interpretation can be generalized to relationships between Y and more than one X.

Figure 6-6 illustrates the two extreme cases for r^2, $r^2 = 0$ and $r^2 = 1$. In the former case, *none* of the variability in Y is explained by X: The scatter diagram suggests no linear relationship between X and Y. When $r^2 = 1$, *all* of the variability in Y is explained when X is known: The sample data points all lie on the fitted regression line.

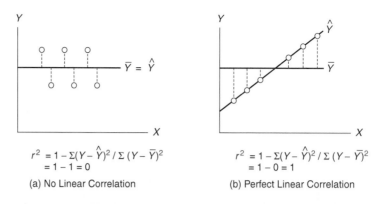

$$r^2 = 1 - \Sigma(Y - \hat{Y})^2 / \Sigma(Y - \bar{Y})^2$$
$$= 1 - 1 = 0$$

(a) No Linear Correlation

$$r^2 = 1 - \Sigma(Y - \hat{Y})^2 / \Sigma(Y - \bar{Y})^2$$
$$= 1 - 0 = 1$$

(b) Perfect Linear Correlation

FIGURE 6-6   Extreme Values for r^2

HYPOTHESIS TESTING

The fitted regression line is produced by a *sample* of X–Y values. The statistical model for simple linear regression suggests the straight-line relationship between Y and X holds for *all* choices of X–Y pairs. That is, there is a true relation between X and Y of the form $\mu_y = \beta_0 + \beta_1 X$. Given the sample evidence, can we conclude the true relation holds for all X and Y?

Consider the hypothesis

$$H_0: \beta_1 = 0$$

where β_1 is the slope of the population regression line. Notice that if this hypothesis is true, there is no relation between Y and X in the population. Failing to reject H_0 means that in spite of the fact that the sample has produced a fitted line with a nonzero value for b_1, we must conclude there is not sufficient evidence to indicate Y is related to X. That is, we cannot rule out the possibility that the population regression line is flat (horizontal).[9]

How could β_1 be zero while b_1 is nonzero? Consider Figure 6-7, where a population of data points is shown from which a sample of five has been selected (sampled data points are indicated by x). As this scatter diagram suggests, if enough sample data points are selected, it will become obvious that the population of data points has a regression line with a zero slope. However, in the random sample of five data points, points were selected that lie fairly close to an upward-trending regression line. It might be erroneously concluded from this evidence that X and Y are related in a positive linear way. However, if the hypothesis $\beta_1 = 0$ is tested with the sample data, the forecaster will probably not be able to reject it.

If $H_0: \beta_1 = 0$ is true, the *test statistic t* with value $t = \dfrac{b_1}{s_{b_1}}$ has a *t* distribution with $df = n - 2$. Here s_{b_1} is the estimated standard deviation (or standard error) of b_1 given by $s_{b_1} = s_{y \cdot x} / \sqrt{\Sigma(X - \bar{X})^2}$.

This result provides a way to test $H_0: \beta_1 = 0$, as the next example illustrates.

---

[9] A flat population regression line (i.e., $\beta_1 = 0$) is also equivalent to the statement $H_0: \rho = 0$, where ρ is the population correlation coefficient.

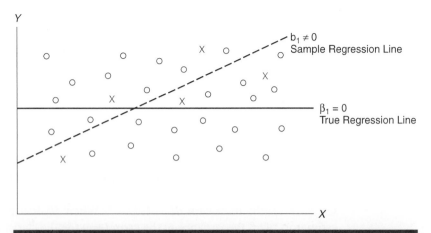

FIGURE 6-7   Population and Sample Data Points

Example 6.8
Mr. Bump would like to test

$$H_0: \beta_1 = 0 \text{ (no linear relation)}$$

versus

$$H_1: \beta_1 \neq 0 \text{ (a linear relation with a nonzero slope)}$$

He computes[10]

$$s_{b_1} = s_{y \cdot x} \bigg/ \sqrt{\Sigma(X - \bar{X})^2} = 2.72 \bigg/ \sqrt{.824} = 3.00$$

and forms the ratio (test statistic)

$$t = \frac{b_1}{s_{b_1}} = \frac{-14.54}{3.00} = -4.8$$

Is the value $t = -4.8$ an unusual result if H_0 is true? Mr. Bump checks the t table with $n - 2 = 8$ degrees of freedom and finds

$$t_{.005} = 3.355$$
$$t_{.025} = 2.306$$

Because $|t| = 4.8 > 3.355$, Mr. Bump rejects H_0 at the 1% level of significance. He concludes his regression is significant because $t = -4.8$ is highly unlikely if H_0 is true. A t value of this magnitude would occur less than one time in 100 if there were no linear relation between Y and X.

For very large sample sizes, it is possible to reject H_0 and conclude there is a linear relation between Y and X even though r^2 may be small, say 10%. Similarly, for small samples and a very large r^2, say 95%, it is possible to conclude the regression is significant. A small r^2 means the fitted regression equation is unlikely to have much predictive power. On the other hand, a high r^2 with a very small sample size

---

[10] The values used in the following calculation were computed earlier in this chapter.

may leave the analyst uncomfortable and require more sample evidence before the fitted function is used for forecasting. There can be a difference between statistical significance and practical significance. At times, judgment coupled with subject matter knowledge is necessary to determine if a fitted regression function is likely to be a useful forecasting tool.

An alternative test of H_0: $\beta_1 = 0$ is available from the ANOVA table.

If the assumptions of the statistical model for linear regression are appropriate and if the null hypothesis H_0: $\beta_1 = 0$ is true, the ratio

$$F = \frac{\text{Regression mean square}}{\text{Error mean square}} = \frac{MSR}{MSE} \tag{6.15}$$

has an F distribution with $df = 1, n - 2$. When H_0 is true, MSR and MSE are each estimators of σ^2, the variance of the error term ε in the statistical model for straight-line regression. On the other hand, if H_1: $\beta_1 \neq 0$ is true, the numerator in the F ratio tends to be larger than the denominator. Large F ratios, then, are consistent with the alternative hypothesis.

In the straight-line regression model, the test of the hypotheses H_0: $\beta_1 = 0$ versus H_1: $\beta_1 \neq 0$ can be based on the F ratio $F = \dfrac{MSR}{MSE}$ with $df = 1, n - 2$. At level α, the rejection region is $F > F_\alpha$.

As discussed in the next chapter, the F test can be extended to check the significance of regression models with more than one independent variable.

Example 6.9

Table 6-7 is the ANOVA table for Mr. Bump's data. From this table,

$$F = \frac{MSR}{MSE} = \frac{174.19}{7.43} = 23.4$$

and with $\delta_1 = 1$ and $\delta_2 = 8$ degrees of freedom,

$$F_{.05} = 5.32$$
$$F_{.01} = 11.26$$

Because $F = 23.4 > 11.26$, H_0: $\beta_1 = 0$ is rejected at the 1% level. The regression is significant.

It is no accident that the results of the F test are consistent with the results of the t test in Example 6.8. In fact, within rounding error,

$$F = 23.4 = (-4.8)^2 = t^2$$

Moreover,

$$F_{.01} = 11.26 = (3.355)^2 = (t_{.005})^2$$

So, for a given significance level, the t test rejects H_0: $\beta_1 = 0$ whenever the F test rejects and vice versa. This relationship between the t and F tests holds only for the straight-line regression model.

The F statistic can also be expressed in terms of the coefficient of determination r^2:

$$F = \frac{r^2(n-2)}{1-r^2} \qquad \textbf{(6.16)}$$

Everything else being equal, the value of F increases as r^2 increases. As more of the variation in Y is explained by the fitted regression function, the more likely the regression is judged significant by the F test.

ANALYSIS OF RESIDUALS

Fitting a model by least squares, constructing prediction intervals and testing hypotheses, does not complete a regression study. These steps are only half the story: the inferences that can be made *when the assumed model is adequate*. In most studies, it is not obvious that a particular model is correct. Inferences can be seriously misleading if the assumptions made in the model formulation are grossly incompatible with the data. It is essential to check the data carefully for indications of any violation of the assumptions. Recall that the assumptions for the straight-line regression model are:

1. The underlying relation is linear.
2. The errors are independent.
3. The errors have constant variance.
4. The errors are normally distributed.

The information on variation that cannot be explained by the fitted regression function is contained in the residuals $e = Y - \hat{Y}$. To check the merits of a tentative model, we can examine the residuals by plotting them in various ways.

1. Plot a histogram of the residuals.
2. Plot the residuals against the fitted values.
3. Plot the residuals against the explanatory variable.
4. Plot the residuals over time if the data are chronological.

A histogram of the residuals provides a check on the normality assumption. Typically, moderate departures from a bell-shaped curve do not impair the conclusions from tests or prediction intervals based on the t distribution, particularly if the data set is large. A violation of the normality assumption alone is ordinarily not as serious as a violation of any of the other assumptions.

If a plot of the residuals against the fitted values indicates that the general nature of the relationship between Y and X forms a curve rather than a straight line, a suitable transformation of the data may reduce a nonlinear relation to one that is approximately linear. Variable transformations are considered in a later section of this chapter.

A transformation may also help to stabilize the variance. Figure 6-8 shows a residual plot indicating that the spread of the residuals increases as the magnitude of the fitted values increases. That is, the variability of the data points about the least squares line is larger for large responses than it is for small responses, which implies that the constant variance assumption may not hold. In this situation, relating the logarithm of Y to X may produce residual variation that is more consistent with a constant variance.

The assumption of independence is the most critical. Lack of independence can drastically distort the conclusions drawn from t tests. The independence assumption is particularly risky for time series data—the data frequently arising in business and economic forecasting problems.

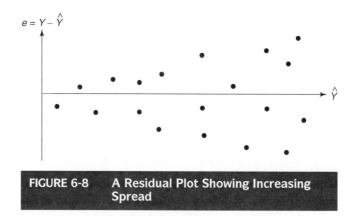

FIGURE 6-8   A Residual Plot Showing Increasing Spread

For time series residuals, that is, for residuals produced by using regression methods on time-ordered data, independence can be checked with a plot of the residuals over time. There should be no systematic pattern, such as a string of high values followed by a string of low values. In addition, calculating the sample autocorrelations of the residuals can check independence:

$$r_k(e) = \frac{\sum\limits_{t=k+1}^{n} e_t e_{t-k}}{\sum\limits_{t=1}^{n} e_t^2} \qquad k = 1, 2, \ldots, K \qquad \textbf{(6.17)}$$

where n is the number of residuals and K is typically $n/4$. Independence is indicated if the residual autocorrelation coefficients are uniformly small (each in the interval $0 \pm 2/\sqrt{n}$) for all lags k.

Example 6.10

Using the fitted values and residuals shown in Table 6-6, Mr. Bump constructed a histogram of the residuals, and a plot of the residuals against the fitted values. The results are displayed in Figure 6-9.

The histogram is centered at zero, and although it is symmetric, it doesn't appear to be bell-shaped. However, with only 10 observations, a histogram such as the one pictured in Figure 6-9 is not unusual for normally distributed data. The normal assumption appears to be reasonable.

The points in the normal probability plot in the first row of Figure 6-9 lie nearly along a straight line. As we pointed out in Chapter 2, this straight line-like behavior suggests a good fit between the data (in this case, the residuals) and a normal distribution. The normal probability plot suggests there is no reason to doubt the normal assumption.

The second plot in the first row of Figure 6-9 also looks good. When the residuals are plotted against the fitted values, the spread about zero in the vertical direction should be about the same for all values along the horizontal axis. That is, the magnitudes of the residuals for small fitted values should be about the same as the magnitudes of the residuals for intermediate fitted values and about the same as the magnitudes of the residuals for large fitted values. This ideal behavior suggests two things: (1) The underlying relation between Y and X is linear, and (2) the error variability is constant (Y's at different values of X have the same spread about the regression line).

Mr. Bump is pleased that the plot of the residuals versus the fitted values is not "bowed," for example, a string of positive residuals followed by a string of negative residuals, followed by a string of positive residuals. This behavior would suggest a nonlinear relation between

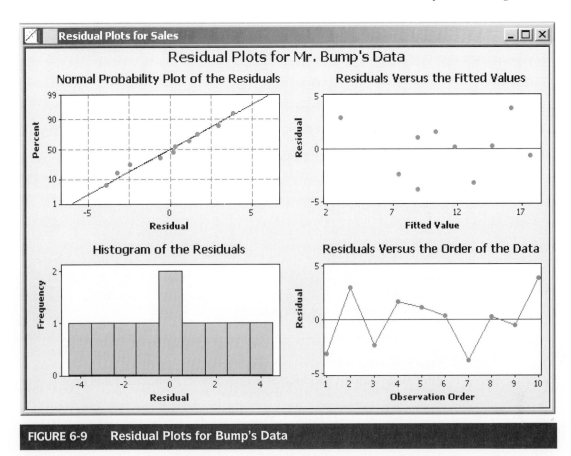

FIGURE 6-9   Residual Plots for Bump's Data

Y and *X*. He is also pleased his plot did not have the cone-shaped appearance of the plot in Figure 6-8 that indicates nonconstant (increasing) variability.

Although the *Y*'s are weekly sales of milk, the weeks were selected at random and were not ordered in time. Consequently, plotting the residuals over time or computing the residual autocorrelations was not appropriate.

Mr. Bump is satisfied with his residual analysis. He feels his straight-line regression model adequately describes the relation between weekly sales volume and price.

COMPUTER OUTPUT

Mr. Bump's regression analysis problem (data from Table 6-1) is run on Minitab (see the "Minitab Applications" section at the end of this chapter for instructions) and the output is presented in Table 6-8.

To explain the terminology used in the computer output, definitions and computations are presented in the following list. These definitions and calculations are keyed to Table 6-8.

1. Correlation $= -.86$. The sample correlation coefficient (r) indicates the relationship between *X* and *Y*, or price and sales, respectively.
2. Regression coefficient (Coef) $= -14.54$. This value (b_1) is the change in *Y* (sales) when *X* (price) increases by one unit. When price increases \$1, estimated sales decrease by 14,540 units.

TABLE 6-8	Minitab Output for Bump's Data

```
Correlations (Pearson)

        Y

X -.863     (1) and (12)

Regression Analysis

The regression equation is

Sales (Y)=32.1-14.5 Price (X)      (5) and (2)

Predictor      Coef      SE Coef        T          P
Constant     32.136 (5)    4.409       7.29       0.000
Price (X)    -14.539 (2)   3.002 (3)  -4.84 (4)   0.001 (7)

S=2.725 (6)      R-Sq=74.6% (8)       R-Sq(adj)=71.4% (9)

Analysis of Variance

Source          DF     SS          MS         F          P
Regression       1    174.18      174.18     23.45 (13)  0.001
Residual Error   8     59.42 (10)   7.43 (6)
Total            9    233.60 (11)
```

3. Standard error of regression coefficient (SE Coef) = 3.0. This value is the estimated standard deviation of the regression coefficient value (b_1).

$$s_{b_1} = s_{y \cdot x} \bigg/ \sqrt{\Sigma(X - \bar{X})^2} = 2.725 \bigg/ \sqrt{.824} = 2.725/.908 = 3.002$$

4. Computed t value (T) = −4.84. The computed t value is used to test whether the population regression coefficient β_1 is significantly different from zero.

$$s_{b_1} = 3.002$$

$$t = \frac{b_1}{s_{b_1}} = \frac{-14.54}{3.002} = -4.84$$

5. Constant (Coef) = 32.14. This value is the Y intercept (b_0). Therefore, the entire regression equation is

$$\hat{Y} = 32.14 - 14.54X$$

6. Std. error of estimate (S) = 2.725. The standard error of the estimate indicates that the Y values fall typically about 2.725 units from the regression line.

$$s_{y \cdot x} = \sqrt{\frac{\Sigma(Y - \hat{Y})^2}{n - 2}} = \sqrt{\frac{SSE}{n - 2}} = \sqrt{MSE} = \sqrt{7.43} = 2.725$$

7. The *p*-value (P), .001, is the probability of obtaining a t value as large as $|t| = |-4.84| = 4.84$ by chance if H_0: $\beta_1 = 0$ is true. Because the *p*-value is extremely small, it is concluded that the regression slope coefficient is significantly different from 0.

8. *r* squared = .746. The fitted regression line explains 74.6% of the sales volume variance.

$$r^2 = \frac{SSR}{SST} = 1 - \frac{SSE}{SST} = 1 - \frac{59.42}{233.60} = 1 - .254 = .746$$

9. Adjusted *r* squared = .714. The r^2 is adjusted for the appropriate degrees of freedom.

$$\bar{r}^2 = 1 - \frac{\Sigma(Y - \hat{Y})^2/(n-2)}{\Sigma(Y - \bar{Y})^2/(n-1)} = 1 - \frac{SSE/(n-2)}{SST/(n-1)} = 1 - \frac{59.42/8}{233.60/9}$$

$$= 1 - \frac{7.428}{25/956} = 1 - .286 = .714$$

10. Residual (Error) sum of squares = 59.42. The sum of squares residual is the sum of squared differences between the actual *Y*'s and the predicted *Y*'s ($\hat{Y}$'s).

$$SSE = \Sigma(Y - \hat{Y})^2 = 59.42$$

11. Total sum of squares = 233.60. This value is the sum of the squared deviations of the *Y*'s from their mean.

$$SST = \Sigma(Y - \bar{Y})^2 = 233.60$$

12. Correlation matrix. This matrix gives the correlation among all variables in the analysis. Because only two variables, *X* and *Y*, are involved, there is only one correlation coefficient (−.863).

13. Analysis of variance and *F* ratio. The *F* ratio (23.45 = 174.18/7.43) in this ANOVA (analysis of variance) table tests the null hypothesis that the regression is not significant; that is, H_0: $\beta_1 = 0$. A large *F* value will allow rejection of this hypothesis, suggesting a *significant* regression. The *F* value (23.45) becomes larger as a larger portion of the total sum of squared deviations (*SST*) is explained by the regression. In this case the tabulated *F* value ($df = 1, 8$; $\alpha = .01$) is 11.26. Thus the hypothesis of no significant regression is rejected at the 1% significance level because $F = 23.45 > 11.26$. (See Example 6.9.)

VARIABLE TRANSFORMATIONS

Although the simple linear regression model assumes a straight-line relationship between *Y* and *X*, in general a linear regression model refers to a model that is linear in the unknown β's. So long as the regression function is linear in the β's (for example, β_1^2 is not present), the predictor variables (the *X*'s) can take various forms and the standard regression methodology is still appropriate. Regression models then can be used to model complex relationships between *Y* and *X* (or several *X*'s) or to model a straight-line relationship between *Y* and some function (transformation) of *X*.

When a scatter diagram indicates there is a nonlinear relationship between *Y* and *X*, there are two basic approaches for dealing with this case. The first is to fit the data with a regression function that plots as a curve and use the fitted relationship for forecasting purposes. The second approach involves the transformation of the *X* variable to another form so that the resulting relationship with *Y* is linear.

Four of the most common transformations (functions) that are used to generate new predictor variables are the reciprocal, the log, the square root, and the square:

$$\frac{1}{X}, \qquad \log(X), \qquad \sqrt{X}, \qquad X^2$$

When these variables are each plotted against Y, the hope is that the nonlinear relationship between Y and X will become a linear relationship between Y and one of the transformed X's. If so, Y and this new variable can be treated using the straight-line model discussed in this chapter, including calculation of the correlation coefficient and the fitted regression equation.

In the following example, Minitab (see "Minitab Applications" at the end of the chapter) is used to plot a simple X and Y relationship that appears to be nonlinear. The program is then instructed to calculate the four transformations described previously. These variables are then each plotted against Y to produce the data plots shown.

Example 6.11

Gilbert Garcia owns a chain of hardware stores in Chicago, Illinois. He is interested in predicting his monthly sales using knowledge of the corresponding monthly advertising expenditures. Gil suspects that sales will increase as the amount spent on advertising increases. However, he also believes that after a certain point sales will begin to increase at a slower rate. Gil feels that after spending a certain amount on advertising, he will reach a point where there will be little to gain in sales by further spending on advertising.

Gil selected a random sample of 14 months of data from company records. The data appear in Figure 6-10 and a scatter diagram of the data is shown in Figure 6-11. Gil notes that sales do appear to level off after a certain amount is spent on advertising. He fits the linear regression equation shown in Figure 6-12 and notes that the equation explains 77.7% of the variability in sales.

A plot of the residuals versus the fitted values from the straight-line fit is shown in Figure 6-13. This plot indicates that a straight line does not adequately describe the relation between sales and advertising expenditures. The residuals are all negative for small predicted values, they are all positive for midlevel predicted values, and they are all negative

FIGURE 6-10   Data for Example 6.11

Fig6-10.MTW ***

↓	C1	C2	C3	C4	C5	C6	C7	C8	C9	C10	C11	C1
	Sales	Expenditures	LOGX	SQRTX	X*X	1/X						
1	1.1	3.9	1.36098	1.97484	15.21	0.256410						
2	1.7	4.9	1.58924	2.21359	24.01	0.204082						
3	2.6	7.6	2.02815	2.75681	57.76	0.131579						
4	2.4	6.8	1.91692	2.60768	46.24	0.147059						
5	2.3	5.9	1.77495	2.42899	34.81	0.169492						
6	2.9	9.1	2.20827	3.01662	82.81	0.109890						
7	0.4	3.4	1.22378	1.84391	11.56	0.294118						
8	3.2	11.6	2.45101	3.40588	134.56	0.086207						
9	3.3	14.1	2.64617	3.75500	198.81	0.070922						
10	3.1	14.9	2.70136	3.86005	222.01	0.067114						
11	3.2	10.5	2.35138	3.24037	110.25	0.095238						
12	3.0	9.9	2.29253	3.14643	98.01	0.101010						
13	3.7	17.1	2.83908	4.13521	292.41	0.058480						
14	3.3	12.4	2.51770	3.52136	153.76	0.080645						
15												

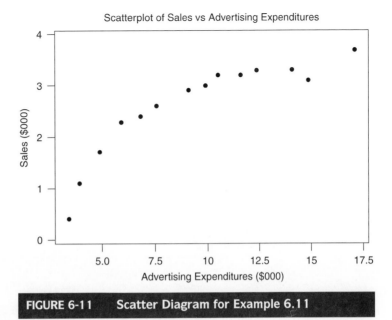

FIGURE 6-11   **Scatter Diagram for Example 6.11**

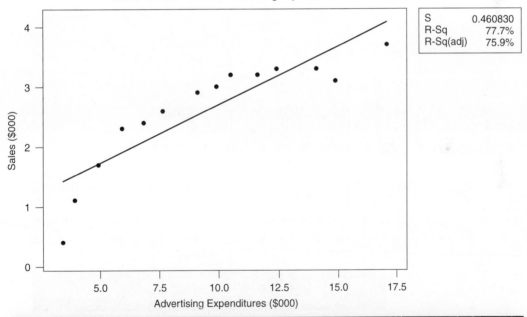

FIGURE 6-12   **Fitted Regression Line for Example 6.11**

again for large predicted values. The residuals are not uniformly distributed about the estimated regression line. Clearly, a straight line does not capture the curvature in the data.

Next, Gil transforms the advertising expenditures variable to the log of X (see Figure 6-10). Then he plots the relationship between sales and the log of advertising expenditures in Figure 6-14. The relationship is still slightly curvilinear.

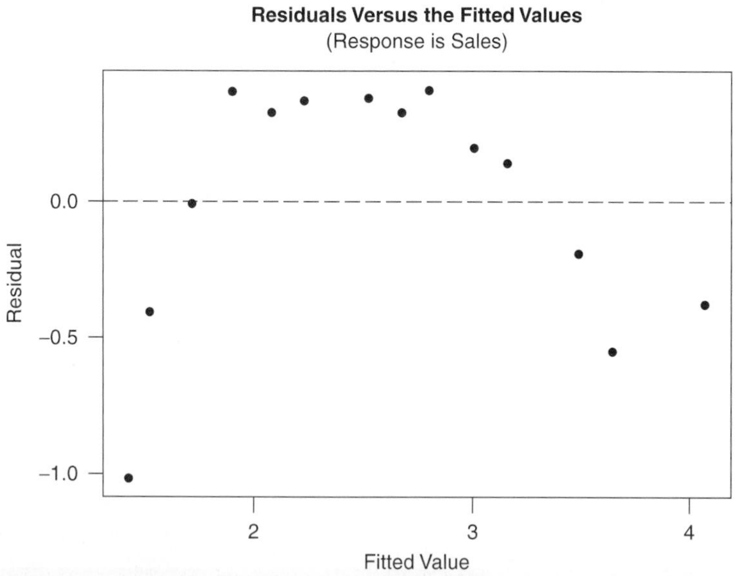

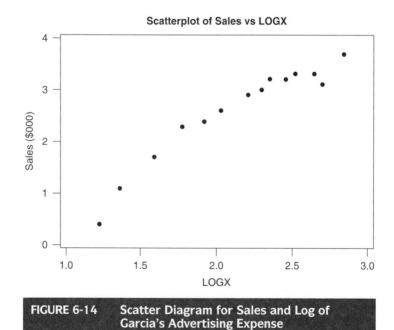

Residuals Versus the Fitted Values
(Response is Sales)

FIGURE 6-13   Plot of Residuals Versus Fitted Values for Straight-Line Fit

Scatterplot of Sales vs LOGX

FIGURE 6-14   Scatter Diagram for Sales and Log of Garcia's Advertising Expense

Gil transforms the advertising expenditures variable to the square root of X (see Figure 6-10). After plotting this relationship, as shown in Figure 6-15, he concludes that the fit is still not linear.

Figure 6-16 shows the relationship between sales and the advertising expenditures squared variable. Again, a linear relationship has not been found.

Finally, Gil transforms the advertising expenditures variable to the reciprocal of X (see Figure 6-10). Figure 6-17 shows that sales and the reciprocal of expenditures are linearly

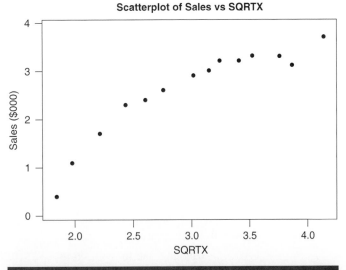

FIGURE 6-15   Scatter Diagram for Sales and Square Root of Garcia's Advertising Expense

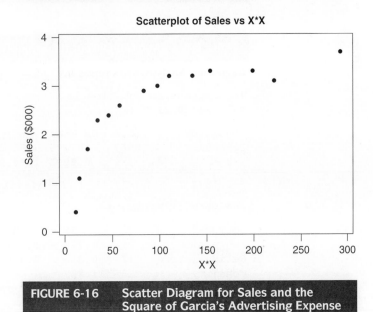

FIGURE 6-16   Scatter Diagram for Sales and the Square of Garcia's Advertising Expense

related. Using Minitab, he determines the fitted equation $\hat{Y} = 4.29 - 12.7(1/X)$ as shown in Table 6-9, and sees that r^2 is equal to 98.1%. A residual analysis indicates the model relating sales to the reciprocal of advertising expenditures is appropriate.

GROWTH CURVES

Growth curves were introduced in Chapter 5 (see Figure 5-7) in our discussion of modeling the trend in the decomposition of a time series. Often the trend (long-term

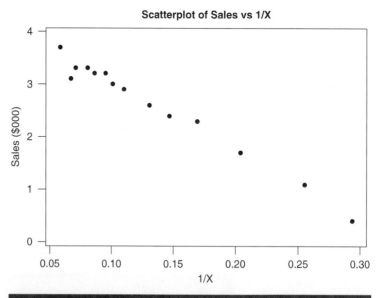

FIGURE 6-17   **Scatter Diagram for Sales and the Reciprocal of Garcia's Advertising Expense**

TABLE 6-9   Minitab Output for Example 6.11

Regression Analysis: Sales versus 1/X

```
The regression equation is
Sales=4.29-12.7 1/X

Predictor        Coef    SE Coef         T      P
Constant      4.28587    0.07695     55.69  0.000
1/X          -12.7132     0.5092    -24.97  0.000

S=0.1342     R-Sq=98.1%      R-Sq(adj)=98.0%

Analysis of Variance

Source          DF        SS        MS        F      P
Regression       1    11.221    11.221   623.44  0.000
Residual Error  12     0.216     0.018
Total           13    11.437
```

change) is of interest in itself. A forecaster, for example, might be interested in projecting the cost per computer transaction well into the future without regard to the technology that might bring about changes in this cost. As another example, a life insurance analyst might be interested in long-term projections of the life expectancy at birth for the U.S. population without regard to the economic and environmental conditions that might be responsible for changes in life expectancy.

Growth curves are curvilinear relations between each variable of interest and time. Growth curves are typically fit to annual data when long-term forecasts are required. Even though inaccurate forecasts are likely when growth curves fit to historical data are extrapolated to predict the future, this forecasting method can be of great benefit to managers because it concentrates attention on the long-term aspects of the business. Moreover, growth curves indicate the annual rate of growth that must be maintained in order to reach projected future levels. This annual growth rate may or may not be reasonable and can be debated in executive retreat or "think tank" sessions.

If a variable measured over time increases by the same *percentage* each time period, it is said to exhibit *exponential growth*. If a variable increases by the same *amount* each time period, it is said to exhibit *linear growth*. Sometimes a simple transformation will convert a variable having exponential growth to a variable with linear growth. If this is the case, the regression methods discussed in this chapter can be used to model exponential growth.

For example, suppose a variable Y, measured annually, follows the exponential trend curve (see Equation 5.6):

$$Y = b_0 \, b_1^t$$

Here $100(b_1 - 1)\%$ is the year-to-year percentage increase in Y. Taking the logarithms of both sides of the exponential trend equation gives

$$\log Y = \log(b_0 \, b_1^t) = \log b_0 + t \log b_1 = \tilde{b}_0 + \tilde{b}_1 t$$

So $\log Y$ versus time (t) plots as a straight line with slope $\tilde{b}_1 = \log b_1$ and intercept $\tilde{b}_0 = \log b_0$. Log Y increases by a constant amount $\tilde{b}_1$ from one year to the next. As the next example illustrates, forecasts of Y and an estimate of the growth rate b_1 can be obtained from the straight-line equation relating $\log Y$ to t.

Example 6.12

Jill Johnson, an administrative assistant at a major university, is pleased with the acceptance of an Internet-based course registration system. She has collected the data in Table 6-10 and sees that the growth in system usage has been phenomenal. If the present rate of growth continues, the entire campus should be registering for courses online within a year, and the old telephone course registration system can be eliminated completely.

The data in Table 6-10 show the numbers of students using the Internet-based course registration system for the 1998–2002 period. The last column in the table contains the logarithms to the base 10 of the numbers of users.

Jill has had some experience with simple linear regression and wonders if this methodology can be used to forecast the number of users for 2003 to provide her with an estimate of the annual growth rate. A plot of the number of users versus year (see Figure 6-18(a)) quickly suggests to Jill that a simple linear regression model is not appropriate for her data. The growth in usage appears to be exponential with an annual percentage increase of about 70% per year. The increase in the number of users from year to year, however, is quite different. The increases in magnitudes range from a low of 2,500 over the 1998–1999 period to a high of 10,000 over the 2001–2002 period.

Jill has always been good at manipulating logarithms, and remembers that a constant percentage change in a variable over some time period is equivalent to a constant increase in magnitude in the log of the variable over the same time period. With this in mind, Jill transforms the numbers of online course registration users by taking their logarithms, and plots log(users) versus year (see Figure 6-18(b)).

TABLE 6-10	Data for Example 6.12		
Year	*Time*	*Users*	*Log(Users)*
1998	1	3000	3.477
1999	2	5500	3.740
2000	3	9000	3.954
2001	4	16500	4.217
2002	5	26500	4.423

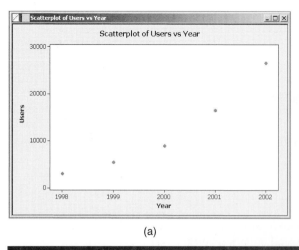
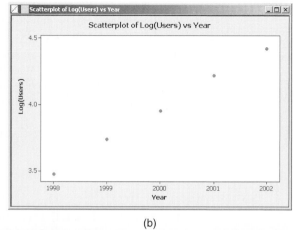

(a)   (b)

FIGURE 6-18   Scatter Diagrams of Jill Johnson's Data for Example 6.12

As she suspected, when the numbers of users have been transformed by taking their logarithms, exponential growth is converted to linear growth. The curvature representing exponential growth in Figure 6-18(a) has been straightened out in Figure 6-18(b) by the logarithmic transformation. In Figure 6-18(b), the increase in the magnitude of log(users) from year to year is roughly the same, about .23 per year. Jill fits a straight line to the data in Figure 6-18(b) with log(users) as the dependent variable Y and time (t) as the independent variable. The results are shown in Figure 6-19.

Using the fitted equation $\log \hat{Y} = 3.252 + .2369t$ with $t = 6$ for year 2003, Jill computes the forecast

$$\log \hat{Y}_{2003} = 3.252 + .2369(6) = 4.673$$
$$\hat{Y}_{2003} = 10^{4.673} = 47,100$$

Jill predicts 47,100 students will use the Internet course registration system in 2003. The university's total enrollment is limited to about 44,000 students, so Jill concludes that all students are likely to use the new course registration system and that the old telephone system can be discontinued.

Finally, Jill estimates the annual growth rate in on-line course registration users to be

$$100(\text{antilog}(.2369) - 1)\% = 100(10^{.2369} - 1)\% = 100(1.725 - 1)\% = 72.5\%$$

Jill recognizes that with the cap on university enrollment, it doesn't make sense to extrapolate the growth in online course registration users beyond 2003.

In some situations, a straight-line growth curve can be fit directly to the original data.

Example 6.13
A company interested in servicing the health needs of elderly persons is interested in a long-term projection of U.S. longevity at birth so it can formulate long-term corporate strategy. It finds projections for this variable from 1970 to 1997 in the *Statistical Abstract of the United States*. These data are shown in Table 6-11. After coding the years as $1 = 1970, 2 = 1971, \ldots, 28 = 1997$, and keying the data into Minitab, the Regression-Fitted Line Plot routine produces the graph shown in Figure 6-20.

The company is not interested in examining the reasons for the obvious increase in longevity over the past several years but rather in projecting the fitted regression line far into the future. Neither is it interested in speculating about whether the upward trend will continue, or by what means such an increase might be achieved. It merely wants to complete the statement, "If present trends continue, the life expectancy at birth will reach Y at X years in the future." It chooses the year 2050 ($X = 53$ years beyond 1997) as its target

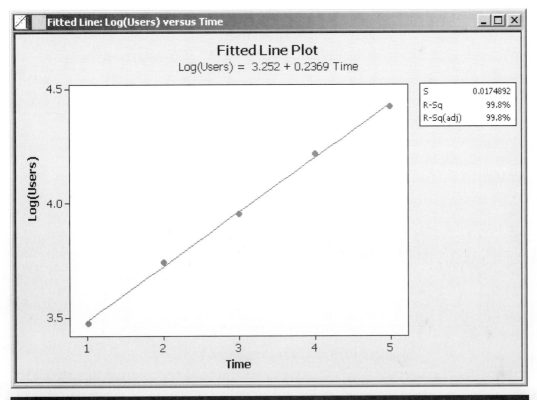

FIGURE 6-19   Fitted Regression Line for Example 6.12

TABLE 6-11	Expectation of Life at Birth, Total Population, United States		
1970	70.8	1984	74.7
1971	71.2*	1985	74.7
1972	71.5*	1986	74.7
1973	71.9*	1987	74.9
1974	72.4*	1988	74.9
1975	72.6	1989	75.1
1976	72.8*	1990	75.4
1977	73.0*	1991	75.5
1978	73.3*	1992	75.8
1979	73.5*	1993	75.5
1980	73.7	1994	75.7
1981	74.1*	1995	75.8
1982	74.5	1996	76.1
1983	74.6	1997	76.5

*Interpolated.

Source: Statistical Abstract of the United States, 119th Edition, 1999.

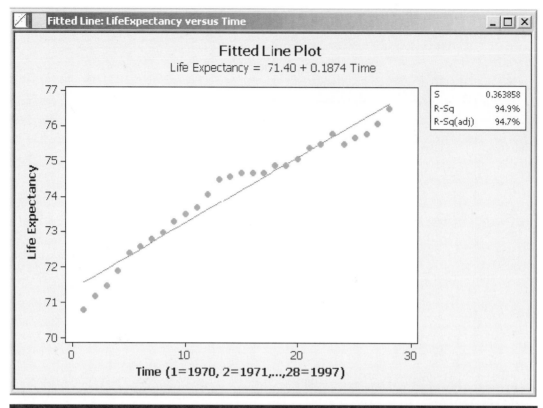

FIGURE 6-20   **Fitted Regression Line for Example 6.13**

future year. Using $28 + 53 = 81$ as the value for Time in the regression equation shown in Figure 6-20 and solving for Y, the company arrives at life expectancy of 86.6 years. This age obviously represents a substantial increase in longevity over the next many years and the company begins working on strategic plans to take advantage of this increased expected lifetime.

APPLICATION TO MANAGEMENT

Regression analysis is the most widely used statistical tool employed by management when there is a need to evaluate the impact of a single independent variable on a dependent variable. Regression analysis, along with correlation analysis, helps the forecaster characterize the relationships among variables. The forecaster can determine both the importance and the direction of the relationship between variables.

Most problems utilizing regression analysis involve the more sophisticated version called *multiple regression analysis* (to be described in the next chapter) because most relationships involve the study of the relation between a dependent variable and more than just one independent variable. Nevertheless, simple regression and correlation analysis are often useful. A few examples of multiple regression situations follow:

- *Product consumption.* A manufacturer might try to forecast how much beer a person drinks per week from looking at variables such as income, age, education, and demographic class.
- *Sales.* A retailer might try to forecast the sales of a product for one store versus another on the basis of price differentials, the relative income of the surrounding

community, the relative friendliness of store personnel, and the number and strength of competitors in each market.

- *Stock prices.* A stock analyst for a regional brokerage firm might try to forecast the price of a new issue for a local firm on the basis of the regional economy, income, population, and visibility of the firm.
- *Bad debts.* An accountant might try to forecast the bad debt a firm might encounter in the next fiscal quarter on the basis of number of people unemployed, outstanding credit, interest rates, and expected sales.
- *Employment needs.* A personnel director of a large manufacturing firm might try to forecast the coming year's staffing requirements from the average age of its employees, its wage scale compared with that of the surrounding community, expected new sales contracts, and the availability of competitive jobs.
- *Shopping center demand.* The manager of a new shopping center might try to anticipate demand by analyzing the income of the surrounding community, the size of the population, and the proximity and size of competitive shopping centers.

Once the relationship between the independent and the dependent variables is determined, management can, in some cases, try to control the dependent variable with this knowledge. For instance, suppose that a marketing manager determines that there is a significant positive relationship between advertising expenditures and sales. The regression equation might be

$$\text{Sales} = \$43,000 + .3\,(\text{Advertising expenditures})$$

From this equation the marketing manager can try to control sales by increasing or decreasing advertising by the amount that would maximize profits. Whenever the manager has control over the independent variable, there is the opportunity for possible partial control of the dependent variable. The regression equation and the coefficient of determination help management determine if such control is worthwhile.

Glossary

Coefficient of determination. The coefficient of determination measures the percentage of variability in Y that can be explained through knowledge of the variability (differences) in the independent variable X.

Fitted regression line. A fitted regression line is the line that best fits a collection of X–Y data points. It minimizes the sum of the squared distances from the points to the line as measured in the vertical, or Y, direction.

Standard error of the estimate. The standard error of the estimate measures the amount by which the actual Y values differ from the estimated values $\hat{Y}$. It is an estimate of the standard deviation of the error term ε in the simple linear regression model.

Key Formulas

Method of least squares: slope formula

$$b_1 = \frac{n\Sigma XY - \Sigma X \Sigma Y}{n\Sigma X^2 - (\Sigma X)^2} = \frac{\Sigma(X - \bar{X})(Y - \bar{Y})}{\Sigma(X - \bar{X})^2} \qquad \textbf{(6.2)}$$

Method of least squares: Y-intercept formula

$$b_0 = \frac{\Sigma Y}{n} - \frac{b_1 \Sigma X}{n} = \bar{Y} - b_1 \bar{X} \qquad \textbf{(6.3)}$$

Relation between slope coefficient and correlation coefficient

$$b_1 = \frac{\sqrt{\Sigma(Y - \bar{Y})^2}}{\sqrt{\Sigma(X - \bar{X})^2}} \, r \tag{6.4}$$

Fitted regression equation

$$\hat{Y} = b_0 + b_1 X \tag{6.6}$$

Standard error of estimate: definitional formula

$$s_{y \cdot x} = \sqrt{\frac{\Sigma(Y - \hat{Y})^2}{n - 2}} \tag{6.7}$$

Standard error of estimate: computational formula

$$s_{y \cdot x} = \sqrt{\frac{\Sigma Y^2 - b_0 \Sigma Y - b_1 \Sigma XY}{n - 2}} \tag{6.8}$$

Standard error of the forecast

$$s_f = s_{y \cdot x} \sqrt{1 + \frac{1}{n} + \frac{(X - \bar{X})^2}{\Sigma(X - \bar{X})^2}} \tag{6.9}$$

Prediction interval

$$\hat{Y} \pm t s_f \tag{6.10}$$

Large-sample 95% prediction interval

$$\hat{Y} \pm 2 s_f \tag{6.11}$$

Sum of squares and degrees of freedom decomposition

$$
\begin{aligned}
SST \quad &= \quad SSR \quad + \quad SSE \\
\Sigma(Y - \bar{Y})^2 &= \Sigma(\hat{Y} - \bar{Y})^2 + \Sigma(Y - \hat{Y})^2
\end{aligned} \tag{6.12}
$$
$$df: \quad n - 1 = \quad 1 \quad + \quad (n - 2) \tag{6.13}$$

Coefficient of determination

$$r^2 = \frac{\Sigma(\hat{Y} - \bar{Y})^2}{\Sigma(Y - \bar{Y})^2} = 1 - \frac{\Sigma(Y - \hat{Y})^2}{\Sigma(Y - \bar{Y})^2} \tag{6.14}$$

***t* statistic for testing H_0: $\beta_1 = 0$**

$$t = \frac{b_1}{s_{b_1}} \qquad \text{(see shaded box on page 226)}$$

Standard error of the regression coefficient

$$s_{b_1} = s_{y \cdot x} \Big/ \sqrt{\Sigma(X - \bar{X})^2} \qquad \text{(see shaded box on page 226)}$$

F statistic

$$F = \frac{\textit{Regression mean square}}{\textit{Error mean square}} = \frac{MSR}{MSE} \qquad (6.15)$$

Relation of F statistic to coefficient of determination

$$F = \frac{r^2(n - 2)}{1 - r^2} \qquad (6.16)$$

Residual autocorrelation coefficient

$$r_k(e) = \frac{\displaystyle\sum_{t=k+1}^{n} e_t e_{t-k}}{\displaystyle\sum_{t=1}^{n} e_t^2} \qquad k = 1, 2, \ldots, K \qquad (6.17)$$

Problems

Note: Most of the following problems contain data that are to be manipulated using regression analysis procedures. Although it is possible, even useful, to work one or two of these by hand, it is important for you to learn how to use computer software to solve such problems. In the next chapter you will learn about multiple regression analysis, in which it is not feasible to solve the problems by hand. You should become familiar with regression analysis software while solving the following problems. If you have access to Minitab or Excel, see the section at the end of this chapter for instructions on their use.

1. Which of the following situations is inconsistent?
   a. $\hat{Y} = 499 + .21X$ and $r = .75$
   b. $\hat{Y} = 100 + .9X$ and $r = -.70$
   c. $\hat{Y} = -20 + 1X$ and $r = .40$
   d. $\hat{Y} = -7 - 4X$ and $r = -.90$

2. AT&T (American Telephone and Telegraph) earnings in billions are estimated using GNP (gross national product). The regression equation is $\hat{Y} = .078 + .06X$ where GNP is measured in billions of dollars.
   a. Interpret the slope.
   b. Interpret the Y intercept.

3. Consider the data in Table P-3, where $X =$ weekly advertising expenditures and $Y =$ weekly sales.
   a. Does a significant relationship exist between advertising expenditures and sales?
   b. State the prediction equation.
   c. Forecast sales for an advertising expenditure of $50.
   d. What percentage of the variation in sales can be explained with the prediction equation?
   e. State the amount of unexplained variation.

TABLE P-3			
Y	X	Y	X
$1250	$41	$1300	$46
1380	54	1400	62
1425	63	1510	61
1425	54	1575	64
1450	48	1650	71

TABLE P-4			
Time Required for Checkout (minutes)	Value of Purchase (dollars)	Time Required for Checkout (minutes)	Value of Purchase (dollars)
3.6	30.6	1.8	6.2
4.1	30.5	4.3	40.1
.8	2.4	.2	2.0
5.7	42.2	2.6	15.5
3.4	21.8	1.3	6.5

   f. State the amount of total variation.

4. The times required to check out customers in a supermarket and the corresponding values of purchases are shown in Table P-4. Answer parts a, b, e, and f of Problem 3 by using these data. Give a point estimate and a 99% interval estimate for Y if $X = 3.0$.

5. Lori Franz, maintenance supervisor for the Baltimore Transit Authority, would like to determine whether there is a positive relationship between the annual maintenance cost of a bus and its age. If a relationship exists, Lori feels that she can do a better job of forecasting the annual bus maintenance budget. She collects the data shown in Table P-5.
   a. Plot a scatter diagram.
   b. What kind of relationship exists between these two variables?
   c. Compute the correlation coefficient.
   d. Determine the least squares line.
   e. Test for the significance of the slope coefficient at the .05 significance level. Is the correlation significant? Explain.
   f. Forecast the annual maintenance cost for a 5-year-old bus.

TABLE P-5		
Bus	Maintenance Cost ($) Y	Age (years) X
1	859	8
2	682	5
3	471	3
4	708	9
5	1094	11
6	224	2
7	320	1
8	651	8
9	1049	12

TABLE P-6		
Week	Number of Books Sold Y	Feet of Shelf Space X
1	275	6.8
2	142	3.3
3	168	4.1
4	197	4.2
5	215	4.8
6	188	3.9
7	241	4.9
8	295	7.7
9	125	3.1
10	266	5.9
11	200	5.0

TABLE P-7					
City	Number of Mail Orders Received (thousands) Y	Number of Catalogs Distributed (thousands) X	City	Number of Mail Orders Received (thousands) Y	Number of Catalogs Distributed (thousands) X
A	24	6	G	18	15
B	16	2	H	18	3
C	23	5	I	35	11
D	15	1	J	34	13
E	32	10	K	15	2
F	25	7	L	32	12

6. Andrew Vazsonyi is the manager of the Spendwise supermarket chain. He would like to be able to forecast paperback book sales (books per week) based on the amount of shelf display space (feet) provided. Andrew gathers data for a sample of 11 weeks as shown in Table P-6.

a. Plot a scatter diagram.

b. What kind of relationship exists between these two variables?

c. Compute the correlation coefficient.

d. Determine the least squares line.

e. Test for the significance of the slope coefficient at the .10 significance level. Is the correlation significant? Explain.

f. Plot the residuals versus the fitted values. Based on this plot, is the simple linear regression model appropriate for these data?

g. Forecast the paperback book sales for a week during which 4 feet of shelf space are provided.

7. Information supplied by a mail-order business for 12 cities is shown in Table P-7.

a. Determine whether a significant linear relationship exists between these two variables. (Test at the .05 significance level.)

b. Determine the fitted regression line.

c. Calculate the standard error of estimate.

d. Determine the ANOVA table.

e. What percentage of the variation in mail orders is explained by the number of catalogs distributed?

TABLE P-8			
Yearly Investment (thousands of dollars)	*Average Interest Rate (%)*	*Yearly Investment (thousands of dollars)*	*Average Interest Rate (%)*
1060	4.8	2050	3.8
940	5.1	2070	3.7
920	5.9	2030	4.5
1110	5.1	1780	4.9
1590	4.8	1420	6.2

   f. Test to determine whether the regression slope coefficient is significantly different from zero. (Use the .01 significance level.)

   g. Test for the significance of the regression using the F statistic from the ANOVA
table. (Use the .01 significance level.) Is the result consistent with the result in
part f? Should it be?

   h. Forecast the number of mail orders received when 10,000 catalogs are distributed with a 90% prediction interval.

  8. In a study of investments and interest rates, the data in Table P-8 were observed
during 10 years.

   a. Is the relationship between these variables significant?

   b. Can an effective prediction equation be developed?

   c. If 5 years from now the average interest rate is 4%, can yearly investment be
forecast?

   d. Calculate and interpret r^2.

   e. Discuss correlation and causation in this example.

  9. The ABC Investment Company is in the business of making bids on investments
offered by various firms that desire additional financing. ABC has tabulated its bid
on the last 25 issues bid in terms of the bid's percentage of par value. The bid of
ABC's major competitor, as a percentage of par value, is also tabulated on these
issues. ABC now wonders if it is using the same rationale in preparing bids as its
competitor. In other words, could ABC's bid be used to forecast the competitor's
bid? If not, then the competitor must be evaluating issues differently. The data are
given in Table P-9.

   a. To what extent are the two firms using the same rationale in preparing their
bids?

   b. Forecast the competitor's bid if ABC bids 101% of par value. Give both a point
estimate and an interval prediction.

   c. Under part b, what is the probability of ABC winning this particular bid (lowest
bid wins)?

 10. Evaluate the following statements:

   a. A high r^2 means a significant regression.

   b. A very large sample size in a regression problem will always produce useful
results.

 11. Ed Bogdanski, owner of the American Precast Company, has hired you as a
part-time analyst. Ed was extremely pleased when you determined that there is
a positive relationship between the number of building permits issued and the
amount of work available to his company. Now he wonders if it is possible to use
knowledge of interest rates on first mortgages to predict the number of building
permits that will be issued each month. You collect a random sample of 9 months
of data as shown in Table P-11.

TABLE P-9					
Issue	*ABC Bid*	*Competitor Bid*	*Issue*	*ABC Bid*	*Competitor Bid*
1	99.035	100.104	14	100.542	99.936
2	104.358	105.032	15	96.842	95.834
3	99.435	99.517	16	99.200	99.863
4	96.932	95.808	17	101.614	102.010
5	98.904	98.835	18	99.501	99.432
6	101.635	101.563	19	100.898	99.965
7	100.001	101.237	20	97.001	96.838
8	98.234	99.123	21	100.025	100.804
9	93.849	94.803	22	103.014	104.300
10	99.412	100.063	23	98.702	99.010
11	99.949	99.564	24	101.834	100.936
12	104.012	103.889	25	102.903	103.834
13	99.473	99.348			

TABLE P-11		
Month	*Building Permits* Y	*Interest Rate (%)* X
1	786	10.2
2	494	12.6
3	289	13.5
4	892	9.7
5	343	10.8
6	888	9.5
7	509	10.9
8	987	9.2
9	187	14.2

a. Plot the data on a scatter diagram.
b. Determine the fitted regression function.
c. Test for the significance of the slope coefficient at the .05 significance level.
d. When the interest rate increases by 1%, what is the average decrease in the number of building permits issued?
e. Compute the coefficient of determination.
f. Write a sentence that Ed can understand interpreting the number computed in part e.
g. Write Ed a memo explaining the results of your analysis.

12. Consider the population of 140 observations that are presented in Table P-12. The Marshall Printing Company wishes to estimate the relationship between the number of copies produced by an offset printing technique (X) and the associated direct labor cost (Y).

    Select a random sample of 20 observations.

a. Construct a scatter diagram.
b. Compute the sample correlation coefficient.
c. Determine the fitted regression line.
d. Plot the fitted line on the scatter diagram.
e. Compute the standard error of estimate.
f. Compute the coefficient of determination and interpret its value.
g. Test the hypothesis that the slope, β_1, of the population regression line is zero.

TABLE P-12

OBS.	Y	X	OBS.	Y	X	OBS.	Y	X
(1)	1.0	10	(48)	2.2	180	(95)	2.0	330
(2)	0.9	10	(49)	2.4	180	(96)	2.4	340
(3)	0.8	10	(50)	1.6	180	(97)	2.2	340
(4)	1.3	20	(51)	1.8	190	(98)	2.0	340
(5)	0.9	20	(52)	4.1	190	(99)	2.5	350
(6)	0.6	30	(53)	2.0	190	(100)	2.8	350
(7)	1.1	30	(54)	1.5	200	(101)	2.3	350
(8)	1.0	30	(55)	2.1	200	(102)	2.7	350
(9)	1.4	40	(56)	2.5	200	(103)	2.8	360
(10)	1.4	40	(57)	1.7	220	(104)	3.1	360
(11)	1.2	40	(58)	2.0	220	(105)	2.5	370
(12)	1.7	50	(59)	2.3	220	(106)	2.9	370
(13)	0.9	50	(60)	1.8	220	(107)	2.6	370
(14)	1.2	50	(61)	1.3	230	(108)	3.0	380
(15)	1.3	50	(62)	1.6	230	(109)	3.2	380
(16)	0.7	60	(63)	2.8	230	(110)	2.9	390
(17)	1.0	60	(64)	2.2	230	(111)	2.6	390
(18)	1.3	70	(65)	2.6	230	(112)	2.5	390
(19)	1.5	70	(66)	1.4	240	(113)	2.7	400
(20)	2.0	70	(67)	1.6	240	(114)	3.1	400
(21)	0.8	80	(68)	1.7	240	(115)	2.4	400
(22)	0.6	80	(69)	1.5	250	(116)	3.0	400
(23)	1.8	80	(70)	2.2	250	(117)	3.4	420
(24)	1.0	90	(71)	2.5	250	(118)	3.5	420
(25)	2.0	100	(72)	2.4	260	(119)	3.1	420
(26)	0.5	100	(73)	2.0	260	(120)	2.9	420
(27)	1.5	100	(74)	2.7	260	(121)	2.8	430
(28)	1.3	110	(75)	2.0	270	(122)	3.3	430
(29)	1.7	110	(76)	2.2	270	(123)	2.5	440
(30)	1.2	110	(77)	2.4	270	(124)	2.8	440
(31)	0.8	110	(78)	1.8	280	(125)	2.4	450
(32)	1.0	120	(79)	2.8	290	(126)	2.6	450
(33)	1.8	120	(80)	2.2	290	(127)	3.0	450
(34)	2.1	120	(81)	2.4	290	(128)	3.4	460
(35)	1.5	130	(82)	2.1	290	(129)	3.0	460
(36)	1.9	130	(83)	1.9	290	(130)	3.3	470
(37)	1.7	140	(84)	2.4	300	(131)	3.4	470
(38)	1.2	150	(85)	2.5	300	(132)	3.1	470
(39)	1.4	150	(86)	2.9	300	(133)	3.6	480
(40)	2.1	150	(87)	2.0	300	(134)	3.0	480
(41)	0.9	160	(88)	1.9	310	(135)	2.9	480
(42)	1.1	160	(89)	2.5	310	(136)	3.2	480
(43)	1.7	160	(90)	2.6	310	(137)	2.6	490
(44)	2.0	160	(91)	3.2	320	(138)	3.8	490
(45)	1.6	170	(92)	2.8	320	(139)	3.3	490
(46)	1.9	170	(93)	2.4	320	(140)	2.9	500
(47)	1.7	170	(94)	2.5	320			

TABLE P-13		

Batch	Number of Defectives Y	Batch Size X
1	4	25
2	8	50
3	6	75
4	16	100
5	22	125
6	27	150
7	36	175
8	49	200
9	53	225
10	70	250
11	82	275
12	95	300
13	109	325

h. Calculate a point estimate and a 90% prediction interval for the direct labor cost if the project involves 250 copies.

i. Examine the residuals. Does it appear as if a simple linear regression model is appropriate for these data? Explain.

13. Harry Daniels is a quality control engineer for the Specific Electric Corporation. Specific manufactures electric motors. One of the steps in the manufacturing process involves the use of an automatic milling machine to produce slots in the shafts of the motors. Each batch of shafts is tested, and all shafts that do not meet required dimensional tolerances are discarded. The milling machine must be readjusted at the beginning of each new batch because its cutter head wears slightly during production. Harry is assigned the job of forecasting how the size of a batch affects the number of defective shafts in the batch so that he can select the best batch size. He collects the following data for the average batch size of 13 batches, shown in Table P-13, and assigns you to analyze it.

a. Plot the data on a scatter diagram.

b. Fit a simple linear regression model.

c. Test for the significance of the slope coefficient.

d. Examine the residuals.

e. Develop a curvilinear model by fitting a simple linear regression model to some transformation of the independent variable.

f. Test for the significance of the slope coefficient of the transformed variable.

g. Examine the residuals.

h. Forecast the number of defectives for a batch size of 300.

i. Which of the models in parts b and e do you prefer?

j. Write Harry a memo summarizing your results.

14. The data in Table P-14 were collected as part of a study of real estate property evaluation. The numbers are observations on X = assessed value (in thousands of dollars) on the city assessor's books and Y = market value (selling price in thousands of dollars) for $n = 30$ parcels of land that sold in a particular calendar year in a certain geographical area.

a. Plot the market value against the assessed value as a scatter diagram.

b. Assuming a simple linear regression model, determine the least squares line relating market value to assessed value.

252   CHAPTER 6   *Simple Linear Regression*

TABLE P-14

Parcel	Assessed	Market	Parcel	Assessed	Market
1	68.2	87.4	16	74.0	88.4
2	74.6	88.0	17	72.8	93.6
3	64.6	87.2	18	80.4	92.8
4	80.2	94.0	19	74.2	90.6
5	76.0	94.2	20	80.0	91.6
6	78.0	93.6	21	81.6	92.8
7	76.0	88.4	22	75.6	89.0
8	77.0	92.2	23	79.4	91.8
9	75.2	90.4	24	82.2	98.4
10	72.4	90.4	25	67.0	89.8
11	80.0	93.6	26	72.0	97.2
12	76.4	91.4	27	73.6	95.2
13	70.2	89.6	28	71.4	88.8
14	75.8	91.8	29	81.0	97.4
15	79.2	94.8	30	80.6	95.4

c. Determine r^2 and interpret its value.
d. Is the regression significant? Explain.
e. Predict the market value of a property with an assessed value of 90.5. Is there any danger in making this prediction?
f. Examine the residuals. Can you identify any observations that have a large influence on the location of the least squares line?

15. Player costs (X) and operating expenses (Y) for $n = 26$ major league baseball teams for the 1990–1991 season are given in Table P-15. (All data are in millions of dollars.)
   a. Assuming a simple linear regression model, determine the equation for the fitted straight line.
   b. Determine r^2 and comment on the strength of the linear relation.
   c. Test for the significance of the regression with a level of significance of .10.
   d. Can we conclude that, as a general rule, operating expenses are about twice player costs? Discuss.
   e. Forecast operating expenses, with a large-sample 95% prediction interval, if player costs are $30.5 million.
   f. Using the residuals as a guide, identify any unusual observations. That is, do some teams have unusually low or unusually high player costs as a component of operating expenses?

16. Table P-16 contains data on newsprint consumption (Y) during a particular year and number of families in the city (X) for a sample of $n = 23$ cities.
   a. Plot newsprint consumptions against number of families as a scatter diagram.
   b. Is a simple linear regression model appropriate for the data in Table P-16? Be sure your answer includes an analysis of the residuals.
   c. Consider a log transformation of newsprint consumption, and a simple linear regression model relating $Y = $ Log(newsprint consumption) to $X = $ number of families. Fit this model.
   d. Examine the residuals from the regression in part c. Which model, the one in part b or the one in part c, is better? Justify your answer.
   e. Using the fitted function in part c, forecast the amount of newsprint consumed in a year if a city has 10,000 families.

TABLE P-15

Team	Player Costs X	Operating Expenses Y
1	29.8	59.6
2	36.0	72.0
3	35.2	70.4
4	29.7	62.4
5	35.4	70.8
6	15.8	39.5
7	18.0	60.0
8	23.2	46.4
9	29.0	58.0
10	20.7	47.6
11	30.4	60.8
12	21.7	43.4
13	39.2	66.6
14	34.3	61.7
15	33.3	53.3
16	27.1	48.8
17	24.4	48.8
18	12.1	31.5
19	24.9	49.8
20	31.1	54.4
21	20.4	40.8
22	24.1	48.2
23	17.4	41.8
24	26.4	50.2
25	19.5	46.8
26	21.8	43.6

TABLE P-16

City	Newsprint Consumption Y	Number of Families X	City	Newsprint Consumption Y	Number of Families X
1	961	8,600	13	878	8,330
2	469	6,870	14	637	9,010
3	556	9,880	15	3,291	11,790
4	1,252	12,370	16	2,470	18,910
5	902	6,920	17	916	8,550
6	1,399	13,760	18	525	8,850
7	1,877	7,450	19	1,159	8,540
8	921	6,700	20	1,138	6,910
9	494	7,420	21	979	7,060
10	530	6,930	22	1,899	10,920
11	488	7,400	23	5,022	14,800
12	1,253	7,420			

f. Can you think of other variables that are likely to influence the amount of newsprint consumed in a year?

17. Outback Steakhouse grew explosively during its first years of operation. The number of Outback Steakhouse locations for the period 1988–1993 are given in the following chart.

TABLE P-18

Year	Time	Copy Centers
1990	1	1
1991	2	2
1992	3	2
1993	4	6
1994	5	10
1995	6	16
1996	7	25
1997	8	41
1998	9	60
1999	10	97
2000	11	150
2001	12	211
2002	13	382
2003	14	537

Years	1988	1989	1990	1991	1992	1993
Number of locations	2	9	23	49	87	137

Source: Outback Steakhouse.

    a. Does there appear to be linear or exponential growth in the number of steakhouses?

    b. Estimate the annual growth rate for Outback Steakhouse over the 1988–1993 period.

    c. Forecast the number of Outback locations for 2003. Does this number seem reasonable? Explain.

18. On The Double, a chain of campus copy centers, began operations with a single store in 1990. The number of copy centers in operation, Y, is recorded for fourteen consecutive years in Table P-18.

    a. Plot number of copy centers versus year. Has On The Double experienced linear or exponential growth?

    b. Determine the annual growth rate for On The Double.

    c. Predict the number of copy centers in operation in 2010. Does this number seem reasonable? Why or why not?

CASES

CASE 6-1   TIGER TRANSPORT

Tiger Transport Company is a trucking firm that moves household goods locally and across the country. Its current concern involves the price charged for moving small loads over long distances. It has rates it is happy with for full truckloads; these rates are based on the variable costs of driver, fuel, and maintenance, plus overhead and profit. When a truck is less than fully loaded, however, there is some question about the proper rate to be charged on goods needed to fill the truck. To forecast future fuel needs and prepare long-range budgets, Tiger would like to determine the cost of adding cargo to a partially filled truck.

Tiger feels that the only additional cost incurred if cargo is added to the truck is the cost of additional fuel because the miles per gallon of the truck would be lowered. As one of the factors used to determine rates for small loads, the company would like to know its out-of-pocket cost associated with these additional fuel costs.

You are a recent business school graduate working in the cost accounting department, and you are assigned the job of investigating this matter and advising top management on the considerations necessary for a sound rate decision. You begin by assuming that all trucks are the same; in fact, they are nearly identical in terms of size, gross-weight capacity, and engine size. You also assume that every driver will get the same truck mileage over a long trip. Tiger's chief accountant feels that these assumptions are reasonable.

You are then left with only one variable that might affect the miles per gallon of long-haul trucks: cargo weight. You find that the accounting department has records for every trip made by a Tiger truck over the past several years. These records include the total cargo weight, the distance covered, and the number of gallons of diesel fuel used. A ratio of these last two figures is the miles per gallon for the trip.

You select trips made over the past 4 years as your population; there are a total of 5,428 trips. You then select 40 random numbers from a random number table, and because the trips are recorded one after another, you assign the number 1 to the first

recorded trip, 2 to the second, and so on. Your 40 random numbers thus produce a random selection of 40 trips to be examined. The cargo weight and miles per gallon for these trips are recorded and appear in Table 6-12.

Your desktop computer has software with a regression analysis package, so you can fit a simple linear regression model to the data in Table 6-12. The resulting printout appears in Table 6-13.

In studying the printout of Table 6-13, you decide that the sample data have produced a useful regression equation. This conclusion is based on a relatively high r^2 (76%), a large negative t value (-10.9), and a high F value (119). From the printout, you write down the equation of the fitted line

$$\hat{Y} = 8.8484 - .0604X$$

where Y is measured in miles per gallon and X is measured in thousands of pounds. The slope of the regression equation ($-.0604$) is interpreted as follows: *Each additional 1,000 pounds of cargo reduces the mileage of a truck by an average of .0604 mile per gallon.*

Tiger is currently paying approximately $1.25 per gallon for diesel fuel. You can, therefore, calculate the cost of hauling an additional 1,000 pounds of cargo 100 miles, as follows:

From Table 6-12, mean miles per gallon = 4.7

$$\text{Cost of 100 miles} = \frac{100(1.25)}{4.7} = \$26.60$$

Cost of same trip with an additional 1,000 pounds

$$\frac{100(1.25)}{(4.7 - .0604)} = \$26.94$$

TABLE 6-12   Data for Trip Cargo Weight (thousands of pounds) and Miles per Gallon for Tiger Transport for Case 6-1

Weight	Miles per Gallon	Weight	Miles per Gallon	Weight	Miles per Gallon	Weight	Miles per Gallon
60	5.3	58	4.9	63	5.0	63	5.0
55	5.0	60	5.1	65	4.9	62	4.9
80	4.0	74	4.5	72	4.6	77	4.6
72	4.2	80	4.3	81	4.0	76	4.5
75	4.5	53	5.9	64	5.3	51	5.7
63	5.1	61	5.5	78	4.4	74	4.2
48	7.2	80	3.5	62	4.9	78	4.3
79	3.9	68	4.1	83	3.8	50	6.1
82	3.8	76	4.5	79	4.1	79	4.3
72	4.4	75	4.4	61	4.8	55	4.7

TABLE 6-13   Regression Analysis Output for Tiger Transport

Regression Analysis: MPG versus Weight

```
The regression equation is
MPG=8.85-0.0604 Weight

Predictor        Coef    SE Coef        T       P
Constant       8.8484     0.3840    23.04   0.000
Weight      -0.060399   0.005538   -10.91   0.000


S=0.3534    R-Sq=75.8%    R-Sq(adj)=75.1%

Analysis of Variance

Source          DF      SS       MS       F       P
Regression       1  14.853   14.853  118.93   0.000
Residual Error  38   4.746    0.125
Total           39  19.599
```

Thus,

Incremental cost of 1,000 pounds carried 100 miles = $.34

You now believe you have completed part of your assignment, namely, determination of the out-of-pocket costs associated with adding cargo weight to a less-than-full truck. You realize, of course, that other factors bear on a rate decision for small loads.

Assignment

Prepare a memo for Tiger's top management that summarizes the analysis. Include comments on the extent to which your work will improve forecasts for fuel needs and truck revenue. ■

CASE 6-2   BUTCHER PRODUCTS, INC.

Gene Butcher is owner and president of Butcher Products, Inc., a small company that makes fiberglass ducting for electrical cable installations. Gene has been studying the number of duct units manufactured per day over the past two and a half years and is concerned about the wide variability in this figure. To forecast production output, costs, and revenues properly, Gene needs to establish a relationship between output and some other variable.

Based on his experience with the company, Gene is unable to come up with any reason for the variability in output until he begins thinking about weather conditions. His reasoning is that the outside temperature may have something to do with the productivity of his workforce and the daily output achieved.

He randomly selects several days from his records and records the number of ducting units produced for each of these days. He then goes to the local weather bureau and, for each of the selected days, records the high temperature for the day. He is then ready to run a correlation study between these two figures when he realizes that output would probably be related to deviation from an ideal temperature rather than the temperature itself. That is, he thinks that a day that is either too hot or too cold would have a negative effect on production when compared with a day that has an ideal temperature. He decides to convert his temperature readings to deviations from 65 degrees Fahrenheit, a temperature he understands is ideal in terms of generating high worker output. His data appear as follows: Y represents the number of units produced, while X represents the absolute difference (negative signs eliminated) between the day's high temperature and 65 degrees:

TABLE 6-14	Regression Analysis Output for Butcher Products, Inc.

Regression Analysis: Y versus X

```
The regression equation is
Y=552-8.91 X

Predictor        Coef   SE Coef       T      P
Constant       552.04     22.85   24.16  0.000
X              -8.911      1.453   -6.13  0.000

S=59.41     R-Sq=64.2%       R-Sq(adj)=62.5%

Analysis of Variance

Source             DF       SS       MS      F      P
Regression          1   132758   132758  37.62  0.000
Residual Error     21    74109     3529
Total              22   206866
```

Y	X	Y	X
485	12	327	15
512	10	308	25
625	3	603	8
585	4	321	35
318	27	426	5
405	10	410	12
379	18	515	2
497	12	498	7
316	27	357	17
351	20	429	8
525	4	401	12
395	11		

Gene performs a regression analysis using his company's computer and the Minitab software program. Gene is pleased to see the results of his regression analysis as presented in Table 6-14. The *t* values are high, indicating that both coefficients in the sample regression equation (552 and −8.9) are significant: For both, the *p*-values for the *t* test are very small.

Turning to *r*-squared, Gene is somewhat disappointed to find that this value, although satisfactory, is not as high as he had hoped (64.2%). However, he decides that it is high enough to begin thinking about ways to increase daily production levels. ∎

QUESTIONS

1. How many units would you forecast for a day in which the high temperature is 89 degrees?
2. How many units would you forecast for a day in which the high temperature is 41 degrees?
3. Based on the results of the regression analysis as shown earlier, what action would you advise Gene to take in order to increase daily output?
4. Do you think Gene has developed an effective forecasting tool?

CASE 6-3   ACE MANUFACTURING

Ace Manufacturing Company employs several thousand people in the manufacture of keyboards, equipment cases, and cables for the small-computer industry. The president of Ace has recently become concerned with the absentee rate among the company's employees and has asked the personnel department to look into this matter. Personnel realizes that an effective method of forecasting absenteeism would greatly strengthen its ability to plan properly.

Bill McGone, the personnel director, decides to take a look at a few personnel folders in an attempt to size up the problem. He decides to randomly select 15 folders and record the number of absent days during the past fiscal year along with employee age. After reading an article in a recent personnel journal, he believes that age may have a significant effect on absenteeism. If he finds that age and absent days show a good correlation in his small sample, he intends to take a sample of 200 or 300 folders and formulate a good prediction equation.

The following table contains the data values collected in the initial sample. Y represents the number of absent days during the past fiscal year, while X represents employee age.

Y	X	Y	X
3	25	9	56
4	36	12	60
7	41	8	51
4	27	5	33
3	35	6	37
3	31	2	31
5	35	2	29
7	41		

∎

QUESTIONS

1. How well are absent days and age correlated? Can this correlation be generalized to the entire workforce?
2. What is the forecasting equation for absent days using age as a predictor variable?
3. What percentage of the variability in absent days can be explained through knowledge of age?
4. Is there a significant relation between absent days and age? In answering this question, use proper statistical procedures to support your answer.
5. Suppose a newly hired person is 24 years old. How many absent days would you forecast for this person during the fiscal year?
6. Should Bill McGone proceed to take a large sample of company employees based on the preliminary results of his sample?
7. Has an effective forecasting method been developed?

CASE 6-4   MR. TUX

John Mosby has heard that regression analysis is often used to forecast time series variables and, because he has a personal computer with a regression software package, decides to give it a try. The monthly sales volumes for Mr. Tux for the years 1989 through 1996 are the dependent variable. As a first try, he decides to use the period number as the predictor, or X, variable. His first Y sales value, $6,028, will have an X value 1, the second will have an X value of 2, and so on. His reasoning is that the upward trend he knows exists in his data will be accounted for by using an ever-rising X value to explain his sales data.

After he performs the regression analysis on his computer, John records the following values:

$$t = 11.01 \qquad r^2 = .563$$
$$F = 121.14 \qquad \hat{Y} = -6,495 + 2,729.2X$$

The high t value indicates to John that his fitted regression line slope (2,729.2) is significant; that is, he rejects the null hypothesis that the slope of the population regression line is zero. The high F value is consistent with this result (John recalls that $F = t^2$ for straight-line regression), and the null hypothesis that the regression is not significant must be rejected.

John is disappointed with the relatively low r^2 (56.3%). He had hoped for a higher value so that his simple regression equation could be used to accurately forecast his sales. He realizes that this low value must be due to the seasonality of his monthly sales, a fact he knew before he began his forecasting efforts. Considerable seasonal variation would result in monthly data points that do not cluster about the linear regression line, resulting in an unsatisfactory r-squared value.

Another thing troubles John about his regression results. On the printout is the statement:

Durbin-Watson = .99. He does not understand this statement and calls the statistics professor he had in college. After he describes the values on his regression printout, the professor says, "I have a class to teach right now, but your low Durbin-Watson statistic means that one of the assumptions of regression analysis does not hold." ■

QUESTIONS

1. Comment on John's belief that his monthly sales are highly seasonal and, therefore, lead to a "low" r-squared value.
2. What is your opinion regarding the adequacy of John's forecasting method?
3. How do John's data violate one of the assumptions of regression analysis?

CASE 6-5   CONSUMER CREDIT COUNSELING

The Consumer Credit Counseling (CCC) operation was described in Chapter 1 (Case 1-2). The executive director, Marv Harnishfeger, concluded that the most important variable that CCC needed to forecast was the number of new clients that would be seen for the rest of 1993. Marv provided Dorothy Mercer with monthly data for the number of new clients seen by CCC for the period January 1985 through March 1993 (see Case 3-3). In Case 3-3 Dorothy used autocorrelation analysis to explore the data pattern. In Case 4-3 she used moving average and exponential smoothing methods to forecast for the rest of 1993.

Dorothy wondered if regression analysis could be used to develop a good forecasting model. She asked Marv if he could think of any potential predictor variables. Marv felt that the number of people on food stamps might be related to the number of new clients seen.

Dorothy could only find data for the number of people on food stamps from January 1989 to December 1992:

```
1989  24,450 24,761 25,397 25,617 25,283 25,242
      25,163 25,184 25,417 25,411 25,565 26,543
1990  26,784 27,044 27,567 28,080 28,142 28,412
      28,161 27,936 28,423 28,366 29,029 29,035
1991  29,254 29,962 30,499 30,879 30,995 31,356
      30,863 31,288 31,492 31,577 31,912 32,050
1992  32,383 32,625 33,499 34,076 34,191 33,788
      33,556 33,751 33,777 33,769 34,077 34,232
```

Marv was also acquainted with a business activity index computed for the county by the local Economic Development Council. The business activity index was an indicator of the relative changes in overall business conditions for the region. The data for this index follow. ■

Year	Jan.	Feb.	Mar.	Apr.	May	June	July	Aug.	Sept.	Oct.	Nov.	Dec.
1985	110	108	105	104	104	102	103	101	102	102	99	99
1986	102	105	106	107	105	106	105	105	103	105	103	101
1987	108	105	105	108	104	108	105	105	103	105	104	104
1988	104	109	109	103	103	104	99	102	101	101	102	102
1989	107	106	109	105	104	103	103	106	105	106	107	99
1990	103	106	110	108	110	105	105	106	107	107	111	112
1991	114	116	118	119	118	120	120	121	119	121	119	120
1992	122	118	123	118	118	120	122	120	122	123	124	122
1993	125	125	130									

QUESTIONS

1. Determine whether there is a significant relationship between the number of new clients seen and the number of people on food stamps and/or the business activity index. Don't forget the possibility of data transformations.
2. Develop a regression equation and use it to forecast the number of new clients for the first 3 months of 1993.
3. Compare the results of your forecast with the actual observations for the first 3 months of 1993.
4. Would the business activity index be a good predictor of the number of new clients?
5. The data consist of a time series; does this mean the independence assumption has been violated?
6. Assume that you developed a good regression equation. Would you be able to use this equation to forecast for the rest of 1993? Explain your answer.

CASE 6-6   AAA WASHINGTON

An overview of AAA Washington was provided in Case 5-5 when students were asked to prepare a time series decomposition of the emergency road service calls received by the club over 5 years. The time series decomposition performed in Case 5-5 showed that the pattern Mr. DeCoria had observed in emergency road service call volume was probably somewhat cyclical in nature. Mr. DeCoria would like to be able to predict emergency road service call volume for future years.

Other research done by the club discovered several factors that have an impact on emergency road service call volume. Among these factors are average daily temperature and the amount of rainfall received in a day. This research has shown that emergency road service calls increase as rainfall increases and as average daily temperature falls. The club also believes that the total number of emergency road service calls it receives is dependent on the number of members in the club. Finally, Mr. DeCoria feels that the number of calls received is related to the general economic cycle. Unemployment rate for Washington State is used as a good surrogate measurement for the general state of Washington's economy. Data on unemployment rate, the average monthly temperature, monthly rainfall, and the number of members in the club have been gathered and are presented in Table 6-15.

A conversation with the manager of the emergency road service call center has led to two important observations: (1) auto makers seem to design cars to operate best at 65 degrees Fahrenheit, and (2) call volume seems to increase more sharply when the average temperature drops a few degrees from an average temperature in the 30s than it does when a similar drop occurs with an average temperature in the 60s. This information suggests that the effect of temperature on emergency road service is nonlinear.

Assignment

1. Run four simple linear regression models using total number of emergency road service calls as the dependent variable and unemployment rate, temperature, rainfall, and number of members as the four independent variables. Would any of these independent variables be useful for predicting total number of emergency road service calls?
2. Create a new temperature variable and relate it to emergency road service. Remember that temperature is a relative scale and that the selection of the zero point is arbitrary. If vehicles are designed to operate best at 65 degrees Fahrenheit, then every degree above or below 65 degrees should make vehicles operate less reliably. To accomplish a transformation of the temperature data that simulates this effect, begin by subtracting 65 from the average monthly temperature values. This repositions "zero" to 65 degrees Fahrenheit. Should absolute values of this new temperature variable be used?

TABLE 6-15	Data for AAA Washington for Case 6-6				
Year	*Month*	*Calls*	*Rate*	*Temp.*	*Rain*	*Members*
1988	May	20002	5.7867	55.1	3.75	—
	June	21591	5.7592	59.0	1.95	—
	July	22696	5.5718	63.8	0.89	—
	August	21509	5.2939	63.8	0.51	384746
	September	22123	5.4709	59.1	2.31	388652
	October	21449	5.5049	54.6	3.12	392241
	November	23475	5.8630	45.4	8.42	393115
	December	23529	6.1349	41.0	4.44	392631
1989	January	23327	7.5474	40.3	4.30	396975
	February	24050	7.8157	34.3	3.18	395186
	March	24010	7.1390	43.2	6.57	397791
	April	19735	6.2637	52.5	2.39	397764
	May	20153	5.8332	55.3	2.83	399348
	June	19512	5.8077	62.4	1.30	401949
	July	19892	5.6713	62.9	0.83	404866
	August	20326	5.4977	63.5	1.53	405341
	September	19378	5.2989	60.9	0.32	407479
	October	21263	5.6028	51.9	3.44	405430
	November	21443	5.9143	46.2	7.24	412134
	December	23366	5.0000	41.8	4.72	415342
1990	January	23836	6.1917	41.8	9.55	416255
	February	23336	6.3775	38.9	5.73	423001
	March	22003	5.7234	46.3	3.40	428559
	April	20155	4.7792	51.7	2.91	431429
	May	20070	4.5715	54.9	2.15	434675
	June	19588	4.3899	59.8	3.55	435864
	July	20804	4.2559	66.7	0.59	437969
	August	19644	3.9359	66.4	1.33	440565
	September	17424	3.9048	61.9	0.24	441936
	October	20833	4.4294	50.4	1.17	448595
	November	22490	5.1523	45.8	10.66	446291
	December	24861	5.5102	33.9	7.93	446455
1991	January	23441	6.8901	37.9	4.40	445392
	February	19205	7.0308	46.9	5.42	445787
	March	20386	6.7186	43.4	4.35	445746
	April	19988	6.1280	49.1	5.69	446430
	May	19077	5.8146	54.3	2.12	450001
	June	19141	5.9480	58.2	1.61	452303
	July	20883	5.9026	65.4	0.51	456551
	August	20709	5.7227	66.0	2.80	455747
	September	19647	5.6877	60.9	0.20	456764
	October	22013	6.2922	51.0	1.70	462340
	November	22375	7.0615	46.2	6.50	460492
	December	22727	7.4370	42.4	3.45	465361
1992	January	22367	8.4513	43.0	7.26	465492
	February	21155	8.7699	46.0	3.59	466775
	March	21209	8.0728	48.9	1.47	467168
	April	19286	7.2392	52.7	4.35	464575
	May	19725	7.0461	58.3	0.60	459019
	June	20276	7.0478	63.6	1.84	463665

TABLE 6-15	*(Continued)*					
Year	*Month*	*Calls*	*Rate*	*Temp.*	*Rain*	*Members*
1992	July	20.795	7.1080	64.9	1.41	463775
(cont.)	August	21126	6.7824	65.0	1.01	466230
	September	20251	6.7691	58.4	2.16	—
	October	22069	7.5896	53.2	2.55	—
	November	23268	7.9908	44.8	6.23	—
	December	26039	8.2460	37.8	4.38	—
1993	January	26127	9.5301	34.9	4.08	—
	February	20067	9.2790	—	—	—
	March	19673	8.6802	—	—	—
	April	19142	7.7815	—	—	—

3. Develop a scatter diagram. Is there a linear relationship between calls and the new temperature variable?

4. If a nonlinear relationship exists between calls and the new temperature variable, develop the best model. ■

Minitab Applications

The problem. In Example 6.2, Mr. Bump wanted to run a regression analysis with the data shown in Table 6-1.

Minitab Solution

1. Enter the data from Table 6-1 onto the worksheet: gallons of milk sales go in column C1 and selling price into column C2.
2. In order to run a regression model, click on the following menus:

```
Stat>Regression>Regression
```

3. The Regression dialog box shown in Figure 6-21 appears.

   a. Sales is selected as the Response or dependent variable.
   b. Price is selected as the Predictor or independent variable.

4. In order to store residuals and Y estimates, click on storage.
   The Regression—Storage dialog box shown in Figure 6-22 appears.

   a. Click on Residuals under Diagnostic Measures to store the residuals in C3.
   b. Click on Fits under Characteristics of Estimated Equation to store the predicted values of Y in C4.
   c. Click OK to close the Regression—Storage dialog box.

5. In order to run residual plots, click on Graphs in the Regression dialog box.
   The Regression—Graphs dialog box shown in Figure 6-23 appears.

   a. Click on Four in one to include all four graphs.
   b. Click OK to close Regression—Graphs dialog box.
   c. Click OK on the Regression dialog box; the regression analysis displayed in Table 6-8 is presented in the session window (see p. 232) and the graph shown in Figure 6-9 (see p. 231) appears on the screen.

The problem. In Example 6.11, Gilbert Garcia wanted to forecast sales using advertising expenditures.

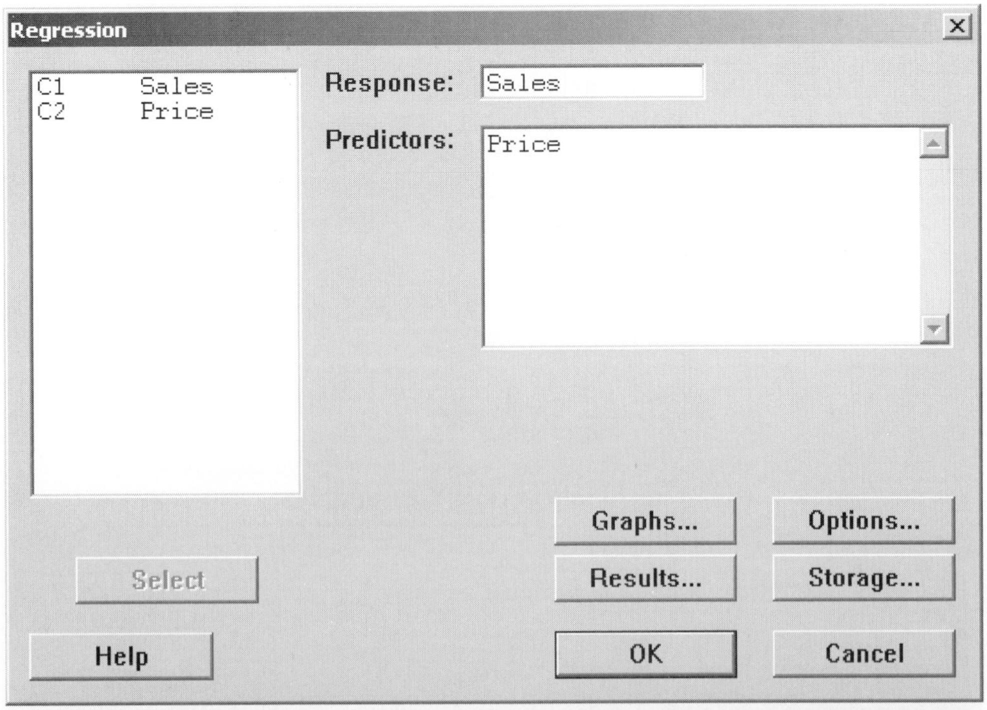

Regression   ☒

| C1 | Sales | **Response:** | Sales |
| C2 | Price | | |

Predictors: Price

Graphs...   Options...

Select

Results...   Storage...

Help   OK   Cancel

FIGURE 6-21   Minitab Regression Dialog Box

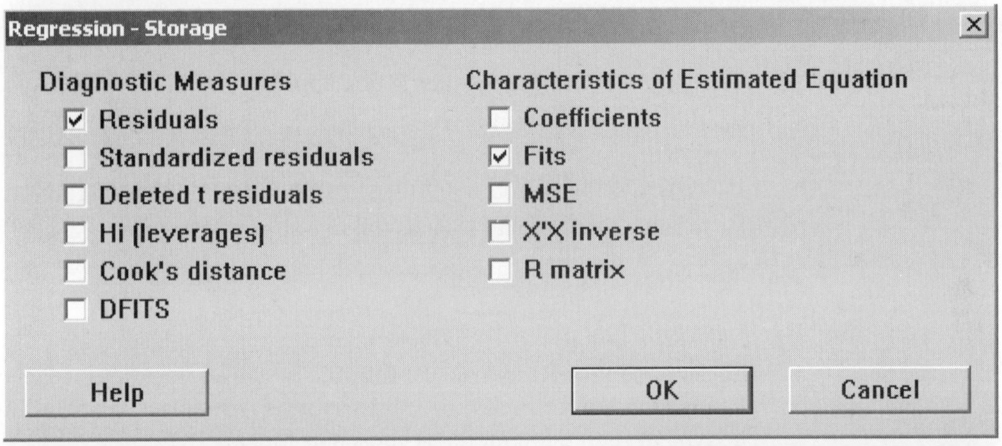

Regression - Storage   ☒

Diagnostic Measures	Characteristics of Estimated Equation
☑ Residuals	☐ Coefficients
☐ Standardized residuals	☑ Fits
☐ Deleted t residuals	☐ MSE
☐ Hi (leverages)	☐ X'X inverse
☐ Cook's distance	☐ R matrix
☐ DFITS	

Help   OK   Cancel

FIGURE 6-22   Minitab Regression—Storage Dialog Box

Minitab Solution

1. Enter the data from Figure 6-10 onto the worksheet (see p. 234): Sales go in column C1 and Advertising Expenditures into column C2.
2. In order to develop the scatter diagram shown in Figure 6-11, click:

```
Graph>Scatterplot
```

3. A choice of Scatterplots appears.
   Select simple and click OK.

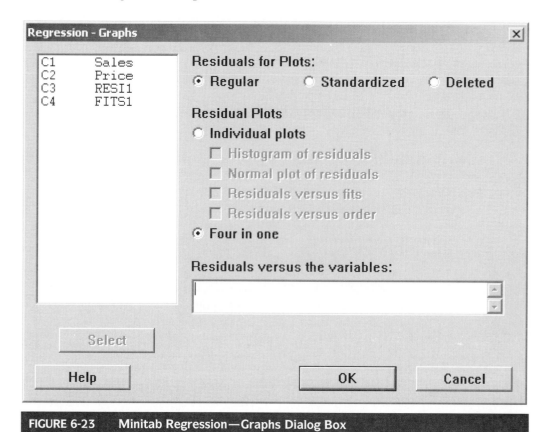

FIGURE 6-23   Minitab Regression—Graphs Dialog Box

4. The Scatterplot—Data Source dialog box appears.

    a. Select C1, Sales, as the *Y* variable, and C2, Advertising Expenditures, as the *X* variable.
    b. Click OK and the scatter diagram shown in Figure 6-11 will appear.

5. In order to run a fitted model such as the one shown in Figure 6-12, click:

    ```
    Stat>Regression>Fitted Line Plot
    ```

6. The Fitted Line Plot dialog box appears.

    a. The dependent or Response (*Y*) variable is Sales.
    b. The independent or Predictor (*X*) variable is Advertising Expenditures.
    c. The type of regression model is chosen as Linear.
    d. Click OK. The results are shown in Figure 6-12.

7. Next, convert the *X* variable to the natural log of *X* by clicking on the following menus:

    ```
    Calc>Calculator
    ```

8. The Calculator dialog box shown in Figure 6-24 appears.

    a. Enter C3 in the space next to Store result in variable.
    b. In order to perform the transformation, Natural log is highlighted on the Functions: screen.
    c. Select is clicked and the LOGE (number) under Select appears in the Expression: space.

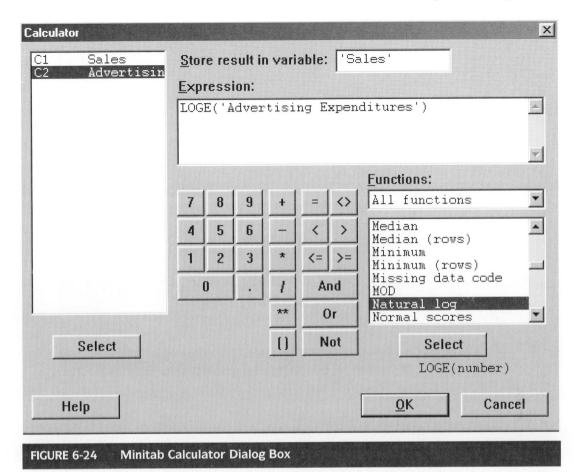

FIGURE 6-24   Minitab Calculator Dialog Box

    d. Because Advertising Expenditures is the variable to be transformed, it replaces "number" in this expression.

    e. OK is clicked and the Natural log of X appears in C3 of the data worksheet.

9. Transformations for the square root of X, the square of X, and the reciprocal of X are also accomplished using the Calculator dialog box.

10. The complete Minitab worksheet is presented in Figure 6-10.

Excel Applications

The problem. In the Bump situation, Example 6.1, regression analysis is used to determine whether selling price could be used to forecast weekly sales of gallons of milk.

Excel Solution

1. Enter Weekly sales (see Table 6-1 on p. 211) into A1 through A10 and selling price into B1 through B10 of the worksheet (see Figure 6-26).

2. Click on the following menus to perform regression analysis:

```
Tools>Data Analysis
```

3. The Data Analysis dialog box appears. Under Analysis Tools, choose Regression and click OK. The Regression dialog box shown in Figure 6-25 appears.

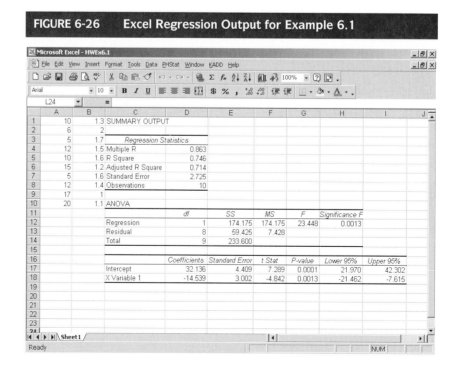

FIGURE 6-25   Excel Regression Dialog Box

a. Enter A1:A10 in the Input Y Range.
b. Enter B1:B10 in the Input X Range.
c. Click Output Range and enter C1 in the next space.
d. Click OK and the output presented in Figure 6-26 appears.

FIGURE 6-26   Excel Regression Output for Example 6.1

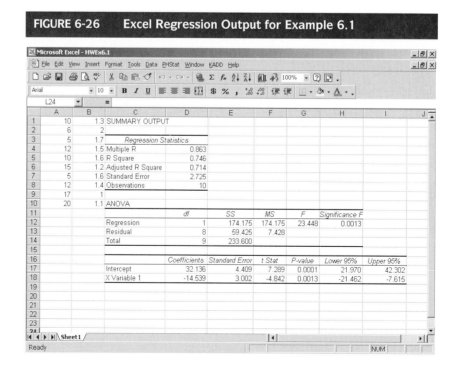

References

Dielman, T. *Applied Regression Analysis for Business and Economics*, Third Edition. Pacific Grove, CA: Duxbury, 2001.

Draper, N., and H. Smith. *Applied Regression Analysis*, Third Edition. New York: John Wiley & Sons, 1998.

Flaherty, W. P. "Using Regression Analysis to Pick the Best Targets." *M&A* (March–April 1991):47–49.

Frees, E. E. *Data Analysis Using Regression Models: The Business Perspective*. Upper Saddle River, NJ: Prentice Hall, 1996.

Johnson, R. A., and D. W. Wichern. *Business Statistics: Decision Making with Data*. New York: John Wiley & Sons, 1997.

Neter, J., W. Wasserman, M. Kutner, and C. Nachtsheim. *Applied Linear Regression Models*, Third Edition. Homewood, IL: Richard D. Irwin, 1996.

CHAPTER

7

MULTIPLE REGRESSION ANALYSIS

In simple linear regression the relationship between a single independent variable and a dependent variable is investigated. The relationship between two variables frequently allows one to accurately predict the dependent variable from knowledge of the independent variable. Unfortunately, many real-life forecasting situations are not so simple. More than one independent variable is usually necessary in order to predict a dependent variable accurately. Regression models with more than one independent variable are called *multiple regression models*. Most of the concepts introduced in simple linear regression carry over to multiple regression. However, some new concepts arise because more than one independent variable is used to predict the dependent variable.

> *Multiple regression* involves the use of more than one independent variable to predict a dependent variable.

SEVERAL PREDICTOR VARIABLES

As an example, return to the problem in which sales volume of gallons of milk is forecast from knowledge of price per gallon. Mr. Bump is faced with the problem of making a prediction that is not entirely accurate. He can explain almost 75% of the differences in gallons of milk sold by using one independent variable. Thus, 25% $(1 - r^2)$ of the total variation is unexplained. In other words, from the sample evidence Mr. Bump knows 75% of what he must know to forecast sales volume perfectly. To do a more accurate job of forecasting, he needs to find another predictor variable that will enable him to explain more of the total variation. If Mr. Bump can reduce the unexplained variation, his forecast will involve less uncertainty and be more accurate.

A search must be conducted for another independent variable that is related to sales volume of gallons of milk. However, this new independent, or predictor, variable cannot relate too highly with the independent variable (price per gallon) already in use. If the two independent variables are highly related to each other, they will explain the same variation, and the addition of the second variable will not improve the forecast.[1] In fields such as econometrics and applied statistics, there is a great deal of concern with this problem of inter-correlation among independent variables, often referred to as

---

[1] Interrelated predictor variables essentially contain much of the same information and, therefore, do not contribute "new" information about the behavior of the dependent variable. Ideally, the effects of separate predictor variables on the dependent variable should be unrelated to one another.

multicollinearity. The simple solution to the problem of two highly related independent variables is to *not* use both of them together. The multicollinearity problem will be discussed later in this chapter.

CORRELATION MATRIX

Mr. Bump decides that advertising expense might help improve his forecast of weekly sales volume. He investigates the relationships among advertising expense, sales volume, and price per gallon by examining a correlation matrix. The *correlation matrix* is constructed by computing the simple correlation coefficients for each combination of pairs of variables.

An example of a correlation matrix is illustrated in Table 7-1. The correlation coefficient that indicates the relationship between variables 1 and 2 is represented as r_{12}. Note that the first subscript, 1, also refers to the row and the second subscript, 2, refers to the column in the table. This approach allows one to determine, at a glance, the relationship between any two variables. Of course, the correlation between, say, variables 1 and 2 is exactly the same as the correlation between variables 2 and 1; that is, $r_{12} = r_{21}$. Therefore, only half of the correlation matrix is necessary. In addition, the correlation of a variable with itself is always 1 so that, for example, $r_{11} = r_{22} = r_{33} = 1$.

Mr. Bump runs his data on the computer, and the correlation matrix shown in Table 7-2 results. An investigation of the relationships among advertising expense, sales volume, and price per gallon indicates that the new independent variable should contribute to improved prediction. The correlation matrix shows that advertising expense has a high positive relationship ($r_{13} = .89$) to the dependent variable, sales volume, and a moderate negative relationship ($r_{23} = -.65$) to the independent variable, price per gallon. This combination of relationships should permit advertising expenses to explain some of the total variation of sales volume that is not already being explained by price per gallon. As will be seen, when both price per gallon and advertising expense are used to estimate sales volume, R^2 increases to 93.2%.

The analysis of the correlation matrix is an important initial step in the solution of any problem involving multiple independent variables.

TABLE 7-1	Correlation Matrix		
		Variables	
Variables	*1*	*2*	*3*
1	r_{11}	r_{12}	r_{13}
2	r_{21}	r_{22}	r_{23}
3	r_{31}	r_{32}	r_{33}

TABLE 7-2	Correlation Matrix for Bump's data		
		Variables	
	Sales	*Price*	*Advertising*
Variables	*1*	*2*	*3*
Sales, 1	1.00	−.86	.89
Price, 2		1.00	−.65
Advertising, 3			1.00

MULTIPLE REGRESSION MODEL

In simple regression the dependent variable can be represented by Y and the independent variable by X. In multiple regression analysis X's with subscripts are used to represent the independent variables. The dependent variable is still represented by Y, and the independent variables are represented by $X_1, X_2, \ldots, X_k$. Once the initial set of independent variables has been determined, the relationship between Y and these X's can be expressed as a *multiple regression model*.

In the multiple regression model the mean response is taken to be a linear function of the explanatory variables,

$$\mu_Y = \beta_0 + \beta_1 X_1 + \beta_2 X_2 + \cdots + \beta_k X_k \tag{7.1}$$

This expression is the *population multiple regression function*. As was the case with simple linear regression, we cannot directly observe the population regression function because the observed values of Y vary about their means. Each combination of values for all of the X's defines the mean for a subpopulation of responses Y. We assume that the Y's in each of these subpopulations are normally distributed about their means with the same standard deviation σ.

The data for simple linear regression consist of observations (X_i, Y_i) on the two variables. In multiple regression, the data for each case consist of an observation on the response and an observation on each of the independent variables. The ith observation on the jth predictor variable is denoted by X_{ij}. With this notation, data for multiple regression have the form given in Table 7-3. It is convenient to refer to the data for the ith case as simply the ith observation. With this convention, n is the number of observations and k is the number of predictor variables.

Statistical Model for Multiple Regression

The response Y is a random variable that is related to the independent (predictor) variables $X_1, X_2, \ldots, X_k$ by

$$Y = \beta_0 + \beta_1 X_1 + \beta_2 X_2 + \cdots + \beta_k X_k + \varepsilon$$

where:

1. For the ith observation, $Y = Y_i$ and $X_1, X_2, \ldots, X_k$ are set at values $X_{i1}, X_{i2}, \ldots, X_{ik}$.

TABLE 7-3	Data Structure for Multiple Regression			

	Predictor Variables			*Response*
Case	X_1	X_2	X_k	Y
1	X_{11}	X_{12}	X_{1k}	Y_1
2	X_{21}	X_{22}	X_{2k}	Y_2
.	.	. ...	.	.
.		. ...		.
i	X_{i1}	X_{i2}	X_{ik}	Y_i
.	.	. ...	.	.
.		. ...		.
n	X_{n1}	X_{n2}	X_{nk}	Y_n

2. The ε's are error components that represent the deviations of the response from the true relation. They are unobservable random variables accounting for the effects of other factors on the response. The errors are assumed to be independent and each is normally distributed with mean 0 and unknown standard deviation σ.
3. The regression coefficients $\beta_0, \beta_1, \ldots, \beta_k$ that together locate the regression function are unknown.

Given the data, the regression coefficients can be estimated using the principle of least squares. The least squares estimates are denoted by $b_0, b_1, \ldots, b_k$ and the estimated regression function by

$$\hat{Y} = b_0 + b_1 X_1 + \cdots + b_k X_k \qquad \textbf{(7.2)}$$

The residuals $e = Y - \hat{Y}$ are estimates of the error component and similar to the simple linear regression situation; the correspondence between population and sample is

$$\text{Population:} \quad Y = \beta_0 + \beta_1 X_1 + \beta_2 X_2 + \cdots + \beta_k X_k + \varepsilon$$
$$\text{Sample:} \quad Y = b_0 + b_1 X_1 + b_2 X_2 + \cdots + b_k X_k + e$$

The calculations in multiple regression analysis are ordinarily performed using computer software packages such as Excel and Minitab (see the "Applications" sections at the end of the chapter).

Example 7.1

For the data shown in Table 7-4, Mr. Bump considers a multiple regression model relating sales volume (Y) to price (X_1) and advertising (X_2)

$$Y = \beta_0 + \beta_1 X_1 + \beta_2 X_2 + \varepsilon$$

Mr. Bump determines the fitted regression function

$$\hat{Y} = 16.41 - 8.25 X_1 + .59 X_2$$

The least squares values $b_0 = 16.41$, $b_1 = -8.25$, and $b_2 = .59$ minimize the sum of squared errors

$$SSE = \sum_i (Y_i - b_0 - b_1 X_{i1} - b_2 X_{i2})^2 = \sum_i (Y_i - \hat{Y}_i)^2$$

for all possible choices of b_0, b_1, and b_2. Here the best-fitting function is a plane (see Figure 7-1). The data points are plotted in three dimensions along the Y, X_1, and X_2 axes. The points fall above and below the plane in such a way that $\Sigma(Y - \hat{Y})^2$ is a minimum.

The fitted regression function can be used to forecast next week's sales. If plans call for a price per gallon of \$1.50 and advertising expenditures of \$1,000, the forecast is 9.935 thousands of gallons; that is,

$$\hat{Y} = 16.41 - 8.25 X_1 + .59 X_2$$
$$\hat{Y} = 16.41 - 8.25(1.5) + .59(10) = 9.935$$

TABLE 7-4	Bump's Data for Example 7.1		
Week	Sales (thousands) Y	Price per Gallon X_1	Advertising (hundreds of dollars) X_2
1	10	$1.30	9
2	6	2.00	7
3	5	1.70	5
4	12	1.50	14
5	10	1.60	15
6	15	1.20	12
7	5	1.60	6
8	12	1.40	10
9	17	1.00	15
10	20	1.10	21
Totals	112	14.40	114
Means	11.2	1.44	11.4

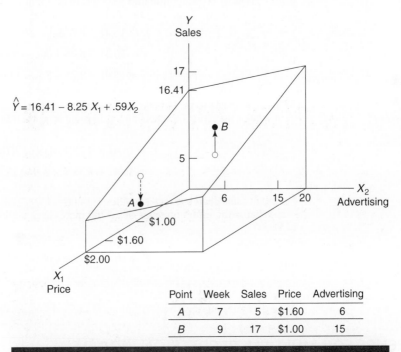

Point	Week	Sales	Price	Advertising
A	7	5	$1.60	6
B	9	17	$1.00	15

$$\hat{Y} = 16.41 - 8.25\,X_1 + .59X_2$$

FIGURE 7-1   Fitted Regression Plane for Bump's Data

INTERPRETING REGRESSION COEFFICIENTS

Consider the interpretation of b_0, b_1, and b_2 in Mr. Bump's fitted regression function. The value b_0 is again the Y intercept. However, now it is interpreted as the value of $\hat{Y}$ when both X_1 and X_2 are equal to zero. The coefficients b_1 and b_2 are referred to as the *partial,* or *net, regression coefficients.* Each measures the average change in Y per unit change in the relevant independent variables. However, because the simultaneous influence of all independent variables on Y is being measured by the regression function, the partial, or net, effect of X_1 (or any other X) must be measured apart from any influence of other variables. Therefore, it is said that b_1 measures the average change in Y per unit change in X_1, holding the other independent variables constant.

> The *partial*, or *net*, *regression coefficient* measures the average change in the dependent variable per unit change in the relevant independent variable, holding the other independent variables constant.

In the present example, the b_1 value of -8.25 indicates that each increase of 1 cent in a gallon of milk when advertising expenditures are held *constant* reduces the quantity purchased by an average of 82.5 gallons. Similarly, the b_2 value of .59 means that if advertising expenditures are increased by \$100 when the price per gallon is held constant, then sales volume will increase an average of 590 gallons.

Example 7.2

To illustrate the net effects of individual X's on the response, consider the situation in which price is to be \$1.00 per gallon and \$1,000 is to be spent on advertising. Then

$$\hat{Y} = 16.41 - 8.25X_1 + .59X_2$$
$$= 16.41 - 8.25(1.00) + .59(10)$$
$$= 16.41 - 8.25 + 5.9 = 14.06$$

Sales are forecast to be 14,060 gallons of milk.

What is the effect on sales of a 1-cent price increase if \$1,000 is still spent on advertising?

$$\hat{Y} = 16.41 - 8.25(1.01) + .59(10)$$
$$= 16.41 - 8.3325 + 5.9 = 13.9775$$

Note that sales decrease by 82.5 gallons ($14.06 - 13.9775 = .0825$).

What is the effect on sales of a \$100 increase in advertising if price remains constant at \$1.00?

$$\hat{Y} = 16.41 - 8.25(1.00) + .59(11)$$
$$= 16.41 - 8.25 + 6.49 = 14.65$$

Note that sales increase by 590 gallons ($14.65 - 14.06 = .59$).

INFERENCE FOR MULTIPLE REGRESSION MODELS

Inference for multiple regression models is analogous to that for simple linear regression. The least squares estimates of the model parameters, their estimated standard errors, t statistics used to examine the significance of individual terms in the regression model, and an F statistic to check the significance of the regression are all provided in output from standard statistical software packages. Determining these quantities by hand for a multiple regression analysis of any size is not practical, and the computer must be used for calculations.

As in Chapter 6, any observation Y can be written

$$\text{Observation} = \text{Fit} + \text{Residual}$$

or

$$Y = \hat{Y} + (Y - \hat{Y})$$

where

$$\hat{Y} = b_0 + b_1 X_1 + b_2 X_2 + \cdots + b_k X_k$$

is the fitted regression function. Recall that $\hat{Y}$ is an estimate of the population regression function. It represents that part of Y explained by the relation of Y with the X's. The residual $Y - \hat{Y}$ is an estimate of the error component of the model. It represents that part of Y not explained by the predictor variables.

The sum of squares decomposition and the associated degrees of freedom are

$$\Sigma(Y - \bar{Y})^2 = \Sigma(\hat{Y} - \bar{Y})^2 + \Sigma(Y - \hat{Y})^2$$

$$SST \quad = \quad SSR \quad + \quad SSE$$

$$df: n - 1 = \quad k \quad + n - k - 1 \tag{7.3}$$

The total variation in the response, SST, consists of two components: SSR, the variation explained by the predictor variables through the estimated regression function, and SSE, the unexplained or error variation. The information in Equation 7.3 can be set out in an analysis of variance (ANOVA) table, which is discussed in a section to follow.

Standard Error of the Estimate

The standard error of the estimate is the standard deviation of the residuals. It measures the typical scatter of the Y values about the fitted regression function.[2] The standard error of the estimate is

$$s_{y \cdot x's} = \sqrt{\frac{\Sigma(Y - \hat{Y})^2}{n - k - 1}} = \sqrt{\frac{SSE}{n - k - 1}} = \sqrt{MSE} \tag{7.4}$$

where

$$n = \text{number of observations}$$
$$k = \text{number of independent variables in the regression}$$
$$\quad\quad \text{function}$$
$$SSE = \Sigma(Y - \hat{Y})^2 = \text{residual sum of squares}$$
$$MSE = SSE/(n - k - 1) = \text{residual mean square}$$

> The *standard error of the estimate* measures the amount the actual values (Y) differ from the estimated values ($\hat{Y}$). For relatively large samples, we would expect about 67% of the differences $Y - \hat{Y}$ to be within $s_{y \cdot x's}$ of 0 and about 95% of these differences to be within $2s_{y \cdot x's}$ of 0.

Example 7.3
The quantities required to calculate the standard error of the estimate for Mr. Bump's data are given in Table 7-5.

---

[2] The standard error of the estimate is an estimate of σ, the standard deviation of the error term ε in the multiple regression model.

			TABLE 7-5	**Residuals from the Model for Bump's Data in Example 7.1**		

Y	X_1	X_2	Predicted Y ($\hat{Y}$) Using $\hat{Y} = 16.406 - 8.248X_1 + .585X_2$	Residual $(Y - \hat{Y})$	$(Y - \hat{Y})^2$
10	1.30	9	10.95	−.95	.90
6	2.00	7	4.01	1.99	3.96
5	1.70	5	5.31	−.31	.10
12	1.50	14	12.23	−.23	.05
10	1.60	15	11.99	−1.99	3.96
15	1.20	12	13.53	1.47	2.16
5	1.60	6	6.72	−1.72	2.96
12	1.40	10	10.71	1.29	1.66
17	1.00	15	16.94	.06	.00
20	1.10	21	19.62	.38	.14
			Totals	.00	15.90

The standard error of the estimate is

$$s_{y \cdot x's} = \sqrt{\frac{15.90}{10 - 2 - 1}} = \sqrt{2.27} = 1.51$$

With a single predictor, X_1 = price, the standard error of the estimate was $s_{y \cdot x} = 2.72$ (see Chapter 6). With the additional predictor, X_2 = advertising, Mr. Bump has reduced the standard error of the estimate by almost 50%. The differences between the actual volumes of milk sold and their forecasts obtained from the fitted regression equation are considerably smaller with two predictor variables than they were for a single predictor. That is, the two-predictor equation comes a lot closer to reproducing the actual Y's than the single-predictor equation.

Significance of the Regression

The analysis of variance (ANOVA) table based on the decomposition of the total variation in Y (*SST*) into its explained (*SSR*) and unexplained (*SSE*) parts (see Equation 7.3) is given in Table 7-6.

Consider the hypothesis $H_0: \beta_1 = \beta_2 = \cdots = \beta_k = 0$. This hypothesis means that Y is not related to any of the X's (the coefficient attached to every X is zero). A test of H_0 is referred to as a test of the *significance of the regression*. If the regression model assumptions are appropriate and H_0 is true, the ratio

$$F = \frac{MSR}{MSE}$$

has an F distribution with $df = k, n - k - 1$. Thus, the F ratio can be used to test the significance of the regression.

		TABLE 7-6	**ANOVA Table for Multiple Regression**	

Source	Sum of Squares	df	Mean Square	F Ratio
Regression	SSR	k	$MSR = SSR/k$	$F = \dfrac{MSR}{MSE}$
Error	SSE	$n - k - 1$	$MSE = SSE/(n - k - 1)$	
Total	SST	$n - 1$		

In simple linear regression, there is only one predictor variable. Consequently, testing for the significance of the regression using the F ratio from the ANOVA table is equivalent to the two-sided t test of the hypothesis that the slope of the regression line is 0. For multiple regression, the t tests (to be introduced shortly) examine the significance of *individual* X's in the regression function, and the F test examines the significance of *all* the X's collectively.

F Test for the Significance of the Regression

In the multiple regression model, the hypotheses

$$H_0: \beta_1 = \beta_2 = \cdots = \beta_k = 0$$
$$H_1: at\ least\ one\ \beta_j \neq 0$$

are tested by the F ratio

$$F = \frac{MSR}{MSE}$$

with $df = k, n - k - 1$. At significance level α, the rejection region is

$$F > F_\alpha$$

where F_α is the upper α percentage point of an F distribution with $\delta_1 = k$, $\delta_2 = n - k - 1$ degrees of freedom.

The *coefficient of determination R^2* is given by

$$R^2 = \frac{SSR}{SST} = \frac{\Sigma(\hat{Y} - \bar{Y})^2}{\Sigma(Y - \bar{Y})^2}$$

$$= 1 - \frac{SSE}{SST} = 1 - \frac{\Sigma(Y - \hat{Y})^2}{\Sigma(Y - \bar{Y})^2} \qquad (7.5)$$

and has the same form and interpretation as r^2 does for simple linear regression. It represents the proportion of variation in the response Y explained by the relationship of Y with the X's.

A value of $R^2 = 1$ says that all the observed Y's fall exactly on the fitted regression function. All of the variation in the response is explained by the regression. A value of $R^2 = 0$ says that $\hat{Y} = \bar{Y}$, that is, $SSR = 0$, and none of the variation in Y is explained by the regression. In practice, $0 \leq R^2 \leq 1$, and the value of R^2 must be interpreted relative to the extremes, 0 and 1.

The quantity

$$R = \sqrt{R^2} \qquad (7.6)$$

is called the *multiple correlation coefficient* and is the correlation between the responses Y and the fitted values $\hat{Y}$. Because the fitted values predict the responses, R is always positive so that $0 \leq R \leq 1$.

For multiple regression

$$F = \frac{R^2}{1 - R^2}\left(\frac{n - k - 1}{k}\right) \tag{7.7}$$

so, everything else equal, significant regressions (large F ratios) are associated with relatively large values for R^2.

The coefficient of determination (R^2) can always be increased by adding an additional independent variable X to the regression function, even if this additional variable is not important.[3] For this reason, some analysts prefer to interpret R^2 adjusted for the number of terms in the regression function. The *adjusted coefficient of determination*, $\bar{R}^2$, is given by

$$\bar{R}^2 = 1 - (1 - R^2)\left(\frac{n - 1}{n - k - 1}\right) \tag{7.8}$$

Like R^2, $\bar{R}^2$ is a measure of the proportion of variability in the response Y explained by the regression. It can be shown that $0 \leq \bar{R}^2 \leq R^2$. When the number of observations n is large relative to the number of independent variables k, $\bar{R}^2 \approx R^2$. If $k = 0$, $\hat{Y} = \bar{Y}$ and $\bar{R}^2 = R^2$. In many practical situations, there is not much difference between the magnitudes of $\bar{R}^2$ and R^2.

Example 7.4
Using the total sum of squares in Table 6-7 and the residual sum of squares from Example 7.3, the sum of squares decomposition for Mr. Bump's problem is

$$SST = SST + SSE$$
$$\Sigma(Y - \bar{Y})^2 = \Sigma(\hat{Y} - \bar{Y})^2 + \Sigma(Y - \hat{Y})^2$$
$$233.6 = 217.7 + 15.9$$

Hence, using both forms of Equation 7.5 to illustrate the calculations,

$$R^2 = \frac{217.7}{233.6} = 1 - \frac{15.9}{233.6} = .932$$

and the multiple correlation coefficient is $R = \sqrt{R^2} = \sqrt{.932} = .965$.

Here about 93% of the variation in sales volume is explained by the regression, that is, the relation of sales to price and advertising expenditures. In addition, the correlation between sales and fitted sales is about .965, indicating close agreement between the actual and predicted values. A summary of the analysis of Bump's data to this point is given in Table 7-7.

Individual Predictor Variables

The coefficient of an individual X in the regression function measures the partial, or net, effect of that X on the response Y holding the other X's in the equation constant. If the regression is judged significant, it is of interest to examine the significance of the individual predictor variables. The issue is: Given the other X's, is the effect of this particular X important, or can this X term be dropped from the regression function? This question can be answered by examining an appropriate t value.

---

[3] Here not important means not significant. That is, the coefficient of X is not significantly different from 0 (see the "Individual Predictor Variable" section that follows).

TABLE 7-7 Summary of the Analysis of Bump's Data		
Variables Used to Explain Variability in Y	R^2	$\Sigma(Y - \hat{Y})^2$
None	.00	233.6
Price	.75	59.4
Price and advertising expense	.93	15.9

If H_0: $\beta_j = 0$ is true, the *test statistic t* with value $t = b_j/s_{b_j}$ has a t distribution with $df = n - k - 1$.[4]

To judge the significance of the jth term, $j = 0, 1, \ldots, k$, in the regression function, the test statistic t is compared with a percentage point of a t distribution with $n - k - 1$ degrees of freedom. For an α level test of

$$H_0: \beta_j = 0$$
$$H_1: \beta_j \neq 0$$

we reject H_0 if $|t| > t_{\alpha/2}$. Here $t_{\alpha/2}$ is the upper $\alpha/2$ percentage point of a t distribution with $df = n - k - 1$. Some care must be exercised in dropping predictor variables from the regression function that are judged to be insignificant by the t test (H_0: $\beta_j = 0$ cannot be rejected). If the X's are related (multicollinear), the least squares coefficients and the corresponding t values can change, sometimes appreciably, if a single X is deleted from the regression function. For example, an X that was previously insignificant may become significant. Consequently, if there are several small (insignificant) t values, predictor variables should be deleted one at a time (starting with the variable having the smallest t value) rather than in bunches. The process stops when the regression is significant and all the predictor variables have large (significant) t statistics.

Forecast of a Future Response

A forecast $\hat{Y}^*$ of a future response Y for new values of the X's, say $X_1 = X_1^*$, $X_2 = X_2^*, \ldots, X_k = X_k^*$, is given by evaluating the fitted regression function at the X^*'s

$$\hat{Y}^* = b_0 + b_1 X_1^* + b_2 X_2^* + \cdots + b_k X_k^* \tag{7.9}$$

With confidence level $1 - \alpha$, a prediction interval for Y takes the form

$$\hat{Y}^* \pm t_{\alpha/2} \times \text{(standard error of forecast)}$$

The standard error of the forecast is a complicated expression, but the standard error of the estimate $s_{y \cdot x's}$ is an important component. In fact, if n is large and all the X's are quite variable, an *approximate* $100(1 - \alpha)\%$ prediction interval for a new response Y is

$$(\hat{Y}^* - t_{\alpha/2}\, s_{y \cdot x's}, \, \hat{Y}^* + t_{\alpha/2}\, s_{y \cdot x's}) \tag{7.10}$$

---

[4] Here b_j is the least squares coefficient for the jth predictor variable, X_j, and s_{b_j} is its estimated standard deviation (standard error). These two statistics are ordinarily obtained with computer software such as Minitab.

COMPUTER OUTPUT

The computer output for Bump's problem is presented in Table 7-8. Examination of this output leads to the following observations (explanations are keyed to Table 7-8).

1. The regression coefficients are -8.25 for price and $.585$ for advertising expense. The fitted regression equation is $\hat{Y} = 16.4 - 8.25X_1 + .585X_2$.
2. The regression equation explains 93.2% of the variation in sales volume.
3. The standard error of the estimate is 1.507 gallons. This value is a measure of the amount the actual values differ from the fitted values.
4. In Chapter 6 the regression slope coefficient was tested to determine whether it was different from zero. In this case, the large t statistic of -3.76 for the price variable X1 and its small p-value (.007) indicate the coefficient of price is significantly different from zero (reject $H_0: \beta_1 = 0$). Given the advertising variable X2 in the regression function, price cannot be dropped from the regression function. Similarly, the large t statistic 4.38 for the advertising variable X2 and its small p-value (.003) indicate that the coefficient of advertising is significantly different from zero (reject $H_0: \beta_2 = 0$). Given the price variable X1 in the regression function, the advertising variable cannot be dropped from the regression function. (As a reference point for the magnitude of the t values, with 7 degrees of freedom, Appendix Table C-3 gives $t_{.01} = 2.998$). In summary, the coefficients of both predictor variables are significantly different from zero.
5. The p-value, .007, is the probability of obtaining a t value at least as large as -3.76 if the hypothesis $H_0: \beta_1 = 0$ is true. Because this probability is extremely small, H_0 is unlikely to be true and it is rejected. The coefficient of price is significantly different from zero. The p-value, .003, is the probability of obtaining a t value at least as large as 4.38 if $H_0: \beta_2 = 0$ is true. Because a t value of this magnitude is extremely unlikely, H_0 is rejected. The coefficient of advertising is significantly different from zero.

TABLE 7-8   Minitab Output for Bump's Data

```
Correlations (Pearson)

        Y           X1
X1   -0.863
X2    0.891    -0.654 (6)

Regression Analysis

The regression equation is
Ŷ = 16.4 - 8.25X1 + 0.585X2  (1)

Predictor    Coef         SE Coef      T            P
Constant     16.406 (1)    4.343       3.78         0.007
X1           -8.248 (1)    2.196      -3.76 (4)     0.007 (5)
X2            0.5851 (1)   0.1337      4.38 (4)     0.003 (5)

S = 1.507 (3)     R-Sq = 93.2% (2)     R-Sq(adj) = 91.2% (9)

Analysis of Variance

Source          DF       SS          MS        F          P
Regression       2    217.70 (7)   108.85    47.92 (8)   0.000
Residual Error   7     15.90 (7)     2.27
Total            9    233.60 (7)
```

6. The correlation matrix was demonstrated in Table 7-2.
7. The sum of squares decomposition, $SST = SSR + SSE$ (sum of squares total = sum of squares regression + sum of squares error), was given in Example 7.4.
8. The computed F value (47.92) is used to test for the significance of the regression. The large F ratio and its small p-value (.000) show the regression is significant (reject H_0: $\beta_1 = \beta_2 = 0$). The F ratio is computed from

$$F = \frac{MSR}{MSE} = \frac{108.85}{2.27} = 47.92$$

As a reference for the magnitude of the F ratio, Appendix Table C-5 gives the upper 1% point of an F distribution with 2 and 7 degrees of freedom as $F_{.01} = 9.55$. The regression function explains a significant amount of the variability in sales Y.
9. The computation for the corrected or adjusted R^2, $\bar{R}^2$, is

$$\bar{R}^2 = 1 - (1 - R^2)\left(\frac{n-1}{n-k-1}\right)$$

$$= 1 - (1 - .932)\left(\frac{10-1}{10-2-1}\right) = 1 - (.068)(1.286) = .912$$

DUMMY VARIABLES

Consider the following example.

Example 7.5
Suppose an analyst wishes to investigate how well a particular aptitude test predicts job performance. Eight women and seven men have taken the test, which measures manual dexterity in using the hands with tiny objects. Each subject then went through a month of intensive training as electronics assemblers, followed by a month at actual assembly, during which their productivity was evaluated by an index having values ranging from 0 to 10 (zero means unproductive).

The data are shown in Table 7-9. A scatter diagram is presented in Figure 7-2. Each female worker is represented by a 0 and each male by a 1.

It is immediately evident from observing Figure 7-2 that the relationship of this aptitude test to job performance follows two distinct patterns, one applying to women and the other to men.

It is sometimes necessary to determine how a dependent variable is related to an independent variable when a *qualitative* factor is influencing the situation. This relationship is accomplished by creating a *dummy variable*. There are many ways to identify quantitatively the classes of a qualitative variable. The values 0 and 1 are used in this text.

Dummy, or indicator, *variables* are used to determine the relationship between qualitative independent variables and a dependent variable.

The dummy variable technique is illustrated in Figure 7-3. The data points for females are shown as 0's; the 1's represent males. Two parallel lines are constructed for the scatter diagram. The top one fits the data for females; the bottom line fits the male data points.

Each of these lines was obtained from a fitted regression function of the form

$$\hat{Y} = b_0 + b_1 X_1 + b_2 X_2$$

	TABLE 7-9	**Electronics Assemblers Dummy Variable Data for Example 7.5**	

Subject	Job Performance Rating Y	Aptitude Test Score X_1	Gender X_2
1	5	60	0 (F)
2	4	55	0 (F)
3	3	35	0 (F)
4	10	96	0 (F)
5	2	35	0 (F)
6	7	81	0 (F)
7	6	65	0 (F)
8	9	85	0 (F)
9	9	99	1 (M)
10	2	43	1 (M)
11	8	98	1 (M)
12	6	91	1 (M)
13	7	95	1 (M)
14	3	70	1 (M)
15	6	85	1 (M)
Total	87	1093	

$\bar{Y}_F$ = Mean female job performance rating = 5.75
$\bar{Y}_M$ = Mean male job performance rating = 5.86
$\bar{X}_F$ = Mean female aptitude test score = 64
$\bar{X}_M$ = Mean male aptitude test score = 83

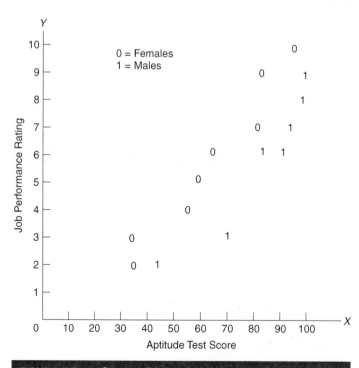

FIGURE 7-2   Scatter Diagram for Data in Example 7.5

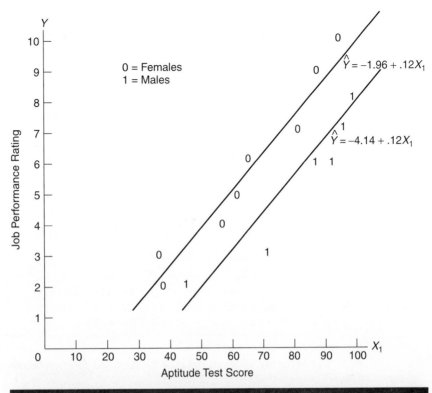

FIGURE 7-3 **Regression Lines Corresponding to Dummy Variables in Example 7.5**

where

$X_1 =$ test score

$X_2 = \begin{cases} 0 \text{ for females} \\ 1 \text{ for males} \end{cases}$ dummy variable

The single equation is equivalent to the following two equations

$$\hat{Y} = b_0 + b_1 X_1 \qquad\qquad\qquad \text{for females}$$
$$\hat{Y} = b_0 + b_1 X_1 + b_2 = (b_0 + b_2) + b_1 X_1 \qquad \text{for males}$$

Note that b_2 represents the effect of a male on job performance and that b_1 represents the effect of differences in aptitude test scores (the b_1 value is assumed to be the same for both males and females). The important point is that one multiple regression equation will yield the two estimated lines shown in Figure 7-3. The top line is the estimated relation for females, and the lower line is the estimated relation for males. One might envisage X_2 as a "switching" variable that is "on" when an observation is made for a male and "off" for a female.

Example 7.6

The estimated multiple regression equation for the data of Example 7.5 is shown in the Minitab computer output in Table 7-10. It is

$$\hat{Y} = -1.96 + .12X_1 - 2.18X_2$$

TABLE 7-10	Minitab Output for Example 7.6

Correlations: Ratings, Test, Gender

```
          Rating    Test
Test       0.876
Gender     0.021   0.428
```

Regression Analysis: Rating versus Test, Gender
```
The regression equation is
Rating = -1.96 + 0.120Test -2.18Gender

Predictor        Coef   SE Coef       T       P
Constant      -1.9565    0.7068   -2.77   0.017
Test           0.12041   0.01015  11.86   0.000
Gender        -2.1807    0.4503   -4.84   0.000

S = 0.7863   R-Sq = 92.1%    R-Sq(adj) = 90.8%

Analysis of Variance

Source          DF       SS       MS       F       P
Regression       2   86.981   43.491   70.35   0.000
Residual Error  12    7.419    0.618
Total           14   94.400
```

For the two values (0 and 1) of X_2, the fitted equation becomes

$$\hat{Y} = -1.96 + .12X_1 - 2.18(0) = -1.96 + .12X_1 \qquad \text{for females}$$

and

$$\hat{Y} = -1.96 + .12X_1 - 2.18(1) = -4.14 + .12X_1 \qquad \text{for males}$$

These equations may be interpreted in the following way: The regression coefficient value $b_1 = .12$, which is the slope of each of the lines, is the estimated average increase in performance rating for each one-unit increase in aptitude test score. This coefficient applies to both males and females.

The other regression coefficient, $b_2 = -2.18$, applies only to males. For a male test taker, the estimated job performance rating is reduced, relative to female test takers, by 2.18 units when the aptitude score is held constant.

An examination of the means of the Y and X_1 variables, classified by gender, helps one understand this result. Table 7-9 shows that the mean job performance ratings were approximately equal for males, 5.86, and females, 5.75. However, the males scored significantly higher (83) on the aptitude test than did the females (64). Therefore, if two applicants, one male and one female, took the aptitude test and both scored 70, the female's estimated job performance rating would be 2.18 points higher than the male's, because

$$\text{Female:} \quad \hat{Y} = -1.96 + .12X_1 = -1.96 + .12(70) = 6.44$$

$$\text{Male:} \quad \hat{Y} = -4.14 + .12X_1 = -4.14 + .12(70) = 4.26$$

A look at the correlation matrix in Table 7-10 provides some interesting insights. A strong linear relationship exists between job performance and the aptitude test because $r_{12} = .876$. If the aptitude test score alone was used to predict performance, it would explain about 77% ($.876^2 = .767$) of the variation in job performance scores.

The correlation coefficient $r_{13} = .02$ indicates virtually no relationship between gender and job performance. This conclusion is also evident from the fact that the mean performance ratings for males and females are nearly equal (5.86 versus 5.75). At first glance, one might conclude that knowledge of whether an applicant is male or female is not useful information.

However, the moderate relationship, $r_{23} = .428$, between gender and aptitude test score indicates that the test might discriminate between sexes. Males seem to do better on the test than do females (83 versus 64). Perhaps some element of strength is required on the test that is not required on the job.

When both test results and gender are used to forecast job performance, 92% of the variance is explained. This result suggests that both variables make a valuable contribution to predicting performance. The aptitude test explains 77% of the variance, and gender used in conjunction with the aptitude test scores adds another 15%. The computed t statistics, 11.86 and -4.84, for aptitude test score and gender indicate that both predictor variables should be included in the final regression function.

MULTICOLLINEARITY

In many regression problems, data are routinely recorded rather than generated from preselected settings of the independent variables. In these cases, the independent variables are frequently linearly dependent. For example, in appraisal work, the selling price of homes may be related to predictor variables such as age, living space in square feet, number of bathrooms, number of rooms other than bathrooms, lot size, and an index of construction quality. Living space, number of rooms, and number of bathrooms should certainly "move together." If one of these variables increases, the others will generally increase.

If this linear dependence is less than perfect, the least squares estimates of the regression model coefficients can still be obtained. However, these estimates tend to be unstable—their values can change dramatically with slight changes in the data—and inflated—their values are larger than expected. In particular, individual coefficients may have the wrong sign, and the t statistics for judging the significance of individual terms may all be insignificant, yet the F test will indicate the regression is significant. Finally, the calculation of the least squares estimates is sensitive to rounding errors.

A linear relation between two or more independent variables is called *multicollinearity*. The strength of the multicollinearity is measured by the *variance inflation factor (VIF)*.[5]

$$VIF_j = \frac{1}{1 - R_j^2} \qquad j = 1, 2, \ldots, k \qquad \textbf{(7.11)}$$

Here R_j^2 is the coefficient of determination from the regression of the jth *independent* variable on the remaining $k-1$ independent variables. For $k = 2$ independent variables, R_j^2 is the square of their sample correlation r.

If the jth predictor variable X_j is not related to the remaining X's, $R_j^2 = 0$ and $VIF_j = 1$. If there is a relationship, then $VIF_j > 1$. For example, when R_j^2 is equal to .90, $VIF_j = 1/(1 - .90) = 10$.

A *VIF* near 1 suggests that multicollinearity is not a problem for that independent variable. Its estimated coefficient and associated t value will not change much as the other independent variables are added or deleted from the regression equation. A *VIF* much greater than 1 indicates that the estimated coefficient attached to that independent variable is unstable. Its value and associated t statistic may change considerably as the other independent variables are added or deleted from the regression equation. A large *VIF* means, essentially, that there is redundant information among the predictor variables. The information being conveyed by a variable with a large *VIF* is already

---

[5]The variance inflation factor (*VIF*) get its name from the fact that $s_{b_j} \propto VIF_j$. The estimated standard deviation (standard error) of the least squares coefficient b_j increases as VIF_j increases.

being explained by the remaining predictor variables. Thus multicollinearity makes interpreting the effect of an individual predictor variable on the response (dependent variable) difficult.

Example 7.7

A large component of the cost of owning a newspaper is the cost of newsprint. Newspaper publishers are interested in factors that determine annual newsprint consumption. In one study (see Johnson and Wichern, 1997), data on annual newsprint consumption (Y), the number of newspapers in a city (X_1), the logarithm[6] of the number of families in a city (X_2), and the logarithm of total retail sales in a city (X_3) were collected for $n = 15$ cities. The correlation array for the three predictor variables and the Minitab output from a regression analysis relating newsprint consumption to the predictor variables is given in Table 7-11.

The F statistic (18.54) and its p-value (.000) clearly indicate the regression is significant. The t statistic for each of the independent variables is small with a relatively large p-value. It must be concluded, for example, that the variable LnFamily is not significant provided the other predictor variables remain in the regression function. This suggests that the term $\beta_2 X_2$ can be dropped from the regression function if the remaining terms $\beta_1 X_1$ and $\beta_3 X_3$ are retained. Similarly, it appears as if $\beta_3 X_3$ can be dropped if $\beta_1 X_1$ and $\beta_2 X_2$ remain in the regression function. The t value (1.69) associated with papers is marginally significant but the term $\beta_1 X_1$ might also be dropped if the other predictor variables remain in the equation. Here the regression is significant but each of the predictor variables is not significant. Why?

The *VIF* column in Table 7-11 provides the answer. Because *VIF* = 1.7 for Papers, this predictor variable is very weakly related (*VIF* near 1) to the remaining predictor variables, LnFamily and LnRetSales. The *VIF* = 7.4 for LnFamily is relatively large, indicating this variable is linearly related to the remaining predictor variables. In addition, the *VIF* = 8.1 for LnRetSales indicates that LnRetSales is related to the remaining predictor variables. Because Papers is weakly related to LnFamily and LnRetSales, the relationship among the predictor variables is, essentially, the relationship between LnFamily and LnRetSales. In

---

TABLE 7-11   Minitab Output for Example 7.7—Three Predictor Variables

```
Correlations: Papers, LnFamily, LnRetSales
          Papers   LnFamily
LnFamily   0.600
LnRetSal   0.643    0.930

Regression Analysis: Newsprint versus Papers, LnFamily, LnRetSales
The regression equation is
Newsprint = -56388 + 2385Papers + 1859LnFamily + 3455LnRetSales

Predictor     Coef   SE Coef      T      P    VIF
Constant    -56388     13206  -4.27  0.001
Papers        2385      1410   1.69  0.119   1.7
LnFamily      1859      2346   0.79  0.445   7.4
LnRetSales    3455      2590   1.33  0.209   8.1

S = 1849   R-Sq = 83.5%   R-Sq(adj) = 79.0%

Analysis of Variance

Source          DF         SS        MS      F      P
Regression       3  190239371  63413124  18.54  0.000
Residual Error  11   37621478   3420134
Total           14  227860849
```

---

[6]Logarithms of the number of families and the total retail sales are used to make the numbers less positively skewed and more manageable.

TABLE 7-12   Minitab Output for Example 7.7—Two Predictor Variables

```
Regression Analysis: Newsprint versus Papers, LnRetSales
The regression equation is
Newsprint = -59766 + 2393 Papers + 5279 LnRetSales

Predictor      Coef   SE Coef       T      P   VIF
Constant     -59766     12304   -4.86  0.000
Papers         2393      1388    1.72  0.110   1.7
LnRetSales     5279      1171    4.51  0.001   1.7

S = 1820    R-Sq = 82.5%     R-Sq(adj) = 79.6%

Analysis of Variance

Source          DF         SS        MS      F      P
Regression       2  188090489  94045244  28.38  0.000
Residual Error  12   39770360   3314197
Total           14  227860849
```

---

fact, the sample correlation between LnFamily and LnRetSales is $r = .93$, showing strong linear association.

The two variables LnFamily and LnRetSales are very similar in their ability to explain newsprint consumption. We need only one, not both, in the regression function. The Minitab output from a regression analysis with LnFamily (smallest t statistic) deleted from the regression function is shown in Table 7-12.

Notice that the coefficient of Papers is about the same for the two regressions. The coefficients of LnRetSales, however, are considerably different (3,455 for $k = 3$ predictors and 5,279 for $k = 2$ predictors). Also, for the second regression, the variable LnRetSales is clearly significant ($t = 4.51$ with p-value $= .001$). With Papers in the model, LnRetSales is an additional important predictor of newsprint consumption. The R^2's for the two regressions are nearly the same, approximately .83, as are the standard errors of the estimates, $s_{y \cdot x's} = 1,849$ and $s_{y \cdot x's} = 1,820$, respectively. Finally, the common $VIF = 1.7$ for the two predictors in the second model indicates multicollinearity is no longer a problem. As a residual analysis confirms, for the variables considered, the regression of Newsprint on Papers and LnRetSales is entirely adequate.

If estimating the separate effects of the predictor variables is important and multicollinearity appears to be a problem, what should be done? There are several ways to deal with severe multicollinearity, as follows. None of them may be completely satisfactory or feasible.

- Create new X variables, and call them $\tilde{X}$, by scaling all the independent variables according to the formula

$$\tilde{X} = \frac{X_{ij} - \bar{X}_j}{\sqrt{\sum_i (X_{ij} - \bar{X}_j)^2}} \qquad j = 1, 2, \ldots, k; \quad i = 1, 2, \ldots, n \qquad \textbf{(7.12)}$$

These new variables will each have a sample mean of 0 and the same sample standard deviation. The regression calculations with the new X's are less sensitive to round-off error in the presence of severe multicollinearity.

- Identify and eliminate one or more of the redundant independent variables from the regression function. (This approach was used in Example 7.7.)

- Consider estimation procedures other than least squares.[7]
- Regress the response Y on linear combinations of the X's that are uncorrelated.[8]
- Carefully select potential independent variables at the beginning of the study. Try to avoid variables that "say the same thing."

SELECTING THE "BEST" REGRESSION EQUATION

How does one develop the best multiple regression equation to forecast a variable of interest? The *first step* involves the selection of a complete set of potential predictor variables. Any variable that might add to the accuracy of the forecast should be included. In the selection of a final equation, one is usually faced with the dilemma of providing the most accurate forecast for the smallest cost. In other words, when choosing predictor variables to include in the final equation, the analyst must evaluate them by using the following two *opposed* criteria:

1. The analyst wants the equation to include as many useful predictor variables as possible.[9]
2. Given that it costs money to obtain and monitor information on a large number of X's, the equation should include as few predictors as possible. The simplest equation is usually the best equation.

The selection of the best regression equation usually involves a compromise between these extremes, and personal judgment will be a necessary part of any solution.

After a seemingly complete list of potential predictors has been compiled, the *second step* is to screen out the independent variables that do not seem appropriate. An independent variable (1) may not be fundamental to the problem (there should be some plausible relation between the dependent variable and an independent variable), (2) may be subject to large measurement errors, (3) may duplicate other independent variables (multicollinearity), or (4) may be difficult to measure accurately (accurate data are unavailable or costly).

The *third step* is to shorten the list of predictors so as to obtain a "best" selection of independent variables. In the next section, techniques currently in use are discussed. None of the search procedures can be said to yield the "best" set of independent variables. Indeed, there is often no unique "best" set. To add to the confusion, the various techniques do not all necessarily lead to the same final prediction equation. The entire variable selection process is extremely subjective. The primary advantage of automatic-search procedures is that analysts can then focus their judgments on the pivotal areas of the problem.

To demonstrate various search procedures, a simple example is presented that has five potential independent variables.

Example 7.8

Pam Weigand, the personnel manager of the Zurenko Pharmaceutical Company, is interested in forecasting whether a particular applicant will become a good salesperson. She decides to use the first month's sales as the dependent variable (Y), and she chooses to analyze the following independent variables:

---

[7] Alternative procedures for estimating the regression parameters are beyond the scope of this book. The interested reader should consult Draper and Smith (1998).

[8] Again, the procedures for creating linear combinations of the X's that are uncorrelated are beyond the scope of this book. Draper and Smith (1998) contains a discussion of these techniques.

[9] Recall that whenever a new predictor variable is added to a multiple regression equation, R^2 increases. Therefore, it is important that a new predictor variable make a *significant* contribution to the regression equation.

X_1 = selling aptitude test
X_2 = age, in years
X_3 = anxiety test score
X_4 = experience, in years
X_5 = high school GPA (grade point average)

Pam collects the data shown in Table 7-13, and she assigns the task of obtaining the "best" set of independent variables for forecasting sales ability to her analyst.

The first step is to obtain a correlation matrix for all the variables from a computer program. This matrix will provide essential knowledge about the basic relationships among the variables.

Examination of the correlation matrix in Table 7-14 reveals that the selling aptitude test, age, experience, and GPA are positively related to sales ability and have potential as good predictor variables. The anxiety test score shows a low negative correlation with sales, and it is probably not an important predictor. Further analysis indicates that GPA and age, and experience and age, are moderately correlated. It is the presence of these interrelationships that must be dealt with in attempting to find the best possible set of explanatory variables.

Two procedures are demonstrated: all possible regressions and stepwise regression.

TABLE 7-13	Zurenko Pharmaceutical Company Data for Example 7.8				
One Month's Sales (units)	Aptitude Test Score	Age (years)	Anxiety Test Score	Experience (years)	High School GPA
44	10	22.1	4.9	0	2.4
47	19	22.5	3.0	1	2.6
60	27	23.1	1.5	0	2.8
71	31	24.0	.6	3	2.7
61	64	22.6	1.8	2	2.0
60	81	21.7	3.3	1	2.5
58	42	23.8	3.2	0	2.5
56	67	22.0	2.1	0	2.3
66	48	22.4	6.0	1	2.8
61	64	22.6	1.8	1	3.4
51	57	21.1	3.8	0	3.0
47	10	22.5	4.5	1	2.7
53	48	22.2	4.5	0	2.8
74	96	24.8	.1	3	3.8
65	75	22.6	.9	0	3.7
33	12	20.5	4.8	0	2.1
54	47	21.9	2.3	1	1.8
39	20	20.5	3.0	2	1.5
52	73	20.8	.3	2	1.9
30	4	20.0	2.7	0	2.2
58	9	23.3	4.4	1	2.8
59	98	21.3	3.9	1	2.9
52	27	22.9	1.4	2	3.2
56	59	22.3	2.7	1	2.7
49	23	22.6	2.7	1	2.4
63	90	22.4	2.2	2	2.6
61	34	23.8	.7	1	3.4
39	16	20.6	3.1	1	2.3
62	32	24.4	.6	3	4.0
78	94	25.0	4.6	5	3.6

TABLE 7-14	Correlations: Sales, Aptitude, Age, Anxiety, Exp., GPA				

	Sales	Aptitude	Age	Anxiety	Exp.
Aptitude	0.676				
	0.000				
Age	0.798	0.228			
	0.000	0.226			
Anxiety	−0.296	−0.222	−0.287		
	0.112	0.238	0.124		
Exp.	0.550	0.350	0.540	−0.279	
	0.002	0.058	0.002	0.136	
GPA	0.622	0.318	0.695	−0.244	0.312
	0.000	0.087	0.000	0.193	0.093

Cell Contents:
Pearson correlation
P-Value

All Possible Regressions

The procedure calls for the investigation of all possible regression equations that involve the potential independent variables. The analyst starts with an equation containing no independent variables and analyzes every possible combination in order to select the best set of predictors.

Different criteria for comparing the various regression equations may be used with the *all possible regressions approach*. Only the R^2 technique, which involves four steps, is discussed here.

The procedure first requires the fitting of every possible regression model that involves the dependent variable and any number of independent variables. Each independent variable can either be, or not be, in the equation (two possible outcomes), and this fact is true for every independent variable. Altogether there are 2^k equations (where k equals the number of independent variables). So if there are eight independent variables to consider ($k = 8$), then $2^8 = 256$ equations must be examined.

The second step in the procedure is to divide the equations into sets according to the number of parameters to be estimated.

Example 7.9
The results from all the possible regression runs for the Zurenko Pharmaceutical Company example are presented in Table 7-15. Note that Table 7-15 is divided into six sets of regression equation outcomes. This breakdown coincides with the number of parameters contained in each equation.

The third step involves the selection of the best independent variable (or variables) for each parameter grouping. The equation with the highest R^2 is considered best. The best equation from each set listed in Table 7-15 is presented in Table 7-16.

The fourth step involves making the subjective decision, "Which equation is the best?" On the one hand, the analyst desires the highest R^2 possible; on the other hand, he or she wants the simplest equation possible. The all possible regressions approach assumes that the number of data points n exceeds the number of parameters $k + 1$.

Example 7.10
The analyst is attempting to find the point at which adding additional independent variables for the Zurenko Pharmaceutical problem is not worthwhile because it leads to a very small increase in R^2. The results in Table 7-16 clearly indicate that adding variables after test

TABLE 7-15 R^2 Values for All Possible Regressions for Zurenko Pharmaceutical, Example 7.9

Independent Variables Used	Number of Parameters	Error Degrees of Freedom	R^2
None	1	29	0000
X_1	2	28	.4570
X_2	2	28	.6370
X_3	2	28	.0880
X_4	2	28	.3020
X_5	2	28	.3870
X_1, X_2	3	27	.8948
X_1, X_3	3	27	.4790
X_1, X_4	3	27	.5690
X_1, X_5	3	27	.6410
X_2, X_3	3	27	.6420
X_2, X_4	3	27	.6570
X_2, X_5	3	27	.6460
X_3, X_4	3	27	.3240
X_3, X_5	3	27	.4090
X_4, X_5	3	27	.5270
X_1, X_2, X_3	4	26	.8951
X_1, X_2, X_4	4	26	.8948
X_1, X_2, X_5	4	26	.8953
X_1, X_3, X_4	4	26	.5750
X_1, X_3, X_5	4	26	.6460
X_1, X_4, X_5	4	26	.7010
X_2, X_3, X_4	4	26	.6590
X_2, X_3, X_5	4	26	.6500
X_2, X_4, X_5	4	26	.6690
X_3, X_4, X_5	4	26	.5310
X_1, X_2, X_3, X_4	5	25	.8951
X_1, X_2, X_3, X_5	5	25	.8955
X_1, X_2, X_4, X_5	5	25	.8953
X_1, X_3, X_4, X_5	5	25	.7010
X_2, X_3, X_4, X_5	5	25	.6710
X_1, X_2, X_3, X_4, X_5	6	24	.8955

TABLE 7-16 Best Regression Equations for Zurenko Pharmaceutical, Example 7.9

Number of Parameters	Independent Variables	Error Degrees of Freedom	R^2
1	None	29	0000
2	X_2	28	.6370
3	X_1, X_2	27	.8948
4	X_1, X_2, X_5	26	.8953
5	X_1, X_2, X_3, X_5	25	.8955
6	X_1, X_2, X_3, X_4, X_5	24	.8955

(X_1) and age (X_2) is not necessary. Therefore, the final fitted regression equation is of the form

$$\hat{Y} = b_0 + b_1 X_1 + b_2 X_2$$

and it explains 89.48% of the variation in Y.

The all possible regressions procedure is best summed up by Draper and Smith (1998):

> In general the analysis of all regressions is quite unwarranted. While it means that the investigator has "looked at all possibilities" it also means he has examined a large number of regression equations that intelligent thought would often reject out of hand. The amount of computer time used is wasteful and the sheer physical effort of examining all the computer printouts is enormous when more than a few variables are being examined. Some sort of selection procedure that shortens this task is preferable. (p. 333)

Stepwise Regression

The stepwise regression procedure adds one independent variable at a time to the model, one step at a time. A large number of independent variables can be handled on the computer in one run when using this procedure.

Stepwise regression can best be described by listing the basic steps (algorithm) involved in the computations.

1. All possible *simple* regressions are considered. The predictor variable that explains the largest significant proportion of the variation in Y (has the largest correlation with the response) is the first variable to enter the regression equation.
2. The next variable to enter the equation is the one (out of those not included) that makes the largest significant contribution to the regression sum of squares. The significance of the contribution is determined by an F test. The value of the F statistic that must be exceeded before the contribution of a variable is deemed significant is often called the *F to enter*.
3. Once an additional variable has been included in the equation, the individual contributions to the regression sum of squares of the other variables *already in the equation* are checked for significance using F tests. If the F statistic is less than a value called the *F to remove*, the variable is deleted from the regression equation.
4. Steps 2 and 3 are repeated until all possible additions are nonsignificant and all possible deletions are significant. At this point, the selection stops.

> *Stepwise regression* permits predictor variables to enter or leave the regression function at different stages of its development. An independent variable is removed from the model if it doesn't continue to make a significant contribution when a new variable is added.

The user of a stepwise regression program supplies the values that decide when a variable is allowed to enter and when a variable is removed. Because the F statistics used in stepwise regression are such that $F = t^2$, where t is the t statistic for checking the significance of a predictor variable, $F = 4$ (corresponding to $|t| = 2$) is a common choice for both the F to enter and the F to remove. An *F to enter* of 4 is essentially equivalent to testing for the significance of a predictor variable at the 5% level. The

Minitab stepwise program allows the user to choose an alpha level to enter and to remove variables instead of F. An alpha to enter of .05 is approximately equivalent to using an $F = 4$.

The result of the stepwise procedure is a model that contains only independent variables with t values that are significant at the specified level. However, because of the step-by-step development, there is no guarantee that stepwise regression will select, for example, the best three variables for prediction. In addition, an automatic selection method is not capable of indicating when transformations of variables are useful, nor does it necessarily avoid a multicollinearity problem. Finally, stepwise regression cannot create important variables that are not supplied by the user. It is necessary to think carefully about the collection of independent variables that is supplied to a stepwise regression program.

The stepwise procedure is illustrated in Example 7.11.

Example 7.11

Let's "solve" the Zurenko problem using stepwise regression.

Pam examines the correlation matrix shown in Table 7-14 and decides that, when she runs the stepwise analysis, the age variable will enter the model first because it has the largest correlation with sales ($r_{1,3} = .798$) and will explain 63.7% ($.798^2$) of the variation in sales.

She notes that the aptitude test score will probably enter the model second because it is strongly related to sales ($r_{1,2} = .676$) but not highly related to the age variable ($r_{2,3} = .228$) already in the model.

Pam also notices that the other variables will probably not qualify as good predictor variables. The anxiety test score will not be a good predictor because it is not well related to sales ($r_{1,4} = -.296$). The experience and GPA variables might have potential as good predictor variables ($r_{1,5} = .550$) and ($r_{1,6} = .622$). However, both of these predictor variables have a potential multicollinearity problem with the age variable ($r_{3,5} = .540$) and ($r_{3,6} = .695$).

The Minitab commands to run a stepwise regression analysis for this example are demonstrated in the "Minitab Applications" section at the end of the chapter. The output from this stepwise regression run is shown in Table 7-17. The stepwise analysis proceeds according to the steps that follow.

TABLE 7-17	Stepwise Regression: Sales versus Aptitude, Age, Anxiety, Exp., GPA	

Alpha-to-Enter: 0.05 Alpha-to-Remove: 0.05

Response is Sales on 5 predictors, with N = 30

Step	1	2
Constant	−100.85	−86.79
Age	6.97	5.93
T-Value	7.01	10.60
P-Value	0.000	0.000
Aptitude		0.200
T-Value		8.13
P-Value		0.000
S	6.85	3.75
R-Sq	63.70	89.48
R-Sq(adj)	62.41	88.70
C-p	57.4	0.2

Step 1.   The model after Step 1 is

$$\text{Sales} = -100.85 + 6.97 \,(\text{Age})$$

As Pam thought, the age variable entered the model first and explains 63.7% of the sales variance. Because the p-value of .000 is less than the alpha value of .05, age is added to the model. Remember that the p-value is the probability of obtaining a t statistic as large as 7.01 by chance alone. The Minitab decision rule is to enter a variable if the p-value is less than alpha.

Note that $t = 7.01 > 2.048$, the upper .025 point of a t distribution with 28 ($n - k - 1 = 30 - 1 - 1$) degrees of freedom. So, at the .05 significance level, the hypothesis $H_0: \beta_1 = 0$ is rejected in favor of $H_1: \beta_1 \neq 0$. Because $t^2 = F$ or $2.048^2 = 4.19$, an F *to enter* of 4 is also essentially equivalent to testing for the significance of a predictor variable at the 5% level. In this case, because the coefficient of the age variable is clearly significantly different from zero, age enters the regression equation, and the procedure now moves to Step 2.

Step 2.   The model after Step 2 is

$$\text{Sales} = -86.79 + 5.93 \,(\text{Age}) + 0.200 \,(\text{Aptitude})$$

This model explains 89.48% of the variation in sales.

The null and alternative hypotheses to determine whether the aptitude test score's regression coefficient is significantly different from zero are

$$H_0: \beta_2 = 0$$
$$H_1: \beta_2 \neq 0$$

Again, the p-value of .000 is less than the alpha value of .05 and aptitude is added to the model. The aptitude test score's regression coefficient is significantly different from zero, and the probability that this occurred by chance sampling error is approximately zero. This result means that the aptitude test score is an important variable when used in conjunction with age.

The critical t statistic based on 27 ($n - k - 1 = 30 - 2 - 1$) degrees of freedom is 2.052.[10] The computed t ratio found on the Minitab output is 8.13, which is greater than 2.052. Using the t test approach, the null hypothesis is also rejected.

Note that the p-value for the age variable's t statistic, .000, remains very small. Age is still a significant predictor of Sales. The procedure now moves on to Step 3.

Step 3.   The computer now considers adding a third predictor variable given that X_1 (Age) and X_2 (Aptitude) are in the regression equation. None of the remaining independent variables is significant (has a p-value less than .05) when run in combination with X_1 and X_2, so the stepwise procedure is completed.

Pam's final model selected by the stepwise procedure is the two-predictor variable model given in Step 2.

Final Notes on Stepwise Regression

The stepwise regression technique is extremely easy to use. Unfortunately, it is also extremely easy to misuse. Analysts developing a regression model often produce a large set of potential independent variables and then let the stepwise procedure determine which ones are significant. The problem is that when a large set of independent variables is analyzed, many t tests are performed, and it is likely that a type I error (adding a nonsignificant variable) will result. That is, the final model might contain a variable that is not linearly related to the dependent variable and entered the model just by chance.

---

[10] Again, since $2.052^2 = 4.21$, using an F *to enter* of 4 is roughly equivalent to testing for the significance of a predictor variable at the .05 level.

As mentioned previously, another problem involves the initial selection of potential independent variables. When these variables are selected, higher-order terms (curvilinear, nonlinear, and interaction) are often omitted to keep the number of variables manageable. Consequently, several important variables may be initially omitted from the model. It becomes obvious that an analyst's intuitive choice of the initial independent variables is critical to the development of a successful regression model.

REGRESSION DIAGNOSTICS AND RESIDUAL ANALYSIS

A regression analysis is not complete until one is convinced the model is an adequate representation of the data. It is imperative to examine the adequacy of the model *before* it becomes part of the decision-making apparatus.

An examination of the residuals is a crucial component of the determination of model adequacy. Several residual plots designed to check the regression model assumptions were introduced in Chapter 6. Also, if regression models are used with time series data (to be discussed in Chapter 8), it is important to compute the residual autocorrelations to check the independence assumption. Inferences (and decisions) made with models that do not approximately conform to the regression assumptions can be grossly misleading. For example, it may be concluded that the manipulation of a predictor variable will produce a specified change in the response when, in fact, it will not. It may be concluded that a forecast is very likely (95% confidence) to be within 2% of the future response when, in fact, the actual confidence is much less, and so forth.

In this section, some additional tools that can be used to evaluate a regression model will be discussed. These tools are designed to identify observations that are outlying or extreme (observations that are well separated from the remainder of the data). Outlying observations are often hidden by the fitting process and may not be easily detected from an examination of residual plots. Yet they can have a major role in determining the fitted regression function. It is important to study outlying observations to decide whether they should be retained or eliminated and, if retained, whether their influence should be reduced in the fitting process or the regression function revised.

A measure of the influence of the ith data point on the location of the fitted regression function is provided by the *leverage* h_{ii}. The leverage depends only on the predictors; it does not depend on the response Y. For simple linear regression with one predictor variable X,

$$h_{ii} = \frac{1}{n} + \frac{(X_i - \bar{X})^2}{\Sigma(X_i - \bar{X})^2}$$

With k predictors, the expression for the ith leverage is more complicated; however, one can show that $0 < h_{ii} < 1$, and that the mean leverage is $\bar{h} = (k+1)/n$.

If the ith data point has high leverage (h_{ii} is close to 1), the fitted response $\hat{Y}_i$ at these X's is almost completely determined by Y_i, with the remaining data having very little influence. The high-leverage data point is also an outlier among the X's (far from other combinations of X values).[11] A rule of thumb suggests that h_{ii} is large enough to merit checking if $h_{ii} \geq 3(k+1)/n$.

The detection of outlying or extreme Y values is based on the size of the residuals $e = Y - \hat{Y}$. Large residuals indicate a Y value that is "far" from its fitted, or predicted,

---

[11]The converse is not necessarily true. That is, an outlier among the X's may not be a high-leverage data point.

value $\hat{Y}$. A large residual will show up in a histogram of the residuals as a value far (in either direction) from zero. A large residual will show up in a plot of the residuals versus the fitted values as a point far above or below the horizontal axis.

Software packages such as Minitab flag data points with extreme Y values by computing "standardized" residuals and identifying points with large standardized residuals.

One standardization is based on the fact that the residuals have estimated standard deviations

$$s_{e_i} = s_{y \cdot x's} \sqrt{1 - h_{ii}}$$

where $s_{y \cdot x's} = \sqrt{MSE}$ is the standard error of the estimate and h_{ii} is the leverage associated with the ith data point. The *standardized residual*[12] is then

$$\frac{e_i}{s_{e_i}} = \frac{e_i}{s_{y \cdot x's} \sqrt{1 - h_{ii}}} \tag{7.13}$$

The standardized residuals all have variance 1. A standardized residual is considered large (the response extreme) if

$$\left| \frac{e_i}{s_{e_i}} \right| > 2$$

The Y values corresponding to data points with large standardized residuals can heavily influence the location of the fitted regression function.

Example 7.12

Chief executive officer (CEO) salaries in the United States are of interest because of their relationship to salaries in international firms and to salaries of top professionals outside corporate America. Also, for an individual firm, the CEO compensation directly, or indirectly, influences the salaries of managers in the positions below CEO. CEO salary varies greatly from firm to firm, but data suggest that salary can be explained in terms of a firm's sales and the CEO's amount of experience, educational level, and ownership stake in the firm. In one study, 50 firms were used to develop a multiple regression model linking CEO compensation to several predictor variables such as sales, profits, age, experience, professional background, educational level, and ownership stake.

After eliminating unimportant predictor variables, the final fitted regression function was

$$\hat{Y} = 5.52 - .467X_1 + .263X_2$$

where

Y = Logarithm of CEO compensation
X_1 = Indicator variable for educational level
X_2 = Logarithm of company sales

Minitab identified three observations from this regression analysis that have either large standardized residuals or large leverage.

---

[12] Some software packages may call the standardized residual given by Equation 7.13 the *Studentized* residual.

Unusual Observations

Obs	Educate	LnComp	Fit	StDev Fit	Residual	St Resid
14	1.00	6.0568	7.0995	0.0949	-1.0427	-2.09R
25	0.00	8.1342	7.9937	0.2224	0.1405	0.31X
33	0.00	6.3969	7.3912	0.2032	-0.9943	-2.13R

R denotes an observation with a large standardized residual.
X denotes an observation whose X value gives it large
     influence.

Observations 14 and 33 have large standardized residuals. The fitted regression function is predicting (log) compensation that is too large for these two CEOs. An examination of the full data set shows that these CEOs each own relatively large percentages of their companies' stock. Case 14 owns more than 10% of the company's stock, and case 33 owns more than 17% of the company's stock. These individuals are receiving much of their remuneration through long-term compensation, such as stock incentives, rather than through annual salary and bonuses. Because the amount of stock owned (or stock value) is not included as a variable in the regression function, it cannot be used to adjust the prediction of compensation determined by CEO education and company sales. Although education and (log) sales do not predict the compensation of these two CEOs as well as the others, there appears to be no reason to eliminate them from consideration.

Observation 25 is singled out because the leverage for this data point is greater than $3(k+1)/n = 3(3)/50 = .18$. This CEO has no college degree (Educate = 0) but is with a company with relatively large sales (LnSales = 9.394). The combination (0, 9.394) is far from the point $(\bar{X}_1, \bar{X}_2)$; therefore, it is an outlier among the pairs of X's. The response associated with these X's will have a large influence on the determination of the fitted regression function. (Notice that the standardized residual for this data point is small, indicating that the predicted, or fitted, log compensation is close to the actual value.) This particular CEO has 30 years of experience as a CEO, more experience than all but one of the CEOs in the data set. This observation is influential but there is no reason to delete it.

Leverage tells us if an observation has unusual predictors, and a standardized residual tells us if an observation has an unusual response. These quantities can be combined into one overall measure of influence known as *Cook's distance*. Cook's distances can be printed out in most statistical software packages, but additional discussion is beyond the scope of this book.[13]

FORECASTING CAVEATS

We finish this discussion of multiple regression with some general comments. These comments are oriented toward the practical application of regression analysis.

Overfitting

Overfitting refers to the development of a regression model that, to a large extent, matches the eccentricities of the sample data under analysis.

When an overfitted model is applied to new sets of data selected from the same population, it does not forecast as well as the initial fit might suggest.

Overfitting is more likely to occur when the sample size is small, especially if a large number of independent variables are included in the model. Some practitioners have

---

[13] A good discussion of Cook's distance is contained in Draper and Smith (1998).

suggested that there should be at least 10 observations for each independent variable. (If there are four independent variables, a sample size n of at least 40 is suggested.)

One way to guard against overfitting is to develop the regression function from one part of the data and then apply it to a "holdout" segment. Use the fitted regression function to forecast the holdout responses and calculate the forecast errors. If the forecast errors are substantially larger than the fitting errors as measured by, say, comparable mean squared errors, then overfitting has occurred.

Useful Regressions, Large F Ratios

A regression that is statistically significant is not necessarily useful. With a relatively large sample size (i.e., n large relative to k, the number of predictors), it is not unusual to get a significant F ratio and a small R^2. That is, the regression is significant yet it explains only a small proportion of the variation in the response. One rule of thumb suggests that with a significance level of .05, the F ratio should be at least four times the corresponding critical value before the regression is likely to be of much use for prediction purposes.[14]

The "four times" criterion comes from arguing that the range of the predictions (over all the X's) should be about four times the (average) prediction error before the regression is likely to yield a worthwhile interpretation.[15]

As an example, with $k = 3$ predictors, $n = 25$ observations, and a significance level of .05, the computed F from the ANOVA table would have to exceed the critical value $F = 3.07$ (see Table C-6 with $\delta_1 = k = 3$, $\delta_2 = n - k - 1 = 21$ degrees of freedom) for the regression to be significant. (Using Equation 7.7, the critical $F = 3.07$ corresponds to an R^2 of about 30%, not a particularly large number.) However, the "four times" rule suggests that the computed F should exceed $4(3.07) = 12.28$ for the regression to be worthwhile from a practical point of view.

APPLICATION TO MANAGEMENT

Multiple regression analysis has been used extensively to help forecast the economic activity of the various segments of the economy. Many of the reports and forecasts about the future of our economy that appear in the *Wall Street Journal, Fortune, Business Week*, and other similar journals are based on econometric (regression) models. The U.S. government makes wide use of regression analysis in predicting future revenues, expenditures, income levels, interest rates, birth rates, unemployment, and Social Security benefits requirements, as well as a multitude of other events. In fact, almost every major department of the U.S. government makes use of the tools described in this chapter.

Similarly, business entities have adopted and, when necessary, modified regression analysis to help in the forecasting of future events. Few firms can survive in today's environment without a fairly accurate forecast of tomorrow's sales, expenditures, capital requirements, and cash flows. Although small or less sophisticated firms may be able to get by with intuitive forecasts, larger or more sophisticated firms have turned to regression analysis to study the relationships among several variables and to determine how these variables are likely to affect their future.

Unfortunately, the acclaim that regression analysis receives for its usefulness as a tool in predicting the future tends to overshadow an equally important asset: its ability

---

[14] Some authors argue that the "four times" rule is not enough and should be replaced by a "ten times" criterion.

[15] This assumes that no other defect is detected in the fit.

to help evaluate and control the present. Because a fitted regression equation provides the researcher with both *strength* and *direction* information, management can evaluate and change current strategies.

Suppose, for example, a manufacturer of jams wants to know where to direct its marketing efforts when introducing a new flavor. Regression analysis can be used to help determine the profile of heavy users of jams. For instance, a company might try to predict the number of flavors of jam a household might have at any one time on the basis of a number of independent variables, such as the following:

Number of children living at home
Age of children
Gender of children
Home ownership versus rental
Time spent shopping
Income

Even a superficial reflection on the jam example quickly leads the researcher to realize that regression analysis has numerous possibilities for use in market segmentation studies. In fact, many companies use regression to study market segments to determine which variables seem to have an impact on market share, purchase frequency, product ownership, and product and brand loyalty, as well as many other areas.

Agricultural scientists use regression analysis to explore the relationship between product yield (e.g., number of bushels of corn per acre) and fertilizer type and amount, rainfall, temperature, days of sun, and insect infestation. Modern farms are equipped with various computers complete with software packages to help them in this process.

Medical researchers use regression analysis to seek links between blood pressure and independent variables such as age, social class, weight, smoking habits, and race. Doctors explore the impact of communications, number of contacts, and age of patient on patient satisfaction with service.

Personnel directors explore the relationship of employee salary levels to geographic location, unemployment rates, industry growth, union membership, industry type, or competitive salaries. Financial analysts look for causes of high stock prices by analyzing dividend yields, earnings per share, stock splits, consumer expectation of interest rates, savings levels, and inflation rates.

Advertising managers frequently try to study the impact of advertising budgets, media selection, message copy, advertising frequency, or spokesperson choice on consumer attitude change. Similarly, marketers attempt to determine sales from advertising expenditures, price levels, competitive marketing expenditures, and consumer disposable income as well as a wide variety of other variables.

A final example further illustrates the versatility of regression analysis. Real estate site location analysts have found that regression analysis can be very helpful in pinpointing geographic areas of over- and under-penetration of specific types of retail stores. For instance, a hardware store chain might look for a potential city in which to locate a new store by developing a regression model designed to predict hardware sales in any given city. Researchers could concentrate their efforts on those cities where the model predicts higher sales than actually achieved (as can be determined by many sources). The hypothesis is that sales of hardware are not up to potential in these cities.

In summary, regression analysis has provided management with a powerful and versatile tool for studying the relationships between a dependent variable and multiple independent variables. The goal is to better understand and control present events as well as to better predict future events.

Glossary

Dummy variables. Dummy variables are used to determine the relationships between qualitative independent variables and a dependent variable.

Multicollinearity. Multicollinearity is the situation in which independent variables in a multiple regression equation are highly intercorrelated.

Multiple regression. Multiple regression involves the use of more than one independent variable to predict a dependent variable.

Overfitting. Overfitting refers to adding independent variables to the regression function that account for (almost) all the eccentricities of the sample data under analysis.

Partial, or net, regression coefficient. The partial, or net, regression coefficient measures the average change in the dependent variable per unit change in the relevant independent variable, holding other independent variables constant.

Standard error of the estimate. The standard error of the estimate is the standard deviation of the residuals. It measures the amount the actual values (Y) differ from the estimated values $(\hat{Y})$.

Stepwise regression. Stepwise regression is a procedure for selecting the "best" regression function by adding or deleting a single independent variable at different stages of its development.

Key Formulas

Population multiple regression function

$$\mu_Y = \beta_0 + \beta_1 X_1 + \beta_2 X_2 + \cdots + \beta_k X_k \tag{7.1}$$

Estimated (fitted) regression function

$$\hat{Y} = b_0 + b_1 X_1 + \cdots + b_k X_k \tag{7.2}$$

Sum of squares decomposition and associated degrees of freedom

$$\begin{aligned} \Sigma(Y - \bar{Y})^2 &= \Sigma(\hat{Y} - \bar{Y})^2 + \Sigma(Y - \hat{Y})^2 \\ SST \;\;&=\;\; SSR \;\;+\;\; SSE \\ df: n - 1 \;\;&=\;\; k \;\;+\; n - k - 1 \end{aligned} \tag{7.3}$$

Standard error of the estimate

$$s_{y \cdot x's} = \sqrt{\frac{\Sigma(Y - \hat{Y})^2}{n - k - 1}} = \sqrt{\frac{SSE}{n - k - 1}} = \sqrt{MSE} \tag{7.4}$$

F statistic for testing the significance of the regression

$$F = \frac{MSR}{MSE} \qquad \text{(see box on page 277)}$$

Coefficient of determination

$$R^2 = \frac{SSR}{SST} = \frac{\Sigma(\hat{Y} - \bar{Y})^2}{\Sigma(Y - \bar{Y})^2}$$

$$= 1 - \frac{SSE}{SST} = 1 - \frac{\Sigma(Y - \hat{Y})^2}{\Sigma(Y - \bar{Y})^2} \tag{7.5}$$

Multiple correlation coefficient

$$R = \sqrt{R^2} \tag{7.6}$$

Relation between F statistic and R^2

$$F = \frac{R^2}{1 - R^2} \left(\frac{n - k - 1}{k} \right) \tag{7.7}$$

Adjusted coefficient of determination

$$\bar{R}^2 = 1 - (1 - R^2) \left(\frac{n - 1}{n - k - 1} \right) \tag{7.8}$$

t statistic for testing H_0: $\beta_j = 0$

$$t = \frac{b_j}{s_{b_j}} \qquad \text{(see shaded box on page 279)}$$

Forecast of a future value

$$\hat{Y}^* = b_0 + b_1 X_1^* + b_2 X_2^* + \cdots + b_k X_k^* \tag{7.9}$$

Large-sample prediction interval for a future response

$$(\hat{Y}^* - t_{\alpha/2}\, s_{y \cdot x's}, \hat{Y}^* + t_{\alpha/2}\, s_{y \cdot x's}) \tag{7.10}$$

Variance inflation factor

$$VIF_j = \frac{1}{1 - R_j^2} \qquad j = 1, 2, \ldots, k \tag{7.11}$$

Standardized independent variable values

$$\tilde{X} = \frac{X_{ij} - \bar{X}_j}{\sqrt{\sum_i (X_{ij} - \bar{X}_j)^2}} \qquad j = 1, 2, \ldots, k; \quad i = 1, 2, \ldots, n \tag{7.12}$$

Standardized residual

$$\frac{e_i}{s_{e_i}} = \frac{e_i}{s_{y \cdot x's} \sqrt{1 - h_{ii}}} \tag{7.13}$$

Problems

1. What are the characteristics of a good predictor variable?

2. What are the assumptions associated with the multiple regression model?

3. What does the partial, or net, regression coefficient measure in multiple regression?

4. What does the standard error of the estimate measure in multiple regression?

5. Your estimated multiple regression equation is $\hat{Y} = 7.52 + 3X_1 - 12.2X_2$. Predict the value of Y if $X_1 = 20$ and $X_2 = 7$.

TABLE P-7

	Variable Number					
Variable Number	1	2	3	4	5	6
1	1.00	.55	.20	−.51	.79	.70
2		1.00	.27	.09	.39	.45
3			1.00	.04	.17	.21
4				1.00	−.44	−.14
5					1.00	.69
6						1.00

6. Explain each of the following concepts:
   a. Correlation matrix
   b. R^2
   c. Multicollinearity
   d. Residual
   e. Dummy variable
   f. Stepwise regression

7. Most computer solutions for multiple regression begin with a correlation matrix. Examining this matrix is often the first step when analyzing a regression problem that involves more than one independent variable. Answer the following questions concerning the correlation matrix given in Table P-7.
   a. Why are all the entries on the main diagonal equal to 1?
   b. Why is the bottom half of the matrix below the main diagonal blank?
   c. If variable 1 is the dependent variable, which independent variables have the highest degree of linear association with variable 1?
   d. What kind of association exists between variables 1 and 4?
   e. Does this correlation matrix show any evidence of multicollinearity?
   f. In your opinion, which variable or variables will be included in the best forecasting model? Explain.
   g. If the data given in the preceding correlation matrix are run on a stepwise program, which independent variable (2, 3, 4, 5, or 6) will be the first to enter the regression function?

8. Jennifer Dahl, supervisor of the Circle O discount chain, would like to forecast the time it takes to check out a customer. She decides to use the following independent variables: number of purchased items and the total amount of the purchase. She collects data for a sample of 18 customers, shown in Table P-8.
   a. Determine the best regression equation.
   b. When an additional item is purchased, what is the average increase in the checkout time?
   c. Compute the residual for customer 18.
   d. Compute the standard error of the estimate.
   e. Interpret part d in terms of the variables used in this problem.
   f. Compute a forecast of the checkout time if a customer purchases 14 items that amount to $70.
   g. Compute a 95% interval estimate for your prediction in part f.
   h. What should Jennifer conclude?

9. Table P-9 contains data on food expenditures, annual income, and family size for a sample of 10 families.

TABLE P-8

Customer	Checkout Time (minutes) Y	Amount (dollars) X_1	Number of Items X_2
1	3.0	36	9
2	1.3	13	5
3	.5	3	2
4	7.4	81	14
5	5.9	78	13
6	8.4	103	16
7	5.0	64	12
8	8.1	67	11
9	1.9	25	7
10	6.2	55	11
11	.7	13	3
12	1.4	21	8
13	9.1	121	21
14	.9	10	6
15	5.4	60	13
16	3.3	32	11
17	4.5	51	15
18	2.4	28	10

TABLE P-9

Family	Annual Food Expenditures ($100's) Y	Annual Income ($1,000's) X_1	Family Size X_2
A	24	11	6
B	8	3	2
C	16	4	1
D	18	7	3
E	24	9	5
F	23	8	4
G	11	5	2
H	15	7	2
I	21	8	3
J	20	7	2

a. Construct the correlation matrix for the three variables in Table P-9. Interpret the correlations in the matrix.

b. Fit a multiple regression model relating food expenditures to income and family size. Interpret the partial regression coefficients of income and family size. Do they make sense?

c. Compute the variance inflation factors (*VIF*) for the independent variables. Is multicollinearity a problem for these data? If so, how might you modify the regression model?

10. Beer sales at the Shapiro One-Stop Store are analyzed by using temperature and number of people (age 21 or over) on the street as independent variables. A random sample of 20 days is selected and three variables are measured.

TABLE P-10	Minitab Output

Correlations (Pearson)

```
         Y          X1
X1    0.827
X2    0.822     0.680
```

Regression Analysis

The regression equation is
Y = -26.7 + .782 X1 + .068X2

Predictor	Coef	SE Coef	T	P
Constant	-26.706			
X1	.78207	.22694		
X2	.06795	.02026		

S =   R-Sq =   R-Sq(adj)=

Analysis of Variance

Source	DF	SS	MS	F
Regression	2	11589.035	5794.516	36.11
Residual Error	17	2727.914	160.466	
Total	19	14316.949		

Y = Number of six-packs of beer sold each day
X_1 = Daily high temperature
X_2 = Daily traffic count

The data are analyzed using a multiple regression analysis. The partial computer output appears in Table P-10.

a. Analyze the correlation matrix.
b. Test the significance of the partial regression coefficients at the .01 significance level.
c. Forecast the volume of beer sold if the high temperature is 60 degrees and the traffic count is 500 people.
d. Calculate R^2, and interpret its meaning in terms of this problem.
e. Calculate the standard error of the estimate.
f. Explain how beer sales are affected by an increase of one degree in the high temperature.
g. State your conclusions for this analysis concerning the accuracy of the forecasting equation and also the contributions of the independent variables.

11. A taxi company is interested in the relationship between mileage, measured in miles per gallon, and the age of cars in its fleet. The 12 fleet cars are the same make and size and in good operating condition as a result of regular maintenance. The company employs both male and female drivers, and it is believed that some of the variability in mileage may be due to differences in driving techniques between the groups of drivers of opposite gender. In fact, other things being equal, women tend to get better mileage than men. Data are generated by randomly assigning the 12 cars to five female and seven male drivers and computing miles per gallon after 300 miles. The data appear in Table P-11.
   a. Construct a scatter diagram with Y as the vertical axis and X_1 as the horizontal axis. Identify the points corresponding to male and female drivers, respectively.

TABLE P-11

Y (MPG)	X_1 (Age of car)	X_2 (Gender: 0 = male, 1 = female)
22.3	3	0
22.0	4	1
23.7	3	1
24.2	2	0
25.5	1	1
21.1	5	0
20.6	4	0
24.0	1	0
26.0	1	1
23.1	2	0
24.8	2	1
20.2	5	0

TABLE P-12

Region	Annual Sales (millions) Y	Number of Retail Outlets X_1	Number of Automobiles Registered (millions) X_2
1	52.3	2011	24.6
2	26.0	2850	22.1
3	20.2	650	7.9
4	16.0	480	12.5
5	30.0	1694	9.0
6	46.2	2302	11.5
7	35.0	2214	20.5
8	3.5	125	4.1
9	33.1	1840	8.9
10	25.2	1233	6.1
11	38.2	1699	9.5

b. Fit the regression model

$$Y = \beta_0 + \beta_1 X_1 + \beta_2 X_2 + \varepsilon$$

and interpret the least squares coefficient b_2.

c. Compute the fitted values for each of the (X_1, X_2) pairs, and plot the fitted values on the scatter diagram. Draw straight lines through the fitted values for male drivers and female drivers, respectively. Specify the equations for these two straight lines.

d. Suppose gender is ignored. Fit the simple linear regression model $Y = \beta_0 + \beta_1 X_1 + \varepsilon$, and plot the fitted straight line on the scatter diagram. Is it important to include the effects of gender in this case? Explain.

12. The sales manager of a large automotive parts distributor, Hartman Auto Supplies, wants to develop a model to forecast as early as May the total annual sales of a region. If regional sales can be forecast, then the total sales for the company can be forecast. The number of retail outlets in the region stocking the company's parts and the number of automobiles registered for each region as of May 1 are the two independent variables investigated. The data appear in Table P-12.

a. Analyze the correlation matrix.
b. How much error is involved in the prediction for region 1?
c. Forecast the annual sales for region 12, given 2,500 retail outlets and 20.2 million automobiles registered.
d. Discuss the accuracy of the forecast made in part c.
e. Show how the standard error of the estimate was computed.
f. Give an interpretation of the partial regression coefficients. Are these regression coefficients sensible?
g. How can this regression equation be improved?

13. The sales manager of Hartman Auto Supplies decides to investigate a new independent variable, personal income by region (see Problem 12). The data for this new variable are presented in Table P-13.
a. Does personal income by region make a contribution to the forecasting of sales?
b. Forecast annual sales for region 12 for personal income of $40 billion, using all three independent variables.
c. Discuss the accuracy of the forecast made in part b.
d. Which independent variables would you include in your final forecast model? Why?

14. The Nelson Corporation decides to develop a multiple regression equation to forecast sales performance. A random sample of 14 salespeople is interviewed and given an aptitude test. In addition, an index of effort expended is calculated for each salesperson on the basis of a ratio of the mileage on his or her company car to the total mileage projected for adequate coverage of territory. Regression analysis yields the following results:

$$\hat{Y} = 16.57 + .65\ X_1 + 20.6\ X_2$$
$$\qquad\qquad (.05)\qquad (1.69)$$

The quantities in parentheses are the standard errors of the partial regression coefficients. The standard error of the estimate is 3.56. The standard deviation of the sales variable is $s_y = 16.57$. The variables are

$$Y = \text{Sales performance, in thousands}$$
$$X_1 = \text{Aptitude test score}$$
$$X_2 = \text{Effort index}$$

a. Are the partial regression coefficients significantly different from zero, at the .01 significance level?
b. Interpret the partial regression coefficient for the effort index.

TABLE P-13

Region	Personal Income (billions)	Region	Personal Income (billions)
1	$98.5	7	67.6
2	31.1	8	19.7
3	34.8	9	67.9
4	32.7	10	61.4
5	68.8	11	85.6
6	94.7		

c. Forecast the sales performance for a salesperson who has an aptitude test score of 75 and an effort index of .5.

d. Calculate the sum of squared residuals $\Sigma(Y - \hat{Y})^2$.

e. Calculate the total sum of squares $\Sigma(Y - \bar{Y})^2$.

f. Calculate R^2 and interpret it in terms of this problem.

g. Calculate the adjusted coefficient of determination $\bar{R}^2$.

15. We might expect credit card purchases to differ from cash purchases at the same store. Table P-15 contains daily gross cash sales and number of items sold for cash purchases, and daily gross credit card sales and number of items sold for credit card purchases at the same consignment store for 25 consecutive days.

a. Make a scatter diagram of daily gross sales Y versus items sold X_1 for cash purchases. Using a separate plot symbol or color, add daily gross sales and items sold for credit card purchases. Visually compare the relationship between sales and number of items sold for cash with that for credit card purchases.

b. Define the dummy variable

$$X_2 = \begin{cases} 1 \text{ if cash purchase} \\ 0 \text{ if credit card purchase} \end{cases}$$

and fit the regression model

$$Y = \beta_0 + \beta_1 X_1 + \beta_2 X_2 + \varepsilon$$

TABLE P-15

Day	Gross Cash	Number of Items	Gross Credit Card	Number of Items
1	$348	55	$148	4
2	42	8	111	6
3	61	9	62	7
4	94	16	0	0
5	60	11	39	5
6	165	26	7	1
7	126	27	143	26
8	111	19	27	5
9	26	5	14	2
10	109	18	71	12
11	180	27	116	21
12	212	36	50	9
13	58	10	13	2
14	115	20	105	16
15	15	8	19	3
16	97	15	44	14
17	61	10	0	0
18	85	15	24	3
19	157	24	144	10
20	88	15	63	11
21	96	19	0	0
22	202	33	14	3
23	108	23	0	0
24	158	21	24	4
25	176	43	253	28

   c. Analyze the fit in part b. Be sure to include an analysis of the residuals. Are you happy with your model?

   d. Using the fitted model from part b, generate a forecast of daily sales for an individual that purchases 25 items and pays cash. Construct a large-sample 95% prediction interval for daily sales.

   e. Describe the nature of the fitted function in part b. Do you think it is better to fit two separate straight lines to the data in Table P-15, one straight line for the cash sales and another straight line for the credit card sales? Discuss.

16. Cindy Lawson just bought a major league baseball team. She has been receiving a lot of advice concerning what she should do to create a winning ballclub. Cindy asks you to study this problem and write a report. You decide to use multiple regression analysis to determine which statistics are important in developing a winning team (measured by the number of games won during the 1991 season). You gather the following statistics from the *Sporting News 1992 Baseball Yearbook*, as shown in Table P-16, and run it on a stepwise regression program.

   a. Discuss the importance of each variable.

   b. What equation should Cindy use to forecast wins?

   c. Write a report for Cindy.

   d. Collect data from the most recent *Sporting News Baseball Yearbook* or other source of baseball statistics. Run a stepwise regression and compare your results.

17. Ms. Haight, a real estate broker, wishes to forecast the importance of four factors in determining the prices of lots. She accumulates data on price, area, elevation,

TABLE P-16

Team	Wins	ERA	SO	BA	Runs	HR	SB
Giants	75	4.03	905	.246	649	141	95
Mets	77	3.56	1028	.244	640	117	153
Cubs	77	4.03	927	.253	695	159	123
Reds	74	3.83	997	.258	689	164	124
Pirates	98	3.44	919	.263	768	126	124
Cardinals	84	3.69	822	.255	651	68	202
Phillies	78	3.86	988	.241	629	111	92
Astros	65	4.00	1033	.244	605	79	125
Dodgers	93	3.06	1028	.253	665	108	126
Expos	71	3.64	909	.246	579	95	221
Braves	94	3.49	969	.258	749	141	165
Padres	84	3.57	921	.244	636	121	101
Red Sox	84	4.01	999	.269	731	126	59
White Sox	87	3.79	923	.262	758	139	134
Yankees	71	4.42	936	.256	674	147	109
Tigers	84	4.51	739	.247	817	209	109
Orioles	67	4.59	868	.254	686	170	50
Brewers	83	4.14	859	.271	799	116	106
Indians	57	4.23	862	.254	576	79	84
Blue Jays	91	3.50	971	.257	684	133	148
Mariners	83	3.79	1003	.255	702	126	97
Rangers	85	4.47	1022	.270	829	177	102
Athletics	84	4.57	892	.248	760	159	151
Royals	82	3.92	1004	.264	727	117	119
Angels	81	3.69	990	.255	653	115	94
Twins	95	3.69	876	.280	776	140	107

TABLE P-17

			Variable		
Variable	Price	Area	Elevation	Slope	View
Price	1.00	.59	.66	.68	.88
Area		1.00	.04	.64	.41
Elevation			1.00	.13	.76
Slope				1.00	.63
View					1.00

TABLE P-18

X_1	X_2	X_3	Y	X_1	X_2	X_3	Y
87	85	2.7	91	93	60	3.2	54
100	84	3.3	90	92	69	3.1	63
91	82	3.5	83	100	86	3.6	96
85	60	3.7	93	80	87	3.5	89
56	64	2.8	43	100	96	3.8	97
81	48	3.1	75	69	51	2.8	50
77	67	3.1	63	80	75	3.6	74
86	73	3.0	78	74	70	3.1	58
79	90	3.8	98	79	66	2.9	87
96	69	3.7	99	95	83	3.3	57

and slope, and rates the view for 50 lots. She runs the data on a correlation program and obtains the correlation matrix given in Table P-17. Ms. Haight then runs the data on a stepwise multiple regression program.

a. Determine which variable would enter the model first, second, third, and last.

b. Which variable or variables will be included in the best prediction equation?

18. The scores X_1 and X_2 for two within-term examinations, the current grade point average (GPA) X_3, and the final exam score Y for 20 students in a business statistics class are listed in Table P-18.

a. Fit a multiple regression model to predict the final exam score from the scores on the within-term exams and GPA. Is the regression significant? Explain.

b. Predict the final exam score for a student with within-term exam scores of 86 and 77, and a GPA of 3.4.

c. Compute the *VIF*s and examine the *t* statistics for checking the significance of the individual predictor variables. Is multicollinearity a problem? Explain.

d. Compute the mean leverage. Are any of the observations high-leverage data points?

e. Compute the standardized residuals. Identify any observation with a large standardized residual. Does the fitted model under- or over-predict the response for these observations?

19. Refer to the data in Table P-18. Find the "best" regression model using the stepwise regression procedure and the all possible regressions procedure. Compare the results. Are you confident using a regression model to predict the final exam score with fewer than the original three independent variables?

20. Recall Example 7.12. The full data set related to CEO compensation is contained in Appendix D. (See p. 517.) Use stepwise regression to select the "best" model with $k = 3$ predictor variables. Fit the stepwise model and interpret the estimated

coefficients. Examine the residuals. Identify and explain any influential observations. If you had to choose between this model and the $k = 2$ predictor model discussed in Example 7.12, which one would you choose? Why?

CASES

CASE 7-1   THE BOND MARKET[16]

Judy Johnson, vice president of finance of a large, private, investor-owned utility in the Northwest, was faced with a financing problem. The company needed money both to pay off short-term debts coming due and to continue construction of a coal-fired plant.

Judy's main concern was estimating the 10- or 30-year bond market; the company needed to decide whether to use equity financing or long-term debt. To make this decision, the utility needed a reliable forecast of the interest rate it would pay at the time of bond issuance.

Judy called a meeting of her financial staff to discuss the bond market problem. One member of her staff, Ron Peterson, a recent M.B.A. graduate, said he thought a multiple regression model could be developed to forecast the bond rates. The vice president was not familiar with multiple regression, so she steered the discussion in another direction. After an hour of unproductive interaction, Judy then asked Ron to have a report on her desk the following Monday.

Ron knew that the key to the development of a good forecasting model is the identification of independent variables that relate to the interest rate paid by utilities at the time of bond issuance. After discussing the problem with various people at the utility, Ron decided to investigate the following variables: A utility's bond rating (Moody's), a utility's ratio of earnings to fixed charges, U.S. Treasury Bond rates, bond maturity (10 or 30 years), and the prime lending rate at time of issuance.

Ron gathered data he believed might correlate with bond interest rates for utility bond issues during two previous years. At first he was uncertain how to handle the utility bond rating. He finally decided to consider only utilities with the same or a slightly higher rating than that of his company. This decision provided him with a sample of 93 issues to analyze.

But he was still worried about the validity of using the bond ratings as interval data. He called his former statistics professor and learned that dummy variables would solve the problem. Thus he coded the bond ratings in the following way:

$X_1 = 1$ if utility bond rating is A; 0 otherwise
$X_2 = 1$ if utility bond rating is AA; 0 otherwise

If the utility bond rating is BAA, both X_1 and X_2 are 0. The next step was for Ron to select a multiple regression program from the computer library and input the data. The following variables were included in the full-model equation:

Variable 1: $Y =$ Interest rate paid by utility at the time of bond issuance
Variable 2: $X_1 = 1$ if utility's bond rating is A
Variable 3: $X_2 = 1$ if utility's bond rating is AA
Variable 4: $X_3 =$ Utility's ratio of earnings to fixed charges
Variable 5: $X_4 =$ U.S. treasury bond rates (for 10 and 30 years) at the time of bond issuance
Variable 6: $X_5 =$ Bond maturity (10 or 30 years)
Variable 7: $X_6 =$ Prime lending rate at the time of issuance

The actual data are presented in Appendix B.

Ron decided to analyze the correlation matrix shown in Table 7-18. He was not surprised to find a high positive relationship between the interest rate paid by the utility at the time of bond issuance and the U.S. treasury bond rate, $r = .883$. He also expected a fairly high positive relationship between the dependent variable and the prime lending rate ($r = .596$). He was not too surprised to discover that these two predictor variables were also related to each other (potential multicollinearity, $r = .713$).

[16]The data for this case study was provided by an Eastern Washington University M.B.A. student, Dorothy Mercer. The analysis was done by M.B.A. students Tak Fu, Ron Hand, Dorothy Mercer, Mary Lou Redmond, and Harold Wilson.

TABLE 7-18	Correlation Matrix for Bond Market Study					
	Correlations (Pearson)					
	Interest Rate	*A*	*AA*	*Ratio*	*Bond Rates*	*Maturity*
A	−0.347					
AA	−0.173	−0.399				
Ratio	0.097	0.037	0.577			
Bond rates	0.883	−0.256	0.291	0.253		
Maturity	−0.221	0.278	0.010	0.094	−0.477	
Prime	0.596	−0.152	0.342	0.255	0.713	−0.314

The negative relationship between the dependent variable and length of bond maturity (10 or 30 years), $r = -.221$, was also a result that made sense to Ron.

Next, Ron ran a full model containing all the predictor variables. Examination of the computed t values and the p-values, which are presented in Table 7-19, indicated that perhaps the variable of ratio of earnings to fixed charges and certainly the prime interest rate were not making a contribution to the forecast of the interest rate paid by the utility at the time of bond issuance.

Ron concluded that the utility's ratio of earnings to fixed charges was not related to the dependent variable ($r = .097$) and that the prime lending rate was collinear with the U.S. Treasury Bond rates ($r = .713$). He decided to eliminate both the ratio and prime variables. The results of the computer run for this model are shown in Table 7-20.

The p-values were significant for each of the independent variables.

Ron's report to Judy included the following comments:

1. The best model, Interest rate $= -1.28 - .929$A $- 1.18$AA $+ 1.23$ Bond rates $+ 0.0615$ Maturity, explained 90.6% of the interest rate variation.
2. The standard error of the estimate is .53. Thus, about 95% of the actual dependent variable values would lie within $2(.53) = 1.06$ of a given forecast.
3. The regression coefficients are significant and appear to be reliable.

Ron was very pleased with his effort and felt that Judy would also be pleased. ∎

QUESTION

1. What questions do you think Judy will have for Ron?

TABLE 7-19	Full-Model Run for Bond Market Study

```
Regression Analysis

The regression equation is
Interest Rates = -1.03 - 0.829 A - 0.889 AA - 0.242 Ratio + 1.26 Bond Rates
                + 0.0628 Maturity - 0.0031 Prime

Predictor       Coef    SE Coef       T       P
Constant     -1.0263     0.6572   -1.56   0.122
A            -0.8285     0.1342   -6.17   0.000
AA           -0.8894     0.2248   -3.96   0.000
Ratio        -0.2417     0.1135   -2.13   0.036
Rates         1.25753    0.05964  21.08   0.000
Maturity      0.062839   0.006589  9.54   0.000
Prime        -0.00313    0.02720  -0.12   0.909
```

TABLE 7-19   (Continued)

```
S = 0.5235       R-Sq = 91.1%      R-Sq(adj) = 90.5%
```

Analysis of Variance

Source	DF	SS	MS	F	P
Regression	6	240.907	40.151	146.52	0.000
Residual Error	86	23.567	0.274		
Total	92	264.474			

Unusual Observations

Obs	A	Rate	Fit	St Dev Fit	Residual	St Resid
64	1.00	15.5000	13.7645	0.1627	1.7355	3.49R
66	1.00	11.3000	13.4780	0.1357	-2.1780	-4.31R
67	1.00	12.3800	13.7897	0.1297	-1.4097	-2.78R
68	1.00	12.1500	13.7097	0.0947	-1.5597	-3.03R

R denotes an observation with a large standardized residual.

TABLE 7-20   Final Model for Bond Market Study

Regression Analysis

The regression equation is
Interest Rates = -1.28 - 0.929 A - 1.18 AA + 1.23 Bond Rates +
0.0615 Maturity

Predictor	Coef	SE Coef	T	P
Constant	-1.2765	0.6554	-1.95	0.055
A	-0.9293	0.1264	-7.35	0.000
AA	-1.1751	0.1781	-6.60	0.000
Rates	1.23308	0.05964	26.81	0.000
Maturity	0.061474	0.006649	9.25	0.000

```
S = 0.5310     R-Sq = 90.6%     R-Sq(adj) = 90.2%
```

Analysis of Variance

Source	DF	SS	MS	F	P
Regression	4	239.665	59.916	212.53	0.000
Residual Error	88	24.809	0.282		
Total	92	264.474			

Unusual Observations

Obs	A	Rate	Fit	St Dev Fit	Residual	St Resid
64	1.00	15.5000	13.6956	0.0894	1.8044	3.45R
66	1.00	11.3000	13.6462	0.0898	-2.3462	-4.48R
67	1.00	12.3800	13.6462	0.0898	-1.2662	-2.42R
68	1.00	12.1500	13.6462	0.0898	-1.4962	-2.86R

R denotes an observation with a large standardized residual.

CASE 7-2   AAA WASHINGTON

An overview of AAA Washington was provided in Case 5-5 when students were asked to prepare a time series decomposition of the emergency road service calls received by the club over five years. The analysis performed in Case 5-5 showed that the pattern in emergency road service call volume was probably somewhat cyclical in nature. In Case 6-6, four variables were investigated: unemployment rate, average daily temperature, amount of rainfall, and number of members in the club. Average daily temperature and unemployment rate were determined to be significant variables. Amount of rainfall and number of members in the club were not significant variables.

A conversation with the manager of the emergency road service call center led to two important observations: (1) auto makers seem to design cars to operate best at 65 degrees Fahrenheit, and (2) call volume seems to increase more sharply when the average temperature drops a few degrees from an average temperature in the 30s than it does when a similar drop occurs with an average temperature in the 60s. This information suggested that the affect of temperature on emergency road service was nonlinear.

Mr. DeCoria has observed that the cyclical trend of the time series seems to be lagging behind the general economic cycle. He has suggested that the unemployment rate for Washington State would be a good surrogate measurement for the general state of Washington's economy. Data on the average monthly temperature and the Washington State unemployment rate are presented in Table 7-21.

TABLE 7-21	Data for AAA Washington for Case 7-2			
Year	*Month*	*Calls*	*Rate*	*Temp*
1987	June		6.9940	
	July		6.8137	
	August		6.3648	
	September		6.5435	
	October		6.7826	
	November		6.9225	
	December		7.1560	
1988	January		7.9143	
	February		7.7576	
	March		7.0641	
	April		6.0977	
	May	20002	5.7867	55.1
	June	21591	5.7592	59.0
	July	22696	5.5718	63.8
	August	21509	5.2939	63.8
	September	22123	5.4709	59.1
	October	21449	5.5049	54.6
	November	23475	5.8630	45.4
	December	23529	6.1349	41.0
1989	January	23327	7.5474	40.3
	February	24050	7.8157	34.3
	March	24010	7.1390	43.2
	April	19735	6.2637	52.5
	May	20153	5.8332	55.3
	June	19512	5.8077	62.4
	July	19892	5.6713	62.9
	August	20326	5.4977	63.5
	September	19378	5.2989	60.9
	October	21263	5.6028	51.9

TABLE 7-21	(Continued)			
Year	*Month*	*Calls*	*Rate*	*Temp*
1989 (*cont.*)	November	21443	5.9143	46.2
	December	23366	5.0000	41.8
1990	January	23836	6.1917	41.8
	February	23336	6.3775	38.9
	March	22003	5.7234	46.3
	April	20155	4.7792	51.7
	May	20070	4.5715	54.9
	June	19588	4.3899	59.8
	July	20804	4.2559	66.7
	August	19644	3.9359	66.4
	September	17424	3.9048	61.9
	October	20833	4.4294	50.4
	November	22490	5.1523	45.8
	December	24861	5.5102	33.9
1991	January	23441	6.8901	37.9
	February	19205	7.0308	46.9
	March	20386	6.7186	43.4
	April	19988	6.1280	49.1
	May	19077	5.8146	54.3
	June	19141	5.9480	58.2
	July	20883	5.9026	65.4
	August	20709	5.7227	66.0
	September	19647	5.6877	60.9
	October	22013	6.2922	51.0
	November	22375	7.0615	46.2
	December	22727	7.4370	42.4
1992	January	22367	8.4513	43.0
	February	21155	8.7699	46.0
	March	21209	8.0728	48.9
	April	19286	7.2392	52.7
	May	19725	7.0461	58.3
	June	20276	7.0478	63.6
	July	20795	7.1080	64.9
	August	21126	6.7824	65.0
	September	20251	6.7691	58.4
	October	22069	7.5896	53.2
	November	23268	7.9908	44.8
	December	26039	8.2460	37.8
1993	January	26127	9.5301	34.9

Assignment

1. Develop a multiple regression equation using unemployment rate and average monthly temperature to predict emergency road service calls.
2. Create a new temperature variable and relate it to emergency road service. Remember that temperature is a relative scale and that the selection of the zero point is arbitrary. If vehicles are designed to operate best at 65 degrees Fahrenheit, then every degree above or below 65 degrees should make vehicles operate less reliably. To accomplish a transformation of the temperature data that simulates this effect, begin by subtracting 65 from the average monthly temperature values. This repositions "zero" to 65 degrees Fahrenheit. Should absolute values of this new temperature variable be used?
3. Transform the new average temperature variable so it is linearly related to service calls.

4. Create a new unemployment rate variable and relate it to emergency road service. Give unemployment a lagged effect on emergency road service by using unemployment rate for the month: (1) three months prior to the current month and (2) 11 months prior to the current month as the data for the unemployment independent variable. Which model is the best for prediction? Are the signs on the coefficients for the independent variables what you would expect them to be? Are the coefficients of the independent variables significantly different from zero?

5. Develop a multiple regression equation using the transformed average temperature variable created in step 3 and the lagged variable created in step 4. Is this a good model? Have any of the underlying assumptions been violated? ∎

CASE 7-3   FANTASY BASEBALL (A)

It was February and John Hanke, a retired professor of statistics, was preparing for another fantasy baseball season. In past years his fellow players had always teased him about using his knowledge of statistics to gain an advantage. Unfortunately, it had never been true. Teaching, researching, publishing, and committee work had kept him far too busy. Now, having recently retired, he finally had the time to apply his knowledge of statistics to the annual rotisserie draft. In this type of fantasy league, each manager has $260 with which to bid on and purchase 23 players (14 hitters and 9 pitchers). Each team would then be ranked (based on actual player statistics from the season) in eight statistical categories. Dr. Hanke was very concerned with choosing players who would perform well on three out of the four pitching categories. In past years his pitching staffs, especially starting pitchers, had been the laughing stock of the league. The 2000 season was going to be different. He intended to develop models to accurately forecast pitching performances for starting pitchers.

The three categories that Hanke wished to research were wins (WINS), earned run average (ERA), and walks and hits given up per innings pitched (Br/IP). He had spent a considerable amount of time downloading baseball statistics for starting pitchers from the 1999 season.[17] He intended to develop a multiple regression model to forecast each of the three categories of interest. He had often preached to his students that the initial variable selection was the most important aspect of developing a regression model. He knew that if he didn't have good predictor variables, he wouldn't end up with useful prediction equations. After a considerable amount of work, Dr. Hanke chose the six variables that follow. He also decided to include only starting pitchers who had pitched at least 100 innings during the season. The data for the 138 starting pitchers selected is presented in Table 7-22.

TABLE 7-22	Pitching Statistics for 138 Starting Pitchers for Case 7-3						
Pitcher		Tm	ERA	Br/IP	Ctl	K/9	HR/9	OBA
1	Alvarez, W.	TAM	4.22	1.49	1.6	7.2	1.2	254
2	Anderson, B.	ARI	4.57	1.32	2.7	5.2	1.2	275
3	Appier, K.	OAK	5.17	1.50	1.6	5.6	1.2	274
4	Arrojo, R.	TAM	5.20	1.58	1.8	6.9	1.5	284
5	Ashby, A.	SD	3.80	1.25	2.4	5.8	1.1	253
6	Astacio, P.	COL	5.04	1.44	2.8	8.1	1.5	276
7	Baldwin, J.	CHW	5.11	1.51	1.5	5.6	1.5	274
8	Batista, M.	MON	4.90	1.52	1.6	6.4	0.7	271
9	Belcher, T.	ANA	6.74	1.62	1.1	3.5	1.8	303
10	Benes, A.	ARI	4.82	1.50	1.7	6.4	1.5	272

---

[17]Baseball pitching statistics were downloaded from Ron Shandler's BaseballHQ Web site at *www. BaseballHQ.com.*

TABLE 7-22   (Continued)

Pitcher		Tm	ERA	Br/IP	Ctl	K/9	HR/9	OBA
11	Benson, K.	PIT	4.08	1.36	1.7	6.4	0.7	243
12	Bergman, S.	ATL	5.22	1.56	1.5	3.8	0.8	306
13	Blair, W.	DET	6.85	1.59	1.9	5.5	1.9	302
14	Bohanon, B.	COL	6.21	1.66	1.3	5.5	1.4	291
15	Bottenfield, K.	STL	3.98	1.50	1.4	5.9	1.0	262
16	Brock, C.	SF	5.51	1.55	1.9	6.4	1.5	286
17	Brown, K.	LA	3.00	1.07	3.7	7.9	0.7	222
18	Burba, D.	CLE	4.25	1.40	1.8	7.1	1.2	247
19	Burkett, J.	TEX	5.63	1.56	2.1	5.9	1.1	300
20	Byrd, P.	PHI	4.61	1.38	1.5	4.8	1.5	261
21	Carpenter, C.	TOR	4.38	1.50	2.2	6.4	1.0	288
22	Clemens, R.	NYY	4.62	1.47	1.8	7.8	1.0	253
23	Clement, M.	SD	4.50	1.53	1.6	6.7	0.9	265
24	Colon, B.	CLE	3.95	1.27	2.1	7.1	1.1	236
25	Cone, D.	NYY	3.45	1.32	2.0	8.2	1.0	225
26	Cordova, F.	PIT	4.44	1.40	1.7	5.5	0.9	262
27	Daal, O.	ARI	3.66	1.25	1.9	6.2	0.9	231
28	Dempster, R.	FLA	4.71	1.63	1.4	7.7	1.3	254
29	Dreifort, D.	LA	4.80	1.42	1.8	7.1	1.0	254
30	Elarton, S.	HOU	3.48	1.24	2.8	8.8	0.6	235
31	Erickson, S.	BAL	4.81	1.49	1.1	4.1	1.1	266
32	Escobar, K.	TOR	5.69	1.63	1.6	6.7	1.0	285
33	Estes, S.	SF	4.92	1.58	1.4	7.0	0.9	261
34	Farnsworth, K.	CHC	5.05	1.48	1.3	4.8	1.9	269
35	Fassero, J.	TEX	7.21	1.86	1.4	6.6	2.0	313
36	Fernandez, A.	FLA	3.38	1.25	2.2	5.8	0.6	247
37	Finley, C.	ANA	4.43	1.37	2.1	8.4	1.0	240
38	Garcia, F.	SEA	4.07	1.47	1.9	7.6	0.8	259
39	Gardner, M.	SF	6.47	1.43	1.5	5.6	1.7	259
40	Glavine, T.	ATL	4.12	1.46	1.7	5.3	0.7	275
41	Gooden, D.	CLE	6.26	1.69	1.3	6.9	1.4	274
42	Guzman, J.	CIN	3.74	1.40	1.8	7.0	1.3	249
43	Halama, J.	SEA	4.22	1.39	1.9	5.3	1.0	270
44	Halladay, R.	TOR	3.92	1.58	1.0	4.9	1.1	264
45	Hampton, M.	HOU	2.90	1.28	1.8	6.7	0.5	228
46	Harnisch, P.	CIN	3.68	1.25	2.1	5.5	1.1	247
47	Hawkins, L.	MIN	6.67	1.71	1.7	5.3	1.5	319
48	Haynes, J.	OAK	6.34	1.68	1.2	5.9	1.3	276
49	Helling, R.	TEX	4.85	1.43	1.5	5.4	1.7	263
50	Hentgen, P.	TOR	4.79	1.46	1.8	5.3	1.4	279
51	Heredia, G.	OAK	4.81	1.31	3.4	5.3	1.0	281
52	Hermanson, D.	MON	4.21	1.36	2.1	6.0	0.8	263
53	Hernandez, O.	NYY	4.12	1.28	1.8	6.6	1.0	230
54	Hernandez, L.	SF	4.65	1.52	1.9	6.5	1.0	281
55	Hershiser, O.	NYM	4.58	1.41	1.2	4.5	0.7	251
56	Hill, K.	ANA	4.78	1.60	1.0	5.3	1.0	256
57	Hitchcock, S.	SD	4.12	1.35	2.6	8.5	1.3	252
58	Holt, C.	HOU	4.66	1.52	2.0	6.3	0.7	287
59	Hudson, T.	OAK	3.24	1.34	2.1	8.7	0.5	233
60	Irabu, H.	NYY	4.84	1.34	2.9	7.1	1.4	267
61	Jimenez, J.	STL	5.85	1.50	1.6	6.2	0.9	267
62	Johnson, R.	ARI	2.49	1.02	5.2	12.1	1.0	207

	TABLE 7-22	(Continued)						

Pitcher		Tm	ERA	Br/IP	Ctl	K/9	HR/9	OBA
63	Johnson, J.	BAL	5.47	1.52	1.3	5.6	1.3	263
64	Karl, S.	MIL	4.79	1.60	1.1	3.4	1.0	299
65	Kile, D.	COL	6.62	1.76	1.1	5.5	1.6	288
66	Leiter, A.	NYM	4.23	1.42	1.7	6.8	0.8	252
67	Lieber, J.	CHC	4.08	1.34	4.0	8.2	1.2	276
68	Lima, J.	HOU	3.58	1.22	4.3	6.8	1.1	263
69	Loaiza, E.	TEX	4.57	1.40	1.9	5.8	0.7	267
70	Maddux, G.	ATL	3.57	1.35	3.7	5.6	0.7	287
71	Martinez, P.	BOS	2.07	0.92	8.5	13.2	0.4	205
72	Mays, J.	MIN	4.37	1.44	1.7	6.1	1.3	264
73	Meadows, B.	FLA	5.61	1.52	1.3	3.6	1.6	292
74	Mercker, K.	BOS	4.81	1.64	1.3	5.6	1.1	282
75	Millwood, K.	ATL	2.68	1.00	3.5	8.1	0.9	201
76	Milton, E.	MIN	4.50	1.23	2.6	7.1	1.2	240
77	Mlicki, D.	DET	4.61	1.46	1.7	5.4	1.1	274
78	Moehler, B.	DET	5.05	1.47	1.8	4.9	1.0	286
79	Morgan, M.	TEX	6.24	1.66	1.3	3.9	1.6	310
80	Moyer, J.	SEA	3.87	1.24	2.9	5.4	0.9	261
81	Mulholland, T.	ATL	4.39	1.45	1.8	4.4	1.1	288
82	Mussina, M.	BAL	3.50	1.28	3.3	7.6	0.7	259
83	Nagy, C.	CLE	4.95	1.47	2.1	5.6	1.2	287
84	Navarro, J.	CHW	6.11	1.74	1.0	4.2	1.6	307
85	Neagle, D.	CIN	4.29	1.21	1.9	6.2	1.9	226
86	Nomo, H.	MIL	4.55	1.43	2.1	8.2	1.4	252
87	Nunez, V.	FLA	4.08	1.38	1.6	7.2	0.9	231
88	Ogea, C.	PHI	5.63	1.51	1.3	4.1	1.9	281
89	Olivares, O.	OAK	4.17	1.45	1.0	3.7	0.8	266
90	Oliver, D.	STL	4.27	1.38	1.6	5.5	0.7	256
91	Oquist, M.	OAK	5.39	1.58	1.4	5.7	1.2	278
92	Ortiz, R.	SF	3.82	1.52	1.3	7.1	1.0	238
93	Park, C.	LA	5.24	1.59	1.7	8.1	1.4	268
94	Parque, J.	CHW	5.14	1.67	1.4	5.8	1.2	293
95	Parris, S.	CIN	3.51	1.37	1.7	6.0	1.1	249
96	Pavano, C.	MON	5.63	1.46	2.0	6.1	0.7	278
97	Person, R.	PHI	4.68	1.51	1.6	8.5	1.5	243
98	Pettitte, A.	NYY	4.71	1.60	1.4	5.7	0.9	279
99	Ponson, S.	BAL	4.71	1.46	1.4	4.8	1.5	270
100	Portugal, M.	BOS	5.52	1.47	1.9	4.7	1.7	290
101	Radke, B.	MIN	3.75	1.30	2.8	5.0	1.2	273
102	Rapp, P.	BOS	4.13	1.48	1.3	5.5	0.8	256
103	Reed, R.	NYM	4.59	1.41	2.2	6.3	1.4	272
104	Reynolds, S.	HOU	3.85	1.24	5.3	7.7	0.9	270
105	Reynoso, A.	ARI	4.37	1.47	1.2	4.3	1.1	267
106	Ritchie, T.	PIT	3.50	1.30	2.0	5.6	0.9	252
107	Rogers, K.	NYM	4.20	1.41	1.8	5.8	0.7	266
108	Rosado, J.	KC	3.85	1.29	2.0	6.1	1.0	245
109	Rueter, K.	SF	5.42	1.49	1.7	4.6	1.4	289
110	Rupe, R.	TAM	4.56	1.36	1.7	6.1	1.1	247
111	Saberhagen, B.	BOS	2.95	1.12	7.4	6.1	0.8	260
112	Schilling, C.	PHI	3.55	1.13	3.5	7.6	1.2	232
113	Schmidt, J.	PIT	4.20	1.43	1.7	6.3	1.0	261

TABLE 7-22	(Continued)							
Pitcher		*Tm*	*ERA*	*Br/IP*	*Ctl*	*K/9*	*HR/9*	*OBA*
114	Schourek, P.	PIT	5.34	1.57	1.9	7.5	1.6	280
115	Sele, A.	TEX	4.79	1.53	2.7	8.2	0.9	290
116	Sirotka, M.	CHW	4.00	1.40	2.2	5.4	1.0	279
117	Smoltz, J.	ATL	3.19	1.12	3.9	7.5	0.7	236
118	Snyder, J.	CHW	6.69	1.67	1.4	4.7	1.9	307
119	Sparks, S.	ANA	5.44	1.68	0.9	4.5	1.3	277
120	Stottlemyre, T.	ARI	4.09	1.44	1.9	6.6	1.1	264
121	Suppan, J.	KC	4.54	1.36	1.7	4.5	1.2	267
122	Tapani, K.	CHC	4.83	1.35	2.2	4.8	0.8	275
123	Thompson, J.	DET	5.13	1.48	1.4	5.3	1.5	268
124	Thurman, M.	MON	4.06	1.31	1.6	5.2	1.0	247
125	Tomko, B.	CIN	4.92	1.37	2.2	6.9	1.6	258
126	Trachsel, S.	CHC	5.57	1.41	2.3	6.5	1.4	274
127	Valdes, I.	LA	3.99	1.33	2.5	6.3	1.4	264
128	Vazquez, J.	MON	5.02	1.34	2.2	6.6	1.2	255
129	Villone, R.	CIN	4.24	1.32	1.3	6.1	0.5	215
130	Weaver, J.	DET	5.57	1.42	2.0	6.3	1.5	270
131	Wells, D.	TOR	4.83	1.33	2.7	6.6	1.2	267
132	Williams, W.	SD	4.41	1.37	1.9	5.9	1.4	260
133	Witasick, J.	KC	5.58	1.73	1.2	5.8	1.3	293
134	Witt, B.	TAM	5.85	1.72	1.3	6.1	1.1	288
135	Wolf, R.	PHI	5.57	1.59	1.7	8.6	1.5	263
136	Woodard, S.	MIL	4.52	1.38	3.3	5.8	1.1	288
137	Wright, J.	CLE	6.08	1.66	1.2	6.1	1.2	270
138	Yoshii, M.	NYM	4.40	1.30	1.8	5.4	1.3	248

TABLE 7-23	**Correlations: ERA, Br/IP, Ctl, K/9, HR/9, OBA**

```
         ERA     Br/IP    Ctl      K/9      HR/9
Br/IP   0.819
        0.000

Ctl    -0.798  -0.701                                Cell Contents: Pearson correlation
        0.000   0.000                                              P-Value

K/9    -0.429  -0.416   0.573
        0.000   0.000   0.000

HR/9    0.649   0.438  -0.305  -0.245
        0.000   0.000   0.000   0.004

OBA     0.745   0.747  -0.329  -0.576   0.432
        0.000   0.000   0.000   0.000   0.000
```

ERA: Earned run average, or the number of earned runs allowed per game (nine innings pitched)

Br/IP: Base runners per inning, or the number of walks plus hits given up per inning pitched

Ctl: Control ratio (strikeouts/walks)

K/9: How many batters a pitcher strikes out per game (nine innings pitched)

HR/9: Opposition home runs per game (nine innings pitched)

OBA: Opposition batting average

TABLE 7-24   Minitab Regression Output Using All of the Predictor Variables: Fantasy Baseball (A) Case 7-3

Regression Analysis: ERA versus Br/IP, Ctl, K/9, HR/9, OBA

The regression equation is

ERA = -3.06 + 2.56 Br/IP - 0.0610 Ctl + 0.0184 K/9 + 0.899 HR/9 + 0.0114 OBA

Predictor	Coef	SE Coef	T	P	VIF
Constant	-3.0583	0.6704	-4.56	0.000	
Br/IP	2.5578	0.6555	3.90	0.000	8.2
Ctl	-0.06105	0.08060	- 0.76	0.450	5.5
K/9	0.01837	0.04709	0.39	0.697	3.4
HR/9	0.8990	0.1225	7.34	0.000	1.3
OBA	0.011355	0.004160	2.73	0.007	6.4

S = 0.4276   R-Sq = 79.8%   R-Sq(adj) = 79.0%

Analysis of Variance

Source	DF	SS	MS	F	P
Regression	5	95.186	19.037	104.13	0.000
Residual Error	132	24.132	0.183		
Total	137	119.317			

TABLE 7-25   Minitab Final Regression Output for Forecasting ERA Fantasy Baseball (A) Case 7-3

Regression Analysis: ERA versus Ctl, K/9, HR/9, OBA

The regression equation is

ERA = -3.26 - 0.327 Ctl + 0.137 K/9 + 0.902 HR/9 + 0.0252 OBA

Predictor	Coef	SE Coef	T	P	VIF
Constant	-3.2624	0.7032	-4.64	0.000	
Ctl	-0.32655	0.04546	-7.18	0.000	1.6
K/9	0.13651	0.03795	3.60	0.000	2.0
HR/9	0.9023	0.1289	7.00	0.000	1.3
OBA	0.025224	0.002275	11.09	0.000	1.7

S = 0.4499   R-Sq = 77.4%   R-Sq(adj) = 76.8%

Analysis of Variance

Source	DF	SS	MS	F	P
Regression	4	92.402	23.100	104.13	0.000
Residual Error	133	26.915	0.202		
Total	137	119.317			

The next step in the analysis was the creation of the correlation matrix shown in Table 7-23. Dr. Hanke found the relationship between ERA and Br/IP, .819, to be extremely interesting. If he could purchase pitchers who performed well on one of these measures, they should also perform well on the other. Table 7-24 shows the regression output when all the independent variables, including Br/IP, were used to predict ERA. The $VIF = 8.2$ for the Br/IP variable is large, indicating that this variable is linearly related to the remaining predictor variables and multicollinearity is a problem. Examination of Table 7-25 shows the result when the Br/IP variable is left out of the model. The R^2 is 77.4%, and the equation looks good. The t statistic for each of the predictor variables is large with a very small

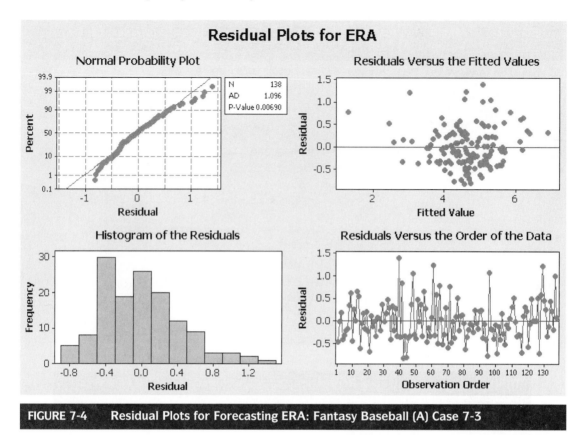

FIGURE 7-4   Residual Plots for Forecasting ERA: Fantasy Baseball (A) Case 7-3

p-value. The *VIF*s are relatively small for the four predictors, indicating that multicollinearity is no longer a problem.

Dr. Hanke decides that he has a good model and develops the residual plots shown in Figure 7-4. ∎

QUESTIONS

1. Comment on the model that Dr. Hanke developed to forecast earned run average (ERA). Examine the residual plots shown in Figure 7-4 and determine whether this model is valid.

2. Are there any nonlinear relationships between the predictor variables and earned run average? If so, develop a new model including the appropriate variable transformation.

3. Develop a model to forecast Br/IP.

CASE 7-4   FANTASY BASEBALL (B)[18]

Now that Dr. Hanke feels that he has successfully developed models for forecasting both ERA and Br/IP, he is ready to tackle WINS.[19] However, the

expert consensus indicates the project is doomed to failure. Comments found on Ron Shandler's BaseballHQ Web site indicated: "There's no way

---

[18] Case 7-4 is based on a model developed by Ron Shandler's BaseballHQ.com.

[19] Baseball pitching statistics were downloaded from Ron Shandler's BaseballHQ Web site at *www.BaseballHQ.com.*

to project pitchers accurately from year to year" (Bill James); "Your most valuable commodity is a starting pitcher you can count on. The only problem is, you can't count on any of them" (Peter Golenbock); "Where else in the realm of fantasy sports can you have worse odds on success than from the wonderful world of the pitcher?" (Rod Beaton); "Starting pitchers are the most unreliable, unpredictable, unpleasant group of people in the world, statistically speaking, that is" (John Benson).

Dr. Hanke investigated and found a statistical model that could be used. According to Ron Shandler's BaseballHQ.com, four variables had an important impact on pitching win totals. They were:

1. Team offense
2. Pitching effectiveness
3. Bullpen support
4. Team defense

He was ready to develop a predictor database.

To project a team's offense, he chose runs scored by a team (RUNS)[20] as the most important variable. In order to indicate how good a team was overall, Dr. Hanke chose team wins (TmWINS). The six variables used in Case 7-3 were used to indicate a pitcher's effectiveness: earned run average, or the number of earned runs allowed per game (nine innings pitched) (ERA), base runners per inning, or the number of walks plus hits given up per innings pitched (Br/IP), control ratio (strikeouts/walks) (Ctl), opposition home runs per game (nine innings pitched) (HR/9), opposition batting average (OBA), and how many batters a pitcher strikes out per game (nine innings pitched) (K/9). For team defense, he used the total number of team errors (ERR). For bullpen support, he tried four variables: adjusted runs prevented (ARP),[21] bullpen support (Bsupp), saves (Sv), and save opportunities (SvOpp).

The data for the six pitching variables are presented in Table 7-22. The data for the rest of the variables are presented in Table 7-26. ∎

TABLE 7-26	Team Statistics for 138 Starting Pitchers for Case 7-4							
Pitcher		*WINS*	*Tm WINS*	*Runs*	*Errors*	*ARP*	*Bsupp*	*Saves*	*Sv Opp*
1	Alvarez, W.	9	69	772	135	17.1	0.95	45	63
2	Anderson, B.	8	100	908	104	37.3	0.14	42	65
3	Appier, K.	16	87	893	122	11.4	0.96	48	76
4	Arrojo, R.	7	69	772	135	17.1	0.95	45	63
5	Ashby, A.	14	74	710	129	41.3	0.17	43	60
6	Astacio, P.	17	72	906	118	10.7	0.66	33	51
7	Baldwin, J.	12	75	777	136	21.3	0.58	39	58
8	Batista, M.	8	68	718	160	18.1	1.08	44	66
9	Belcher, T.	6	70	711	106	34.7	0.40	37	58
10	Benes, A.	13	100	908	104	37.3	0.14	42	65
11	Benson, K.	11	78	775	147	23.7	0.08	34	52
12	Bergman, S.	5	103	840	111	47.5	0.18	45	63
13	Blair, W.	3	69	747	106	7.9	0.66	33	44
14	Bohanon, B.	12	72	906	118	10.7	0.66	33	51
15	Bottenfield, K.	18	75	809	132	44.6	0.90	38	62
16	Brock, C.	6	86	872	105	1.8	0.38	42	67
17	Brown, K.	18	77	793	137	13.9	0.47	37	53
18	Burba, D.	15	97	1,009	106	14.3	0.90	46	70
19	Burkett, J.	9	95	945	119	50.5	0.38	47	67
20	Byrd, P.	15	77	841	100	11.5	0.06	32	47
21	Carpenter, C.	9	84	883	106	5.4	0.09	39	60

---

[20] Statistics for RUNS, TmWINS, Sv, and SvOpp are from SportsTicker® and appear at *www.sportsline.com/baseball/mlb/stats.*

[21] Statistics for ARP and Bsupp were found in a section by Michael Wolverton at *www.Baseballprospectus.com.*

TABLE 7-26   (Continued)

Pitcher		WINS	Tm WINS	Runs	Errors	ARP	Bsupp	Saves	Sv Opp
22	Clemens, R.	14	98	900	111	40.7	0.21	50	67
23	Clement, M.	10	74	710	129	41.3	0.17	43	60
24	Colon, B.	18	97	1,009	106	14.3	0.90	46	70
25	Cone, D.	12	98	900	111	40.7	0.21	50	67
26	Cordova, F.	8	78	775	147	23.7	0.08	34	52
27	Daal, O.	16	100	908	104	37.3	0.14	42	65
28	Dempster, R.	7	64	691	127	71.2	0.73	33	53
29	Dreifort, D.	13	77	793	137	13.9	0.47	37	53
30	Elarton, S.	9	97	823	106	35.4	0.38	48	63
31	Erickson, S.	15	78	851	89	16.9	0.32	33	58
32	Escobar, K.	14	84	883	106	5.4	0.09	39	60
33	Estes, S.	11	86	872	105	1.8	0.38	42	67
34	Farnsworth, K.	5	67	747	139	49.3	0.32	32	58
35	Fassero, J.	5	95	945	119	50.5	0.38	47	67
36	Fernandez, A.	7	64	691	127	71.2	0.73	33	53
37	Finley, C.	12	70	711	106	34.7	0.40	37	58
38	Garcia, F.	17	79	859	113	64.1	0.57	40	60
39	Gardner, M.	5	86	872	105	1.8	0.38	42	67
40	Glavine, T.	14	103	840	111	47.5	0.18	45	63
41	Gooden, D.	3	97	1,009	106	14.3	0.90	46	70
42	Guzman, J.	11	96	865	105	84.8	0.07	55	78
43	Halama, J.	11	79	859	113	64.1	0.57	40	60
44	Halladay, R.	8	84	883	106	5.4	0.09	39	60
45	Hampton, M.	22	97	823	106	35.4	0.38	48	63
46	Harnisch, P.	16	96	865	105	84.8	0.07	55	78
47	Hawkins, L.	10	63	686	92	13.2	0.12	34	52
48	Haynes, J.	7	87	893	122	11.4	0.96	48	76
49	Helling, R.	13	95	945	119	50.5	0.38	47	67
50	Hentgen, P.	11	84	883	106	5.4	0.09	39	60
51	Heredia, G.	13	87	893	122	11.4	0.96	48	76
52	Hermanson, D.	9	68	718	160	18.1	1.08	44	66
53	Hernandez, O.	17	98	900	111	40.7	0.21	50	67
54	Hernandez, L.	8	86	872	105	1.8	0.38	42	67
55	Hershiser, O.	13	97	853	68	58.8	0.15	49	69
56	Hill, K.	4	70	711	106	34.7	0.40	37	58
57	Hitchcock, S.	12	74	710	129	41.3	0.17	43	60
58	Holt, C.	5	97	823	106	35.4	0.38	48	63
59	Hudson, T.	11	87	893	122	11.4	0.96	48	76
60	Irabu, H.	11	98	900	111	40.7	0.21	50	67
61	Jimenez, J.	5	75	809	132	44.6	0.90	38	62
62	Johnson, R.	17	100	908	104	37.3	0.14	42	65
63	Johnson, J.	8	78	851	89	16.9	0.32	33	58
64	Karl, S.	11	74	815	127	5.0	0.75	40	69
65	Kile, D.	8	72	906	118	10.7	0.66	33	51
66	Leiter, A.	13	97	853	68	58.8	0.15	49	69
67	Lieber, J.	10	67	747	139	49.3	0.32	32	58
68	Lima, J.	21	97	823	106	35.4	0.38	48	63
69	Loaiza, E.	9	95	945	119	50.5	0.38	47	67
70	Maddux, G.	19	103	840	111	47.5	0.18	45	63
71	Martinez, P.	23	94	836	127	59.9	0.75	50	76
72	Mays, J.	6	63	686	92	13.2	0.12	34	52

TABLE 7-26   (*Continued*)

Pitcher		WINS	Tm WINS	Runs	Errors	ARP	Bsupp	Saves	Sv Opp
73	Meadows, B.	11	64	691	127	71.2	0.73	33	53
74	Mercker, K.	8	94	836	127	59.9	0.75	50	76
75	Millwood, K.	18	103	840	111	47.5	0.18	45	63
76	Milton, E.	7	63	686	92	13.2	0.12	34	52
77	Mlicki, D.	14	69	747	106	7.9	0.66	33	44
78	Moehler, B.	10	69	747	106	7.9	0.66	33	44
79	Morgan, M.	13	95	945	119	50.5	0.38	47	67
80	Moyer, J.	14	79	859	113	64.1	0.57	40	60
81	Mulholland, T.	10	103	840	111	47.5	0.18	45	63
82	Mussina, M.	18	78	851	89	16.9	0.32	33	58
83	Nagy, C.	17	97	1,009	106	14.3	0.90	46	70
84	Navarro, J.	8	75	777	136	21.3	0.58	39	58
85	Neagle, D.	9	96	865	105	84.8	0.07	55	78
86	Nomo, H.	12	74	815	127	5.0	0.75	40	69
87	Nunez, V.	7	64	691	127	71.2	0.73	33	53
88	Ogea, C.	6	77	841	100	11.5	0.06	32	47
89	Olivares, O.	15	87	893	122	11.4	0.96	48	76
90	Oliver, D.	9	75	809	132	44.6	0.90	38	62
91	Oquist, M.	9	87	893	122	11.4	0.96	48	76
92	Ortiz, R.	18	86	872	105	1.8	0.38	42	67
93	Park, C.	13	77	793	137	13.9	0.47	37	53
94	Parque, J.	9	75	777	136	21.3	0.58	39	58
95	Parris, S.	11	96	865	105	84.8	0.07	55	78
96	Pavano, C.	6	68	718	160	18.1	1.08	44	66
97	Person, R.	10	77	841	100	11.5	0.06	32	47
98	Pettitte, A.	14	98	900	111	40.7	0.21	50	67
99	Ponson, S.	12	78	851	89	16.9	0.32	33	58
100	Portugal, M.	7	94	836	127	59.9	0.75	50	76
101	Radke, B.	12	63	686	92	13.2	0.12	34	52
102	Rapp, P.	6	94	836	127	59.9	0.75	50	76
103	Reed, R.	11	97	853	68	58.8	0.15	49	69
104	Reynolds, S.	16	97	823	106	35.4	0.38	48	63
105	Reynoso, A.	10	100	908	104	37.3	0.14	42	65
106	Ritchie, T.	15	78	775	147	23.7	0.08	34	52
107	Rogers, K.	10	97	853	68	58.8	0.15	49	69
108	Rosado, J.	10	64	856	125	59.6	1.17	29	60
109	Rueter, K.	15	86	872	105	1.8	0.38	42	67
110	Rupe, R.	8	69	772	135	17.1	0.95	45	63
111	Saberhagen, B.	10	94	836	127	59.9	0.75	50	76
112	Schilling, C.	15	77	841	100	11.5	0.06	32	47
113	Schmidt, J.	13	78	775	147	23.7	0.08	34	52
114	Schourek, P.	4	78	775	147	23.7	0.08	34	52
115	Sele, A.	18	95	945	119	50.5	0.38	47	67
116	Sirotka, M.	11	75	777	136	21.3	0.58	39	58
117	Smoltz, J.	11	103	840	111	47.5	0.18	45	63
118	Snyder, J.	9	75	777	136	21.3	0.58	39	58
119	Sparks, S.	5	70	711	106	34.7	0.40	37	58
120	Stottlemyre, T.	6	100	908	104	37.3	0.14	42	65
121	Suppan, J.	10	64	856	125	59.6	1.17	29	60
122	Tapani, K.	6	67	747	139	49.3	0.32	32	58
123	Thompson, J.	9	69	747	106	7.9	0.66	33	44

TABLE 7-26   (Continued)

Pitcher		WINS	Tm WINS	Runs	Errors	ARP	Bsupp	Saves	Sv Opp
124	Thurman, M.	7	68	718	160	18.1	1.08	44	66
125	Tomko, B.	5	96	865	105	84.8	0.07	55	78
126	Trachsel, S.	8	67	747	139	49.3	0.32	32	58
127	Valdes, I.	9	77	793	137	13.9	0.47	37	53
128	Vazquez, J.	9	68	718	160	18.1	1.08	44	66
129	Villone, R.	9	96	865	105	84.8	0.07	55	78
130	Weaver, J.	9	69	747	106	7.9	0.66	33	44
131	Wells, D.	17	84	883	106	5.4	0.09	39	60
132	Williams, W.	12	74	710	129	41.3	0.17	43	60
133	Witasick, J.	9	64	856	125	59.6	1.17	29	60
134	Witt, B.	7	69	772	135	17.1	0.95	45	63
135	Wolf, R.	6	77	841	100	11.5	0.06	32	47
136	Woodard, S.	11	74	815	127	5.0	0.75	40	69
137	Wright, J.	8	97	1,009	106	14.3	0.90	46	70
138	Yoshii, M.	12	97	853	68	58.8	0.15	49	69

QUESTION

1. The expert consensus indicates the project is doomed to failure. Are the experts right?

Minitab Applications

The problem.   In Example 7.11 Pam Weigand wanted to run stepwise regression on the data for the Zurenko Pharmaceutical Company to forecast which applicant would become a good salesperson.

Minitab Solution

1. If the data are on file, open the file (TAB 7-13) using the following menus:

   ```
   File>Open Worksheet
   ```

   If the data are not on file, enter them on the worksheet. To run stepwise regression, click on the following menus:

   ```
   Stat>Regression>Stepwise
   ```

2. The Stepwise Regression dialog box shown in Figure 7-5 appears.
   a. The dependent or Response variable is C1 or Sales.
   b. The predictor variables are C2–C6 or Aptitude-GPA.
   c. Click Methods to provide the alpha level.
3. The Stepwise–Methods dialog box shown in Figure 7-6 appears.
   a. Click Use alpha values.
   b. Click Stepwise (forward and backward).
   c. Change the alpha to enter and alpha to remove from .15 to .05.
   d. Click OK and then OK on the Stepwise Regression dialog box. The results are shown in Table 7-17.

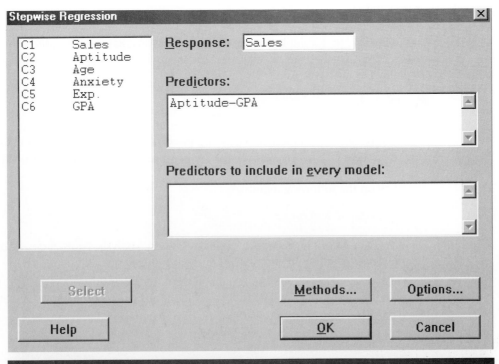

FIGURE 7-5   Minitab Stepwise Regression Dialog Box

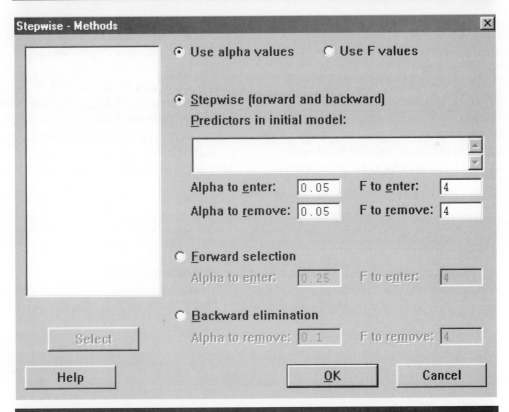

FIGURE 7-6   Minitab Stepwise–Methods Dialog Box

Excel Applications

The problem. In Example 7.1, multiple regression analysis was used to determine whether selling price and advertising expense could be used to forecast weekly sales for gallons of milk (see Table 7-4 on p. 273).

Excel Solution

1. Enter the label Price in A1, Adv. in B1, and Sales in C1. Enter selling price into A3 through A12, advertising expense into B3 through B12, and weekly sales into C3 through C12 of the worksheet. The two-predictor variables must be in adjacent columns to the left.

2. Click on the following menus:

    ```
    Tools>Data Analysis
    ```

3. The Data Analysis dialog box appears. Under Analysis Tools choose Regression. The Regression dialog box shown in Figure 6-25 appears. (See p. 266.)

    a. Enter A3 to A12 in The Input *Y* Range.
    b. Enter B3 to C12 in The Input *X* Range for the two-predictor variables, selling price, and advertising expense.
    c. The Output Range begins in D1.
    d. Click OK and the output appears.

References

Belsley, D. A. *Conditioning, Diagnostics, Collinearity and Weak Data in Regression.* New York: John Wiley & Sons, 1991.

Dielman, T. *Applied Regression Analysis for Business and Economics*, Third Edition. Pacific Grove, CA: Duxbury, 2001.

Draper, N. R., and H. Smith. *Applied Regression Analysis*, Third Edition. New York: John Wiley & Sons, 1998.

Frees, E. E. *Data Analysis Using Regression Models: The Business Perspective.* Upper Saddle River, NJ: Prentice Hall, 1996.

Johnson, R. A., and D. W. Wichern. *Business Statistics: Decision Making with Data.* New York: John Wiley & Sons, 1997.

Neter, J., W. Wasserman, M. Kutner, and C. Nachtsheim. *Applied Linear Regression Models*, Third Edition. Homewood, IL: Richard D. Irwin, 1996.

CHAPTER
8

REGRESSION WITH TIME SERIES DATA

Many business and economic applications of forecasting involve time series data. Regression models can be fit to monthly, quarterly, or yearly data using the techniques described in previous chapters. However, because data collected over time tend to exhibit trends, seasonal patterns, and so forth, observations in different time periods are related or autocorrelated. That is, for time series data, the sample of observations cannot be regarded as a random sample. Problems of interpretation can arise when standard regression methods are applied to observations that are related to one another over time. Fitting regression models to time series data must be done with considerable care.

TIME SERIES DATA AND THE PROBLEM OF AUTOCORRELATION

The regression models discussed in Chapters 6 and 7 assume that the errors, ε, are independent (or uncorrelated) random variables. This means that the different values of the response variable Y can be related to the values of the predictor variables, the X's, but not to one another. The usual interpretations of the results of a regression analysis depend heavily on the assumption of independence.

With time series data, the assumption of independence rarely holds. Consider the annual base price for a particular model of a new car. Can you imagine the chaos that would exist if the new car prices from one year to the next were indeed unrelated to (independent of) one another? In such a world, prices would be determined like numbers drawn from a random number table. Knowledge of the price in one year would not tell you anything about the price in the next year. In the real world, price in the current year is related to (correlated with) the price in the previous year and maybe the price two years ago, and so forth. That is, the prices in different years are autocorrelated; they are not independent.

> *Autocorrelation* exists when successive observations over time are related to one another.

Autocorrelation can occur because the effect of a predictor variable on the response is distributed over time. For example, an increase in salary may affect your consumption (or saving) not only in the current period but also in several future periods. A change in price may affect sales in the current period and in future periods. A current labor contract may affect the cost of production for some time to come. Over time, relationships tend to be dynamic (evolving), not static.

327

From a forecasting perspective, autocorrelation is not all bad. If values of a response Y in one time period are related to Y values in previous time periods, then previous Y's can be used to predict future Y's.[1] In a regression framework, autocorrelation is handled by "fixing up" the standard regression model. To accommodate autocorrelation, sometimes it is necessary to change the mix of predictor variables or the form of the regression function. More typically, however, autocorrelation is handled by changing the nature of the error term.

A common kind of autocorrelation, often called *first-order serial correlation*, is one in which the error term in the current time period is directly related to the error term in the previous time period. In this case, with the subscript t representing time, the simple linear regression model takes the form

$$Y_t = \beta_0 + \beta_1 X_t + \varepsilon_t \qquad (8.1)$$

with

$$\varepsilon_t = \rho\varepsilon_{t-1} + v_t \qquad (8.2)$$

where

   $\varepsilon_t =$ the error at time t

   $\rho =$ the parameter (lag 1 autocorrelation coefficient) that measures correlation
   between adjacent error terms

   $v_t =$ normally distributed independent error term with mean 0 and variance σ_v^2

Equation 8.2 says that the level of one error term (ε_{t-1}) directly affects the level of the next error term (ε_t). The magnitude of the autocorrelation coefficient ρ, where $-1 \leq \rho < 1$, indicates the strength of the serial correlation. If ρ is zero there is no serial correlation, and the error terms are independent ($\varepsilon_t = v_t$).

Figure 8-1 illustrates the effect of positive serial correlation in a simple linear regression model. Suppose the true relation between Y and X, indicated by the solid line in the figure, is increasing over time. If the first Y value is above the true regression line, then the next several Y values are likely to be above the line because of the positive autocorrelation (first error is positive, so second error is likely to be positive, and so forth). Eventually, there may be a sequence of Y's below the true regression line (a negative error is likely to be followed by negative error). The data are "tilted" relative to the true X, Y relationship. However, the least square line, by its very nature, will pass through the observations as indicated by the dotted line in the figure. Using the dotted line to make inferences about the solid line, or using the dotted line to generate forecasts of future Y's, could be very misleading.

It should also be clear for Figure 8-1 that the scatter about the least squares line is tighter than it is about the true regression line. Consequently, the standard error of the estimate, $s_{y \cdot x}$, will underestimate the variability of the Y's about the true regression line or, equivalently, underestimate the standard deviation σ of the error term ε.

Strong autocorrelation can make two unrelated variables appear to be related. Standard regression procedures applied to observations on these variables can produce a significant regression. In this case, the estimated relationship is spurious, and an examination of the residuals will ordinarily reveal the problem. However, with an uncritical application of standard procedures, the spurious regression may go undetected with a serious misinterpretation of the results.

---

[1] This idea is considered again in a later section of this chapter when autoregressive models are discussed, and is developed more fully in Chapter 9.

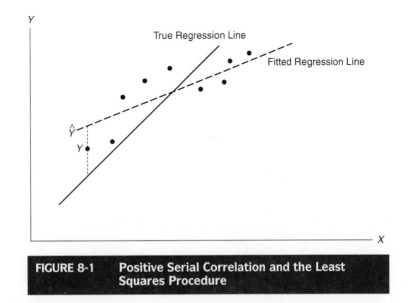

FIGURE 8-1   Positive Serial Correlation and the Least Squares Procedure

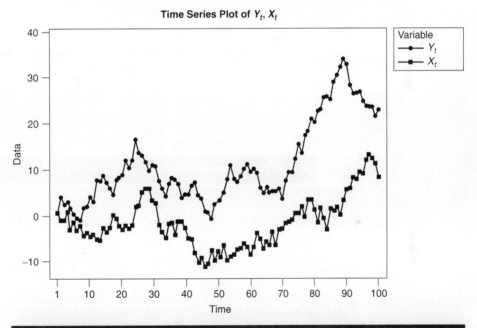

FIGURE 8-2   Time Series Plots of Two Unrelated Series, Y_t (top) and X_t (bottom)

Example 8.1

Figure 8-2 contains plots of two computer-generated time series, Y_t and X_t. These two series were formed in such a way that the first series (Y_t) is not related to the second series (X_t).[2] At the same time, each sequence of observations is highly autocorrelated. The

---

[2] The first series was constructed by selecting a random sample of 100 values from a normal distribution with mean 0 and standard deviation 2, and then forming partial sums. For example, the first observation in the series was the first value selected in the sample, the second observation in the series was the sum of the first

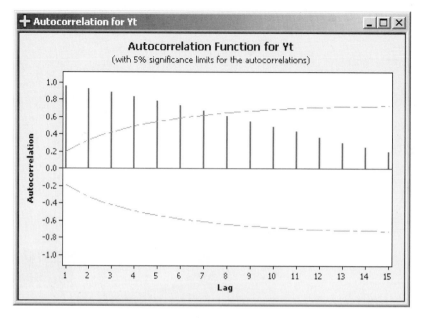

Autocorrelation Function: Yt

Lag	ACF	T	LBQ	Lag	ACF	T	LBQ
1	0.959355	9.59	94.83	9	0.543683	1.61	584.51
2	0.923743	5.48	183.64	10	0.486047	1.40	611.29
3	0.878880	4.12	264.86	11	0.427587	1.21	632.24
4	0.833189	3.38	338.62	12	0.360773	1.01	647.33
5	0.783946	2.87	404.61	13	0.299414	0.83	657.84
6	0.730737	2.48	462.55	14	0.245812	0.68	665.01
7	0.666258	2.13	511.24	15	0.199546	0.55	669.78
8	0.601754	1.84	551.38				

FIGURE 8-3   Autocorrelations for the Y_t Series

autocorrelations for the first series are shown in Figure 8-3. The autocorrelations for the second series (not shown) are very similar.

Figure 8-2 indicates that the two time series appear to move together. In fact, it might be possible to relate the first (top) series to the second (bottom) series using a simple linear regression model. A scatter diagram of the data is shown in Figure 8-4 along with the least squares line. The estimated regression is significant ($F = 83.08$, p-value $= .000$), with X_t explaining about 46% of the variability in Y_t. Yet the Y_t series was generated independently of the X_t series; that is, the X's were not used to generate the Y's. The estimated regression in this case is spurious.

An examination of the residuals would reveal problems with this regression analysis. For example, the residual autocorrelations are large for several lags, indicating the assumption of independent errors is wrong, and the initial regression model should be modified. In this case, if the modification is done correctly the spurious relation between Y_t and X_t would disappear.

If regression models are used with autocorrelated (time series) data, it is especially important to examine the residuals. If not, it is possible to reach conclusions that are not justified. The fault is not with the least squares procedure. The fault lies in applying

---

two values, the third observation was the sum of the first three values, and so forth. The second series was constructed in the same way, beginning with a *different* random sample of 100 values from the same normal distribution.

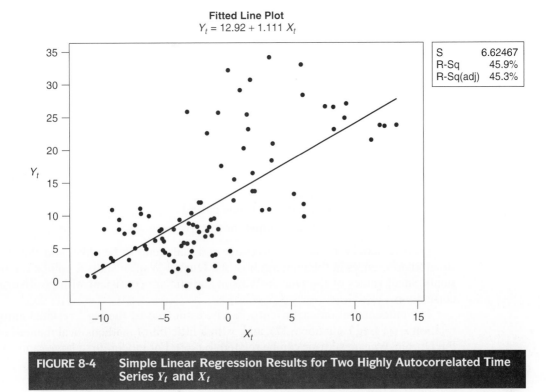

FIGURE 8-4   Simple Linear Regression Results for Two Highly Autocorrelated Time Series Y_t and X_t

the standard regression model in a situation that does not correspond to the usual regression assumptions. The technical problems that arise include:

1. The standard error of the estimate can seriously underestimate the variability of the error terms.
2. The usual inferences based on the t and F statistics are no longer strictly applicable.
3. The standard errors of the regression coefficients underestimate the variability of the estimated regression coefficients. Spurious regressions can result.

DURBIN-WATSON TEST FOR SERIAL CORRELATION

One approach that is used frequently to determine if serial correlation is present is the *Durbin-Watson test*.[3] The test involves the determination of whether the autocorrelation parameter ρ shown in Equation 8.2 is zero. Consider

$$\varepsilon_t = \rho \varepsilon_{t-1} + v_t$$

The hypotheses to be tested are

$$H_0: \rho = 0$$
$$H_1: \rho > 0$$

The alternative hypothesis is $\rho > 0$ because business and economic time series tend to show positive autocorrelation.

---

[3] See Durbin and Watson (1951). This test is not directly applicable if the regression equation does not contain a constant term.

If a regression model does not properly account for autocorrelation, the residuals will be autocorrelated. So, the Durbin-Watson test is carried out using the residuals from the regression analysis.

The Durbin-Watson statistic is defined as

$$DW = \frac{\sum_{t=2}^{n}(e_t - e_{t-1})^2}{\sum_{t=1}^{n}e_t^2} \tag{8.3}$$

where

$e_t = Y_t - \hat{Y}_t = $ the residual for time period t

$e_{t-1} = Y_{t-1} - \hat{Y}_{t-1} = $ the residual for time period $t - 1$

For positive serial correlation, successive residuals tend to be alike, and the sum of squared differences in the numerator of the Durbin-Watson statistic will be relatively small. Small values of the Durbin-Watson statistic are consistent with positive serial correlation.

The autocorrelation coefficient ρ can be estimated by the lag 1 residual autocorrelation $r_1(e)$ (see Equation 6.17), and, with a little bit of mathematical maneuvering, the Durbin-Watson statistic can be related to $r_1(e)$. For moderate to large samples,

$$DW = 2(1 - r_1(e)) \tag{8.4}$$

Because $-1 < r_1(e) < 1$, Equation 8.4 shows that $0 < DW < 4$. For $r_1(e)$ close to 0, the *DW* statistic will be close to 2. Positive lag 1 residual autocorrelation is associated with *DW* values less than 2, and negative lag 1 residual autocorrelation is associated with *DW* values above 2.

A useful, but sometimes not definitive, test for serial correlation can be performed by comparing the calculated value of the Durbin-Watson statistic with lower (d_L) and upper (d_U) bounds. The decision rules are:

1. When the Durbin-Watson statistic is larger than the upper (d_U) bound, the autocorrelation coefficient ρ is equal to zero (there is no positive autocorrelation).
2. When the Durbin-Watson statistic is smaller than the lower (d_L) bound, the autocorrelation coefficient ρ is greater than zero (there is positive autocorrelation).
3. When the Durbin-Watson statistic lies within the lower and upper bounds, the test is inconclusive (we don't know whether there is positive autocorrelation).

The *Durbin-Watson test* is used to determine whether positive autocorrelation is present.

> If $DW > d_U$, conclude H_0: $\rho = 0$
> If $DW < d_L$, conclude H_0: $\rho > 0$
> If *DW* lies within the lower and upper bounds ($d_L \leq DW \leq d_U$), the test is inconclusive.

The critical bounds for d_L and d_U are given in Appendix Table C-6. To find the appropriate d_L and d_U, the analyst needs to know the sample size, level of significance, and the number of independent variables. In the Durbin-Watson table in Appendix C, the sample size is given in the left-hand column, and the number of independent variables is determined from the top of each column. If three independent variables were used, for instance, one would look in the $k = 3$ column.[4]

As indicated in Equation 8.4, one can infer the sign and magnitude of the lag 1 residual autocorrelation coefficient from the *DW* statistic and vice versa. Thus for situations in which the Durbin-Watson test is inconclusive, the significance of the serial correlation can be investigated by comparing $r_1(e)$ with $\pm 2/\sqrt{n}$.[5] If $r_1(e)$ falls in the interval $0 \pm 2/\sqrt{n}$, we conclude that the autocorrelation is small and can be ignored.

Example 8.2
Suppose an analyst is engaged in forward planning for Reynolds Metals Company, an aluminum producer, and wishes to establish a quantitative basis for projecting future sales. Because the company sells regionally, a measure of disposable personal income for the region should be closely related to sales. Table 8-1 shows sales and income for the period from 1976 to 1996. Also shown in the table are the columns necessary to calculate the *DW* statistic (see "Minitab Applications" at end of the chapter). The residuals come from a least squares line fit to the data as shown in Figure 8-5.

TABLE 8-1	Reynolds Metals Sales Data and the Durbin-Watson Calculations				

Year	Sales Y_t	Income X_t	Residuals e_t	$e_t - e_{t-1}$	$(e_t - e_{t-1})^2$	e_t^2
1976	295	273.4	−76.36	—	—	5,830.85
1977	400	291.3	−47.53	28.83	831.17	2,259.10
1978	390	306.9	−123.91	−76.38	5,833.90	15,353.69
1979	425	317.1	−132.32	−8.41	70.73	17,508.58
1980	547	336.1	−91.16	41.16	1,694.15	8,310.15
1981	555	349.4	−139.76	−48.60	2,361.96	19,532.86
1982	620	362.9	−132.20	7.56	57.15	17,476.84
1983	720	383.9	−121.56	10.64	113.21	14,776.83
1984	880	402.8	−41.98	79.58	6,332.98	1,762.32
1985	1,050	437.0	−17.51	24.47	598.78	306.60
1986	1,290	472.2	72.71	90.22	8,139.65	5,286.74
1987	1,528	510.4	148.16	75.45	5,692.70	21,951.39
1988	1,586	544.5	61.06	−87.10	7,586.41	3,728.32
1989	1,960	588.1	249.53	188.47	35,520.94	62,265.22
1990	2,118	630.4	227.54	−21.99	483.56	51,774.45
1991	2,116	685.9	−10.62	−238.16	56,720.19	112.78
1992	2,477	742.8	108.26	118.88	14,132.45	11,720.23
1993	3,199	801.3	581.33	473.07	223,795.22	337,944.57
1994	3,702	903.1	651.16	69.83	4,876.23	424,009.35
1995	3,316	983.6	−77.38	−728.54	530,770.53	5,987.66
1996	2,702	1,076.7	−1,087.54	−1,010.16	1,020,423.23	1,182,743.25
				Totals	1,926,035.14	2,210,641.78

---

[4] It is also possible to test for negative autocorrelation. In this case H_1: $\rho < 0$ and the test statistic *DW* is compared to $4 - d_L$ and $4 - d_U$. The null hypothesis H_0: $\rho = 0$ is rejected if $DW > 4 - d_L$ and not rejected if $DW < 4 - d_U$. The test is inconclusive for *DW* between $4 - d_U$ and $4 - d_L$.

[5] If there is no autocorrelation, the standard error of $r_1(e)$ is approximately $1/\sqrt{n}$ (see the discussion of autocorrelation in Chapter 3 and the discussion of residual autocorrelation in Chapter 6).

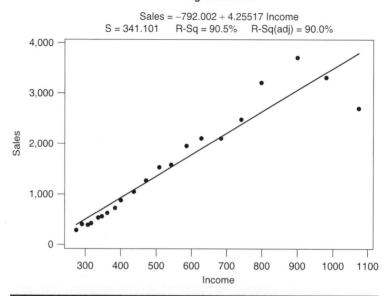

Regression Plot

Sales = −792.002 + 4.25517 Income
S = 341.101   R-Sq = 90.5%   R-Sq(adj) = 90.0%

FIGURE 8-5   Regression Plot for Reynolds Metals Data

Before using the least squares line for forecasting, the analyst performs the Durbin-Watson test for positive serial correlation. The computations for the last three columns for 1977 are:

$$e_t - e_{t-1} = -47.53 - (-76.36) = 28.83$$
$$(e_t - e_{t-1})^2 = 28.83^2 = 831.17$$
$$e_t^2 = (-47.53)^2 = 2,259.1$$

The Durbin-Watson statistic is computed as

$$DW = \frac{\sum\limits_{t=2}^{21}(e_t - e_{t-1})^2}{\sum\limits_{t=1}^{21}e_t^2} = \frac{1,926,035.14}{2,210,641.78} = .87$$

Using a .01 level of significance for a sample of $n = 21$ and $k = 1$ independent variable, one obtains

$$d_L = .97$$
$$d_U = 1.16$$

$DW = .87$ falls below $d_L = .97$, so the null hypothesis H_0: $\rho = 0$ is rejected, and it is concluded that the errors are positively correlated ($\rho > 0$). The regression model should be modified before it is used for forecasting.

SOLUTIONS TO AUTOCORRELATION PROBLEMS

After autocorrelation has been discovered in a regression of time series data, it is necessary to remove it, or model it, before the regression function can be evaluated for its effectiveness. The appropriate method for treating serial correlation depends on what caused it in the first place. Autocorrelation can arise because of a specification error such as an omitted variable, or it can arise because the independent error terms are correlated in an otherwise correctly specified model.

The solution to the problem of serial correlation begins with an evaluation of the model specification. Is the functional form correct? Were any important variables omitted? Are there effects that might have some pattern over time that could have introduced autocorrelation into the errors?

Because a major cause of autocorrelated errors in the regression model is the omission of one or more key variables, the best approach to solving the problem is to find them. This effort is sometimes referred to as improving the model specification. Model specification involves not only finding the important predictor variables but also entering these variables in the regression function in the right way. Unfortunately, it is not always possible to improve the model specification because an important missing variable may not be quantifiable or, if it is quantifiable, the data may not be available. For example, one may suspect that business investment in future periods is related to the attitude of potential investors. However, it is difficult to quantify the variable "attitude." Nevertheless, whenever possible, the model should be specified in accordance with theoretically sound insight.

Only after the specification of the equation has been carefully reviewed should the possibility of an adjustment be considered. Several techniques for eliminating autocorrelation will be discussed.

One approach to eliminating autocorrelation is to add an omitted variable to the regression function that explains the association in the response from one period to the next.

Another approach involves the general notion of differencing. In this approach, the regression model is specified in terms of *changes* rather than *levels*. So, for example, using the Reynolds Metals data, the change in sales from one year to the next (the change is 105 for the period 1976 to 1977) is related to the corresponding change in income (17.9 for the period 1976 to 1977). On occasion, the original variables may be expressed in terms of logarithms, and changes in the logarithms are used in the regression. This procedure is equivalent to regressing the *percentage change* in the response on the percentage changes in the predictor variables. Finally, instead of using simple or first differences in the regression model, it may be the case that *generalized differences* are required to eliminate autocorrelation.

The autoregressive model approach to eliminating autocorrelation generates predictor variables by using the response variable Y lagged one or more periods. In the first-order autoregressive model case, the only predictor variable is the Y variable lagged one time period. Using the Reynolds Metals data again, the value used to predict 1977 sales is the sales for 1976 (295).

The next examples illustrate these methods for eliminating autocorrelation.

Model Specification Error (Omitting a Variable)

Example 8.3 shows how incorporating a missing variable can eliminate serial correlation.

Example 8.3

The Novak Corporation wishes to develop a forecasting model for the projection of future sales. Because the corporation has outlets throughout the region, disposable personal income on a region-wide basis is chosen as a possible predictor variable. Table 8-2 shows Novak sales for 1980 to 1996. The table also shows disposable personal income and the unemployment for the region.

TABLE 8-2	Novak Corporation Sales Data for Examples 8.3 and 8.6				
Row	*Year*	*Sales (Y)*	*Income*	*Rate*	*Y-Lagged*
1	1980	8.0	336.1	5.5	—
2	1981	8.2	349.4	5.5	8.0
3	1982	8.5	362.9	6.7	8.2
4	1983	9.2	383.9	5.5	8.5
5	1984	10.2	402.8	5.7	9.2
6	1985	11.4	437.0	5.2	10.2
7	1986	12.8	472.2	4.5	11.4
8	1987	13.6	510.4	3.8	12.8
9	1988	14.6	544.5	3.8	13.6
10	1989	16.4	588.1	3.6	14.6
11	1990	17.8	630.4	3.5	16.4
12	1991	18.6	685.9	4.9	17.8
13	1992	20.0	742.8	5.9	18.6
14	1993	21.9	801.3	5.6	20.0
15	1994	24.9	903.1	4.9	21.9
16	1995	27.3	983.6	5.6	24.9
17	1996	29.1	1076.7	8.5	27.3

TABLE 8-3	Minitab Output for Novak Sales and Disposable Personal Income for Example 8.3

Regression Analysis: Sales versus Income

```
The regression equation is
Sales = -1.50 + 0.0292 Income

Predictor        Coef     SE Coef        T       P
Constant      -1.5046      0.3290    -4.57   0.000
Income      0.0291916   0.0005129    56.92   0.000

S = 0.4767      R-Sq = 99.5%      R-Sq(adj) = 99.5%

Analysis of Variance

Source          DF       SS       MS        F       P
Regression       1   736.15   736.15  3239.89   0.000
Residual Error  15     3.41     0.23
Total           16   739.56

Durbin-Watson statistic = 0.72
```

From Table 8-3, the Durbin-Watson statistic is .72, and using a significance level of .01 with $n = 17$ and $k = 1$, Appendix Table C-6 gives

$$d_L = .87$$
$$d_U = 1.10$$

Because $DW = .72 < d_L = .87$, positive serial correlation is indicated. A key variable that accounts for the remaining association in sales from one year to the next may be missing from the model. This result may be true even though the Minitab output says that disposable income explains 99.5% of the variability in sales.

TABLE 8-4   Minitab Output for Novak Sales, Disposable Income, and Unemployment Rate for Example 8.3

```
Regression Analysis: Sales versus Income, Rate
The regression equation is
Sales = -0.014 + 0.0297 Income - 0.350 Rate

Predictor         Coef      SE Coef        T       P
Constant       -0.0140       0.2498    -0.06   0.956
Income       0.0297492    0.0002480   119.96   0.000
Rate          -0.34987      0.04656    -7.51   0.000

S = 0.2199     R-Sq = 99.9%      R-Sq(adj) = 99.9%

Analysis of Variance

Source            DF        SS        MS        F       P
Regression         2    738.88    369.44  7637.91   0.000
Residual Error    14      0.68      0.05
Total             16    739.56

Durbin-Watson statistic = 1.98
```

The unemployment rate may be an important missing predictor of sales. Table 8-4 shows the results of the regression analysis when the unemployment rate is added to the model.

The fitted model now explains 99.9% of the variability in sales. Although the intercept is not significant, refitting the model without the intercept leaves the Durbin-Watson statistic of 1.98 essentially unchanged.

With a .01 level of significance, $n = 17$ and $k = 2$, Appendix Table C-6 gives

$$d_L = .77$$
$$d_U = 1.25$$

Because $DW = 1.98 > d_U = 1.25$, there is no evidence of serial correlation.

The function $\hat{Y} = -.014 + .03X_1 - .35X_2$ can be used to predict Novak sales with the knowledge that the errors are independent.[6] Expert estimates of disposable personal income ($1,185 million) and the unemployment rate (7.8%) for the region are used to generate a forecast of Novak sales for 1997. The forecast is

$$\hat{Y} = -.014 + .03(1,185) - .35(7.8) = 32.8$$

or $32.8 million.

Regression with Differences

For highly autocorrelated data, modeling changes rather than levels can often eliminate the serial correlation. That is, instead of formulating the regression equation in terms of Y and $X_1, X_2, \ldots, X_k$, the regression equation is written in terms of the differences, $Y'_t = Y_t - Y_{t-1}$ and $X'_{t1} = X_{t1} - X_{t-1,1}$, $X'_{t2} = X_{t2} - X_{t-1,2}$, and so forth. Differences should be considered when the Durbin-Watson statistic associated with the regression involving the original variables is close to 0.[7]

---

[6] The usual residual plots indicate there is no reason to doubt any of the regression model assumptions.

[7] An autocorrelation pattern for the Y variable or the X variables such as the one pictured in Figure 8-3 (see page 330) also indicates that a regression function with differences may eliminate (or greatly reduce) problems caused by serial correlation.

One rationale for differencing comes from the following argument. Suppose Equations 8.1 and 8.2 hold so that

$$Y_t = \beta_0 + \beta_1 X_t + \varepsilon_t$$

with

$$\varepsilon_t = \rho\varepsilon_{t-1} + v_t$$

where

ρ = correlation between consecutive errors
v_t = random error
$v_t = \varepsilon_t$ when $\rho = 0$

The model holds for any time period, so

$$Y_{t-1} = \beta_0 + \beta_1 X_{t-1} + \varepsilon_{t-1}$$

Multiplying this equation on both sides by ρ and then subtracting equals from equals in Equation 8.1 gives

$$Y_t = \beta_0 + \beta_1 X_t + \varepsilon_t \qquad \text{(Equation 8.1)}$$
$$\rho Y_{t-1} = \rho\beta_0 + \rho\beta_1 X_{t-1} + \rho\varepsilon_{t-1} \qquad \text{(multiply } Y_{t-1} \text{ by } \rho)$$
$$Y_t - \rho Y_{t-1} = \beta_0 - \rho\beta_0 + (\beta_1 X_t - \rho\beta_1 X_{t-1}) + (\varepsilon_t - \rho\varepsilon_{t-1}) \qquad \text{(subtract)}$$

or

$$Y_t' = \beta_0(1 - \rho) + \beta_1 X_t' + v_t \tag{8.5}$$

where the "prime" indicates the *generalized differences*

$$Y_t' = Y_t - \rho Y_{t-1}$$
$$X_t' = X_t - \rho X_{t-1} \tag{8.6}$$

The model in Equation 8.5 has errors v_t that are independently distributed with mean equal to zero and a constant variance. Thus the usual regression methods can be applied to this model.

If the correlation between consecutive errors is strong (ρ near 1), the generalized differences are essentially simple, or first, differences

$$Y_t' = Y_t - Y_{t-1}$$
$$X_t' = X_t - X_{t-1} \tag{8.7}$$

and the intercept term in the model (8.5) is near zero (disappears).

Using regression models constructed with generalized differences can frequently eliminate serial correlation. If the serial correlation is especially strong, simple differences can be used. Example 8.1 shows what can happen if strong autocorrelation is ignored.

Example 8.4

Fred Gardner is engaged in forecasting Sears Roebuck sales in thousands of dollars for the western region. He has chosen disposable personal income for the region as his independent variable. Relating sales to disposable income using a log linear regression model will also allow Fred to estimate the income elasticity of sales. The elasticity measures the percentage change in sales for a 1% change in income.

The log linear regression model assumes that income is related to sales by the equation

$$Sales = \gamma(Income)^{\beta_1}$$

Taking the natural logarithms of both sides of the foregoing equation gives

$$Ln(Sales) = Ln\,\gamma + \beta_1 Ln(Income)$$

Adding an error term to account for the influence of variables other than income on sales, the previous expression becomes a *log linear regression model* of the form

$$Ln\,Y_t = \beta_0 + \beta_1 Ln\,X_t + \varepsilon_t \qquad\qquad (8.8)$$

where

$Ln\,Y_t = Ln(Sales) = $ natural logarithm of sales
$Ln\,X_t = Ln(Income) = $ natural logarithm of income
$\varepsilon_t = $ the error term
$\beta_0 = Ln\,\gamma = $ the intercept coefficient
$\beta_1 = $ the slope coefficient $= $ the income elasticity of sales

Table 8-5 shows Sears sales, disposable income, their logarithms, and the differences in the logarithms of sales and disposable income for the 1976–1996 period.

TABLE 8-5	Sears Sales and U.S. Disposable Income 1976–1996, Along with Transformed Data, for Example 8.4					
	Sales (thousands)	*Income (millions)*			*Differences*	
Year	Y_t	X_t	**Ln** Y_t	**Ln** X_t	Y'_t	X'_t
1976	3,307	273.4	8.1038	5.6109	—	—
1977	3,556	291.3	8.1764	5.6744	.0726	.0634
1978	3,601	306.9	8.1890	5.7265	.0126	.0522
1979	3,721	317.1	8.2218	5.7592	.0328	.0327
1980	4,036	336.1	8.3030	5.8174	.0813	.0582
1981	4,134	349.4	8.3270	5.8562	.0240	.0388
1982	4,268	362.9	8.3589	5.8941	.0319	.0379
1983	4,578	383.9	8.4290	5.9504	.0701	.0563
1984	5,093	402.8	8.5356	5.9984	.1066	.0481
1985	5,716	437.0	8.6510	6.0799	.1154	.0815
1986	6,357	472.2	8.7573	6.1574	.1063	.0775
1987	6,769	510.4	8.8201	6.2352	.0628	.0778
1988	7,296	544.5	8.8951	6.2999	.0750	.0647
1989	8,178	588.1	9.0092	6.3769	.1141	.0770
1990	8,844	630.4	9.0875	6.4464	.0783	.0695
1991	9,251	685.9	9.1325	6.5307	.0450	.0844
1992	10,006	742.8	9.2109	6.6104	.0785	.0797
1993	11,200	801.3	9.3237	6.6862	.1127	.0758
1994	12,500	903.1	9.4335	6.8058	.1098	.1196
1995	13,101	983.6	9.4804	6.8912	.0470	.0854
1996	13,640	1,076.7	9.5208	6.9817	.0403	.0904

A portion of the Minitab output showing the regression of Ln(Sales) on Ln(Income) is shown in Table 8-6. Fred notices that 99.2% of the variability in the logarithm of Sears sales for the western region can be explained by its relationship with the logarithm of disposable income for the same region. The regression is highly significant. In addition, the income elasticity is estimated to be $b_1 = 1.117$ with a standard error of $s_{b_1} = .023$. However, the Durbin-Watson statistic of .50 is small and less than $d_L = .97$, the lower .01 level critical value for $n = 21$ and $k = 1$. Fred concludes that the correlation between successive errors is positive and large (close to 1).

Because of the large serial correlation, Fred decides to model the changes (differences) in the logarithms of sales and income, respectively. He understands that the slope coefficient in the model for the differences is the same slope coefficient as the one in the original model involving the logarithms; therefore, he can still estimate the income elasticity directly. The intercept coefficient in the regression model for the differences is likely to be small and is omitted. The Minitab results for the changes are shown in Table 8-7.

Table 8-7 shows that the regression is significant. The income elasticity is estimated to be $b_1 = 1.010$ with a standard error of $s_{b_1} = .093$. The elasticity estimate b_1 did not change too much from the first regression (a 1% increase in disposable income leads to an approximate 1% increase in annual sales in both cases), but its current standard error ($s_{b_1} = .093$) is about four times as large as the previous standard error ($s_{b_1} = .023$). The previous standard error is likely to understate the true standard error due to the serial correlation.

Checking the Durbin-Watson statistic for $n = 20$, $k = 1$ and a significance level of .05, Fred finds that $d_L = 1.20 < DW = 1.28 < d_U = 1.41$, so the test for positive serial correlation is inconclusive. However, a check of the residual autocorrelations, shown in Figure 8-6, indicates that they are all well within their two standard error limits (the dashed lines in the figure) for the first few lags. Fred concludes that serial correlation has been eliminated and he will use the fitted equation for forecasting.

To use the final model for forecasting, Fred writes

$$\hat{Y}'_t = 1.01 X'_t \quad \text{where} \quad \begin{aligned} \hat{Y}'_t &= \text{Ln}\,\hat{Y}_t - \text{Ln}\,\hat{Y}_{t-1} \\ X'_t &= \text{Ln}\,X_t - \text{Ln}\,X_{t-1} \end{aligned}$$

TABLE 8-6   Minitab Output for the Regression of the Logarithms of Sears Sales on the Logarithms of Disposable Income for Example 8.4

```
Regression Analysis: Ln(Sales) versus Ln(Income)
The regression equation is
Ln(Sales) = 1.82 + 1.12 Ln(Income)

Predictor        Coef    SE Coef        T        P
Constant       1.8232     0.1434    12.71    0.000
Ln(Income)    1.11727    0.02305    48.47    0.000

S = 0.04368      R-Sq = 99.2%        R-Sq(adj) = 99.2%

Analysis of Variance

Source            DF        SS       MS         F        P
Regression         1    4.4821   4.4821   2349.13    0.000
Residual Error    19    0.0363   0.0019
Total             20    4.5184

Durbin-Watson statistic = 0.50
```

TABLE 8-7	Minitab Output for the Regression of the Changes in Logarithms of Sears Sales on the Changes in Logarithms of Disposable Income for Example 8.4

Regression Analysis: Change in Ln(Sales) versus Change in Ln(Income)

The regression equation is
Change in Ln(Sales) = 1.01 Change in Ln(Income)

Predictor	Coef	SE Coef	T	P
Noconstant				
Change in Ln(Income)	1.00989	0.09304	10.85	0.000

S = 0.02975

Analysis of Variance

Source	DF	SS	MS	F	P
Regression	1	0.10428	0.10428	117.83	0.000
Residual Error	19	0.01681	0.00088		
Total	20	0.12109			

Durbin-Watson statistic = 1.28

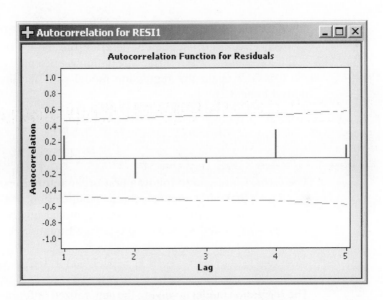

Autocorrelation Function: RESI1

Lag	ACF	T	LBQ
1	0.274432	1.23	1.74
2	-0.257852	-1.08	3.37
3	-0.065264	-0.26	3.48
4	0.349965	1.38	6.85
5	0.160779	0.58	7.61

FIGURE 8-6	The Residual Autocorrelations for the Regression Analysis in Table 8-7

Substituting for $\hat{Y}_t'$ and X_t' and rearranging terms,

$$\text{Ln}\,\hat{Y}_t' = \text{Ln}\,\hat{Y}_{t-1}' + 1.01(\text{Ln}\,X_t - \text{Ln}\,X_{t-1}) \qquad \textbf{(8.9)}$$

The forecast for Sears sales in 1997 is obtained by setting $t = 22$:

$$\text{Ln}\,\hat{Y}_{22}' = \text{Ln}\,\hat{Y}_{21}' + 1.01(\text{Ln}\,X_{22} - \text{Ln}\,X_{21})$$

Sales in 1996 are known, so $\hat{Y}_{21} = Y_{21} = 13{,}640$. Disposable income for 1996 is known, so $X_{21} = 1{,}076.7$. To continue, Fred needs disposable income for 1997. An economist familiar with the western region sends Fred an estimate of \$1,185 million for 1997 disposable income. Fred uses this expert's estimate and sets $X_{22} = 1{,}185$. The forecasting equation becomes

$$\text{Ln}\,\hat{Y}_{22} = \text{Ln}\,(13{,}640) + 1.01(\text{Ln}\,(1{,}185) - \text{Ln}\,(1{,}076.7))$$

$$= 9.5208 + 1.01(7.0775 - 6.9817) = 9.6176$$

or, taking antilogs,

$$\hat{Y}_{22} = e^{9.6176} = 15{,}027$$

Fred's forecast of Sears 1997 sales for the western region is \$15,027 thousands. Fred can use Equation 8.9 and the procedure described earlier to generate forecasts for the years 1998, 1999 and so forth, but to do so he needs estimates of disposable personal incomes for these years.

Autocorrelated Errors and Generalized Differences

The objective is to adequately describe the nature of the relationship between the variables Y and X when serial correlation is present.

Consider again the regression model with serially correlated errors (see Equations 8.1 and 8.2):

$$Y_t = \beta_0 + \beta_1 X_t + \varepsilon_t$$

$$\varepsilon_t = \rho \varepsilon_{t-1} + v_t$$

The errors ε_t are said to follow a first-order autoregressive, or AR(1), model.[8]

Recall that, after some algebraic manipulation, the system of equations above can be written as a simple linear regression model involving the generalized differences $Y_t' = Y_t - \rho Y_{t-1}$ and $X_t' = X_t - \rho X_{t-1}$ (see Equation 8.5):

$$Y_t' = \beta_0(1 - \rho) + \beta_1 X_t' + v_t$$

The regression model involving the generalized differences is specifically constructed to eliminate serial correlation in the errors. The errors v_t are assumed to be independent and normally distributed with mean 0 and constant variance σ_v^2. Consequently, it seems reasonable to fit this model directly using the principle of least squares. However, the autocorrelation coefficient ρ is unknown, so Y_t' and X_t' cannot be determined. Therefore, the model cannot be fit using ordinary least squares.

There are two general approaches to estimating the parameters, β_0 and β_1, of primary interest. One approach is to use the model corrected for serial correlation (Equation 8.5) and estimate the parameters β_0, β_1, and ρ directly using a numerical technique called *nonlinear least squares*. This approach uses a search routine to find

---

[8] First-order autoregressive models are formally introduced in the next section of this chapter and discussed again in Chapter 9.

```
Equation: LSVAR   Workfile: SEARS DATA HW                    _ □ ✕
View Procs Objects   Print Name Freeze   Estimate Forecast Stats Resids

Dependent Variable: SALES
Method: Least Squares
Date: 07/08/02   Time: 12:41
Sample: 1976 1996
Included observations: 21
```

Variable	Coefficient	Std. Error	t-Statistic	Prob.
C	-524.3323	188.4470	-2.782386	0.0119
INCOME	14.04963	0.318500	44.11184	0.0000

R-squared	0.990330	Mean dependent var	7102.476
Adjusted R-squared	0.989821	S.D. dependent var	3404.744
S.E. of regression	343.5060	Akaike info criterion	14.60668
Sum squared resid	2241931.	Schwarz criterion	14.70616
Log likelihood	-151.3701	F-statistic	1945.854
Durbin-Watson stat	0.630087	Prob(F-statistic)	0.000000

FIGURE 8-7   **E-Views Output for the Regression of Sears Sales on Disposable Income for Example 8.5**

the parameter values that minimize the error sum of squares Σv_t^2. The other approach is to estimate ρ, use the estimate $\hat{\rho}$ to construct the generalized differences, and then fit the model involving the generalized differences using ordinary least squares.[9]

The next example illustrates the nonlinear least squares approach using output from E-Views, a popular software package for econometric modeling.

Example 8.5
The Sears data are given in Table 8-5. Ordinary least squares is used to fit a simple linear regression model relating sales to disposable personal income. The E-Views output is shown in Figure 8-7. From Figure 8-7, the fitted regression equation is

$$\hat{Y}_t = -524.33 + 14.05X_t$$

where

$$b_1 = 14.04$$
$$s_{b_1} = .319$$
$$t = b_1/s_{b_1} = 44.11$$
$$r^2 = .99$$
$$DW = .63$$

[9] A discussion of techniques for estimating ρ and accounting for serial correlation is available in Pindyck and Rubinfeld (1998).

```
┌─────────────────────────────────────────────────────────────────┐
│ ▣ Equation: LSARVAR  Workfile: SEARS DATA HW       _ □ X          │
├─────────────────────────────────────────────────────────────────┤
│ View│Procs│Objects│  Print│Name│Freeze│  Estimate│Forecast│Stats│Resids│ │
├─────────────────────────────────────────────────────────────────┤
│ Dependent Variable: SALES                                      ▲  │
│ Method: Least Squares                                             │
│ Date: 07/08/02   Time: 13:38                                      │
│ Sample(adjusted): 1977 1996                                       │
│ Included observations: 20 after adjusting endpoints               │
│ Convergence achieved after 151 iterations                         │
├─────────────────────────────────────────────────────────────────┤
│   Variable      Coefficient   Std. Error    t-Statistic    Prob.  │
├─────────────────────────────────────────────────────────────────┤
│      C          54483.00      3344949.      0.016288      0.9872   │
│   INCOME        9.262387      7.240644      1.279221      0.2180   │
│    AR(1)        0.997245      0.170084      5.863238      0.0000   │
├─────────────────────────────────────────────────────────────────┤
│ R-squared            0.995227   Mean dependent var    7292.250    │
│ Adjusted R-squared   0.994666   S.D. dependent var    3377.322    │
│ S.E. of regression   246.6659   Akaike info criterion 13.99143    │
│ Sum squared resid    1034349.   Schwarz criterion     14.14079    │
│ Log likelihood       -136.9143  F-statistic           1772.444    │
│ Durbin-Watson stat   1.121974   Prob(F-statistic)     0.000000  ▼ │
└─────────────────────────────────────────────────────────────────┘
```

FIGURE 8-8   E-Views Output for the Regression of Generalized Differences of Sears Sales on Generalized Differences of Disposable Income for Example 8.5

The *DW* statistic is close to zero, indicating a positive autocorrelation.[10] At this point, we allow for serial correlated [AR(1)] errors and fit the model involving the generalized differences

$$Y'_t = \beta_0(1 - \rho) + \beta_1 X'_t + v_t$$

with $Y'_t = Y_t - \rho Y_{t-1}$ and $X'_t = X_t - \rho X_{t-1}$. E-Views is used to estimate the parameters in this model directly. The E-Views output is shown in Figure 8-8.

The fitted regression function is

$$\hat{Y}'_t = 54{,}483(1 - .997) + 9.26X'_t$$

where

$$\hat{\rho} = .997$$
$$\hat{Y}'_t = Y_t - .997Y_{t-1}, \quad X'_t = X_t - .997X_{t-1}$$
$$b_0 = 54{,}483, \quad b_1 = 9.26$$
$$s_{b_1} = 7.241$$
$$t = b_1/s_{b_1} = 1.28$$
$$DW = 1.12$$

The value of the Durbin-Watson statistic, 1.12, is in the "inconclusive" region at the .01 level. Note that the estimates of the slope coefficient in the two regressions are similar

---

[10] For $n = 21$, $k = 1$, and $\alpha = .01$, $d_L = .97$. Since $DW = .63 < d_L = .97$, we reject H_0: $\rho = 0$ in favor of H_1: $\rho > 0$.

(14.05 and 9.26). However, the standard error associated with b_1 in the second regression is considerably larger than the corresponding standard error in the first regression (7.241 versus .319). Thus the t statistic for testing the significance of the slope coefficient in the second regression is much smaller than it is in the first regression (1.28 versus 44.11). In fact, the p-value associated with the t statistic in the second regression is .218, indicating the slope coefficient is not significantly different from zero. The strong serial correlation has little effect on the estimate of the slope coefficient in the relation between Y and X. However, the strong (positive) serial correlation does result in severe underestimation of the standard error of the estimated slope coefficient. Indeed, one reason for adjusting for serial correlation is to avoid making mistakes of inference because of t values that are too large.

Finally, $\hat{\rho} = .997$ is very close to 1, which suggests that the relationship between Y and X might be represented by a simple linear regression model in the differences $Y'_t = Y_t - Y_{t-1}$ and $X'_t = X_t - X_{t-1}$. This issue is explored in Problem 8.17.

Autoregressive Models

Autocorrelation implies that values of the dependent variable in one time period are linearly related to values of the dependent variable in another time period. Thus one way to solve the problem of serial correlation is to model the association in different time periods directly, which can be done in a regression framework by using the dependent variable lagged one or more time periods as the predictor or independent variables. Regression models formulated in this way are called *autoregressive models*. The first-order autoregressive model is written

$$Y_t = \beta_0 + \beta_1 Y_{t-1} + \varepsilon_t \qquad \textbf{(8.10)}$$

where the errors ε_t are assumed to have the usual regression model properties. After this model has been fit to the data by least squares, the forecasting equation becomes

$$\hat{Y}_t = b_0 + b_1 Y_{t-1} \qquad \textbf{(8.11)}$$

> An *autoregressive model* expresses a forecast as a function of previous values of the time series.

Autoregressive models are a subset of the autoregressive integrated moving average (ARIMA) models discussed in more detail in Chapter 9.

Example 8.6

The Novak Corporation sales data introduced in Example 8.3 and shown in Table 8-2 (see p. 336) will be used to demonstrate the development of an autoregressive model. Note that after sales were lagged as shown in Table 8-2, one year of data is lost because Novak sales for 1979 are not known. The sample size is $n = 16$ instead of $n = 17$. A first-order autoregressive model is developed with Novak sales lagged one year (Y-lagged) as the predictor variable.

The Minitab output that results from fitting the autoregressive model to the Novak sales data is shown in Table 8-8. A forecast for 1997 sales and the 95% prediction interval is also shown in the table.

The forecast of Novak sales for 1997 is \$31.722 million. This figure is computed, within rounding error, as follows:

$$\hat{Y} = b_0 + b_1 Y_{t-1} = -.109 + 1.094 Y_{t-1}$$
$$\hat{Y}_{18} = -.109 + 1.094 Y_{18-1} = -.109 + 1.094 Y_{17}$$
$$\hat{Y}_{18} = -.109 + 1.094(29.1) = 31.726$$

TABLE 8-8	Minitab Output for Novak Corporation Sales: Autoregressive Model Fit for Example 8.6

```
Regression Analysis: Sales versus Y-Lagged

The regression equation is
Sales = -0.109 + 1.09 Y-Lagged

Predictor       Coef   SE Coef       T      P
Constant     -0.1093    0.3367   -0.32  0.750
Y-Lagged      1.09388   0.02063   53.01  0.000

S = 0.4875   R-Sq = 99.5%   R-Sq(adj) = 99.5%

Analysis of Variance

Source           DF       SS       MS        F      P
Regression        1   667.73   667.73  2810.16  0.000
Residual Error   14     3.33     0.24
Total            15   671.05

Predicted Values for New Observations

New Obs     Fit   SE Fit      95% CI             95% PI
1        31.722    0.311  (31.055,32.390)   (30.482,32.963)
```

The Durbin-Watson test cannot be used in this example. When a lagged dependent variable is included in the regression as a predictor variable, the Durbin-Watson statistic is biased toward 2. Instead, a test for serial correlation can be based on the Durbin-Watson h statistic.[11]

The intercept coefficient in this regression is small and not significantly different from zero. Rerunning the regression without an intercept term leaves the estimate of the slope coefficient, and subsequent forecasts, essentially unchanged.

When regression analysis is applied to time series data, the residuals are frequently autocorrelated. The term *serial correlation* is sometimes used to refer to this situation. Regression analysis assumes that the errors are independent, which can cause problems. The R^2 for a regression with data containing serial correlation can be artificially high; furthermore, the standard errors of the regression coefficients can be seriously underestimated and the corresponding t statistics inflated.

One cause of autocorrelated residuals is the omission of one or more key predictor variables. This omission usually means that an important part of the dependent variable variation has not been adequately explained. One solution to this problem is to search for the missing variable(s) to include in the model. Other solutions are to consider regression models with differenced data, or autoregressive models.

TIME SERIES DATA AND THE PROBLEM OF HETEROSCEDASTICITY

The variability in some time series tends to increase with the level of the series. The Cavanaugh Company sales time series shown in Figure 5-1 and discussed in Example 5.2 is one example. Variability can increase if a variable is growing at a

---

[11] The h test for serial correlation is described in Pindyck and Rubinfeld (1998).

constant rate rather than a constant amount over time. Non-constant variability is called *heteroscedasticity*.

In a regression framework, heteroscedasticity occurs if the variance of the error term, ε, is not constant. If the variability for recent time periods is larger than it was for past time periods, the standard error of the estimate, $s_{y \cdot x'}$s, underestimates the current standard deviation of the error term. If the standard deviation of the estimate is then used to set forecast limits for future observations, these limits can be too narrow for the stated confidence level.

Sometimes the problem of heteroscedasticity can be solved by simple transformations of the data. For example, in the case of two variables, the log linear model shown in Equation 8.8 might be used to reduce the heteroscedasticity. Also, if the variables are expressed as dollar amounts, converting current dollars to constant dollars (see the discussion of price deflation in Chapter 5) may overcome the problem of increasing error variability.

Example 8.7

Consider again the Reynolds Metals sales data introduced in Example 8.2 and shown in Table 8-1. (See p. 333.) The result of a simple linear regression of sales on disposable personal income is given in Figure 8-5. A time sequence plot of the residuals from this regression is pictured in Figure 8-9.

In addition to the positive autocorrelation in the residuals (string of negative residuals followed by string of positive residuals; see the discussion in Example 8.2), it is clear from Figure 8-9 that the size of the residuals is increasing over time. One approach to this problem is to try a log linear model (Equation 8.8) for the Reynolds Metals data.

The results of a log linear model fit are given in Figure 8-10. Comparing Figure 8-10 with Figure 8-5, it can be seen that the residuals (deviations from the fitted line) for the log linear regression are more uniform in size throughout the time period under study, but the fitted

FIGURE 8-9   Time Sequence Plot of Residuals from Regression of Sales on Disposable Income: Reynolds Metals Data

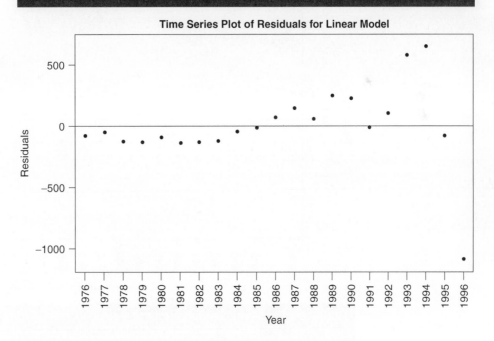

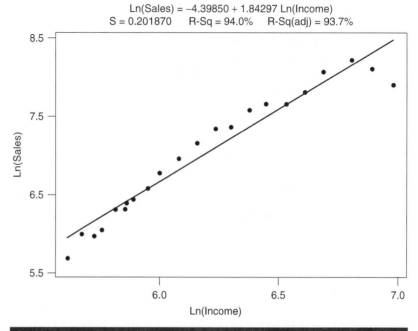

Regression Plot

Ln(Sales) = −4.39850 + 1.84297 Ln(Income)
S = 0.201870   R-Sq = 94.0%   R-Sq(adj) = 93.7%

FIGURE 8-10   Regression Plot of Log Linear Model Fit to Reynolds Metals Data

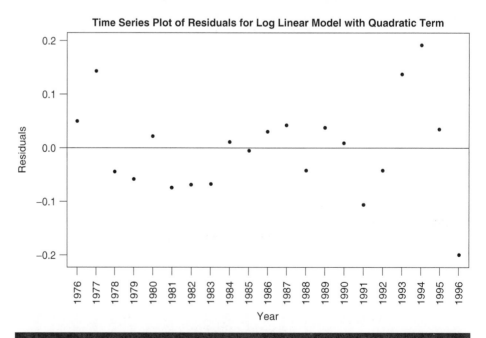

Time Series Plot of Residuals for Log Linear Model with Quadratic Term

FIGURE 8-11   Time Sequence Plot of Residuals from Fitting Log Linear Model with Quadratic Term to Reynolds Metal Data

straight line does not capture the curvature in the data. An additional predictor variable $X_2 = X_1^2 = (\text{Ln Income})^2$ was added and the model[12]

$$\text{Ln Sales} = \beta_0 + \beta_1 \text{Ln Income} + \beta_2 (\text{Ln Income})^2 + \varepsilon$$

fit to the data. A time sequence plot of the residuals from this regression is displayed in Figure 8-11.

The residuals in Figure 8-11 appear to be randomly distributed about zero with constant variability. It appears as if the final regression adequately represents the Reynolds Metals data. For this model there is no reason to doubt the error term assumptions.

USING REGRESSION TO FORECAST SEASONAL DATA

Decomposition models for time series with seasonal patterns were discussed in Chapter 5. A regression model for representing seasonal data that is closely aligned with an additive decomposition is given next. In this model the seasonality is handled by using *dummy variables* in the regression function.

A seasonal model for quarterly data with a time trend is

$$Y_t = \beta_0 + \beta_1 t + \beta_2 S_2 + \beta_3 S_3 + \beta_4 S_4 + \varepsilon_t \tag{8.12}$$

where

$$Y_t = \text{the variable to be forecast}$$
$$t = \text{the time index}$$
$$S_2 = \text{a dummy variable that is 1 for the second quarter of the year;}$$
$$\text{0 otherwise}$$
$$S_3 = \text{a dummy variable that is 1 for the third quarter of the year;}$$
$$\text{0 otherwise}$$
$$S_4 = \text{a dummy variable that is 1 for the fourth quarter of the year;}$$
$$\text{0 otherwise}$$
$$\varepsilon_t = \text{errors assumed to be independent and normally distributed}$$
$$\text{with mean zero and constant variance}$$
$$\beta_0, \beta_1, \beta_2, \beta_3, \beta_4 = \text{coefficients to be estimated}$$

Note that the four levels of the qualitative variable (quarter or season) are described with only three dummy variables. The final quarter (the first quarter in this case) is handled by the intercept term β_0. To see this, for first-quarter data $S_2 = S_3 = S_4 = 0$, and the expected level is

$$E(Y_t) = \beta_0 + \beta_1 t$$

For second-quarter data $S_2 = 1$, $S_3 = S_4 = 0$, and the expected level is

$$E(Y_t) = \beta_0 + \beta_1 t + \beta_2 = (\beta_0 + \beta_2) + \beta_1 t$$

Similar patterns emerge for the third and fourth quarters.

In model (8.12), different quarters give different intercept terms. The trend and seasonal pattern are modeled as a series of straight lines, one for each quarter. The four lines are postulated to have the same slope but different intercepts. The regression coefficients for the dummy variables represent changes in the intercept relative to

[12] A regression model with predictor variables $X, X^2, X^3, \ldots$ is called a *polynomial regression model*.

the intercept for the first-quarter β_0. If there is a seasonal pattern but no trend, Equation 8.12 applies with $\beta_1 = 0$.

Example 8.8

James Brown, forecaster for the Washington Water Power Company, is trying to forecast electrical usage for residential customers for the third and fourth quarters of 1996. He knows the data are seasonal and decides to use Equation 8.12 to develop a forecasting equation. He gathers quarterly data from 1980 through the second quarter of 1996. The data for electrical usage, measured in millions of kilowatt-hours, are given in Table 8-9.

James creates dummy variables, S_2, S_3, and S_4, representing the second, third, and fourth quarters, respectively. The data for the four quarters of 1980 are given in Table 8-10.

TABLE 8-9	Electrical Usage Data for Washington Water Power Company, 1980–1996, for Example 8.8

Year	Quarter	Kilowatt-Hours (millions)	Year	Quarter	Kilowatt-Hours (millions)
1980	1	1071	1989	1	1036
	2	648		2	612
	3	480		3	503
	4	746		4	710
1981	1	965	1990	1	952
	2	661		2	628
	3	501		3	534
	4	768		4	733
1982	1	1065	1991	1	1085
	2	667		2	692
	3	486		3	568
	4	780		4	783
1983	1	926	1992	1	928
	2	618		2	655
	3	483		3	590
	4	757		4	814
1984	1	1047	1993	1	1018
	2	667		2	670
	3	495		3	566
	4	794		4	811
1985	1	1068	1994	1	962
	2	625		2	647
	3	499		3	630
	4	850		4	803
1986	1	975	1995	1	1002
	2	623		2	887
	3	496		3	615
	4	728		4	828
1987	1	933	1996	1	1003
	2	582		2	706
	3	490			
	4	708			
1988	1	953			
	2	604			
	3	508			
	4	708			

Source: Washington Water Power Annual Report, various years.

TABLE 8-10	Data for Four Quarters of 1980 for Example 8.8		
Y_t	S_2	S_3	S_4
1071	0	0	0
648	1	0	0
480	0	1	0
746	0	0	1

TABLE 8-11   Computer Output for Washington Water Power, Example 8.8

```
The regression equation is
Hours = 968 + 0.938 Time - 342 2nd Qt. - 472 3rd Qt. - 230 4th Qt.

Predictor      Coef   SE Coef        T      P
Constant     968.39     16.88    57.38  0.000
Time         0.9383    0.3377     2.78  0.007
2nd Qt.     -341.94     17.92   -19.08  0.000
3rd Qt.     -471.60     18.20   -25.91  0.000
4th Qt.     -230.23     18.20   -12.65  0.000

S = 52.25     R-Sq = 92.4%      R-Sq(adj) = 91.9%

Analysis of Variance

Source          DF        SS       MS        F      P
Regression       4   2012975   503244   184.34  0.000
Residual Error  61    166526     2730
Total           65   2179502

Durbin-Watson statistic = 1.48

New Obs     Fit  SE Fit      95.0% CI            95.0% PI
1        559.65   17.39  (524.87, 594.43)  (449.54, 669.76)

Values of Predictors for New Observations
New Obs   Time   2nd Qt.   3rd Qt.   4th Qt.
1         67.0      0         1         0
```

The Minitab commands to run the seasonal analysis are shown in the "Minitab Applications" section at the end of the chapter.

The results are shown in Table 8-11.

The fitted seasonal regression model is

$$\hat{Y}_t = 968 + .938t - 342S_2 - 472S_3 - 230S_4$$

where $S_2 = $ 2ndQt., $S_3 = $ 3rdQt., and $S_4 = $ 4thQt. James notes that the model explains 92.4% of the variability in electrical usage for residential customers measured in kilowatt-hours. The forecast for the third quarter of 1996 is

Third quarter: Hours $= 968 + .938(67) - 342(0) - 472(1) - 230(0) = 559$

The forecast for the fourth quarter of 1996 is

Fourth quarter: Hours $= 968 + .938(68) - 342(0) - 472(0) - 230(1) = 802$

James sees that the forecasts for the different quarters will lie along four straight lines. The lines will all have the same slope (.938), but the intercepts will change depending on the quarter. The first-quarter forecasts will lie along a line with intercept 968. Second-quarter forecasts will lie along a line with intercept $968 - 342 = 626$. The intercept for third-quarter forecasts will be $968 - 472 = 496$, and the intercept for fourth-quarter forecasts will be $968 - 230 = 738$. James is pleased that the forecasting model captures the seasonal pattern and slight upward trend observed in the series. Within a given year, forecasts of electrical usage will be highest for the first quarter, lower for the second quarter, lowest for the third quarter, and second highest for the fourth quarter.

ECONOMETRIC FORECASTING

When regression analysis is applied to economic data, the predictions developed from such models are referred to as *economic forecasts*. However, because economic theory frequently suggests that the values taken by the quantities of interest are determined through the simultaneous interaction of different economic forces, it may be necessary to model this interaction with a set of simultaneous equations. This idea leads to the construction of *simultaneous equation econometric models*, which involve individual equations that look like regression equations. However, in a simultaneous system the individual equations are related, and the econometric model allows the *joint determination* of a *set of dependent variables* in terms of several independent variables. This contrasts with the usual regression situation in which a single equation determines the expected value of one dependent variable in terms of the independent variables.

A simultaneous equation econometric model determines jointly the values of a set of dependent variables, called *endogenous variables* by econometricians, in terms of the values of independent variables, called *exogenous variables*. The values of the exogenous variables are assumed to influence the endogenous variables but not the other way around. A complete simultaneous equation model will involve the same number of equations as endogenous variables.

Simultaneity in the econometric system creates some problems that require special statistical treatment. A full treatment of econometric models is beyond the scope of this book.[13] However, a two-equation model will illustrate some of the concepts.

Economic theory holds that, in equilibrium, the quantity supplied is equal to the quantity demanded at a particular price. That is, the quantity demanded, the quantity supplied, and price are determined simultaneously. In one study of the price elasticity of demand, the model was specified as

$$Q_t = \alpha_0 + \alpha_1 P_t + \alpha_2 I_t + \alpha_3 T_t + \varepsilon_t$$
$$P_t = \beta_0 + \beta_1 Q_t + \beta_2 L_t + v_t$$

where

Q_t = a measure of the demand (quantity sold)

P_t = a measure of price (deflated dollars)

I_t = a measure of income per capita

T_t = a measure of temperature

L_t = a measure of labor cost

ε_t, v_t = independent error terms that are not correlated with each other

Notice in this model that the price and quantity variables P_t and Q_t appear in both equations. In the first equation, quantity sold is partially determined by price and, in

---

[13] An introductory account of simultaneous equation econometric models is available in Pindyck and Rubinfeld (1998).

the second equation, price is partially determined by quantity sold. Price and quantity are endogenous variables the values of which are determined within the system. The remaining variables, income and temperature in the first equation and labor cost in the second equation, are exogenous variables, the values of which are determined outside the system. Given adequate estimates for the coefficients in the model (the identification problem), forecasts of, say, future demand (sales) can be generated. Of course, to estimate future demand, future values of the exogenous variables must be specified or estimated from outside the system. In addition, future values of the price variable must be determined.

Large-scale econometric models are being used today to model the behavior of specific firms within an industry, selected industries within the economy, and the total economy. Econometric models can include any number of simultaneous multiple regression-like equations. Econometric models are used to understand how the economy works and to generate forecasts of key economic variables. Econometric models are important aids in policy formulation.

APPLICATION TO MANAGEMENT

The applications described in Chapter 5 are also appropriate for this chapter. The techniques described in this chapter permit the analyst to detect and correct for the problem of serial correlation, and thus to develop better forecasting models. The net result is that management or economists can deal with a far greater variety of time-dependent data and feel confident that the predictions are sound. Areas in which these techniques are particularly helpful include the following:

Sales forecasting
Stock and bond price projections
Raw materials cost projections
New-product penetration projections
Personnel needs estimates
Advertising–sales relationship studies
Inventory control

Because these applications involve variables that evolve over time, the variables are likely to be autocorrelated. Forecasting models based on the techniques presented in this chapter should provide more reliable forecasts than some of the techniques considered earlier that ignore autocorrelation.

Glossary

Autocorrelation (serial correlation). Autocorrelation exists when successive observations over time are related to one another.

Autoregressive model. An autoregressive model expresses a forecast as a function of previous values of the time series.

Durbin-Watson test. A test used to determine whether autocorrelation is present.

Key Formulas

Simple linear regression model

$$Y_t = \beta_0 + \beta_1 X_t + \varepsilon_t \tag{8.1}$$

First-order serial correlation

$$\varepsilon_t = \rho \varepsilon_{t-1} + v_t \tag{8.2}$$

Durbin-Watson statistic

$$DW = \frac{\sum_{t=2}^{n} (e_t - e_{t-1})^2}{\sum_{t=1}^{n} e_t^2} \tag{8.3}$$

Relation of Durbin-Watson statistic to lag 1 residual autocorrelation (*n* large)

$$DW = 2(1 - r_1(e)) \tag{8.4}$$

Transformed simple linear regression model

$$Y_t' = \beta_0(1 - \rho) + \beta_1 X_t' + v_t \tag{8.5}$$

Generalized differences

$$Y_t' = Y_t - \rho Y_{t-1}$$
$$X_t' = X_t - \rho X_{t-1} \tag{8.6}$$

Simple or first differences

$$Y_t' = Y_t - Y_{t-1}$$
$$X_t' = X_t - X_{t-1} \tag{8.7}$$

Log linear regression model

$$\text{Ln } Y_t = \beta_0 + \beta_1 \text{Ln } X_t + \varepsilon_t \tag{8.8}$$

Forecasting equation for the differenced form of log linear regression model

$$\text{Ln } \hat{Y}_t' = \text{Ln } \hat{Y}_{t-1}' + b_1(\text{Ln } X_t - \text{Ln } X_{t-1}) \tag{8.9}$$

First-order autoregressive model

$$Y_t = \beta_0 + \beta_1 Y_{t-1} + \varepsilon_t \tag{8.10}$$

Forecasting equation for first-order autoregressive model

$$\hat{Y}_t = b_0 + b_1 Y_{t-1} \tag{8.11}$$

Seasonal model with dummy variables for quarterly data

$$Y_t = \beta_0 + \beta_1 t + \beta_2 S_2 + \beta_3 S_3 + \beta_4 S_4 + \varepsilon_t \tag{8.12}$$

Standardized coefficients (see Case 8-2)

$$B = b\left(\frac{s_x}{s_y}\right) \tag{8.13}$$

Problems

1. Why is serial correlation a problem when time series data are analyzed?

2. What is a major cause of serial correlation?

3. Which underlying regression assumption is violated most frequently when time series variables are analyzed?

4. Which statistic is commonly used to detect serial correlation?

5. You test for serial correlation at the .01 level with 32 residuals from a regression with two independent variables. If the calculated Durbin-Watson statistic is equal to 1.0, what is your conclusion?

6. You test for serial correlation at the .05 level with 61 residuals from a regression with one independent variable. If the calculated Durbin-Watson statistic is equal to 1.6, what is your conclusion?

7. Suggest ways to solve the problem of serial correlation.

8. How does an autoregressive model work?

9. Tamson Russell, an economist working for the government, is trying to determine the demand function for passenger car motor fuel in the United States. Tamson developed a model that used the actual price of a gallon of regular gasoline to predict motor fuel consumed per year. She was able to explain 83.5% of the variation in fuel consumption with her model. Tamson has decided to add a variable representing the population of the United States to the model. Determine whether serial correlation is a problem. The data are shown in Table P-9.

10. Decision Science Associates has been asked to do a feasibility study for a proposed destination resort to be located within half a mile of the Grand Coulee Dam. Mark Craze is not happy with the regression model that used the price of a regular gallon of gasoline to predict the number of visitors to the Grand Coulee Dam Visitors Center. After plotting the data on a scatter diagram, Mark decides to use a dummy variable to represent significant celebrations in the general area. Mark uses a 1 to represent a celebration and a 0 to represent no celebration. Note that the 1 in 1974 represents the Expo '74 World's Fair celebrated in Spokane, Washington, the 1 in 1983 represents the celebration of the fiftieth anniversary of the construction of Grand Coulee Dam, and the 1 in 1986 represents the World's Fair held in Vancouver, Canada. Mark also decides to use time as a predictor variable. The data are shown in Table P-10. Write a report for Mark to present to his boss. Indicate whether serial correlation is a problem. Also indicate what additional information would be important in deciding whether to recommend that the destination resort be built.

11. Jim Jackson, a rate analyst for the Washington Water Power Company, is preparing for a rate case and needs to forecast electric residential revenue for 1996. Jim decides to investigate three potential predictor variables: residential use per kilowatt-hour (kWh), residential charge per kWh (cents/kWh), and number of residential electric customers. He collects data from 1968 to 1995. The data are

TABLE P-9

Year	Motor Fuel Consumed by Cars (billions of gallons) Y	Price of Gasoline X_1	U.S. Population (millions) X_2
1973	78.8	.39	211.9
1974	75.1	.53	213.9
1975	76.4	.57	216.0
1976	79.7	.59	218.0
1977	80.4	.62	220.2
1978	81.7	.63	222.6
1979	77.1	.86	225.1
1980	71.9	1.19	227.7
1981	71.0	1.33	230.1
1982	70.1	1.26	232.5
1983	69.9	1.22	234.8
1984	68.7	1.21	236.3
1985	69.3	1.16	238.5
1986	71.4	.92	240.7
1987	70.6	.95	242.8
1988	71.7	.95	245.1

Source: Statistical Abstract of the United States, various years.

TABLE P-10

Year	Number of Visitors Y	Time X_1	Price of Gasoline X_2	Celebration X_3
1973	268,528	1	.39	0
1974	468,136	2	.53	1
1975	390,129	3	.57	0
1976	300,140	4	.59	0
1977	271,140	5	.62	0
1978	282,752	6	.63	0
1979	244,006	7	.86	0
1980	161,524	8	1.19	0
1981	277,134	9	1.31	0
1982	382,343	10	1.22	0
1983	617,737	11	1.16	1
1984	453,881	12	1.13	0
1985	471,417	13	.86	0
1986	654,147	14	.90	1

Source: Grand Coulee Dam Visitors Center and *Statistical Abstract of the United States*, 1988.

shown in Table P-11. Jim testified before the Idaho Rate Commission and was asked if serial correlation was a problem. He didn't know the answer and has asked you to write a response to the commission's question.

12. Paul Raymond, president of Washington Water Power, is worried about the possibility of a takeover attempt and the fact that the number of common shareholders has been decreasing since 1983. He instructs you to study the number of common

TABLE P-11

Year	Revenue (millions) Y	Use per kWh X₁	Charge (cents/kWh) X₂	Number of Customers X₃
1968	19.3	10,413	1.33	139,881
1969	20.4	11,129	1.29	142,806
1970	20.9	11,361	1.25	146,616
1971	21.9	11,960	1.21	151,640
1972	23.4	12,498	1.19	157,205
1973	24.5	12,667	1.19	162,328
1974	25.8	12,857	1.21	166,558
1975	30.5	13,843	1.29	170,317
1976	33.3	14,223	1.33	175,536
1977	37.2	14,427	1.42	181,553
1978	42.5	14,878	1.52	188,325
1979	48.8	15,763	1.59	194,237
1980	55.4	15,130	1.84	198,847
1981	64.3	14,697	2.17	201,465
1982	78.9	15,221	2.55	203,444
1983	86.5	14,166	2.97	205,533
1984	114.6	14,854	3.70	208,574
1985	129.7	14,997	4.10	210,811
1986	126.1	13,674	4.34	212,865
1987	132.0	13,062	4.71	214,479
1988	138.1	13,284	4.82	215,610
1989	141.2	13,531	4.81	217,164
1990	143.7	13,589	4.81	219,968
1991	149.2	13,800	4.84	223,364
1992	146.1	13,287	4.83	227,575
1993	153.9	13,406	4.91	233,795
1994	146.9	12,661	4.84	239,733
1995	156.8	12,434	4.98	253,364

Source: "Financial and Operating Supplement," Washington Water Power Annual Report, various years.

shareholders since 1968 and forecast for 1996. You decide to investigate three potential predictor variables: earnings per share (common), dividends per share (common), and payout ratio. You collect the data from 1968 to 1995 as shown in Table P-12.

a. Run these data on the computer and find the best prediction model.

b. Is serial correlation a problem in this model?

c. If serial correlation is a problem, write a memo to Paul that discusses various solutions to the autocorrelation problem and includes your final recommendation.

13. Thompson Airlines has determined that 5% of the total number of U.S. domestic airline passengers fly on Thompson planes. You are given the task of forecasting the number of passengers who will fly on Thompson Airlines in 2004. The data are presented in Table P-13.

a. Develop a time series regression model, using time as the independent variable and the number of passengers as the dependent variable.

b. Are the error terms for this model dispersed in a random manner?

TABLE P-12

Year	Common Shareholders Y	Earnings per Share X_1	Dividends per Share X_2	Payout Ratio X_3
1968	26,472	1.68	1.21	72
1969	28,770	1.70	1.28	73
1970	29,681	1.80	1.32	73
1971	30,481	1.86	1.36	72
1972	30,111	1.96	1.39	71
1973	31,052	2.02	1.44	71
1974	30,845	2.11	1.49	71
1975	32,012	2.42	1.53	63
1976	32,846	2.79	1.65	55
1977	32,909	2.38	1.76	74
1978	34,593	2.95	1.94	61
1979	34,359	2.78	2.08	75
1980	36,161	2.33	2.16	93
1981	38,892	3.29	2.28	69
1982	46,278	3.17	2.40	76
1983	47,672	3.02	2.48	82
1984	45,462	2.46	2.48	101
1985	45,599	3.03	2.48	82
1986	41,368	2.06	2.48	120
1987	38,686	2.31	2.48	107
1988	37,072	2.54	2.48	98
1989	36,968	2.70	2.48	92
1990	34,348	3.46	2.48	72
1991	34,058	2.68	2.48	93
1992	34,375	2.74	2.48	91
1993	33,968	2.88	2.48	86
1994	34,120	2.56	2.48	97
1995	33,138	2.82	2.48	88

Source: "Financial and Operating Supplement," Washington Water Power Annual Report, various years.

c. Transform the number-of-passengers variable so that the error terms will be randomly dispersed.
d. Run a computer program for the transformed model developed in part c.
e. Are the error terms independent for the model run in part d?
f. If the error terms are dependent, what problems are involved with using this model?
g. Forecast the number of Thompson Airlines passengers for 2004.

14. Thomas Furniture Company concludes that production scheduling can be improved by developing an accurate method of predicting quarterly sales. The company analyst, Mr. Estes, decides to investigate the relationship between housing construction permits and furniture sales in the Springfield area. Estes feels that permits will lead sales by one or two quarters. In addition, he wonders if seasons affect furniture sales. Estes decides to consider another independent variable:

$$X_2 = \begin{cases} 0 \text{ if first- or second-quarter sales} \\ 1 \text{ if third- or fourth-quarter sales} \end{cases}$$

TABLE P-13

Year	Number of Passengers (thousands)	Year	Number of Passengers (thousands)	Year	Number of Passengers (thousands)	Year	Number of Passengers (thousands)
1979	22.8	1986	45.4	1993	79.9	2000	144.8
1980	26.1	1987	46.3	1994	96.3	2001	147.9
1981	29.4	1988	45.8	1995	109.0	2002	150.1
1982	34.5	1989	48.0	1996	116.0	2003	151.9
1983	37.6	1990	54.6	1997	117.2		
1984	40.3	1991	61.9	1998	124.9		
1985	39.5	1992	69.9	1999	136.6		

TABLE P-14

Year	Quarter	Sales (thousands) Y	Permits X_1	Year	Quarter	Sales (thousands) Y	Permits X_1
1999	3		19	2002	1	120	72
	4		3		2	150	31
2000	1	120	35		3	660	19
	2	80	11		4	270	14
	3	400	11	2003	1	200	75
	4	200	16		2	280	41
2001	1	75	32		3	800	17
	2	120	10		4	320	10
	3	270	12	2004			
	4	155	21				

The data are given in Table P-14.
a. Develop a regression model that uses housing construction permits as the predictor variable.
b. Test for autocorrelation in this model.
c. Develop a regression model that uses both permits and the seasonal dummy as predictor variables.
d. Is there a significant seasonal pattern in these data? (Test at the .05 level.)
e. Is there an autocorrelation problem with the multiple regression model developed in part c? If so, how might it be corrected?
f. Using the model from part c, forecast Thomas Furniture Company sales for the four quarters of 2004.

15. National Presto is a manufacturer of small electrical appliances, including pressure cookers, heaters, canners, fry pans, griddles, roaster ovens, deep fryers, corn poppers, can openers, coffee makers, slicers, hand mixers, and portable ranges. Its quarterly sales dollars in millions are shown in Table P-15. Presto has mainly a Christmas business, so there is a strong seasonal effect. Develop a multiple regression model using dummy variables to forecast sales for the third and fourth quarters of 1996. Write a report summarizing your results.

16. The data in Table P-16 show seasonally adjusted quarterly sales for Dickson Corporation and for the entire industry for 20 quarters.
a. Fit a linear regression model, obtain the residuals, and plot the residuals against time. What do you find?

TABLE P-15

			Quarter	
Year	1	2	3	4
1985	16.3	17.7	28.1	34.3
1986	17.3	16.7	32.2	42.3
1987	17.4	16.9	30.9	36.5
1988	17.5	16.5	28.6	45.5
1989	24.3	24.2	33.8	45.2
1990	20.6	18.7	28.1	59.6
1991	19.5	22.5	38.3	81.2
1992	24.9	17.5	26.8	59.1
1993	22.4	14.3	24.7	57.2
1994	16.2	16.5	35.5	59.8
1995	18.0	15.9	28.0	57.3
1996	17.1	17.0		

Source: The Value Line Investment Survey (New York: Value Line, 1996), p. 132.

TABLE P-16

Year	Quarter	Dickson Sales (thousands) Y	Industry Sales (millions) X_1	Year	Quarter	Dickson Sales (thousands) Y	Industry Sales (millions) X_1
1998	1	83.8	31.8	2000	3	98.2	37.1
	2	85.6	32.5		4	97.2	36.6
	3	87.8	33.2	2001	1	100.1	37.6
	4	86.1	32.4		2	102.6	38.3
1999	1	89.6	33.8		3	105.4	39.3
	2	91.0	34.3		4	107.9	40.2
	3	93.9	35.3	2002	1	110.1	41.1
	4	94.6	35.7		2	111.1	41.4
2000	1	96.4	36.4		3	110.1	41.1
	2	96.0	36.3		4	111.1	41.4

b. Calculate the Durbin-Watson statistic and determine whether autocorrelation exists.

c. Estimate the regression coefficient β_1 using generalized differences. (Estimate ρ with the lag 1 residual autocorrelation coefficient.)

d. Compare the standard errors of the two estimates of β_1 obtained using the original data and the generalized differences. Which estimate is more accurate? Explain.

17. Refer to Example 8.5. Using the Sears data in Table 8-5, convert the sales and disposable income values to simple differences. That is, create the numbers $Y'_t = Y_t - Y_{t-1}$ and $X'_t = X_t - X_{t-1}$. Fit a simple linear regression model to the differenced data. Compare your results to the results obtained by the method of generalized differences in Example 8.5. Did you expect them to be much different? Explain.

TABLE P-18

Year	Personal Savings Y	Personal Income X	Year	Personal Savings Y	Personal Income X	Year	Personal Savings Y	Personal Income X
1935	2	60	1942	28	123	1949	9	207
1936	4	69	1943	33	151	1950	13	279
1937	4	74	1944	37	165	1951	18	257
1938	1	68	1945	30	171	1952	19	273
1939	3	73	1946	15	179	1953	20	288
1940	4	78	1947	7	191	1954	19	290
1941	11	96	1948	13	210			

18. A study is done in an attempt to relate personal savings to personal income (in billions of dollars) for the time period from 1935 to 1954. The data are given in Table P-18.

   a. Fit a simple linear regression model to the data in Table P-18 using personal income to predict personal savings. Specifically: (1) Test for the significance of the regression slope coefficient at the $\alpha = .01$ level; (2) test for the significance of the regression using the F test (at $\alpha = .01$); (3) calculate r^2 and interpret this quantity; and (4) test for autocorrelation (at $\alpha = .05$). Should you modify your conclusions in parts 1 and 2? How can the model be improved?

   b. Construct a dummy variable X_2 for the war years. Let $X_2 = 0$ for peacetime and $X_2 = 1$ for wartime. The war years are from 1941 to 1945. Fit a multiple linear regression model using personal income and the war years dummy variable as predictor variables for personal savings. Evaluate the results. Specifically: (1) Test to determine whether knowledge of the war years makes a significant contribution to the prediction of personal savings beyond that provided by personal income (set $\alpha = .01$); and (2) test for autocorrelation. Is the multiple regression model better than the simple linear regression model of part a? Discuss.

19. Circuit City Inc. is a retailer of video and audio equipment and other consumer electronics and office products. Recently, sales have been weak, declining by a total of 5% in December. Among the reasons were a fiercely competitive retailing environment among consumer-electronics sellers, price deflation in many products, a slump in store traffic, and sluggish demand for most computer hardware items. Jim Lowe has the task of forecasting sales for fiscal year 2003. Jim has access to estimates provided by *The Value Line Investment Survey* (see Table P-19); however, he is afraid that they are optimistic.

   a. Which forecasting models should Jim investigate?

   b. Would an autoregressive model be appropriate?

   c. How would Jim determine whether serial correlation is a problem for an autoregressive model?

   d. Develop an autoregressive model for Jim.

   e. How do the estimates for 2003 for this model compare with Value Line's?

   f. Can you tell whether serial correlation is a problem in this model?

TABLE P-19

Fiscal Year	May 31	Aug 31	Nov 30	Feb 28
1996	1742	1806	1999	2897[b]
1997	1851	1948	2039	3156
1998	2078	2369	2222	3289
1999	2205	2423	2495	3476
2000	2449	2566	2336	3177
2001	1882	2037	2280	3391
2002	2118	2221	2422	3239
2003	**2150**[a]	**2350**[a]	**2600**[a]	**3400**[a]

[a]Value Line estimates 2003.
[b]Fiscal year ends last day of February of following calendar year.

Source: The Value Line Investment Survey (New York: Value Line, 2002), p. 1725.

CASES

CASE 8-1   COMPANY OF YOUR CHOICE

A company's health can be examined every month, quarter, and/or year with measurements on an array of variables. For any one of these variables, there may be several other variables that can provide insights into its behavior and that can be used as predictor variables in a forecasting equation.

The purpose of this case is to simulate the identification of an important time series variable for a company of your choice and then to analyze the patterns in the data using autocorrelation analysis. In addition, you can use an appropriate computer program to develop an equation that can be used to forecast future values of your time series variable.

Assignment

1. Identify a company or organization that interests you. The company can be a local or national company that has published records, including the measurement of time series variables. Identify a key variable for your chosen company and record its values for several years, quarters, or months.

2. Either by hand or with a computer (see the CB Predictor application in Chapter 9), calculate several autocorrelation coefficients and plot the autocorrelation function.

3. Based on the pattern of the autocorrelation function, describe the patterns in your time series.

4. Compute the first differences for your data and construct the autocorrelation function for the differenced data. Describe the resulting patterns in the time series of first differences.

5. Identify several potential predictor variables for your dependent variable. You may use company records and other data sources in this process.

6. Develop a forecasting equation for your dependent variable using one or more of the identified predictor variables.

7. Examine the residuals from your fitted model. In particular, check for autocorrelation. Once you are satisfied with your forecasting equation, generate forecasts for the next six time periods. If possible, compare your forecasts with the actual values. ■

CASE 8-2 BUSINESS ACTIVITY INDEX FOR SPOKANE COUNTY

Prior to 1973 Spokane County, Washington, had no up-to-date measurement of general business activity. What happens in this area as a whole, however, affects every local business, government agency, and individual. Plans and policies made by an economic unit would be incomplete without some reliable knowledge about the recent performance of the economy of which the unit is a component part. A Spokane business activity index should serve as a vital input in the formulation of strategies and decisions in private as well as in public organizations.

A business activity index is an indicator of the relative changes in overall business conditions within a specified region. At the national level, the Gross National Product (measured by the U.S. Department of Commerce) and the Industrial Production Index (by the Federal Reserve Board) are generally considered excellent indicators. Each of these series is based on thousands of pieces of information, the collecting, editing, and computing of which are costly and time-consuming undertakings. For a local area such as Spokane County, Washington, a simplified version, capable of providing reasonably accurate and current information at moderate cost, is very desirable.

Multiple regression can be used to construct a business activity index. There are three essential questions with which the construction of such an index must deal:

- What are the components of the index?
- Do these components adequately represent the changes in overall business conditions?
- What weight should be assigned to each of the chosen components?

Answers to these questions can be obtained through regression analysis.

Dr. Shik Chun Young, professor of economics at Eastern Washington University, is attempting to develop a business activity index for Spokane County. Young selects personal income as the dependent variable. At the county level, personal income is judged as the best available indicator of local business conditions. Personal income measures the total income received by households before personal taxes are paid. Because productive activities are typically remunerated by monetary means, personal income may indeed be viewed as a reasonable proxy for the general economic performance. Why, then, is it necessary to construct another index if personal income can serve as a good business activity indicator? Unfortunately, personal income data at the county level are estimated by the U.S. Department of Commerce on an annual basis and are released 16 months too late. Consequently, these data are of little use for short-term planning. Young's task is to establish an up-to-date business activity index.

The independent variables are drawn from those local data that are readily available on a monthly basis. Currently, about 50 series of such monthly data are available, ranging from employment, bank activities, and real estate transactions to electrical consumption. If each series were to be included in the regression analysis, the effort would yield low productivity because only a handful of these series would be statistically significant. Therefore, some knowledge of the relationship between personal income and the available data is necessary in order to determine which independent variables are to be included in the regression equation. From Young's knowledge of the Spokane economy, the following 10 series are selected:

X_1, total employment
X_2, manufacturing employment
X_3, construction employment
X_4, wholesale and retail trade employment
X_5, service employment
X_6, bank debits
X_7, bank demand deposits
X_8, building permits issued
X_9, real estate mortgages
X_{10}, total electrical consumption

The first step in the analysis is to fit the model

$$E(Y) = \beta_0 + \beta_1 X_1 + \beta_2 X_2 + \cdots + \beta_{10} X_{10}$$

where

$$Y = \text{personal income}$$
$$\beta_0 = Y \text{ intercept}$$
$$\beta_1, \beta_2, \ldots, \beta_{10} = \text{coefficients of the respective independent variables}$$

When the preceding model is fit to the data, the adjusted $\bar{R}^2$ is .96, which means that the 10 variables used together explain 96% of the variability in the dependent variable, personal income. However, other regression statistics indicate problems. First, of these 10 independent variables only three have a computed t value significant at the .05 level, namely, total employment, service employment, and total bank debits. Second, the correlation matrix shows a high degree of interdependence among several of the independent variables—multicollinearity.[14] For example, the total employment and bank debits have a correlation coefficient of .88; total electricity consumption and the bank demand deposits, .76; and building permits issued and real estate mortgages, .68. Third, a test for autocorrelation using the Durbin-Watson statistic of .91 indicates that successive values of the dependent variable are positively correlated. Of course, autocorrelation is rather common in time series data; in general, observations in the same series tend to be related to one another.

Because one of the basic assumptions in regression analysis is that the observations of the dependent variable are random, Young chooses to deal with the autocorrelation problem first. He decides to calculate first differences, or changes, in an attempt to minimize the interdependence among the observations in each of the time series. The 10 independent variables are now measured by the difference between the periods rather than by the absolute value for each period. To allow the sets of data to be distinguished, a new designation for the independent variables is used:

ΔX_1, change in total employment

ΔX_2, change in manufacturing employment

ΔX_3, change in construction employment

ΔX_4, change in wholesale and retail trade employment

ΔX_5, change in service employment

ΔX_6, change in bank debits

ΔX_7, change in demand deposits

ΔX_8, change in building permits issued

ΔX_9, change in real estate mortgages

ΔX_{10}, change in total electrical consumption

The regression model becomes

$$E(\Delta Y) = \beta_0 + \beta_1 \Delta X_1 + \beta_2 \Delta X_2 + \cdots + \beta_{10} \Delta X_{10}$$

where

$$\Delta Y = \text{change in personal income}$$
$$\beta_0 = \Delta Y \text{ intercept}$$
$$\beta_1, \beta_2, \ldots, \beta_{10} = \text{coefficients of the respective independent variables}$$

A regression run using this model, based on the first-difference data, produces a Durbin-Watson statistic of 1.71. It indicates that no serious autocorrelation remains.

The next step is to determine which of the 10 variables are significant predictors of the dependent variable. The dependent variable ΔY is regressed against several possible combinations of the 10 potential predictors in order to select the best equation. The criteria used in the selection are:

- A satisfactorily high adjusted $\bar{R}^2$
- Low correlation coefficients among the independent variables
- Significant (at the .05 level) coefficients for each of the independent variables

After careful scrutiny of the regression results, Young finds that the equation containing ΔX_4, ΔX_5, and ΔX_{10} as independent variables best meets the foregoing criteria.

However, Young reasons that (in addition to commercial and industrial uses) total electrical consumption includes residential consumption, which should not have a significant relation to business activity in the near term. To test this hypothesis, Young subdivides the total electrical consumption into four variables:

---

[14]Some care must be exercised in interpreting a correlation between two time series variables because autocorrelation in the individual series can produce spurious correlation; see Example 8.1.

TABLE 8-12	Young's Regression Variables	
Equation	*Independent Variables*	*Dependent Variable*
A	$\Delta X_4, \Delta X_5, \Delta X_{11}$	ΔY
B	$\Delta X_4, \Delta X_5, \Delta X_{12}$	ΔY
C	$\Delta X_4, \Delta X_5, \Delta X_{13}$	ΔY
D	$\Delta X_4, \Delta X_5, \Delta X_{14}$	ΔY

ΔX_{11}, change in residential electricity use

ΔX_{12}, change in commercial electricity use

ΔX_{13}, change in industrial electricity use

ΔX_{14}, change in commercial and industrial electricity use

All four variables, combined with ΔX_4 and ΔX_5, are used to produce the four new regression equations (see Table 8-12).

Statistical analysis indicates that Equation D in Table 8-12 is the best. Compared with the previous equation that contains ΔX_4, ΔX_5, and ΔX_{10} as independent variables, Equation A is the only one that shows a deterioration in statistical significance. This result confirms Young's notion that commercial and industrial electricity uses are better predictors of personal income than total electrical consumption, which includes residential electricity use.

Therefore, Equation D is selected as the final regression equation, and the results are

$$\Delta \hat{Y} = -1.86 + 17.10\Delta X_4 + 23.01\Delta X_5 + .007\Delta X_{14}$$
$$\quad\quad\quad\quad (4.07) \quad\quad\quad (5.61) \quad\quad\quad (.002)$$

$$n = 15 \quad\quad\quad F = 26.26$$
$$DW = 1.77 \quad\quad \bar{R}^2 = .835$$

The figures in parentheses below the regression coefficients are the standard errors of the estimated coefficients. The t values of the coefficients are 4.20, 4.10, and 3.50 for ΔX_4, ΔX_5, and ΔX_{14}, respectively. The $\bar{R}^2$ indicates that nearly 84% of the variance in change in personal income is explained by the three independent variables. The Durbin-Watson (DW) statistic shows that autocorrelation is not a problem. In addition, the correlation coefficient matrix of Table 8-13 demonstrates a low

TABLE 8-13	Correlation Coefficient Matrix		
	ΔX_4	ΔX_5	ΔX_{14}
ΔX_4	1.00	.45	.11
ΔX_5	.45	1.00	.12
ΔX_{14}	.11	.12	1.00

level of interdependence among the three independent variables.

For index construction purposes, the independent variables in the final regression equation become the index components. The weights of the components can be determined from the regression coefficients. (Recall that the regression coefficient represents the average change in the dependent variable for a one-unit increase in the independent variable.) However, because the variables in the regression equation are not measured in the same units (for example, ΔY is measured in thousands of dollars and ΔX_{14} in thousands of kilowatt-hours), the regression coefficients must be transformed into relative values. This transformation is accomplished by computing their *standardized*, or B, *coefficients*.

$$B = b\left(\frac{s_x}{s_y}\right) \tag{8.13}$$

where

$b =$ the independent variable's regression coefficient

$s_x =$ the independent variable's standard deviation

$s_y =$ the dependent variable's standard deviation

The values of all these statistics are typically available from the regression computer output. Hence, the standardized coefficients of the three independent variables are

$$B_4 = .4959$$
$$B_5 = .4833$$
$$B_{14} = .3019$$
$$\overline{\quad\quad\quad}$$
$$\text{Total} = 1.2811$$

Because the sum of the weights in an index must be 100%, the standardized coefficients are normalized as shown in Table 8-14.

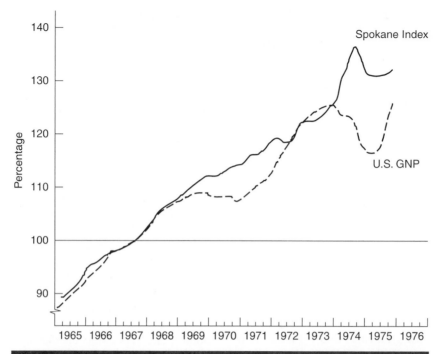

FIGURE 8-12   Spokane County Business Activity Index and the U.S. GNP, in Constant Dollars (1967 = 100).

TABLE 8-14	Standardized Coefficients
Component	*Weight*
ΔX_4	$\dfrac{.4959}{1.2811} = .3871$
ΔX_5	$\dfrac{.4833}{1.2811} = .3772$
ΔX_{14}	$\dfrac{.3019}{1.2811} = .2357$
	Total = 1.000

After the components and their respective weights have been determined, the following steps give the index:

1. Compute the percentage change of each component since the base period.
2. Multiply the percentage change by the appropriate weight.
3. Sum the weighted percentage changes obtained in Step 2.

The completed Spokane County activity index is compared with the U.S. GNP, in constant dollars (1967 = 100), in Figure 8-12. ∎

QUESTIONS

1. Why did Young choose to solve the autocorrelation problem first?
2. Would it have been better to eliminate multicollinearity first and then tackle autocorrelation?
3. How does the small sample size affect the analysis?
4. Should the regression done on the first differences have been through the origin?
5. Is there any potential for the use of lagged data?
6. What conclusions can be drawn from a comparison of the Spokane County business activity index and the GNP?

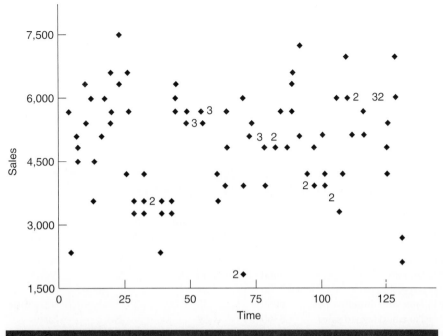

FIGURE 8-13   Restaurant Sales, January 1981 – December 1982

CASE 8-3   RESTAURANT SALES[15]

Jim Price, who was working on his M.B.A. degree, worked at a small restaurant near Marquette University in Milwaukee, Wisconsin. One day the restaurant manager asked Jim to report to her office. She indicated that she was very interested in forecasting weekly sales and wanted to know whether Jim would help. Jim had just taken an advanced statistics course, and he said that he would enjoy the challenge.

Jim asked the restaurant manager to provide him with whatever historical records she had available. She indicated that the restaurant compiled the previous week's sales every Monday morning. Jim began his analysis by obtaining weekly sales data from the week ending Sunday, January 1, 1981 through the week ending Sunday, December 29, 1982—a total of 104 observations.

The mean weekly sales for the 104 weeks turned out to be $4,862. Figure 8-13 is a graph of the weekly sales over time. The graph indicates that weekly sales were quite volatile, ranging from $1,870 to $7,548, with very little trend. Because Jim had recently completed a course on regression analysis,

he decided to use weekly sales as the dependent variable and see if he could find some useful independent, or predictor, variables.

Jim tested three predictors. The first predictor was time. The second predictor was a dummy variable indicating whether or not Marquette University was in full session that week ($0 =$ not in full session, $1 =$ in full session). Examination of the sales data in Figure 8-13 revealed that weekly sales always dropped when Marquette was not in full session, namely, during the Christmas break, the spring break, and the summer break. Jim was not surprised; the restaurant is located near Marquette's campus and most of its customers are members of the Marquette community. The third predictor Jim tried was sales lagged one week because examination of Figure 8-13 indicated that sales for two adjacent weeks were frequently similar.

Jim computed the simple correlations among the three potential predictors and the dependent variable, weekly sales. The results are presented in the correlation matrix shown in Table 8-15. As Jim

---

[15] Case 8-3 was contributed by Frank G. Forst, Marquette University, Milwaukee, Wisconsin.

| TABLE 8-15 | Restaurant Sales Correlation Matrix for Case 8-3 | | | |

	Current Sales	Time	Dummy Variable	Sales Lagged One Week
Current sales	1.000	.049	.772	.580
Time		1.000	−.048	.120
Dummy variable			1.000	.490
Lagged sales				1.000

| TABLE 8-16 | Restaurant Regression Models for Case 8-3 | | | |

Model Predictor(s)	R^2	Durbin-Watson Statistic	Autocorrelation Significant at the .05 Level?	Amount of Collinearity
(1) Time	.0024	.81	Yes	None
(2) Dummy	.5960	1.30	Yes	None
(3) Lagged sales	.3360	1.89		None
(4) Time and dummy sales	.6030	1.32		Very little
(5) Time and lagged sales	.3360	1.89	No	Little
(6) Dummy and lagged sales	.6490	1.74	No	Little
(7) Time, dummy, and lagged sales	.6510	1.73	No	Moderate

expected, there was almost no trend in the weekly sales as indicated by the correlation coefficient of .049. However, the dummy variable was strongly correlated with current sales, $r = .772$; in other words, whether or not Marquette University is in full session has good potential as a predictor of the current week's sales. The current week's sales were moderately related, $r = .580$, to sales lagged one week. However, Jim also noticed that the dummy variable was moderately related, $r = .490$, to sales lagged one week.

Jim experimented with several regression models. The results of the various regression models are presented in Table 8-16. Because the sales data have almost no trend, the predictor "time" adds very little predictive power to the regression model. Note that model 4 has only a slightly higher R^2 than model 2, and that the errors from both models appear to have a significant amount of autocorrelation. Models 3 and 5 have the same R^2, whereas model 7 has only a slightly higher R^2 than model 6. On the other hand, the predictor "lagged sales" adds a fair amount of predictive power to a regression model. Finally, model 6 has a higher R^2 than model 2 without a significant amount of autocorrelation.

Jim decided to select regression model 6 to forecast weekly sales for the following reasons:

1. Model 6 had the second largest R^2, only .002 below that of model 7.
2. The parameters of model 6 were each significantly different from zero at the .01 level.
3. Autocorrelation is not a problem for model 6.
4. Model 6 is simpler than model 7 and does not have as much multicollinearity.

The fitted regression function that Jim used was

$$\hat{Y} = 2,614.3 + 1,610.7 \text{ (dummy variable)}$$
$$+ .2605 \text{ (lagged sales)}$$

R^2 means that 64.9% of the variation in weekly sales can be explained by whether Marquette was in full session and by the previous week's sales. The regression equation implies that the weekly sales average is about \$1,611 higher when Marquette is in full session, holding the previous week's sales constant.

Jim was pleased with his effort but wondered if another type of forecasting model might not be more effective. For this reason he decided to take a forecasting course. ∎

QUESTIONS

1. Is autocorrelation significant for models (3) and (4)? (Test at the .05 level.)
2. Was Jim's use of a dummy variable correct?
3. Was it correct for Jim to use lagged sales as a predictor variable?
4. Do you agree with Jim's conclusions?
5. Would another type of forecasting model be more effective for forecasting weekly sales?

CASE 8-4   MR. TUX

John Mosby has run a simple regression analysis using time as the predictor variable and observed a disappointing r^2 of .563 (see the Mr. Tux case at the end of Chapter 6). Because he knows that his sales data have a strong seasonal component, he decides to fit a seasonal multiple regression model.

John created 11 dummy variables for the seasonal effect. Because the Mr. Tux data are monthly, he coded S1 as 1 if the data were January, 0 otherwise. John did this for each month ending with S11, which was 1 for November and 0 otherwise.

John ran a model using all 12 predictor variables: one for time and the other 11 representing the monthly seasonal effect. The results are shown in Table 8-17.

John hand-calculated the *MAPE* for the last 12 months of data and found it to be 21.25%. He is not sure whether he has a good model.

TABLE 8-17   Minitab Output for Mr. Tux Seasonal Regression Model for Case 8-4

```
Regression Analysis: Sales Versus Time, S1,...

The regression equation is
Sales = - 35023 + 2752 Time = 48459 S1 - 29808 S2 + 21681 S3 + 199019 S4
        + 139212 S5 + 57713 S6 + 21689 S7 + 74014 S8 + 7872 S9 - 9009 S10
        - 25050 S11
```

Predictor	Coef	SE Coef	T	P
Constant	-35023	15441	-2.27	0.026
Time	2752.4	141.0	19.52	0.000
S1	48459	19059	-2.54	0.013
S2	-29808	19048	-1.56	0.121
S3	21681	19039	1.14	0.258
S4	119019	19030	6.25	0.000
S5	139212	19022	7.32	0.000
S6	57713	19015	3.04	0.003
S7	21689	19009	1.14	0.257
S8	74014	19005	3.89	0.000
S9	7872	19001	0.41	0.680
S10	-9009	18998	-0.47	0.637
S11	-25050	18997	-1.32	0.191

```
S = 37992.3    R-Sq = 87.7%    R-Sq(adj) = 85.9%
```

Analysis of Variance

Source	DF	SS	MS	F	P
Regression	12	8.55392E+11	71282630871	49.38	0.000
Residual Error	83	1.19804E+11	1443416727		
Total	95	9.75195E+11			

```
Durbin-Watson statistic = 1.41
```

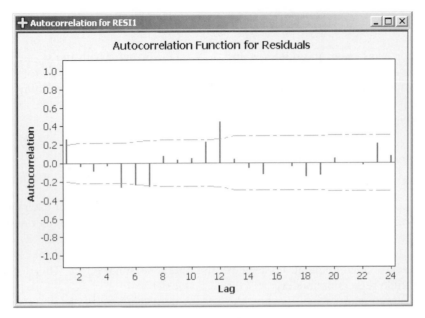

Autocorrelation Function: Residuals

Lag	ACF	T	LBQ	Lag	ACF	T	LBQ
1	0.260241	2.55	6.71	13	0.040709	0.28	57.33
2	-0.039905	-0.37	6.87	14	-0.060195	-0.41	57.75
3	-0.091961	-0.84	7.72	15	-0.129158	-0.88	59.68
4	-0.030178	-0.28	7.81	16	-0.006461	-0.04	59.69
5	-0.266888	-2.43	15.18	17	-0.044247	-0.30	59.92
6	-0.241385	-2.07	21.27	18	-0.150021	-1.01	62.64
7	-0.258015	-2.12	28.31	19	-0.136353	-0.91	64.91
8	0.074975	0.59	28.91	20	0.048747	0.32	65.20
9	0.034480	0.27	29.04	21	-0.006104	-0.04	65.21
10	0.051103	0.40	29.32	22	-0.022500	-0.15	65.27
11	0.229282	1.79	35.14	23	0.208753	1.38	70.89
12	0.443214	3.36	57.14	24	0.079236	0.51	71.71

FIGURE 8-14   Autocorrelation Function for Mr. Tux Seasonal Regression Model Residuals

The model explains 87.7% of the sales variable variance. However, a *MAPE* of over 20% seems high. Next, John generated the autocorrelations for the residuals of the model, which are shown in Figure 8-14.

The residual autocorrelations have a spike at lag 12, the seasonal lag. Somewhat dissatisfied with the results of his seasonal regression model, John decided to try an autoregressive model to forecast his monthly sales (the data appeared in the Mr. Tux case at the end of Chapter 2).

John knows that his data have a strong seasonal component, so he decides to try to model this component using an autoregressive model with the Y values lagged 12 months. John is unable to use the first 12 months of his sales data, but because he started with 96 periods, this still leaves him with a sample size of 84. The Minitab output is shown in Table 8-18.

Assignment

Write a memo to John with a careful analysis of the results of his two attempts to develop a seasonal forecasting model. Which model is better? Be sure your discussion includes an evaluation of model fit, potential forecast accuracy, and any remaining problems, for example, autocorrelation. ∎

TABLE 8-18	Minitab Output for Mr. Tux Seasonal Autoregressive Model for Case 8-4

Regression Analysis: Sales versus Y-Lagged

```
The regression equation is
Sales = 24786 + 1.07 Y-Lagged

84 cases used, 12 cases contain missing values

Predictor      Coef   SE Coef        T      P
Constant      24786      5322     4.66  0.000
Y-Lagged    1.06807   0.03803    28.08  0.000

S = 30784.9   R-Sq = 90.6%   R-Sq(adj) = 90.5%

Analysis of Variance

Source          DF          SS          MS        F      P
Regression       1  7.47470E+11  7.47470E+11   788.71  0.000
Residual Error  82  77712386803    947712034
Total           83  8.25183E+11

Durbin-Watson statistic = 1.829
```

CASE 8-5   CONSUMER CREDIT COUNSELING

The Consumer Credit Counseling (CCC) operation was described in Chapters 1 (Case 1-2) and 3 (Case 3-3).

The executive director, Marv Harnishfeger, concluded that the most important variable CCC needed to forecast was the number of new clients to be seen in the rest of 1993. Marv provided Dorothy Mercer monthly data for the number of new clients seen by CCC for the period January 1985 through March 1993 (see Case 3-3). In Case 3-3, Dorothy used autocorrelation analysis to explore the data pattern. In Case 6-5, she tried both the number of people on food stamps and a business activity index to develop a regression model to forecast the rest of 1993.

Dorothy was not happy with the results of her regression model. She decided to try multiple regression and asked Marv to think of other variables that might be related to the number of clients seen. Marv indicated that she might try the number of bankruptcies filed and the number of building permits issued.

Data for the number of bankruptcies filed from January 1986 to December 1992 are shown in Table 8-19, and the number of building permits issued from January 1986 to December 1992 are shown in Table 8-20.

Dorothy developed a multiple regression model that used the number of people on food stamps, the business activity index, the number of bankruptcies filed, and the number of building permits issued. She also created a model based solely on the assumption that the data were seasonal.

Dorothy has recently been informed that serial correlation is often a problem when regression is performed with time series data. She is worried that some of the regression models developed to predict the number of clients seen were affected by this condition.

Because she liked the report you submitted that used the time series decomposition analysis model, she has assigned you the task of checking on this situation.

TABLE 8-19		Bankruptcies, January 1986 to December 1992									
1986	160	170	140	173	162	160	150	145	134	155	145	152
1987	171	206	173	195	165	177	168	165	131	169	166	157
1988	174	162	196	178	169	170	143	177	192	195	164	146
1989	180	149	200	165	168	177	143	180	169	170	160	161
1990	172	146	185	143	156	173	140	160	131	169	152	135
1991	136	167	179	181	166	151	165	129	132	162	140	140
1992	130	165	172	145	129	166	146	143	127	186	157	94

TABLE 8-20		Building Permits Issued, January 1986 to December 1992									
1986	49	60	149	214	191	193	161	174	168	203	111	64
1987	44	76	137	145	150	168	168	170	158	146	104	48
1988	32	32	127	149	128	178	132	164	152	92	121	77
1989	61	48	108	161	200	204	164	175	200	171	153	79
1990	111	92	166	189	245	261	207	238	198	247	164	108
1991	67	118	205	253	296	300	284	282	282	261	237	130
1992	133	210	298	334	312	333	311	327	352	387	243	140

You vaguely remember developing an autoregressive model at one point in your educational experience and ask Dorothy if she would like to have you look into that possibility. She decides that it would be a good way for you to spend your time.

Assignment

Analyze the significance of the variables in Dorothy's regression model. Develop a regression model (be sure to include additive dummy variables for the seasonal component if necessary) and use it to forecast the number of new clients for the first three months of 1993. Compare your forecasts with the actual observations.

Develop an autoregressive model and generate forecasts for the first three months of 1993. Which model (multiple regression or autoregression) do you feel is the better candidate for generating forecasts for the rest of 1993? Write Dorothy a memo that provides her with the information she has requested concerning the problem of serial correlation. Include an analysis of the results of your efforts to develop an appropriate model to forecast the number of new clients for the remainder of 1993. ■

CASE 8-6   AAA WASHINGTON[16]

An overview of AAA Washington was provided in Case 5-5 when students were asked to prepare a time series decomposition of the emergency road service calls received by the club over five years. The time series decomposition performed in Case 5-5 showed that the pattern Michael DeCoria had observed in emergency road service call volume was probably cyclical in nature. Michael would like to be able to predict the cyclical effect on emergency road service call volume for future years.

Other research done by the club discovered several factors that have an impact on emergency road service call volume. Among these factors are average daily temperature and the amount of rainfall received in a day. This research has shown that emergency road service calls increase as rainfall increases and as average daily temperature falls. The club also believes that the total number of emergency road service calls it receives is dependent on the number of members in the club.

---

[16]This case was provided by Steve Branton, former student and M.B.A. graduate, Eastern Washington University.

Michael has observed that the cyclical trend of the time series seems to be lagging behind the general economic cycle. He has suggested that the unemployment rate for Washington State would be a good surrogate measurement for the general state of Washington's economy. Data on the average monthly temperature, monthly rainfall, and Washington State unemployment rate have been gathered and are presented in Table 8-21. A conversation with the manager of the emergency road service call center has led to two important observations: (1) Automakers seem to design cars to operate best at 65 degrees Fahrenheit, and (2) call volume seems to increase more sharply when the average temperature drops a few degrees from an average temperature in the 30s than it does when a similar drop occurs with an average temperature in the 60s. This information suggests that the effect of temperature on emergency road service is nonlinear.

In Case 6-6 four linear regression models using total number of emergency road service calls as the dependent variable and unemployment rate, temperature, rainfall, and number of members as the four independent variables were investigated. The temperature variable was transformed by subtracting 65 degrees from the average monthly temperature values. A nonlinear relationship was then researched.

In Case 7-2 a multiple regression model was developed. Variables such as rainfall, number of members, the exponentially transformed average monthly temperature, and the unemployment rate lagged 11 months were tested.

Assignment

1. Which regression model is the best for prediction? Are the signs on the coefficients for the independent variables what you would expect them to be? Are the coefficients of the independent variables significantly different from zero?
2. Is serial correlation a problem?
3. Prepare a memo to Mr. DeCoria recommending the regression model you believe is most appropriate for predicting the cyclical nature of emergency road service call volume. ∎

TABLE 8-21	Data for AAA Washington for Case 8-6					
Year	*Month*	*Calls*	*Rate*	*Temperature*	*Rainfall*	*Members*
1987	June	—	6.9940	—	—	—
	July	—	6.8137	—	—	—
	August	—	6.3648	—	—	—
	September	—	6.5435	—	—	—
	October	—	6.7826	—	—	—
	November	—	6.9225	—	—	—
	December	—	7.1560	—	—	—
1988	January	—	7.9143	—	—	—
	February	—	7.7576	—	—	—
	March	—	7.0641	—	—	—
	April	—	6.0977	—	—	—
	May	20,002	5.7867	55.1	3.75	—
	June	21,591	5.7592	59.0	1.95	—
	July	22,696	5.5718	63.8	0.89	—
	August	21,509	5.2939	63.8	0.51	384,746
	September	22,123	5.4709	59.1	2.31	388,652
	October	21,449	5.5049	54.6	3.12	392,241
	November	23,475	5.8630	45.4	8.42	393,115
	December	23,529	6.1349	41.0	4.44	392,631
1989	January	23,327	7.5474	40.3	4.30	396,975
	February	24,050	7.8157	34.3	3.18	395,186
	March	24,010	7.1390	43.2	6.57	397,791
	April	19,735	6.2637	52.5	2.39	397,764
	May	20,153	5.8332	55.3	2.83	399,348
	June	19,512	5.8077	62.4	1.30	401,949

				TABLE 8-21 (Continued)		
Year	Month	Calls	Rate	Temperature	Rainfall	Members
	July	19,892	5.6713	62.9	0.83	404,866
	August	20,326	5.4977	63.5	1.53	405,341
	September	19,378	5.2989	60.9	0.32	407,479
	October	21,263	5.6028	51.9	3.44	405,430
	November	21,443	5.9143	46.2	7.24	412,134
	December	23,366	5.0000	41.8	4.72	415,342
1990	January	23,836	6.1917	41.8	9.55	416,255
	February	23,336	6.3775	38.9	5.73	423,001
	March	22,003	5.7234	46.3	3.40	428,559
	April	20,155	4.7792	51.7	2.91	431,429
	May	20,070	4.5715	54.9	2.15	434,675
	June	19,588	4.3899	59.8	3.55	435,864
	July	20,804	4.2559	66.7	0.59	437,969
	August	19,644	3.9359	66.4	1.33	440,565
	September	17,424	3.9048	61.9	0.24	441,936
	October	20,833	4.4294	50.4	1.17	448,595
	November	22,490	5.1523	45.8	10.66	446,291
	December	24,861	5.5102	33.9	7.93	446,455
1991	January	23,441	6.8901	37.9	4.40	445,392
	February	19,205	7.0308	46.9	5.42	445,787
	March	20,386	6.7186	43.4	4.35	445,746
	April	19,988	6.1280	49.1	5.69	446,430
	May	19,077	5.8146	54.3	2.12	450,001
	June	19,141	5.9480	58.2	1.61	452,303
	July	20,883	5.9026	65.4	0.51	456,551
	August	20,709	5.7227	66.0	2.80	455,747
	September	19,647	5.6877	60.9	0.20	456,764
	October	22,013	6.2922	51.0	1.70	462,340
	November	22,375	7.0615	46.2	6.50	460,492
	December	22,727	7.4370	42.4	3.45	465,361
1992	January	22,367	8.4513	43.0	7.26	465,492
	February	21,155	8.7699	46.0	3.59	466,775
	March	21,209	8.0728	48.9	1.47	467,168
	April	19,286	7.2392	52.7	4.35	464,575
	May	19,725	7.0461	58.3	0.60	459,019
	June	20,276	7.0478	63.6	1.84	463,665
	July	20,795	7.1080	64.9	1.41	463,775
	August	21,126	6.7824	65.0	1.01	466,230
	September	20,251	6.7691	58.4	2.16	—
	October	22,069	7.5896	53.2	2.55	—
	November	23,268	7.9908	44.8	6.23	—
	December	26,039	8.2460	37.8	4.38	—
1993	January	26,127	9.5301	34.9	4.08	—
	February	20,067	9.2790	—	—	—
	March	19,673	8.6802	—	—	—
	April	19,142	7.7815	—	—	—
	May	—	7.4338	—	—	—
	June	—	7.3701	—	—	—
	July	—	7.2442	—	—	—

— = Data not available.

CASE 8-7   ALOMEGA FOOD STORES

In Example 1.1 Julie Ruth collected monthly sales data on her company along with several other variables she thought might be related to sales. Her forecasting efforts using these data along with Minitab are detailed in cases at the end of Chapters 2, 3, and 5. Her desire to improve the accuracy of her forecasts suggested the use of multiple regression.

Julie recognized from her decomposition analysis of sales that her data had a strong seasonal component (see Case 5-6). Because she also felt that sales were influenced by the amounts spent on newspaper and TV advertising (see Case 2-3), she decided to run a regression relating sales to newspaper advertising (Papers), TV advertising (TV), and eleven 0–1

dummy variables, with December serving as the base month, to account for the monthly seasonal effects. Some of the Minitab output from Julie's regression run is shown in Table 8-22.

Julie was quite pleased to see an R^2 value of about 91%, a significant improvement over the r-squared value for the regression model containing the single predictor TV (review the regression results in Case 2-3). Moreover, the variance inflation factor (*VIF*) for each of the predictor variables was small, and the Durbin-Watson statistic was close to 2.

Julie realized that an examination of the residuals was required before she could be completely pleased with her results, and she intended to do a complete residual analysis before proposing her

---

TABLE 8-22   Minitab Output for Julie Ruth's Regression Model for Alomega Sales

```
Regression Analysis: Sales versus Paper, TV,...

The regression equation is
Sales = 184393 + 0.363 Paper + 0.315 TV + 200847 Dum1 + 55491 Dum2
        + 199556 Dum3 + 100151 Dum4 + 190293 Dum5 + 135441 Dum6
        + 156609 Dum7 + 51586 Dum8 + 183619 Dum9 + 109096 Dum10
        + 96206 Dum11
```

Predictor	Coef	SE Coef	T	P	VIF
Constant	184393	23402	7.88	0.000	
Paper	0.36319	0.06854	5.30	0.000	2.1
TV	0.31530	0.03638	8.67	0.000	1.6
Dum1	200847	39151	5.13	0.000	2.7
Dum2	55491	32399	1.71	0.096	1.8
Dum3	199556	34147	5.84	0.000	2.0
Dum4	100151	32388	3.09	0.004	1.8
Dum5	190293	32822	5.80	0.000	1.9
Dum6	135441	32581	4.16	0.000	1.9
Dum7	156609	32699	4.79	0.000	1.9
Dum8	51586	32420	1.59	0.121	1.8
Dum9	183619	36522	5.03	0.000	2.3
Dum10	109096	32439	3.36	0.002	1.8
Dum11	96206	32417	2.97	0.005	1.8

```
S = 45801.4    R-Sq = 90.8%    R-Sq(adj) = 87.3%
```

Analysis of Variance

Source	DF	SS	MS	F	P
Regression	13	7.06412E+11	54339402344	25.90	0.000
Residual Error	34	71324031968	2097765646		
Total	47	7.77736E+11			

```
Durbin-Watson statistic = 2.274
```

regression model as a useful tool for forecasting sales.

Julie liked the fact that the predictors Papers and TV were under the company control. Values of these variables could then be chosen in advance to generate forecasts of future sales.

Julie is almost ready to confront her tormentor Jackson Tilson, but she has a few more loose ends to wrap up. ■

QUESTIONS

1. Julie has collected data on other variables that were not included in her multiple regression model. Should one or more of these other variables be included in her model? More generally, how can Julie be sure she has the "right" set of predictor variables?
2. Assuming there are no additional important predictor variables, are you satisfied with Julie's forecasting model? How would you "sell" the model to management (and Jackson Tilson)?
3. How might Julie's model be used to determine future amounts spent on newspaper and TV advertising?
4. What conditions might prompt Julie to reexamine her regression model or, perhaps, to look for another method of forecasting sales?

Minitab Applications

The problem. In Example 8.8, James Brown is trying to forecast electrical usage by residential customers for the third and fourth quarters of 1996 for Washington Water Power.

Minitab Solution

1. Enter the variable Hours from Table 8-9 into column C1. Enter time in column C2 $(1, 2, 3, \ldots 66)$. Enter the dummy variables as shown in Table 8-10 into columns C3, C4, and C5.
2. In order to run the seasonal regression model, click on the following menus:

```
Stat>Regression>Regression
```

3. The Regression dialog box similar to the one shown in Figure 6-21 appears.
   a. Hours is selected as the Response or dependent variable.
   b. Time-4th Qt. are entered as the Predictor or independent variables.
   c. Click Options to obtain the Regression–Options dialog box.
4. The Regression–Options dialog box shown in Figure 8-15 appears.
   a. Click on the Durbin-Watson statistic box.
   b. In the space under Prediction intervals for new observations, type the new observations for third quarter: 67 0 1 0.
   c. Click OK and then OK on the Regression dialog box. The results displayed in Table 8-11 are presented in the session window.

   Note that in Example 8.4, Fred Gardner developed a regression model through the origin (there was no Y intercept). In order to run this type of model, click off the check mark in the Fit intercept box shown in Figure 8-15.

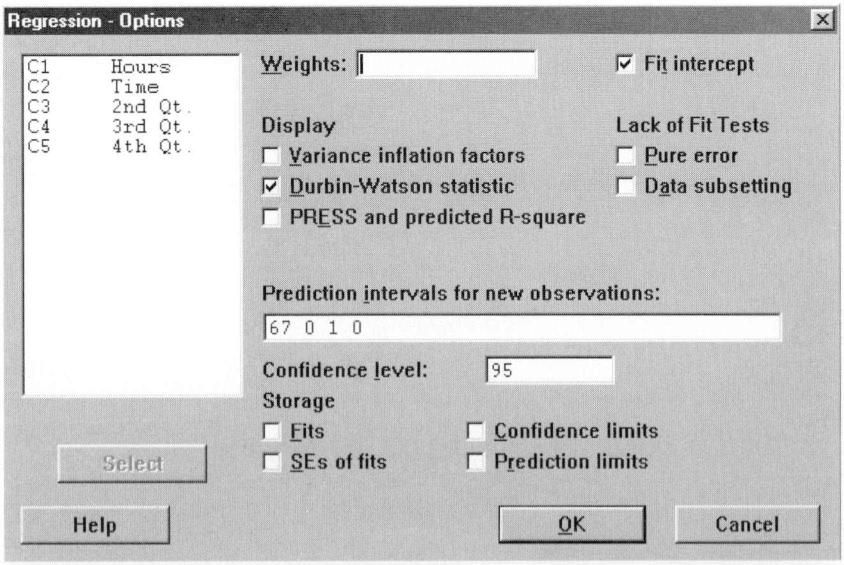

FIGURE 8-15   Minitab Regression—Options Dialog Box

Excel Applications

The problem. In Example 8.6, a first-order autoregressive model was developed for the Novak Corporation sales data.

Excel Solution

1. Enter the Minitab file that contains the data shown in Table 8-2 (see p. 336) and highlight the Sales column. Click on the following menus:

   `Edit>Copy Cells`

   Now enter your Excel spreadsheet, highlight A3, and click on the following menus:

   `Edit>Paste`

   The data for Sales appears in column A. After the heading for this column is entered in the first row the spreadsheet looks like Figure 8-16 without the lagged variable.
2. In order to create the Sales variable Lagged one period, position the mouse at A3 and highlight through A19. Click on the following menus:

   `Edit>Copy`

   Now highlight B4 and click:

   `Edit>Paste`

   The result appears in Figure 8-16.
3. Click on the following menus to run the autoregressive model:

   `Tools>Data Analysis`

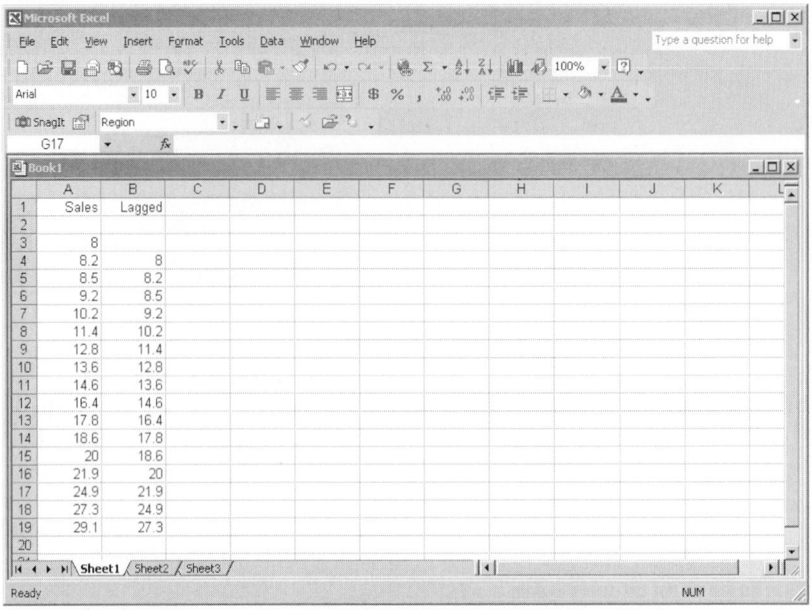

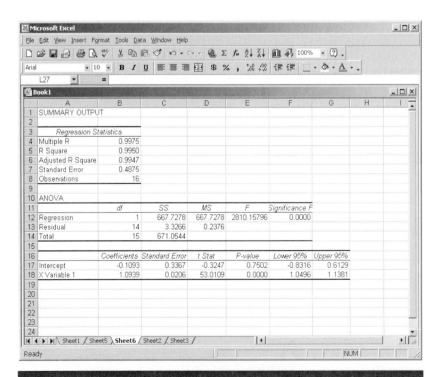

FIGURE 8-16   **Excel Spreadsheet after Lagging a Variable Sales One Period**

FIGURE 8-17   **Excel Output for an Autoregressive Model**

The Data Analysis dialog box appears. Under Analysis Tools choose Regression. The Regression dialog box was shown in Figure 6-25.

a. Enter A4:A19 in the Input Y Range.
b. Enter B4:B19 in the Input X Range.
c. Click the button next to New Worksheet Ply.
d. Click OK, and the output appears as displayed in Figure 8-17.

References

Diebold, F. X. *Elements of Forecasting*, Third Edition. Cincinnati, OH: South-Western, 2004.

Durbin, J., and G. S. Watson. "Testing for Serial Correlation in Least Squares Regression II." *Biometrika* 38 (1951): 159–178.

King, J. L., and D. A. Bessler. "A Comparison of Multivariate Forecasting Procedures for Economic Time Series." *International Journal of Forecasting* 1(1) (1985): 5–24.

Kleinbaum, D., L. Kupper, K. Muller, and A. Nizam. *Applied Regression Analysis and Other Multivariable Methods*, Third Edition. Pacific Grove, CA: Duxbury, 1998.

Newbold, P., and T. Bos. *Introductory Business and Economic Forecasting*, Second Edition. Cincinnati, OH: South-Western, 1994.

Pindyck, R. S., and D. L. Rubinfeld. *Econometric Models and Economic Forecasts*, Fourth Edition. New York: McGraw-Hill, 1998.

Young, R. M. "Forecasting with an Econometric Model: The Issue of Judgemental Adjustment." *Journal of Forecasting* 1(2) (1982): 189–204.

9

THE BOX-JENKINS (ARIMA) METHODOLOGY

Several approaches for analyzing and forecasting time series have been discussed. In Chapter 4, smoothing was introduced and time series forecasts were generated by a particular smoothing (averaging) mechanism. In Chapter 5, time series were decomposed into trend, seasonal, and irregular components, and forecasts were produced by extrapolating the estimated trend and seasonality. In Chapter 8, regression models appropriate for time series data were considered. Forecasts of the dependent variable Y generated from these models ordinarily require forecasts of future values of the independent variables, the X's.

This chapter introduces a class of models that can produce accurate forecasts based on a description of historical patterns in the data. Autoregressive integrated moving average (ARIMA) models are a class of linear models that is capable of representing *stationary* as well as *nonstationary* time series. Recall that stationary processes vary about a fixed level, and nonstationary processes have no natural constant mean level. The autoregressive models discussed in Chapter 8 are actually a special subset of ARIMA models that are useful for modeling stationary time series.

ARIMA models do not involve independent variables in their construction. Rather, they make use of the information in the series itself to generate forecasts. For example, an ARIMA model for monthly sales would project the historical sales pattern to produce a forecast of next month's sales.

ARIMA models rely heavily on autocorrelation patterns in the data. The methodology for identifying, fitting, and checking appropriate ARIMA models was greatly advanced by the work of two statisticians, G. E. P. Box and G. M. Jenkins. For this reason, ARIMA modeling and forecasting is often referred to as the Box-Jenkins methodology.

BOX-JENKINS METHODOLOGY

The *Box-Jenkins methodology* of forecasting is different from most methods because it does not *assume* any particular pattern in the historical data of the series to be forecast. It uses an iterative approach of identifying a possible model from a general class of models. The chosen model is then checked against the historical data to see whether it accurately describes the series. The model fits well if the residuals are generally small, randomly distributed, and contain no useful information. If the specified model is *not* satisfactory, the process is repeated using a new model designed to improve on the original one. This iterative procedure continues until a satisfactory model is found. At that point, the model can be used for forecasting. Figure 9-1 illustrates the Box-Jenkins model-building strategy.

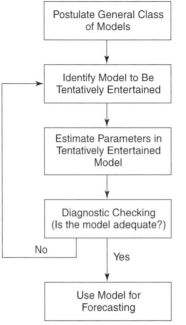

Source: Box, G. E. P., Jenkins, G. M., and G. C. Reinsel, *Time Series Analysis: Forecasting and Control* (3rd ed.), Upper Saddle River, New Jersey: Prentice Hall, 1994, p.17. Reprinted with permission.

FIGURE 9-1   Flow Diagram for the Box-Jenkins Model-Building Strategy

The initial selection of an ARIMA model is based on an examination of a plot of the time series (to observe its general character) and an examination of its autocorrelations for several time lags. Specifically, the pattern of sample autocorrelations calculated from the time series is matched with the known autocorrelation pattern associated with a particular ARIMA model. This matching is done for both autocorrelations and partial autocorrelations.[1] Theoretical autocorrelation coefficients for some of the more common ARIMA models are shown in Figures 9-2, 9-3, and 9-4. The significance of the patterns shown in these figures will be evident later in the chapter.

> The *Box-Jenkins methodology* refers to a set of procedures for identifying, fitting, and checking ARIMA models with time series data. Forecasts follow directly from the form of the fitted model.

In selecting a model, remember that the autocorrelations calculated from the data will not exactly match any set of theoretical autocorrelations associated with an ARIMA model. Autocorrelations calculated from the data are subject to sampling variation. However, you should be able to adequately match most time series data with an ARIMA model. If the initial selection is not quite right, inadequacies will show up in an analysis of the residuals (model checking), and the original model can be modified. As you gain experience, this iterative model-building task becomes much easier.

---

[1] A partial autocorrelation at time lag k is the correlation between Y_t and Y_{t-k}, the responses for period t and $t - k$ respectively, after adjusting for the effects of the intervening values, $Y_{t-1}, Y_{t-2}, \ldots, Y_{t-k+1}$. Partial autocorrelations are derived and discussed in Newbold and Bos (1994) and Box, Jenkins, and Reinsel (1994).

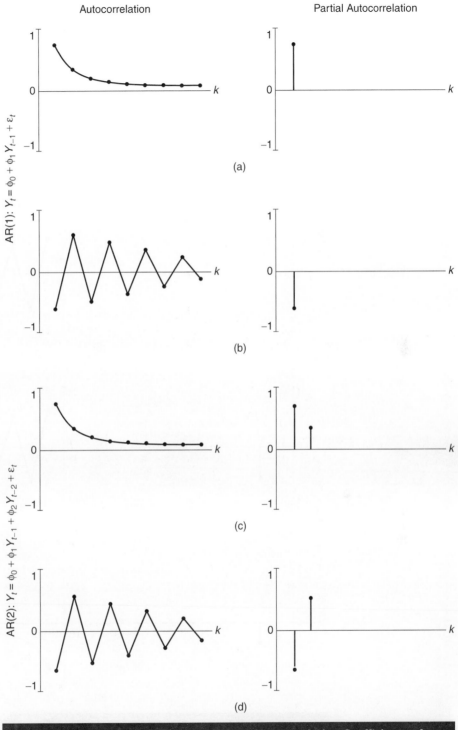

FIGURE 9-2   Autocorrelation and Partial Autocorrelation Coefficients of AR(1) and AR(2) Models

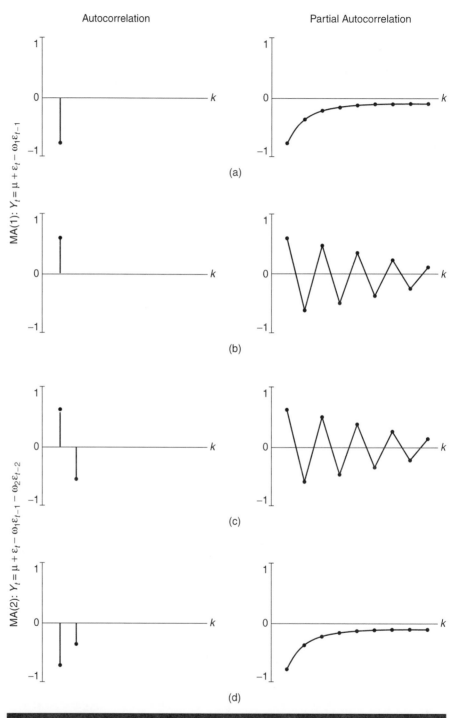

FIGURE 9-3   **Autocorrelation and Partial Autocorrelation Coefficients of MA(1) and MA(2) Models**

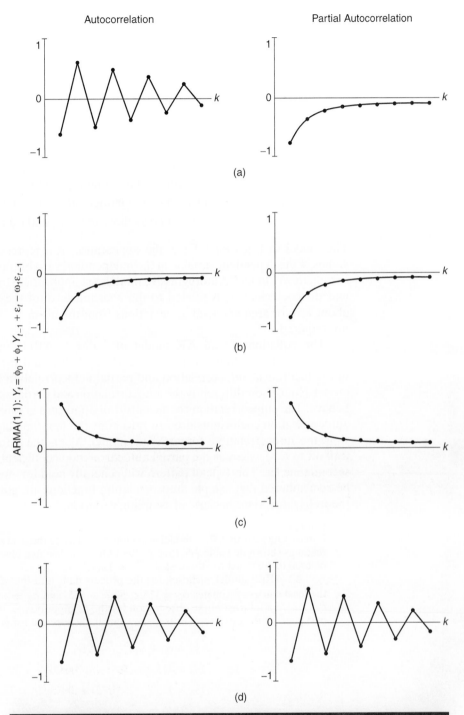

Autocorrelation   Partial Autocorrelation

(a)

(b)

(c)

(d)

FIGURE 9-4   Autocorrelation and Partial Autocorrelation Coefficients of a Mixed ARMA(1,1) Model

Autoregressive Models

A first-order autoregressive model was introduced in Chapter 8. A pth-order autoregressive model takes the form

$$Y_t = \phi_0 + \phi_1 Y_{t-1} + \phi_2 Y_{t-2} + \cdots + \phi_p Y_{t-p} + \varepsilon_t \tag{9.1}$$

where

$$Y_t = \text{response (dependent) variable at time } t$$
$$Y_{t-1}, Y_{t-2}, \ldots, Y_{t-p} = \text{response variable at time lags } t-1, t-2, \ldots, t-p,$$
$$\text{respectively; these } Y\text{'s play the role of independent variables}$$
$$\phi_0, \phi_1, \phi_2, \ldots, \phi_p = \text{coefficients to be estimated}[2]$$
$$\varepsilon_t = \text{error term at time } t \text{ that represents the effects of variables not}$$
$$\text{explained by the model; the assumptions about the error term}$$
$$\text{are the same as those for the standard regression model}$$

The model in Equation 9.1 has the appearance of a regression model with lagged values of the dependent variable in the independent variable positions, hence the name *autoregressive model*. Autoregressive models are appropriate for stationary time series, and the coefficient ϕ_0 is related to the constant level of the series. If the data vary about zero or are expressed as deviations from the mean $Y_t - \bar{Y}$, the coefficient ϕ_0 is not required.

The equations of an AR model of order 1, AR(1) model, and of order 2, AR(2) model, are shown in Figure 9-2. Figure 9-2(a) and (b) illustrate the behavior of the theoretical autocorrelation and partial autocorrelation functions for an AR(1) model. Notice how differently the autocorrelation and partial autocorrelation functions behave. The autocorrelation coefficients trail off to zero gradually, whereas the partial autocorrelation coefficients drop to zero after the first time lag. Figure 9-2(c) and (d) show the autocorrelations for an AR(2) model. Again, the autocorrelation coefficients trail off to zero, whereas the partial autocorrelation coefficients drop to zero after the second time lag. This type of pattern will generally hold for any AR(p) model. It must be remembered that sample autocorrelation functions are going to differ from these theoretical functions because of sampling variation.

Example 9.1

Forecasting with an AR(2) model is demonstrated using the data set consisting of 75 process readings shown in Table 9-5. (See p. 398.) Only the last five observations in Table 9-5 will be used to construct the forecast shown in Table 9-1.

An AR(2) model is chosen for the process data, and the Minitab program computes the least squares estimates $\hat{\phi}_0 = 115.2$, $\hat{\phi}_1 = -.535$, and $\hat{\phi}_2 = .0055$. Suppose that at time $t-1 = 75$ a forecast of the observation for the next period $t = 76$ is required. Because the best guess of the error term is its mean value 0, the forecast for period $t = 76$ is

$$\hat{Y}_t = \hat{\phi}_0 + \hat{\phi}_1 Y_{t-1} + \hat{\phi}_2 Y_{t-2}$$
$$\hat{Y}_{76} = 115.2 - .535 Y_{75} + .0055 Y_{74}$$
$$\hat{Y}_{76} = 115.2 - .535(72) + .0055(99) = 77.2$$

For autoregressive models, forecasts depend on observed values in previous time periods. For AR(2) models, forecasts of the next value depend on the observations in the two previous time periods. For AR(3) models, forecasts of the next value depend on observations in the three previous time periods, and so forth.

---

[2] The coefficient ϕ_0 is related to the mean μ of the process by $\phi_0 = \mu(1 - \phi_1 - \phi_2 - \cdots - \phi_p)$.

TABLE 9-1	Forecasting with an AR(2) Autoregressive Model for Example 9.1			
Period	**Time** t	**Values** Y_t	**Forecasts** $\hat{Y}_t$	**Residuals** e_t
$t-5$	71	90	76.4	13.6
$t-4$	72	78	67.5	10.5
$t-3$	73	87	74.0	13.0
$t-2$	74	99	69.1	29.9
$t-1$	75	72	62.7	9.3
t	76		77.2	

Moving Average Models

A qth-order moving average model takes the form

$$Y_t = \mu + \varepsilon_t - \omega_1\varepsilon_{t-1} - \omega_2\varepsilon_{t-2} - \cdots - \omega_q\varepsilon_{t-q} \tag{9.2}$$

where

$$Y_t = \text{response (dependent) variable at time } t$$
$$\mu = \text{constant mean of the process}$$
$$\omega_1, \omega_2, \ldots, \omega_q = \text{coefficients to be estimated}$$
$$\varepsilon_t = \text{error term that represents the effects of variables not explained}$$
by the model; the assumptions about the error term are the
same as those for the standard regression model
$$\varepsilon_{t-1}, \varepsilon_{t-2}, \ldots, \varepsilon_{t-q} = \text{errors in previous time periods that, at time } t, \text{ are incorporated}$$
in the response Y_t

Equation 9.2 is similar to Equation 9.1 except that the dependent variable Y_t depends on previous values of the errors rather than on the variable itself. Moving average (MA) models provide forecasts of Y_t based on a linear combination of a finite number of past errors, whereas autoregressive (AR) models forecast Y_t as a linear function of a finite number of past values of Y_t.

The term *moving average* for the model in Equation 9.2 is historical and should not be confused with the moving average procedures discussed in Chapter 4. Here *moving average* refers to the fact that the deviation of the response from its mean, $Y_t - \mu$, is a linear combination of current and past errors, and as time moves forward, the errors involved in this linear combination move forward as well.

$$Y_t - \mu = \varepsilon_t - \omega_1\varepsilon_{t-1} - \omega_2\varepsilon_{t-2} - \cdots - \omega_q\varepsilon_{t-q}$$
$$Y_{t+1} - \mu = \varepsilon_{t+1} - \omega_1\varepsilon_t - \omega_2\varepsilon_{t-1} - \cdots - \omega_q\varepsilon_{t-q+1}$$

The weights $\omega_1, \omega_2, \ldots, \omega_q$ do not necessarily sum to 1 and may be positive or negative, although they are each preceded by a minus sign in the specification of the model.

Figure 9-3 shows the equations of a moving average model of order 1, MA(1) model, and of order 2, MA(2) model. Error terms can be added sequentially to get an MA(q) model, where q is the number of past error terms to be included in the forecast of the next observation. Figure 9-3(a) and (b) also illustrate the behavior of the theoretical autocorrelation and partial autocorrelation coefficients for the MA(1) model. Note how fortunate it is that the autocorrelation and partial autocorrelation functions

	TABLE 9-2	Forecasting with an MA(2) Moving Average Model for Example 9.2		
Period	Time t	Values Y_t	Forecasts $\hat{Y}_t$	Residuals e_t
$t-5$	71	90	76.1	13.9
$t-4$	72	78	69.1	8.9
$t-3$	73	87	75.3	11.7
$t-2$	74	99	72.0	27.0
$t-1$	75	72	64.3	7.7
t	76		80.6	

of AR and MA models behave very differently. The autocorrelation coefficients for the MA(1) model drop to zero after the first time lag, whereas the partial autocorrelation coefficients trail off to zero gradually. Furthermore, the autocorrelation coefficients for the MA(2) model are zero after the second time lag, whereas the partial autocorrelations trail off gradually [see Figure 9-3(c) and (d)]. Again, it must be mentioned that sample autocorrelation functions are going to differ from these theoretical functions because of sampling variation.

Example 9.2

The 75 process readings given in Table 9-5 can be used to demonstrate forecasting with an MA(2) model. Forecasting is demonstrated using only the last five observations shown in Table 9-2.

An MA(2) model is selected, and the Minitab program computes the least squares estimates[3] of the model coefficients getting $\hat{\mu} = 75.4$, $\hat{\omega}_1 = .5667$, and $\hat{\omega}_2 = -.3560$. Again, suppose that at time $t - 1 = 75$ a forecast of the observation in period $t = 76$ is required. Because at time $t - 1$, the best guess of the error term in the next period is its mean value 0, and the best guesses of errors in the current and previous time periods are the corresponding residuals, the forecast for period $t = 76$ is

$$\hat{Y}_t = \hat{\mu} - \hat{\omega}_1 e_{t-1} - \hat{\omega}_2 e_{t-2}$$

$$\hat{Y}_{76} = 75.4 - .5667 e_{75} + .3560 e_{74}$$

$$\hat{Y}_{76} = 75.4 - .5667(7.7) + .3560(27) = 80.6$$

Notice that the two residuals e_{75} and e_{74} are substituted for the errors ε_{75} and ε_{74} in the computation of the forecast for period 76. To compute forecasts from moving average models, errors corresponding to time periods that have already occurred are replaced by residuals for those time periods. The number of residuals involved in the forecast of the next observation is equal to the order of the moving average model.

Autoregressive Moving Average Models

A model with autoregressive terms can be combined with a model having moving average terms to get a "mixed" autoregressive–moving average model. It is convenient to use the notation ARMA(p, q), where p is the order of the autoregressive part and

---

[3] Least squares estimates for coefficients in moving average models, or models involving moving average terms, must be obtained iteratively using a nonlinear least squares algorithm. Using an initial starting point, a nonlinear least squares algorithm generates improved coefficient estimates that have a smaller sum of squared errors. Estimates are continually improved until the sum of squared errors cannot be made appreciably smaller. Although autoregressive models can be fit with standard regression packages, least squares estimates of the coefficients in autoregressive models are often obtained using a nonlinear least squares procedure.

q is the order of the moving average part, to represent these models. An ARMA(p, q) model has the general form

$$Y_t = \phi_0 + \phi_1 Y_{t-1} + \phi_2 Y_{t-2} + \cdots + \phi_p Y_{t-p} + \varepsilon_t - \omega_1 \varepsilon_{t-1} - \omega_2 \varepsilon_{t-2} - \cdots - \omega_q \varepsilon_{t-q}$$

$$(9.3)$$

ARMA(p, q) models can describe a wide variety of behaviors for stationary time series.[4] Forecasts generated by an ARMA(p, q) model will depend on current and past values of the response Y as well as current and past values of the errors (residuals) e.

Figure 9-4 shows the equation of an ARMA$(1, 1)$ model and the possible behaviors of the theoretical autocorrelations and partial autocorrelations. In this case, both the autocorrelations and partial autocorrelations die out; neither cuts off.

Summary

The autocorrelation and partial autocorrelation patterns for autoregressive–moving average processes can be summarized as follows:

	Autocorrelations	*Partial Autocorrelations*
MA(q)	Cut off after the order q of the process	Die out
AR(p)	Die out	Cut off after the order p of the process
ARMA(p, q)	Die out	Die out

The numbers of autoregressive and moving average terms (orders p and q) in an ARMA model are determined from the patterns of the sample autocorrelations and partial autocorrelations and the values of the model selection criteria that are discussed in a later section of this chapter. In practice, the values of p and q each rarely exceed 2.

IMPLEMENTING THE MODEL-BUILDING STRATEGY

As shown in Figure 9-1, the Box-Jenkins approach uses an iterative model-building strategy that consists of selecting an initial model (model identification), estimating the model coefficients (parameter estimation), and analyzing the residuals (model checking). If necessary, the initial model is modified and the process is repeated until the residuals indicate no further modification is necessary. At this point, the fitted model can be used for forecasting.

The steps in the model-building strategy are examined in some detail next.

Step 1: Model Identification

1. The first step in model identification is to determine whether the series is stationary, that is, whether the time series appears to vary about a fixed level. It is useful to look at a plot of the series along with the sample autocorrelation function. A nonstationary time series is indicated if the series appears to grow or decline over time and the sample autocorrelations fail to die out rapidly. The time series pictured in Figure 8-2 are nonstationary, and the pattern of sample autocorrelations shown in Figure 8-3 is typical for a nonstationary series. (See p. 330.)

---

[4]Notice that when $q = 0$, the ARMA$(p, 0)$ model reduces to a pure autoregressive model of order p. Similarly, when $p = 0$, the ARMA$(0, q)$ model is a pure moving average model of order q.

If the series is not stationary, it can often be converted to a stationary series by differencing. That is, the original series is replaced by a series of differences. An ARMA model is then specified for the differenced series. In effect, the analyst is modeling changes rather than levels.

As an example, suppose the original series Y_t is generally increasing over time, but the first differences $\Delta Y_t = Y_t - Y_{t-1}$ vary about a fixed level. It may be appropriate to model the stationary differences using an ARMA model of, say, order $p = 1$ and $q = 1$. In this case the model is[5]

$$\Delta Y_t = \phi_1 \Delta Y_{t-1} + \varepsilon_t - \omega_1 \varepsilon_{t-1}$$

or

$$(Y_t - Y_{t-1}) = \phi_1 (Y_{t-1} - Y_{t-2}) + \varepsilon_t - \omega_1 \varepsilon_{t-1}$$

In some cases, it may be necessary to difference the differences before stationary data are obtained. Simple differencing is done twice and the stationary data are

$$\Delta^2 Y_t = \Delta(\Delta Y_t) = \Delta(Y_t - Y_{t-1}) = Y_t - 2Y_{t-1} + Y_{t-2}$$

Differencing is done until a plot of the data indicates the series varies about a fixed level, and the sample autocorrelations die out fairly rapidly. The number of differences required to achieve stationarity is denoted by d.

Models for nonstationary series are called autoregressive *integrated* moving average models and denoted by ARIMA(p, d, q).[6] Here p indicates the order of the autoregressive part, d indicates the amount of differencing, and q indicates the order of the moving average part. If the original series is stationary, $d = 0$ and the ARIMA models reduce to the ARMA models. Consequently, from this point on, the ARIMA(p, d, q) notation is used to indicate models for both stationary $(d = 0)$ and nonstationary $(d > 0)$ time series.

Although ARIMA models involve differences, forecasts for the original series can always be computed directly from the fitted model.

2. Once a stationary series has been obtained, the analyst must identify the form of the model to be used.

This second part of step 1 is accomplished by comparing the autocorrelations and partial autocorrelations computed from the data to the theoretical auto-correlations and partial autocorrelations for the various ARIMA models. The theoretical correlations for some of the more common ARIMA models are shown in Figures 9-2, 9-3, and 9-4 for help in selecting an appropriate model.

Each ARIMA model has a unique set of autocorrelations and partial autocor-relations, and the analyst should be able to match the corresponding sample values to one of the theoretical patterns.

There may be some ambiguity in determining an appropriate ARIMA model from the patterns of the sample autocorrelations and partial autocorrelations. Thus the initial model selection should be regarded as tentative. Analyses can be done during Steps 2 and 3 to determine if the model is adequate. If not, an alternative model can be tried. With a little practice, the analyst should become more adept at identifying an adequate model.

---

[5] When an ARMA model is used for a differenced series, the constant term ϕ_0 may not be required.

[6] The term *integrated* means the differences must be summed (or integrated) to get the original series.

Remember, if sample autocorrelations die out exponentially to zero and sample partial autocorrelations cut off, the model will require autoregressive terms. If the sample autocorrelations cut off and the sample partial autocorrelations die out, the model will require moving average terms. If both sample autocorrelations and sample partial autocorrelations die out, both autoregressive and moving average terms are indicated. By counting the number of significant sample autocorrelations and partial autocorrelations, the orders of the MA and AR parts can be determined. To judge their significance, both the sample autocorrelations and sample partial autocorrelations are usually compared with $\pm 2/\sqrt{n}$ where n is the number of observations in the time series. These limits work well when n is large.

All things being equal, simple models are preferred to complex models. This is known as the *principle of parsimony*. With a limited amount of data, it is relatively easy to find a model with a large number of parameters that fits the data well. However, forecasts from such a model are likely to be poor because much of the variation in the data due to random error is being modeled. The goal is to develop the simplest model that provides an adequate description of the major features of the data.

The *principle of parsimony* refers to the preference for simple models over complex ones.

Step 2: Model Estimation

1.   Once a tentative model has been selected, the parameters for that model must be estimated.

     The parameters in ARIMA models are estimated by minimizing the sum of squares of the fitting errors. These least squares estimates must, in general, be obtained using a nonlinear least squares procedure. A nonlinear least squares procedure is simply an algorithm that finds the minimum of the sum of squared errors function. After the least squares estimates and their standard errors are determined, t values can be constructed and interpreted in the usual way. Parameters that are judged significantly different from zero are retained in the fitted model; parameters that are not significant are dropped from the model. For example, suppose an ARIMA$(1, 0, 1)$ has been fit to a time series of 100 observations and the fitted equation is

$$\hat{Y}_t = 33.4 \;+\; .25 Y_{t-1} \;-\; .5 \hat{\varepsilon}_{t-1}$$
$$\phantom{\hat{Y}_t = }(7.02)\quad (.17)\qquad\;\; (.21)$$

where the numbers in parentheses under the estimated coefficients are their standard errors. Because the t ratio for the coefficient of the autoregressive term is $t = .25/.17 = 1.47$ with a p-value of .14, the hypothesis $H_0 : \phi_1 = 0$ is not rejected, and this term could be deleted from the model. An ARIMA$(0, 0, 1)$ model—that is, an MA(1) model—could then be fit to the data.

2.   In addition, the *residual mean square error*, an estimate of the variance of the error ε_t, is computed.

     The residual mean square error is defined as[7]

$$s^2 = \frac{\displaystyle\sum_{t=1}^{n} e_t^2}{n-r} = \frac{\displaystyle\sum_{t=1}^{n} (Y_t - \hat{Y}_t)^2}{n-r} \tag{9.4}$$

---

[7] The square root of s^2, $s = \sqrt{s^2}$, is analogous to the standard error of the estimate (see Equation 7.4).

where
$$e_t = Y_t - \hat{Y}_t = \text{the residual at time } t$$
$$n = \text{the number of residuals}$$
$$r = \text{the total number of parameters estimated}$$

The residual mean square error is useful for assessing fit and comparing different models. It is also used to calculate forecast error limits.

Step 3: Model Checking

Before using the model for forecasting, it must be checked for adequacy. Basically, a model is adequate if the residuals cannot be used to improve the forecasts. That is, the residuals should be random.

1. Many of the same residual plots that are useful in regression analysis can be developed for the residuals from an ARIMA model. A histogram and a normal probability plot (to check for normality) and a time sequence plot (to check for outliers) are particularly helpful.
2. The individual residual autocorrelations should be small and generally within $\pm 2/\sqrt{n}$ of zero. Significant residual autocorrelations at low lags or seasonal lags suggest the model is inadequate and a new or modified model should be selected.
3. The residual autocorrelations as a group should be consistent with those produced by random errors.

An overall check of model adequacy is provided by a chi-square (χ^2) test based on the Ljung-Box Q statistic. This test looks at the sizes of the residual autocorrelations as a group. The test statistic Q is

$$Q_m = n(n+2) \sum_{k=1}^{m} \frac{r_k^2(e)}{n-k} \qquad (9.5)$$

which is approximately distributed as a chi-square random variable with $m - r$ degrees of freedom, where r is the total number of parameters estimated in the ARIMA model. In Equation 9.5,

$$r_k(e) = \text{the residual autocorrelation at lag } k$$
$$n = \text{the number of residuals}$$
$$k = \text{the time lag}$$
$$m = \text{the number of time lags to be tested}$$

If the p-value associated with the Q statistic is small (say, p-value $< .05$), the model is considered inadequate. The analyst should consider a new or modified model and continue the analysis until a satisfactory model has been determined.

Judgment plays a large role in the model-building effort. Two simple competing models may adequately describe the data, and a choice may be made on the basis of the nature of the forecasts. In addition, a few large residuals may be ignored if they can be explained by unusual circumstances, and the model is adequate for the remainder of the observations.

Step 4: Forecasting with the Model

1. After an adequate model has been found, forecasts for one period or several periods into the future can be made.

Prediction intervals based on the forecasts can also be constructed. In general, for a given confidence level, the longer the forecast lead time, the larger the prediction interval. This is sensible because the uncertainty is expected to be greater for a forecast of a distant value than it is for a forecast of, say, the next observation. Calculating forecasts and prediction intervals is tedious and best left to the computer. Computer programs that fit ARIMA models generate forecasts and prediction intervals at the analyst's request.

2. As more data become available, the same ARIMA model can be used to generate revised forecasts from another time origin.

3. If the pattern of the series appears to be changing over time, the new data may be used to re-estimate the model parameters or, if necessary, to develop an entirely new model.

It is a good idea to monitor the forecast errors. If the magnitudes of the most recent errors tend to be consistently larger than previous errors, it may be time to reevaluate the model. At this point, another iteration of the model-building strategy may be required. The same holds true if the recent forecast errors tend to be consistently positive (underpredicting) or negative (overpredicting).

Example 9.3

The Cameron Consulting Corporation specializes in portfolio investment services. Lynn Stephens, the company analyst, was assigned the task of developing more sophisticated techniques for forecasting Dow Jones averages. Lynn recently attended a workshop on Box-Jenkins methodology and decided to try the technique on the Transportation Index. Table 9-3 represents 65 daily closing averages of the Transportation Index during the summer months.

Lynn began the analysis by looking at a plot of the data shown in Figure 9-5. There appeared to be an upward trend in the series. Her next step in identifying a tentative model was to look at the sample autocorrelations of the data shown in Figure 9-6. When Lynn observed that the first several autocorrelations were persistently large and trailed off to zero rather slowly, she recognized that her original observation was correct and that this time series was nonstationary and did not vary about a fixed level.

Lynn decided to difference the data to see if she could eliminate the trend and create a stationary series. A plot of the differenced data (not shown) appears to vary about a fixed level. In fact, the sample mean of the differences was 1.035. The sample autocorrelations

TABLE 9-3   Daily Closing Averages of the Transportation Index for Example 9.3

Time Period	Closing Average	Time Period	Closing Average	Time Period	Closing Average	Time Period	Closing Average	Time Period	Closing Average
1	222.34	15	223.07	29	246.74	43	249.76	57	268.21
2	222.24	16	225.36	30	248.73	44	251.66	58	272.16
3	221.17	17	227.60	31	248.83	45	253.41	59	272.79
4	218.88	18	226.82	32	248.78	46	252.04	60	275.03
5	220.05	19	229.69	33	249.61	47	248.78	61	278.49
6	219.61	20	229.30	34	249.90	48	247.76	62	281.75
7	216.40	21	228.96	35	246.45	49	249.27	63	285.70
8	217.33	22	229.99	36	247.57	50	247.95	64	286.33
9	219.69	23	233.05	37	247.76	51	251.41	65	288.57
10	219.32	24	235.00	38	247.81	52	254.67		
11	218.25	25	236.17	39	250.68	53	258.62		
12	220.30	26	238.31	40	251.80	54	259.25		
13	222.54	27	241.14	41	251.07	55	261.49		
14	223.56	28	241.48	42	248.05	56	264.95		

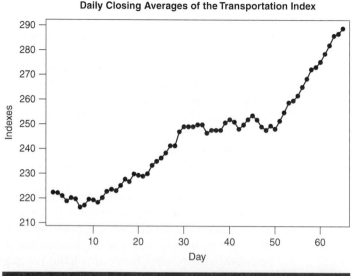

FIGURE 9-5   Daily Closing Averages of the Dow Jones Transportation Index

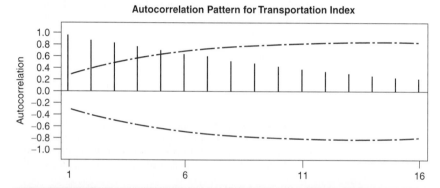

FIGURE 9-6   Sample Autocorrelation Function for the Transportation Index

for the differences are shown in Figure 9-7. The sample partial autocorrelations for the differences are displayed in Figure 9-8.

Lynn was perplexed. Comparing the autocorrelations with their error limits, the only significant autocorrelation was at lag 1. Similarly, only the lag 1 partial autocorrelation was significant. The autocorrelations appear to cut off after lag 1, indicating MA(1) behavior. At the same time, the partial autocorrelations appear to cut off after lag 1, indicating AR(1) behavior. Neither pattern appears to die out in a declining manner at low lags. Lynn decides to fit both ARIMA(1, 1, 0) and ARIMA(0, 1, 1) models to the Transportation Index. She decides to include a constant term in each model to allow for the fact that the series of differences appears to vary about a level greater than zero. If Y_t denotes the Transportation Index, then the differenced series is $\Delta Y_t = Y_t - Y_{t-1}$ and Lynn's models are

$$\text{ARIMA}(1, 1, 0): \quad \Delta Y_t = \phi_0 + \phi_1 \Delta Y_{t-1} + \varepsilon_t$$

$$\text{ARIMA}(0, 1, 1): \quad \Delta Y_t = \mu + \varepsilon_t - \omega_1 \varepsilon_{t-1}$$

The Minitab outputs for Lynn's models are shown in Table 9-4. The residual autocorrelations for the ARIMA(1, 1, 0) model fit are shown in Figure 9-9.

Autocorrelation Pattern for Transportation Index Differenced

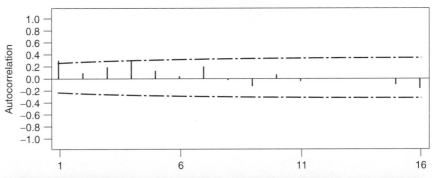

FIGURE 9-7   Sample Autocorrelation Function for the First Differences of the Transportation Index

Partial Autocorrelations for Transportation Data Differenced

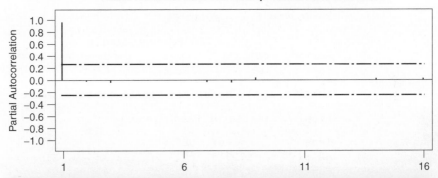

FIGURE 9-8   Sample Partial Autocorrelations for the First Differences of the Transportation Index

Both models fit the data equally well. The residual mean squares (MS) are

$$\text{ARIMA}(1, 1, 0): \quad s^2 = 3.536$$
$$\text{ARIMA}(0, 1, 1): \quad s^2 = 3.538$$

Lynn also notices that the constant in the ARIMA(0, 1, 1) model is estimated to be $\hat{\mu} = 1.038$, (essentially) the sample mean of the differences.

Figure 9-9 shows there is no significant residual autocorrelation for the ARIMA(1, 1, 0) model. Although the residual autocorrelation function for the ARIMA(0, 1, 1) model is not shown, the results are similar. The Ljung-Box Q_m statistics computed for groups of lags $m = 12, 24, 36$, and 48 are not significant as indicated by the large p-values for either model. Lynn decides that either model is adequate. Moreover, the one-step-ahead forecasts provided by the two models are nearly the same.

To resolve her dilemma, Lynn opts for the ARIMA(1, 1, 0) model on the basis of its slightly better fit. She checks the forecast for period 66 for this model as follows.

$$Y_t - Y_{t-1} = \phi_0 + \phi_1(Y_{t-1} - Y_{t-2}) + \varepsilon_t$$

or

$$Y_t = Y_{t-1} + \phi_0 + \phi_1(Y_{t-1} - Y_{t-2}) + \varepsilon_t$$

TABLE 9-4	Minitab Output for ARIMA(1, 1, 0) and ARIMA(0, 1, 1) Models Fit to Transportation Index

ARIMA(1, 1, 0): Model for Transportation Index

```
Final Estimates of Parameters
Type          Coef   SE Coef      T       P
AR 1        0.2844   0.1221    2.33   0.023
Constant    0.7408   0.2351    3.15   0.003

Differencing: 1 regular difference
Number of observations: Original series 65, after differencing 64
Residuals:  SS = 219.223 (backforecasts excluded)
            MS = 3.536 DF = 62

Modified Box-Pierce (Ljung-Box) Chi-Square statistic
Lag               12      24      36      48
Chi-Square      11.8    29.1    37.1    48.1
DF                10      22      34      46
P-Value        0.297   0.141   0.328   0.389

Forecasts from period 65

                     95 Percent Limits
Period  Forecast    Lower     Upper    Actual
66       289.948   286.262   293.634
```

ARIMA(0, 1, 1): Model for Transportation Index

```
Final Estimates of Parameters

Type           Coef   SE Coef       T       P
MA 1        -0.2913   0.1226    -2.38   0.021
Constant     1.0381   0.3035     3.42   0.001

Differencing: 1 regular difference
Number of observations: Original series 65, after differencing 64
Residuals:  SS = 219.347 (backforecasts excluded)
            MS = 3.538 DF = 62

Modified Box-Pierce (Ljung-Box) Chi-Square statistic
Lag               12      24      36      48
Chi-Square      11.6    32.0    41.0    51.4
DF                10      22      34      46
P-Value        0.310   0.077   0.189   0.270

Forecasts from period 65
                     95 Percent Limits
Period  Forecast    Lower     Upper    Actual
66       290.053   286.366   293.740
```

so with $\hat{\phi}_0 = .741$ and $\hat{\phi}_1 = .284$ the forecasting equation becomes

$$\hat{Y}_{66} = Y_{65} + .741 + .284(Y_{65} - Y_{64})$$
$$= 288.57 + .741 + .284(288.57 - 286.23) = 289.947$$

The forecast agrees with the result in Table 9-4. The prediction interval for the actual value in period 66 calculated by Minitab is (286.3, 293.6).

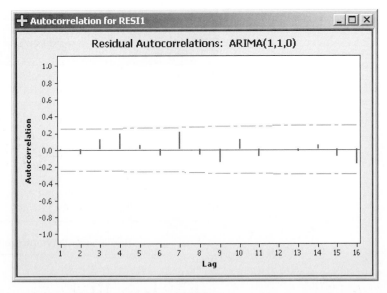

Autocorrelation Function: RESI1

Lag	ACF	T	LBQ	Lag	ACF	T	LBQ
1	-0.002164	-0.02	0.00	9	-0.155310	-1.12	10.09
2	-0.054880	-0.44	0.21	10	0.119656	0.85	11.21
3	0.126703	1.01	1.32	11	-0.087686	-0.61	11.82
4	0.192990	1.52	3.94	12	0.005717	0.04	11.83
5	0.053912	0.41	4.15	13	-0.024945	-0.17	11.88
6	-0.069976	-0.53	4.50	14	0.052536	0.37	12.11
7	0.215477	1.62	7.94	15	-0.083232	-0.58	12.71
8	-0.062525	-0.45	8.24	16	-0.170800	-1.18	15.28

FIGURE 9-9   Residual Autocorrelations: ARIMA(1, 1, 0) Model Fit to Transportation Index

Example 9.4

The analyst for Atron Corporation, Jim White, had a time series of readings for a process that needed to be forecast. The data are shown in Table 9-5. The readings are plotted in Figure 9-10. Jim believed that the Box-Jenkins methodology might work best for these data.

Jim began to identify a tentative model by looking at the plot of the data and the sample autocorrelations shown in Figure 9-11. The time series of readings appears to vary about a fixed level of around 80, and the autocorrelations die out rapidly toward zero. Jim concluded that the time series is stationary.

The first sample autocorrelation coefficient (−.53) is significantly different from zero at the 5% level because it lies outside the range

$$0 \pm 2\frac{1}{\sqrt{n}} = 0 \pm 2\frac{1}{\sqrt{75}} = 0 \pm 2(.115) = 0 \pm .23$$

The autocorrelation at lag 2 is close to significant at the 5% level and opposite in sign from the lag 1 autocorrelation r_1. The remaining autocorrelations are small and well within their individual error limits. The pattern of the autocorrelations suggests either an AR(1) model [see Figure 9-2(b)] or, perhaps, an MA(2) model if the autocorrelations cut off (are zero) after lag 2. Jim decided to examine the sample partial autocorrelations shown in Figure 9-12.

Jim noticed that the first partial autocorrelation (−.53) was significantly different from zero, but none of the other partial autocorrelations approached significance.[8] Jim feels

---

[8] The value of the first partial autocorrelation is equal to the value of the first autocorrelation (both are −.53). This is a characteristic of a first-order autoregressive process.

TABLE 9-5		Readings for the Atron Process for Example 9.4 (read by columns)					
60.0	99.0	75.0	79.5	61.5	88.5	72.0	90.0
81.0	25.5	78.0	64.5	81.0	51.0	66.0	78.0
72.0	93.0	66.0	99.0	76.5	85.5	73.5	87.0
78.0	75.0	97.5	72.0	84.0	58.5	66.0	99.0
61.5	57.0	60.0	78.0	57.0	90.0	73.5	72.0
78.0	88.5	97.5	63.0	84.0	60.0	103.5	
57.0	76.5	61.5	66.0	73.5	78.0	60.0	
84.0	82.5	96.0	84.0	78.0	66.0	81.0	
72.0	72.0	79.5	66.0	49.5	97.5	87.0	
67.8	76.5	72.0	87.0	78.0	64.5	73.5	

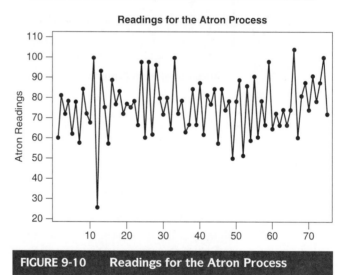

FIGURE 9-10   Readings for the Atron Process

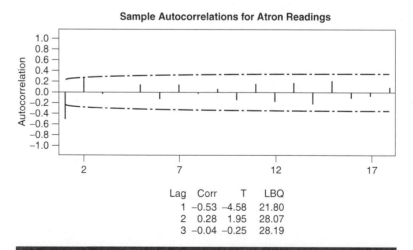

Lag	Corr	T	LBQ
1	−0.53	−4.58	21.80
2	0.28	1.95	28.07
3	−0.04	−0.25	28.19

FIGURE 9-11   Sample Autocorrelation Function for the Atron Readings

Partial Autocorrelations for the Atron Readings

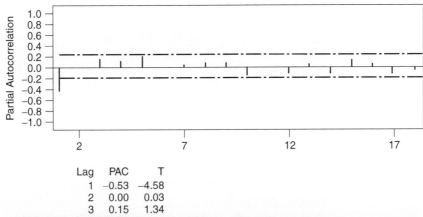

Lag	PAC	T
1	−0.53	−4.58
2	0.00	0.03
3	0.15	1.34

FIGURE 9-12   Sample Partial Autocorrelations for the Atron Readings

the autocorrelations and partial autocorrelations suggest an AR(1) [or, equivalently, an ARIMA(1, 0, 0)] model but, to play safe, he decides to fit an MA(2) [ARIMA(0, 0, 2)] model as well. If both models are adequate, he will decide the issue using the principle of parsimony.

Table 9-6 shows the results of using Minitab to fit the AR(1) and MA(2) models to the readings for the Atron process. A constant term is included in both models to allow for the fact that the readings vary about a level other than zero.[9]

Both models appear to fit the data well. The estimated coefficients are significantly different from zero. The mean square errors are similar:

$$\text{MA(2): } s^2 = 135.1$$
$$\text{AR(1): } s^2 = 137.9$$

The one- and two-step-ahead forecasts from the two models are somewhat different, but the three-step-ahead (period 78) forecasts are nearly the same. For a fixed forecast origin, forecasts for stationary processes will eventually equal the estimated mean level. In this case, the mean level is estimated to be approximately $\hat{\mu} = 75$ for both models.

The Ljung-Box (modified Box-Pierce) Q_m statistic is not significant for collections of lags $m = 12, 24, 36,$ and 48 for either model. The residual autocorrelations for the AR(1) model are shown in Figure 9-13. The individual residual autocorrelations are small and well within their error limits. The residual autocorrelation function for the MA(2) model is similar. For each model, there is no reason to believe the errors are not random.

Because the AR(1) model has two parameters (including the constant term) and the MA(2) model has three parameters (including the constant term), Jim appeals to the principle of parsimony and decides to use the simpler AR(1) model to forecast future readings.

The AR(1) forecasting equation is[10]

$$\hat{Y}_t = 115.842 + (-.538)Y_{t-1} = 115.842 - .538Y_{t-1}$$

so, for period 76,

$$\hat{Y}_{76} = 115.842 - .538Y_{75} = 115.842 - .538(72) = 77.11$$

---

[9] If the data had been expressed as deviations from the sample mean, a constant term would not be required in either model.

[10] The error term ε_t is dropped because, for the forecast $\hat{Y}_t$, the best guess of ε_t is zero.

TABLE 9-6   Minitab Output for MA(2) and AR(1) Models for the Atron Readings

ARIMA(0,0,2) Model: Atron readings

Final Estimates of Parameters

Type	Coef	SE Coef	T	P
MA 1	0.5667	0.1107	5.12	0.000
MA 2	−0.3560	0.1146	−3.11	0.003
Constant	75.410	1.061	71.08	0.000
Mean	75.410	1.061		

Number of observations: 75
Residuals: SS = 9724.97 (backforecasts excluded)
            MS = 135.07 DF = 72

Modified Box-Pierce (Ljung-Box) Chi-Square statistic

Lag	12	24	36	48
Chi-Square	7.0	23.8	31.8	46.9
DF	9	21	33	45
P-Value	0.638	0.305	0.526	0.394

Forecasts from period 75

		95 Percent Limits		
Period	Forecast	Lower	Upper	Actual
76	80.648	57.864	103.431	
77	78.169	51.982	104.356	
78	75.410	47.996	102.825	

ARIMA(1,0,0) Model: Atron readings

Final Estimates of Parameters

Type	Coef	SE Coef	T	P
AR 1	−0.5379	0.0986	−5.46	0.000
Constant	115.842	1.356	85.44	0.000
Mean	75.3269	0.8817		

Number of observations: 75
Residuals: SS = 10065.2 (backforecasts excluded)
            MS = 137.9 DF = 73

Modified Box-Pierce (Ljung-Box) Chi-Square statistic

Lag	12	24	36	48
Chi-Square	9.3	29.9	37.3	58.3
DF	10	22	34	46
P-Value	0.503	0.121	0.319	0.105

Forecasts from period 75

		95 Percent Limits		
Period	Forecast	Lower	Upper	Actual
76	77.116	54.097	100.136	
77	74.364	48.227	100.502	
78	75.845	48.872	102.817	

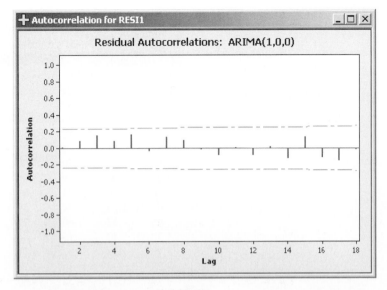

Autocorrelation Function: RESI1

Lag	ACF	T	LBQ	Lag	ACF	T	LBQ
1	0.011666	0.10	0.01	10	-0.087622	-0.69	8.61
2	0.086969	0.75	0.61	11	0.013357	0.11	8.62
3	0.152240	1.31	2.47	12	-0.086323	-0.68	9.31
4	0.091121	0.77	3.14	13	0.022431	0.18	9.35
5	0.164081	1.37	5.36	14	-0.125549	-0.98	10.85
6	-0.035253	-0.29	5.47	15	0.131885	1.02	12.52
7	0.137130	1.11	7.07	16	-0.112050	-0.85	13.75
8	0.097466	0.78	7.88	17	-0.160319	-1.21	16.31
9	-0.021834	-0.17	7.93	18	-0.022964	-0.17	16.36

FIGURE 9-13   Autocorrelation Function for the Residuals of the AR(1) Model

Moreover, the two-step-ahead forecast is

$$\hat{Y}_{77} = 115.842 - .538\hat{Y}_{76} = 115.842 - .538(77.11) = 74.36$$

Jim was pleased to see that these results agreed with those on the Minitab output.

Example 9.5

Jim White was happy with the results of his forecasts for the time series of readings shown in Table 9-5. He decided to use the Box-Jenkins methodology to attempt to forecast the errors (deviations from target) resulting from the quality control of a manufacturing process under his administration. The data are given in Table 9-7, and the time series of errors is plotted in Figure 9-14.

Jim began the identification process by examining the plot of the error time series and by checking the autocorrelations and partial autocorrelations shown in Figures 9-15 and 9-16. The time series plot and the autocorrelation functions indicate the series is stationary. Because there is one significant autocorrelation of −.50 at lag 1 and the autocorrelations at the remaining lags are each small and well within their error limits, the sample autocorrelations appear to cut off after lag 1. Beginning with a significant partial autocorrelation at lag 1, the first three sample partial autocorrelations are all negative and decay toward zero. The behaviors of the sample autocorrelations and sample partial autocorrelations look much like the theoretical quantities for an MA(1) [ARIMA(0, 0, 1)] process shown in Figure 9-3(a). Jim is convinced his series could be represented by an MA(1) model.

TABLE 9-7	Errors for Atron Quality Control (read by columns)			
−.23	−.20	−1.93	−.97	.10
.63	−.21	1.87	.83	−.62
.48	.91	−.97	−.33	2.27
−.83	−.36	.46	.91	−.62
−.03	.48	2.12	−1.13	.74
1.31	.61	−2.11	2.22	−.16
.86	−1.38	.70	.80	1.34
−1.28	−.04	.69	−1.95	−1.83
0	.90	−.24	2.61	.31
−.63	1.79	.34	.59	1.13
.08	−.37	.60	.71	−.87
−1.30	.40	.15	−.84	1.45
1.48	−1.19	−.02	−.11	−1.95
−.28	.98	.46	1.27	−.51
−.79	−1.51	−.54	−.80	−.41
1.86	.90	.89	−.76	.49
.07	−1.56	1.07	1.58	1.54
.09	2.18	.20	−.38	−.96

Errors (Deviations from Target) for Atron Quality Control

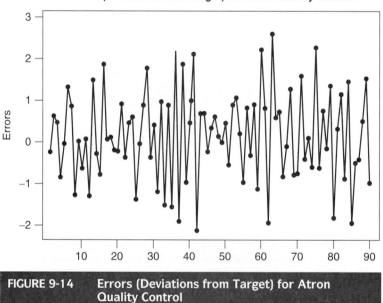

FIGURE 9-14	Errors (Deviations from Target) for Atron Quality Control

Jim used Minitab to fit an MA(1) model to his data. The results are displayed in Table 9-8. The parameters in the MA(1) model are estimated to be $\hat{\mu} = .1513$ and $\hat{\omega}_1 = .5875$. Each is significantly different from zero. The residual autocorrelations shown in Figure 9-17 and the Ljung-Box (modified Box-Pierce) chi-square statistics indicate the errors are random.

The MA(1) forecasting equation is

$$\hat{Y}_t = \hat{\mu} - \hat{\omega}_1\varepsilon_{t-1} = .1513 - .5875\varepsilon_{t-1}$$

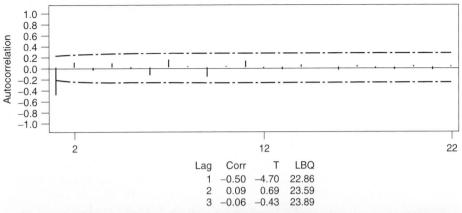

Autocorrelation Pattern for Atron Quality Control

Lag	Corr	T	LBQ
1	−0.50	−4.70	22.86
2	0.09	0.69	23.59
3	−0.06	−0.43	23.89

FIGURE 9-15   Sample Autocorrelations for Atron Quality Control

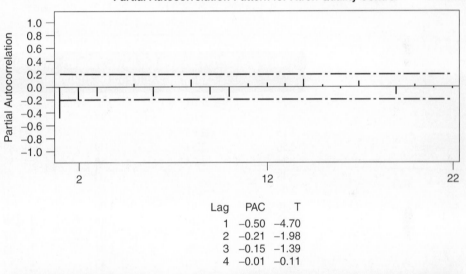

Partial Autocorrelation Pattern for Atron Quality Control

Lag	PAC	T
1	−0.50	−4.70
2	−0.21	−1.98
3	−0.15	−1.39
4	−0.01	−0.11

FIGURE 9-16   Sample Partial Autocorrelations for Atron Quality Control

where ε_{t-1} is estimated by the corresponding residual e_{t-1}. To forecast the error (deviation from target) for period 91, the residual for period 90, $e_{90} = -.4804$, is required. Jim computes

$$\hat{Y}_{91} = .1513 - .5875(-.4804) = .4335$$

Jim's forecast of the quality control error in period 92 is simply the estimated mean of the series because, at forecast origin $t = 90$, the best guess of the error term in period 91, ε_{91}, is zero. So,

$$\hat{Y}_{92} = .1513 - .5875(0) = .1513$$

Jim was happy to see that his calculated forecasts agreed with those from Minitab.

TABLE 9-8	Minitab Output for MA(1) Model for Atron Quality Control

```
ARIMA(0,0,1) Model: Atron Quality Control

Final Estimates of Parameters
Type          Coef   SE Coef      T      P
MA 1        0.5875   0.0864    6.80   0.000
Constant   0.15129  0.04022    3.76   0.000
Mean       0.15129  0.04022

Number of observations: 90
Residuals:   SS = 74.4933 (backforecasts excluded)
             MS = 0.8465 DF = 88

Modified Box-Pierce (Ljung-Box) Chi-Square statistic
Lag               12     24     36     48
Chi-Square       9.1   10.8   17.3   31.5
DF                10     22     34     46
P-Value        0.524  0.977  0.992  0.950


Forecasts from period 90
                     95 Percent Limits
Period  Forecast      Lower    Upper   Actual
91       0.43350    -1.37018  2.23719
92       0.15129    -1.94064  2.24322
```

TABLE 9-9	Errors for Ed Jones' Quality Control for Example 9.6 (read by columns)

.77	1.04	−2.46	−.73	−.23
.33	1.02	−.37	.10	1.05
2.15	−2.03	.80	−1.47	−.66
2.50	−2.54	.49	−.89	.25
1.36	−.23	.50	−.53	−.63
.48	.49	.07	−.20	.91
2.05	−.87	1.92	−.70	−.21
−1.46	.61	1.00	−.27	.24
−1.13	.20	2.16	.39	.05
−2.85	.98	.04	−.07	.85
−2.67	.78	1.91	.89	1.55
−2.71	.80	.43	.37	.40
−1.30	.86	−.32	−.75	1.82
−.88	1.72	−.48	−1.24	.81
−.07	.15	−.13	−.62	.28
−1.47	−1.15	−2.26	−.54	1.06

Example 9.6

The analyst for Atron Corporation, Jim White, was delighted with the forecasts of the quality control errors that he developed using the Box-Jenkins methodology discussed in Example 9.5. Jim met his old friend Ed Jones at a conference and told him about his success. Ed had been struggling with a similar application and decided to give Box-Jenkins a try. Ed's data are given in Table 9-9 and a time series plot of the data is shown in Figure 9-18.

The plot of the series and the sample autocorrelations, shown in Figure 9-19, suggest that the series of quality control errors is stationary. The errors appear to vary about a fixed level of zero, and the autocorrelations die out rather quickly.

Ed noticed the first two autocorrelations were significantly different from zero and, perhaps more importantly, the autocorrelations for the first few time lags fell off toward

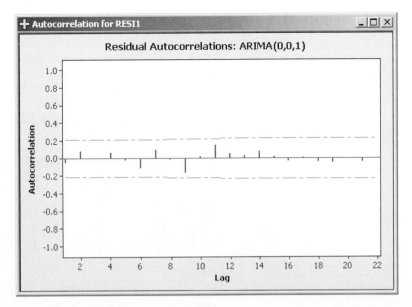

Autocorrelation Function: RESI1

Lag	ACF	T	LBQ	Lag	ACF	T	LBQ
1	-0.049843	-0.47	0.23	12	0.056395	0.49	9.08
2	0.076340	0.72	0.78	13	0.022413	0.20	9.14
3	0.003799	0.04	0.78	14	0.075709	0.66	9.76
4	0.063375	0.60	1.17	15	0.015967	0.14	9.79
5	-0.029768	-0.28	1.25	16	-0.036527	-0.32	9.94
6	-0.112420	-1.05	2.50	17	0.006337	0.05	9.94
7	0.101193	0.94	3.52	18	-0.040046	-0.35	10.13
8	-0.017494	-0.16	3.55	19	-0.051729	-0.45	10.44
9	-0.169055	-1.55	6.47	20	-0.003963	-0.03	10.44
10	0.015437	0.14	6.50	21	-0.039909	-0.35	10.63
11	0.146365	1.31	8.74	22	0.002874	0.02	10.63

FIGURE 9-17   Autocorrelation Function for the Residuals of the MA(1) Model

zero much like the theoretical pattern for an AR(1) process [see Figure 9-2(a)]. Ed also examined the sample partial autocorrelations shown in Figure 9-20. As he suspected, the partial autocorrelations seemed to cut off after the significant partial autocorrelation at lag 1.[11] Taken together, the sample autocorrelation and sample partial autocorrelation patterns were consistent with an AR(1) process, and Ed felt comfortable fitting an AR(1) [ARIMA(1, 0, 0)] model to his time series of errors (deviations from target).

The Minitab output for Ed's initial attempt with the Box-Jenkins methodology is given in Table 9-10. Because the sample mean of the error series is extremely small (close to zero) compared with its standard deviation, Ed did not include a constant term in his AR(1) model.

The parameter in the AR(1) model is estimated to be $\hat{\phi}_1 = .501$, and it is significantly different from zero ($t = 5.11$). The residual mean square error is $s^2 = 1.0998$. Plots of the residuals (not shown), the Ljung-Box chi-square statistics, and the residual autocorrelations displayed in Figure 9-21 suggest the AR(1) model is adequate. There is no reason to doubt the usual error term assumptions.

The AR(1) forecasting equation is

$$\hat{Y}_t = .501Y_{t-1}$$

---

[11] Ed attributed the significant partial autocorrelation at lag 5 to sampling error because he could find no physical reason why the quality control errors five time periods apart should be correlated.

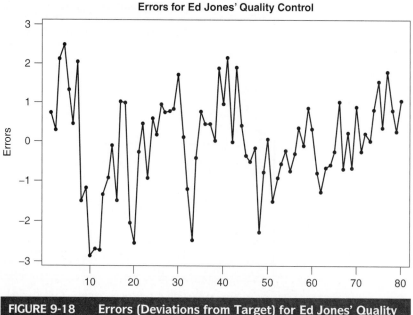

FIGURE 9-18   Errors (Deviations from Target) for Ed Jones' Quality Control

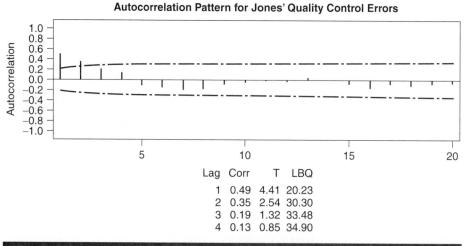

FIGURE 9-19   Sample Autocorrelations for Ed Jones' Quality Control

so the forecasts for time periods 81 and 82 are

$$\hat{Y}_{81} = .501Y_{80} = .501(1.06) = .531$$
$$\hat{Y}_{82} = .501\hat{Y}_{81} = .501(.531) = .266$$

Ed's computed forecasts agree with the one- and two-step-ahead forecasts generated by Minitab.

Because it was his first experience with the Box-Jenkins methodology, Ed decided to fit a slightly more complex model to see if the results would confirm his choice of an AR(1) model for his data. He decided to add an additional parameter and fit an ARMA(1, 1)

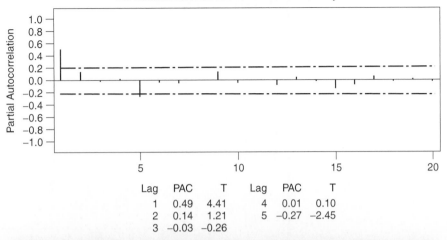

Partial Autocorrelations for Ed Jones' Quality Control

Lag	PAC	T	Lag	PAC	T
1	0.49	4.41	4	0.01	0.10
2	0.14	1.21	5	−0.27	−2.45
3	−0.03	−0.26			

FIGURE 9-20   Sample Partial Autocorrelations for Ed Jones' Quality Control

TABLE 9-10   Minitab Output for AR(1) Model for Ed Jones' Quality Control

```
ARIMA(1,0,0) Model: Ed Jones' Quality Control Errors

Final Estimates of Parameters
Type    Coef  SE Coef     T       P
AR 1  0.5008   0.0980   5.11   0.000

Number of observations: 80
Residuals:   SS = 86.8808 (backforecasts excluded)
             MS = 1.0998 DF = 79

Modified Box-Pierce (Ljung-Box) Chi-Square statistic
Lag             12      24      36      48
Chi-Square    10.7    19.5    36.2    44.2
DF              11      23      35      47
P-Value      0.468   0.669   0.410   0.591

Forecasts from period 80
                    95 Percent Limits
Period  Forecast      Lower     Upper    Actual
81       0.53088   −1.52498   2.58673
82       0.26588   −2.03340   2.56515
```

[ARIMA(1, 0, 1)] model to the quality control errors. He reasoned that if his AR(1) model was correct, the moving average parameter in the ARMA(1, 1) model should not be significant.

Table 9-11 shows the output for the ARMA(1, 1) model fit to Ed's series. Ed was pleased to see that the MA(1) parameter was not significantly different from zero ($t = 1.04$), implying that this term is not needed. Of course, because it is a slightly more general model than the AR(1) model, it still adequately represents the data as indicated by $s^2 = 1.0958$ and the random behavior of the residuals.

Example 9.7

Jill Blake, the analyst for the ISC Corporation, was asked to develop forecasts for the closing prices of ISC stock. The stock had been languishing for some time with little growth,

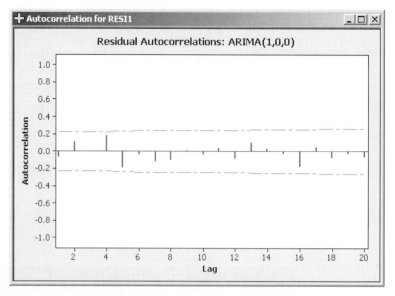

Autocorrelation Function: RESI1

Lag	ACF	T	LBQ	Lag	ACF	T	LBQ
1	-0.069795	-0.62	0.40	11	0.044251	0.36	10.00
2	0.113142	1.01	1.48	12	-0.085789	-0.69	10.71
3	0.002175	0.02	1.48	13	0.100085	0.80	11.69
4	0.178268	1.57	4.22	14	0.029426	0.23	11.77
5	-0.187692	-1.60	7.31	15	-0.029028	-0.23	11.86
6	-0.039199	-0.32	7.44	16	-0.179254	-1.42	15.15
7	-0.117368	-0.97	8.68	17	0.047315	0.37	15.38
8	-0.103656	-0.85	9.66	18	-0.075845	-0.59	15.99
9	0.013443	0.11	9.68	19	-0.027833	-0.21	16.08
10	-0.037854	-0.31	9.81	20	-0.070332	-0.54	16.62

FIGURE 9-21   Autocorrelation Function for the Residuals of the AR(1) Model

and senior management wanted some projections to discuss with the board of directors. The ISC stock prices are plotted in Figure 9-22 and listed in Table 9-12.

The plot of the stock prices suggests the series is stationary. It appears from Figure 9-22 as if the stock prices vary about a fixed level of approximately 250.

Jill believes the Box-Jenkins methodology might suit her purpose and immediately generates the sample autocorrelations and sample partial autocorrelations for the stock price series. The results are displayed in Figures 9-23 and 9-24.

Jill notices that the sample autocorrelations alternate in sign and decline to zero for low lags. The sample partial autocorrelations are similar but clearly cut off (are zero) after lag 2. Jill remembers the possible patterns for the theoretical autocorrelations and partial autocorrelations for an AR(2) process [see Figure 9-2(d)] and decides that the corresponding sample quantities are consistent with one of these patterns. She identifies an AR(2) [ARIMA(2, 0, 0)] model for her data.

Jill uses Minitab to estimate the parameters in her model. She includes a constant term to allow for a nonzero level. The output is shown in Table 9-13.

The parameter estimates are $\hat{\phi}_0 = 284.9$, $\hat{\phi}_1 = -.324$, and $\hat{\phi}_2 = .219$. The estimated coefficient $\hat{\phi}_2$ is not significant ($t = 1.75$) at the 5% level but is significant at the 10% level. Jill decides to keep this parameter in her model. The residual mean square is $s^2 = 2808$, and the residual autocorrelations given in Figure 9-25 are each well within their two standard error limits. In addition, the values of the Ljung-Box Q_m statistics for $m = 12, 24, 36$, and 48 are all small. Jill decides her model is adequate.

Jill uses her model to generate forecasts for periods 66 and 67 as follows.

**TABLE 9-11   Minitab Output for ARIMA(1, 0, 1) Model for Ed Jones'
Quality Control**

`ARIMA(1, 0, 1) Model: Ed Jones' Errors`

```
Final Estimates of Parameters
Type    Coef  SE Coef      T       P
AR 1  0.6671   0.1628   4.10   0.000
MA 1  0.2204   0.2121   1.04   0.302

Number of observations: 80
Residuals:   SS = 85.4710 (backforecasts excluded)
             MS = 1.0958 DF = 78

Modified Box-Pierce (Ljung-Box) Chi-Square statistic
Lag             12      24      36      48
Chi-Square     8.8    17.5    32.2    38.7
DF              10      22      34      46
P-Value      0.547   0.737   0.555   0.770

Forecasts from period 80
                  95 Percent Limits
Period  Forecast     Lower     Upper   Actual
81       0.52814  -1.52399   2.58027
82       0.35230  -1.89526   2.59985
```

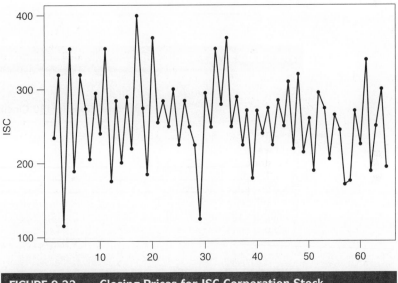

Closing Prices for ISC Corporation Stock

FIGURE 9-22   Closing Prices for ISC Corporation Stock

From forecast origin $t = 65$ the forecast for period 66 is generated by the equation

$$\hat{Y}_t = \hat{\phi}_0 + \hat{\phi}_1 Y_{t-1} + \hat{\phi}_2 Y_{t-2}$$

so

$$\hat{Y}_{66} = 284.9 + (-.324)Y_{65} + .219 Y_{64}$$
$$= 284.9 - .324(195) + .219(300) = 287.4$$

TABLE 9-12	Closing Prices for ISC Corporation Stock for Example 9.7 (read by columns)			
235	200	250	270	275
320	290	225	240	205
115	220	125	275	265
355	400	295	225	245
190	275	250	285	170
320	185	355	250	175
275	370	280	310	270
205	255	370	220	225
295	285	250	320	340
240	250	290	215	190
355	300	225	260	250
175	225	270	190	300
285	285	180	295	195

Autocorrelation Pattern for ISC Closing Stock Prices

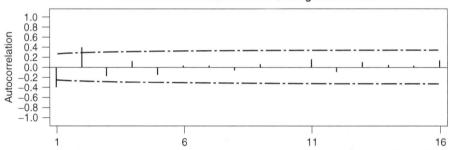

FIGURE 9-23   Sample Autocorrelations for the ISC Stock Prices

Partial Autocorrelations for ISC Closing Stock Prices

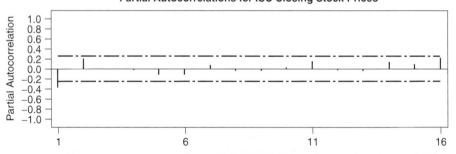

FIGURE 9-24   Sample Partial Autocorrelations for the ISC Stock Prices

Similarly,

$$\hat{Y}_{67} = 284.9 + (-.324)\hat{Y}_{66} + .219 Y_{65}$$

$$= 284.9 - .324(287.4) + .219(195) = 234.5$$

The results agree with those shown in the Minitab output in Table 9-13. For stationary series, the 95% prediction limits are approximately

$$\hat{Y} \pm 2s \qquad\qquad\qquad (9.6)$$

TABLE 9-13   Minitab Output for AR(2) Model for ISC Stock Prices

```
ARIMA(2,0,0) Model: ISC Closing Stock Prices

Final Estimates of Parameters
Type          Coef  SE Coef       T       P
AR 1       -0.3243   0.1246   -2.60   0.012
AR 2        0.2192   0.1251    1.75   0.085
Constant  284.903    6.573    43.34   0.000
Mean      257.828    5.949

Number of observations: 65
Residuals:  SS = 174093 (backforecasts excluded)
            MS = 2808 DF = 62

Modified Box-Pierce (Ljung-Box) Chi-Square statistic
Lag                12      24      36      48
Chi-Square        6.3    13.3    18.2    29.1
DF                  9      21      33      45
P-Value         0.707   0.899   0.983   0.969

Forecasts from period 65
                    95 Percent Limits
Period   Forecast     Lower     Upper   Actual
66        287.446   183.565   391.328
67        234.450   125.244   343.656
```

---

where $\hat{Y}$ is the forecast and s is the square root of the mean square error. For example, the approximate 95% prediction limits for period 66 are

$$287.4 \pm 2\sqrt{2808} = 287.4 \pm 106 \qquad \text{or} \qquad (181.4, 393.4)$$

This interval is close to the 95% interval given by Minitab for period 66 in Table 9-13.

Final Comments

In ARIMA modeling, it is *not* good practice to include AR and MA parameters to "cover all the possibilities" suggested by the sample autocorrelation and sample partial autocorrelation functions. That is, when in doubt, start with a model containing few rather than many parameters. The need for additional parameters will be evident from an examination of the residual autocorrelations and partial autocorrelations. If MA behavior is apparent in the residual autocorrelations and partial autocorrelations, add an MA parameter and fit the revised model. If the residual autocorrelations look like those of an AR process, add an AR term and refit the model.

Least squares estimates of autoregressive and moving average parameters in ARIMA models tend to be highly correlated. When there are more parameters than necessary, this leads to "tradeoffs" among the parameters and unstable models that can produce poor forecasts.

To summarize, it is good practice to start with a small number of clearly justifiable parameters and add one parameter at a time as needed. On the other side, if parameters in a fitted ARIMA model are not significant (as judged by their t ratios), delete one parameter at a time and refit the model. Because of the high correlation among estimated parameters, it may be the case that a previously nonsignificant parameter becomes significant.

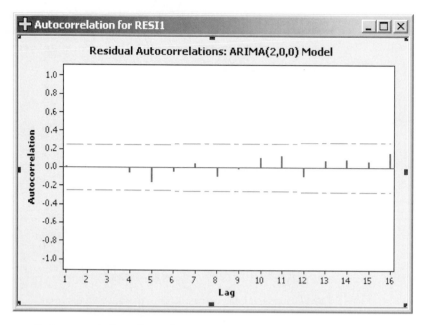

Autocorrelation Function: RESI1

Lag	ACF	T	LBQ	Lag	ACF	T	LBQ
1	0.010050	0.08	0.01	9	-0.023229	-0.18	3.40
2	-0.010389	-0.08	0.01	10	0.100117	0.77	4.20
3	-0.004837	-0.04	0.02	11	0.124524	0.95	5.45
4	-0.060200	-0.49	0.27	12	-0.103614	-0.78	6.33
5	-0.160907	-1.29	2.15	13	0.072227	0.54	6.77
6	-0.049459	-0.39	2.33	14	0.078554	0.58	7.29
7	0.041586	0.32	2.46	15	0.066695	0.49	7.68
8	-0.108359	-0.85	3.36	16	0.155047	1.14	9.82

FIGURE 9-25   Autocorrelation Function for the Residuals of the AR(2) Model

Model Selection Criteria

ARIMA models are identified (selected) by looking at a plot of the series and by matching sample autocorrelation and sample partial autocorrelation patterns with the known theoretical patterns of ARIMA processes. However, there is some subjectivity involved in this procedure, and it is possible that two (or more) initial models may be consistent with the patterns of the sample autocorrelations and partial autocorrelations. Moreover, after estimation and checking, both models may adequately represent the data. If the models contain the same number of parameters, the model with the smallest mean square error s^2 is ordinarily preferred. (This was the case for Lynn Stephens in Example 9.3.) If the models contain different numbers of parameters, the parsimony principle leads to the selection of the simpler model. However, the model with more parameters may have an appreciably smaller mean square error.

An approach to model selection that considers both the model fit and the number of parameters has been developed. The information criterion of Akaike,[12] or *AIC*,

[12] See H. Akaike, "A New Look at the Statistical Model Identification," *IEEE Trans. Automatic Control* AC-19 (1974): 716–723.

selects the best model from a group of candidate models as the one that minimizes

$$AIC = \ln \hat{\sigma}^2 + \frac{2}{n}r \qquad (9.7)$$

where

$\ln$ = the natural log
$\hat{\sigma}^2$ = the residual sum of squares divided by the number of observations
n = the number of observations (residuals)
r = the total number of parameters (including the constant term) in the ARIMA model

The Bayesian information criterion developed by Schwarz,[13] or *BIC*, selects the model that minimizes

$$BIC = \ln \hat{\sigma}^2 + \frac{\ln n}{n}r \qquad (9.8)$$

The second term in both *AIC* and *BIC* is a "penalty factor" for including additional parameters in the model. Because the *BIC* criterion imposes a greater penalty for the number of parameters than does the *AIC* criterion, use of minimum *BIC* for model selection will result in a model whose number of parameters is no greater than that chosen by *AIC*. Often, the two criteria produce the same result.

AIC and *BIC* should be viewed as additional procedures to assist in model selection. They should not be used as substitutes for a careful examination of the sample autocorrelations and partial autocorrelations.

Example 9.8
In Example 9.4, Jim White found that two ARIMA models appeared to provide an adequate description of the readings for the Atron Corporation process. One was an AR(1) model with $r = 2$ estimated parameters (including a constant term) and $\hat{\sigma}^2 = 10,065/75 = 134.2$. The second model was an MA(2) model with $r = 3$ parameters (including a constant term) and $\hat{\sigma}^2 = 9,725/75 = 129.7$. Jim computed the *AIC* and *BIC* criteria as follows.

AR(1):
$$AIC = \ln(134.2) + \frac{2}{75}(2) = 4.8993 + .0533 = 4.9526$$
$$BIC = \ln(134.2) + \frac{\ln(75)}{75}(2) = 4.8993 + .1151 = 5.0144$$

MA(2):
$$AIC = \ln(129.7) + \frac{2}{75}(3) = 4.8652 + .0800 = 4.9452$$
$$BIC = \ln(129.7) + \frac{\ln(75)}{75}(3) = 4.8652 + .1727 = 5.0379$$

The AIC and *BIC* give conflicting results. The *AIC* is smallest for the MA(2) model, whereas the *BIC* is smallest for the AR(1) model. Jim remembers that the *BIC* will not select a model with more parameters than the *AIC* because of the larger penalty for additional parameters. Jim was happy to see his initial choice of the AR(1) model, based on the parsimony principle, was supported by the BIC criterion.

---

[13] See G. Schwarz, "Estimating the Dimension of a Model," *Annuals of Statistics* 6 (1978): 461–464.

Models for Seasonal Data

Seasonal data have a distinct pattern that repeats itself every year. The monthly sales of the Cavanaugh Company shown in Figure 5-1 (see p. 160) always peak in the late fall (October and November). For monthly data with an annual seasonal pattern, observations for the same months in different years should be correlated. That is, January in one year should be similar to January in the next year, February one year should be similar to February the next year, and so forth. So, not only are observations within the year related to one another (correlated), observations between years are related to one another (correlated). If the length of the seasonal period is S, so that $S = 12$ for monthly data and $S = 4$ for quarterly data, the autocorrelations and partial autocorrelations for seasonal processes are nonzero at low lags (within-year association) and at lags that are multiples of the seasonal period S (between-year association). The interpretations of the autocorrelations and partial autocorrelations at the seasonal lags are the same as the interpretation of the autocorrelations and partial autocorrelations at low lags. Seasonal ARIMA models contain regular autoregressive and moving average terms that account for the correlation at low lags and seasonal autoregressive and moving average terms that account for the correlation at the seasonal lags. In addition, for nonstationary seasonal series, an additional seasonal difference is often required to completely specify the model.

The next examples illustrate the development of seasonal ARIMA models. The same model-building strategy used for nonseasonal models is used for seasonal models. After an adequate model has been established, it can be used for forecasting.

Example 9.9

Kathy Fisher has been given the responsibility for forecasting sales for the Keytron Corporation. Kathy has been able to collect 115 consecutive months of sales data. The data begin in January 1987 and are shown in Table 9-14.

Kathy examined the time series plot in Figure 9-26 and noticed the pronounced seasonal pattern along with a general upward trend. She felt the series was nonstationary and decided to develop a seasonal ARIMA model for her data.

Kathy began the model identification step by looking at the sample autocorrelations shown in Figure 9-27. Kathy saw that the autocorrelations at the small lags appeared to cut off after lag 1, although there was a small blip at lag 3. Kathy also saw that the

TABLE 9-14	Sales of the Keytron Corporation for Example 9.9 (read by columns)					
1736.8	1627.6	1895.4	1768.0	2202.2	1708.2	2288.0
1297.4	1575.6	1822.6	1840.8	2449.2	806.0	2275.0
559.0	1682.2	2054.0	1804.4	2090.4	2028.0	2581.8
1455.6	1710.8	1544.4	2007.2	2184.0	2236.0	2540.2
1526.2	1853.8	600.6	2067.0	2267.2	2028.0	2519.4
1419.6	1788.8	1604.2	2048.8	1705.6	2100.8	2267.2
1484.6	1822.4	1796.6	2314.0	962.0	2327.0	2615.6
1651.0	1838.2	1822.6	2072.2	1929.2	2225.6	2163.2
1661.4	1635.4	1835.6	1952.6	2202.2	2321.8	899.6
1851.2	618.8	1944.8	2134.6	1903.2	2275.0	2210.0
1617.2	1593.8	2009.8	1799.2	2337.4	2171.0	2376.4
1614.6	1898.0	2116.4	756.6	2022.8	2431.0	2259.4
1757.6	1911.0	1994.2	1890.2	2225.6	2165.8	2584.4
1302.6	1695.0	1895.4	2256.8	2441.4	780.0	
572.0	1757.6	1947.4	2111.2	2113.8	2056.6	
1458.6	1944.8	1770.6	2080.0	2035.8	2340.0	
1567.8	2108.6	626.6	2191.8	2152.8	2033.2	

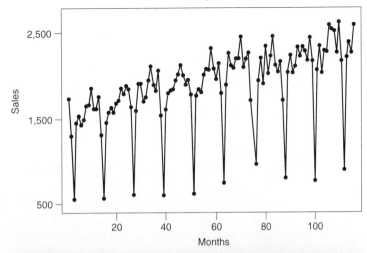

FIGURE 9-26   Sales of the Keytron Corporation

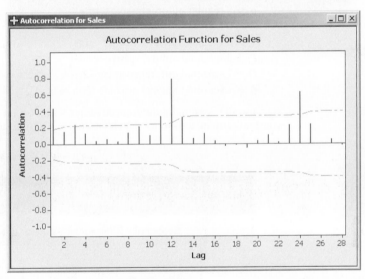

Autocorrelation Function: Sales

Lag	ACF	T	LBQ	Lag	ACF	T	LBQ
1	0.431371	4.63	21.96	15	0.127275	0.74	156.77
2	0.153911	1.41	24.78	16	0.039851	0.23	156.99
3	0.237841	2.14	31.58	17	-0.031030	-0.18	157.12
4	0.128583	1.11	33.58	18	-0.012252	-0.07	157.14
5	0.041549	0.36	33.79	19	-0.049556	-0.29	157.48
6	0.061352	0.53	34.26	20	0.041444	0.24	157.73
7	0.028549	0.24	34.36	21	0.107932	0.62	159.39
8	0.136014	1.16	36.69	22	0.026250	0.15	159.49
9	0.212966	1.80	42.44	23	0.227137	1.30	167.04
10	0.105905	0.87	43.88	24	0.635500	3.59	226.75
11	0.332651	2.71	58.20	25	0.238127	1.22	235.23
12	0.791934	6.08	140.12	26	0.000420	0.00	235.23
13	0.324223	1.94	153.99	27	0.050577	0.26	235.62
14	0.067091	0.39	154.59	28	-0.025580	-0.13	235.72

FIGURE 9-27   Sample Autocorrelations for the Keytron Corporation Sales

autocorrelations at the seasonal lags, 12, 24, and 36 (not shown) were large and failed to die out quickly. This suggested the series was nonstationary and confirmed the impression Kathy had from the time series plot. Before continuing, Kathy decided to difference the series with respect to the seasonal lag to see if she could convert the nonstationary series to a stationary one.

The seasonal difference for period $S = 12$ is defined as

$$\Delta_{12} = Y_t - Y_{t-12}$$

For Keytron sales, the first seasonal difference that can be computed is

$$Y_{13} - Y_1 = 1757.6 - 1736.8 = 20.8$$

The remaining seasonal differences are computed, and the series consisting of the seasonal differences of sales is shown in Figure 9-28.

The sample autocorrelations and sample partial autocorrelations for the differenced series are given in Figures 9-29 and 9-30, respectively. Figure 9-28 indicates that the seasonally differenced data are stationary and seem to vary about a level of roughly 100. The autocorrelations have one significant spike at lag 12 (cuts off), and the sample partial autocorrelations have significant spikes at lags 12 and 24 that get progressively smaller (die out). This behavior suggests an MA(1) term at the seasonal lag 12.

Kathy identifies an ARIMA$(0, 0, 0)(0, 1, 1)_{12}$ model for her sales data. This notation means the model has

$p = 0$ regular autoregressive terms
$d = 0$ regular differences
$q = 0$ regular moving average terms
$P = 0$ seasonal autoregressive terms
$D = 1$ seasonal difference at lag 12
$Q = 1$ seasonal moving average term at lag 12

Because the seasonally differenced series varies about a nonzero level, Kathy includes a constant term in her model. The identified model has the form

$$Y_t - Y_{t-12} = \mu + \varepsilon_t - \Omega_1 \varepsilon_{t-12} \qquad \textbf{(9.9)}$$

FIGURE 9-28   Seasonally Differenced Sales for the Keytron Corporation

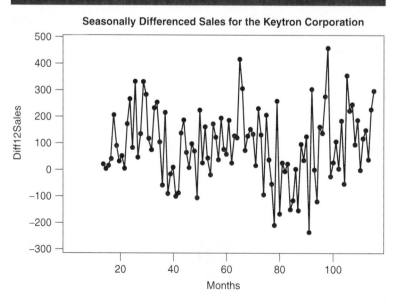

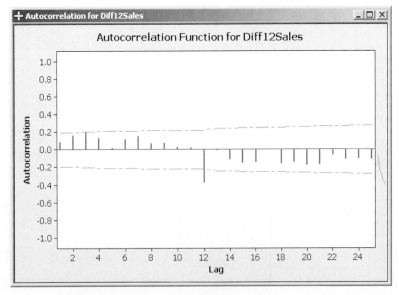

Autocorrelation Function: Diff12Sales

Lag	ACF	T	LBQ	Lag	ACF	T	LBQ
1	0.082290	0.84	0.72	14	-0.111889	-0.90	34.33
2	0.164373	1.66	3.61	15	-0.159221	-1.28	37.45
3	0.206938	2.03	8.24	16	-0.146828	-1.16	40.13
4	0.128010	1.21	10.03	17	0.000677	0.01	40.13
5	0.018390	0.17	10.07	18	-0.161582	-1.26	43.45
6	0.117004	1.09	11.60	19	-0.144594	-1.11	46.14
7	0.156824	1.44	14.37	20	-0.178727	-1.36	50.31
8	0.064878	0.59	14.85	21	-0.173436	-1.29	54.27
9	0.074454	0.67	15.48	22	-0.068707	-0.50	54.90
10	0.028748	0.26	15.58	23	-0.116692	-0.85	56.74
11	0.023747	0.21	15.65	24	-0.109328	-0.79	58.38
12	-0.379941	-3.40	32.80	25	-0.112515	-0.81	60.14
13	-0.009173	-0.07	32.81				

FIGURE 9-29   Sample Autocorrelations for the Seasonally Differenced Sales for Keytron Corporation

where μ is the mean level of the seasonally differenced process and Ω_1 is the seasonal moving average parameter.

Kathy uses Minitab to estimate the parameters in her model, compute the residual autocorrelations, and generate forecasts. The output is shown in Table 9-15. The residual autocorrelations are given in Figure 9-31 and forecasts for the next 12 months are appended to the end of the sales series in Figure 9-32.

Kathy was pleased to see her initial model fit the data very well. The Ljung-Box chi-square statistics, for groups of lags $m = 12, 24, 36$, and 48, were clearly not significant as evidenced by their large p-values. The residual autocorrelations were uniformly small with no apparent pattern. Kathy was ready to use her fitted model to verify the forecasts produced by Minitab.

The estimated parameters were $\hat{\mu} = 85.457$ and $\hat{\Omega}_1 = .818$. Using these values, Equation 9.9 can be solved for Y_t to give

$$Y_t = Y_{t-12} + 85.457 + \varepsilon_t - .818\varepsilon_{t-12}$$

To forecast sales for period 116, Kathy sets $t = 116$ and notes that, at the time she is making the forecast, her best guess of ε_{116} (the error for the next period) is zero. Thus the forecasting equation is

$$\hat{Y}_{116} = Y_{104} + 85.457 - .818e_{104}$$

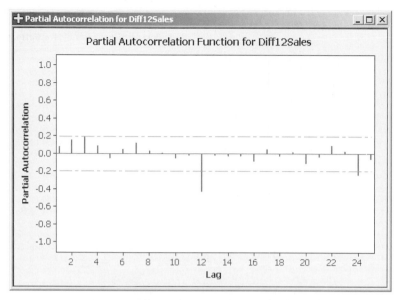

Partial Autocorrelation Function: Diff12Sales

Lag	PACF	T	Lag	PACF	T
1	0.082290	0.84	14	-0.036679	-0.37
2	0.158675	1.61	15	-0.036390	-0.37
3	0.188491	1.91	16	-0.091175	-0.93
4	0.086124	0.87	17	0.048016	0.49
5	-0.053533	-0.54	18	-0.036175	-0.37
6	0.052428	0.53	19	0.012596	0.13
7	0.125409	1.27	20	-0.113143	-1.15
8	0.033422	0.34	21	-0.037869	-0.38
9	0.007631	0.08	22	0.089451	0.91
10	-0.056774	-0.58	23	0.024185	0.25
11	-0.024356	-0.25	24	-0.248846	-2.53
12	-0.436449	-4.43	25	-0.064072	-0.65
13	-0.022329	-0.23			

FIGURE 9-30 Sample Partial Autocorrelations for the Seasonally Differenced Sales for Keytron Corporation

where $e_{104} = -72.418$ is the residual (estimated error) for period 104.

$$\hat{Y}_{116} = 2275 + 85.457 - .818(-72.418) = 2419.7$$

Similarly,

$$\hat{Y}_{117} = Y_{105} + 85.457 - .818e_{105}$$

$$\hat{Y}_{117} = 2581.8 + 85.457 - .818(199.214) = 2504.3$$

Kathy's forecasts agreed with those from the Minitab output. She was convinced she understood how to use the fitted model to produce forecasts. Kathy was delighted with the forecasts of sales for the next 12 months shown in Figure 9-32. The forecasts seemed to be entirely consistent with the behavior of the series. She felt they captured the seasonal pattern and the growth in sales quite well.

Example 9.10
In Example 3.5, Perkin Kendell, analyst for Outboard Marine Corporation, used autocorrelation analysis to conclude that quarterly sales were seasonal. He has decided to forecast sales for 1997 using the Box-Jenkins methodology. The data were plotted in Figure 3-14.

TABLE 9-15   Minitab Output for ARIMA(0, 0, 0)(0, 1, 1)$_{12}$ Model for Keytron Sales

`ARIMA(0,0,0)(0,1,1)`$_{12}$ `Model: Keytron Sales`

```
Final Estimates of Parameters
Type          Coef  SE Coef       T       P
SMA 12      0.8180   0.0881    9.28   0.000
Constant    85.457    2.910   29.36   0.000

Differencing: 0 regular, 1 seasonal of order 12
Number of observations: Original series 115, after differencing 103
Residuals:   SS = 1172652 (backforecasts excluded)
             MS = 11610 DF = 101
```

```
Modified Box-Pierce (Ljung-Box) Chi-Square statistic
Lag             12      24      36      48
Chi-Square    12.5    27.1    34.6    46.4
DF              10      22      34      46
P-Value      0.250   0.209   0.439   0.456
```

```
Forecasts from period 115
                  95 Percent Limits
Period  Forecast     Lower    Upper  Actual
116      2419.69   2208.46  2630.93
117      2504.31   2293.07  2715.54
```

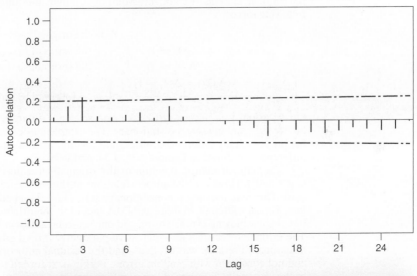

Residual Autocorrelations: ARIMA(0, 0, 0) (0, 1, 1)$_{12}$

FIGURE 9-31   Autocorrelation Function for the Residuals for the ARIMA(0, 0, 0)(0, 1, 1)$_{12}$ Model

(See page 73.) The time series plot shows a pretty clear seasonal pattern with, perhaps, a slight upward trend.

Perkin began his analysis by looking at the sample autocorrelations for the original series and the series' various differences. Perkin's friend, an expert in Box-Jenkins methodology, told him this was a good idea whenever there was a possibility the series was nonstationary. Once the simplest model suggested by an autocorrelation pattern has been

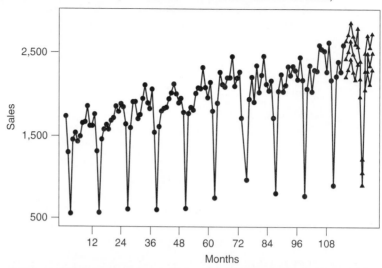

FIGURE 9-32   Sales and Forecasts for the Next 12 Months for Keytron Corporation

tentatively identified, the identification can be confirmed by examining the sample partial autocorrelations. Perkin has Minitab compute the autocorrelation functions for the following series:

$$Y_t = \text{the original sales series}$$
$$\Delta Y_t = Y_t - Y_{t-1} = \text{the series of first (regular) differences}$$
$$\Delta_4 Y_t = Y_t - Y_{t-4} = \text{the series of seasonal differences of order } S = 4$$
$$\begin{bmatrix} \Delta\Delta_4 Y_t = \Delta(\Delta_4 Y_t) = \Delta(Y_t - Y_{t-4}) \\ = Y_t - Y_{t-1} - Y_{t-4} + Y_{t-5} \end{bmatrix} = \begin{array}{l}\text{the series consisting of a seasonal difference} \\ \text{followed by a regular difference}\end{array}$$

On occasion, it is necessary to take one seasonal difference and one regular difference before the resulting series is stationary. The sample autocorrelations for the original series, for the seasonally differenced series, and for the series with one regular and one seasonal difference are shown in Figures 9-33, 9-34, and 9-35.

The autocorrelation function of the original series has (significantly) large spikes at lags 1 and 4. However, the autocorrelations at the seasonal lags 4, 8, and 12 decay toward zero. This may indicate a nonstationary series and the need for a seasonal difference. In fact, Perkin's attempt to fit an ARIMA model to the original series with a constant term, one regular moving average term, and one seasonal autoregressive term was not successful. The estimated seasonal autoregressive parameter turned out to be close to one (implying a seasonal difference was needed), and the residual autocorrelations were generally large and not consistent with random errors. Perkin next turned to the autocorrelation function of the seasonally differenced series in Figure 9-34.

The autocorrelations for the seasonally differenced data are large at low lags and decline rather slowly in the form of a wavelike pattern. Perkin decided the series may still be nonstationary and felt that a regular difference in addition to the seasonal difference may be required to achieve stationarity. Consequently, he had Minitab produce the sample autocorrelations for the first differenced and seasonally differenced sales in Figure 9-35.

Examining the autocorrelations in Figure 9-35, Perkin noticed only two significant values at lags 1 and 8. In addition, he saw that the autocorrelations for the first two lags alternated in sign. Perkin felt that an ARIMA model with a regular autoregressive term and, perhaps, a seasonal moving average term at lag 8 might be appropriate. Before continuing, Perkin wanted to confirm his initial choice by examining the partial autocorrelations for the first differenced and seasonally differenced series.

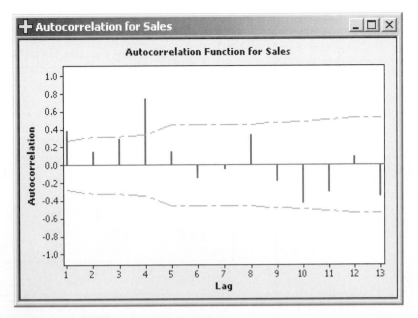

Autocorrelation Function: Sales

Lag	ACF	T	LBQ	Lag	ACF	T	LBQ
1	0.392861	2.83	8.50	8	0.346975	1.51	57.72
2	0.153945	0.97	9.83	9	-0.182601	-0.76	59.90
3	0.293782	1.82	14.77	10	-0.434729	-1.80	72.53
4	0.743520	4.34	47.11	11	-0.315031	-1.23	79.33
5	0.150655	0.67	48.47	12	0.091203	0.35	79.91
6	-0.153008	-0.67	49.90	13	-0.353274	-1.34	88.90
7	-0.046978	-0.21	50.04				

FIGURE 9-33 Sample Autocorrelations for Outboard Marine Corporation Sales

The sample partial autocorrelations are shown in Figure 9-36 for the first differenced and seasonally differenced data. The partial autocorrelations seemed to cut off after the first lag, consistent with the AR(1) behavior he observed in the autocorrelations, and there was a significant partial autocorrelation at lag 8.

Perkin was not sure how to handle the seasonal parameters, so he decided to keep it simple and fit an ARIMA$(1, 1, 0)(0, 1, 0)_4$ model. This model allows for one regular and one seasonal difference at lag 4, a regular autoregressive term, but no seasonal autoregressive or moving average coefficients. A plot of the series after differencing showed it varied about zero, so no constant term was included in the model. Perkin reasoned if seasonal parameters were needed, the evidence would show up in the residual autocorrelations from his initial model.

The output for the ARIMA$(1, 1, 0)(0, 1, 0)_4$ model is shown at the top of Table 9-16, and the residual autocorrelations are shown at the beginning of Figure 9-37. The model seemed to fit fairly well with an estimated AR(1) coefficient of $\hat{\phi}_1 = -.352$ and a residual mean square error of $s^2 = 1041.3$. However, a significant spike occurred at lag 8 in the residual autocorrelations, and the Ljung-Box statistic for the first $m = 12$ lags was $Q_{12} = 19.7$ with a p-value of .05. The latter suggests that, as a group, the first 12 residual autocorrelations are larger than would be expected for random errors.

Perkin decides to modify his initial model and include moving average terms corresponding to the seasonal lags 4 and 8. The evidence suggests that only the term at lag 8 is necessary; however, the Minitab program requires including seasonal AR or MA parameters

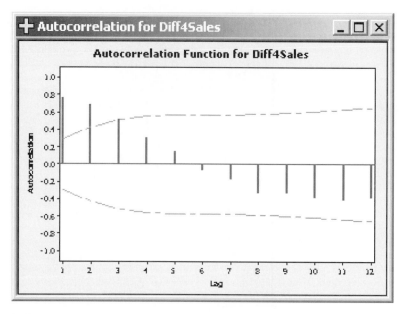

Autocorrelation Function: Diff4Sales

Lag	ACF	T	LBQ	Lag	ACF	T	LBQ
1	0.768185	5.32	30.13	7	-0.171085	-0.60	77.70
2	0.693331	3.25	55.21	8	-0.333127	-1.16	84.36
3	0.514793	2.01	69.35	9	-0.338294	-1.14	91.40
4	0.303188	1.10	74.36	10	-0.392484	-1.29	101.13
5	0.152404	0.54	75.66	11	-0.407611	-1.30	111.90
6	-0.075474	-0.26	75.98	12	-0.387217	-1.19	121.90

FIGURE 9-34   Sample Autocorrelations for Outboard Marine Corporation Sales Seasonally Differenced

in the model up to and including the highest multiple of the seasonal lag that is needed. In this case, the seasonal lag is $S = 4$ and a moving average parameter at lag $2 \times 4 = 8$ is needed.

Perkin uses Minitab to fit an ARIMA$(1, 1, 0)(0, 1, 2)_4$ model to his data.[14] The output is shown in Table 9-16 (bottom), and the residual autocorrelations are given in Figure 9-37 (see p. 426). Perkin is pleased with the results. The residual mean square error has been reduced to $s^2 = 716.3$, and the residual autocorrelations, as judged by the individual values and the Ljung-Box chi-square statistics, are consistent with random errors. Residual plots (not shown) suggest that the other error term assumptions are appropriate.

To gain additional experience with the Box-Jenkins methodology, Perkin wants to check the forecasts of sales for the next two quarters shown on the Minitab output. Using parameter estimates in place of the true values, the final model is

$$W_t = -.351W_{t-1} + \varepsilon_t - .239\varepsilon_{t-4} - .672\varepsilon_{t-8}$$

where

$$W_t = \Delta\Delta_4 Y_t = Y_t - Y_{t-1} - Y_{t-4} + Y_{t-5}$$

---

[14]The Minitab commands to run the ARIMA$(1, 1, 0)(0, 1, 2)_4$ model are demonstrated at the end of this chapter.

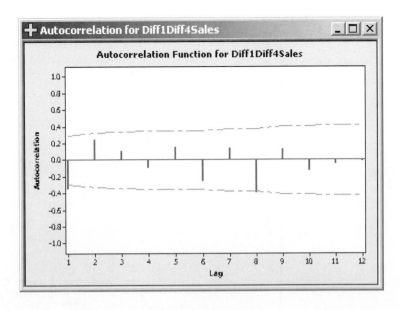

Autocorrelation Function: Diff1Diff4Sales

Lag	ACF	T	LBQ	Lag	ACF	T	LBQ
1	-0.347173	-2.38	6.03	7	0.147388	0.80	16.47
2	0.248695	1.53	9.20	8	-0.398618	-2.14	25.86
3	0.106003	0.62	9.79	9	0.127499	0.63	26.84
4	-0.093888	-0.55	10.26	10	-0.126568	-0.62	27.84
5	0.158168	0.91	11.63	11	-0.053319	-0.26	28.02
6	-0.252819	-1.44	15.22	12	-0.021388	-0.10	28.05

FIGURE 9-35   Sample Autocorrelations for Outboard Marine Corporation Sales First Differenced and Seasonally Differenced

is the differenced series. At forecast origin $t - 1$, the forecasting equation, written in terms of the Y's, takes the form

$$\hat{Y}_t = Y_{t-1} + Y_{t-4} - Y_{t-5} - .351(Y_{t-1} - Y_{t-2} - Y_{t-5} + Y_{t-6}) - .239e_{t-4} - .672e_{t-8}$$

where e_{t-4} and e_{t-8} are the residuals (estimated errors) for periods $t - 4$ and $t - 8$ respectively.

The forecast of sales for period 53 is

$$\hat{Y}_{53} = Y_{52} + Y_{49} - Y_{48} - .351(Y_{52} - Y_{51} - Y_{48} + Y_{47}) - .239e_{49} - .672e_{45}$$
$$\hat{Y}_{53} = 281.4 + 232.1 - 338.2 - .351(281.4 - 291.0 - 338.2 + 329.6) - .239(-1.726)$$
$$\qquad - .672(18.898)$$
$$= 169.4$$

and the forecast for period 54 is

$$\hat{Y}_{54} = \hat{Y}_{53} + Y_{50} - Y_{49} - .351(\hat{Y}_{53} - Y_{52} - Y_{49} + Y_{48}) - .239e_{50} - .672e_{46}$$
$$\hat{Y}_{54} = 169.4 + 285.6 - 232.1 - .351(169.4 - 281.4 - 232.1 + 338.2) - .239(-37.040)$$
$$\qquad - .672(4.781)$$
$$= 230.6$$

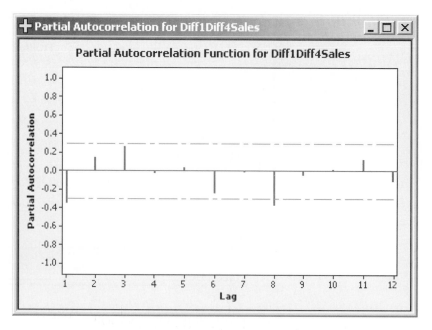

Partial Autocorrelation Function: Diff1Diff4Sales

Lag	PACF	T	Lag	PACF	T
1	-0.347173	-2.38	7	-0.020174	-0.14
2	0.145731	1.00	8	-0.376537	-2.58
3	0.267607	1.83	9	-0.043690	-0.30
4	-0.026767	-0.18	10	0.012654	0.09
5	0.036594	0.25	11	0.124850	0.86
6	-0.238699	-1.64	12	-0.111552	-0.76

FIGURE 9-36   Sample Partial Autocorrelations for Outboard Marine Corporation Sales First Differenced and Seasonally Differenced

Perkin was happy to see his calculated forecasts agreed with those produced by Minitab. Forecasts for the next four quarters are plotted in Figure 9-38. The forecasts seem reasonable. The pattern of the forecasts is much like the historical pattern. Perkin felt his forecasting effort was a success and planned on recommending the Box-Jenkins methodology to his colleagues.

Simple Exponential Smoothing and an ARIMA Model

Several ARIMA models produce forecasts that are the same or nearly the same as the smoothing methods discussed in Chapter 4. To illustrate one case, consider the ARIMA$(0, 1, 1)$ model

$$Y_t - Y_{t-1} = \varepsilon_t - \omega_1 \varepsilon_{t-1} \tag{9.10}$$

Suppose the forecast origin is t and a forecast of Y_{t+1} is required. Substituting $t + 1$ for t in Equation 9.10 and solving for Y_{t+1} gives

$$Y_{t+1} = Y_t + \varepsilon_{t+1} - \omega_1 \varepsilon_t$$

TABLE 9-16	Minitab Output for ARIMA(1, 1, 0)(0, 1, 0)$_4$ Model (top) and ARIMA(1, 1, 0)(0, 1, 2)$_4$ Model (bottom) for Outboard Marine Sales

```
ARIMA(1,1,0)(0,1,0)₄ Model: Outboard Marine Sales

Final Estimates of Parameters
Type      Coef   SE Coef       T       P
AR 1   -0.3520    0.1384   -2.54   0.014

Differencing: 1 regular, 1 seasonal of order 4
Number of observations: Original series 52, after differencing 47
Residuals:   SS = 47898.3 (backforecasts excluded)
             MS = 1041.3 DF = 46

Modified Box-Pierce (Ljung-Box) Chi-Square statistic
Lag                 12      24      36    48
Chi-Square        19.7    23.7    32.1     *
DF                  11      23      35     *
P-Value          0.050   0.420   0.608     *

ARIMA(1,1,0)(0,1,2)₄ Model: Outboard Marine Sales

Final Estimates of Parameters
Type      Coef   SE Coef       T       P
AR 1   -0.3511    0.1423   -2.47   0.018
SMA 4   0.2382    0.1339    1.78   0.082
SMA 8   0.6730    0.1403    4.80   0.000

Differencing: 1 regular, 1 seasonal of order 4
Number of observations: Original series 52, after differencing 47
Residuals:   SS = 31518.1 (backforecasts excluded)
             MS = 716.3 DF = 44

Modified Box-Pierce (Ljung-Box) Chi-Square statistic
Lag                 12      24      36    48
Chi-Square         8.4    10.7    22.0     *
DF                   9      21      33     *
P-Value          0.493   0.969   0.927     *

Forecasts from period 52
                   95 Percent Limits
Period  Forecast    Lower     Upper   Actual
53       169.386  116.917   221.854
54       230.533  167.987   293.080
```

Because, at time t, the best guess of ε_{t+1} is zero, and ε_t is estimated by the residual $e_t = Y_t - \hat{Y}_t$, the forecasting equation is

$$\hat{Y}_{t+1} = Y_t - \omega_1(Y_t - \hat{Y}_t) = (1 - \omega_1)Y_t + \omega_1\hat{Y}_t \qquad (9.11)$$

Let $\alpha = 1 - \omega_1$, and Equation 9.11 is identical to the simple exponential smoothing Equation 4.13

$$\hat{Y}_{t+1} = \alpha Y_t + (1 - \alpha)\hat{Y}_t$$

Forecasting using simple exponential smoothing is equivalent to generating forecasts using an ARIMA(0, 1, 1) model with parameter $\omega_1 = 1 - \alpha$. Note that the ARIMA(0, 1, 1) model represents a nonstationary process. Simple exponential smoothing should work well for those time series that can be adequately described by an ARIMA$(0, 1, 1)$ model. For those time series that cannot be adequately described by this model, forecasts generated by exponential smoothing may not be particularly good.

For simple exponential smoothing, the parameter α is usually restricted to the range $0 < \alpha < 1$. The moving average parameter ω_1 in the ARIMA$(0, 1, 1)$ model is restricted to the range $-1 < \omega_1 < 1$ so, strictly speaking, the two forecasting methods are equivalent for positive values of the parameters α and ω_1.

Advantages and Disadvantages of ARIMA Models

The Box-Jenkins approach to time series analysis is a very powerful tool for providing accurate short-range forecasts. ARIMA models are quite flexible and can represent a wide range of characteristics of time series that occur in practice. Formal procedures for testing the adequacy of the model are available. Moreover, forecasts and prediction intervals follow directly from the fitted model.

However, ARIMA modeling has some drawbacks.

1. A relatively large amount of data is required. It should be recognized that if the data are seasonal with, say, a seasonal period of $S = 12$, then monthly observations for one year essentially constitute one data point (one look at the seasonal pattern),

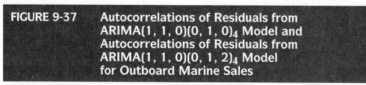

FIGURE 9-37   Autocorrelations of Residuals from ARIMA(1, 1, 0)(0, 1, 0)$_4$ Model and Autocorrelations of Residuals from ARIMA(1, 1, 0)(0, 1, 2)$_4$ Model for Outboard Marine Sales

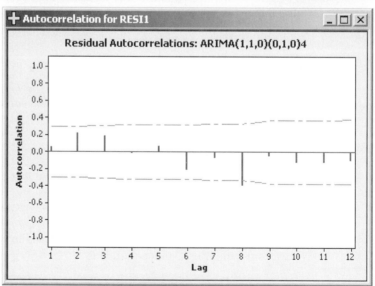

Autocorrelation Function: RESI1

Lag	ACF	T	LBQ	Lag	ACF	T	LBQ
1	0.054510	0.37	0.15	7	-0.070930	-0.43	7.59
2	0.222343	1.52	2.68	8	-0.393430	-2.38	16.73
3	0.193279	1.26	4.63	9	-0.043829	-0.24	16.85
4	-0.017583	-0.11	4.65	10	-0.126685	-0.69	17.85
5	0.065878	0.42	4.89	11	-0.129403	-0.69	18.92
6	-0.207367	-1.30	7.30	12	-0.107972	-0.57	19.69

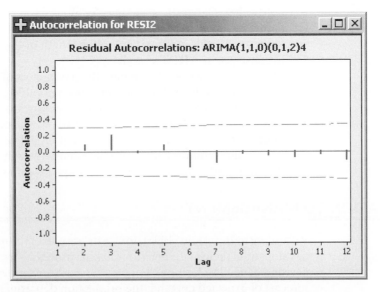

Autocorrelation Function: RESI2

Lag	ACF	T	LBQ	Lag	ACF	T	LBQ
1	-0.013785	-0.09	0.01	7	-0.152917	-0.96	6.72
2	0.086619	0.59	0.39	8	-0.042170	-0.26	6.83
3	0.203811	1.39	2.57	9	-0.060928	-0.37	7.05
4	-0.031045	-0.20	2.62	10	-0.080110	-0.49	7.45
5	0.085412	0.56	3.02	11	-0.044302	-0.27	7.58
6	-0.204742	-1.33	5.37	12	-0.113216	-0.69	8.42

FIGURE 9-37   *(Continued)*

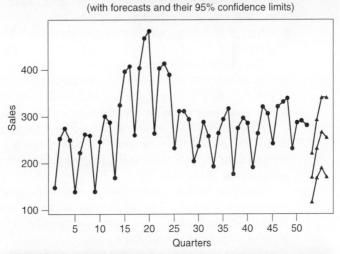

FIGURE 9-38   **Forecasts for the Next Four Quarters from ARIMA$(1, 1, 0)(0, 1, 2)_4$ Model for Outboard Marine Sales**

not twelve. Generally speaking, for nonseasonal data, about 40 observations or more are required to develop an ARIMA model. For seasonal data, about six to ten years of data—depending on the length of the seasonal period—are required to construct an ARIMA model.

2. There are no easy ways to update the parameters of an ARIMA model as new data become available, as there are in some smoothing methods. The model has to be periodically completely refitted, and, sometimes, a new model must be developed.

3. The construction of a satisfactory ARIMA model often requires a large investment of time and other resources. The costs of model development, computer run time, and storage requirements can be substantially higher for ARIMA models than for the more traditional forecasting techniques such as smoothing.

APPLICATION TO MANAGEMENT

According to Bernstein (1996), forecasts are one of the most important inputs managers develop to aid them in the decision-making process. Virtually every important operating decision depends to some extent on a forecast. Inventory accumulation is related to the forecast of expected demand; the production department has to schedule employment needs and raw materials orders for the next month or two; the finance department must arrange short-term financing for the next quarter; the personnel department must determine hiring and layoff requirements. The list of forecasting applications is quite lengthy.

Executives are keenly aware of the importance of forecasting. Indeed, a great deal of time is spent studying trends in economic and political affairs and how events might affect demand for products and/or services. One issue of interest is the importance executives place on quantitative forecasting methods versus forecasts based strictly on their judgments. This issue is especially sensitive when events that have a significant impact on demand are involved. One problem with quantitative forecasting methods is that they depend on historical data. For this reason they are probably least effective in calling the turn that often results in sharply higher or lower demand.

One type of problem that business managers frequently face is the need to prepare short-term forecasts for a number of different items. A typical example is the manager who must schedule production on the basis of some forecast of demand for several hundred different products in a product line. The techniques that are used most frequently in this situation are the smoothing methods.

The major advantage of exponential smoothing is its low cost and simplicity. It may not be as accurate as more sophisticated methods, such as general ARIMA modeling. However, when forecasts are needed for inventory systems containing thousands of items, smoothing methods are often the only reasonable approach.

Forecasting from a time series perspective depends on the assumption that the future will be like the past, and that past patterns can be described adequately. Time series techniques are most useful for forecasting variables that fluctuate in some stable pattern over time.

The Box-Jenkins methodology is a very powerful tool for providing accurate short-range forecasts. Managers must be aware that building a satisfactory ARIMA model with the Box-Jenkins technique requires a fair amount of historical data and a high investment in the analyst's time.

Appropriate applications for Box-Jenkins methodology are many. ARIMA models have been used as follows:

- Estimate a change in price structure in the U.S. telephone industry
- Investigate the relationship among ammonia concentration, flow rate, and temperature in rivers

- Forecast annual stock volume
- Forecast the number of active oil wells
- Analyze the number of private housing units started
- Analyze the daily observations on percent advances of number of issues traded
- Analyze the competition between rail and airline routes
- Forecast employment
- Analyze a large number of energy time series for a utility company
- Analyze the effect of promotions on the sales of consumer products
- Forecast different categories of product quality assurance

Glossary

Box-Jenkins methodology. The Box-Jenkins methodology refers to a set of procedures for identifying, fitting, and checking ARIMA models with time series data. Forecasts follow directly from the form of the fitted model.

Principle of parsimony. The principle of parsimony refers to the preference for simple models over complex ones.

Key Formulas

ARIMA model: pth-order autoregressive model

$$Y_t = \phi_0 + \phi_1 Y_{t-1} + \phi_2 Y_{t-2} + \cdots + \phi_p Y_{t-p} + \varepsilon_t \tag{9.1}$$

ARIMA model: qth-order moving average model

$$Y_t = \mu + \varepsilon_t - \omega_1 \varepsilon_{t-1} - \omega_2 \varepsilon_{t-2} - \cdots - \omega_q \varepsilon_{t-q} \tag{9.2}$$

ARIMA model: ARMA(p,q) model

$$Y_t = \phi_0 + \phi_1 Y_{t-1} + \phi_2 Y_{t-2} + \cdots + \phi_p Y_{t-p} + \varepsilon_t - \omega_1 \varepsilon_{t-1} - \omega_2 \varepsilon_{t-2} - \cdots - \omega_q \varepsilon_{t-q} \tag{9.3}$$

Residual mean square error

$$s^2 = \frac{\sum_{t=1}^{n} e_t^2}{n-r} = \frac{\sum_{t=1}^{n}(Y_t - \hat{Y}_t)^2}{n-r} \tag{9.4}$$

Ljung-Box (Modified Box-Pierce) Q statistic

$$Q_m = n(n+2) \sum_{k=1}^{m} \frac{r_k^2(e)}{n-k} \tag{9.5}$$

Approximate prediction intervals for stationary series

$$\hat{Y} \pm 2s \tag{9.6}$$

Akaike information criterion (*AIC*)

$$AIC = \ln \hat{\sigma}^2 + \frac{2}{n} r \tag{9.7}$$

Bayesian (Schwarz) information criterion (*BIC*)

$$BIC = \ln \hat{\sigma}^2 + \frac{\ln n}{n} r \qquad (9.8)$$

Seasonal moving average model (monthly data)

$$Y_t - Y_{t-12} = \mu + \varepsilon_t - \Omega_1 \varepsilon_{t-12} \qquad (9.9)$$

ARIMA(0, 1, 1) model

$$Y_t - Y_{t-1} = \varepsilon_t - \omega_1 \varepsilon_{t-1} \qquad (9.10)$$

ARIMA(0, 1, 1) model forecasting equation in exponential smoothing form

$$\hat{Y}_{t+1} = Y_t - \omega_1(Y_t - \hat{Y}_t) = (1 - \omega_1)Y_t + \omega_1 \hat{Y}_t \qquad (9.11)$$

Problems

1. a. For a sample of 100 observations of random data, calculate a 95% confidence interval for the autocorrelation coefficient at any lag.
    b. If all the autocorrelation coefficients are within their individual 95% confidence intervals and they show no particular pattern, what conclusion about the process can be drawn?
    c. If the first three autocorrelations are all positive, significantly different from zero, and, in general, the autocorrelation pattern declines to zero, what conclusion can be drawn about the process?
    d. A process is observed quarterly. If the autocorrelations r_4, r_8, and r_{12} are significantly different from zero, what conclusion can be drawn?

2. Suppose the following time series model has been fit to historical data and found to be an adequate model.

$$Y_t = 35 + \varepsilon_t + .25\varepsilon_{t-1} - .30\varepsilon_{t-2}$$

The first four observations are $Y_1 = 32.5$, $Y_2 = 36.6$, $Y_3 = 33.3$, and $Y_4 = 31.9$. Assuming $\hat{Y}_1 = 35$ and $\varepsilon_0 = 0$, calculate forecasts for periods 5, 6, and 7 if period 4 is the forecast origin.

3. A time series model has been fit and checked with historical data yielding

$$Y_t = 50 + .45Y_{t-1} + \varepsilon_t$$

Suppose at time $t = 60$, the observation is $Y_{60} = 57$.
    a. Determine forecasts for periods 61, 62, and 63 from origin 60.
    b. Suppose the observed value of Y_{61} is 59. Update the forecasts for periods 62 and 63.
    c. Suppose the estimate for the variance of the error term is $s^2 = 3.2$. Compute a 95% prediction interval about the forecast for period 61.

TABLE P-4		
Model	*Autocorrelations*	*Partial Autocorrelations*
MA		
AR		
ARMA		

4. Fill in the missing information in Table P-4, indicating whether the theoretical autocorrelations and partial autocorrelations die out or cut off for these models.

5. Given the graphs in Figure P-5a–c of the sample autocorrelations and the sample partial autocorrelations, tentatively identify an ARIMA model from each pair of graphs.

6. An ARIMA$(1, 1, 0)$ model [AR(1) model for first differences] is fit to observations of a time series. The first 12 residual autocorrelations are shown in Figure P-6. The model was fit with a constant.
   a. Based on an inspection of the residual autocorrelations, does the model appear to be adequate? Why or why not?
   b. If you decide the model is not adequate, indicate how it might be modified to eliminate any inadequacy.

7. Chips Bakery has been having trouble forecasting the demand for its special high-fiber bread and would like your assistance. Data for the weekly demand, and the autocorrelations of the original data and various differences of the data, are shown in Tables P-7A–D.
   a. Inspect the autocorrelation plots and suggest a tentative model for these data. How did you decide on this model? (Note: Do not difference more than necessary. Too much differencing is indicated if low lag sample autocorrelations tend to increase in magnitude.)
   b. Using a computer program for ARIMA modeling, fit and check your identified model with the bread demand data.
   c. Write down the equation for forecasting the demand for high-fiber bread for period 53.
   d. Using a computer program for ARIMA modeling, forecast the demand for high-fiber bread for the next four periods from forecast origin 52. Also, construct 95% prediction intervals.

8. Table P-8 contains a time series with 126 observations. Using a computer program for ARIMA modeling, obtain a plot of the data, the sample autocorrelations, and the sample partial autocorrelations. Develop an appropriate ARIMA model and generate forecasts for the next three time periods from forecast origin $t = 126$.

9. Table P-9 contains a time series of 80 observations. Using a computer program for ARIMA modeling, obtain a plot of the data, the sample autocorrelations, and the sample partial autocorrelations. Develop an appropriate ARIMA model and generate forecasts for the next three time periods from forecast origin $t = 80$.

10. Table P-10 contains a time series of 80 observations. Using a computer program for ARIMA modeling, obtain a plot of the data, the sample autocorrelations, and the sample partial autocorrelations. Develop an appropriate ARIMA model and generate forecasts for the next three time periods from forecast origin $t = 80$.

11. Table P-11 contains a time series of 96 monthly observations. Using a computer program for ARIMA modeling, obtain a plot of the data, the sample

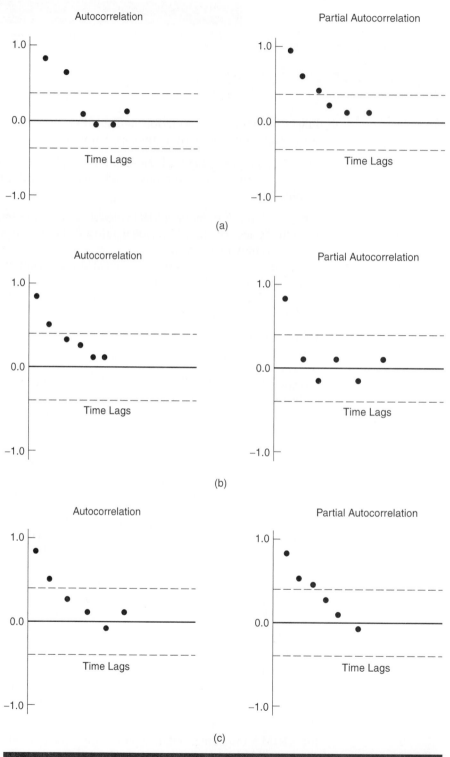

FIGURE P-5   Sample Autocorrelations and Sample Partial
Autocorrelations

Residual Autocorrelations: ARIMA(1, 1, 0)

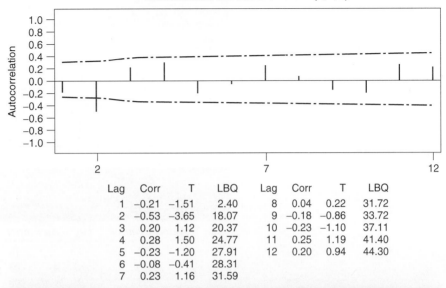

Lag	Corr	T	LBQ	Lag	Corr	T	LBQ
1	−0.21	−1.51	2.40	8	0.04	0.22	31.72
2	−0.53	−3.65	18.07	9	−0.18	−0.86	33.72
3	0.20	1.12	20.37	10	−0.23	−1.10	37.11
4	0.28	1.50	24.77	11	0.25	1.19	41.40
5	−0.23	−1.20	27.91	12	0.20	0.94	44.30
6	−0.08	−0.41	28.31				
7	0.23	1.16	31.59				

FIGURE P-6	Autocorrelations for the Residuals of an ARIMA(1, 1, 0) Model

TABLE P-7A	Weekly Sales Demand for High-Fiber Bread (in thousands)						
Week	*Demand*	*Week*	*Demand*	*Week*	*Demand*	*Week*	*Demand*
1	22.46	14	30.21	27	39.29	40	47.31
2	20.27	15	30.09	28	39.61	41	50.08
3	20.97	16	33.04	29	41.02	42	50.25
4	23.68	17	31.21	30	42.52	43	49.00
5	23.25	18	32.44	31	40.83	44	49.97
6	23.48	19	34.73	32	42.15	45	52.52
7	24.81	20	34.92	33	43.91	46	53.39
8	25.44	21	33.37	34	45.67	47	52.37
9	24.88	22	36.91	35	44.53	48	54.06
10	27.38	23	37.75	36	45.23	49	54.88
11	27.74	24	35.46	37	46.35	50	54.82
12	28.96	25	38.48	38	46.28	51	56.23
13	28.48	26	37.72	39	46.70	52	57.54

TABLE P-7B	Sample Autocorrelations for Original Data		
Lag	*Autocorrelation*	*Lag*	*Autocorrelation*
1	.94	7	.59
2	.88	8	.53
3	.82	9	.48
4	.77	10	.43
5	.71	11	.38
6	.65	12	.32

TABLE P-7C	Autocorrelations for the First-Differenced Series		
Lag	Autocorrelation	Lag	Autocorrelation
1	−.40	7	.20
2	−.29	8	−.03
3	.17	9	−.03
4	.21	10	−.23
5	−.22	11	.21
6	−.05	12	.14

TABLE P-7D	Autocorrelations for the Second-Differenced Series		
Lag	Autocorrelation	Lag	Autocorrelation
1	−.53	7	.16
2	−.10	8	−.05
3	.11	9	.06
4	.18	10	−.23
5	−.20	11	.16
6	−.04	12	.13

TABLE P-8										
t	Y_t	t	Y_t	t	Y_t	t	Y_t	t	Y_t
1	60.9	27	54.2	53	56.9	79	51.6	105	52.9
2	64.2	28	50.9	54	58.9	80	48.2	106	56.9
3	64.2	29	52.2	55	58.2	81	47.6	107	51.6
4	59.6	30	57.6	56	60.9	82	50.2	108	48.2
5	62.2	31	51.6	57	51.6	83	58.2	109	47.6
6	60.9	32	46.9	58	54.9	84	65.6	110	50.2
7	54.2	33	51.6	59	66.2	85	53.6	111	58.2
8	56.9	34	57.6	60	57.6	86	55.6	112	65.6
9	58.2	35	60.2	61	48.9	87	61.6	113	53.6
10	56.2	36	64.2	62	46.2	88	57.6	114	55.6
11	60.9	37	62.2	63	50.9	89	56.2	115	61.6
12	56.9	38	53.6	64	57.6	90	60.9	116	57.6
13	55.6	39	50.9	65	54.9	91	57.6	117	56.2
14	52.2	40	54.2	66	51.6	92	51.6	118	60.9
15	58.2	41	56.2	67	50.2	93	56.2	119	57.6
16	62.9	42	59.6	68	50.9	94	52.2	120	51.6
17	57.6	43	66.2	69	56.9	95	50.2	121	56.2
18	58.9	44	57.6	70	50.2	96	56.9	122	52.2
19	59.6	45	48.9	71	54.2	97	56.9	123	50.2
20	55.6	46	50.9	72	58.2	98	50.2	124	56.9
21	60.2	47	60.2	73	56.9	99	54.2	125	56.9
22	62.2	48	64.2	74	55.6	100	58.2	126	50.2
23	58.2	49	56.9	75	64.2	101	56.9		
24	51.6	50	56.9	76	58.2	102	55.6		
25	50.9	51	63.6	77	52.9	103	64.2		
26	59.6	52	58.2	78	56.9	104	58.2		

TABLE P-9

t	Y_t	t	Y_t	t	Y_t	t	Y_t
1	61	21	50	41	59	61	57
2	50	22	69	42	49	62	56
3	62	23	53	43	64	63	53
4	47	24	57	44	55	64	55
5	64	25	52	45	48	65	55
6	40	26	66	46	61	66	66
7	76	27	47	47	47	67	49
8	38	28	67	48	58	68	57
9	75	29	51	49	46	69	50
10	41	30	57	50	58	70	68
11	74	31	55	51	57	71	42
12	47	32	64	52	52	72	77
13	72	33	48	53	62	73	30
14	47	34	65	54	46	74	88
15	62	35	52	55	72	75	37
16	57	36	65	56	37	76	88
17	56	37	47	57	71	77	32
18	53	38	68	58	33	78	90
19	58	39	48	59	71	79	31
20	61	40	61	60	47	80	85

TABLE P-10

t	Y_t	t	Y_t	t	Y_t	t	Y_t
1	91.5	21	181.5	41	125.1	61	155.6
2	93.0	22	183.0	42	119.0	62	169.3
3	106.8	23	167.8	43	117.4	63	173.8
4	109.8	24	143.3	44	115.9	64	170.8
5	114.4	25	132.7	45	94.5	65	158.6
6	106.8	26	134.2	46	90.0	66	151.0
7	105.2	27	134.2	47	135.7	67	151.0
8	115.9	28	126.6	48	114.4	68	158.6
9	123.5	29	122.0	49	106.8	69	169.3
10	131.2	30	131.2	50	91.5	70	199.8
11	138.8	31	151.0	51	96.1	71	222.7
12	140.3	32	161.7	52	106.8	72	233.3
13	120.5	33	163.2	53	108.3	73	250.1
14	125.1	34	163.2	54	93.0	74	271.4
15	134.2	35	152.5	55	93.0	75	273.0
16	138.8	36	131.2	56	120.5	76	273.0
17	152.5	37	122.0	57	131.2	77	269.9
18	164.7	38	126.6	58	129.6	78	260.8
19	161.7	39	129.6	59	143.3	79	260.8
20	163.2	40	125.1	60	151.0	80	266.9

TABLE P-11

t	Y_t	t	Y_t	t	Y_t	t	Y_t
1	97,575	26	106,650	51	149,850	76	166,950
2	97,755	27	122,550	52	149,850	77	181,500
3	105,825	28	124,650	53	160,350	78	173,925
4	104,700	29	128,925	54	161,325	79	174,450
5	110,700	30	126,038	55	153,225	80	179,475
6	108,060	31	129,300	56	159,375	81	180,300
7	111,825	32	127,050	57	149,325	82	177,975
8	114,525	33	125,025	58	157,200	83	174,525
9	108,375	34	129,675	59	163,350	84	220,650
10	117,900	35	134,250	60	190,650	85	152,625
11	117,600	36	161,475	61	141,600	86	143,100
12	142,800	37	115,350	62	136,725	87	164,925
13	109,500	38	111,750	63	158,625	88	167,175
14	103,995	39	134,025	64	163,050	89	181,725
15	119,250	40	134,325	65	173,925	90	174,150
16	121,200	41	140,175	66	165,900	91	174,675
17	123,900	42	144,300	67	226,650	92	179,700
18	124,350	43	143,475	68	175,050	93	180,525
19	125,775	44	143,700	69	164,700	94	178,200
20	126,900	45	140,325	70	167,625	95	174,750
21	121,650	46	144,375	71	171,225	96	220,875
22	126,600	47	149,175	72	203,550		
23	124,350	48	182,400	73	152,400		
24	152,400	49	132,900	74	142,875		
25	108,150	50	133,950	75	164,700		

TABLE P-12

Period	IBM	Period	IBM	Period	IBM	Period	IBM
Jan. 6	267	Apr. 7	241	Jul. 7	258	Oct. 6	279
13	267	14	244	14	259	13	287
20	268	21	254	21	268	20	276
27	264	28	262	28	276	27	273
Feb. 3	263	May 5	261	Aug. 4	285	Nov. 3	270
10	260	12	265	11	288	10	264
17	256	19	261	18	295	17	261
24	256	26	261	25	297	24	268
Mar. 2	252	Jun. 2	257	Sep. 1	292	Dec. 1	270
10	245	9	268	8	299	8	276
17	243	16	270	15	294	15	274
24	240	23	266	22	284	22	284
31	238	30	259	29	277	29	304

autocorrelations, and the sample partial autocorrelations. Develop an appropriate ARIMA model and generate forecasts for the next 12 time periods from forecast origin $t = 96$.

12. The data in Table P-12 are weekly stock prices for IBM stock.
    a. Using a program for ARIMA modeling, obtain a plot of the data, the sample autocorrelations, and the sample partial autocorrelations. Use this information to tentatively identify an appropriate ARIMA model for this series.
    b. Is the IBM series stationary? What correction would you recommend if the series is nonstationary?
    c. Fit an ARIMA model to the IBM series. Interpret the result. Are successive changes random?
    d. Perform diagnostic checks to determine the adequacy of your fitted model.
    e. After a satisfactory model has been found, forecast the IBM stock price for the first week of January of the next year. How does your forecast differ from the naive forecast, which says that the forecast for the first week of January is the price for the last week in December (current price)?

13. The data in Table P-13 are closing stock quotations for the DEF Corporation for 150 days. Determine the appropriate ARIMA model and forecast the stock price five days ahead from forecast origin $t = 145$. Compare your forecasts with the actual prices using the *MAPE*. How accurate are your forecasts?

TABLE P-13

Period	DEF	Period	DEF	Period	DEF
1	136.0	29	136.0	57	134.4
2	132.8	30	142.4	58	140.8
3	130.4	31	140.0	59	137.6
4	128.8	32	144.8	60	132.8
5	136.8	33	140.0	61	136.8
6	135.2	34	139.2	62	135.2
7	134.4	35	139.2	63	132.8
8	139.2	36	136.8	64	144.0
9	136.8	37	140.8	65	137.6
10	136.0	38	141.6	66	138.4
11	133.6	39	139.2	67	136.0
12	139.2	40	142.4	68	135.2
13	137.6	41	140.8	69	138.4
14	139.2	42	140.0	70	134.4
15	139.2	43	132.0	71	138.4
16	136.0	44	142.4	72	139.2
17	138.4	45	138.4	73	141.6
18	137.6	46	138.4	74	134.4
19	139.2	47	136.8	75	135.2
20	134.4	48	139.2	76	136.0
21	136.8	49	135.2	77	135.2
22	139.2	50	138.4	78	136.0
23	139.2	51	140.8	79	132.8
24	140.0	52	135.2	80	133.6
25	139.2	53	133.6	81	134.4
26	140.8	54	134.4	82	133.6
27	139.2	55	134.4	83	131.2
28	138.4	56	137.6	84	132.0

TABLE P-13			(Continued)		
Period	DEF	Period	DEF	Period	DEF
85	131.2	107	129.6	129	137.6
86	132.8	108	132.8	130	137.6
87	132.0	109	135.2	131	140.0
88	133.6	110	132.0	132	135.2
89	131.2	111	132.8	133	135.2
90	131.2	112	132.8	134	135.2
91	129.6	113	136.0	135	136.0
92	131.2	114	136.8	136	132.0
93	130.4	115	136.8	137	133.6
94	131.2	116	133.6	138	134.4
95	136.0	117	134.4	139	133.6
96	135.2	118	130.4	140	133.6
97	136.8	119	132.8	141	132.8
98	136.8	120	134.4	142	132.0
99	133.6	121	135.2	143	136.0
100	135.2	122	136.8	144	133.6
101	136.0	123	134.4	145	133.6
102	137.6	124	136.0	146	135.2
103	131.2	125	137.6	147	139.2
104	136.0	126	138.4	148	136.8
105	136.0	127	137.6	149	136.0
106	133.6	128	138.4	150	134.4

TABLE P-14					
Period	Observation	Period	Observation	Period	Observation
1	101	25	64	49	78
2	84	26	58	50	83
3	54	27	44	51	87
4	39	28	26	52	64
5	26	29	24	53	44
6	40	30	18	54	24
7	99	31	16	55	29
8	148	32	17	56	73
9	147	33	21	57	138
10	134	34	28	58	154
11	106	35	30	59	119
12	83	36	51	60	102
13	76	37	62	61	79
14	63	38	57	62	53
15	57	39	46	63	40
16	37	40	40	64	27
17	32	41	32	65	31
18	22	42	23	66	56
19	20	43	20	67	78
20	23	44	18	68	114
21	30	45	24	69	140
22	50	46	33	70	112
23	61	47	52	71	82
24	59	48	66	72	80

TABLE P-14	(Continued)				
Period	*Observation*	*Period*	*Observation*	*Period*	*Observation*
73	70	79	71	85	63
74	55	80	110	86	46
75	37	81	112	87	32
76	23	82	93	88	23
77	20	83	75	89	53
78	39	84	60	90	90

14. The data in Table P-14 are the number of weekly automobile accidents for the years 1996 to 1997 in Havana County. Determine the appropriate ARIMA model and forecast accidents for the 91st week. Comment on the accuracy of your forecast.

15. Table P-15 gives the 120 monthly observations on the price in cents per bushel of corn in Omaha, Nebraska. Determine the best ARIMA model for these data. Generate forecasts of the price of corn for the next 12 months. Comment on the pattern of the forecasts.

TABLE P-15					
t	Y_t	*t*	Y_t	*t*	Y_t
1	125	30	128	59	358
2	126	31	130	60	359
3	126	32	129	61	333
4	129	33	139	62	310
5	132	34	131	63	293
6	136	35	131	64	285
7	139	36	166	65	284
8	137	37	159	66	283
9	155	38	163	67	291
10	144	39	158	68	312
11	142	40	165	69	288
12	153	41	206	70	280
13	159	42	252	71	255
14	160	43	215	72	258
15	156	44	238	73	266
16	153	45	249	74	271
17	151	46	250	75	272
18	158	47	250	76	265
19	150	48	275	77	281
20	129	49	292	78	294
21	117	50	304	79	300
22	112	51	301	80	284
23	109	52	265	81	282
24	126	53	271	82	250
25	123	54	289	83	231
26	121	55	319	84	247
27	123	56	377	85	252
28	125	57	350	86	250
29	128	58	378	87	253

TABLE P-15		(*Continued*)			
t	Y_t	t	Y_t	t	Y_t
88	255	99	256	110	239
89	236	100	253	111	251
90	221	101	250	112	261
91	204	102	232	113	268
92	187	103	221	114	304
93	187	104	214	115	285
94	182	105	221	116	274
95	210	106	225	117	281
96	221	107	224	118	259
97	222	108	228	119	270
98	236	109	233	120	251

16. Use the Box-Jenkins methodology to model and forecast the monthly sales of the Cavanaugh Company given in Table P-14 in Problem 14 of Chapter 5. (Hint: Consider a log transformation before modeling these data.)

17. Use the Box-Jenkins methodology to model and forecast the quarterly sales of Disney Company given in Table P-16 in Problem 16 of Chapter 5. (Hint: Consider a log transformation before modeling these data.)

18. Use the Box-Jenkins methodology to model and forecast the monthly gasoline demand of Yukong Oil Company shown in Table P-17 in Problem 17 of Chapter 5.

CASES

CASE 9-1 RESTAURANT SALES

This case refers to the data and situation for the restaurant sales discussed in Case 8-3. Jim Price has now completed a course in forecasting and is anxious to apply the Box-Jenkins methodology to the restaurant sales data. These data, shown in Table 9-17A, begin with the week ending Sunday, January 4, 1981, and continue through the week ending Sunday, December 26, 1982. Table 9-17B contains new data for the week ending January 2, 1983 through the week ending October 30, 1983. ■

TABLE 9-17A		Restaurant Sales: Old Data for Case 9-1			
Week Ending	*Sales ($)*	*Week Ending*	*Sales ($)*	*Week Ending*	*Sales ($)*
1/4/81	1,688	3/8/81	3,460	5/10/81	4,103
1/11/81	2,514	3/15/81	4,517	5/17/81	6,594
1/18/81	5,843	3/22/81	5,188	5/24/81	5,742
1/25/81	4,912	3/29/81	5,944	5/31/81	3,714
2/1/81	5,133	4/5/81	5,842	6/7/81	3,399
2/8/81	4,563	4/12/81	6,589	6/14/81	3,376
2/15/81	5,416	4/19/81	5,447	6/21/81	3,627
2/22/81	6,416	4/26/81	7,548	6/28/81	4,201
3/1/81	5,879	5/3/81	6,403	7/5/81	3,515

TABLE 9-17A		(Continued)			
Week Ending	Sales ($)	Week Ending	Sales ($)	Week Ending	Sales ($)
7/12/81	3,645	1/10/82	1,870	7/11/82	3,885
7/19/81	3,416	1/17/82	3,962	7/18/82	4,209
7/26/81	3,565	1/24/82	5,973	7/25/82	3,614
8/2/81	2,428	1/31/82	5,009	8/1/82	3,722
8/9/81	3,292	2/7/82	5,328	8/8/82	4,307
8/16/81	3,460	2/14/82	5,014	8/15/82	3,322
8/23/81	6,212	2/21/82	4,986	8/22/82	5,962
8/30/81	6,057	2/28/82	5,213	8/29/82	6,784
9/6/81	5,739	3/7/82	4,807	9/5/82	6,069
9/13/81	5,560	3/14/82	3,964	9/12/82	5,897
9/20/81	5,335	3/21/82	5,201	9/19/82	5,916
9/27/81	5,305	3/28/82	4,863	9/26/82	4,998
10/4/81	5,364	4/4/82	5,019	10/3/82	5,111
10/11/81	5,511	4/11/82	4,868	10/10/82	5,612
10/18/81	5,698	4/18/82	5,777	10/17/82	5,906
10/25/81	5,382	4/25/82	6,543	10/24/82	6,010
11/1/81	5,629	5/2/82	6,352	10/31/82	5,937
11/8/81	5,617	5/9/82	5,837	11/7/82	6,004
11/15/81	5,742	5/16/82	7,162	11/14/82	5,959
11/22/81	3,747	5/23/82	4,997	11/21/82	4,223
11/29/81	4,159	5/30/82	4,063	11/28/82	4,679
12/6/81	4,853	6/6/82	3,942	12/5/82	5,307
12/13/81	5,607	6/13/82	4,011	12/12/82	6,101
12/20/81	3,946	6/20/82	3,999	12/19/82	6,896
12/27/81	1,919	6/27/82	4,794	12/26/82	2,214
1/3/82	1,898	7/4/82	4,956		

TABLE 9-17B		Restaurant Sales: New Data for Case 9-1			
Week Ending	Sales ($)	Week Ending	Sales ($)	Week Ending	Sales ($)
1/2/83	2,431	4/17/83	6,357	7/31/83	3,558
1/9/83	2,796	4/24/83	7,273	8/7/83	3,791
1/16/83	4,432	5/1/83	8,678	8/14/83	3,946
1/23/83	5,714	5/8/83	7,418	8/21/83	3,054
1/30/83	5,324	5/15/83	10,388	8/28/83	6,893
2/6/83	5,011	5/22/83	4,940	9/4/83	8,037
2/13/83	5,336	5/29/83	4,195	9/11/83	6,884
2/20/83	4,999	6/5/83	3,895	9/18/83	7,143
2/27/83	5,340	6/12/83	3,762	9/25/83	8,318
3/6/83	5,009	6/19/83	3,739	10/2/83	6,871
3/13/83	5,590	6/26/83	3,975	10/9/83	6,514
3/20/83	3,308	7/3/83	4,634	10/16/83	6,656
3/27/83	6,558	7/10/83	4,891	10/23/83	6,484
4/3/83	4,991	7/17/83	3,463	10/30/83	6,125
4/10/83	6,952	7/24/83	3,536		

QUESTIONS

1. What is the appropriate Box-Jenkins model to use on the original data?
2. What are your forecasts for the first four weeks of January 1983?
3. How do these forecasts compare with actual sales?
4. How does your Box-Jenkins model compare to the regression models used in Chapter 8?
5. Would you use the same Box-Jenkins model if the new data were combined with the old data?

CASE 9-2   MR. TUX

John Mosby has decided to try the Box-Jenkins method for forecasting his monthly sales data. He understands that this procedure is much more complex than the simpler methods he has been trying. He also knows that more accurate forecasts are possible using this advanced method. Also, he has access to the Minitab computer program that can fit ARIMA models. Because he already has the data collected and stored in his computer, he decides to give it a try.

John decides to use his entire data set, consisting of 96 months of sales data. John knows that an

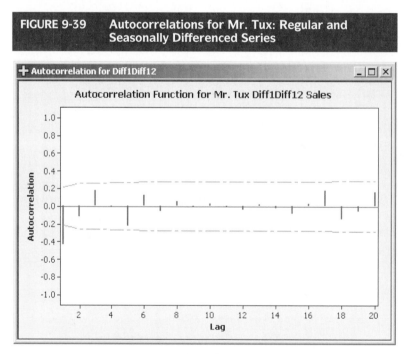

FIGURE 9-39   Autocorrelations for Mr. Tux: Regular and Seasonally Differenced Series

Autocorrelation Function for Mr. Tux Diff1Diff12 Sales

Autocorrelation Function: Diff1Diff12

Lag	ACF	T	LBQ	Lag	ACF	T	LBQ
1	-0.434972	-3.96	16.28	11	-0.006051	-0.04	26.96
2	-0.119297	-0.93	17.52	12	-0.037127	-0.27	27.09
3	0.177448	1.36	20.29	13	0.024916	0.18	27.16
4	-0.013968	-0.10	20.31	14	-0.025145	-0.18	27.22
5	-0.223625	-1.68	24.84	15	-0.081508	-0.58	27.91
6	0.126474	0.92	26.30	16	0.028684	0.20	28.00
7	-0.053425	-0.38	26.57	17	0.184183	1.31	31.62
8	0.054957	0.39	26.85	18	-0.148161	-1.03	34.01
9	-0.006380	-0.05	26.85	19	-0.059354	-0.41	34.39
10	0.032094	0.23	26.95	20	0.165452	1.14	37.46

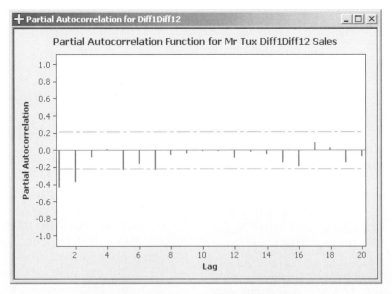

Partial Autocorrelation Function: Diff1Diff12

Lag	PACF	T	Lag	PACF	T
1	-0.434972	-3.96	11	-0.009411	-0.09
2	-0.380486	-3.47	12	-0.091044	-0.83
3	-0.086077	-0.78	13	-0.021219	-0.19
4	0.013655	0.12	14	-0.051663	-0.47
5	-0.232666	-2.12	15	-0.144650	-1.32
6	-0.163070	-1.49	16	-0.191300	-1.74
7	-0.237648	-2.17	17	0.089113	0.81
8	-0.061466	-0.56	18	0.032755	0.30
9	-0.042868	-0.39	19	-0.142079	-1.29
10	-0.010757	-0.10	20	-0.075125	-0.68

**FIGURE 9-40   Partial Autocorrelations for Mr. Tux:
Regular and Seasonally Differenced Series**

ARIMA model can handle the seasonal structure in his time series as well as model the month-to-month correlation.

John computed the sample autocorrelation function for his data in Case 3-2 (see Figure 3-25 on p. 93) and determined that his data were trending (nonstationary). He then computed the autocorrelation function for the first differences of his sales data. The result is shown in Figure 3-26 on p. 93. From this plot, John immediately noticed the significant spikes at lags 12 and 24, indicating seasonality and, perhaps, the need for a seasonal difference. The sample autocorrelation function for the data after a regular (first) difference and a seasonal difference is displayed in Figure 9-39. The sample partial autocorrelations for the differenced data are shown in Figure 9-40. ■

QUESTIONS

1. Discuss the problems, if any, of explaining the Box-Jenkins method to John's banker and others on his management team.

2. Given the autocorrelations in Figure 9-39 and the partial autocorrelations in Figure 9-40, what regular (nonseasonal) terms might John include in an ARIMA model for Mr. Tux sales? What seasonal terms might be included in the model?

3. Using a program for ARIMA modeling, fit and check an ARIMA model for Mr. Tux sales. Generate forecasts for the next 12 months.

CASE 9-3   CONSUMER CREDIT COUNSELING

The Consumer Credit Counseling (CCC) operation was described in Chapters 1 (Case 1-2) and 3 (Case 3-3).

The executive director, Marv Harnishfeger, concluded that the most important variable that CCC needed to forecast was the number of new clients that would be seen for the rest of 1993. Marv provided Dorothy Mercer with monthly data for the number of new clients seen by CCC for the period January 1985 through March 1993 (see Case 3-3).

Dorothy was very happy with your forecasting work so far. However, you are not completely satisfied and decide that now is the time to really impress her. You tell her that she should try one

of the most powerful techniques used in forecasting, the Box-Jenkins methodology and ARIMA models. Dorothy has never heard of Box-Jenkins but is willing to have you give it a try.

Assignment

1. Write Dorothy a memo that explains the Box-Jenkins methodology.
2. Develop an ARIMA model using the Box-Jenkins methodology, and forecast the monthly number of new clients for the rest of 1993.
3. Write Dorothy a second memo that summarizes the results of this analysis. ∎

CASE 9-4   THE LYDIA E. PINKHAM MEDICINE COMPANY[15]

The Lydia E. Pinkham Medicine Company was a family-owned concern whose income was derived largely from the sale of Lydia Pinkham's Vegetable Compound. Perhaps students today could use some of the compound to relieve stress; unfortunately, it is no longer sold. Lydia Pinkham's picture was on the label, and the compound was marketed to women. Ads for the compound included this invitation: "Write freely and fully to Mrs. Pinkham, at Lynn, Mass., and secure the advice which she offers free of charge to all women. This is the advice that has brought sunshine into many homes which nervousness and irritability had nearly wrecked." In fact, the company ensured that a female employee answered every letter. Women *did* write to Mrs. Pinkham. Their claims included this one: "Without [Lydia Pinkham's Vegetable Compound] I would by this time have been dead or, worse, insane . . . I had given up on myself; as I had tried so many things, I

believed nothing would ever do me any good. But, thanks to your medicine, I am now well and strong; in fact, another person entirely." This testimonial and others were reproduced in print ads for the compound.

The unique nature of the company—one dominant product that accounted for most of the company's sales, no sales staff, and a large proportion of sales revenues invested in advertising—and the availability of data on both sales and advertising led the Committee on Price Determination of the National Bureau of Economic Research (NBER) in 1943 to recommend that the data be subjected to thorough analysis. The research was not undertaken for several years.[16] Analysts have studied the data using causal models that include the advertising data and other economic variables (similar to those presented in Chapter 8). However, several researchers have suggested that Box-Jenkins approaches using

---

[15] This case was contributed by Dr. Susan C. White, George Washington University, Washington, D.C. For more information, see Susan C. White, "Predicting Time Series with Neural Networks versus Statistical Models: The Lydia Pinkham Data." *Proceedings of the 24th Annual Conference of the Decision Sciences Institute, Southwest Region*, 1993, 108–110.

[16] See Palda (1964).

only the sales data provide comparable, or even superior, predictions when compared with the causal approaches.[17] The sales data are appealing to study for two reasons:

1. The product itself was unchanged for the span of the data; that is, there are no shifts in the series caused by changes in the product.
2. There was no change in the sales force over the span of the data, and the proportion of revenues spent on advertising was fairly constant. Thus there are no shifts in the data caused by special promotions or other marketing phenomena.

Typically, actual data are not this "clean" in terms of product and marketing continuity.

The task at hand, then, is to determine which Box-Jenkins (ARIMA) model is the "best" for these data. The model will be developed using the 1907–1948 data and tested using the 1949–1960 data shown in Table 9-18.

MODEL IDENTIFICATION

A computer program capable of ARIMA modeling was used to examine the data for 1907 through 1948; the data for 1949 through 1960 are used to examine the forecasting ability of the selected model. Preliminary tests suggest that the data are stationary (that is, there is no apparent trend), so differencing is not employed. After examining the autocorrelations and partial autocorrelations, it was determined that an AR model was most appropriate for the data. [The autocorrelations (ACF) and partial autocorrelations (PACF) for 10 periods are given in Table 9-19.] The autocorrelations and partial autocorrelations seemed to be consistent with those of an AR(2) process. To verify the order p of the AR component, Akaike's information criterion (*AIC*; see Equation 9.7) was used with autoregressive models of orders $p = 1, 2$, and 3. The *AIC* leads to the choice of an AR(2) model for the Lydia Pinkham data.

MODEL ESTIMATION AND TESTING OF MODEL ADEQUACY

A computer program was used to estimate the parameters (including a constant term) of the AR(2)

model using the data for 1907 through 1948. The resulting model is

$$Y_t = 178.6 + 1.423Y_{t-1} - .521Y_{t-2} + \varepsilon_t$$
$$\quad\quad\quad (.137) \quad\quad\quad (.136)$$

where the numbers in parentheses beneath the autoregressive coefficients are their estimated standard deviations. Each autoregressive coefficient is significantly different from zero for any reasonable significance level. The residual autocorrelations were all small and each was within its 95% error limits. The Ljung-Box chi-square statistics had p-values of .63, .21, and .64 for groups of lags $m = 12, 24$, and 36, respectively. The AR(2) model appears to be adequate for the Lydia Pinkham sales data.

FORECASTING WITH THE MODEL

The final step in the analysis of the AR(2) model for these data is to forecast the values for 1949 through 1960 one period ahead. (For example, data through 1958 are used in computing the forecast for 1959). The forecasting equation is

$$\hat{Y}_t = 178.6 + 1.423Y_{t-1} - .521Y_{t-2}$$

The one-step-ahead forecasts and the forecast errors are shown in Table 9-20.

In addition to the one-step-ahead forecasts, some accuracy measures were computed. The forecasts from the AR(2) model have a mean absolute percentage error (*MAPE*) of 6.9% and a mean absolute deviation (*MAD*) of $113 (thousands of current dollars). These figures compare favorably to the accuracy measures from the causal models developed by other researchers.

SUMMARY AND CONCLUSIONS

A parsimonious (smallest number of parameters) AR(2) model has been fit to the Lydia Pinkham data for the years 1907 through 1948. This model has produced fairly accurate one-step-ahead forecasts for the years 1949 through 1960. ∎

---

[17] See Kyle (1978).

TABLE 9-18	Lydia E. Pinkham Medicine Data				
Year	Sales (thousands of current dollars)	Year	Sales (thousands of current dollars)	Year	Sales (thousands of current dollars)
1907	1016	1925	3438	1943	2602
1908	921	1926	2917	1944	2518
1909	934	1927	2359	1945	2637
1910	976	1928	2240	1946	2177
1911	930	1929	2196	1947	1920
1912	1052	1930	2111	1948	1910
1913	1184	1931	1806	1949	1984
1914	1089	1932	1644	1950	1787
1915	1087	1933	1814	1951	1689
1916	1154	1934	1770	1952	1866
1917	1330	1935	1518	1953	1896
1918	1980	1936	1103	1954	1684
1919	2223	1937	1266	1955	1633
1920	2203	1938	1473	1956	1657
1921	2514	1939	1423	1957	1569
1922	2726	1940	1767	1958	1390
1923	3185	1941	2161	1959	1397
1924	3352	1942	2336	1960	1289

TABLE 9-19		
Lag k	ACF	PACF
1	0.915	0.915
2	0.765	−0.440
3	0.597	−0.061
4	0.424	−0.124
5	0.243	−0.168
6	0.059	−0.141
7	−0.099	0.024
8	−0.240	−0.170
9	−0.356	−0.036
10	−0.440	−0.040

QUESTIONS

1. After this analysis was completed, the figure for sales in 1961 became available: $1,426. What is the model's forecast for 1961? If this year were added to the testing data set, what would the revised *MAPE* and *MAD* be?

2. There is some evidence that the Lydia Pinkham data may be nonstationary. For example, the sample autocorrelations tend to be large (persist) for several lags. Difference the data.

Construct a time series plot of the differences. Using Minitab or a similar program, fit an ARIMA(1, 1, 0) model to annual sales for 1907 to 1948. Generate one-step-ahead forecasts for the years 1949 to 1960. Which model, AR(2) or ARIMA(1, 1, 0), do *you* think is better for the Lydia Pinkham data?

3. The Lydia Pinkham data are interesting due to the unique (unchanging) nature of the product

TABLE 9-20

Year	Actual	Forecast	Error
1949	1984	1896.4	87.6
1950	1787	2006.7	−219.7
1951	1689	1687.8	1.2
1952	1866	1651.0	215.0
1953	1896	1953.9	−57.9
1954	1684	1904.4	−220.4
1955	1633	1587.1	45.9
1956	1657	1625.0	32.0
1957	1569	1685.7	−116.7
1958	1390	1548.0	−158.0
1959	1387	1339.1	−47.9
1960	1289	1442.3	−153.3

and marketing for the 54-year period represented. What factors might affect annual sales data for automobiles and copper over this same period? Why?

For further reading on the Lydia E. Pinkham Medicine Company and Lydia Pinkham, see Sarah Stage, *Female Complaints: Lydia Pinkham and the Business of Women's Medicine* (New York: Norton, 1979).

CASE 9-5   CITY OF COLLEGE STATION

The City of College Station relies on monthly sales tax revenue to fund operations. The sales tax revenue generates accounts for, approximately, 44% of the total General Fund budget. It is important to be able to forecast the amount of sales tax revenue the city will receive each month from the state of Texas, so that only the amount of funds equal to the anticipated expenditures is deposited in a checking account. The excess funds can be placed in an account drawing interest.

Charles Lemore, an analyst for the city, was asked to develop a forecasting model for monthly sales tax revenue. Charles has recently completed a forecasting course at the local university and decides to try the Box-Jenkins methodology. He begins by looking at the data and the sample autocorrelation and sample partial autocorrelation functions.

The monthly sales tax revenues (in thousands of dollars) for the period January 1991 to November 1999 are listed in Table 9-21. A time series plot of revenues is given in Figure 9-41.

A strong seasonal component is evident in a plot of the series and in the sample autocorrelations and sample partial autocorrelations shown in Figure 9-42 and Figure 9-43, respectively. The autocorrelations at multiples of lag 3 suggest that there is a within-year quarterly seasonal pattern (the second monthly payment to the city within any quarter is relatively large) as well as an annual pattern. In addition, the series contains a clear upward trend.

Charles decides to difference the revenue series with respect to the seasonal period $S = 12$. The sample autocorrelations for the seasonally differenced series are shown in Figure 9-44. A plot of the seasonally differenced series (not shown) appears to vary about a constant level of about 50.

Charles is ready to fit and check an ARIMA model for the sales tax revenue series, but he needs your help. He would also like to generate forecasts for the next 12 months once he has an adequate model. ∎

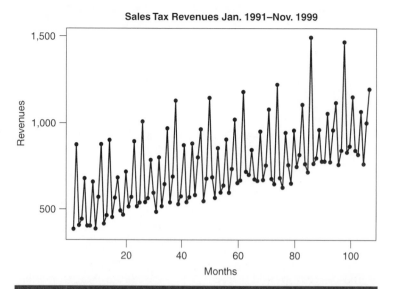

FIGURE 9-41   City of College Station Sales Tax Revenues

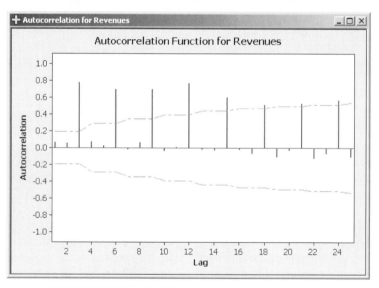

Autocorrelation Function: Revenues

Lag	ACF	T	LBQ	Lag	ACF	T	LBQ
1	0.065295	0.68	0.47	14	-0.028273	-0.13	255.29
2	0.052000	0.54	0.77	15	0.598940	2.68	300.77
3	0.778231	7.99	68.69	16	-0.024427	-0.10	300.85
4	0.069311	0.48	69.23	17	-0.073904	-0.31	301.56
5	0.027452	0.19	69.32	18	0.515622	2.16	336.40
6	0.693138	4.79	124.80	19	-0.109377	-0.44	337.98
7	-0.022330	-0.13	124.86	20	-0.034739	-0.14	338.14
8	0.066637	0.39	125.38	21	0.527036	2.12	375.81
9	0.694694	4.01	182.81	22	-0.126835	-0.49	378.02
10	-0.042753	-0.22	183.03	23	-0.075273	-0.29	378.81
11	0.008252	0.04	183.04	24	0.571783	2.20	424.75
12	0.766130	3.88	255.10	25	-0.111329	-0.41	426.51
13	-0.027366	-0.12	255.19				

FIGURE 9-42   Sample Autocorrelations for Sales Tax Revenues

QUESTIONS

1. Develop an ARIMA model for sales tax revenue using the Box-Jenkins methodology.
2. Using your model, generate forecasts of revenue for the next 12 months. Append these forecasts to the end of the series and plot the results. Are you happy with the pattern of the forecasts?
3. Write a brief memo summarizing your findings.

TABLE 9-21

Year	Jan.	Feb.	Mar.	Apr.	May	Jun.	July	Aug.	Sept.	Oct.	Nov.	Dec.
1991	382	872	408	443	679	406	409	662	388	570	879	417
1992	468	895	457	568	685	492	465	713	518	572	891	519
1993	544	1005	543	568	785	596	488	799	518	644	968	544
1994	691	1125	531	576	868	541	571	876	579	801	960	546
1995	675	1139	684	564	851	595	641	902	596	735	1014	652
1996	663	1174	714	698	842	675	665	948	670	753	1073	676
1997	646	1219	680	628	943	756	649	951	742	814	1100	759
1998	715	1487	763	793	955	780	777	1052	775	957	1117	757
1999	839	1459	828	862	1147	840	814	1064	766	997	1187	

FIGURE 9-43   Sample Partial Autocorrelations for Sales Tax Revenues

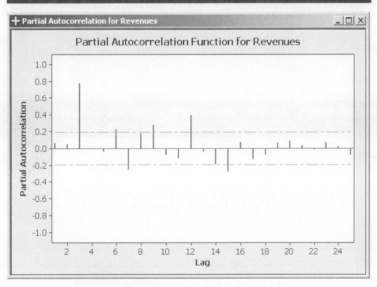

Partial Autocorrelation Function: Revenues

Lag	PACF	T	Lag	PACF	T
1	0.065295	0.68	14	-0.189410	-1.96
2	0.047941	0.50	15	-0.285778	-2.96
3	0.776959	8.04	16	0.072095	0.75
4	-0.002013	-0.02	17	-0.130604	-1.35
5	-0.036516	-0.38	18	-0.082646	-0.85
6	0.224379	2.32	19	0.065410	0.68
7	-0.256006	-2.65	20	0.091950	0.95
8	0.177547	1.84	21	0.028949	0.30
9	0.278791	2.88	22	-0.017353	-0.18
10	-0.078668	-0.81	23	0.072479	0.75
11	-0.123788	-1.28	24	0.022790	0.24
12	0.396276	4.10	25	-0.079367	-0.82
13	-0.042746	-0.44			

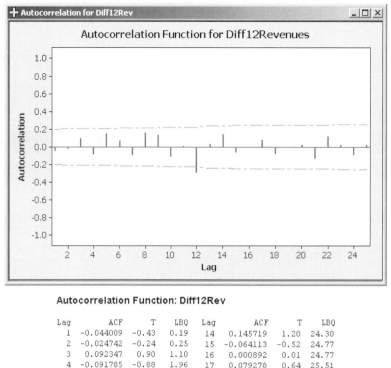

Autocorrelation Function: Diff12Rev

Lag	ACF	T	LBQ	Lag	ACF	T	LBQ
1	-0.044009	-0.43	0.19	14	0.145719	1.20	24.30
2	-0.024742	-0.24	0.25	15	-0.064113	-0.52	24.77
3	0.092347	0.90	1.10	16	0.000892	0.01	24.77
4	-0.091785	-0.88	1.96	17	0.079278	0.64	25.51
5	0.153888	1.47	4.38	18	-0.078264	-0.63	26.25
6	0.068941	0.64	4.87	19	-0.008088	-0.06	26.26
7	-0.099190	-0.92	5.90	20	0.026202	0.21	26.34
8	0.162988	1.50	8.72	21	-0.138299	-1.11	28.72
9	0.138474	1.25	10.77	22	0.117117	0.92	30.45
10	-0.108053	-0.96	12.04	23	0.023113	0.18	30.52
11	0.007556	0.07	12.05	24	-0.093960	-0.74	31.67
12	-0.295737	-2.60	21.76	25	0.023869	0.19	31.74
13	0.033589	0.28	21.88				

FIGURE 9-44   Sample Autocorrelations for the Seasonally Differenced Sales Tax Revenues

CASE 9-6   UPS AIR FINANCE DIVISION

The Air Finance Division is one of several divisions within United Parcel Service Financial Corporation, a wholly owned subsidiary of United Parcel Service (UPS). The Air Finance Division has the responsibility of providing financial services to the company as a whole with respect to all jet aircraft acquisitions. In addition, this division also provides financing to independent outside entities for aviation purchases as a separate and distinct operation. Historically, the non-UPS financing segment of the Air Finance Division has provided a higher rate of return

and greater fee income than the UPS segment; however, it is more costly to pursue.

Funding forecasts for the non-UPS market segment of the Air Finance Division have been highly subjective and not as reliable as the forecasts for other segments. Table 9-22 lists 10 years of monthly funding requirements for the non-UPS Air Finance Division segment. These data were collected from management reports during the period January 1989 through December 1998, and are the month-end figures in millions of dollars.

The data in Table 9-22 are plotted in Figure 9-45. The funding requirement time series has a strong seasonal component along with a general upward trend. The sample autocorrelations and sample partial autocorrelations are shown in Figures 9-46 and 9-47, respectively.

The Box-Jenkins methodology will be used to develop an ARIMA model for forecasting future funding requirements for the non-UPS segment of the Air Finance Division.

Because of the nonstationary character of the time series, the autocorrelations and partial autocorrelations for various differences of the series are examined. The autocorrelation function for the series with one regular difference and one seasonal difference of order $S = 12$ is shown in Figure 9-48. That is, these autocorrelations are computed for the differences

$$W_t = \Delta \Delta_{12} Y_t = \Delta (Y_t - Y_{t-12})$$
$$= Y_t - Y_{t-1} - Y_{t-12} + Y_{t-13}$$

TABLE 9-22											
Year	*Jan.*	*Feb.*	*Mar.*	*Apr.*	*May*	*Jun.*	*July*	*Aug.*	*Sept.*	*Oct.*	*Nov.*	*Dec.*
1989	16.2	16.7	18.7	18.8	20.6	22.5	23.3	23.8	22.3	22.3	22.1	23.6
1990	20.1	21.6	21.6	21.9	23.4	25.9	26.0	26.2	24.7	23.5	23.4	23.9
1991	20.0	20.4	20.9	21.6	23.2	25.6	26.6	26.3	23.7	22.2	22.7	23.6
1992	20.2	21.1	21.5	22.2	23.4	25.7	26.3	26.2	23.6	22.8	22.8	23.3
1993	21.0	21.7	22.2	23.1	24.8	26.6	27.4	27.1	25.3	23.6	23.5	24.7
1994	21.2	22.5	22.7	23.6	25.1	27.6	28.2	27.7	25.7	24.3	23.7	24.9
1995	21.8	21.9	23.1	23.2	24.2	27.2	28.0	27.6	25.2	24.1	23.6	24.1
1996	20.7	22.0	22.5	23.6	25.2	27.6	28.2	28.0	26.3	25.9	25.9	27.1
1997	22.9	23.8	24.8	25.4	27.0	29.9	31.2	30.7	28.9	28.3	28.0	29.1
1998	25.6	26.5	27.2	27.9	29.4	31.8	32.7	32.4	30.4	29.5	29.3	30.3

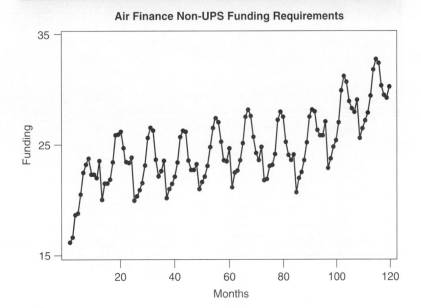

FIGURE 9-45   Funding Requirements for Non-UPS Segment of Air Finance Division

There is clearly a significant spike at lag 12 in the sample autocorrelations shown in Figure 9-48. This suggests an ARIMA model for the W_t's (the process with a regular difference and a seasonal difference) that has a moving average term at the seasonal lag 12. Consequently, an ARIMA$(0, 1, 0)(0, 1, 1)_{12}$ model might be a good initial choice for the funding requirements data. ■

QUESTIONS

1. Using Minitab or equivalent software, fit an ARIMA$(0, 1, 0)(0, 1, 1)_{12}$ model to the data in Table 9-22. Do you think a constant term is required in the model? Explain.
2. Is the model suggested in part 1 adequate? Discuss with reference to residual plots, residual autocorrelations, and the Ljung-Box chi-square statistics. If the model is not adequate, modify

and refit the initial model until you feel you have achieved a satisfactory model.
3. Using the model you have developed in part 2, generate forecasts for the funding requirements for the next 12 months.
4. Write a report summarizing your findings. Include in your report a plot of the original series and the forecasts.

FIGURE 9-46   Sample Autocorrelations for Funding Requirements

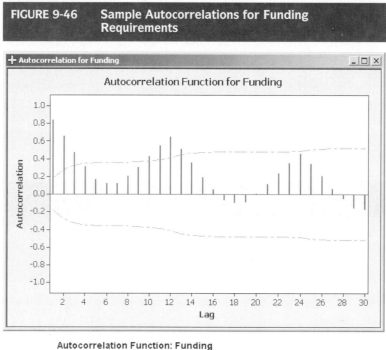

Autocorrelation Function for Funding

Autocorrelation Function: Funding

Lag	ACF	T	LBQ	Lag	ACF	T	LBQ
1	0.837546	9.17	86.30	16	0.051635	0.21	385.19
2	0.653627	4.62	139.31	17	-0.070460	-0.29	385.90
3	0.471450	2.86	167.12	18	-0.101867	-0.42	387.38
4	0.309926	1.76	179.24	19	-0.090741	-0.38	388.58
5	0.167326	0.93	182.80	20	0.006750	0.03	388.59
6	0.119600	0.66	184.64	21	0.114121	0.47	390.51
7	0.118763	0.65	186.47	22	0.233914	0.97	398.68
8	0.208453	1.14	192.15	23	0.353911	1.45	417.59
9	0.308387	1.67	204.69	24	0.457769	1.85	449.55
10	0.428652	2.27	229.15	25	0.340459	1.34	467.41
11	0.546265	2.77	269.23	26	0.202990	0.78	473.83
12	0.649303	3.10	326.37	27	0.061054	0.23	474.41
13	0.511713	2.27	362.20	28	-0.056059	-0.22	474.91
14	0.355561	1.51	379.66	29	-0.156711	-0.60	478.86
15	0.192224	0.80	384.81	30	-0.175532	-0.67	483.88

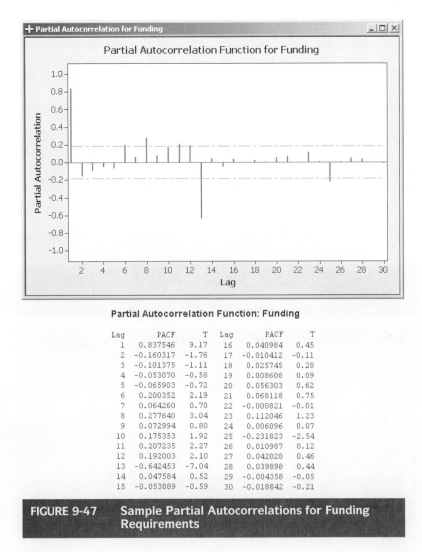

Partial Autocorrelation Function: Funding

Lag	PACF	T	Lag	PACF	T
1	0.837546	9.17	16	0.040984	0.45
2	-0.160317	-1.76	17	-0.010412	-0.11
3	-0.101375	-1.11	18	0.025745	0.28
4	-0.053070	-0.58	19	0.008608	0.09
5	-0.065903	-0.72	20	0.056303	0.62
6	0.200352	2.19	21	0.068118	0.75
7	0.064260	0.70	22	-0.000821	-0.01
8	0.277640	3.04	23	0.112046	1.23
9	0.072994	0.80	24	0.006096	0.07
10	0.175353	1.92	25	-0.231823	-2.54
11	0.207235	2.27	26	0.010987	0.12
12	0.192003	2.10	27	0.042028	0.46
13	-0.642453	-7.04	28	0.039898	0.44
14	0.047584	0.52	29	-0.004358	-0.05
15	-0.053889	-0.59	30	-0.018842	-0.21

FIGURE 9-47   Sample Partial Autocorrelations for Funding Requirements

CASE 9-7   AAA WASHINGTON

An overview of AAA Washington was provided in Case 5-5 when students were asked to prepare a time series decomposition of the emergency road service calls received by the club over five years. The time series decomposition performed in Case 5-5 showed that the pattern Michael DeCoria had observed in emergency road service call volume was probably cyclical in nature. Michael would like to be able to predict the cyclical effect on emergency road service call volume for future years.

In Case 6-6 four linear regression models using total number of emergency road service calls as

the dependent variable and unemployment rate, temperature, rainfall, and number of members as the four independent variables were investigated. The temperature variable was transformed by subtracting 65 degrees from the average monthly temperature values. A nonlinear relationship was then researched.

In Case 7-2 a multiple regression model was developed. Variables such as rainfall, number of members, the exponentially transformed average monthly temperature, and the unemployment rate lagged 11 months were tested.

In Case 8-6 the multiple regression model developed in Case 7-2 was checked for serial correlation and a model recommended to Michael DiCoria that was believed to be most appropriate for predicting the cyclical nature of emergency road service call volume.

Michael is still not satisfied. The model presented in Case 8-6 only explained about 71 percent of the variance of the emergency road service call volume variable. He has asked you to try the Box-Jenkins methodology to forecast the road call volume data presented in Table 9-23. You decide to divide the data set into two sections. The values from May of 1988 through December 1992 will be the initialization, or fitting, section, and the first four months of 1993 will be the test, or forecasting, section.

Assignment
Develop an ARIMA model for the emergency road service call volume data. Write Michael DeCoria a memo summarizing your findings. ■

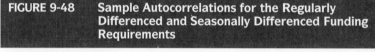

FIGURE 9-48   Sample Autocorrelations for the Regularly Differenced and Seasonally Differenced Funding Requirements

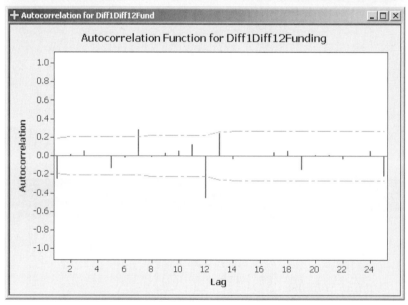

Autocorrelation Function: Diff1Diff12Fund

Lag	ACF	T	LBQ	Lag	ACF	T	LBQ
1	-0.249318	-2.58	6.84	14	-0.040666	-0.31	53.68
2	0.015515	0.15	6.87	15	-0.008993	-0.07	53.69
3	0.049961	0.49	7.15	16	-0.000199	-0.00	53.69
4	-0.004556	-0.04	7.15	17	0.035883	0.27	53.86
5	-0.138456	-1.35	9.34	18	0.052056	0.39	54.21
6	-0.026264	-0.25	9.42	19	-0.152044	-1.14	57.28
7	0.279279	2.67	18.52	20	0.004204	0.03	57.28
8	-0.017412	-0.16	18.55	21	0.009024	0.07	57.29
9	0.027132	0.24	18.64	22	-0.040388	-0.30	57.52
10	0.052554	0.47	18.97	23	-0.005729	-0.04	57.52
11	0.121755	1.09	20.77	24	0.052168	0.39	57.90
12	-0.453775	-4.02	46.05	25	-0.221294	-1.63	64.87
13	0.244586	1.90	53.47				

TABLE 9-23		Emergency Road Call Volume by Month for Case 9-7			
Year	Month	Calls	Year	Month	Calls
1988	May	20,002		November	22,490
	June	21,591		December	24,861
	July	22,696	1991	January	23,441
	August	21,509		February	19,205
	September	22,123		March	20,386
	October	21,449		April	19,988
	November	23,475		May	19,077
	December	23,529		June	19,141
1989	January	23,327		July	20,883
	February	24,050		August	20,709
	March	24,010		September	19,647
	April	19,735		October	22,013
	May	20,153		November	22,375
	June	19,512		December	22,727
	July	19,892	1992	January	22,367
	August	20,326		February	21,155
	September	19,378		March	21,209
	October	21,263		April	19,286
	November	21,443		May	19,725
	December	23,366		June	20,276
1990	January	23,836		July	20,795
	February	23,336		August	21,126
	March	22,003		September	20,251
	April	20,155		October	22,069
	May	20,070		November	23,268
	June	19,588		December	26,039
	July	20,804	1993	January	26,127
	August	19,644		February	20,067
	September	17,424		March	19,673
	October	20,833		April	19,142

Minitab Applications

The problem. In Example 9.10 Perkin Kendell, an analyst for the Outboard Marine Corporation, wants to forecast sales for 1997.

Minitab Solution

1. If the data are stored in a file, open it using the following menus:

   ```
   File>Open Worksheet
   ```

   If the data are not on file, enter them on the worksheet.
2. To compute the autocorrelations for the variable sales click:

   ```
   Stat>Time Series>Autocorrelation
   ```

3. The Autocorrelation Function dialog box that was shown in Figure 3-28 appears.
   a. Double-click on the variable Sales and it will appear to the right of Series.
   b. Click OK and Figure 9-33 will appear.

4. In order to seasonally difference the data click on the following menus:

`Stat>Time Series>Differences`

5. The Differences dialog box that was shown in Figure 3-29 appears.
   a. Double-click on the Variable Sales and it will appear to the right of Series.
   b. Tab to Store differences in: and enter C2.
   c. Tab to Lag: and enter a 4. Click OK and the fourth differences will appear in column 2 beginning in row 5.
6. Label the C2 variable Diff4Sales. To compute the autocorrelations for this variable, repeat step 2 using Diff4Sales as the variable to the right of Series:.
7. To compute the first differences for the Diff4Sales variable, repeat step 5 storing the differences in C3 and using a Lag: of 1.
8. Label the C3 variable Diff1Diff4Sales. To compute the autocorrelations for this variable, repeat step 2 using Diff1Diff4Sales as the variable to the right of Series:.
9. To compute the partial autocorrelations for the variable Diff1Diff4Sales click:

`Stat>Time Series>Partial Autocorrelation`

10. The Partial Autocorrelation Function dialog box that is similar to Figure 3-28 appears.
    a. Double-click on the variable Diff1Diff4Sales and it will appear to the right of Series.
    b. Click OK and Figure 9-36 will appear.
11. In order to run an ARIMA(1, 1, 0)(0, 1, 2) model click on the following menus:

`Stat>Time Series>ARIMA`

12. The ARIMA dialog box shown in Figure 9-49 appears.
    a. Double-click on the variable Sales and it will appear to the right of Series.
    b. Click the box to the left of Fit seasonal model and indicate 4 to the right of Period:.
    c. Under Nonseasonal place a 1 to the right of Autoregressive:, a 1 to the right of Difference:, and a 0 to the right of Moving average:.
    d. Under Seasonal place a 0 to the right of Autoregressive:, a 1 to the right of Difference:, and a 2 to the right of Moving average:.
    e. Because the data have been differenced, click off the box for Include constant term in model.
    f. Click Forecast and the ARIMA–Forecast dialog box appears. In order to forecast two periods into the future place a 2 to the right of Lead:. Click OK.
    g. Click Storage and the ARIMA–Storage dialog box appears. Click on the box next to Residuals and then click OK. Click OK on the ARIMA dialog box and the bottom portion of Table 9-16 appears.
    h. To compute the autocorrelations for the residuals, repeat step 2 using RES1 as the variable to the right of Series:.
13. In order to develop a time series plot that includes a forecast, click Graphs on the ARIMA dialog box and the ARIMA–Graphs dialog box shown in Figure 9-50 appears.
    a. Click on the box next to the left of time Series Plot.
    b. An alternative method for obtaining the autocorrelations for the residuals is to click on the box to the left of ACF of residuals.
    c. Click OK. Click OK on the ARIMA dialog box and Figure 9-38 appears.

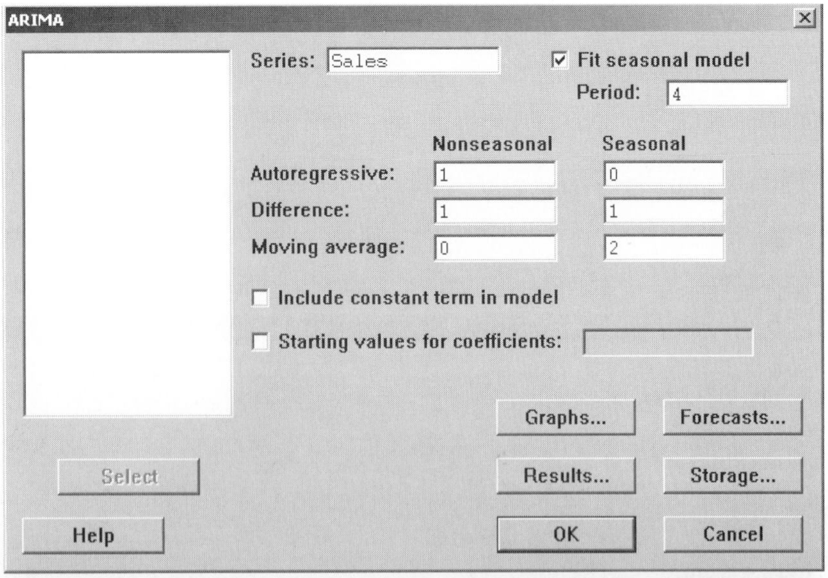

FIGURE 9-49   Minitab ARIMA Dialog Box

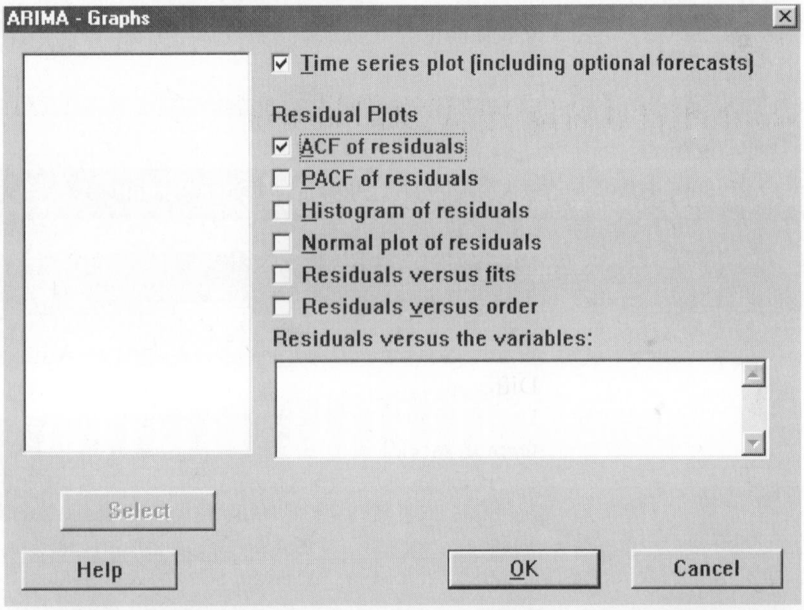

FIGURE 9-50   Minitab ARIMA—Graphs Dialog Box

Excel Applications: CB Predictor

The problem. In Chapter 3, Excel was used to compute autocorrelation coefficients and a correlogram for the data presented in Table 3-1. (See p. 61.) In this section CB Predictor will be demonstrated using the daily closing averages of the Dow Jones Transportation Index shown in Table 9-3.

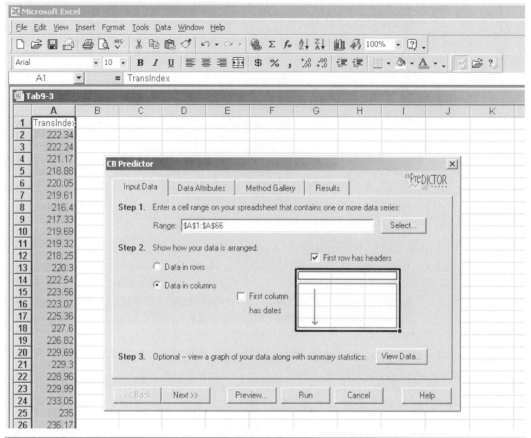

FIGURE 9-51   CB Predictor Dialog Box—Input Data Screen

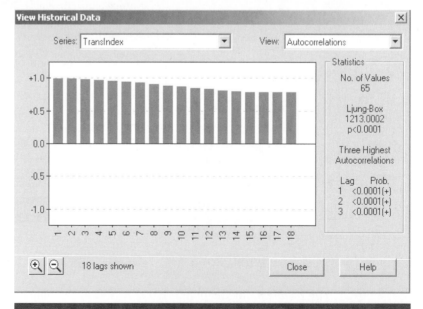

FIGURE 9-52   CB Predictor View Historical Data Screen

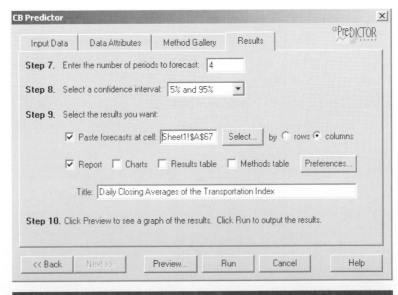

FIGURE 9-53   CB Predictor Results Data Screen

CB Predictor Solution

1. Install CB Predictor from the CD included with this text. You may elect to have CB Predictor load each time you open Excel. If so, the CB Predictor icons will appear on the menu bar. If not, click the box corresponding to

   `Tools>Add-Ins`

   The Add-Ins dialog box appears. Select CB Predictor and click OK. CB Predictor will appear on the menu bar.

2. Open the data file in Excel by clicking on the following menus:

   `File>Open`

   In the Open dialog box enter Tab9-3 to the right of File name:. Click Open and the data from Table 9-3 will appear.

3. Put the cursor over Indices—renamed TransIndex for Figure 9-51—and click on CB Predictor. The CB Predictor dialog box shown in Figure 9-51 appears with the data already entered in the Range: box.

4. In Step 3, click View Data and select Autocorrelations in the View box on the View Data Screen. The screen shown in Figure 9-52 appears.

5. The numerical values of the autocorrelations[18] and the *p*-values associated with the *t* statistics for testing for significant autocorrelation at a given lag are printed out as part of the Report output in CB predictor. Consequently, it is necessary to complete the model and forecast specification steps in CB Predictor (Steps 4–9). The CB Predictor screen at Step 9 is shown in Figure 9-53.

6. In Step 9, select Report and click Preferences. When the Preferences screen appears, click the Autocorrelations box and then click OK.

---

[18]CB Predictor computes the autocorrelation coefficient at a given lag using the Pearson definition of correlation given in Equation 2.10 with the lagged series Y_{t-k} playing the role of the X observations in this equation. Consequently, the numerical values of the CB Predictor autocorrelations will differ from the autocorrelations r_k given by Equation 3.1. However, the differences will be small for large n.

Tab9-3

Report for Daily Closing Averages of the Transportation Index
Created: 3/10/2003 at 1:09:22 PM

Summary:
    Number of series: 1
    Periods to forecast: 4
    Seasonality: none
    Error Measure: RMSE

Series: TransIndex   **Range: A2:A66**

    Method: Double Moving Average
    Parameters:
        Periods: 3
    Error: 2.3581

    Series Statistics:
        Mean: 244.176
        Std. Dev.: 19.320
        Minimum: 216.4
        Maximum: 288.57
        Ljung-Box: 1213.0002

    Autocorrelations:

Lag	Correlation	Probability
1	0.9953	0.0000
2	0.9881	0.0000
3	0.9804	0.0000
4	0.9706	0.0000
5	0.9573	0.0000
6	0.9421	0.0000
7	0.9266	0.0000
8	0.9064	0.0000
9	0.8857	0.0000
10	0.8672	0.0000
11	0.8490	0.0000
12	0.8317	0.0000
13	0.8124	0.0000
14	0.7973	0.0000
15	0.7866	0.0000
16	0.7848	0.0000

FIGURE 9-54   **CB Predictor Report Output for the Dow Jones Transportation Index Data**

7. After completing Step 9, select Run and the Report output shown in Figure 9-54 appears. This output can be edited like an Excel spreadsheet. The autocorrelations and their *p*-values are printed below the descriptive statistics information in the Report. The value of the Ljung-Box statistic is also displayed.

References

Akaike, H. "A New Look at the Statistical Model Identification." *IEEE Transactions Automatic Control* AC-19 (1974): 716–723.

Bernstein, P. *Against the Gods: The Remarkable Story of Risk.* New York: John Wiley & Sons, 1996.

Box, G. E. P., G. M. Jenkins, and G. C. Reinsel. *Time Series Analysis: Forecasting and Control,* Third Edition. Upper Saddle River, NJ: Prentice Hall, 1994.

DeLurgio, S. A. *Forecasting Principles and Applications.* New York: McGraw-Hill, 1998.

Diebold, F. X. *Elements of Forecasting*, Third Edition. Cincinnati, OH: South-Western, 2004.

Jenkins, G., and G. McLeod. *Case Studies in Time Series Analysis.* Lancaster, UK: Gwilym Jenkins & Partners Ltd., 1982.

Kyle, P. W. "Lydia Pinkham Revisited: A Box-Jenkins Approach." *Journal of Advertising Research* 18(2) (1978): 31–39.

Makridakis, S., S. C. Wheelwright, and R. J. Hyndman. *Forecasting Methods and Applications,* Third Edition. New York: John Wiley & Sons, 1998.

Montgomery, D. S., and L. A. Johnson. *Forecasting and Time Series Analysis.* New York: McGraw-Hill, 1976.

Newbold, P., and T. Bos. *Introductory Business & Economic Forecasting*, Second Edition. Cincinnati, OH: South-Western, 1994.

O'Donovan, T. M. *Short Term Forecasting: An Introduction to the Box-Jenkins Approach.* New York: John Wiley & Sons, 1983.

Pack, D. J. "In Defense of ARIMA Modeling." *International Journal of Forecasting* 6(2) (1990): 211–218.

Palda, K. S. *The Measurement of Cumulative Advertising Effects.* Upper Saddle River, NJ: Prentice Hall, 1964.

Pindyck, R. S., and D. L. Rubinfeld. *Econometric Models and Economic Forecasts,* Fourth Edition. New York: McGraw-Hill, 1998.

Quenouille, M. H. "The Joint Distribution of Serial Correlation Coefficients." *Annals of Mathematical Statistics* 20 (1949): 561–571.

Schwarz, G. "Estimating the Dimension of a Model." *Annals of Statistics* 6 (1978): 461–464.

CHAPTER

10

JUDGMENTAL FORECASTING AND FORECAST ADJUSTMENTS

The forecasting techniques covered in this book all involve the manipulation of historical data to produce predictions, or forecasts, of important variables of interest. The discussions in previous chapters were concerned with complex data analyses and perhaps implied that the forecaster's judgment was not involved. In fact, as emphasized in Chapter 1, the use of good judgment is an essential component of all good forecasting techniques. Good judgment is required in deciding on the data that are relevant to the problem and in interpreting the results of the data analysis process, and sometimes constitutes a major portion of the analysis itself.

This chapter discusses some of the important forecasting elements that are adjuncts or supplements for the methodical manipulation of such historical data. In Chapter 11, several considerations regarding the management of the forecasting process are described.

In many forecasting situations, only the analysis of historical data is used to generate the final forecast; the judgment or opinion of the analyst is not injected into the process. This book is concerned primarily with such forecasting techniques and, as a result, with short- and intermediate-term forecasts. Such forecasts are the essential concern of most levels of management in an organization and are associated with most of the critical decisions that must be made.

These forecasting procedures rely on the manipulation of historical data and assume a past and a future that are indistinguishable except for the specific variables identified as affecting the likelihood of future outcomes. This assumption precludes a substantive shift in the technological base of the society, an assumption that many recent developments suggest is erroneous. Consider, for example, the introduction and proliferation of high-speed, inexpensive personal computers, cellular phones, hand-held personal data assistants, and so forth.

In some forecasting situations, the analyst supplements the data analysis process after considering the unusual circumstances of the situation or after recognizing that past history is not an accurate predictor of the future. The amount of judgment injected into the forecasting process is increased if the historical data are few in number or are judged to be partially irrelevant. In the extreme case, it may be the analyst's opinion that no historical data are directly relevant to the forecasting process. Under these conditions, forecasts based purely on the opinions of "experts" are used to formulate the forecast or scenario for the future.

Interestingly, research has shown that, when historical data are available, the judgmental modification of the forecasts produced by analytical methods reduces the accuracy of the forecasts. This finding may be attributed to some bias on the part of the forecaster, possibly because of a tendency to be overly optimistic or to underestimate future uncertainty. It has also been shown that using a judgment component in the forecasting process increases the forecasting cost.[1]

When little or no relevant historical data are available to assist in the forecasting process, judgment must be relied on if forecasts, or predictions, about the future are desired. Because such situations often arise, especially for top management, techniques have been developed to improve the accuracy of such forecasts by using available executive judgment to the best advantage. The use of these techniques is worthy of consideration because executives frequently consider their own judgment superior to other methods of predicting the future. As Makridakis states, "People prefer making forecasts judgmentally. They believe that their knowledge of the product, market, and customers as well as their insight and inside information gives them a unique ability to forecast judgmentally."[2]

Several questions follow, and each suggests the use of imagination and brainstorming rather than complete reliance on the collection and manipulation of historical data. For each question, one of the forecasting techniques discussed in this chapter can provide a company's management team with valuable insights into its firm's future operating environment.

- What will be the age distribution of the United States in the year 2025?
- To what extent will U.S. citizens work in the home 25 years from now?
- What cities will be the major population and business centers in 20 years?
- To what extent will the United States depend on other countries for the manufacture of key consumer items?
- To what extent will shopping from home using television and computers or other electronic devices be popular in 20 years?
- What kinds of recreation will occupy U.S. citizens in the year 2025?
- How much leisure time will the average U.S. citizen have in the 21st century?
- Will the United States begin pulling back from its commitments around the globe over the next 25 years? If so, in what ways will this affect U.S. business?

The techniques discussed in this chapter are sometimes called *judgmental forecasting* methods because judgment is the primary or sole component of the process. Some of them are also referred to as technological forecasting methods; they frequently deal with projecting the effects of technological changes into the uncertain future. The remainder of this chapter outlines some of the commonly used forecasting methods in which the judgment of the forecaster is the primary ingredient.[3]

THE DELPHI METHOD

When experts are gathered in a single meeting location and asked about the future, group dynamics can sometimes distort the process and result in a consensus that may not be carefully thought out by all participants. The Delphi method, first used by an Air-Force-funded RAND Corporation project in the 1950s, attempts to remove the group dynamic aspect from the deliberations of the forecasters. In the first round of the method, the experts reply in writing to the questions posed by the investigating team. The team then summarizes the comments of the participants and mails them

---

[1] Makridakis (1986), p. 45.

[2] Makridakis (1986), p. 63.

[3] For an organized outline of many forecasting methods including judgment forecasting, see Georgoff and Murdick (1986).

back. Participants are then able to read the reactions of the others and to either defend their original views or modify them based on the views of others.

This process continues through two or three rounds until the investigators are satisfied that many viewpoints have been developed and carefully considered. Participants may then be invited to meet to share and debate their viewpoints. At the conclusion of this process, the investigating team should have good insight into the future and can begin to plan their organization's posture accordingly.

As Rowe and Wright (1999) point out:

> Delphi is not a procedure designed to challenge statistical or model-based procedures, against which human judgment is generally shown to be inferior: it is intended for use in judgment and forecasting situations in which pure model-based statistical methods are not practical or possible because of the lack of appropriate historical/economic/technical data, ...

Any Delphi procedure has four key features. These are *anonymity, iteration, controlled feedback*, and the *aggregation of group response*. Anonymity is achieved through the use of questionnaires either administered by hand, by mail, over the phone, or via a computer network. When experts express their opinions privately, they are free from group social pressures and can concentrate only on the merits of each idea, proposal, or situation. Moreover, with the iteration of the questionnaire over a number of rounds, the participating experts are given the opportunity to change their opinions without losing face in the eyes of the remaining (anonymous) group members.

After each iteration of the questionnaire, the opinions of each expert are briefly summarized, and each group member is informed of the positions of their anonymous colleagues. Consequently, feedback contains the opinions and judgments of all group members and not just the most vocal. After the final round, the group judgment is summarized (often using descriptive statistics such as an average or quartiles describing the range) so that each judgment receives equal weight.

The first round of the Delphi method is often unstructured, allowing the experts free rein to identify, and comment on, those issues they see as important. The monitor team then consolidates these issues into a single set of structured statements (the questionnaire) from which the opinions and judgments of the Delphi panelists may be gathered in a quantitative manner in subsequent rounds. The results from each round are summarized and provided to each expert for further consideration. After the second round, members are given the opportunity to change prior opinions based on the provided feedback. In most applications of the Delphi technique, the number of rounds rarely exceeds three. Empirical studies of the Delphi method suggest that accuracy increases over Delphi rounds, and that Delphi panelists tend to be more accurate than unstructured interacting groups.

Example 10.1

Applied Biosystems supplies life science firms and research institutions with a host of products and services for: researching genes and proteins; studying how drugs interact with the body's systems and genetic makeup; testing food and the environment for contaminants; and performing DNA-based identification. In the early years of the company, instrument systems and other equipment generated most of the sales revenue. In recent years, the consumable (reagents, services, assays) side of the business has been growing rapidly, and consumables now account for about half of the company's revenue. Applied Biosystems does most of its business in the United States but is considering expanding its presence in Europe, Japan, and Australia, where it currently has relatively small percentages of the biosystems equipment market. Before committing to the capital expenditures associated with global expansion, the company is interested in developing forecasts of sales growth in Europe, Japan, and Australia for the next 10 years. With little historical sales data in these regions to guide it, Applied Biosystems has decided to hire three experts familiar with life science research and general international economic conditions.

Expert A is a geneticist who has extensive experience with the pharmaceutical industry and has spent some time studying the growth of genetically linked research in Europe. Expert B is a noted economist and has extensive experience studying, in particular, the economy of Japan. Expert C, a native of Australia, has spent some time working at the European head-quarters of the World Health Organization in the Health Technologies and Pharmaceuticals area. She currently works as a consultant to Australia's government and industry.

Applied Biosystems would like a forecast of the growth in sales for both its equipment and consumable groups over the next 10 years in each of Europe, Japan, and Australia. To begin, each expert was asked to provide his or her estimates of sales growth for the instrumentation/equipment and consumables groups by region over the next 10 years. Each expert was provided with a current level of annual sales and estimated market share by group for Europe, Japan, and Australia. For the money budgeted, Applied Biosystems was able to obtain the commitment of the three experts for two rounds of reports. The anonymous (to each other) experts, located in different parts of the world, were connected to the project manager at Applied Biosystems by computer.

The results after the first round are summarized in Table 10-1.

In the first round, Expert A does not see much sales growth for the products and services of Applied Biosystems in Europe over the next 10 years. Although genetically linked research in Europe is likely to grow substantially, the competition from European firms, and non-European firms with a strong presence in the biologicals market, is likely to limit the opportunities for Applied Biosystems in spite of its excellent reputation. Similarly, Expert A sees relatively limited growth for Applied Biosystems equipment/instrumentation in Japan because of the tendency of Japanese researchers to use the excellent Japanese equipment. He does, however, feel there is a chance for appreciable growth in consumable sales in Japan. Expert A does not have an opinion about the growth of Applied Biosystems sales in Australia.

Expert B sees limited growth for Applied Biosystems equipment/instrumentation sales in Europe and Japan but a substantial growth opportunity in Australia, although the Australian market as a whole is relatively small. Expert B is a little more optimistic about European sales growth than Expert A, but both agree the sales growth, particularly in consumables, is likely to be small for a 10-year period. Expert B feels there is likely to be tremendous growth in sales for both equipment/instrumentation and consumables in Australia, with the growth in consumable sales particularly attractive. Expert B feels Applied Biosystems has no major competitors in Australia, and the Australian commitment to nurturing a healthy lifestyle and maintaining a quality environment will remain strong.

Expert C is more uncertain about equipment/instrumentation sales growth in Europe than Experts A and B and suggests a reasonable wide range of 0% to 150%. Her forecast of consumable sales growth for Europe, although more optimistic than Experts A and B, is still relatively small. Expert C has no opinion about Applied Biosystems sales growth in Japan. She is very "bullish" on potential sales growth of Applied Biosystems products and services in her native country of Australia. Her sales growth estimates are large for both equipment/instrumentation and consumables, and of the same order of magnitude as those of Expert B.

TABLE 10-1	Results from the First Round of the Delphi Method		
	Expert A	*Expert B*	*Expert C*
Equipment/Instrumentation			
—Europe	+10% to +40%	+30% to +70%	+0% to +150%
Consumables—Europe	+5% to +15%	+10% to +25%	+20% to +60%
Equipment/Instrumentation			
—Japan	+0% to +50%	−10% to +40%	—
Consumables—Japan	+40% to +100%	+50% to +200%	—
Equipment/Instrumentation			
—Australia	—	+100% to +200%	+150% to +300%
Consumables—Australia	—	+200% to +400%	+200% to +400%

The information in Table 10-1 was supplied to each of the experts, and a second round of sales growth forecasts was solicited. Each expert had the opportunity to adjust their initial forecasts after viewing the results of the first round. Expert A's opinions remained essentially unchanged. Expert B adjusted his sales growth range for equipment/instrumentation in the European market to +20% to +60%, a slight downward adjustment. He also adjusted the upper limit of his range for consumable sales growth in the Japanese market down to +150%. He left his sales growth forecasts for the Australian market unchanged.

Expert C adjusted the ranges of her sales growth forecasts for the European market to

Equipment/Instrumentation—Europe	+10% to +90%
Consumables—Europe	+15% to +40%

She left her forecasts for Australia unchanged.

A final phone call to the Delphi panelists with the results of the second round did not yield any additional adjustments. With the results of the Delphi exercise in hand, Applied Biosystems decided to maintain their current presence in Europe with more emphasis on equipment/instrumentation sales. In Japan, the company decided to launch a major marketing effort to increase the sales of products in their consumable groups, with the possibility of partnering with a Japanese firm to help with the sales and distribution efforts. Australia appeared to represent a major opportunity, but the overall market is small and Applied Biosystems decided to do a little more cost-benefit analysis before committing to the Australian market.

The advantage of the Delphi method is that noted experts can be asked to carefully consider the subject of interest and to reply thoughtfully to the viewpoints of others without the interference of group dynamics. The result, if the process is handled carefully, may be a good consensus of the future along with several alternative scenarios.[4]

SCENARIO WRITING

Scenario writing involves defining the particulars of an uncertain future by writing a "script" for the environment of an organization over many years in the future. New technology, population shifts, and changing consumer demands are among the factors that are considered and woven into this speculation to provoke the thinking of top management.

A most likely scenario is usually written along with one or more less likely, but possible, scenarios. By considering the posture of the company for each of these possible future environments, top management is in a better position to react to actual business environment changes as they occur and to recognize the long-range implications of subtle changes that might otherwise go unnoticed. In this way, the organization is in a better position to maintain its long-term profitability rather than concentrate on short-term profits and ignore the changing technological environment in which it operates.

The scenario-writing process is often followed by a discussion phase, sometimes by a group other than the one that developed the scenarios. Discussion among the groups can then be used to defend and modify viewpoints so that a solid consensus and alternative scenarios are developed. For example, scenarios might be developed by a company's planning staff and then discussed by the top management team. Even if none of the scenarios are subsequently proven to be totally true, this process encourages the long-range thinking of the top management team and better prepares it to recognize and react to important environmental changes.

---

[4] For a detailed description of the Delphi method, see Parente and Anderson-Parente (1987).

Example 10.2

A company that manufactures industrial telephone and television cables decides to conduct a scenario-writing exercise prior to its annual weekend retreat. Each member of the retreat group is asked to write three scenarios that might face the company 5 years from now: a worst-case, a most-likely, and a best-case scenario. After these writing assignments are completed, and just before the weekend retreat, the president and his senior vice president summarize the contributions into the following three scenarios on which they intend to focus the group's discussion during the two-day retreat:

1. Internet usage continues to grow rapidly but slowly moves away from cable in favor of satellite access. Even telephone service relies increasingly on noncable means, as does home television reception. The company sees its sales and profits on a nonending decline and will soon be out of business.
2. Internet and home television service continues to grow rapidly but is provided by several sources. Satellite service is widely used, but buried cables continue to be an integral part of high-tech service, especially in large cities, both in private housing and industrial applications. The company's leadership in cable development and deployment results in increased sales and profits.
3. Due to technical problems and security issues, satellite usage for the Internet and television service declines until it is used primarily in rural areas. Cable service grows rapidly in both residential and industrial applications, and the company prospers as its well-positioned products and industry leadership result in industry dominance.

The company president and senior vice president intend to have extensive discussions on each of these three scenarios. They want to have long-range strategies developed that will accommodate all future possibilities and believe that focusing on these three cases will energize both themselves and their management team.

COMBINING FORECASTS

A developing branch of forecasting study involves the combination of two or more forecasting methods to produce the final forecasts. An issue of the *International Journal of Forecasting* contained a special section on this new technique. Portions of the abstracts of three articles in this issue illustrate the developing nature of combining forecasts:

1. According to Armstrong (1989), research from over 200 studies demonstrates that combining forecasts produces consistent but modest gains in accuracy. However, this research does not define well the conditions under which combining is most effective nor how methods should be combined in each situation.
2. Mahoud (1989) indicates that the amount of research on combining forecasts is substantial. Yet relatively little is known about when and how managers combine forecasts. Important managerial issues that require further study include managerial adjustment of quantitative forecasts, the use of expert systems in combining forecasts, and analyses of the costs of combining forecasts.
3. Considerable literature has accumulated over the years regarding the combination of forecasts. The primary conclusion of this line of research, according to Clemen (1989), is that forecast accuracy can be substantially improved through the combination of multiple individual forecasts. This paper provides a review and annotated bibliography of that literature.

Example 10.3

A company that makes parts for large farm tractors wants to forecast the number of these units that will be sold over the next 10 years. From this forecast it will develop strategies to remain competitive in its business. Specifically, the company is concerned about its plant capacity. A forecast of future business would help it greatly both in developing expansion plans and in dealing with its sources of financial support.

After an extensive data collection and forecasting effort, the company is faced with deciding which of two forecasts to accept. Although they are not too far apart for most

TABLE 10-2		Combining Forecasts	
Year in Future	*Professional Forecast*	*In-House Forecast*	*Final Forecast*
1	328	335	329.8
2	342	340	341.5
3	340	345	341.3
4	348	350	348.5
5	350	352	350.5
6	360	355	358.8
7	366	365	365.8
8	371	370	370.8
9	385	375	382.5
10	390	385	388.8

years, there are some differences. A professional forecasting firm with a solid track record generated the first forecast. The methods this firm used are unknown to company management, but they have been told the process was "mathematically sophisticated." The second forecast resulted from an executive retreat attended by top management along with marketing staff familiar with the expectations of its customers.

After discussions with company executives, the president decides to combine the two forecasts. These discussions tended to favor the professional forecast over the in-house forecast, so the president decides to weight the former 75% and the latter 25%. Table 10-2 shows the two forecasts for each of the next 10 years in units sold, in thousands, followed by the combined forecast. Each final forecast was computed by multiplying the first forecast by .75, the second by .25, and adding them together. For example, for year 1, the combined forecast is given by

$$(.75)328 + (.25)335 = 329.75$$

Notice that the final forecasts fall between the professional and in-house forecasts, but they are closer to the professional forecasts because the professional forecasts received the greater weight.

One of the benefits of combining forecasts is to minimize the effects of bias, that is, giving undue weight to a particular forecasting method. One strategy is to combine different forecasts by simply averaging the individual forecasts produced by different methods. If $\hat{Y}_{11}, \hat{Y}_{12}, \ldots, \hat{Y}_{1m}$ are one-step-ahead forecasts produced by m different methods, then the one-step-ahead combined forecast, $\hat{Y}_{1C}$, obtained by simple averaging is

$$\hat{Y}_{1C} = \frac{\hat{Y}_{11} + \hat{Y}_{12} + \cdots + \hat{Y}_{1m}}{m} \qquad (10.1)$$

Similar results hold for other forecast lead times.

As in Example 10.2, forecasts can be combined with unequal weights. In this case, each one-step-ahead forecast $\hat{Y}_{1i}$ receives weight $0 < w_i < 1$, where $\Sigma w_i = 1$. So, with m one-step-ahead forecasts produced by m different methods, the combined forecast $\hat{Y}_{1C}$ is

$$\hat{Y}_{1C} = w_1 \hat{Y}_{11} + w_2 \hat{Y}_{12} + \cdots + w_m \hat{Y}_{1m} \qquad (10.2)$$

where

$$\sum_{i=1}^{m} w_i = 1$$

There is no change in the weights as the forecast lead time changes. For example, the combined forecast two steps ahead, $\hat{Y}_{2C}$, would be computed like the combined forecast in Equation 10.2 with the two-step-ahead forecasts for each method replacing the one-step-ahead forecasts. The fact that the weights sum to 1 ensures that the combined forecast will be somewhere between the smallest and largest values of the individual forecasts.

There are several procedures for determining the weights w_i. If a record of past performance for each forecasting method is available, the weights can be taken to be inversely proportional to the sum of squared forecasting errors. Alternatively, the weights can be obtained by regression methods. Additional discussion of the procedures for combining forecasts is available in Newbold and Bos (1994).

In the coming years, further research will likely be conducted on the advantages of combining forecasts, along with the techniques for doing so. The objective of such combinations will be to develop accurate forecasts that are cost-effective.

FORECASTING AND NEURAL NETWORKS

Conventional forecasting methods, such as those discussed in this book, rely on historical data to develop a model and use it to project the variables of interest into the future. These projected values become the forecasts that are then used to develop plans for the business. In these models, it is assumed that the future will be exactly like the past, except for those variables specifically recognized by the model.

Conventional models sometimes make assumptions about the form of population distributions, assumptions that may or may not be subject to verification. Interval estimates using a regression model, for example, assume that the underlying population follows a normal distribution.

The developing field of artificial intelligence attempts to duplicate the processes of the human brain and nervous system using the computer. Although this field originated in biology and psychology, it is rapidly advancing into other areas, including business and economics. The three main thrusts of artificial intelligence are language processing, robotics, and artificial neural networks. This last field has the most commercial applications, including forecasting.

In neural networks, many examples are programmed into the computer, examples that capture the full range of past relationships among all variables that might affect the outcome of the dependent variables. The neural network program then assimilates these examples and attempts to develop the underlying relationships by "learning" as it goes along. This learning process, also called *training*, is analogous to a human trainee learning on the job.

A few forecasting researchers have noticed the similarity between neural network techniques and conventional forecasting methods that attempt to find variables to successfully predict the dependent variable. The theoretical advantage of neural networking as a forecasting tool is that relationships need not be specified in advance because the method involves learning about relationships using the examples provided. Also, neural networks do not require any assumptions about underlying population distributions and, unlike many conventional forecasting methods, they can operate with incomplete data.[5]

---

[5] Although neural networks do not produce judgmental forecasts in the usual sense, neural net forecasts are distinct from the data-based procedures discussed in Chapters 4–9 and so are included in this chapter. A neural network is an attempt to put the human thought process on a computer. Moreover, considerable judgment is required to use a neural network effectively.

A successful neural network application is sometimes called *plug compatible*. This means that the neural network program can quickly and easily replace the existing model, such as regression analysis, without disruption. An improvement in performance, such as more accurate forecasts, can sometimes be achieved with a minimal impact on ongoing operations. Neural networks are especially valuable when inputs are highly correlated or missing, or when the systems are highly nonlinear.

Following are some examples of the successful use of neural networks in practical settings. NeuralWare, Inc., a commercial supplier of neural network software, provided these examples.[6]

- A Kodak plant in Texas reduced costs by $3 million per year while maintaining product yield and quality. It began by collecting historical operating data, which were used to train a neural network to forecast the quality of the product as a function of the various process parameters.
- One of the classic problems in interpreting seismic signals for oil exploration is finding the first evidence of the shock wave from sensor recordings. Traditional signal processing methods have not been very successful in correctly identifying this first evidence—only 30% for one algorithm. Several oil companies have used a network program to correctly identify the first wave, with Amoco claiming a 95% success rate. This has had a major impact on their ability to improve the processing of seismic data for reservoir modeling.
- A German manufacturer of automotive electric fan motors used master inspectors to determine whether a completed motor was too noisy or exhibited "funny" sounds. A neural network took one week to learn from a master inspector and is currently doing the noise test work. The financial impact is a uniformly higher-quality product with fewer complaints from customers. The master inspectors have been released from this high-stress job to concentrate on other quality improvement tasks in the factory.
- Since 1989, a neural network has been used to determine the suitability of customers for instant credit from a loan company.
- Several companies have discovered that neural networks can be used to develop indicators useful in trading. Results of the systems indicate that neural network trading indicators, coupled with appropriate trading strategies, can consistently make money in the marketplace.
- The U.S. Air Force is using a neural network to forecast component failures in Air Force jets. A variety of data was collected on each aircraft, and the network was trained to predict the likelihood of specific failures in specific planes. These results are used for part stocking and preventive maintenance.
- A commercial product has been developed to forecast the outcome of horse races. The system requires the user to input specific information about the horses in a race. It wins 80% of the time that it decides the odds favor betting.

With examples such as these currently enjoying practical success, it is not hard to imagine a neural network system successfully forecasting monthly sales volume, employee absentee rate, or the prime interest rate. Freed from the confining restrictions of specifying relationships in advance and assuming population distributions, such networks have great potential for accurate forecasting as their use gains wider acceptance. As an example of a neural network application, see Case 10-2 at the end of this chapter.

---

[6] NeuralWare, Inc., Penn Center West, Building IV, Suite 227, Pittsburgh, PA 15276.

SUMMARY OF JUDGMENTAL FORECASTING

A potential danger in using most of the forecasting methods discussed in this text is that they involve the manipulation of historical data to generate the forecast. This practice is a valid procedure if the forecast is for the near-term future but becomes increasingly suspect as the distance of the forecasting horizon increases. The methods discussed in this chapter are valuable additions to the forecaster's arsenal when the particular concern of top management, the long-term forecast of the company's environment, is being considered.

Several authors have fascinated the general public with their speculations about the long-term trends currently developing in our society and the future they portend along with the managerial skills that will be needed to cope with them. Among the more provocative are:

- Bill Gates, *The Road Ahead* (Viking, 1995)
- Rowan Gibson (editor), Alvin Toffler, and Heidi Toffler, *Rethinking the Future: Rethinking Business, Principles, Competition, Control and Complexity, Leadership, Markets and the World* (Nicholas Breasley, 1999)
- Di Kamp, *The 21st Century Manager: Future-Focused Skills for the Next Millennium* (Kogan Page, 1999)
- Chuck Martin, *Net Future: The 7 Cybertrends That Will Drive Your Business, Create New Wealth, and Define Your Future* (McGraw-Hill, 1998)
- Alvin Toffler, *Future Shock* (New York: Random House, 1970)
- Alvin Toffler, *The Third Wave* (New York: Bantam Books, 1980)
- John Naisbitt, *Megatrends* (New York: Warner Books, 1982)
- John Naisbitt and Patricia Aburdene, *Megatrends 2000* (New York: William Morrow, 1990)
- John Naisbitt (audio tape), *Eight Asian Megatrends That Are Reshaping the World* (Simon & Schuster Books, 1996)
- John Naisbitt, *Global Paradox* (Avon, 1995)
- Jim Taylor, Watts Wacker, and Howard Means, *The 500-Year Delta: What Happens After What Comes Next* (Harperbusiness, 1998)

The references above make for interesting reading, even though some of them are 20 to 30 years old, because these authors have a unique ability to speculate about the future in provocative ways. A more formal approach to the kinds of changes they write about is called *technological forecasting* and is becoming an increasingly important field for many firms. This is because an estimated 25% of existing technology is replaced every year. Obviously, even a very sophisticated manipulation of historical data to produce forecasts can miss the mark by a wide margin under these circumstances. Consider, for example, the following developing fields. As these technologies unfold, the impact on many firms will be considerable.

- Artificial intelligence
- Genetic engineering
- Bioelectricity
- Multisensory robotics
- Lasers
- Fiber optics
- Microwaves
- Advanced satellites

- Solar energy
- Superconductors

PricewaterhouseCoopers produces an internal publication, *Technology Forecast*, available to the general public. This annual document analyzes key information technologies and forecasts their directions in the next 1 to 3 years. This is an example of one company's intense concern about technological advances and their effects on society as well as on their own firm.

The rate of technological development increases the need for managers to be increasingly alert to change. Still, historical patterns can provide at least some clues to the future in almost every business. As stressed in Chapter 1, there needs to be a prudent mix of appropriate historical data manipulation, along with the judicious use of judgment and experience, if useful forecasts are to be generated.

OTHER TOOLS USEFUL IN MAKING JUDGMENTS ABOUT THE FUTURE

A number of tools have been developed to assist decision makers in the process of weighing information about the future and making the best possible decisions. One set of tools is frequently discussed in textbooks and journal articles under the general heading of "decision making" or sometimes "decision making under uncertainty." When managers are faced with the task of making decisions in the face of uncertainty, their ability to forecast becomes a critical element in the decision-making process.

When the analysis of historical data has been completed, the decision maker must make a judgment regarding alterations in the firm's course of action. In other words, the analyst must weave the results of the forecasting process into the firm's existing decision-making procedures. A few of the elements of decision theory that are often relevant at this stage of the process are briefly discussed next.[7]

The concept of *expected value* was described in Chapter 2. Decision makers frequently use it, either explicitly or implicitly. Recall that this concept involves calculating the mean value that a random numerical variable will assume over many trials. In Table 10-3, a discrete random variable X is displayed in a probability distribution; every possible future value that X can assume is shown along with the probability of each.

Notice that the sum of the probabilities in Table 10-3 is 1.00, or 100%, which means that every possible value that X can assume has been identified. In Table 10-3, X represents the number of new major contracts that a firm will sign during the next fiscal

TABLE 10-3	A Probability Distribution
X	$P(X)$
1	.10
2	.20
3	.25
4	.30
5	.15
	1.00

---

[7] For an excellent and very readable book on decision making, see Hammond, Keeney, and Raiffa (1999).

year. The question that is answered by the expected value is: How many new contracts can be expected, on the average, if the probability distribution of Table 10-3 is valid? Equation 10.3 is used to calculate the expected value of a probability distribution such as the one shown in Table 10-3.

$$E(X) = \Sigma X[P(X)] \tag{10.3}$$

where

$E(X)$ = Expected value

X = Values that the random variable can assume

$P(X)$ = Probability of each X occurring

The expected value of Table 10-3 can be calculated using Equation 10.3 as follows:

$$E(X) = 1(.10) + 2(.20) + 3(.25) + 4(.30) + 5(.15) = 3.2$$

The expected value of the probability distribution shown in Table 10-3 is 3.2. If X in this example represents the number of new major contracts for the coming fiscal year, then, on average, if the chances for new contracts remain the same year after year, 3.2 new contracts would be signed. Notice that the value 3.2 is not possible in any one year; only integer values 1, 2, 3, 4, and 5 are possible. Nevertheless, the value 3.2 represents the mean outcome over many trials. Decision makers are frequently interested in expected values and use them as their best forecasts for critical numerical variables in planning for the uncertain future.

Decision theory formally addresses the elements that comprise the decision-making function of business leaders. Expected values are often woven into this more general consideration of decision making. The *decision tree diagram* is used to help the decision maker visualize a complex situation and make rational decisions. Such a decision tree diagram is shown in Figure 10-1.

Figure 10-1 reflects the uncertainty that exists about the nature of future sales and incorporates the decision about whether to build a new plant or repair the old one. The problem is that if the company knew that high demand would result, it would be better off building the new plant; on the other hand, if it knew that low demand would result, profits would be higher if it repaired the old plant. Even in this simple example, the benefit of the tree diagram can be seen: it enables the decision maker to see the various choices available, to identify those uncertainties beyond the firm's control, and to explicitly determine costs, profits, and the probabilities of future events. In more complicated situations, the benefits of the tree diagram and formal decision theory are even more evident.

A statistical concept designed to revise preliminary probabilities on the basis of sample evidence is *Bayes' theorem*. This concept is often applicable in situations in which estimates of the probabilities of unknown future events are determined and then modified after collecting sample evidence. An example is the test market concept used by many manufacturers of consumer products. Such a company might estimate the probability of public acceptance of a new product as being quite high. However, before risking the millions of dollars that a national campaign requires, a test market might be undertaken in areas the company regards as good representative markets. The results of the test market are then used to modify the original estimates of product success, and a decision about introducing the product nationally is made. A simplified version

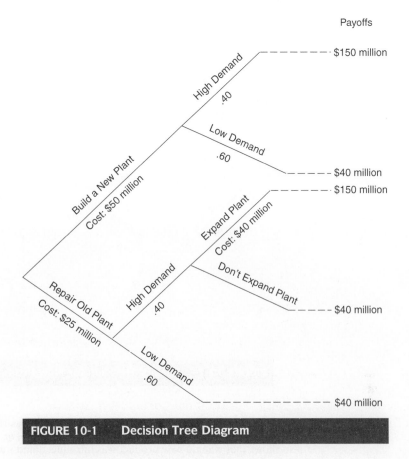

FIGURE 10-1   Decision Tree Diagram

of Bayes' theorem is shown in Equation 10.4.[8]

$$P(A|B) = \frac{P(A)P(B|A)}{P(B)}$$ (10.4)

where

$P(A|B)$ = Probability of event A occurring given that event B has occurred

$P(B)$ = Probability that event B occurs

$P(A)$ = Probability that event A occurs

$P(B|A)$ = Probability of event B occurring given that event A has occurred

Example 10.4

Figure 10-2 reflects a specific application of Bayes' theorem in a test market situation. The management of a large consumer products company needs to decide whether to introduce a new product nationally. They estimate that their new product has a 50% chance of high sales in the national market; that is, $P(H) = .50$. They are considering the use of a test market to determine whether they can do a better job of forecasting high or low sales of the new product. Figure 10-2 shows a decision tree of the test market outcomes.

---

[8] The general statement of Bayes' theorem for n events $A_1, A_2, \ldots, A_n$, each of which can occur in conjunction with another event B, is:

$$P(A_i|B) = \frac{P(A_i)P(B|A_i)}{P(A_1)P(B|A_1) + P(A_2)P(B|A_2) + \cdots + P(A_n)P(B|A_n)} \qquad i = 1, 2, \ldots, n$$

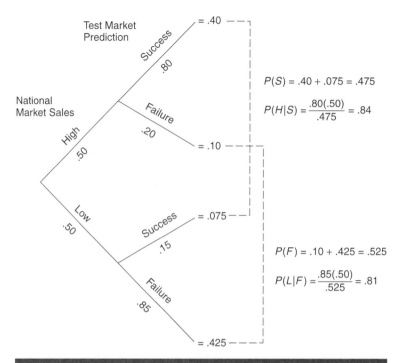

$P(S) = .40 + .075 = .475$

$P(H|S) = \dfrac{.80(.50)}{.475} = .84$

$P(F) = .10 + .425 = .525$

$P(L|F) = \dfrac{.85(.50)}{.525} = .81$

FIGURE 10-2   Bayes' Decision for New-Product Introduction

Past experience shows that when a new product was introduced and high sales were achieved, the test market was successful 80% of the time, or $P(S|H) = .80$. Past experience also shows that when a new product was introduced and low sales were achieved, the test market failed (low sales) 85% of the time, or $P(F|L) = .85$.

Bayes' theorem can be used to compute the probability of the new product being successful in the national market under different test conditions. Figure 10-2 shows the computation of the two probabilities of particular interest:

- If the test market predicts success, there is an 84% chance the product will have high sales nationally. Equivalently,

$$P(H|S) = .84 = .80(.50)/.475 = P(S|H)P(H)/P(S)$$

- If the test market predicts failure, there is an 81% chance the product will have low sales nationally, or

$$P(L|F) = .81 = .85(.50)/.525 = P(F|L)P(L)/P(F)$$

In Example 10.4, a test market would help management decide whether or not to introduce the new product nationally. The test market accuracy is sufficient to change the probability of high sales (or low sales) from the pretest value of 50%. If the test market is successful, the chance of high sales increases to 84%. If the test market is a failure, the chance of low sales increases to 81%. The probabilities were calculated using Bayes' theorem. The decision about product introduction will be much easier to make than it would have been without the test market.

Another useful tool for forecasting is computer simulation. *Simulation* is a set of numerical and programming techniques for modeling situations subject to uncertainty, and conducting sampling experiments on those models using a computer. Each simulation run (replication) produces one possible outcome ("forecast") for the problem being studied. Many runs (replications) allow the decision maker the opportunity to observe the complete set of possible outcomes, as well as their likelihood of occurrence. These computer-generated scenarios can then be summarized and used to make the best decision.

There are many reasons for using simulation instead of mathematical analysis to gather information in an uncertain environment.

- Many realistic representations of actual business systems are much too complex to be analyzed mathematically.
- The primary interest might be to experiment with the system or to find the best levels for the variables that influence the system or to simply study the system. Experimenting with the actual system may be impossible (combat situations) or extremely expensive (design of nuclear generating facilities) or so time-consuming that only one replication is possible.
- The simulation effort is frequently useful in itself because it leads to a better understanding of the system.
- As a tool, simulation carries a certain amount of credibility with management. It is relatively easy to explain to management the efforts involved in a simulation study.

From a business perspective, the chief advantage of a computer simulation exercise is that forecasts of the consequences of various management decisions can be generated before such decisions must be made. Simulation has been used in a wide variety of settings, including modeling of manufacturing operations, workforce scheduling, modeling of investment alternatives, analyzing and pricing sophisticated investment instruments, and modeling passenger flows at an airport terminal.[9] Decision trees such as the one in Figure 10-1 are often part of computer simulation experiments.

Key Formulas

Combined forecast given by simple average

$$\hat{Y}_{1C} = \frac{\hat{Y}_{11} + \hat{Y}_{12} + \cdots + \hat{Y}_{1m}}{m} \tag{10.1}$$

Combined forecast given by weighted average

$$\hat{Y}_{1C} = w_1\hat{Y}_{11} + w_2\hat{Y}_{12} + \cdots + w_m\hat{Y}_{1m} \tag{10.2}$$

Expected value formula

$$E(X) = \Sigma X[P(X)] \tag{10.3}$$

Bayes' theorem

$$P(A|B) = \frac{P(A)P(B|A)}{P(B)} \tag{10.4}$$

---

[9] Good discussions of computer simulation are available in Shela, Ceric, and Tadikamalla (2003), Law and Kelton (2000), and Banks (1998).

TABLE P-1			
Month	Actual Sales	Winters' Forecasts	Regression Forecasts
1	5502	4586	5263
2	6535	5944	6008
3	7390	6706	6832
4	4388	4530	4886
5	4521	5010	4918
6	5679	6574	5630
7	8578	8462	7963
8	7088	6415	5942
9	4839	4457	5156
10	4050	4638	3819

Problems

1. Identify two business situations where the Delphi method might be used to generate forecasts.

2. Consider the actual sales shown in Table P-1, along with one-step-ahead forecasts produced by Winters' method and by a regression model.
   a. Construct the combined forecasts of sales produced by taking a simple average of the forecasts produced by Winters' method and the regression model.
   b. Construct the combined forecasts of sales produced by taking a weighted average of the Winters' forecasts and the regression forecasts with weights $w_1 = .8$ and $w_2 = 1 - w_1 = .2$.
   c. Using the actual sales, determine the *MAPE*'s for the Winters' forecasts and the regression forecasts.
   d. Repeat part c using the combined forecasts from parts a and b. Based on the *MAPE* measure, which set of forecasts do you prefer?

CASES

CASE 10-1   GOLDEN GARDENS RESTAURANT

Sue and Bill Golden have decided to open a restaurant in a city in the Midwest. They have spent over a year researching the area and visiting medium- to high-price restaurants. They definitely believe that there is room for another restaurant and have found a good site that is available at a good price.

In addition, they have contacts with a number of first-class chefs and believe that they can attract one of them to their new restaurant. Their inquiries with local bankers have convinced them that financing will be readily available, given their own financial resources and their expertise in the restaurant business.

The only thing still troubling the Goldens is the atmosphere and motif for their restaurant. They have already conducted a series of three focus groups with area residents who eat out regularly, and no consensus on this matter emerged. They have talked about the matter considerably between themselves but now believe some other opinions would be valuable.

After reading about some of the techniques used in judgmental forecasting, they believe some of them might help them decide on the atmosphere for their new restaurant. They have identified a number of their friends and associates in other cities who would be willing to help them, but the Goldens are not certain how to utilize their talents. ■

=======

QUESTIONS

1. What method would you suggest to the Goldens in utilizing the expertise of their friends to decide on the atmosphere and motif for their new restaurant?

2. Are there any other methods they have overlooked while trying to research this matter?

CASE 10-2   ALOMEGA FOOD STORES

Example 1.1 in Chapter 1 described how Julie Ruth, the president of Alomega Food Stores, collected monthly sales data for her company (see Table 10-4) along with several other variables she thought might be related to sales. The Alomega cases in Chapters 2, 3, 5, and 8 described her efforts to use various Minitab procedures in an attempt to make meaningful forecasts of monthly sales.

In Case 8-7 Julie developed a multiple regression model that explained almost 91 percent of the monthly sales variable variance. She felt good about this model but was especially sensitive to the negative comments made by Jackson Tilson, her production manager, during a recent meeting (see the end of Example 1.1). Tilson said "I've been trying to keep my mouth shut during this meeting, but this is really too much. I think we're wasting a lot of people's time with all this data collection and fooling around with computers. All you have to do is talk with our people on the floor and with the grocery store managers to understand what's going on. I've seen this happen around here before, and here we go again. Some of you people need to turn off your computers, get out of your fancy offices, and talk with a few real people." Julie decided that office politics dictated that she heed Jackson's advice. She consulted with several people including Tilson to determine their opinions of how to forecast sales for January 2003. A large majority felt that using the sales figure for the previous January would provide the best prediction. Likewise, the forecast for February 2003 should be based on the sales figure for February 2002.

TABLE 10-4	Monthly Sales for 27 Alomega Food Stores, 1999–2002, for Case 10-2		
Month	*1999*	*2000*	*2001*	*2002*
Jan.	425,075	629,404	655,748	455,136
Feb.	315,305	263,467	270,483	247,570
Mar.	432,101	468,612	429,480	732,005
Apr.	357,191	313,221	260,458	357,107
May	347,874	444,404	528,210	453,156
Jun.	435,529	386,986	379,856	320,103
Jul.	299,403	414,314	472,058	451,779
Aug.	296,505	253,493	254,516	249,482
Sep.	426,701	484,365	551,354	744,583
Oct.	329,722	305,989	335,826	421,186
Nov.	281,783	315,407	320,408	397,367
Dec.	166,391	182,784	276,901	269,096

Based on this input, Julie developed a naive forecasting model

$$\hat{Y}_{t+1} = Y_{t-11}$$

that used last year's monthly value to predict this year's monthly value. ∎

QUESTIONS

1. How accurate is Julie's naive forecasting model?
2. How does the naive model compare to the multiple regression model developed in Case 8-7?
3. Until Julie can experience each of these two methods in action, she is considering combining forecasts. She feels that this approach would counter office politics and still allow her to use a more scientific approach. Would this be a good idea?
4. Should Julie use a simple average or weighted average approach to combining the forecasts?

CASE 10-3   THE LYDIA E. PINKHAM MEDICINE COMPANY REVISITED[10]

This case demonstrates an actual application of the usage of neural networks to forecast time series data. The authors understand that students have not been provided with the background to completely understand this case. However, we feel that benefits will be derived from experiencing this actual case.

The Lydia E. Pinkham Medicine Company and Lydia Pinkham's Vegetable Compound were introduced in Case 9-4.

During the late 1980s and into the 1990s, there were many attempts to use networks to forecast time series data. Most of the work was in the field of power utilization because power companies need accurate forecasts of hourly demand for their product. However, some research focused on more traditional business time series such as micro- and macroeconomic series, demographic data, and company-specific data. Virtually all this work used a feed-forward network trained using backpropagation. This case will employ this type of network to forecast the Lydia Pinkham sales data. The resulting forecasts will be compared to the forecasts from the AR(2) model presented in Case 9-4.

Figure 10-3 depicts a 2–4–1 feed-forward neural network—the network used for this study. The first number in the 2–4–1 indicates the number of inputs to the network. In this case, the two inputs are Y_{t-1} and Y_{t-2}. (Using the two previous periods to predict the current period is consistent with the AR(2) model, thus both the AR(2) model and the neural network model use the same "information" in computing the one-step-ahead predictions.) The 4 indicates the number of nodes, or processing units, in the hidden layer. (It is termed *hidden* because it is not directly connected to the "outside world," as are the input and output layers.) The number of nodes in the hidden layer is chosen arbitrarily in a sense: Too few hidden nodes restrict the network's ability to "fit" the data, and too many hidden nodes cause the network to memorize the training (or estimation) data. The memorization leads to very poor performance over the testing sample. In this case, the number of nodes in the hidden layer is simply twice the number of inputs. Finally, the one output node gives the one-step-ahead forecast, or Y_t.

---

[10]This case was contributed by Susan C. White, George Washington University, Washington, D.C. For more information, see Susan C. White, "Predicting Time Series with Neural Networks versus Statistical Models: The Lydia Pinkham Data," Proceedings of the 24th Annual Conference of the Decision Sciences Institute, Southwest Region, 1993, 108–110.

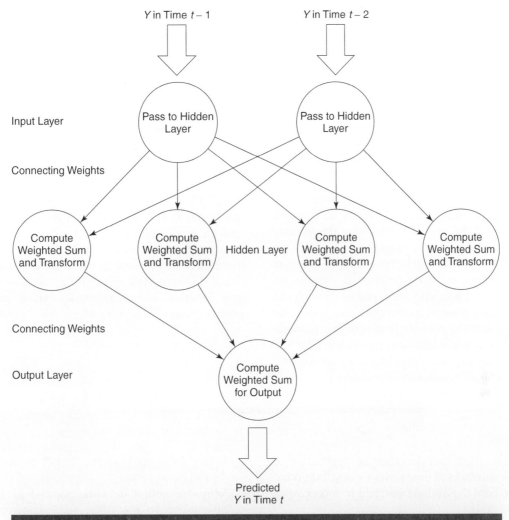

FIGURE 10-3   A 2−4−1 Feed-Forward Network

The neural network computes its output in the following manner: Each of the connecting arcs between nodes in two adjacent layers has an associated weight. Each node in the hidden layer computes a weighted sum of its inputs. (The input layer nodes simply pass the inputs on to the hidden layer.) This weighted sum is then "transformed" in some fashion, such as $Y = 1/(1 + e^{-x})$, where Y is the "transformed" data and X is the weighted sum. The Y is then passed on to the output layer, where each node again computes a weighted sum. This final weighted sum is the output of the network. The network is trained by adjusting all the connecting weights in an iterative fashion.

THE NEURAL NETWORK MODEL

The neural network was trained using BrainMaker,[11] a commercially available PC-based neural network simulation package. For this study, the step size was set to 0.500, and the training tolerance to 0.001. (Other packages might require the user to specify a learning rate and a momentum term.) As in Case 9-4, the first 42 observations are used to train the network; the last 12 are used to assess the performance of the network predicting one step ahead. One problem with using neural networks to forecast time series data is in determining how long to train the network; an over-trained network tends to memorize the training data and perform poorly on the testing

---

[11] BrainMaker, California Scientific Software, 1990.

	Estimation Data			Training Data		
TABLE 10-5	**Lydia E. Pinkham Medicine Neural Network Results for Case 10-3**					
Iterations	*MAD*	*MAPE*	*MSE*	*MAD*	*MAPE*	*MSE*
10,000	189.7	11.06%	51923.0	182.2	11.26%	43441.1
20,000	189.8	10.80%	53926.3	169.6	10.18%	37737.4
50,000	195.0	11.22%	54311.3	176.3	10.51%	41529.7
75,000	196.0	11.40%	54424.2	178.1	10.66%	42758.1
100,000	196.5	11.53%	54725.5	181.9	11.02%	43985.4

data. Thus some researchers have suggested simply stopping the training "early"—before the network has memorized the data. To determine the training effect, the network was trained for 10,000, 20,000, 50,000, 75,000, and 100,000 iterations. (One iteration is the presentation of one observation; this represents 250, 500, 1,250, 1,875, and 2,500 passes through the complete training set, respectively.) This allows the analyst to assess the possible impact of overtraining. (The work was originally done on an Intel 386SX-20 based PC, and the "time" to train for 100,000 iterations was approximately 20 minutes.)

RESULTS

The *MAD*, *MAPE*, and *MSE* for the various neural network models are presented in Table 10-5. They do not compare favorably with the AR(2) model. The author of this case is currently experimenting with a different type of neural network—a radial basis function neural network—which produces results comparable to those of the AR(2) model.[12] ∎

QUESTIONS

1. Find an article that describes an application of neural networks to time series forecasting. What method did the authors use, and how successful was it?
2. If you have access to a neural network program, try to find a network that produces better forecasts than the 2–4–1 network presented here.
3. Why are neural networks viewed as a viable alternative to the other forecasting methods discussed in this text?

References

Armstrong, J. S. "Combining Forecasts: The End of the Beginning or the Beginning of the End?" *International Journal of Forecasting* 5(4) (1989): 585–592.

Balkin, S. D., and J. K. Ord. "Automatic Neural Network Modeling for Univariate Time Series." *International Journal of Forecasting* 16(4) (2000): 509–515.

Banks, J. *Handbook of Simulation*. New York: John Wiley & Sons, 1998.

Bopp, A. E. "On Combining Forecasts: Some Extensions and Results." *Management Science* 31(12) (December 1986): 1492–1497.

Bunn, D., and G. Wright. "Interaction of Judgmental and Statistical Forecasting Methods: Issues and Analysis." *Management Science* 37(5) (May 1991): 501–516.

Clemen, R. T. "Combining Forecasts: A Review and Annotated Bibliography." *International Journal of Forecasting* 5(4) (1989): 559–583.

[12] For further reading on neural networks, see Khanna (1990).

Denton, J. W., "How Good Are Neural Networks for Causal Forecasting?" *Journal of Business Forecasting* 14(2) (Summer 1995): 17–20.

Dull, R. "Delphi Forecasting: Market Research for the 1990's." *Marketing News* (August 1988): 17.

Edmundson, R. H. "Decomposition: A Strategy for Judgmental Forecasting." *Journal of Business Forecasting* 9 (Summer 1990): 305–315.

Georgoff, D. M., and R. G. Murdick. "Manager's Guide to Forecasting." *Harvard Business Review* 1 (January–February 1986): 110–120.

Hammond, J. S., R. L. Keeney, and H. Raiffa. *Smart Choices: A Practical Guide to Making Better Decisions*. Boston: Harvard Business School Press, 1999.

Jain, C. L. *A Managerial Guide to Judgmental Forecasting*. New York: Graceway, 1987, p. 101.

Jain, C. L. "Myths and Realities of Forecasting." *Journal of Business Forecasting* (Fall 1990): 18–22.

Khanna, T. *Foundations of Neural Networks*. Reading, MA: Addison-Wesley, 1990.

Kudlow, L. "The Case for Market-Based Forecasting." *CATO Journal* 12(1) (Spring 1992): 119.

Law, A. M., and W. D. Kelton. *Simulation Modeling and Analysis*, Third Edition. Boston: McGraw-Hill, 2000.

Mahoud, E. "Combining Forecasts: Some Managerial Issues." *International Journal of Forecasting* 5(4) (1989): 599–600.

Makridakis, S. "The Art and Science of Forecasting." *International Journal of Forecasting* 2 (1986): 15–39.

Newbold, P., and T. Bos. *Introductory Business & Economic Forecasting*, Second Edition. Cincinnati, OH: South-Western, 1994.

Parente, F. J., and J. K. Anderson-Parente. "Delphi Inquiry Systems," in *Judgmental Forecasting*, eds. G. Wright and P. Ayton. New York: John Wiley & Sons, 1987, 129–156.

PricewaterhouseCoopers Global Technology Centre. *Technology Forecast* (Current Version). Menlo Park, CA: PricewaterhouseCoopers Global Technology Centre, 2003.

Rowe, G., and G. Wright. "The Delphi Technique as a Forecasting Tool: Issues and Analysis." *International Journal of Forecasting* 15(4) (1999): 353–375.

Seila, A. F., V. Ceric, and P. Tadikamalla. *Applied Simulation Modeling*. Belmont, CA: Brooks/Cole, 2003.

Walden, M. "How to Evaluate and Improve a Forecasting Process." *Journal of Business Forecasting* 15(2) (Summer 1996): 22.

Willard, T. "Forecasting: A Key to Business Success." *Futurist* (July–August 1991): 33–34.

CHAPTER

11

MANAGING THE FORECASTING PROCESS

Chapter 1 introduced the subject of forecasting with suggestions about its usefulness within the modern organization. Modern organizations must develop forecasts to make timely decisions in the face of uncertainty. This process of making educated guesses about the uncertain future (forecasting) usually involves a rational process of extending historical data and experiences into the future. It is now possible to review the basic notions and important points made in Chapter 1 with the benefit of the numerous forecasting techniques covered in the intervening chapters.

THE FORECASTING PROCESS

The forecasting process consists of two distinct phases. One phase occurs on a strategic level, and the other phase occurs on an operational level. On the strategic level, decisions include what to forecast, how to use the forecasts, and who will be responsible for generating the forecasts. The operational phase of forecasting consists of data gathering, forecast generation, and the ongoing evaluation of the forecasts. The forecasting process is like any other process: Left unmanaged and unchecked, it is likely to spiral out of control.

One key point discussed in Chapter 1 is the importance of using good management judgment along with quantitative techniques in developing good forecasts. Good management judgment is indeed important and can now be illustrated using several of the forecasting techniques discussed in previous chapters. A judicious mixture of quantitative techniques with common sense is always necessary if forecasts are to be accurate, understood, and used by the firm's decision makers.

Time series analysis (decomposition) is a good example of a technique involving the necessity of using sound judgment along with an analysis of past history. A company using a time series analysis program with, say, monthly data that yield a historical analysis of trend-cycle variation, seasonal variation, and irregular movements might recombine these three factors to produce a usable forecast of unit sales. Appropriate recombination of these factors requires considerable judgment as to their future behavior. In using the decomposition process, it is important to decide how many historical periods to include in the analysis.

Regression analysis requires judgment along with statistical analysis whenever forecasting takes place. If a multiple regression were conducted using employee job performance rating as the dependent variable and two variables—entry test score and age—as predictor variables, an R-squared value of 60% might be obtained. In addition, the t values for the predictor variables might both be significant along with the regression F value. The forecaster is then tempted to measure the two-predictor

485

variables on each job applicant and use them to predict job performance. However, three additional questions need to be considered. First, is the 60% explained variation sufficient for forecasting purposes? Perhaps "intuitive judgment" on the desirability of hiring a person is a superior method, or perhaps more precision in the forecasting process is needed and other predictor variables should be considered. Second, can it be assumed that future job applicants are essentially identical to those sampled in the regression study? If they differ in any substantive way, the forecasting model may not be valid. Finally, is the cost of the forecasting process justified in terms of benefit received? The company test may be expensive, especially if purchased from an outside testing agency, and must be justified by the benefits of the forecast.

Regression of time series data is a common occurrence in organizations in which tracking important measures of performance on a weekly, monthly, or quarterly basis is conducted. As autocorrelation is a common problem in such studies, an understanding of this condition and its cure becomes vital if the results of such analyses are to be valid in the decision-making process. Unfortunately, such understanding is often lacking; this shortcoming has become an increasing problem with the advent of inexpensive regression analysis software.

The Box-Jenkins techniques discussed in Chapter 9 illustrate a common problem in forecasting discussed in Chapter 1. These procedures are often superior forecasting methods, producing lower forecasting errors in many complex situations. Their disadvantage is that some sophistication is required on the part of the user. If the process that generates the forecasts is totally mysterious to the decision maker, the forecasts may be disregarded in the management of the organization regardless of their precision.

The short-, medium-, and long-term aspects of forecasting techniques as they relate to different levels of management in a firm can be illustrated with time series analysis and technological forecasting. First- and second-line management in a firm might be interested in a time series analysis of monthly unit sales with data collected over the past 4 years. By using judgment regarding the future of the trend-cycle component of this series, sales might be forecast for the next fiscal year and used to schedule monthly production for the factory. Midlevel managers might use the same time series program to analyze annual unit sales data over the past 8 years and forecast them for 5 years into the future. In this case, any long-term component might be ignored in an attempt to plan capital expenditure needs for the factory during this 5-year period. At the same time, top management might be engaged in technological forecasting using the Delphi method along with scenario writing. Their purpose would be to evaluate the company's current position in the market and to search for technology or societal changes that would threaten its market niche over the next 20 years or offer it opportunities not evident in day-to-day operations.

The data analysis techniques discussed in this book are summarized in Table 11-1. This table provides descriptions, points out applications, estimates cost levels, and indicates whether computer capabilities are necessary for the implementation of each technique. Each technique is also referenced to the chapters in which it is discussed. Summaries such as those in Table 11-1 should be viewed as guidelines and not definite statements that cannot be challenged.

MONITORING FORECASTS

Collecting data and selecting an acceptable forecasting technique are only among the first steps in an effective, ongoing forecasting effort. Several steps in the operational phase of the forecasting process have been described in this book, with an emphasis

TABLE 11-1	Forecasting Models				

Method	*Description*	*Applications*	*Cost*	*Computer Necessary?*	*Chapter*
Causal Forecasting Models					
Regression analysis	Explanatory forecasting; assumes a cause-and-effect relationship between the input to a system and its output	Short- and medium-range forecasting of existing products and services; marketing strategies, production, personnel hiring, and facility planning	Low to medium	Usually	6
Multiple regression	Explanatory forecasting; assumes a cause-and-effect relationship between more than one input to a system and its output	Same as above	Low to medium	Yes	7
Time Series Forecasting Models					
Decomposition method	Explanatory forecasting; assumes a cause-and-effect relationship between time and the output of a system; the system is decomposed into its components	Medium-range forecasting for new plant and equipment planning, financing, new-product development, and new methods of assembly; short-range forecasting for personnel, advertising, inventory, financing, and production planning	Low to medium	Yes	5
Moving averages	To eliminate randomness in a time series; forecast based on projection from time series data smoothed by a moving average	Short-range fore-casts for operations such as inventory, scheduling, control, pricing, and timing special promotions; used to compute both the seasonal and cyclical components for the short-term decomposition method	Low	No	4 and 5

TABLE 11-1	*(Continued)*				
			Computer		
Method	*Description*	*Applications*	*Cost*	*Necessary?*	*Chapter*
Exponential smoothing	Similar to moving averages but values weighted exponentially, giving more weight to most recent data	Short-range forecasts for operations such as inventory, scheduling, control, pricing, and timing special promotions	Low	Yes	4
Autoregressive models	Employed with economic variables to account for relationships between adjacent observations in a time series	Short- and medium-range forecasting for economic data ordered in a time series; price, inventory, production, stocks, and sales	Medium	Yes	8 and 9
Box-Jenkins techniques	Does not assume any particular pattern in the historical data of the series to be forecast; uses an iterative approach of identifying and fitting a possibly useful model from a general class of models	Same as above	High	Yes	9
Neural networks	Uses sophisticated computer program to assimilate relevant data and recognize patterns by "learning" as humans do	Increasing use in a variety of forecasting applications; is in development phase	High	Yes	10

on learning the techniques commonly used to generate the actual forecasts. The key operational steps in the forecasting process are summarized in Figure 11-1.

The collection and examination of appropriate historical data were described earlier in this book (Chapter 3), along with considerations in selecting a forecasting technique or model. As suggested by Figure 11-1, the next step is usually to forecast several historical periods where the actual values are known. The resulting errors can be summarized in several ways, as discussed in Chapter 3, and this process is continued until a technique with a sufficient cost-benefit ratio is found. The model is then used to forecast future periods, and the results are incorporated into the firm's decision-making process.

From time to time it is necessary to pause in the forecasting process and reconsider the procedures being used. The usual steps are as follows:

1. The oldest historical values in the data being used by the forecasting technique are discarded and the most recent actual values are added to the data bank.

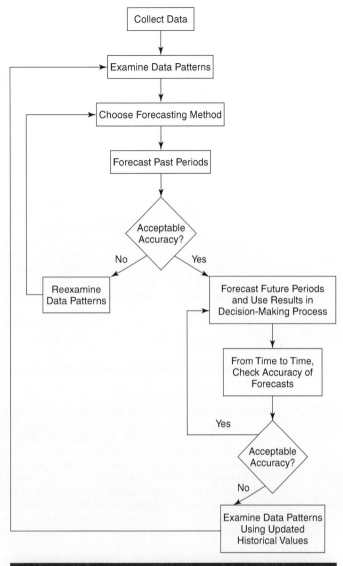

FIGURE 11-1   The Operational Phase of the Forecasting Process

2. Following this data update, the parameters used in the forecasting model are recalculated. For example, the optimum value(s) of the weighting constant(s) used in exponential smoothing may shift, possibly considerably, when more recent data values are added. Or, the coefficients in a regression analysis can change when different data values are fitted with an equation.

3. The forecasting model with new parameters is examined for adequate accuracy. If this accuracy is judged to be sufficient, the model is then used as before until the next update period. If forecasting accuracy is deemed inadequate or marginal, the patterns in the new data can be examined with the possibility of choosing a new forecasting procedure. This process continues until the accuracy of the chosen model, as judged by the accuracy of forecasting periods where the actual values are known, is deemed to be adequate.

The preceding process is summarized in the flow diagram of Figure 11-1 and constitutes the kind of feedback loop commonly found in system designs of all types.

Forecasts are sometimes monitored constantly using a tracking signal, a concept discussed in Chapter 4, following the material on simple exponential smoothing. The idea is to establish limits within which the errors generated by the forecasts are expected to fall if the forecasting process is adequate. So long as the errors fall within these acceptable limits, the forecasting process continues. As soon as an error falls outside the acceptable range, management attention is focused on the forecasting process, and the updating and revision steps outlined earlier are undertaken. This concept is illustrated in Example 11.1.

Example 11.1

Sue Bradley is responsible for forecasting the monthly dollar sales of her company. Sue has chosen a forecasting model that has an error rate acceptable to her managers. Specifically, the standard error of this forecasting process is $935; that is, the forecast and actual values of monthly dollar sales are typically $935 apart.

Sue assumes that forecast errors are normally distributed with a mean of zero and a standard deviation of $935. She makes this assumption after examining a plot of past forecasting errors and finds that they follow a bell-shaped curve about zero. Using a 95% confidence level, she then establishes the following limits within which she expects the forecast error of each month to fall:

$$0 \pm (1.96)(935)$$
$$0 \pm 1,833$$

So Sue expects each monthly forecast to be within $1,833 of the actual value for the month, with 95% confidence. If it is, the forecasting procedure will continue without her attention. But if the error should be greater than $1,833, she will examine both the parameters in her chosen forecasting technique and even consider using another technique.

To monitor the forecasting errors more easily, Sue designs a chart to track them. Over the course of several months, Sue finds two plots that cause her to closely examine her forecasting procedures. The first, shown in Figure 11-2, shows forecasting errors that appear to be randomly distributed, until the most recent period. This large error leads Sue to re-estimate the parameters in her forecasting model after updating her database by adding recent values and discarding the same number of older values. Some time later, a second error plot, Figure 11-3, again causes Sue to look at her forecasting process. Although none of the errors has exceeded her established limits, Sue notes that recent errors do not appear to be randomly distributed. In fact, the errors are increasing in the positive direction, and it is obvious that they will soon be out of control. Sue updates her database and, after carefully examining the data patterns, chooses a new forecasting technique.

FIGURE 11-2   First Data Error Plot for Example 11.1

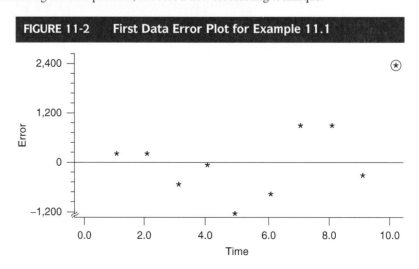

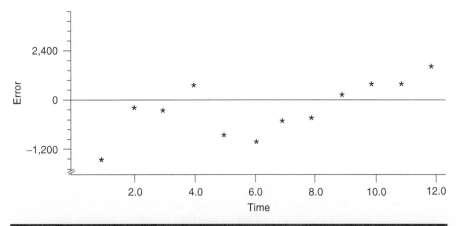

FIGURE 11-3   Second Data Error Plot for Example 11.1

FORECASTING STEPS REVIEWED

In Chapter 1, the point was made several times that sound judgment must be constantly exercised along with quantitative analysis if useful and accurate forecasting is to take place. Several questions were listed that should be raised if management of the forecasting process is to be properly conducted. They are repeated here:

- Why is a forecast needed?
- Who will use the forecast, and what are their specific requirements?
- What level of detail or aggregation is required, and what is the proper time horizon?
- What data are available, and will the data be sufficient to generate the needed forecast?
- What will the forecast cost?
- What level of forecast accuracy can be expected?
- Will the forecast be made in time to help the decision-making process?
- Does the forecaster clearly understand how the forecast will be used in the organization?
- Is a feedback process available to evaluate the forecast after it is made and to adjust the forecasting process accordingly?

When the preceding questions have been properly addressed and answered, the actual forecasting process can begin. Chapter 1 listed the steps followed in such a process:

Data collection
Data reduction or condensation
Model building and evaluation
Model extrapolation (the actual forecast)
Forecast evaluation

To this list of steps might be added another: Feedback after the forecasting process is under way to determine if sufficient accuracy has been obtained and if management is finding the forecast useful and cost-effective in the decision-making process.

Although the primary concern of this book has been with model building or selection of the appropriate forecasting method, it is the authors' hope that the importance of managing the forecasting process has been emphasized as well. The questions listed previously are important in all forecasting situations and must be addressed if useful results are to be obtained. We especially recommend study of the cases at the end of this chapter. They are designed to emphasize the managerial aspects of forecasting.

FORECASTING RESPONSIBILITY

The location of the forecasting process within a firm varies depending on the size of the firm, the importance attached to formal forecasting, and the nature of the firm's management style. The forecasting responsibility falls somewhere on the continuum between a separate forecasting department and forecasting within small management units without reference to other efforts within the firm.

Forecasting staffs are more common in large organizations than in small ones. Large firms can afford to hire the experts needed for sophisticated forecasting and can equip their staffs with modern computing and software capabilities. The advantage of such a centralized effort is that such expertise is available to all units of the organization. The disadvantage is that coordination between the forecasting staff and line managers is often quite difficult to achieve. The forecasting staff may find itself spending more time negotiating with users and explaining its role than in actual forecasting.

At the other extreme is the location of the forecasting process within each unit of the firm without coordination or cooperation across units. The advantage of this process is that there is no misunderstanding between those forecasting and those using the forecasts: They are the same people. Forecasts generated under these conditions tend to be accepted and used in the decision-making process. The disadvantage is that sophistication and, therefore, forecasting accuracy may be difficult to achieve because computer/software availability and technical expertise may not be uniformly spread across many users. It is usually difficult to persuade top management to acquire appropriate hardware and software, for example, when they know they exist in other locations in the company.

Moreover, lack of coordination and cooperation can lead to problems when one unit uses forecasts generated by another unit in the company. If units are not held properly accountable for the quality of the forecasts, biases can result that lead to operational difficulties.

In one forecasting situation, the marketing organization owned the forecasts. Marketing was measured by product availability, which was defined by the percentage of time that a particular product was available for purchase by a customer. However, marketing was not penalized for any excess inventory that might develop as a result of production's reliance on marketing's forecasts. Although those forecasts were based on market conditions, they were at the same time heavily influenced by quota and revenue expectations. Consequently, the marketing group consistently generated optimistic demand forecasts to ensure the product availability that would enable it to meet its revenue targets. On the other hand, the production planning unit was measured both on product availability and excess inventory. This group used statistical methods to buffer against uncertainties and was highly motivated to keep the forecasts accurate and unbiased.

Many organizations attempt to locate the responsibility for forecasting midway between the extremes just mentioned. A small staff of forecasters may be assigned to subunits within the firm to service the needs of several functional areas. The task of such a forecasting staff involves proper coordination with clients as well as the generation of accurate forecasts. Sometimes this forecasting responsibility is combined with other staff functions such as statistical support or computing support.

The advent of inexpensive small computers and forecasting software has moved the forecasting function downward in the organization. It is now possible for managers to have access to sophisticated forecasting tools at a fraction of the cost of such capability just a few years ago. However, the knowledge required to properly use this capability does not come with the hardware or software package; the need to understand the proper use of forecasting techniques has increased as the computing capability has moved out of the hands of the "experts" into those of the users in an organization.

FORECASTING COSTS

Computing hardware and software, plus staff, are the obvious costs involved with creating forecasts. But additional costs are involved that may not be as obvious due to the expenditure of company personnel time as well as money. The time of salaried persons in various departments spent in gathering data for the forecasting process, monitoring the process, and interpreting the results must be considered a cost of forecasting. Such cost must be balanced against the benefits received if rational decisions regarding the usefulness of the resulting forecasts are to be reached.

An alternative to producing forecasts internally is to use consultants for this purpose. This practice is especially appealing if the need for a forecast involves a one-time requirement rather than an ongoing one. In addition, a forecasting requirement beyond the technical capability of company personnel suggests the use of professional consultants. Such outside hiring of forecasting assistance makes the identification of cost an easy matter.

FORECASTING AND THE MIS SYSTEM

The management information systems (MIS's) of modern firms have increased in sophistication and usefulness in recent years. Their primary benefit to the forecasting process involves their enormous capability to collect and record data throughout the organization. The forecaster must resist the temptation to collect data for the forecasting models being used if such data have already been collected and recorded in the company's MIS system.

The rapid development of computer networks within many firms has also increased data access to all users on the network. In addition, large integrative software programs such as SAP[1] have forecasting modules that make use of databases that can be accessed with the program.

Reliance on existing databases is important even if the available data are not in precisely the format or time sequence desired by the forecaster. Modifications in the forecasting model or in the available data should be considered before abandoning the MIS data in favor of collecting new data. This advice presumes, of course, that collecting new data would involve a considerable expenditure of time and money. If the data needed for a forecasting model were easy to obtain in the correct format, these data would be preferable to precollected data that are not in the proper form or that are out of date.

---

[1] SAP, headquartered in Walldorf, Germany, is, at present, the world's largest inter-enterprise software company.

An additional advantage to using data available on the company's MIS or network system is that the forecasting process then becomes a component of this system. As such, it enters the distribution and decision-making network already established by the system and may become more readily incorporated into the company's decision-making process. This situation is in contrast to a forecasting procedure that attempts to infiltrate the decision-making procedures already in use by company managers.

SELLING MANAGEMENT ON FORECASTING

Several factors are important considerations if the forecasts generated within a firm are to become important aspects of the decision-making process. First, it must be recognized that effective managers are interested in practical and useful results. In general, forecasts must meet the needs of such managers; they must provide answers to the series of questions posed earlier in this chapter.

Second, forecasts must be accurate enough to be useful. Good managers will not stay with a forecasting process long, regardless of its sophistication, if accurate results are not generated.

Finally, the cost-benefit instincts of all good managers must be recognized in the forecasting process. The ability to analyze situations in terms of cost incurred versus benefit received is the keystone of an effective management process and must be recognized by the forecasting staff. This situation often creates difficulties between the forecaster and the user. The forecaster must always keep in mind that the end result of the forecasting process is to improve the efficiency of the business, including the bottom-line profit.

THE FUTURE OF FORECASTING

As mentioned in Chapter 1, forecasting continues to gain in importance in modern organizations due to the increasing complexity of the business world along with the availability of lower cost and more powerful computing equipment and software. The continuing competition in the small computer and software areas is obvious to everyone; less obvious may be the long-term trends that slowly change the makeup of the business scene and that exert subtle but powerful pressures on the ways businesspeople operate.

Consider some of the "megatrends" identified by Naisbitt in his book by that title (see several additional references of this kind in Chapter 10). These forces have particular importance to the business world and bring to mind the need for forecasting using modern equipment and software:

Industrial to information society
National to world economy
Short- to long-term thinking
Centralization to decentralization
Either/or to multiple options

Today's economy is an economy of fierce competition on a global basis. Due to the World Wide Web, an abundance of information is available at any time of the day. Changes in the marketplace are swift and sudden, and will likely remain so. Product life cycles continue to shorten. Conducting business electronically (e-business) is a way of life, and transactions over the Web are going to continue to increase.

These trends underline the importance of continuing management development on the part of businesspeople who must deal with the complex issues facing their firms over the next several years. In particular, they emphasize the necessity of developing more and more sophisticated methods of dealing with the uncertainties of future events. They emphasize, in other words, the growing importance of combining good judgment and sophisticated data manipulation methods into sound business forecasting. As Naisbitt's trends and the increasingly dynamic business environment continue to unfold, the ability of business leaders to react quickly and profitably to changing events is brought into sharper focus. The basic business question, "What will happen next?" will assume even greater importance; it is with this question that business forecasting is concerned. New challenges and opportunities for forecasters await.

Problems

1. Write a short response to the following assertions:
   a. Forecasts are always wrong, so why place any emphasis on demand planning?
   b. A good forecasting process is too expensive.
   c. All we need to do is hire a "quantitative type" to do our forecasting.

2. Can you think of any future business trends not discussed in this chapter that may influence the way forecasting is done in the future? Explain briefly.

CASES

CASE 11-1 BOUNDARY ELECTRONICS

Boundary Electronics is a large supplier of electronic products for home use. Among its largest sellers are home video recorders and satellite television systems. Because the company's business has grown so rapidly, Guy Preston, Boundary's president, is concerned that a change in market conditions could alter its sales pattern.

In asking his managers about the future of the company, Guy has discovered two things. First, most of his managers are too busy thinking about the day-to-day problems of meeting growing demand to give much thought to the long-range future. Second, their opinions vary considerably from quite optimistic to quite pessimistic. As president of the company, Guy feels he has an obligation to seriously consider the future environment of his company.

After thinking about this matter, Guy plans a Saturday retreat for the six members of his top management team. He rents a meeting room in a local hotel and arranges for lunch and coffee breaks for the day. When the team meets Saturday morning, he introduces the topic of the day and then instructs each person to prepare a one- or two-page description of the company's operating environment over the next 20 years for each of the following situations:

1. The company's environment will continue essentially as it is now. Products demanded by the market will be modifications of current products, and no new technology will intervene.
2. Major technological changes will render the company's current line of products obsolete. New products will have to be developed to meet the leisure demands of the American population.
3. Between these two extremes, what is the most likely scenario for the company's operating environment?

Guy allows one hour for each team member to develop the scenarios for each of these three situations. During this hour, Guy thinks about the rest of the day and what will happen. He hopes that there will be some provocative ideas developed by his managers and that subsequent discussions will prove lively and interesting. In addition to gaining ideas for his own use, Guy hopes that the day's exercise will help his managers look beyond the company's immediate problems and opportunities and give them a more long-range view of the company. ∎

QUESTIONS

1. What process do you think Guy should use after the hour's writing activities have been completed?

2. Is there some other approach that Guy might have tried, given his objectives?

3. Do you think Guy will accomplish his objectives with the Saturday meeting?

CASE 11-2   BUSBY ASSOCIATES

Jill Tilson was a recent graduate of a university business school when she took a job with Busby Associates, a large exporter of farm equipment. Busby's president noticed a forecasting course on Jill's résumé during the hiring process and decided to start Jill's employment with a forecasting project that had been discussed many times by Busby's top managers.

Busby's president believed there was a strong relationship between the company's export sales

TABLE 11-2	Quarterly Time Series Data for Case 11-2						
	Variable						
Time Period	*1*	*2*	*3*	*4*	*5*	*6*	*7*
1987							
1	18.2	128.3	306.2	110.0	—	—	—
2	19.8	45.8	311.6	109.7	1.6	8.79	18.2
3	20.9	66.1	320.7	109.9	1.1	5.56	19.8
4	22.1	129.7	324.2	109.7	1.2	5.74	20.9
1988							
1	24.0	136.4	331.0	109.4	1.9	8.60	22.1
2	26.0	140.7	337.3	110.5	2.0	8.33	24.0
3	27.7	156.9	342.6	110.6	1.7	6.54	26.0
4	29.7	148.5	352.6	110.9	2.0	7.22	27.7
1989							
1	33.6	189.8	351.5	113.4	3.9	13.13	29.7
2	35.0	168.9	357.6	112.4	1.4	4.17	33.6
3	35.0	154.5	365.2	111.9	0.0	0.00	35.0
4	38.0	174.1	366.3	111.0	3.0	8.57	35.0
1990							
1	40.7	191.3	369.1	111.9	2.7	7.11	38.0
2	42.0	201.2	370.0[a]	112.1	1.3	3.19	40.7

[a] Estimated.
Variable key:
1: Consumer goods, exports, billions of dollars
2: Gross personal savings, billions of dollars
3: National income retail trade, billions of dollars
4: Fixed weight price indices for national defense purchases, military equipment, 1982 = 100
5: Change in dependent variable from previous period
6: Percent change in dependent variable from previous period
7: Dependent variable lagged one period
Source for variables 1 through 4: *Survey of Current Business*, 70, no. 7 (July 1990), U.S. Department of Commerce.

and the national figures for exports. The national figures were readily available from government sources, so Jill's project was to forecast a good, representative export variable. If this effort was successful, Busby's president believed the company would have a powerful tool for forecasting its own export sales.

Jill located the most recent copy of the *Survey of Current Business* in a local library and recorded the quarterly figures for consumer goods exports in billions of dollars. She believed this variable was a good representative of total national exports. Anticipating the possibility of forecasting using regression analysis, she also recorded values for other variables she thought might possibly correlate well with this dependent variable. She ended up with values for four variables for 14 quarters.

She then computed three additional variables from her dependent variable values: Change in Y, percent change in Y, and Y lagged one period. So, as she began to think about various ways to forecast her variable, she had collected the data shown in Table 11-2.

Jill keyed her data into a computer program that performed regression analysis and computed the correlation matrix for her seven variables. After examining this matrix, she chose three regressions with a single predictor variable and six regressions with two predictor variables. She then ran these regressions and chose the one she considered best: It used one predictor (Y lagged one period) with the following results:

$$r\text{-squared} = .98$$

$$t = 25.9$$

$$F = 671.6$$

$$\text{Durbin-Watson} = 2.18$$

The Durbin-Watson table Jill used started at $n = 15$ and her sample size was only 13. So she interpolated the DW critical values and estimated that the upper limit for the autocorrelation test was 1.35. Because her DW statistic was 2.18, she concluded that no autocorrelation was present in her regression. She believed she had found a good predictor variable (Y lagged one period).

Jill realized that her sample size was rather small: 13 quarters. She returned to the *Survey of Current Business* to collect more data points and was disappointed to find that during the years in which

she was interested the definition of her dependent variable changed, resulting in an inconsistent time series. That is, the series took a jump upward halfway through the period that she was studying.

Jill pointed out this problem to her boss, and it was agreed that total merchandise exports could be used as the dependent variable instead of consumer goods exports. Jill found that this variable remained consistent through several issues of the *Survey of Current Business* and that several years of data could be collected. She collected the data shown in Table 11-3, lagged the data one period, and again ran a regression analysis using Y lagged one period as the predictor variable.

This time she again found good statistics in her regression printout, except for the Durbin-Watson statistic. This value was .96 and she concluded that autocorrelation was present because this value is below the lower table value for the Durbin-Watson

TABLE 11-3	Quarterly Time Series Data: Total Merchandise Exports for Case 11-2 (Billions of Dollars)		
Year	Quarter	Y	Y Lagged One Period
1984	1	219.3	—
	2	223.1	219.3
	3	225.9	223.1
	4	228.0	225.9
1985	1	225.0	228.0
	2	221.6	225.0
	3	218.0	221.6
	4	218.6	218.0
1986	1	220.7	218.6
	2	221.4	220.7
	3	225.7	221.4
	4	230.4	225.7
1987	1	234.5	230.4
	2	246.6	234.5
	3	261.6	246.6
	4	281.3	261.6
1988	1	306.7	281.3
	2	319.2	306.7
	3	327.9	319.2
	4	342.8	327.9
1989	1	360.6	342.8
	2	373.2	360.6
	3	367.3	373.2
	4	378.7	367.3
1990	1	394.2	378.7
	2	394.4	394.2

Source: Survey of Current Business, various issues.

test. She tried additional runs by adding the period number and the change in Y as additional predictor variables. But she was unable to find a Durbin-Watson statistic high enough for her to conclude that the autocorrelation had been removed. Jill decided to look at other forecasting techniques to forecast her new dependent variable: total merchandise exports. She used the time series data shown in the Y column of Table 11-3.

Among the computer software available at Busby's was an old forecasting program called Sibyl/Runner. Jill prepared her data for use with this program and began working her way through several forecasting routines. Among these was a procedure that plots the raw data. The quarterly plot of total merchandise exports for the years 1984 through the second quarter of 1990 is shown in Figure 11-4.

After studying Figure 11-4, Jill decided to use only the last 16 data points in her forecasting effort. She reasoned that, beginning with period 9, the series had shown a relatively steady increase, whereas before that period it exhibited an increase and decline. The Sibyl/Runner program warned her about using a low number of data points (16), but she continued after ignoring this warning.

She began her analysis by calling for the Sibyl routine of the program, using only the last 16 data points. The first analysis produced by the program

indicated that there was some pattern to the data, but that there was no seasonality. The program used several forecasting methods to forecast the sample values and printed a table showing the forecast errors as percentages for each method and each period.

After studying these forecast errors, Jill chose three forecasting techniques for further analysis. The three she chose had the lowest percentage forecasting errors and were the following:

Simple exponential smoothing
Holt's linear exponential smoothing, which can accommodate a trend in the data
Quadratic exponential smoothing, which allows for a curved trend line through the data

She then called for forecasts of her data using each technique, with the results shown in Table 11-4.

TABLE 11-4

Technique	Mean Square Error	Optimum Smoothing Constant
Simple exponential	185.5	.999
Holt's linear	81.0	.722
Quadratic exponential	87.7	.485

FIGURE 11-4   Plot of Quarterly Data Values: Total Merchandise Exports, First Quarter of 1984 to Second Quarter of 1990

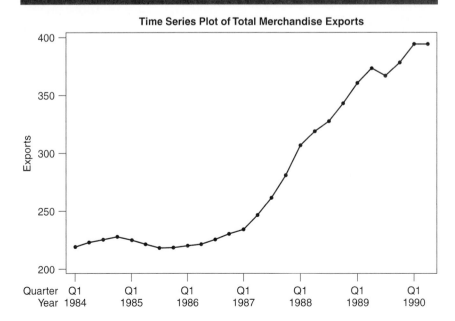

Jill noted that the optimum smoothing constant using simple exponential smoothing was almost 1.00 (.999). Apparently, in order to track through the data in an optimum fashion, the program was basically using each data value to predict the next. This is equivalent to using a simple naive method to forecast, that is, a model that says consecutive differences are random.

Holt's linear exponential smoothing produced the lowest mean square error, so Jill thought she should use that method. She examined the printout for this method further and found that the mean absolute percentage error (*MAPE*) was 2.39% and the mean percentage error (*MPE*), or bias, was .34%. Jill considered these values satisfactory and decided to use Holt's linear exponential smoothing to forecast future values.

Using her chosen method, she asked for forecasts for the next four periods beyond the end of her data. The forecast values are:

Period	Forecast
17	401.27
18	407.30
19	413.34
20	419.38

Jill realized that, with each passing quarter, a new actual value of total merchandise exports would be available and the forecasts for future periods could be updated.

Jill met with her boss to discuss her results. She said that she thought she had a good way to forecast the national variable, total merchandise exports, using exponential smoothing with trend adjustments. Her boss asked her to explain this method, which she did. Her next assignment was to use actual data to verify the hunch of Busby's president that Busby's exports were well correlated with national exports. If she could establish this, Busby would have a good forecasting method for its exports and could use the forecasts to plan future operations. ∎

QUESTIONS

1. Jill did not consider combining the forecasts generated by the three methods she analyzed. How would she go about doing so? What would be the advantages and disadvantages of such action?
2. The optimum smoothing constants used by Holt's linear exponential smoothing were $\alpha = .722$ and $\beta = .722$. As new data come in over the next few quarters, Jill should probably rerun her data to see if these values change. How often do you think she should do this?
3. It's possible that the choice of forecasting method could shift to another technique as new quarterly data are added to the database. Should Jill rerun her entire analysis once in a while to check this? How often should this be done?
4. A colleague of Jill's suggested she try the Box-Jenkins ARIMA methodology. What advice do you have for Jill if she decides to try Box-Jenkins?

CASE 11-3 CONSUMER CREDIT COUNSELING

The Consumer Credit Counseling (CCC) operation was described in Chapters 1 (Case 1-2) and 3 (Case 3-3).

The executive director, Marv Harninshfeger, concluded that the most important variable that CCC needed to forecast was the number of new clients that would be seen for the rest of 1993. Marv provided Dorothy Mercer monthly data for the number of new clients seen by CCC for the period from January 1985 through March 1993 (see Case 3-3).

Dorothy, with your help, has tried several ways to forecast the most important variable. These efforts are outlined in Cases 4-3, 5-3, 6-5, 8-5, and 9-3. Having completed these forecasting attempts, Dorothy decides it is time to summarize these efforts and to attempt to arrive at a method of forecasting the rest of the year.

Assignment

Assume that Dorothy assigns you to help her with this forecasting problem. Write a report that recommends a course of action. Keep in mind that Marv must develop forecasts for the number of clients seen that are as accurate as possible and that he can use in the everyday decision making of the organization. Be specific about what you are recommending to Dorothy and Marv. Remember to consider the issues discussed in this chapter, such as cost. ■

CASE 11-4   MR. TUX

The owner of several Mr. Tux rental outlets, John Mosby, has tried several ways to forecast his most important variable, monthly dollar sales. His efforts are outlined at the end of several chapters in this book. Having completed these forecasting attempts, John decides it is time to summarize his efforts and attempt to arrive at a method of forecasting the future. He realizes that he should update both his data and his method of forecasting at some time in the future, but he needs to choose a way of forecasting sales for the next few months right away.

To begin, John summarizes the results of the methods he has tried so far.

- Case 2-2: Using the annual average to forecast future annual sales might work, but, because John noticed an upward trend, he needs a sound way of extending these averages into the future. Also, John is quite concerned with the seasonal effect because he knows his sales vary considerably by month. His efforts using annual averages are not fruitful.
- Case 3-2: John's use of the Minitab program established that both a trend and seasonal effect existed in his data. Although he knew these elements were there before he started, he was pleased to see that his computer program established them statistically. The program also indicated that several autocorrelation coefficients were outside sampling error limits, indicating to John that both trend and seasonal effects needed to be reflected in his final forecasting model.
- Case 4-2: When John used exponential smoothing, including methods that took account of trend and seasonal factors, the resulting error measurements were unsatisfactory. He realized that these measurements, such as the average error

and average percentage error, resulted from predicting past values of his variable. But because they were so high, he didn't want to use these techniques to predict the unknown future.

- Case 5-2: John finally got some encouraging results using the decomposition method to construct a trend line, seasonal indices, and a cyclical component for his data. He was able to show his banker the seasonal indices and make desired arrangements on his loan payments. He also generated forecasts for the next few months by reassembling his estimated components. However, John was somewhat disturbed by the wide range of his projections.
- Case 6-4: Simple regression analysis was the next technique John tried, using the time period as the independent, or predictor, variable. He reasoned that this variable would account for the trend factor he knew was in his data. This method did not account for the seasonality in sales, and the r-squared value of 56.3% was unsatisfactory.
- Case 8-4: John next tried a multiple regression using both a time period number to reflect trend and a series of dummy variables to account for the seasonal effect (months). His R-squared value of 88% was a considerable improvement over his simple regression, but the forecast error for the last 12 months of his data, as measured by the mean absolute percentage error ($MAPE$), of 21% was unacceptable. With this kind of error, John decided not to use multiple regression. He also tried a seasonal autoregressive model, which resulted in an R-squared value of 90.6%. John was quite pleased with this result.
- Case 9-2: The Box-Jenkins ARIMA methodology bothered John from the outset because he did not totally understand it. He recognized,

however, that his seasonal autoregressive model was a particular ARIMA model. He wanted to know if he could improve on this model. He knew he would have to explain whatever forecasts he came up with to investors and bankers in his attempt to gain capital for expansion, so he wanted a forecasting method that was both accurate and understandable.

In thinking over these efforts, John realized that time was running out and that he must generate forecasts of his monthly revenues soon. He had limited time to try modifications to the methods he used and could think about combining two or more methods. But he did not have time to acquire new software and try completely different methods. As

he wondered what he should do, he looked at one of his favorite sayings posted on his office wall: "Let's do something, even if it's not quite right."

Assignment

Assume you have been hired to help John Mosby with his forecasting problem. Write him a memo that summarizes his efforts to date and that recommends a course of action to him. Keep in mind that John must quickly develop forecasts for monthly sales that are as accurate as possible and that he can use in discussions with investors. Be very specific about what you are recommending to the owner of Mr. Tux. ■

CASE 11-5 ALOMEGA FOOD STORES

Example 1.1 in Chapter 1 described how Julie Ruth, the president of Alomega Food Stores, collected monthly sales data for her company along with several other variables she thought might be related to sales. The Alomega cases in Chapters 2, 3, 5, 8, 9, and 10 described her efforts to use various Minitab procedures in an attempt to make meaningful forecasts of monthly sales.

Julie knew that her technical staff was using the same data to generate good forecasts but didn't know how they were coming along. Also, she really wanted to come up with a good forecasting method on her own. She knew that as the first woman president of Alomega, she had jumped over several potential candidates for the job and that there might be some resentment among her management team. She was especially sensitive to the negative comments made by Jackson Tilson, her production manager, during a recent meeting (see the end of Example 1.1).

In reviewing her efforts, Julie decided to discard the simple regression analysis she performed as summarized in Case 2-3. She was left with a choice between the decomposition analysis described in Case 5-6, the multiple regression described in Case 8-7, or a combination of methods described in Case 10-2. ■

QUESTIONS
1. Suppose you were recently hired by Alomega Food Stores and assigned to assist Julie in developing an effective forecasting method for monthly sales. After reviewing Julie's efforts to date, of the methods she tried, which would you recommend to her?
2. Based on your choice in Question 1, write a detailed memo to Julie outlining your reasons for

your choice, and indicate the extent to which you think this forecasting method would be effective.
3. In addition to choosing among the methods Julie tried, what other forecasting procedures would you suggest? Use Minitab or another forecasting software package to try other methods and compare them with your choice in Question 1.
4. Should Julie combine forecasts?

References

Armstrong, J. S. (Ed.) *Principles of Forecasting: A Handbook for Researchers and Practitioners.* Norwell, MA: Kluwer Academic Publishers, 2001.

Naisbitt, J. *Megatrends.* New York: Warner Books, 1982.

Derivations

Correlation Derivation

$$r = \frac{\Sigma Z_X Z_Y}{n-1} = \Sigma \frac{[(X-\bar{X})/S_X][(Y-\bar{Y})/S_Y]}{n-1}$$

$$= \frac{\Sigma(X-\bar{X})(Y-\bar{Y})}{\sqrt{\Sigma X^2 - n(\Sigma X/n)^2}\sqrt{\Sigma Y^2 - n(\Sigma Y/n)^2}}$$

$$= \frac{n\Sigma(X-\bar{X})(Y-\bar{Y})}{\sqrt{n\Sigma X^2 - (\Sigma X)^2}\sqrt{n\Sigma Y^2 - (\Sigma Y)^2}}$$

$$= \frac{n[\Sigma XY - (\Sigma X\Sigma Y)/n]}{\sqrt{n\Sigma X^2 - (\Sigma X)^2}\sqrt{n\Sigma Y^2 - (\Sigma Y)^2}}$$

$$= \frac{n\Sigma XY - \Sigma X\Sigma Y}{\sqrt{n\Sigma X^2 - (\Sigma X)^2}\sqrt{n\Sigma Y^2 - (\Sigma Y)^2}}$$

Least Squares Derivation

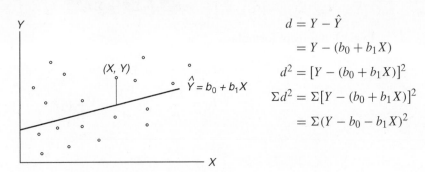

$$d = Y - \hat{Y}$$
$$= Y - (b_0 + b_1 X)$$
$$d^2 = [Y - (b_0 + b_1 X)]^2$$
$$\Sigma d^2 = \Sigma[Y - (b_0 + b_1 X)]^2$$
$$= \Sigma(Y - b_0 - b_1 X)^2$$

Partial Derivatives

$$\frac{\delta\Sigma}{\delta b_1} = 2\Sigma(Y - b_0 - b_1 X)(-X)$$
$$= 2\Sigma(-XY + b_0 X + b_1 X^2)$$

$$\frac{\delta\Sigma}{\delta b_0} = 2\Sigma(Y - b_0 - b_1 X)(-1)$$
$$= 2\Sigma(-Y + b_0 + b_1 X)$$

To obtain minimums, set partials $= 0$

$$\frac{\delta \Sigma}{\delta b_1} = 0 \Rightarrow \quad 2\Sigma(-XY + b_0 X + b_1 X^2) = 0 \qquad\qquad \frac{\delta \Sigma}{\delta b_0} = 0 \Rightarrow \quad 2\Sigma(-Y + b_0 + b_1 X) = 0$$

$$\Sigma(-XY + b_0 X + b_1 X^2) = 0 \qquad\qquad\qquad \Sigma(-Y + b_0 + b_1 X) = 0$$

$$-\Sigma XY + b_0 \Sigma X + b_1 \Sigma X^2 = 0 \qquad\qquad\qquad -\Sigma Y + n b_0 + b_1 \Sigma X = 0$$

Find a b_0 and b_1 such that Σd^2 is a minimum

$$b_0 \Sigma X + b_1 \Sigma X^2 = \Sigma XY \qquad \times n$$

$$n b_0 + b_1 \Sigma X = \Sigma Y \qquad \times \Sigma X$$

Have

$$n b_0 \Sigma X + n b_1 \Sigma X^2 = n \Sigma XY$$

$$n b_0 \Sigma X + b_1 (\Sigma X)^2 = \Sigma X \Sigma Y \qquad \text{subtract}$$

$$\overline{\quad n b_1 \Sigma X^2 - b_1 (\Sigma X)^2 = n \Sigma XY - \Sigma X \Sigma Y \quad}$$

and solve for b_1 to get slope formula

$$b_1 [n \Sigma X^2 - (\Sigma X)^2] = n \Sigma XY - \Sigma X \Sigma Y$$

$$b_1 = \frac{n \Sigma XY - \Sigma X \Sigma Y}{n \Sigma X^2 - (\Sigma X)^2}$$

Solve

$$n b_0 + b_1 \Sigma X = \Sigma Y$$

to get Y intercept formula

$$n b_0 = \Sigma Y - b_1 \Sigma X$$

$$b_0 = \frac{\Sigma Y}{n} - b_1 \frac{\Sigma X}{n} = \bar{Y} - b_1 \bar{X}$$

Data for Case 7-1

14.75	0.00	0.00	2.01	12.57	10.00	20.50	16.13	0.00	0.00	2.80	13.39	10.00	16.50
14.50	0.00	0.00	2.53	12.57	10.00	20.00	15.75	1.00	0.00	4.00	13.35	30.00	16.00
14.13	1.00	0.00	2.10	12.57	10.00	20.00	16.13	0.00	0.00	2.81	13.50	10.00	15.80
14.63	0.00	1.00	4.13	12.14	30.00	20.00	16.25	1.00	0.00	3.38	13.50	30.00	15.80
14.00	1.00	0.00	2.10	12.57	10.00	20.00	16.00	0.00	0.00	2.57	13.50	10.00	15.80
13.38	0.00	1.00	3.97	12.57	10.00	20.00	15.88	0.00	1.00	3.96	13.50	30.00	15.80
14.57	0.00	1.00	3.27	12.14	30.00	20.00	16.50	1.00	0.00	2.67	13.50	30.00	15.80
13.88	1.00	0.00	3.50	13.19	10.00	19.50	16.38	1.00	0.00	3.05	13.50	30.00	15.80
15.38	0.00	0.00	2.85	13.19	10.00	19.50	12.50	1.00	0.00	2.36	10.60	30.00	15.30
15.63	0.00	0.00	1.81	13.12	10.00	18.50	12.25	1.00	0.00	2.54	10.60	30.00	15.30
15.88	1.00	0.00	2.72	12.69	30.00	18.50	14.25	1.00	0.00	2.20	12.13	30.00	15.30
15.00	1.00	0.00	2.43	13.12	10.00	18.00	15.00	1.00	0.00	3.03	12.13	30.00	15.80
16.13	0.00	0.00	3.27	12.69	30.00	18.00	15.25	1.00	0.00	3.24	12.13	30.00	16.50
15.25	0.00	1.00	3.13	12.69	30.00	17.50	16.00	0.00	0.00	1.95	12.34	30.00	17.80
16.00	0.00	0.00	2.55	13.68	10.00	17.00	14.88	1.00	0.00	2.86	12.34	30.00	17.80
16.25	0.00	0.00	2.08	13.68	10.00	17.50	14.75	1.00	0.00	2.64	12.34	30.00	19.00
17.38	0.00	0.00	2.12	13.20	30.00	17.50	15.50	1.00	0.00	2.23	11.40	30.00	20.00
16.35	1.00	0.00	3.40	14.10	10.00	19.00	13.75	1.00	0.00	2.24	11.40	30.00	19.50
17.00	1.00	0.00	2.63	13.60	30.00	19.00	11.30	1.00	0.00	3.24	11.36	30.00	17.50
16.00	0.00	1.00	2.61	14.10	10.00	19.50	12.38	1.00	0.00	1.95	11.36	30.00	17.50
16.63	1.00	0.00	2.06	14.10	10.00	19.50	12.15	1.00	0.00	2.32	11.36	30.00	14.50
16.38	0.00	0.00	2.08	14.10	10.00	20.00	11.75	1.00	0.00	2.45	9.81	30.00	13.00
16.75	1.00	0.00	2.09	13.60	30.00	20.00	12.38	1.00	0.00	1.88	9.81	30.00	13.00
15.13	0.00	1.00	4.29	12.69	30.00	20.00	12.63	0.00	0.00	1.76	9.81	30.00	13.00
16.00	1.00	0.00	2.50	12.96	30.00	20.00	11.13	1.00	0.00	1.99	9.81	30.00	12.50
14.50	0.00	1.00	3.32	13.47	10.00	20.00	11.38	0.00	0.00	2.20	9.78	10.00	12.50
16.25	0.00	0.00	2.95	12.96	30.00	20.00	11.88	1.00	0.00	2.14	9.81	30.00	12.00
16.88	0.00	0.00	1.85	14.28	10.00	20.50	11.75	1.00	0.00	2.61	9.81	30.00	12.00
17.38	0.00	0.00	1.55	13.59	30.00	20.50	13.63	0.00	0.00	1.84	10.24	30.00	11.00
16.00	0.00	1.00	3.33	14.28	10.00	20.50	13.88	0.00	0.00	1.62	11.00	30.00	11.00
16.75	1.00	0.00	2.77	14.94	10.00	20.50	13.00	1.00	0.00	3.56	11.00	30.00	11.00
17.13	0.00	0.00	2.18	14.94	10.00	20.50	12.00	1.00	0.00	2.65	11.10	10.00	11.00
17.50	0.00	1.00	4.21	14.67	30.00	20.50	13.13	1.00	0.00	2.65	11.00	30.00	11.00
17.00	1.00	0.00	2.66	15.32	10.00	19.50	14.27	0.00	0.00	1.80	11.34	30.00	12.30
16.75	0.00	1.00	3.58	15.32	10.00	19.50	14.63	0.00	0.00	1.69	11.34	30.00	12.30
17.20	0.00	1.00	2.96	15.32	10.00	19.50	15.25	0.00	0.00	1.88	11.34	30.00	12.20
18.75	0.00	0.00	1.93	15.32	10.00	19.50	14.25	1.00	0.00	2.77	11.34	30.00	12.30
17.50	0.00	1.00	2.57	14.68	30.00	19.00	13.52	1.00	0.00	2.22	11.75	10.00	13.50
17.50	0.00	0.00	3.18	15.15	10.00	18.00	14.63	1.00	0.00	2.42	11.59	30.00	13.50
18.00	0.00	0.00	1.93	15.15	10.00	18.00	14.75	0.00	0.00	1.77	11.39	30.00	13.50
15.63	0.00	0.00	2.20	13.39	10.00	17.00	14.00	0.00	0.00	2.22	11.75	10.00	13.50
14.75	1.00	0.00	2.21	13.39	10.00	17.00	14.50	0.00	0.00	2.99	11.59	30.00	13.50
15.25	0.00	1.00	3.24	13.35	30.00	16.50	14.25	0.00	0.00	2.22	11.75	10.00	13.50
15.75	1.00	0.00	2.35	13.35	30.00	16.50	14.63	0.00	0.00	1.93	11.75	10.00	14.50
15.25	1.00	0.00	2.11	13.39	10.00	16.50	13.30	1.00	0.00	3.35	12.68	10.00	15.50
15.75	1.00	0.00	2.80	13.35	30.00	16.50	14.50	0.00	0.00	2.21	12.68	10.00	17.00
15.63	0.00	0.00	1.95	13.39	10.00	16.50							

Appendix C

Tables

TABLE C-1   Individual Terms of the Binomial Distribution

n	x	.05	.10	.15	.20	.25	.30	.35	.40	.45	.50	.55	.60	.65	.70	.75	.80	.85	.90	.95
1	0	.9500	.9000	.8500	.8000	.7500	.7000	.6500	.6000	.5500	.5000	.4500	.4000	.3500	.3000	.2500	.2000	.1500	.1000	.0500
	1	.0500	.1000	.1500	.2000	.2500	.3000	.3500	.4000	.4500	.5000	.5500	.6000	.6500	.7000	.7500	.8000	.8500	.9000	.9500
2	0	.9025	.8100	.7225	.6400	.5625	.4900	.4225	.3600	.3025	.2500	.2025	.1600	.1225	.0900	.0625	.0400	.0225	.0100	.0025
	1	.0950	.1800	.2550	.3200	.3750	.4200	.4550	.4800	.4950	.5000	.4950	.4800	.4550	.4200	.3750	.3200	.2550	.1800	.0950
	2	.0025	.0100	.0225	.0400	.0625	.0900	.1225	.1600	.2025	.2500	.3025	.3600	.4225	.4900	.5625	.6400	.7225	.8100	.9025
3	0	.8574	.7290	.6141	.5120	.4219	.3430	.2746	.2160	.1664	.1250	.0911	.0640	.0429	.0270	.0156	.0080	.0034	.0010	.0001
	1	.1354	.2430	.3251	.3840	.4219	.4410	.4436	.4320	.4084	.3750	.3341	.2880	.2389	.1890	.1406	.0960	.0574	.0270	.0071
	2	.0071	.0270	.0574	.0960	.1406	.1890	.2389	.2880	.3341	.3750	.4084	.4320	.4436	.4410	.4219	.3840	.3251	.2430	.1354
	3	.0001	.0010	.0034	.0080	.0156	.0270	.0429	.0640	.0911	.1250	.1664	.2160	.2746	.3430	.4219	.5120	.6141	.7290	.8574
4	0	.8145	.6561	.5220	.4096	.3164	.2401	.1785	.1296	.0915	.0625	.0410	.0256	.0150	.0081	.0039	.0016	.0005	.0001	.0000
	1	.1715	.2916	.3685	.4096	.4219	.4116	.3845	.3456	.2995	.2500	.2005	.1536	.1115	.0756	.0469	.0256	.0115	.0036	.0005
	2	.0135	.0486	.0975	.1536	.2109	.2646	.3105	.3456	.3675	.3750	.3675	.3456	.3105	.2646	.2109	.1536	.0975	.0486	.0135
	3	.0005	.0036	.0115	.0256	.0469	.0756	.1115	.1536	.2005	.2500	.2995	.3456	.3845	.4116	.4219	.4096	.3685	.2916	.1715
	4	.0000	.0001	.0005	.0016	.0039	.0081	.0150	.0256	.0410	.0625	.0915	.1296	.1785	.2401	.3164	.4096	.5220	.6561	.8145
5	0	.7738	.5905	.4437	.3277	.2373	.1681	.1160	.0778	.0503	.0313	.0185	.0102	.0053	.0024	.0010	.0003	.0001	.0000	.0000
	1	.2036	.3281	.3915	.4096	.3955	.3602	.3124	.2592	.2059	.1563	.1128	.0768	.0488	.0284	.0146	.0064	.0022	.0004	.0000
	2	.0214	.0729	.1382	.2048	.2637	.3087	.3364	.3456	.3369	.3125	.2757	.2304	.1811	.1323	.0879	.0512	.0244	.0081	.0011
	3	.0011	.0081	.0244	.0512	.0879	.1323	.1811	.2304	.2757	.3125	.3369	.3456	.3364	.3087	.2637	.2048	.1382	.0729	.0214
	4	.0000	.0004	.0022	.0064	.0146	.0283	.0488	.0768	.1128	.1562	.2059	.2592	.3124	.3601	.3955	.4096	.3915	.3281	.2036
	5	.0000	.0000	.0001	.0003	.0010	.0024	.0053	.0102	.0185	.0312	.0503	.0778	.1160	.1681	.2373	.3277	.4437	.5905	.7738
6	0	.7351	.5314	.3771	.2621	.1780	.1176	.0754	.0467	.0277	.0156	.0083	.0041	.0018	.0007	.0002	.0001	.0000	.0000	.0000
	1	.2321	.3543	.3993	.3932	.3560	.3025	.2437	.1866	.1359	.0938	.0609	.0369	.0205	.0102	.0044	.0015	.0004	.0001	.0000
	2	.0305	.0984	.1762	.2458	.2966	.3241	.3280	.3110	.2780	.2344	.1861	.1382	.0951	.0595	.0330	.0154	.0055	.0012	.0001
	3	.0021	.0146	.0415	.0819	.1318	.1852	.2355	.2765	.3032	.3125	.3032	.2765	.2355	.1852	.1318	.0819	.0415	.0146	.0021
	4	.0001	.0012	.0055	.0154	.0330	.0595	.0951	.1382	.1861	.2344	.2780	.3110	.3280	.3241	.2966	.2458	.1762	.0984	.0305
	5	.0000	.0001	.0004	.0015	.0044	.0102	.0205	.0369	.0609	.0937	.1359	.1866	.2437	.3025	.3560	.3932	.3993	.3543	.2321
	6	.0000	.0000	.0000	.0001	.0002	.0007	.0018	.0041	.0083	.0156	.0277	.0467	.0754	.1176	.1780	.2621	.3771	.5314	.7351
7	0	.6983	.4783	.3206	.2097	.1335	.0824	.0490	.0280	.0152	.0078	.0037	.0016	.0006	.0002	.0001	.0000	.0000	.0000	.0000
	1	.2573	.3720	.3960	.3670	.3115	.2471	.1848	.1306	.0872	.0547	.0320	.0172	.0084	.0036	.0013	.0004	.0001	.0000	.0000
	2	.0406	.1240	.2097	.2753	.3115	.3177	.2985	.2613	.2140	.1641	.1172	.0774	.0466	.0250	.0115	.0043	.0012	.0002	.0000
	3	.0036	.0230	.0617	.1147	.1730	.2269	.2679	.2903	.2918	.2734	.2388	.1935	.1442	.0972	.0577	.0287	.0109	.0026	.0002
	4	.0002	.0026	.0109	.0287	.0577	.0972	.1442	.1935	.2388	.2734	.2918	.2903	.2679	.2269	.1730	.1147	.0617	.0230	.0036
	5	.0000	.0002	.0012	.0043	.0115	.0250	.0466	.0774	.1172	.1641	.2140	.2613	.2985	.3177	.3115	.2753	.2097	.1240	.0406
	6	.0000	.0000	.0001	.0004	.0013	.0036	.0084	.0172	.0320	.0547	.0872	.1306	.1848	.2471	.3115	.3670	.3960	.3720	.2573
	7	.0000	.0000	.0000	.0000	.0001	.0002	.0006	.0016	.0037	.0078	.0152	.0280	.0490	.0824	.1335	.2097	.3206	.4783	.6983
8	0	.6634	.4305	.2725	.1678	.1001	.0576	.0319	.0168	.0084	.0039	.0017	.0007	.0002	.0001	.0000	.0000	.0000	.0000	.0000
	1	.2793	.3826	.3847	.3355	.2670	.1977	.1373	.0896	.0548	.0313	.0164	.0079	.0033	.0012	.0004	.0001	.0000	.0000	.0000

507

TABLE C-1 (*Continued*)

n	x	.05	.10	.15	.20	.25	.30	.35	.40	.45	.50	.55	.60	.65	.70	.75	.80	.85	.90	.95
	2	.0515	.1488	.2376	.2936	.3115	.2965	.2587	.2090	.1569	.1094	.0703	.0413	.0217	.0100	.0038	.0011	.0002	.0000	.0000
	3	.0054	.0331	.0839	.1468	.2076	.2541	.2786	.2787	.2568	.2188	.1719	.1239	.0808	.0467	.0231	.0092	.0026	.0004	.0000
	4	.0004	.0046	.0185	.0459	.0865	.1361	.1875	.2322	.2627	.2734	.2627	.2322	.1875	.1361	.0865	.0459	.0185	.0046	.0004
	5	.0000	.0004	.0026	.0092	.0231	.0467	.0808	.1239	.1719	.2188	.2568	.2787	.2786	.2541	.2076	.1468	.0839	.0331	.0054
	6	.0000	.0000	.0002	.0011	.0038	.0100	.0217	.0413	.0703	.1094	.1569	.2090	.2587	.2965	.3115	.2936	.2376	.1488	.0515
	7	.0000	.0000	.0000	.0001	.0004	.0012	.0033	.0079	.0164	.0312	.0548	.0896	.1373	.1977	.2670	.3355	.3847	.3826	.2793
	8	.0000	.0000	.0000	.0000	.0000	.0001	.0002	.0007	.0017	.0039	.0084	.0168	.0319	.0576	.1001	.1678	.2725	.4305	.6634
9	0	.6302	.3874	.2316	.1342	.0751	.0404	.0207	.0101	.0046	.0020	.0008	.0003	.0001	.0000	.0000	.0000	.0000	.0000	.0000
	1	.2986	.3874	.3679	.3020	.2253	.1556	.1004	.0605	.0339	.0176	.0083	.0035	.0013	.0004	.0001	.0000	.0000	.0000	.0000
	2	.0629	.1722	.2597	.3020	.3003	.2668	.2162	.1612	.1110	.0703	.0407	.0212	.0098	.0039	.0012	.0003	.0000	.0000	.0000
	3	.0077	.0446	.1069	.1762	.2336	.2668	.2716	.2508	.2119	.1641	.1160	.0743	.0424	.0210	.0087	.0028	.0006	.0001	.0000
	4	.0006	.0074	.0283	.0661	.1168	.1715	.2194	.2508	.2600	.2461	.2128	.1672	.1181	.0735	.0389	.0165	.0050	.0008	.0000
	5	.0000	.0008	.0050	.0165	.0389	.0735	.1181	.1672	.2128	.2461	.2600	.2508	.2194	.1715	.1168	.0661	.0283	.0074	.0006
	6	.0000	.0001	.0006	.0028	.0087	.0210	.0424	.0743	.1160	.1641	.2119	.2508	.2716	.2668	.2336	.1762	.1069	.0446	.0077
	7	.0000	.0000	.0000	.0003	.0012	.0039	.0098	.0212	.0407	.0703	.1110	.1612	.2162	.2668	.3003	.3020	.2597	.1722	.0629
	8	.0000	.0000	.0000	.0000	.0001	.0004	.0013	.0035	.0083	.0176	.0339	.0605	.1004	.1556	.2253	.3020	.3679	.3874	.2986
	9	.0000	.0000	.0000	.0000	.0000	.0000	.0001	.0003	.0008	.0020	.0046	.0101	.0207	.0404	.0751	.1342	.2316	.3874	.6302
10	0	.5987	.3487	.1969	.1074	.0563	.0282	.0135	.0060	.0025	.0010	.0003	.0001	.0000	.0000	.0000	.0000	.0000	.0000	.0000
	1	.3151	.3874	.3474	.2684	.1877	.1211	.0725	.0403	.0207	.0098	.0042	.0016	.0005	.0001	.0000	.0000	.0000	.0000	.0000
	2	.0746	.1937	.2759	.3020	.2816	.2335	.1757	.1209	.0763	.0439	.0229	.0106	.0043	.0014	.0004	.0001	.0000	.0000	.0000
	3	.0105	.0574	.1298	.2013	.2503	.2668	.2522	.2150	.1665	.1172	.0746	.0425	.0212	.0090	.0031	.0008	.0001	.0000	.0000
	4	.0010	.0112	.0401	.0881	.1460	.2001	.2377	.2508	.2384	.2051	.1596	.1115	.0689	.0368	.0162	.0055	.0012	.0001	.0000
	5	.0001	.0015	.0085	.0264	.0584	.1029	.1536	.2007	.2340	.2461	.2340	.2007	.1536	.1029	.0584	.0264	.0085	.0015	.0001
	6	.0000	.0001	.0012	.0055	.0162	.0368	.0689	.1115	.1596	.2051	.2384	.2508	.2377	.2001	.1460	.0881	.0401	.0112	.0010
	7	.0000	.0000	.0001	.0008	.0031	.0090	.0212	.0425	.0746	.1172	.1665	.2150	.2522	.2668	.2503	.2013	.1298	.0574	.0105
	8	.0000	.0000	.0000	.0001	.0004	.0014	.0043	.0106	.0229	.0439	.0763	.1209	.1757	.2335	.2816	.3020	.2759	.1937	.0746
	9	.0000	.0000	.0000	.0000	.0000	.0001	.0005	.0016	.0042	.0098	.0207	.0403	.0725	.1211	.1877	.2684	.3474	.3874	.3151
	10	.0000	.0000	.0000	.0000	.0000	.0000	.0000	.0001	.0003	.0010	.0025	.0060	.0135	.0282	.0563	.1074	.1969	.3487	.5987
11	0	.5688	.3138	.1673	.0859	.0422	.0198	.0088	.0036	.0014	.0005	.0002	.0000	.0000	.0000	.0000	.0000	.0000	.0000	.0000
	1	.3293	.3835	.3248	.2362	.1549	.0932	.0518	.0266	.0125	.0054	.0021	.0007	.0002	.0000	.0000	.0000	.0000	.0000	.0000
	2	.0867	.2131	.2866	.2953	.2581	.1998	.1395	.0887	.0513	.0269	.0126	.0052	.0018	.0005	.0001	.0000	.0000	.0000	.0000
	3	.0137	.0710	.1517	.2215	.2581	.2568	.2254	.1774	.1259	.0806	.0462	.0234	.0102	.0037	.0011	.0002	.0000	.0000	.0000
	4	.0014	.0158	.0536	.1107	.1721	.2201	.2428	.2365	.2060	.1611	.1128	.0701	.0379	.0173	.0064	.0017	.0003	.0000	.0000
	5	.0001	.0025	.0132	.0388	.0803	.1321	.1830	.2207	.2360	.2256	.1931	.1471	.0985	.0566	.0268	.0097	.0023	.0003	.0000
	6	.0000	.0003	.0023	.0097	.0268	.0566	.0985	.1471	.1931	.2256	.2360	.2270	.1830	.1321	.0803	.0388	.0132	.0025	.0001
	7	.0000	.0000	.0003	.0017	.0064	.0173	.0379	.0701	.1128	.1611	.2060	.2365	.2428	.2201	.1721	.1107	.0536	.0158	.0014
	8	.0000	.0000	.0000	.0002	.0011	.0037	.0102	.0234	.0462	.0806	.1259	.1774	.2254	.2568	.2581	.2215	.1517	.0710	.0137
	9	.0000	.0000	.0000	.0000	.0001	.0005	.0018	.0052	.0126	.0269	.0513	.0887	.1395	.1998	.2581	.2953	.2866	.2131	.0867
	10	.0000	.0000	.0000	.0000	.0000	.0000	.0002	.0007	.0021	.0054	.0125	.0266	.0518	.0932	.1549	.2362	.3248	.3835	.3293
	11	.0000	.0000	.0000	.0000	.0000	.0000	.0000	.0000	.0002	.0005	.0014	.0036	.0088	.0198	.0422	.0859	.1673	.3138	.5688
12	0	.5404	.2824	.1422	.0687	.0317	.0138	.0057	.0022	.0008	.0002	.0001	.0000	.0000	.0000	.0000	.0000	.0000	.0000	.0000
	1	.3413	.3766	.3012	.2062	.1267	.0712	.0368	.0174	.0075	.0029	.0010	.0003	.0001	.0000	.0000	.0000	.0000	.0000	.0000
	2	.0988	.2301	.2924	.2835	.2323	.1678	.1088	.0639	.0339	.0161	.0068	.0025	.0008	.0002	.0000	.0000	.0000	.0000	.0000
	3	.0173	.0852	.1720	.2362	.2581	.2397	.1954	.1419	.0923	.0537	.0277	.0125	.0048	.0015	.0004	.0001	.0000	.0000	.0000
	4	.0021	.0213	.0683	.1329	.1936	.2311	.2367	.2128	.1700	.1208	.0762	.0420	.0199	.0078	.0024	.0005	.0001	.0000	.0000
	5	.0002	.0038	.0193	.0532	.1032	.1585	.2039	.2270	.2225	.1934	.1489	.1009	.0591	.0291	.0115	.0033	.0006	.0000	.0000
	6	.0000	.0005	.0040	.0155	.0401	.0792	.1281	.1766	.2124	.2256	.2124	.1766	.1281	.0792	.0401	.0155	.0040	.0005	.0000
	7	.0000	.0000	.0006	.0033	.0115	.0291	.0591	.1009	.1489	.1934	.2225	.2270	.2039	.1585	.1032	.0532	.0193	.0038	.0002
	8	.0000	.0000	.0001	.0005	.0024	.0078	.0199	.0420	.0762	.1208	.1700	.2128	.2367	.2311	.1936	.1329	.0683	.0213	.0021
	9	.0000	.0000	.0000	.0001	.0004	.0015	.0048	.0125	.0277	.0537	.0923	.1419	.1954	.2397	.2581	.2362	.1720	.0852	.0173
	10	.0000	.0000	.0000	.0000	.0000	.0002	.0008	.0025	.0068	.0161	.0339	.0639	.1088	.1678	.2323	.2835	.2924	.2301	.0988
	11	.0000	.0000	.0000	.0000	.0000	.0000	.0001	.0003	.0010	.0029	.0075	.0174	.0368	.0712	.1267	.2062	.3012	.3766	.3413
	12	.0000	.0000	.0000	.0000	.0000	.0000	.0000	.0000	.0001	.0002	.0008	.0022	.0057	.0138	.0317	.0687	.1422	.2824	.5404

Source: Table A, pages 464–466 in *Business Statistics: Concepts and Applications* by William J. Stevenson. Copyright © 1978 by William J. Stevenson. Reprinted by permission of Harper & Row, Publishers.

TABLE C-2   **Table of Areas for Standard Normal Probability Distribution**

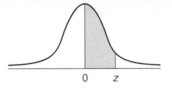

For $z = 1.93$, shaded area is .4732 out of total area of 1.

z	.00	.01	.02	.03	.04	.05	.06	.07	.08	.09
0.0	.0000	.0040	.0080	.0120	.0160	.0199	.0239	.0279	.0319	.0359
0.1	.0398	.0438	.0478	.0517	.0557	.0596	.0636	.0675	.0714	.0753
0.2	.0793	.0832	.0871	.0910	.0948	.0987	.1026	.1064	.1103	.1141
0.3	.1179	.1217	.1255	.1293	.1331	.1368	.1406	.1443	.1480	.1517
0.4	.1554	.1591	.1628	.1664	.1700	.1736	.1772	.1808	.1844	.1879
0.5	.1915	.1950	.1985	.2019	.2054	.2088	.2123	.2157	.2190	.2224
0.6	.2257	.2291	.2324	.2357	.2389	.2422	.2454	.2486	.2518	.2549
0.7	.2580	.2612	.2642	.2673	.2704	.2734	.2764	.2794	.2823	.2852
0.8	.2881	.2910	.2939	.2967	.2995	.3023	.3051	.3078	.3106	.3133
0.9	.3159	.3186	.3212	.3238	.3264	.3289	.3315	.3340	.3365	.3389
1.0	.3413	.3438	.3461	.3485	.3508	.3531	.3554	.3577	.3599	.3621
1.1	.3643	.3665	.3686	.3708	.3729	.3749	.3770	.3790	.3810	.3830
1.2	.3849	.3869	.3888	.3907	.3925	.3944	.3962	.3980	.3997	.4015
1.3	.4032	.4049	.4066	.4082	.4099	.4115	.4131	.4147	.4162	.4177
1.4	.4192	.4207	.4222	.4236	.4251	.4265	.4279	.4292	.4306	.4319
1.5	.4332	.4345	.4357	.4370	.4382	.4394	.4406	.4418	.4429	.4441
1.6	.4452	.4463	.4474	.4484	.4495	.4505	.4515	.4525	.4535	.4545
1.7	.4554	.4564	.4573	.4582	.4591	.4599	.4608	.4616	.4625	.4633
1.8	.4641	.4649	.4656	.4664	.4671	.4678	.4686	.4693	.4699	.4706
1.9	.4713	.4719	.4726	.4732	.4738	.4744	.4750	.4756	.4761	.4767
2.0	.4772	.4778	.4783	.4788	.4793	.4798	.4803	.4808	.4812	.4817
2.1	.4821	.4826	.4830	.4834	.4838	.4842	.4846	.4850	.4854	.4857
2.2	.4861	.4864	.4868	.4871	.4875	.4878	.4881	.4884	.4887	.4890
2.3	.4893	.4896	.4898	.4901	.4904	.4906	.4909	.4911	.4913	.4916
2.4	.4918	.4920	.4922	.4925	.4927	.4929	.4931	.4932	.4934	.4936
2.5	.4938	.4940	.4941	.4943	.4945	.4946	.4948	.4949	.4951	.4952
2.6	.4953	.4955	.4956	.4957	.4959	.4960	.4961	.4962	.4963	.4964
2.7	.4965	.4966	.4967	.4968	.4969	.4970	.4971	.4972	.4973	.4974
2.8	.4974	.4975	.4976	.4977	.4977	.4978	.4979	.4979	.4980	.4981
2.9	.4981	.4982	.4982	.4983	.4984	.4984	.4985	.4985	.4986	.4986
3.0	.49865	.4987	.4987	.4988	.4989	.4989	.4989	.4989	.4990	.4990
4.0	.4999683									

TABLE C-3   Critical Values of *t*

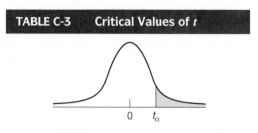

df	$t_{.100}$	$t_{.050}$	$t_{.025}$	$t_{.010}$	$t_{.005}$
1	3.078	6.314	12.706	31.821	63.657
2	1.886	2.920	4.303	6.965	9.925
3	1.638	2.353	3.182	4.541	5.841
4	1.533	2.132	2.776	3.747	4.604
5	1.476	2.015	2.571	3.365	4.032
6	1.440	1.943	2.447	3.143	3.707
7	1.415	1.895	2.365	2.998	3.499
8	1.397	1.860	2.306	2.896	3.355
9	1.383	1.833	2.262	2.821	3.250
10	1.372	1.812	2.228	2.764	3.169
11	1.363	1.796	2.201	2.718	3.106
12	1.356	1.782	2.179	2.681	3.055
13	1.350	1.771	2.160	2.650	3.012
14	1.345	1.761	2.145	2.624	2.977
15	1.341	1.753	2.131	2.602	2.947
16	1.337	1.746	2.120	2.583	2.921
17	1.333	1.740	2.110	2.567	2.898
18	1.330	1.734	2.101	2.552	2.878
19	1.328	1.729	2.093	2.539	2.861
20	1.325	1.725	2.086	2.528	2.845
21	1.323	1.721	2.080	2.518	2.831
22	1.321	1.717	2.074	2.508	2.819
23	1.319	1.714	2.069	2.500	2.807
24	1.318	1.711	2.064	2.492	2.797
25	1.316	1.708	2.060	2.485	2.787
26	1.315	1.706	2.056	2.479	2.779
27	1.314	1.703	2.052	2.473	2.771
28	1.313	1.701	2.048	2.467	2.763
29	1.311	1.699	2.045	2.462	2.756
inf.	1.282	1.645	1.960	2.326	2.576

Source: "Table of Percentage Points of the t-Distribution." Computed by Maxine Merrington, *Biometrika*, vol. 32 (1941), p. 300. Reproduced by permission of Professor D. V. Lindley.

TABLE C-4   Critical Values of Chi-Square

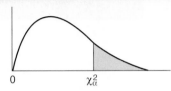

df	$\chi^2_{.995}$	$\chi^2_{.990}$	$\chi^2_{.975}$	$\chi^2_{.950}$	$\chi^2_{.900}$
1	0.0000393	0.0001571	0.0009821	0.0039321	0.0157908
2	0.0100251	0.0201007	0.0506356	0.102587	0.210720
3	0.0717212	0.114832	0.215795	0.351846	0.584375
4	0.206990	0.297110	0.484419	0.710721	1.063623
5	0.411740	0.554300	0.831211	1.145476	1.61031
6	0.675727	0.872085	1.237347	1.63539	2.20413
7	0.989265	1.239043	1.68987	2.16735	2.83311
8	1.344419	1.646482	2.17973	2.73264	3.48954
9	1.734926	2.087912	2.70039	3.32511	4.168216
10	2.15585	2.55821	3.24697	3.94030	4.86518
11	2.60321	3.05347	3.81575	4.57481	5.57779
12	3.07382	3.57056	4.40379	5.22603	6.30380
13	3.56503	4.10691	5.00874	5.89186	7.04150
14	4.07468	4.66043	5.62872	6.57063	7.78953
15	4.60094	5.22935	6.26214	7.26094	8.54675
16	5.14224	5.81221	6.90766	7.96164	9.31223
17	5.69724	6.40776	7.56418	8.67176	10.0852
18	6.26481	7.01491	8.23075	9.39046	10.8649
19	6.84398	7.63273	8.90655	10.1170	11.6509
20	7.43386	8.26040	9.59083	10.8508	12.4426
21	8.03366	8.89720	10.28293	11.5913	13.2396
22	8.64272	9.54249	10.9823	12.3380	14.0415
23	9.26042	10.19567	11.6885	13.0905	14.8479
24	9.88623	10.8564	12.4011	13.8484	15.6587
25	10.5197	11.5240	13.1197	14.6114	16.4734
26	11.1603	12.1981	13.8439	15.3791	17.2919
27	11.8076	12.8786	14.5733	16.1513	18.1138
28	12.4613	13.5648	15.3079	16.9279	18.9302
29	13.1211	14.2565	16.0471	17.7083	19.7677
30	13.7867	14.9535	16.7908	18.4926	20.5992
40	20.7065	22.1643	24.4331	26.5093	29.0505
50	27.9907	29.7067	32.3574	34.7642	37.6886
60	35.5347	37.4848	40.4817	43.1879	46.4589
70	43.2752	45.4418	48.7576	51.7393	55.3290
80	51.1720	53.5400	57.1532	60.3915	64.2778
90	59.1963	61.7541	65.6466	69.1260	73.2912
100	67.3276	70.0648	74.2219	77.9295	82.3581

TABLE C-4	(*Continued*)			
df	$\chi^2_{.100}$	$\chi^2_{.050}$	$\chi^2_{.025}$	$\chi^2_{.010}$	$\chi^2_{.005}$
1	2.70554	3.84146	5.02389	6.63490	7.87944
2	4.60517	5.99147	7.37776	9.21034	10.5966
3	6.25139	7.81473	9.34840	11.3449	12.8381
4	7.77944	9.48773	11.1433	13.2767	14.8602
5	9.23635	11.0705	12.8325	15.0863	16.7496
6	10.6446	12.5916	14.4494	16.8119	18.5476
7	12.0170	14.0671	16.0128	18.4753	20.2777
8	13.3616	15.5073	17.5346	20.0902	21.9550
9	14.6837	16.9190	19.0228	21.6660	23.5893
10	15.9871	18.3070	20.4831	23.2093	25.1882
11	17.2750	19.6751	21.9200	24.7250	26.7569
12	18.5494	21.0261	23.3367	26.2170	28.2995
13	19.8119	22.3621	24.7356	27.6883	29.8194
14	21.0642	23.6848	26.1190	29.1413	31.3193
15	22.3072	24.9958	27.4884	30.5779	32.8013
16	23.5418	26.2962	28.8454	31.9999	34.2672
17	24.7690	27.5871	30.1910	33.4087	35.7185
18	25.9894	28.8693	31.5264	34.8053	37.1564
19	27.2036	30.1435	32.8523	36.1908	38.5822
20	28.4120	31.4104	34.1696	37.5662	39.9968
21	29.6151	32.6705	35.4789	38.9321	41.4010
22	30.8133	33.9244	36.7807	40.2894	42.7956
23	32.0069	35.1725	38.0757	41.6384	44.1813
24	33.1963	36.4151	39.3641	42.9798	45.5585
25	34.3816	37.6525	40.6465	44.3141	46.9278
26	35.5631	38.8852	41.9232	45.6417	48.2899
27	36.7412	40.1133	43.1944	46.9630	49.6449
28	37.9159	41.3372	44.4607	48.2782	50.9933
29	39.0875	42.5569	45.7222	49.5879	52.3356
30	40.2560	43.7729	46.9792	50.8922	53.6720
40	51.8050	55.7585	59.3417	63.6907	66.7659
50	63.1671	67.5048	71.4202	76.1539	79.4900
60	74.3970	79.0819	83.2976	88.3794	91.9517
70	85.5271	90.5312	95.0231	100.425	104.215
80	96.5782	101.879	106.629	112.329	116.321
90	107.565	113.145	118.136	124.116	128.299
100	118.498	124.342	129.561	135.807	140.169

Source: "Tables of the Percentage Points of the χ^2-Distribution," *Biometrika*, vol. 32 (1941), pp. 188–189, by Catherine M. Thompson. Reproduced by permission of Professor D. V. Lindley.

TABLE C-5   Table of *F* Distribution

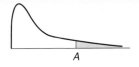

For example, the *F* scale value for $\delta_1 = 3$, $\delta_2 = 10$ corresponding to area .01 in right tail is 6.55.

F value corresponding to area .05 in right tail in lightface type.

F value corresponding to area .01 in right tail in boldface type.

δ_2, Denominator Degrees of Freedom	δ_1, *Numerator Degrees of Freedom*									
	1	*2*	*3*	*4*	*5*	*6*	*7*	*8*	*9*	*10*
1	161	200	216	225	230	234	237	239	241	242
	4,052	**4,999**	**5,403**	**5,625**	**5,764**	**5,859**	**5,928**	**5,981**	**6,022**	**6,056**
2	18.51	19.00	19.16	19.25	19.30	19.33	19.36	19.37	19.38	19.39
	98.49	**99.00**	**99.17**	**99.25**	**99.30**	**99.33**	**99.36**	**99.37**	**99.39**	**99.40**
3	10.13	9.55	9.28	9.12	9.01	8.94	8.88	8.84	8.81	8.78
	34.12	**30.82**	**29.46**	**28.71**	**28.24**	**27.91**	**27.67**	**27.49**	**27.34**	**27.23**
4	7.71	6.94	6.59	6.39	6.26	6.16	6.09	6.04	6.00	5.96
	21.20	**18.00**	**16.69**	**15.98**	**15.52**	**15.21**	**14.98**	**14.80**	**14.66**	**14.54**
5	6.61	5.79	5.41	5.19	5.05	4.95	4.88	4.82	4.78	4.74
	16.26	**13.27**	**12.06**	**11.39**	**10.97**	**10.67**	**10.45**	**10.29**	**10.15**	**10.05**
6	5.99	5.14	4.76	4.53	4.39	4.28	4.21	4.15	4.10	4.06
	13.74	**10.92**	**9.78**	**9.15**	**8.75**	**8.47**	**8.26**	**8.10**	**7.98**	**7.87**
7	5.59	4.74	4.35	4.12	3.97	3.87	3.79	3.73	3.68	3.63
	12.25	**9.55**	**8.45**	**7.85**	**7.46**	**7.19**	**7.00**	**6.84**	**6.71**	**6.62**
8	5.32	4.46	4.07	3.84	3.69	3.58	3.50	3.44	3.39	3.34
	11.26	**8.65**	**7.59**	**7.01**	**6.63**	**6.37**	**6.19**	**6.03**	**5.91**	**5.82**
9	5.12	4.26	3.86	3.63	3.48	3.37	3.29	3.23	3.18	3.13
	10.56	**8.02**	**6.99**	**6.42**	**6.06**	**5.80**	**5.62**	**5.47**	**5.35**	**5.26**
10	4.96	4.10	3.71	3.48	3.33	3.22	3.14	3.07	3.02	2.97
	10.04	**7.56**	**6.55**	**5.99**	**5.64**	**5.39**	**5.21**	**5.06**	**4.95**	**4.85**
11	4.84	3.98	3.59	3.36	3.20	3.09	3.01	2.95	2.90	2.86
	9.65	**7.20**	**6.22**	**5.67**	**5.32**	**5.07**	**4.88**	**4.74**	**4.63**	**4.54**
12	4.75	3.88	3.49	3.26	3.11	3.00	2.92	2.85	2.80	2.76
	9.33	**6.93**	**5.95**	**5.41**	**5.06**	**4.82**	**4.65**	**4.50**	**4.39**	**4.30**
13	4.67	3.80	3.41	3.18	3.02	2.92	2.84	2.77	2.72	2.67
	9.07	**6.70**	**5.74**	**5.20**	**4.86**	**4.62**	**4.44**	**4.30**	**4.19**	**4.10**
14	4.60	3.74	3.34	3.11	2.96	2.85	2.77	2.70	2.65	2.60
	8.86	**6.51**	**5.56**	**5.03**	**4.69**	**4.46**	**4.28**	**4.14**	**4.03**	**3.94**
15	4.54	3.68	3.29	3.06	2.90	2.79	2.70	2.64	2.59	2.55
	8.68	**6.36**	**5.42**	**4.89**	**4.56**	**4.32**	**4.14**	**4.00**	**3.89**	**3.80**
16	4.49	3.36	3.24	3.01	2.85	2.74	2.66	2.59	2.54	2.49
	8.53	**6.23**	**5.29**	**4.77**	**4.44**	**4.20**	**4.03**	**3.89**	**3.78**	**3.69**
17	4.45	3.59	3.20	2.96	2.81	2.70	2.62	2.55	2.50	2.45
	8.40	**6.11**	**5.18**	**4.67**	**4.34**	**4.10**	**3.93**	**3.79**	**3.68**	**3.59**
18	4.41	3.55	3.16	2.93	2.77	2.66	2.58	2.51	2.46	2.41
	8.28	**6.01**	**5.09**	**4.58**	**4.25**	**4.01**	**3.85**	**3.71**	**3.60**	**3.51**
19	4.38	3.52	3.13	2.90	2.74	2.63	2.55	2.48	2.43	2.38
	8.18	**5.93**	**5.01**	**4.50**	**4.17**	**3.94**	**3.77**	**3.63**	**3.52**	**3.43**

TABLE C-5   (*Continued*)

δ_2, Denominator Degrees of Freedom	δ_1, Numerator Degrees of Freedom									
	1	2	3	4	5	6	7	8	9	10
20	4.35	3.49	3.10	2.87	2.71	2.60	2.52	2.45	2.40	2.35
	8.10	**5.85**	**4.94**	**4.43**	**4.10**	**3.87**	**3.71**	**3.56**	**3.45**	**3.37**
21	4.32	3.47	3.07	2.84	2.68	2.57	2.49	2.42	2.37	2.32
	8.02	**5.78**	**4.87**	**4.37**	**4.04**	**3.81**	**3.65**	**3.51**	**3.40**	**3.31**
22	4.30	3.44	3.05	2.82	2.66	2.55	2.47	2.40	2.35	2.30
	7.94	**5.72**	**4.82**	**4.31**	**3.99**	**3.76**	**3.59**	**3.45**	**3.35**	**3.26**
23	4.28	3.42	3.03	2.80	2.64	2.53	2.45	2.38	2.32	2.28
	7.88	**5.66**	**4.76**	**4.26**	**3.94**	**3.71**	**3.54**	**3.41**	**3.30**	**3.21**
24	4.26	3.40	3.01	2.78	2.62	2.51	2.43	2.36	2.30	2.26
	7.82	**5.61**	**4.72**	**4.22**	**3.90**	**3.67**	**3.50**	**3.36**	**3.25**	**3.17**
25	4.24	3.38	2.99	2.76	2.60	2.49	2.41	2.34	2.28	2.24
	7.77	**5.57**	**4.68**	**4.18**	**3.86**	**3.63**	**3.46**	**3.32**	**3.21**	**3.13**

Source: Abridged by permission from *Statistical Methods,* Seventh Edition, by George W. Snedecor and William C. Cochran. Copyright © 1980 by the Iowa State University Press, Ames, Iowa.

TABLE C-6   Durbin-Watson Test Bounds

Level of Significance $\alpha = .05$

n	k = 1		k = 2		k = 3		k = 4		k = 5	
	d_L	d_U	d_L	d_U	d_L	d_U	d_L	d_U	d_L	d_U
15	1.08	1.36	0.95	1.54	0.82	1.75	0.69	1.97	0.56	2.21
16	1.10	1.37	0.98	1.54	0.86	1.73	0.74	1.93	0.62	2.15
17	1.13	1.38	1.02	1.54	0.90	1.71	0.78	1.90	0.67	2.10
18	1.16	1.39	1.05	1.53	0.93	1.69	0.82	1.87	0.71	2.06
19	1.18	1.40	1.08	1.53	0.97	1.68	0.86	1.85	0.75	2.02
20	1.20	1.41	1.10	1.54	1.00	1.68	0.90	1.83	0.79	1.99
21	1.22	1.42	1.13	1.54	1.03	1.67	0.93	1.81	0.83	1.96
22	1.24	1.43	1.15	1.54	1.05	1.66	0.96	1.80	0.86	1.94
23	1.26	1.44	1.17	1.54	1.08	1.66	0.99	1.79	0.90	1.92
24	1.27	1.45	1.19	1.55	1.10	1.66	1.01	1.78	0.93	1.90
25	1.29	1.45	1.21	1.55	1.12	1.66	1.04	1.77	0.95	1.89
26	1.30	1.46	1.22	1.55	1.14	1.65	1.06	1.76	0.98	1.88
27	1.32	1.47	1.24	1.56	1.16	1.65	1.08	1.76	1.01	1.86
28	1.33	1.48	1.26	1.56	1.18	1.65	1.10	1.75	1.03	1.85
29	1.34	1.48	1.27	1.56	1.20	1.65	1.12	1.74	1.05	1.84
30	1.35	1.49	1.28	1.57	1.21	1.65	1.14	1.74	1.07	1.83
31	1.36	1.50	1.30	1.57	1.23	1.65	1.16	1.74	1.09	1.83
32	1.37	1.50	1.31	1.57	1.24	1.65	1.18	1.73	1.11	1.82
33	1.38	1.51	1.32	1.58	1.26	1.65	1.19	1.73	1.13	1.81
34	1.39	1.51	1.33	1.58	1.27	1.65	1.21	1.73	1.15	1.81
35	1.40	1.52	1.34	1.58	1.28	1.65	1.22	1.73	1.16	1.80
36	1.41	1.52	1.35	1.59	1.29	1.65	1.24	1.73	1.18	1.80
37	1.42	1.53	1.36	1.59	1.31	1.66	1.25	1.72	1.19	1.80

TABLE C-6   (*Continued*)

Level of Significance $\alpha = .05$

	k = 1		k = 2		k = 3		k = 4		k = 5	
n	d_L	d_U	d_L	d_U	d_L	d_U	d_L	d_U	d_L	d_U
38	1.43	1.54	1.37	1.59	1.32	1.66	1.26	1.72	1.21	1.79
39	1.43	1.54	1.38	1.60	1.33	1.66	1.27	1.72	1.22	1.79
40	1.44	1.54	1.39	1.60	1.34	1.66	1.29	1.72	1.23	1.79
45	1.48	1.57	1.43	1.62	1.38	1.67	1.34	1.72	1.29	1.78
50	1.50	1.59	1.46	1.63	1.42	1.67	1.38	1.72	1.34	1.77
55	1.53	1.60	1.49	1.64	1.45	1.68	1.41	1.72	1.38	1.77
60	1.55	1.62	1.51	1.65	1.48	1.69	1.44	1.73	1.41	1.77
65	1.57	1.63	1.54	1.66	1.50	1.70	1.47	1.73	1.44	1.77
70	1.58	1.64	1.55	1.67	1.52	1.70	1.49	1.74	1.46	1.77
75	1.60	1.65	1.57	1.68	1.54	1.71	1.51	1.74	1.49	1.77
80	1.61	1.66	1.59	1.69	1.56	1.72	1.53	1.74	1.51	1.77
85	1.62	1.67	1.60	1.70	1.57	1.72	1.55	1.75	1.52	1.77
90	1.63	1.68	1.61	1.70	1.59	1.73	1.57	1.75	1.54	1.78
95	1.64	1.69	1.62	1.71	1.60	1.73	1.58	1.75	1.56	1.78
100	1.65	1.69	1.63	1.72	1.61	1.74	1.59	1.76	1.57	1.78

Level of Significance $\alpha = .01$

	k = 1		k = 2		k = 3		k = 4		k = 5	
n	d_L	d_U	d_L	d_U	d_L	d_U	d_L	d_U	d_L	d_U
15	0.81	1.07	0.70	1.25	0.59	1.46	0.49	1.70	0.39	1.96
16	0.84	1.09	0.74	1.25	0.63	1.44	0.53	1.66	0.44	1.90
17	0.87	1.10	0.77	1.25	0.67	1.43	0.57	1.63	0.48	1.85
18	0.90	1.12	0.80	1.26	0.71	1.42	0.61	1.60	0.52	1.80
19	0.93	1.13	0.83	1.26	0.74	1.41	0.65	1.58	0.56	1.77
20	0.95	1.15	0.86	1.27	0.77	1.41	0.68	1.57	0.60	1.74
21	0.97	1.16	0.89	1.27	0.80	1.41	0.72	1.55	0.63	1.71
22	1.00	1.17	0.91	1.28	0.83	1.40	0.75	1.54	0.66	1.69
23	1.02	1.19	0.94	1.29	0.86	1.40	0.77	1.53	0.70	1.67
24	1.04	1.20	0.96	1.30	0.88	1.41	0.80	1.53	0.72	1.66
25	1.05	1.21	0.98	1.30	0.90	1.41	0.83	1.52	0.75	1.65
26	1.07	1.22	1.00	1.31	0.93	1.41	0.85	1.52	0.78	1.64
27	1.09	1.23	1.02	1.32	0.95	1.41	0.88	1.51	0.81	1.63
28	1.10	1.24	1.04	1.32	0.97	1.41	0.90	1.51	0.83	1.62
29	1.12	1.25	1.05	1.33	0.99	1.42	0.92	1.51	0.85	1.61
30	1.13	1.26	1.07	1.34	1.01	1.42	0.94	1.51	0.88	1.61
31	1.15	1.27	1.08	1.34	1.02	1.42	0.96	1.51	0.90	1.60
32	1.16	1.28	1.10	1.35	1.04	1.43	0.98	1.51	0.92	1.60
33	1.17	1.29	1.11	1.36	1.05	1.43	1.00	1.51	0.94	1.59
34	1.18	1.30	1.13	1.36	1.07	1.43	1.01	1.51	0.95	1.59
35	1.19	1.31	1.14	1.37	1.08	1.44	1.03	1.51	0.97	1.59
36	1.21	1.32	1.15	1.38	1.10	1.44	1.04	1.51	0.99	1.59
37	1.22	1.32	1.16	1.38	1.11	1.45	1.06	1.51	1.00	1.59
38	1.23	1.33	1.18	1.39	1.12	1.45	1.07	1.52	1.02	1.58
39	1.24	1.34	1.19	1.39	1.14	1.45	1.09	1.52	1.03	1.58
40	1.25	1.34	1.20	1.40	1.15	1.46	1.10	1.52	1.05	1.58

TABLE C-6   (*Continued*)

Level of Significance α = .01

	k = 1		k = 2		k = 3		k = 4		k = 5	
n	d_L	d_U	d_L	d_U	d_L	d_U	d_L	d_U	d_L	d_U
45	1.29	1.38	1.24	1.42	1.20	1.48	1.16	1.53	1.11	1.58
50	1.32	1.40	1.28	1.45	1.24	1.49	1.20	1.54	1.16	1.59
55	1.36	1.43	1.32	1.47	1.28	1.51	1.25	1.55	1.21	1.59
60	1.38	1.45	1.35	1.48	1.32	1.52	1.28	1.56	1.25	1.60
65	1.41	1.47	1.38	1.50	1.35	1.53	1.31	1.57	1.28	1.61
70	1.43	1.49	1.40	1.52	1.37	1.55	1.34	1.58	1.31	1.61
75	1.45	1.50	1.42	1.53	1.39	1.56	1.37	1.59	1.34	1.62
80	1.47	1.52	1.44	1.54	1.42	1.57	1.39	1.60	1.36	1.62
85	1.48	1.53	1.46	1.55	1.43	1.58	1.41	1.60	1.39	1.63
90	1.50	1.54	1.47	1.56	1.45	1.59	1.43	1.61	1.41	1.64
95	1.51	1.55	1.49	1.57	1.47	1.60	1.45	1.62	1.42	1.64
100	1.52	1.56	1.50	1.58	1.48	1.60	1.46	1.63	1.44	1.65

k = Number of independent variables.

Source: Reprinted, with permission, from J. Durbin and G. S. Watson, "Testing for Serial Correlation in Least Squares Regression—II," *Biometrika*, vol. 38 (1951), pp. 159–178.

Appendix D

Data Sets and Databases

This appendix contains 18 time series data sets and three multiple regression databases. The first database involves seven variables for 25 campgrounds, the second database has nine financial variables measured on each of 266 U.S. corporations in a recent year,[1] and the third database has 13 variables related to CEO compensation measured on 50 U.S. companies in a recent year.

Data sets are available on the CD included with this book and on the Internet for most text examples, problems, and cases. Each has three versions (Minitab, Excel, and all other programs). In order to access these data sets on the Internet, go to the Prentice Hall Web site *www.prenhall.com/Hanke* and follow the download instructions.

Data Sets

Year	Total Population	Purchasing Power of the Dollar, Consumer Prices	Federal Minimum Wage Rate, Current Dollars
1960	180,671	3.373	1.00
1961	183,691	3.340	1.15
1962	186,538	3.304	1.15
1963	189,242	3.265	1.25
1964	191,889	3.220	1.25
1965	194,303	3.166	1.25
1966	196,560	3.080	1.25
1967	198,712	2.993	1.40
1968	200,706	2.873	1.60
1969	202,677	2.726	1.60
1970	205,052	2.574	1.60
1971	207,661	2.466	1.60
1972	209,896	2.391	1.60
1973	211,909	2.251	1.60
1974	213,854	2.029	2.00
1975	215,973	1.859	2.10
1976	218,035	1.757	2.30
1977	220,239	1.649	2.30
1978	222,585	1.532	2.65
1979	225,055	1.380	2.90
1980	227,726	1.215	3.10
1981	229,966	1.098	3.35
1982	232,188	1.035	3.35
1983	234,307	1.003	3.35

Data Sets (Cont.)

Year	Total Population	Purchasing Power of the Dollar, Consumer Prices	Federal Minimum Wage Rate, Current Dollars
1984	236,348	0.961	3.35
1985	238,466	0.928	3.35
1986	240,651	0.913	3.35
1987	242,804	0.880	3.35
1988	245,021	0.846	3.35
1989	247,342	0.807	3.35
1990	249,948	0.766	3.80
1991	252,639	0.734	4.25
1992	255,374	0.713	4.25
1993	258,083	0.692	4.25
1994	260,599	0.675	4.25
1995	263,044	0.656	4.25
1996	265,463	0.638	4.75
1997	268,008	0.623	5.15
1998	270,561	0.600	

Year	Eastman Kodak Revenue	Money Market Deposits	Cable Television Subscribers
1975	5.0		
1976	5.4		
1977	6.0		
1978	7.0		
1979	8.0		
1980	9.7	400	
1981	10.3	344	
1982	10.8	400	21,000
1983	10.2	685	25,000
1984	10.6	705	30,000
1985	10.6	815	32,000
1986	11.5	941	37,500
1987	13.3	937	41,100
1988	17.0	926	44,000
1989	18.4	894	47,500
1990	18.9	924	50,000
1991	19.4	1,045	51,000
1992	20.2	1,187	53,000
1993	16.3	1,219	55,000
1994	13.7	1,150	57,000
1995	15.3	1,135	58,000
1996	16.2	1,272	60,280
1997		1,397	64,050
1998			64,170

---

[1] We are indebted to Dr. Lynn Stephens of Eastern Washington University for providing these data values.

Household Major Appliances, Industry Shipments, Freezers (thousands)

Year	1983	1984	1985	1986	1987	1988	1989	1990	1991	1992	1993
January	100	109	110	90	84	91	89	98	95	90	78
February	97	100	73	77	82	89	88	79	75	91	121
March	115	94	88	80	105	82	85	87	100	128	130
April	111	97	90	99	97	108	89	90	114	120	119
May	113	118	112	106	106	112	106	103	109	132	112
June	136	134	136	140	136	126	110	126	142	176	158
July	148	153	149	159	137	156	125	155	154	205	167
August	134	133	131	122	138	152	139	136	138	166	156
September	117	106	108	110	109	128	121	123	132	135	137
October	92	87	100	94	87	110	93	101	118	160	
November	78	80	66	72	93	99	84	97	106	138	
December	82	70	75	72	86	94	90	100	125	136	

Beer Production (millions of barrels)

Year	1983	1984	1985	1986	1987	1988	1989	1990	1991	1992	1993
January	14.77	14.15	15.50	15.71	15.60	15.80	15.88	16.46	16.27	15.65	15.36
February	14.53	14.75	14.55	15.21	15.63	15.85	15.29	15.74	15.17	16.10	15.78
March	16.78	17.72	16.76	16.51	17.66	17.12	17.57	17.97	16.08	18.06	17.41
April	18.42	16.81	17.97	17.99	17.42	17.73	17.30	17.48	17.23	18.00	17.44
May	18.17	18.74	18.86	18.67	17.44	18.31	18.41	18.10	18.90	18.89	18.87
June	18.47	18.47	18.23	18.65	18.58	18.58	18.82	18.58	19.16	18.95	18.96
July	18.50	19.12	18.59	18.33	18.09	18.17	18.28	18.25	19.88	18.34	18.51
August	18.27	17.59	17.71	17.06	16.81	17.72	18.88	18.96	18.63	17.55	
September	15.71	14.58	14.54	15.26	15.82	15.78	15.28	16.08	16.11	15.66	
October	15.41	15.14	14.36	15.62	15.50	15.61	15.82	16.62	16.65	16.15	
November	13.62	13.06	13.12	13.53	13.81	14.02	14.78	15.44	14.47	14.43	
December	12.46	12.89	13.13	13.97	13.69	13.22	13.45	13.97	13.64	14.32	

New Prescriptions (thousands)

Year	1994	1995	1996	1997	1998	1999	2000
January	154	200	223	346	518	613	628
February	96	118	104	261	404	392	308
March	73	90	107	224	300	273	324
April	49	79	85	141	210	322	248
May	36	78	75	148	196	189	272
June	59	91	99	145	186	257	634
July	95	167	135	223	247	324	299
August	169	169	121	272	343	404	424
September	210	289	335	445	464	677	548
October	278	347	460	560	680	858	372
November	298	375	488	612	711	895	876
December	245	203	326	467	610	664	676

Seattle, Washington, Daily Bus Ridership for 146 Days on the Pike Street Route

350	339	351	364	369	331	331	340	346	341	357	398	381	367	383	375
353	361	375	371	373	366	382	429	406	403	429	425	427	409	402	409
419	404	429	463	428	449	444	467	474	463	432	453	462	456	474	514
489	475	492	525	527	533	527	522	526	513	564	599	572	587	599	601
611	620	579	582	592	581	630	663	638	631	645	682	601	595	521	521
516	496	538	575	537	534	542	538	547	540	526	548	555	545	594	643
625	616	640	625	637	634	621	641	654	649	662	699	672	704	700	711
715	718	652	664	695	704	733	772	716	712	732	755	761	748	748	750
744	731	782	810	777	816	840	868	872	811	810	762	634	626	649	697
657	549														

Data are read across the table.

Monthly Occupancy Statistics for Motel Nine

Year	1991	1992	1993	1994	1995	1996	1997	1998	1999	2000
January	563	635	647	676	748	795	843	778	895	875
February	599	639	658	748	773	788	847	856	856	993
March	669	712	713	811	814	890	942	939	893	977
April	598	622	688	729	767	797	804	813	875	969
May	580	621	724	701	729	751	840	783	835	872
June	668	676	707	790	749	821	872	828	935	1006
July	499	501	629	594	681	692	656	657	833	832
August	215	220	238	231	241	291	370	310	300	346
September	556	561	613	617	680	727	742	780	791	850
October	587	603	730	691	708	868	847	860	900	914
November	546	626	735	701	694	812	732	780	782	869
December	571	606	652	706	772	800	899	808	880	994

Woodpulp Production (thousands of short tons)

Year	1992	1993	1994	1995	1996
January	5276	5466	5480	5579	5681
February	4919	4821	4988	5033	5254
March	5227	5307	5272	5319	5525
April	5003	5193	5254	5285	5489
May	5004	5087	5156	5188	5320
June	4949	5102	5175	5197	5417
July	5219	5399	5490	5604	5711
August	5265	5301	5366	5357	5419
September	5007	5063	5200	5133	5318
October	5079	5295	5410	5483	5409
November	4974	5021	5123	5186	5310
December	5282	4991	5428	5472	5458

Year	Higher Education Price Index, 1983 = 100	Number of U.S. Farms (thousands)
1970	39.5	
	42.1	
	44.3	
	46.7	
	49.9	
1975	54.3	2521
	57.9	2497
	61.7	2456
	65.8	2436
	70.6	2437
1980	77.5	2440
	85.9	2440
	94.0	2407
	100.0	2379
	104.7	2334
1985	110.5	2293
	115.6	2250
	120.3	2213
	125.8	2197
	133.1	2171
1990	140.8	2140
	148.3	2105
	153.1	2094
	158.2	2040

Year	Average Wellhead Price, Natural Gas (cents per million cubic feet)	Moody's Electric Utility Common Stocks Annual Average Price
1972	18.6	80.20
	21.6	71.21
	30.4	48.26
1975	44.5	51.25
	58.0	60.10
	79.0	67.55
	90.5	63.54
	117.8	60.28
1980	158.8	54.80
	198.2	55.41
	245.7	63.56
	259.3	74.04
	265.5	71.16
1985	248.0	87.24
	194.2	111.11
	166.5	105.90
	169.0	97.99
	169.0	110.45
1990	172.0	112.61
	164.0	126.97
	174.0	
	203.0	

Thousands of Freight Car Loadings, Forest Products

Year	1992	1993	1994	1995	1996
January	17.6	16.9	16.1	15.6	13.2
February	19.0	18.5	15.8	16.7	14.5
March	19.1	18.6	16.0	17.2	14.7
April	18.7	17.9	16.6	16.7	14.1
May	19.1	18.0	16.2	16.3	15.2
June	19.9	17.4	15.8	16.4	15.3
July	18.3	16.4	16.6	13.9	14.9
August	19.1	16.5	15.8	15.9	14.0
September	18.6	16.7	15.6	15.5	15.3
October	18.8	17.0	15.6	15.2	14.4
November	16.7	12.4	14.4	13.9	14.2
December	17.3	16.9	14.3	14.0	15.0

Industrial Price/Earnings Ratio

Year	Quarter	P/E	Year	Quarter	P/E
1986	1	17.56	1990	1	15.80
	2	18.09		2	17.00
	3	16.47		3	14.80
	4	18.73		4	15.90
1987	1	22.16	1991	1	18.80
	2	21.80		2	20.40
	3	20.82		3	23.70
	4	14.09		4	29.20
1988	1	13.61	1992	1	28.40
	2	13.29		2	26.80
	3	12.50		3	26.00
	4	12.35		4	26.00
1989	1	12.46			
	2	13.30			
	3	14.73			
	4	15.40			

CAMPSITE DATA

A group of businesspeople in Spokane is planning to develop a number of campsites in the state. One of their problems is to decide the amount to be charged per day. According to their observations, the fee depends on a number of variables such as whether a swimming pool is accessible and the size of the campground. In an effort to be objective, the following information was collected on 25 campgrounds in Washington (from the Rand McNally Campground Guide for Washington) and a computer analysis completed. The variables analyzed were:

Y = Daily fee (FEE)
X_1 = Number of acres (ACRES)
X_2 = Number of sites (SITES)
X_3 = Whether there were flush toilets or not (TOILET)
X_4 = Whether there was a swimming pool or not (POOL)
X_5 = Whether there were electric hookups or not (HOOKUP)
X_6 = Number of additional recreational facilities (ADD)

Site	Y	X_1	X_2	X_3	X_4	X_5	X_6
1	7.00	40	32	0	0	0	2
2	8.50	20	47	1	0	1	2
3	9.00	45	18	1	1	1	1
4	8.00	110	32	1	0	1	3
5	8.00	30	54	1	0	1	2
6	7.00	50	30	1	0	1	3
7	7.75	35	30	1	0	1	2
8	8.00	18	40	1	0	1	1
9	8.50	23	60	1	1	1	1
10	8.50	9	60	1	0	1	3
11	9.00	52	50	1	1	1	2
12	7.00	25	21	0	0	1	1
13	9.00	250	30	1	0	1	2
14	8.50	140	70	1	1	1	2
15	9.00	120	80	1	1	1	1
16	7.50	60	50	1	1	1	2
17	8.50	120	35	1	0	1	2
18	9.00	173	25	1	1	1	2
19	8.00	100	75	1	0	1	2
20	9.50	134	35	1	1	1	1
21	7.50	114	120	0	1	1	2
22	7.50	2	17	0	0	1	2
23	7.50	32	15	0	1	0	3
24	9.00	25	30	1	1	1	2
25	7.50	66	100	1	0	1	2

Database

Company Number	Sales (millions)	Employees (thousands)	Capital Expenditures (millions)	Intangibles Expenditures (millions)	Cost of Goods Sold (millions)	Labor and Related Expense (millions)	Advertising Expense (millions)	Research and Development Expense (millions)
1	3,221.8008	42.0000	147.9000	30.6000	2,285.2007	599.7998	118.3000	28.0000
2	1,690.6001	20.9050	93.0000	29.1000	1,057.2002	343.2000	114.9000	8.9000
3	2,197.2764	39.0000	66.8670	55.8600	1,387.0679	661.3997	95.5680	11.1820
4	2,357.8206	23.3000	59.5560	69.6080	1,743.7952	25.6320	51.9170	8.5000
5	8,129.0000	35.0000	297.0000	29.0000	7,423.0000	1,178.0000	12.8000	9.2530
6	11,851.0000	23.0000	394.0000	20.0000	10,942.0000	2,556.0000	11.6530	14.6000
7	323.8606	3.9000	2.5900	4.2880	233.5300	22.8350	3.5290	30.7320
8	660.4856	8.3780	10.9840	3.3720	582.2649	25.6250	44.9990	64.8730
9	4,351.1601	50.9120	102.7080	217.0920	4,156.8671	12.8360	66.2640	8.7790
10	985.8357	5.5000	16.6010	29.5900	874.1287	19.5000	112.3860	18.3650
11	3,802.5581	39.6000	206.1020	157.3520	2,997.2703	518.0000	139.7290	16.4130
12	2,576.0464	22.6000	50.6690	47.0790	1,885.9053	349.4910	48.8170	9.5000
13	106.0160	28.0000	1.3120	42.0000	84.6590	35.5550	22.9370	8.7330
14	5,669.8945	46.8810	103.0000	31.1000	4,424.3007	785.0000	141.3000	18.5000
15	319.6570	2.8940	4.5770	2.2090	246.6980	42.8370	87.0000	1.1000
16	511.7217	10.1000	19.5600	27.0000	286.2288	48.9990	1.8700	23.6520
17	884.6189	22.8010	58.0940	33.0000	467.4436	36.5000	16.0350	29.6320
18	166.3750	2.3000	3.9510	5.2890	111.0310	31.0000	4.0230	38.5420
19	59.1310	18.0000	1.1400	14.5000	43.7430	26.3210	90.3250	56.9820
20	136.6970	3.1000	2.0090	18.4930	105.3300	15.8880	46.3000	8.6330
21	767.8799	8.1000	37.4250	18.0560	519.3948	112.1350	21.8470	2.7860
22	61.3280	1.1390	1.3880	26.3250	35.2020	17.3140	2.4270	88.5230
23	445.6387	5.8000	18.9780	12.6000	213.2880	12.1000	62.8060	1.4600

Database (Cont.)

Company Number	Sales (millions)	Employees (thousands)	Capital Expenditures (millions)	Intangibles Expenditures (millions)	Cost of Goods Sold (millions)	Labor and Related Expense (millions)	Advertising Expense (millions)	Research and Development Expense (millions)
24	2,259.6316	16.0270	228.7270	27.3350	1,696.3772	421.8057	116.5990	9.6000
25	624.8040	8.7000	86.4030	2.8080	408.4707	168.0200	33.4700	9.4440
26	329.9578	4.0000	14.9460	8.3710	225.0410	20.9850	12.9790	32.0000
27	308.7327	2.1070	14.8080	43.5920	239.1300	36.5000	18.1220	1.8510
28	598.9507	5.0000	39.7150	27.8920	481.9436	45.0000	39.8230	.7500
29	172.7920	1.5760	1.6590	23.5420	118.7090	48.2000	7.9090	26.3330
30	910.8406	7.0000	14.4610	5.5880	677.2527	7.0000	58.2130	1.8000
31	142.1830	1.6000	5.5880	72.5190	126.9660	1.6000	2.7310	57.2710
32	425.0828	6.8330	72.5190	31.8030	256.2837	6.8330	12.1440	44.1550
33	4,337.9140	36.1000	306.0220	101.4290	2,344.1631	36.1000	270.2576	16.1100
34	271.0076	2.0780	27.1230	6.5030	134.3790	35.7730	20.2540	87.4830
35	209.4520	2.9980	14.4690	14.6060	176.4890	2.0780	1.8970	714.9990
36	62.4180	3.8000	3.7390	7.6680	34.4700	2.9980	44.0500	121.3300
37	4,300.0000	95.5000	412.2886	157.6030	2,108.5503	5.1000	257.6807	11.6440
38	390.6829	5.1000	30.8480	10.8550	225.1080	6.3000	18.3780	33.4770
39	270.0127	6.3000	40.0340	22.4540	189.8000	2.0000	4.9080	43.7430
40	97.9660	2.0600	6.9940	5.2500	64.5920	31.9700	2.5900	18.9700
41	66.4090	12.5261	3.7570	1.0090	57.2310	33.2000	59.1300	14.9460
42	56.5550	3.9000	1.6240	6.9940	44.0550	53.5000	19.5600	1.6590
43	3,267.9551	31.9790	502.0398	45.6140	2,517.7566	754.8977	3.9510	57.7210
44	2,745.7439	43.9680	251.0340	16.1110	1,638.7969	45.0000	161.2000	108.1480
45	2,609.0000	33.2000	248.0001	10.0000	1,874.0000	564.0000	18.0000	83.0000
46	1,677.6016	11.6440	284.6089	87.4830	1,185.9717	24.4530	6.4840	36.1310
47	6,887.6210	53.5000	1,075.1719	84.0390	4,721.9570	1,375.7996	44.0700	231.4690
48	10,584.1990	132.1400	714.2002	22.6000	7,353.5000	3,204.2688	93.4000	377.1001
49	2,912.7644	45.8540	195.2680	45.6430	2,189.5293	879.6548	14.9460	66.0560
50	4,309.5820	66.8000	275.3079	67.3120	2,913.9036	993.3997	1.6590	40.5470
51	1,946.4766	24.4530	121.3300	6.2920	1,403.4976	546.0508	35.2020	40.0810
52	9,254.1171	151.2000	1,431.0906	121.3300	6,187.7851	2,125.2012	95.9510	334.8057
53	5,018.6914	62.8510	479.8997	1.6240	3,478.0989	1,318.0999	9.2530	144.3000
54	1,510.7798	15.3000	207.9320	63.5190	1,157.2117	13.9700	27.6660	39.7150
55	1,560.0750	22.7000	162.5190	61.9380	1,188.9126	18.4340	19.3190	24.7010
56	2,794.0000	37.4000	256.0999	7.3000	1,928.4988	780.7996	18.3650	70.1000
57	921.3689	13.9700	61.9380	18.4340	597.7000	45.1640	19.2020	22.6500
58	1,253.5430	13.0580	66.4310	13.9700	806.6758	236.5000	32.0000	48.6510
59	1,328.1138	13.1160	201.1960	31.2730	851.8938	1.1550	31.2730	33.5620
60	1,314.6299	27.3460	36.9330	43.0750	569.7327	6.4690	174.4610	42.1160
61	7,869.6914	113.3710	687.7998	90.2000	5,580.5976	1,931.5005	76.5000	155.9000
62	73.0550	7.8240	26.5680	20.6650	38.9980	22.8990	43.0750	99.8430
63	108.5090	87.4350	5.6630	37.3860	77.1740	36.9990	90.2000	1.6500
64	1,422.4507	16.5000	100.4700	69.8820	1,060.5420	305.7000	6.3970	25.4520
65	87.4350	7.6550	8.5150	15.3750	51.3970	11.3940	69.8820	2.7200
66	7.8240	9.5280	26.6950	7.7640	6.7860	20.5720	4.2100	52.1780
67	868.7107	15.3400	42.4040	1.2120	686.0518	200.4850	10.4000	22.7240
68	137.3950	2.8750	14.1080	9.7470	112.2350	30.7620	83.1580	1.9000
69	753.8848	6.5480	24.2870	4.2120	596.5076	13.4000	88.8250	6.4200
70	1,445.0166	27.0030	84.1490	99.9080	786.8777	1.9360	39.8650	76.1870
71	3,062.6316	49.6190	67.6310	83.1580	1,446.5227	668.9910	243.0450	74.5240
72	2,450.4285	32.6000	81.9220	88.8250	906.9639	6.7120	423.2698	90.5730
73	141.2580	1.3040	4.5050	6.7300	95.1540	3.7000	9.9040	9.7580

Database (Cont.)

Company Number	Sales (millions)	Employees (thousands)	Capital Expenditures (millions)	Intangibles Expenditures (millions)	Cost of Goods Sold (millions)	Labor and Related Expense (millions)	Advertising Expense (millions)	Research and Development Expense (millions)
74	6.8030	5.1000	9.5230	1.4590	2.3980	12.2490	0.7230	11.9490
75	1,852.0896	25.4000	89.5500	57.7900	672.7947	4.5070	28.4910	148.0770
76	365.7217	4.9030	17.0620	16.7160	217.5420	3.4720	6.7300	11.8950
77	1,981.4397	28.7000	155.8530	141.2700	668.7720	634.0596	55.2940	161.3500
78	2,362.1326	40.7000	110.1000	99.8430	1,055.4187	11.3940	75.7000	113.1280
79	357.0696	5.5500	12.6430	52.1780	141.2700	2.1330	36.8860	18.9510
80	220.3790	3.7000	10.7860	9.7580	67.1220	20.5720	7.1610	6.2610
81	1,082.4927	17.9000	51.3360	52.1780	310.7820	315.8997	114.9660	65.6910
82	848.3799	17.1000	41.2990	11.9490	386.0066	16.0000	40.6150	61.6940
83	1,112.0386	16.5890	74.5790	44.6610	378.7710	7.3000	91.2150	77.3130
84	1,515.8816	37.0000	108.0460	52.3290	758.5320	469.9229	74.5950	61.8300
85	1,328.5508	19.9200	44.6810	6.2850	566.2200	323.7090	36.9560	115.5890
86	2,878.4956	58.0000	182.2670	348.1426	1,247.2339	1.1500	391.6277	85.3970
87	4,312.0507	56.6000	169.2950	66.9970	2,672.3262	6.4600	260.3870	37.6540
88	54.3250	37.3860	1.0660	2.8130	26.5960	4.7670	0.7520	44.6610
89	122.9470	57.1720	13.7480	7.5620	94.6720	17.6580	1.4590	3.8670
90	2,014.7056	31.0000	74.7910	0.0000	700.4778	503.6768	45.0900	21.1460
91	969.8328	18.5170	40.8340	54.2710	448.5286	9.4450	91.2690	8.5670
92	45.3670	8.3500	1.6430	7.0670	15.7310	2.1230	5.1820	52.3290
93	255.1320	3.3000	10.6420	20.2520	131.6750	12.2220	42.5670	6.2850
94	1,710.4700	31.7000	91.5640	54.7540	752.5889	530.2456	239.9010	42.0600
95	365.8809	3.4800	20.0140	6.7300	177.5500	25.8740	16.7100	23.7910
96	33.2650	2.0870	1.5120	4.4840	19.7100	19.7100	1.1550	2.8890
97	53.7460	.5250	2.0870	42.2810	16.1820	16.1800	7.6770	19.7100
98	52.8760	1.1420	2.4190	1.2160	27.1500	27.1500	6.4690	16.1820
99	9.6630	2.4190	12.7460	7.9670	5.6960	5.6950	0.4570	27.1500
100	1,451.6687	29.0000	86.6820	97.2690	505.8267	36.1200	137.7250	30.7620
101	321.3638	4.9110	13.1180	11.0840	268.0159	57.2600	1.1110	13.4000
102	156.4580	2.3500	4.5670	3.8620	114.1930	6.4800	4.7670	5.6960
103	52.1870	.8650	1.5100	20.6490	36.5130	59.3250	18.0150	1.9360
104	447.2100	7.7670	12.7460	41.7940	280.3218	26.8120	9.4400	505.8267
105	86.8170	1.1000	1.2810	19.3850	57.2600	26.6950	2.1230	1.3420
106	1,132.3499	18.0150	16.8570	1.6970	785.0718	36.9240	25.8740	6.7120
107	217.4120	3.2000	4.4840	10.5440	142.6020	57.5790	3.2520	3.7000
108	7.7640	86.6820	1.2810	7.2210	6.4800	9.5280	20.8580	268.0159
109	1,581.8760	20.8580	142.2810	5.8820	1,280.1670	359.0999	1.1000	12.2490
110	201.4650	1.1000	7.9670	1.3370	169.2630	57.5700	7.4000	114.1930
111	198.9010	.9110	9.7470	.4290	164.1940	73.9670	1.8400	36.5130
112	1,497.0076	7.4000	131.9400	6.0210	1,098.2969	99.4080	5.1000	280.3280
113	153.2290	1.8400	11.0840	3.4390	59.2350	9.2800	8.3500	4.5070
114	367.9246	5.1000	20.6490	11.2110	230.1690	73.9670	1.2110	11.3940
115	494.4136	8.3500	19.3850	3.1490	342.9849	6.4690	3.8030	2.1000
116	52.4550	1.2120	7.2210	7.0620	26.8120	4.7670	4.0510	57.2600
117	37.3860	.8200	1.3370	44.3730	26.6950	9.4400	5.6000	785.0718
118	57.7120	13.1190	3.4390	.7160	36.9240	2.1230	7.5620	.9510
119	586.4766	3.8030	44.3730	34.2780	391.3706	25.8740	2.8100	20.5720
120	476.2078	4.0510	34.2780	30.2360	244.7830	99.9080	5.8820	16.0000
121	15.3570	4.5671	16.8570	53.2830	9.5280	29.0000	6.0200	142.6020
122	393.6016	5.6000	30.2360	2.8890	265.3079	9.2800	11.2110	7.3000
123	4,701.1210	7.5620	353.2830	48.6920	3,707.6846	4.9110	3.1490	6.4800

Database (Cont.)

Company Number	Sales (millions)	Employees (thousands)	Capital Expenditures (millions)	Intangibles Expenditures (millions)	Cost of Goods Sold (millions)	Labor and Related Expense (millions)	Advertising Expense (millions)	Research and Development Expense (millions)
124	1,167.8340	2.8100	48.6920	8.4580	1,017.6038	2.3500	7.0620	59.2350
125	12,298.3980	50.7000	1,221.8008	10.4000	9,285.7109	1,016.5000	13.1160	64.6000
126	439.4727	1.9020	65.1100	39.8650	263.8108	51.1480	27.3460	31.2730
127	29,127.0030	108.7000	1,897.0005	9.9040	20,032.0000	78.7700	16.5000	86.0000
128	1,993.6624	8.0000	43.4190	45.7820	1,755.5662	3.5730	31.1370	43.0750
129	4,660.8945	18.1000	636.1238	28.4900	3,675.6895	440.7996	3.4000	11.6000
130	976.4578	8.8280	14.8590	55.2940	879.3516	91.8000	15.3440	90.2000
131	3,834.9324	6.6610	316.7156	68.2690	3,557.4734	7.4050	2.8250	69.8820
132	9,535.7382	42.7800	1,107.3838	75.7000	7,075.1875	971.0000	6.5480	29.7730
133	657.7776	1.2640	56.1460	36.8860	565.0176	14.4700	27.0030	4.2120
134	100.4570	43.0750	44.0680	7.1610	72.7830	22.0310	49.6110	83.1580
135	60,334.5110	130.0000	4,186.9296	40.6150	45,999.0070	3,405.0000	32.6000	290.0000
136	2,150.0000	90.2110	311.7000	91.2150	1,460.7996	57.4030	1.3040	25.1000
137	18,069.0000	58.3000	1,680.0000	74.5900	13,442.0000	1,345.0000	25.4000	88.8250
138	109.7380	69.8870	32.2560	36.9560	97.0130	2.5200	4.9030	6.7300
139	592.7710	3.2520	123.7680	3.8770	420.3206	67.3300	28.7000	1.4590
140	4,642.3945	14.3280	353.5999	33.5620	4,085.0989	324.0000	40.7000	25.0000
141	2,072.4412	11.1480	270.1846	42.1160	1,640.8118	1.2400	5.5500	4.9810
142	4,509.3828	13.3540	502.2720	1.6500	2,838.0845	236.4540	2.0370	12.8000
143	34,736.0030	207.7000	1,760.7100	2.7200	26,053.9060	20.9400	3.7000	16.7160
144	1,191.0337	4.2070	255.6150	1.9000	865.6477	82.6730	0.2670	99.8430
145	312.7300	4.2120	76.5000	6.4200	452.4130	17.0050	17.9000	52.1780
146	1,553.1077	9.1500	343.9539	23.6410	988.8760	185.6600	12.5840	9.7580
147	6,997.7734	30.0080	956.1719	11.2330	4,886.8125	720.5000	17.1000	58.2460
148	513.1880	5.1420	41.9800	41.9800	375.3599	25.0200	11.3330	11.9490
149	28,085.0030	94.8000	2,913.0000	32.5600	20,632.0000	2,344.0000	89.0000	231.0000
150	11,062.8980	34.9740	1,774.3904	43.0250	8,259.7656	1,051.0000	16.5890	114.0000
151	23,232.4060	37.5750	1,049.6729	90.2110	19,964.6050	994.0000	37.0000	89.7370
152	14,961.5000	47.0110	1,744.0364	69.8870	10,046.0000	1,126.7310	19.9200	80.3250
153	5,197.7070	24.1450	762.2510	4.2120	3,336.7566	431.9976	7.7130	15.0520
154	7,428.2343	33.7210	601.1216	6.7310	5,714.3085	9.7320	58.0000	21.0000
155	28,607.5030	67.8410	1,344.3777	10.4000	24,787.6050	1,572.7996	56.6000	52.0000
156	87.6100	6.7310	12.7120	39.8650	74.5510	31.5580	31.0000	44.6610
157	1,165.6736	3.5310	26.6780	9.9040	1,035.7129	6.6000	18.5170	2.4490
158	567.3650	1.5420	97.4910	28.9400	480.5110	23.5230	3.3000	52.3290
159	5,954.9414	16.2970	732.0000	55.9240	4,540.4609	444.8997	31.7000	18.5000
160	368.0940	2.3150	15.0860	2.7160	319.4939	10.6050	3.4800	6.2850
161	751.7327	6.2550	51.1060	13.5380	606.8318	3.5230	6.8000	9.9000
162	895.4087	10.9000	145.5140	9.3840	681.9656	26.3250	39.0000	30.6000
163	1,063.2908	16.1790	51.1480	25.7670	746.2820	12.6000	16.6980	14.6320
164	1,306.0867	19.3970	78.7700	2.7490	1,021.4856	435.2998	23.3000	13.2830
165	140.4440	1.9190	3.5730	55.8600	122.3210	27.3350	35.0000	29.1000
166	4,357.2812	52.1400	110.4470	12.0830	3,540.9612	1,235.0000	3.9000	55.8600
167	263.9048	3.7000	7.4050	27.2080	203.3440	2.8080	8.3780	3.2500
168	6,184.8945	94.5000	398.2000	69.6080	5,224.0000	2,550.0000	50.9120	37.1000
169	257.6509	3.3640	14.4730	7.5700	190.4190	8.3710	5.5000	69.6080
170	50.5150	52.5350	29.1000	29.0000	18.0560	43.5920	39.6000	29.0000
171	419.6470	4.3020	22.0310	20.0000	341.5906	135.6000	22.6000	20.0000
172	1,227.4490	20.0000	57.4030	4.2880	999.7520	27.8920	28.0000	9.0000
173	779.3450	8.8000	22.0670	3.3700	678.4258	229.1270	46.8810	4.2880

Database (Cont.)

Company Number	Sales (millions)	Employees (thousands)	Capital Expenditures (millions)	Intangibles Expenditures (millions)	Cost of Goods Sold (millions)	Labor and Related Expense (millions)	Advertising Expense (millions)	Research and Development Expense (millions)
174	72.1760	1.3000	2.5210	29.5900	50.9650	24.8290	2.8940	3.3700
175	3,248.0076	36.0620	263.6167	19.4460	2,710.3455	974.3379	10.1000	29.5900
176	921.1270	12.6590	67.3340	10.5250	771.0059	23.5420	22.8010	157.3520
177	711.9827	12.5120	133.3850	45.0790	653.8069	351.4700	2.3000	45.0790
178	72.4110	1.0250	1.2400	42.0000	60.0820	93.0000	18.0000	42.0000
179	297.5686	4.1520	20.9420	.8990	248.7160	123.1000	3.1000	31.1000
180	677.8489	6.0700	17.0050	31.1000	613.3047	169.2570	8.1000	2.2090
181	582.6238	1.4000	25.0290	2.2090	474.3450	66.8670	1.1390	27.0000
182	3,750.4109	38.1700	120.8280	27.0000	3,240.7886	1,132.6216	5.8000	33.0000
183	88.8070	2.3330	9.7320	7.2110	66.6540	59.5500	16.0270	5.2890
184	306.9397	2.8000	31.5880	33.0000	220.4980	2.5900	8.7000	14.5000
185	331.7366	5.2000	6.6000	11.0250	295.3848	10.9840	4.0000	18.4930
186	546.9500	8.9000	23.5230	5.2890	439.0479	16.0010	2.1000	18.0560
187	7.5910	30.6000	7.8900	14.5000	5.0480	50.6690	5.0000	26.3250
188	3,479.4573	41.3940	170.3720	18.4930	3,100.5391	1,177.5999	1.5760	15.0500
189	485.6138	6.6580	58.6750	3.5250	335.3318	42.0000	93.0000	1.4320
190	123.2280	2.0450	10.6050	5.2550	96.6630	20.9000	66.8670	12.6000
191	488.2327	4.6500	20.4800	1.1111	402.8457	402.8400	77.0101	22.2426
192	100.7820	1.7030	2.4430	1.6800	88.7960	4.0000	21.0000	28.3032
193	165.7970	4.7660	3.2790	88.0003	120.1080	2.0000	4.0008	18.2022
194	274.8440	3.5500	21.7900	2.9530	213.1860	3.0000	3.7521	24.2628
195	11,049.5000	166.8480	667.7998	55.5000	9,955.3984	4,485.1953	22.0007	52.5000
196	1,154.8477	14.4190	32.2360	4.0800	1,037.4727	424.4556	21.1234	30.3234
197	578.7107	11.4920	26.3000	8.0141	433.8230	1.0111	12.3456	5.3300
198	124.5440	1.8000	4.6280	1.9850	101.5300	23.6630	78.9101	36.3840
199	3,711.2029	63.4000	303.3838	4.5720	2,729.9280	22.0222	91.0111	33.0000
200	124.8600	2.0000	5.2240	2.3200	79.7770	51.0000	21.3141	2.6500
201	2,466.0000	26.8650	161.7000	2.0202	2,028.7996	18.4021	3.2000	14.9000
202	2,829.2991	36.2000	156.8000	27.1000	2,261.0000	930.2000	51.1617	25.2000
203	814.8196	14.8000	48.5520	16.0111	622.9507	204.9000	18.1920	1.4150
204	4,051.7996	46.0000	349.5999	2.6000	3,036.5999	1,215.2996	21.2223	56.6000
205	67.0390	28.0000	3.5010	2.5170	54.9070	66.5620	24.2526	42.4446
206	240.5670	4.0000	5.5670	1.3220	184.1350	61.6900	2.5860	3.0470
207	45.2140	2.0000	1.4110	18.1010	38.0970	62.3201	27.2829	48.5052
208	69.9520	81.0000	33.3333	8.0033	65.4570	52.3302	30.3132	54.5658
209	54.5490	1.1270	1.7720	17.7200	42.5990	42.4444	33.3435	60.6264
210	317.4480	5.7840	12.6650	11.0330	254.1990	80.1010	36.3738	66.6870
211	847.9927	24.0000	85.0240	19.7930	664.9578	34.1021	39.4041	10.4000
212	467.9546	4.8450	13.1650	2.3810	400.5806	4.0999	42.4344	1.0011
213	126.6750	14.0007	7.7490	14.1441	109.6830	50.6410	45.4647	1.0022
214	85.7290	49.0000	2.1610	49.4949	72.8400	9.9901	48.4950	1.0033
215	680.7666	8.2200	19.2340	77.7878	578.8528	9.8175	51.5253	1.3090
216	211.3230	1.5670	4.8350	15.6180	171.4130	65.0000	54.5556	1.8201
217	254.3030	3.1000	2.7620	2.3570	205.8410	42.4381	57.5859	2.0880
218	1,396.8108	29.4160	79.9820	28.2626	1,000.2886	3.8107	16.1580	3.4510
219	3,981.0000	52.9000	188.3000	70.3000	3,120.5999	1,085.7996	75.8000	37.5000
220	3,943.0990	56.5320	259.5000	49.9000	3,352.3008	1,275.7002	60.6162	42.3000

Database (Cont.)

Company Number	Sales (millions)	Employees (thousands)	Capital Expenditures (millions)	Intangibles Expenditures (millions)	Cost of Goods Sold (millions)	Labor and Related Expense (millions)	Advertising Expense (millions)	Research and Development Expense (millions)
221	1,260.2349	17.2880	103.0320	11.4810	1,055.9436	12.0000	63.6465	2.1133
222	973.2527	9.8850	25.4530	5.5580	848.7227	4.0877	66.6768	3.3210
223	19.9060	18.0002	5.6666	1.4100	16.5170	3.3876	69.7071	4.2242
224	66.8260	1.3200	6.1110	88.1388	48.9480	4.5222	72.7374	5.6210
225	178.7460	2.1980	5.5430	138.0000	138.5690	43.4350	75.7677	6.2155
226	26.7510	1.0560	8.8888	211.0113	17.9930	18.1111	78.7980	7.2102
227	20.5750	43.1111	7.7777	82.1003	13.9720	14.2222	81.8283	8.9712
228	51.5960	18.5216	1.6940	1.1620	38.8190	88.9922	81.0077	24.2601
229	106.1150	2.6000	4.6850	9.9210	64.0500	12.4243	77.0222	23.2810
230	8.5160	14.2421	12.0818	12.1402	5.9500	7.8246	22.4443	24.8588
231	308.8916	5.7000	15.8370	13.1402	144.7340	42.4444	47.8877	2.7060
232	753.8069	16.8750	37.4620	3.6210	491.1160	210.0050	16.4370	4.9340
233	41.2960	1.1080	2.5820	12.1213	28.1320	81.8118	12.5456	24.5293
234	145.6840	3.4190	13.3250	1.0087	105.1630	51.7100	51.8196	1.8480
235	51.3130	1.0000	1.5700	8.0025	35.9730	43.4400	21.4231	59.6085
236	21.4070	12.5358	18.7842	5.5554	12.9550	12.8888	37.8286	64.8821
237	585.6597	8.2000	56.0530	80.9960	359.8350	77.9999	13.6920	8.9610
238	516.7239	10.3000	17.9320	9.3610	376.4170	1.1007	5.6670	5.6000
239	316.8147	7.0000	3.9360	12.1314	267.2456	2.0008	86.8686	76.7686
240	509.7000	10.0000	27.0360	15.1617	375.3457	179.9240	85.8686	3.6080
241	341.3887	7.1270	7.1570	8.1819	287.6907	9.0007	86.8888	86.7795
242	33.0660	1.0872	1.9540	9.2021	24.0720	12.7210	83.1111	95.9594
243	200.5920	4.0000	5.3320	20.0290	153.5480	7.6660	82.2222	94.9388
244	184.5810	4.0500	7.2780	10.3570	142.7160	8.7770	22.6665	1.0790
245	217.7520	4.0880	7.3840	10.1146	179.1020	78.3910	44.6621	89.9012
246	386.8118	7.4040	18.4880	47.1213	302.5586	2.9990	18.1716	3.8620
247	69.1530	12.1212	1.6190	48.1415	54.4310	11.3410	15.1413	13.8125
248	81.4650	1.6220	4.1890	16.4950	70.5080	4.4555	12.1110	47.8552
249	329.5518	6.0040	12.2520	8.0540	269.6377	12.1417	9.8765	51.9185
250	36.3870	133.0000	12.7246	51.5355	27.7690	21.8283	4.3210	54.3321
251	344.7937	7.5000	24.7400	57.5982	205.0610	92.9395	8.1234	4.8200
252	22.8030	84.1000	2.1060	83.4952	10.6830	96.9899	5.6788	43.8388
253	196.3030	5.4660	5.9730	99.9242	142.1520	97.9294	12.4582	2.2710
254	31.5660	13.7124	8.1264	10.1115	22.3750	95.0092	14.5220	66.7274
255	108.8580	1.7000	1.2870	92.4445	45.9130	92.6666	1.4330	53.5422
256	83.6260	1.2320	4.1220	55.6677	45.0950	92.5555	13.5620	22.5673
257	390.8726	6.1660	17.3310	40.5880	296.8577	58.2130	18.0000	10.0000
258	363.9839	7.0160	11.2700	11.5610	234.6320	2.7310	6.4860	86.0000
259	52.2620	.4420	5.1030	1.1500	43.5110	12.1440	44.0700	16.0000
260	228.6110	5.6500	1.8370	41.5600	161.4700	20.5400	14.9460	3.0730
261	60.8250	1.5000	1.4910	45.3100	41.6820	1.8970	1.6590	30.7300
262	16.6890	40.5000	57.6000	9.8540	9.8450	18.3700	35.2020	63.5300
263	39.8290	62.1000	3.9900	1.5610	32.6580	4.9080	9.2530	30.0000
264	28.9020	93.4000	1.1040	36.5000	23.1410	2.5900	18.3650	10.0000
265	8.7410	27.0000	55.6000	32.1400	6.3700	59.3100	27.6600	56.6660
266	61.9446	7.0000	35.0470	43.2000	432.3777	160.6660	19.2020	6.3530

Executive (CEO) Compensation Data

Salary ($1,000's)	Bonus ($1,000's)	Other Compens ($1,000's)	Total Compens ($1,000's)	Age	Education*	Professional Backgrnd	Tenure	Exper	Market Valuation ($1,000,000's)	Pct Own	Firm Profits ($1,000,000's)	Firm Sales ($1,000,000's)
173	275	5	453	64	2	3	40	26	54.5	3.14	91	872
1,441	429	78	1,948	55	1	1	23	23	7.6	0.55	145	1,237
1,646	0	89	1,735	47	2	7	5	5	21.7	0.52	-47	1,712
294	325	24	643	65	1	3	29	23	8.9	0.89	44	1,681
1,254	105	102	1,461	63	1	6	23	8	3.6	0.05	201	5,673
325	25	7	357	54	2	5	20	1	0.5	0.06	71	1,117
658	0	11	669	61	2	5	2	2	0.7	0.05	-187	1,475
1,723	289	82	2,094	63	1	3	41	8	5.9	0.04	1,166	10,818
504	69	24	597	57	2	5	27	13	1.4	0.03	377	2,686
822	38	29	889	56	2	1	5	5	0.7	0.03	224	2,201
374	129	11	514	57	2	4	3	3	4.1	0.17	79	661
447	11	8	466	48	2	1	17	1	0.2	0.01	189	1,539
2,781	0	52	2,833	50	1	3	4	4	11.7	0.39	-332	11,663
128	282	17	427	54	1	8	31	15	71.4	10.09	55	2,366
1,782	0	74	1,856	60	2	7	33	3	0.4	0.03	-507	4,864
1,137	423	92	1,652	60	2	1	34	14	11.5	0.06	856	14,949
761	20	1	782	49	2	9	18	9	1.3	0.07	14	5,061
505	0	108	613	56	2	9	8	1	0.1	0.02	-29	1,929
976	448	64	1,488	58	1	3	9	8	9.4	0.56	126	2,643
434	12	1	447	50	2	9	5	1	0.3	0.03	54	1,084
1,010	687	55	1,752	63	1	7	14	14	534.2	3.99	249	5,137
956	1,452	89	2,497	64	0	1	28	28	221.1	3.98	91	844
700	37	31	768	60	2	9	30	8	0.7	0.02	322	2,097
1,813	489	40	2,342	71	1	4	46	34	9.6	0.83	99	835
3,396	0	13	3,409	64	0	9	30	30	29.4	0.31	-99	12,021

2,108	38	98	2,244	64	2	5	41	5	4.0	0.04	30	4,451
597	0	4	601	59	2	4	35	5	0.1	0.12	−85	1,911
616	862	76	1,554	61	1	8	41	17	30.6	2.23	82	1,435
237	221	4	462	61	2	5	25	11	16.8	1.03	27	1,314
571	0	16	587	55	2	4	5	5	1.6	0.17	−76	2,301
269	391	28	688	54	2	9	28	28	1,689.0	34.04	317	3,277
721	101	71	893	60	2	5	36	15	2.0	0.04	417	4,444
328	238	34	600	60	0	7	42	1	85.6	17.66	43	1,214
538	25	7	570	60	1	4	3	3	0.2	0.21	49	804
741	104	9	854	62	1	7	30	3	2.6	0.17	81	669
607	380	47	1,034	51	1	6	23	3	7.0	0.83	82	578
1,044	107	36	1,187	55	2	8	2	1	3.1	1.21	10	1,214
2,409	1,487	143	4,039	55	1	7	32	17	35.2	0.29	715	12,651
287	198	32	517	59	1	8	37	21	181.0	6.70	136	3,180
567	15	34	616	51	2	1	16	9	0.3	0.01	237	2,754
682	0	2	684	62	2	1	36	2	0.8	0.01	−1,086	12,794
1,226	174	56	1,456	52	1	4	30	10	6.0	0.17	98	4,439
952	80	56	1,088	45	2	7	11	11	2.6	0.17	48	415
432	0	12	444	50	2	7	25	3	0.1	0.01	−50	1,569
1,085	440	97	1,622	57	1	8	29	5	9.7	0.19	347	9,886
1,009	117	0	1,126	64	1	3	28	14	3.4	0.21	63	2,545
1,711	182	134	2,027	62	2	2	25	5	3.4	0.04	806	8,379
408	183	9	600	52	2	7	12	2	4.2	0.26	10	21,351
543	13	2	558	62	2	5	34	12	0.2	0.01	265	2,359
278	209	74	561	61	2	6	24	24	15.4	0.95	52	695

* 0 = no college degree; 1 = undergraduate degree; 2 = graduate degree

Index

531